More Tricks of the Game-Programming Gurus

More Tricks of the Game-Programming Gurus

Greg Anderson
Peter Freese
Brenda Garno
Eagle Jones
Tab Julius
Steve Larsen
Andrew Lehrfeld
Erik Lorenzen
Tim Melton
Michael J. Norton
Bob Pendleton
Wayne Russell
Mark Seminatore
Lee Taylor
Keith Weiner
Brad Whitlock

SAMS
PUBLISHING

201 West 103rd Street
Indianapolis, IN 46290

Overview

Contents

About the Authors

Greg Anderson holds a degree in history from Ball State University in Indiana. Currently, he is working as a freelance writer. He is unmarried and resides in Florida.

Peter Freese has been writing software for more than 15 years. He is currently Technical Director for Q Studios, where he is responsible for achieving the best possible performance in 2-D and 3-D graphics engines. He is currently hard at work on Blood, a real-time 3-D action horror game for the PC. Peter has several published games and educational titles to his credit, including Thinkin' Things, Baileys Book House, The Incredible Toon Machine, and Lode Runner: The Legend Continues. Peter lives in the Pacific Northwest with his computer, wife, two daughters, and odd sense of humor. He can be reached via e-mail at pfreese@qstudios.com.

Brenda Garno is a game designer with Sir-tech Software, where she has worked in development and author submissions from 1989 to 1994. Readers are welcome to contact the author at 76711.33@compuserve.com. She will give advice or answers to any questions you may have about submitting games to a developer.

Eagle Jones currently works at InfoStructure, an Internet access provider. In 1994, he participated in space physics research, including development of a neural network. This year, he will work at Intel with the P6 development team. A high school student, Jones also has dual enrollment at college, where he has taken math, physics, and computer science courses, including some graduate-level computer science classes. He may be reached through e-mail at eagle@mind.net.

Tab Julius is a multimedia developer whose company, Penworks Corporation, develops children's educational software for established publishers. He may be reached via e-mail at tab@penworks.com or through CompuServe at 72037,3662.

Steve Larsen is a medical information computer programmer who lives in Sandy, Utah. He has worked or done computer-related research in graphics, Operating Systems, networking, UNIX System Administration, GUI programming, and has had experience in artificial intelligence, robotics, vision, music, and other areas. He is currently finishing his Bachelor of Science degree in Computer Science at the University of Utah. After he completes this obligation, he plans to write his own video game. You may contact Steve via Internet e-mail at: larsen@sunset.cs.utah.edu.

Andrew Lehrfeld coordinates the beta-testing activities at Epic MegaGames, a leading producer of shareware games for the PC. He's been the Beta Test Leader on many projects, including Epic's Jazz Jackrabbit, One Must Fall, Extreme Pinball, and Tyrian. He can be reached online at andy@epicgames.com.

Erik Lorenzen conspires with **Keith Weiner** to take over the world. His job is to help implement the crazy stuff that Keith dreams up. He thinks that no matter its primary purpose, every computer will run games. So he's pushing to develop a game with some of these new technologies, sure to win a place on every hard drive, if not to make a lot of money.

Tim Melton is owner of Melton Productions, a music and sound design service for computer game and software developers. Melton, who is classically trained in piano, has 18 years experience in professional audio recording and sound reinforcement. He can be reached through e-mail at 72134,175.

Michael J. Norton is a full-time programmer who works in Silicon Valley. He holds a Bachelor of Science in Physics with an emphasis on computational physics and computer modeling. His career experience includes work on 386 PC chip sets, VGA hardware and programming, and extensive programming on multi-platform network applications. Currently, he is working on a 3-D multiplayer dungeon engine for Windows 95 that will be available for licensing. He is co-founder of pixelDyne, a small, innovative, game software development company. You can contact Norton on CompuServe at 73164,2436.

Bob Pendleton started learning to program when he was 19 years old. That was 23 years ago and he's still learning to program. Along the way he's picked up a couple of degrees in computer science, done game programming academic research, corporate research, shipped several commercial products, and worked for four start-up companies. Now, he's doing game programming again. He likes to program.

Wayne Russell is a British programmer and writer who has been working with PCs since the days of the IBM XT. His articles on game programming topics have appeared many times in the UK magazine *PC Home*. He may be reached via the Internet at 100430,1236.

Mark Seminatore is president and co-founder of M&E Consulting Enterprises, Ltd., which is a small-business computer consulting firm in Albany, New York. Seminatore has a Masters Degree in Mechanical Engineering and has been programming for more than 15 years. He specializes in numerical analysis, optimization, and high-performance graphics. In his "spare" time, he enjoys the challenge of writing computer games. Seminatore was one of the co-authors of *Tricks of the Game-Programming Gurus* and also has written an article on ray casting for *Dr. Dobb's Journal*. He also has done some consulting on graphics performance with game developers.

Lee Taylor has lived in Allentown, Pennsylvania, his entire life. He started programming in the mid-1980s with a Tandy Color Computer Two. Since then, he has learned many programming languages and techniques. He currently attends Salisbury High School and works at Science Express, a computer bookstore. He can be reached via the Internet at 74213.2334@compuserve.com.

Keith Weiner began his programming habit in 1979, and hasn't been able to quit, even with the help of PROGANON. In lieu of sleep, he plans to conquer the world. Step one of The Plan is to get some of his code running on every computer. He figures that he'll need a lot of leverage, and so he wants to develop technologies for use by other programmers.

Brad Whitlock has headed (for nine years) a company he started that manufactures and markets PC-based programmer productivity tools. In a past life, he was Director of Programming as well as Director of Marketing for UCCEL Corporation. Whitlock also was a Senior Product Manager for Dun & Bradstreet. He has spoken at numerous conferences and seminars on programming productivity and database management systems. Whitlock holds a Bachelor of Arts degree in Economics from UCLA.

Introduction

I will never forget the day I played my first video game—I was instantly hooked! After that first experience, I was determined to learn how to program my own video games.

The first book in this series, *Tricks of the Game-Programming Gurus*, covered many of the basic skills used in game programming. *More Tricks of the Game-Programming Gurus* goes one step further—it provides you with the tools necessary to take your game ideas and turn them into successful, commercial products.

This book covers such advanced game programming topics as story-line development, CD-ROM games, 3-D Super VGA graphics, dazzling digital sound effects, DOS Extendors, and debugging and optimization techniques. Also included are chapters on important topics such as game installation programs, documentation, pre-release testing, and the many legal aspects of computer game publishing.

The topics covered in this book are the ingredients which help to separate popular games like Commanche Maximum Overkill, DOOM, Descent, and Myst from other games on the market. If you have dreams of creating a unique and successful computer game of your own, this book is definitely for you!

Mark Seminatore

The programming information in this book is based on information for developing applications for Windows 95 made public by Microsoft as of 9/9/94. Since this information was made public before the final release of the product, there may have been changes to some of the programming interfaces by the time the product is finally released. We encourage you to check the updated development information that should be part of your development system for resolving issues that might arise.

The end-user information in this book is based on information on Windows 95 made public by Microsoft as of 9/9/94. Since this information was made public before the release of the product, we encourage you to visit your local bookstore at that time for updated books on Windows 95.

If you have a modem or access to the Internet, you can always get up-to-the-minute information on Windows 95 direct from Microsoft on WinNews:

On CompuServe: `GO WINNEWS`

On the Internet:

`ftp://ftp.microsoft.com/PerOpSys/Win_News/Chicago`
`http://www.microsoft.com`

On AOL: keyword `WINNEWS`

On Prodigy: jumpword WINNEWS

On Genie: WINNEWS file area on Windows RTC

You can also subscribe to Microsoft's WinNews electronic newsletter by sending Internet e-mail to news@microsoft.nwnet.com and putting the words SUBSCRIBE WINNEWS in the text of the e-mail.

Getting Started

P A R T

1

Developing Your Story Line

by Gregory Anderson

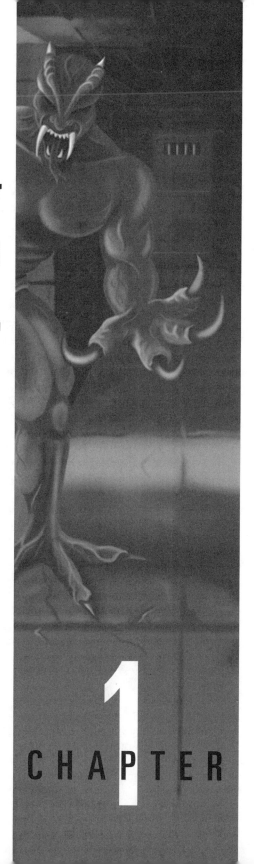

1

CHAPTER

The personal computer industry is booming. Already a billion-dollar baby, the industry is still an infant. There are no signs that the growth will slow any time soon, and many of signs that we have seen only glimmer of what is ultimately possible. Put plainly, 1995 is a great year to get involved in the computer software industry, and a fascinating—not to mention potentially extremely lucrative—place to start is writing computer games. This book will cover the basics of writing computer games, starting with an overview of the kinds of games on the market and how to put a dramatic story together, through the programming skills necessary to get a game on the screen, to the selling and marketing skills essential in getting the game in the hands of consumers. Those who have a good imagination, a grasp of computer basics, a logical mind, and a desire to make a comfortable living should read on. Your future may well await!

Most of this book concerns the technical aspects of producing computer games. That may be the guts of the gaming enterprise, but the real point of the enterprise is to market games the public will buy, and that often requires telling a good story—or several variations on a story. Some computer games, of course, are simply games—computerized versions of board games such as chess or new games designed strictly for computers (such as the ones that allow the players to save the Earth by zapping alien attackers). This chapter, however, will concentrate on the storytelling side of games that explore new worlds or alternate realities. To successfully produce this type of game, a writer must have a firm grasp on the basics of drama and fiction, a handle on the film-format style of writing, a good imagination, and an understanding of the demands of story logic. So, for a few pages, we will leave the programmers to their algorithms.

Homer and Helen

The first requisite for a good computer game that explores a dramatic situation is a dramatic situation. That seems obvious, but it is also important to keep in mind. Virtually all good stories follow the same basic pattern: They have a beginning, a middle, and an end. Take Homer, for example. The beginning of his *Iliad* is the launching of the Greek fleet toward Troy to recover Helen, who the Greeks believed had been abducted and taken to Troy. The middle tells of the Trojan War itself, and the end of *The Iliad* recounts how the Greeks used the Trojan Horse to finally destroy their enemy. Homer's *Iliad*, therefore, has a definite beginning, a middle overflowing with conflict and complications, and an ending with finality. No wonder it still holds up after 3,000 years. Think about any story you've ever heard, read, or seen, and it too will no doubt follow this same simple pattern. Homer probably sang his stories to groups of people gathered around after a hard day's work; creators of computer games are looking to capture much the same kind of audience. To succeed with story-based games, those creators need to master the same techniques Homer did (though having a singing voice is optional).

Dissecting a Simple Bank Heist

Let's look at a simple situation and try to set it up dramatically. There is currently much concern about crime, and especially about how crime is depicted in the media, but we will pick a bank robbery as a situation to examine. Crimes are often dramatized partly because the conflict necessary for drama—the middle of the story—comes ready-made. In our example, in the middle of the story, we might have a old-fashioned bank heist. Or a new-fangled bank heist. Or a bungled bank heist. Or a bank heist pulled off by a group of genetically-enhanced chimpanzees controlled by neo-Nazi animal-rights activists. The exact nature of the robbery will be established at the beginning of the story. Indeed, a writer will often conceive of the middle and end of a story first, and then construct a beginning that leads naturally to the rest. A bank robbery performed by a lone man pushing a crumpled note at a teller could flow from the desperation of being jobless, for example, or perhaps the robber has a sister who needs a kidney transplant, but lacks the necessary money or insurance. The beginning, and the tone, of such a story would certainly be much different from that of a story about Al Capone's gang knocking over a bank in 1930s Chicago.

The beginnings might be different, but the endings of those two situations are not so easily determined. They could be similar—both the lone man and the gang could be caught, possibly shot, or both could make a clean getaway—or, given the different fundamentals of the two stories, the endings could be wildly different. From the core event of a bank robbery, any number of stories could flow, depending upon the characters created and the situations in which the robbery takes place. Whatever is done, however, should make sense within the world created for the story; otherwise the audience, or the game-players, could easily feel hoodwinked.

That's not the way to build a long, lucrative career. In fact, a poorly structured story probably won't even get a writer a first sale. Admittedly, such is not always the case. As special effects get better and better in the film industry, for instance, there has been some tendency in Hollywood to make movies with very thin plots and to allow the "gee-whiz factor" to sell the tickets. Take the recent movie hit, *Ace Ventura: Pet Detective*, for example. It featured truly amazing special effects—as well as the comedic talents of Jim Carrey—but the plot was pure silly. Maybe that's not a disaster in a movie comedy, but in most types of fiction, see-through plots should be avoided. No doubt, as the capabilities of personal computers increase, and as the programmers addressed in this book get better at what they do, there will be a similar tendency in the computer game industry. Thus, the initial emphasis on plain old storytelling in this chapter was meant to be a reminder. Story-based computer games must engage the mind of the player at a deeper level than flight simulators reach, else the player will always roam the wild blue electronic yonder. Characters must be believable and complex; the main character must be likable, or at least compelling; and each story within the game must stand on its own. Writing the scenarios for a story-based game should be like writing any other kind of top-notch fiction. Homer, if he were to return on the crest of some space-time disturbance, should be able to enjoy it.

Producing a Game

We will return to the workings of storytelling shortly, but first it is important to understand how story-game scenarios are written, and how the games are produced. Game scenarios are written in film format, just as movies are. This makes sense, because both games and movies tell stories strictly in scenes; both are oriented to the visual, although the additional audio component obviously is important in movies and will become so in games, particularly storytelling games, as we move ahead. It is important to grasp this point: Unlike a novel, where the author can interrupt the narrative as he or she wishes to interject, emphasize, or expound, the writer of a script in film format must convey everything either visually or through the use of dialogue. Such restrictions make the choice of setting, each physical action by a character, and each word of dialogue something to be carefully considered.

Before going further and linking the tools of the scriptwriter—setting, physical action, and dialogue—to our bank-robbery idea, let's sketch the process by which a computer game of this kind is produced. First, there is the concept for the game. The idea. It could be the writer's idea, or it could be someone else's, but before anything happens, the idea and the writer must meet. We won't go into the technical details of writing in film format, but the basics are not difficult to pick up. When the writer is finished with the script, and the boss is satisfied, the script goes to the art department. (In the real world, the writer is probably working on one part of the script while the artists are working on another part.) The artists then create a storyboard of the script. Remember, scripts are simply collections of organized scenes, so each scene in the script is depicted on the storyboard. Once the boss is happy with the development of the game, the programmers translate the work into the bits, bytes, and instructions that computers understand. (Movies, by the way, are developed much the same way, except that instead of using programs and computers to execute the story, movie producers get to use the likes of Tom Cruise and Julia Roberts.)

Back to the Bank

Now, let's go back to our bank-robbery notion and apply the screenwriter's tools of drama. Take the lone man with the crumpled note. We cannot simply say he's basically a good man trapped by circumstances—even if he is; we must find a way to *show* that. Maybe his hands shake as he hands the teller the note; maybe he refuses to look her in the eye; maybe he apologizes to her after she gives him the money—any of those clues, or all of them combined, could be used to indicate that this fellow really didn't have his heart in robbing banks. Capone's gang would obviously take a completely different attitude during the robbery.

While bank robberies are limited to banks, the setting of a computer game can literally be anywhere and anytime we can imagine. Indeed, that is no doubt a fundamental attraction to these games. They can take the player out of his or her everyday life to explore worlds of the far future or distant past, worlds of pure fantasy or a different part of the world as it is, or any combination of those possibilities. Generally speaking, as long as it is well done, the more complex and imaginative a game is, the better; complexity and imagination are among the keys to keeping players entertained over a period of time. An equally important key, however, is the game's internal story logic. When we have unlimited possibilities, it is easy to shortchange the plotline in favor of more flashy stuff.

The Alamo

Much of a game's internal logic must be in the writer's mind before the first scene is written. This should be fairly clear; as all stories are rooted in the worlds in which they take place, it is important to know how that world works. For example, if we were going to write a game story in which the defenders prevail at the Alamo against the Mexican army, we would first have to know the "world" in which this battle will take place. One obvious way to change the outcome of the battle is to somehow fiddle with the flow of time and give the defenders more advanced weapons, whether submachine guns or phasers. Such a twist, of course, would also have to be convincingly explained. Whatever happened to re-arm the Texans would also have to logically leave the Mexicans with flintlocks. In a fantasy San Antonio, the battle could be fought with potions of horned frog toes and bluebonnet petals, Bowie knives of cold fire, and magical spears made from bull longhorns; but again, some "logically" convincing way for a few men to overcome an army would need to be the key to the story. Even fantasy has to have rules that players can recognize.

Another way to approach an Alamo game would be to write an "alternate history" plot. In this type of game, we would take 1836 Texas as it was, put the defenders within the mission walls as they were, place Santa Ana's army on the plains as it was—and proceed to produce a Texan triumph. (No fair having Davy Crockett simply whip all comers! That wouldn't be logical—and worse, it would make a boring game.) To do an alternate history plot, the writer should be relatively familiar with the actual history surrounding the event to be explored. History, after all, is not the way it is because it could have been no other way. Important events often turn on small events; personalities thrust into the spotlight at critical moments make decisions that have far-reaching consequences. Study the actual history, identify the turning points, and then turn the story in another direction. Identify the key people, and have them make different decisions—consistent with that person's basic character, of course.

The Alamo might be a particular challenge in this area because it was not a close fight; it is difficult to imagine a reasonable alternative to what happened, given the disparity in forces. But as writers we don't have to hang around San Antonio. Sam Houston, commander of the Texan forces at that time, was also well-known to many Indian tribes; he was, in fact, the adopted son of a chief. So, suppose General Sam had persuaded his Indian brothers to act as midwives in the birth of an independent Texas. At that time, both the Kiowa and the Comanche were fierce, powerful tribes in the general area of the Alamo. Could Indian warriors, attacking and harassing the Mexican army, have saved the Alamo defenders? Well, in reality, probably not; there was already enough friction between white and red to preclude any such thing, but we are concerned with writing games that are at least generally plausible and entertaining. The Indian-ally scenario may well fit that bill.

For a less bloody alternative, we could look to General Santa Ana. The General, who was also President of Mexico, liked the ladies. Another possible scenario could have a San Antonio beauty stealing Santa Ana's heart and steering him away from the Alamo. Indeed, Texas legend has it that a local belle was, in fact, distracting the Mexican leader during the early moments of the Battle of San Jacinto, thus allowing Sam Houston to claim the decisive victory that gave Texas independence. Using knowledge of the general history surrounding our subject, we can sometimes find a "twist" to propel an alternate history scenario.

Note the use of the characters and life histories of Houston and Santa Ana in the preceding examples. When doing alternate history scenarios, it is important, and useful, to write within the characters of the historic figures involved even if the story being told never happened in fact. The idea is to create stories that reasonably could have happened; to do that, root the story in the same historical context that gave rise to the actual event, and animate the story with at least the key characters involved. Of course, the writer is free to introduce new characters, even fictional ones, into old stories. Historical novelists have freely used such a device for a long time. A different approach would be to take a historical figure who was on the periphery of the actual event and make that person a key player in the alternate plot. In the Alamo example, perhaps that person could be Andrew Jackson, who was President of the United States at the time the Alamo fell. In fact, Jackson had been the political mentor of Sam Houston in Tennessee, the two remained close, and President Jackson was keenly interested in wresting Texas away from Mexico, so there is a good basis for having the U.S. Cavalry charge to the rescue just as Crockett is reduced to batting away Mexican soldiers with the butt end of his beloved Old Betsy.

This type of game can be educational as well as entertaining. History is ultimately about choices made. By presenting some choices that could have been made, we can throw a slightly different light on what actually occurred. Done carefully and well, we can make people think. So far in the Alamo examples, however, we have concentrated upon producing a Texan victory; there is another side. Suppose Mexico had held Texas through 1840? through 1850? What would that have meant to the flow of U.S. history? Suppose Mexico had prevailed by whatever means in the Mexican-American War of 1846-48? Would a Mexico that included the present American Southwest from Texas to Colorado to California (at least) have become the dominant power in the Western Hemisphere? Remember, the discovery of gold in California was shortly after this time; a few years earlier, and that would've been Mexican gold. How would that have changed the world we know? Would a United States confined to the land east of the Mississippi have finally broken apart over slavery? Well, we have ranged rather far from the Alamo, but a game scenario can do precisely that, as long as each plot is well-structured.

Possibilities Galore

The examples used thus far have largely been alternate history possibilities, and we will return to that area soon, but there are other popular types of story-games, too. Fantasy games, for example. These stories are often written in the hero-on-a-quest pattern. Along the way, the hero runs up against all manner of monsters and evil-doers and saves a beautiful princess from a hideous fate. Usually, the princess also turns out to be the key to the hero's successful completion of his quest. Such a game is often the sword-and-sorcery type, with lots of magic—a natural, given the seemingly magical capabilities of computers. Borrowing from the Greek and Roman myths has been popular in the area. Hercules and Hercules-type heroes are abundant. Also popular are medieval settings complete with dungeons, knights in shining armor, and Merlinesque wizards. This story genre should probably have more heroines undertaking quests than has been traditional, as magic does not rely on physical power and swordsmanship. Whichever, or whatever, gender, however, the same rules about setting and character apply. Both must be consistent within the game, from plot to plot. If a magical apparatus works in one story, it should work in another story unless some reason is given why it will not. Because a magical world will not always work as we would expect, it is especially important for the writer to work out the details before starting to write. Inconsistencies, even in fantasy, will consistently bring forth players' wrath.

There are also science-fiction games galore. Some of these will merge with fantasy, using magic as well as science; others rely more on accepted science and extrapolation based on scientific principles. In this kind of scenario, allowing character development to take a back seat while some interesting science drives the story is risky. Such an approach can work for one story, but we are selling a packet of stories in these games, all rooted in one premise; generally, a character the player can identify with, should be at the center of most plots. Some of the most popular games in this category are no doubt the space-oriented games, whether they concern space exploration, the politics of galactic empire, or defending the Earth from invaders.

If you are writing a game in this area, doing something really original is particularly important, both to sell the game and to avoid being sued for copyright infringement. The 800-pound gorilla in this category is no doubt the *Star Trek* family of games—whether centering upon Captain Kirk and Mister Spock, or Captain Picard and Data, or Commander Sisko and Major Kira. All of that material is taken. Stay well away from Romulans and Ferengis unless you have express permission from the owners of Star Trek. Happily, the universe is an awfully big and varied place, so there is still plenty of room for creative storytellers who want to reach for the stars.

One clear place to start when looking for an idea to be developed into a story game is the history of serials in literature, television, and films. In these areas, we can see one lead character, or group of characters, being used in several different situations over time. Essentially, as your game branches off into its various twists and turns and new plots, writing each scenario will be like writing a new story within a serial. That might be especially true if you write a game in the category we are about to touch upon: crime-solving games and mysteries. Yes, this would be the natural home for the bank-robbery scenarios discussed early in this chapter. More importantly, however, it is also the home for some of the best-known characters and writers of the past 100 years—Sherlock Holmes, Sam Spade, Mike Hammer, Perry Mason, Raymond Chandler, Dashiell Hammett, Agatha Christie. And if we stretch the breadth of this category just a bit, as literary critics and editors do, we can also include the likes of James Bond, John le Carré, and maybe even Indiana Jones, although Indy would probably fit better in the adventure category. Adventures are structured much like the quest games; a hero is generally in search of something.

They differ from the quests in that they don't depend on magic. In an Indiana Jones story, for example, evil sorcerers and magical crowns are replaced by evil Nazis and archaeological treasures. Rich soil indeed.

The fascination that this field has held for people is long-standing, and it can be expected to continue into computer games. Indeed, it already has; certain classic detectives have already been the basis for games. Writing mysteries is its own art, and it is beyond the scope of this chapter; but it is important to note that the writer must establish the "method of operation" of his or her detective before going further. Mike Hammer, for example, has plenty of street smarts, but he is basically a tough guy. He would approach a case very differently than would Sherlock Holmes, and these two characters appeal to different audiences. A Hammer game would likely be action-oriented, with lots of fistfights, bodies, blood liberally splashed around, some gunplay, dialogue peppered with hard-edged one liners, and, of course, gorgeous women with hearts of gold. That is what a Hammer fan would expect. A Holmes game, on the other hand, would stress clue detection, analysis of the evidence, and deductive reasoning to follow the trail of the culprit. Quite possibly, a Holmes story could completely lack gore and violence, though a quick spasm of fisticuffs when Holmes finally confronts the villain would not be inappropriate.

The key to writing a game based upon a individual crimefighter, then, is understanding the character of that crimefighter, whether it is a well-established detective or one of your own creation. (Obviously, before doing a game based upon someone else's work, you must secure the appropriate rights to that character or work, unless it's already in the public domain. A later chapter will deal with legal matters.)

Adult Games

As graphics become more sophisticated and as more imaging of actual people is used, an increasingly popular kind of story game is what we like to call "adult" entertainment. Some people have other names for it. Indeed, bringing up this type of game in the storytelling chapter might be superfluous; historically, adult movies have paid very little attention to plot. On the other hand, literary erotica is not altogether bereft of story, and computer games may well go in that direction, if only to try to avoid problems with pornography laws. The argument has also been made that women are more interested in good stories in this area than men are, so as more homes get computers and more women either buy computer games from stores or download adult games for their own use, storytelling may be increasingly emphasized.

To get a handle on what may sell in this area, especially to women, take a look at today's romance-fiction market. The traditional romance is still out there, in which the leading woman is more stoic in her nature; but the so-called "modern romance" is about a strong, aggressive, often—but not always—professional woman who runs her own life. These women even utter expletives on occasion, and their collective sexual experiences are many and varied. With some rework, these modern romances could be made more appealing to the male player while holding its female audience, thus possibly becoming the mainstream computer erotica of the near future.

Of course, there will always be the more hard-core sex game, but that kind probably has very short scripts and doesn't really apply to this discussion.

Other Possibilities

There are many other genres open to story games as well: Westerns, for example. Although the western's dominance on television is well in the past, the western novel and short story is currently on one of its periodic upticks, and the well-done western movie or television miniseries can still be a success. The Lone Ranger and Marshall Dillon may yet find new homes on the cyber-prairie.

Alternate biographies—placing historical figures in new time frames and exploring how they might react—could be another idea. Weaving some of the world's great myths together and playing with the possibilities might be another. The point is that the computer-game writer is now limited, quite literally, only by his or her imagination and ability to actually execute stories—and the financial rewards of success are potentially vast.

A Deeper Look

We have gone through basic storytelling, some mechanics of how story games operate, with each story being an independent whole yet linked to the other stories in the game, and we've gone through various types of stories. Now let's take a more detailed look at how various scenarios in an actual game fit together. To do that, we will use excerpts from a game for which I wrote the scenarios. This game is an alternate history game which, if it comes out soon, will be well-timed for purposes of marketing. For the past three years, we have been observing various fiiftieth anniversaries in connection with World War II, and the game explores some ways in which the war could have turned out differently. My boss in this endeavor told me to keep the stories realistic and plausible given the time frame of the late 1930s through the mid-1940s (or, as he put it, no flying saucers), so I didn't fool with the technology of the time. (Actually, I did, but it was reasonable fooling, and my boss accepted it.) Instead, I concentrated on the characters involved in the military and political sides of the war, although it is important to understand that there are many ways to approach such a subject. (Introducing flying saucers from outer space into the war could have placed the war in a new perspective, for example.)

Since we have already gone into alternate history possibilities at some length when dealing with the Alamo, we won't stress that area again, except to note how many more possibilities there are in a truly global war than there are in connection with one frontier battle. Rather, we will look at how to present the same (historical, in this case) characters in different lights from story to story within a game while remaining faithful to the core characteristics of that personage. This might seem to be more important in history-related games, but it is equally important to present consistent, coherent fictional characters. We shall also look at creating what I thought of as "forks": turning-off points in which a game story leaves the common trunk to branch off into a new plot.

One of the most dominant figures of the Second World War was Winston Churchill. To this elderly, portly man fell the task of saving the British people from a long, dark night by slaying a Nazi dragon that, upon Churchill's election as Prime Minister, was trampling the Low Countries and opening its jaws, soon to swallow France itself. Britain, led by Churchill, stood alone. Here is approximately how I introduced Churchill into one game scenario, in which Britain ultimately prevails, *without* help from the United States:

Int—Number 10 Downing Street—May 10, 1940—Day

Winston Churchill has just been elected Prime Minister of Great Britain at one of his nation's darkest hours. He is nearing retirement age for most men, fat, cigar smoking, and balding. Churchill is no stranger to government, having been around the top levels of British politics for decades, but the challenge facing him is immense. He is meeting with Lord Halifax, who he retained as Foreign Secretary. Churchill has kept the defense portfolio himself.

Note the film-script format. The first line establishes the physical setting of the upcoming scene. The paragraph or sentence that follows the first line puts the characters into the scene, gives some of the context of the scene, and sets up the dialogue, which I have not included here. Also note that if there is room for only the first line of a scene on a page, you should begin the scene on a new page. Finally, always write in present tense. These are the basics of writing in film format.

Now, let's examine how the paragraph in the scene introduces Churchill in the scenario. We are told he is an experienced politician, well-known to the people and the British ruling class. We are also given a thumbnail sketch of the physical appearance of the man. In this case, that might seem unnecessary, as everyone knows what Churchill looked like at that point, but generally a writer will be creating characters out of the air, and he or she must give the art department some guidance. A quick description is thus provided the first time a new character enters the story. Lord Halifax was not described in the preceding example because he had entered the story earlier; as explained, he was retained by Churchill from Neville Chamberlain's cabinet. The paragraph also tells us that Churchill appointed himself Defense Minister on top of his duties as Prime Minister. The implication of that decision could easily be that Churchill expected his primary responsibility to be leading a war effort. We also learn that Churchill is facing an immense challenge. Hopefully, the story had made that obvious before, but the statement in the paragraph does imply Churchill did not intend to back down. So, in a very few lines, a good bit of a character's looks and outlook can be presented.

The rest of the story is about how the character copes with the challenge before him. In my case, I was twice lucky and once unlucky. Lucky because the material I based the scenarios upon was deep and vast and powerful and filled with extraordinary characters on all sides—all I had to do was keep from mucking it up! Twice lucky because the leaders of World War II, especially

Churchill, tended to be eloquent speakers. As the best of today's politicians are masters of television, so Churchill and Roosevelt, and even Hitler, knew the power of the spoken word because the mass medium of their day was radio. Writing the dialogue for this game, therefore, was easy. I was unlucky in one respect, however. How do you let Churchill lose? How do you let Hitler win? This is an exercise in might-have-beens, remember. In an alternate history, this book could be written in German. Or Japanese. The first step in changing the outcome and creating a new scenario is shading the characters—presenting them in slightly different lights.

Actually, figuring out a way for Britain to lose to the Nazis was not the problem—after all, it nearly happened; the problem was to find a creative way for the end to come. I decided it was impossible to write a story about World War II, certainly within the guidelines I had been given, without having Winston Churchill be the British leader. Squaring the historic Churchill with a German victory, however, posed major problems. Having the Churchill we all know bow down to *der Führer* struck me as unbelievable; hence, anything but the most masterful story that ended in this way would probably fail. I won't reveal how my particular scenario comes out, but it starts by presenting Churchill as he was viewed by many contemporary Englishmen. I used the same scene we examined earlier—more on that shortly—but I gave the description of Churchill a little twist, as follows:

> **Int—Number 10 Downing Street—May 10, 1940—Day**
>
> Winston Churchill has just been elected Prime Minister of Great Britain at one of his nation's darkest hours. He is nearing retirement age for most men, fat, cigar smoking, and balding. Churchill is no stranger to government, having been around the top levels of British politics for decades, but many consider him a political opportunist, hungry for power. He is meeting with Lord Halifax, who he retained as foreign secretary. Churchill has kept the defense portfolio himself.

Do you sense the different tone that a few new words can impart? Churchill has gone from the great political leader to just another politician, at least potentially. As this particular game was based on history, we should note that this paragraph is as historically valid as the earlier version— Churchill had switched parties earlier in his career in an attempt to gain more power, and he had been a consistent critic of his predecessor. Many Brits, therefore, saw his election as Prime Minister as his last grab for glory. The two paragraphs, therefore, present different views of the same man, each chosen to meet the needs of its story. Of course, most games will have purely fictional characters, so such attention to reality will not be necessary. Getting new angles on characters is useful to writers, however; new perspectives can lead to new stories. Plus, when a writer creates more scenarios within a game, as mentioned earlier, it is important to stay within the logic of that game-world. In that sense, the way that these different views of Churchill serve different stories is instructive.

The Plot Tree

Probably the most distinctive element in story-game writing, as opposed to other types of fiction writing, is the branching off of many plots from a single premise and sometimes from a single "trunk" sequence of scenes. These are the scenes that open every story in a game. Remember, these are games, so we should "play the player" a bit. One way to do that is to start every story the same way. Don't give away too much too soon. Keep the player guessing *what* may happen and *when*. This is different advice from that which is given to writers of other types of fiction, where the goal is often to grab the reader on the first page; it springs from the different underlying assumptions of literary fiction and game fiction. In literary fiction—a short story in a magazine, say—a slow start could mean the reader would skip the rest. Worse, it could mean an editor wouldn't buy the story in the first place. In game fiction, however, the writer can assume the players will be familiar with how computer games proceed and enjoy that process; therefore, a player will likely play the game out. None of which means trunk sequences are unimportant, or that the writer gets a free ride in creating or executing trunk scenes. On the contrary, these scenes don't set up just one story, but several stories, so they should be done with care and with an eye to the logical possibilities they open up. My game actually has two trunks—roughly, one for the European Theater, and one for the Pacific—but that is because I wasn't clever enough to merge the two in a reasonable way. Generally, the fewer trunks the better, because that gives the players fewer clues as to what's coming up, which increases the fun for the players, which is, after all, the point.

After the trunk is established, branches must begin to sprout. Actually, the obvious way to proceed is to go ahead and write one story straight through—that will be one story in the game—then go back through it and find places new plots can reasonably be branched off. We don't want to get too wrapped up in this tree metaphor, but note that there is no set distance up a trunk at which branching begins. Some kinds of trees have low branches while others have their first branches well up the trunk. Similarly, branch plots in story games can fork out from the trunk at any time; that decision is up to the writer. There are some things a writer might want to keep in mind in this connection, however. Branching into a new plot from the first scene may be too soon. The idea is to allow the player to feel comfortable in the world created by the game before taking him or her into a new story; establishing that world sufficiently for a new plot to take off will probably require more than one scene. Think about television serials. They don't start off cold. Rather, sometime very early on, they run the opening sequence that plays the show's theme, reintroduces the main characters, and so on, thus easing the viewer back into the world of that show. The trunk sequence can play the same role in computer games. By becoming familiar territory for the player it can ease that player into a new story.

Just as branching too soon is possible, so is branching too late. While we may go on the assumption that most players will play a game out to its conclusion, we should never test that assumption by simply tacking on different endings to the same lengthy story. For late branching to work, the various endings would need to be very special—and absolutely consistent with the rest of the story. Creating such a game might be possible, but one wonders if it would be commercially successful. The clear temptation would be for a player to run the game through once, and thereafter simply skip to the new ending. Such a game would probably not be very satisfying.

Bearing these cautions in mind, branching into new storylines can be done anytime, and the more branching, the better. Further, these branches should not simply go off on their own forever. Intertwine the branches. Take a scene out of one story and put it in another. That will help keep the players guessing about what's going to happen next, plus some clever programmer might be able to get more stories out of a game than the writer had intentionally written! (Who owns the rights to the subsequent storylines—the writer or the programmer? Consult Chapter 17, "Copyrights and Permissions.") Of course, weaving scenes into other storylines must make logical sense. (One note about the "surplus stories" mentioned previously: They probably will not be a major source of extra income to anyone. Whoever owns the legal rights to them, most such accidental plots probably will not make sense, and so they should be guarded against in the final game.) In biology, it may be physically possible for many different species to mate, but any resulting embryo will only rarely be capable of surviving. So it is with plots created when two different stories have the same scene. That scene might make it possible to connect the beginning of one to the ending of the other, but that doth not a viable plot make. Of course, the more "core" scenes that two or more stories share, the greater the likelihood of something coherent and logical coming out. All in all, I think using the same scene or scenes in different plotlines and in different sequences and at different points within a story can keep a player involved. The only requirement, once again, is that whatever the writer comes up with be a dramatic whole that makes sense within the world of the game.

Now, let's take a close look at exactly how to "fork" a story away from the direction it is heading and onto a new branch. Recall how I changed the presentation of Churchill's character? That was not a fork because it did not act upon the plot. It simply alerted my boss, the art department, and possibly the players, depending on how the game is presented, that something was going to change in that scenario. A fork is that change. It works directly upon the plot and turns the story into a different direction. Again, we will use two scenes approximately from my game as examples. You will note that they are action scenes, which makes sense. Action moves plots. First, a little more World War II history. The Battle of Midway in the summer of 1942 is seen by most historians as a major turning point in the Pacific war. The American victory blunted the Japanese offensive then underway, secured Hawaii as a relatively safe American base of operations, and set the stage for the U.S. offensive against the Japanese over the next three years.

Ext—The Skies Around Midway—Day

We *see* the planes from the carriers of the two fleets make contact. The battle is joined. A huge dogfight ensues. We *see* some planes climb into wispy white clouds to gain an advantage; we *see* others dive to the deck below, in order to gain more speed. We *hear* the high whines of the plane engines. We *see* the bright sunlight glint off the red disk on the tail of a Japanese Zero as it maneuvers to get behind an American Mustang. We *see* the yellow tracers rip through the blue sky and into the Mustang. We *see* the resulting fireball of red and yellow trailing black smoke as it crashes into the blue-green water. The scene would be beautiful if it weren't so deadly.

We *see* the fleets begin to close on each other. As the battleships come within range, we *see* the flashes as their big guns open up. We *hear* the booms. We *see* planes strafe opposing ships. We *see* one sailor running along a deck cut in two by tracer bullets. We *see* shells splash close to ships. One Japanese battleship takes a direct hit in its ammunition magazine. We *see* and *hear* the tremendous explosion.

We *see* planes dive-bombing enemy ships. Some bombs hit. We *see* one American battleship set ablaze by Japanese bombs, and one Japanese carrier destroyed by two huge explosions midship. Another Japanese carrier is taken out of the battle as one of its disabled planes attempts to land, but instead we *see* it cartwheel across the deck and explode as it crashes into other planes.

Slowly, the Americans gain control of the skies. As their carriers are put out of action, the Japanese can no longer launch air attacks, and their planes already airborne are forced to ditch in the ocean. Some pilots choose instead to crash into American ships. From behind an American gunner, we *see* him shoot down one such attempt. We *watch* the tracer bullets bore into their target, and we *see* the Zero explode in midair. The fireball falls into the sea just short of the ship. As the Americans press the air attacks and, as the battleships and destroyers push closer under the air cover, the vaunted Japanese Imperial Navy is forced to retreat for the first time in the war.

Quickly, let's note a couple more film-format conventions. When action is about to take place, always put the lead-in verb—*see, hear, watch,* and so forth—in italics. This alerts the art department and special-effects people that their talents will soon be needed. Also notice the line between each paragraph, and understand that, in this format, such descriptive sequences always finish a sentence on a page. If necessary, leave lines blank at the end of one page and begin the uncooperative sentence on the next page.

The substance of the preceding scene is, no doubt, a simplified account of the actual American victory at Midway. Remember, this is fiction writing, so every last detail need not be nailed down; I was more concerned with making the scene work within the game than with historical accuracy down to the last fuselage rivet. Furthermore, taking the "game world" concept to its logical end, whatever actually happened in 1942 is irrelevant. For our purposes, the world created for the game is what counts; in an alternate history game, the history is a guide, a starting place, and an initial common ground between game and reader, but is only one of several possibilities.

Many computer games have been criticized recently for their excessively violent nature, as was mentioned earlier in this chapter, and the preceding scene could certainly be turned into a blood-splattered mess. Even then, however, the pixel horror would be a pale imitation of life and death. While such violence might disturb some people, I know of no way to write a non-violent game based on World War II. Violent scenes may be necessary in other types of stories as well. The key, I would suggest, is to use only as much violence as is necessary to tell a particular story—and no more.

Now let's see how the preceding scene could be altered to fork into a different story:

Ext—The Skies Around Midway—Day

We *see* the planes from the carriers of the two fleets make contact. The battle is joined. A huge dogfight ensues. We *see* some planes climb into wispy white clouds to gain an advantage; we *see* others dive to the deck below, in order to gain more speed. We *hear* the high whines of the plane engines. We *see* the bright sunlight glint off the red disk on the tail of a Japanese Zero as it maneuvers to get behind an American Mustang. We *see* the yellow tracers rip through the blue sky and into the Mustang. We *see* the resulting fireball of red and yellow trailing black smoke as it crashes into the blue-green water. The scene would be beautiful if it weren't so deadly.

We *see* the fleets begin to close on each other. As the battleships come within range, we *see* the flashes as their big guns open up. We *hear* the booms. We *see* planes strafe opposing ships. We *see* one sailor running along a deck cut in two by tracer bullets. We *see* shells splash close to ships. One Japanese battleship takes a direct hit in its ammunition magazine. We *see* and *hear* the tremendous explosion.

We *see* planes dive-bombing enemy ships. Some bombs hit. We *see* one American battleship set ablaze by Japanese bombs, and one Japanese carrier destroyed by two huge explosions midship. Another American ship, a destroyer, is torpedoed. We *see* the destroyer lifted nearly out of the water and split in two. The Zeroes continue to pound American ships and outduel inexperienced American pilots. In one spectacular and terrible second, two Wildcats, their pilots intent upon their Japanese foes, collide in midair. We *see* the white-hot explosion against the bright blue sky, and *watch* as the wreckage gives an American battleship a glancing blow before disappearing under the waves.

Slowly, the American fleet, already crippled by the attack on Pearl Harbor, begins to withdraw.

Under constant attacks by Zeroes and shells from Japanese battleships, what is left of the American Pacific Fleet struggles to preserve itself so that it may defend Hawaii.

The first two paragraphs, as you see, stay the same; they set up the battle and keep the player guessing. Only then do I begin to turn the battle in a different direction. I also tried to use essentially random or accidental occurrences—the loss of the Japanese carriers, the disastrous, cartwheeled landing attempt, the Wildcat collision—to help turn the tide of the battle. From these scenes forward, we have two entirely different stories within the same game. That is what a fork does.

We haven't touched upon writing dialogue yet, mainly because it is largely a matter of feel and therefore is not something that can be learned in a few paragraphs or even a few pages of instruction. The best dialogue flows naturally from the characters speaking it, so examples would be of limited use. However, here are a few points to keep in mind:

- Understand your characters and how they might express themselves. Winston Churchill and Davy Crockett, both known in their times as effective public speakers, no doubt used very different versions of the English language. An innocent young princess would likewise speak and think differently than would an evil queen. Know the differences.

- Be logical. Make sure each reply makes sense when it follows what was said immediately before, given the particular dramatic situation. This doesn't mean every question must be directly answered, of course. People often hedge or dodge or try to slide around a subject they don't want to discuss, and having your characters do that is fine. Remember, however, that each scene should move the story along, and aimless chit-chat probably won't do that. Know what the scene has to accomplish within the story and stick to that goal.

- Follow the conventions of the genre in which you're writing. Fantasies tend towards more formal, poetic language, for example, while a hard-boiled detective game would use a rougher, sharper street talk. Know your area.

- Read dialogue, listen to movies and television shows, and listen to other people talk. Don't write dialogue the way people actually speak, because we all digress, wander, and leave things unsaid when we talk; but write an *approximation* of real dialogue. Listen to the rhythms of speech and words, and try to put that on paper.

- Constantly read the dialogue you've written earlier. If any of it sounds wooden to you, odds are it will cause giggling in the outside world. Unless that is your goal, rewrite. In other words, be aware of how your dialogue might strike others.

Storytelling

Storytelling is probably the true "oldest profession." Before we domesticated sheep, we painted stories of great hunts on cave walls. Before leaving on such hunts, a man had to convince his fellows cavedwellers that he knew where a herd of giant bison awaited. Perhaps the man told his friends that a god had revealed the whereabouts of a herd to him and told him that all his people would eat well if the man led the hunt. Perhaps the man used poetic license. An argument can be made that civilization itself began when people started passing stories, not just survival information, from generation to generation, thus linking ancestors to descendants, the unearthly to the familiar, and morality—or immorality—to human behavior.

Story-based computer games are among the latest ways humans try to connect with the world around them. The technology and programming involved will become more and more sophisticated—as will, no doubt, the stories and their modes of presentation. Profit motives will drive most of the developments, but let me leave the future scriptwriters among you with a question, which could also be a challenge. Imagine that three thousand years from now a human ship of exploration is surveying the system of a bloated red star. When the lonely captain reaches for some connection to humanity, will that hand grasp a crystal of a computer story-game first published in the early twenty-first century—or a well-thumbed volume of Homer?

Designing Your Game for CD-ROM

by Tab Julius

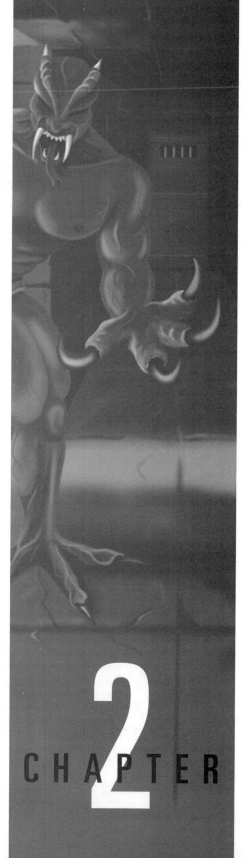

CHAPTER 2

Nowadays, the boxes games come in seem different. Something about them has changed. When you pick them up, they feel lighter. There's just not as much heft to them anymore.

The reason is that there's not much in the box. The stacks of 3.5-inch floppy disks (and sometimes 5.25-inch disks, to boot) are being replaced by a wafer-thin, 1/2-ounce CD-ROMs. A CD-ROM has so much space on it, it's possible to put the instruction manual on it, too.

More and more, the CD-ROM is becoming the *de facto* distribution media, not only for games, but for software in general. Most machines sold nowadays have a CD-ROM drive included. In fact, a machine is more likely to have a CD-ROM drive than a sound card. However, if a new machine *does* have a sound card, it's likely to have a CD-ROM drive also.

CD-ROMs, though, aren't cheap. The drives cost more than the equivalent for floppy disks, as do the CD-ROM versions of the software. What's the appeal then?

First, a CD-ROM holds some 600MB of data, compared to a floppy's insignificant little 1.44MB (which, I might add, we all raved about when it arrived). Not only can you include the program—not just in compressed form, but in full ready-to-execute form—on the disc, but also the manuals, demos for other programs, and lots of extra software, clip art, or whatever you want.

Second, it's difficult to pirate a CD-ROM. To copy the contents onto floppies not only requires a ton of floppies, but it is unlikely to work anyway, since many programs execute off the CD-ROM. To copy the contents to another CD-ROM requires a CD-ROM maker (called a "burner"), which most people don't have, and to copy the contents to your hard disk could require up to 600MB of hard disk space. Hard disk space *is* getting cheaper, but it's not *that* cheap yet.

Third, you can do some things with a CD-ROM that have no equivalent in the world of floppies. That is, you can put digital audio tracks on the disc and have your program play a five-minute wave-file segment right off the disc. Also, the user can pop the CD-ROM into a regular compact-disc player and play the music. (This hasn't always been the case, but new standards are now making it possible).

In addition, the small cost of mass-duplication makes the CD-ROM *very* attractive to packagers. A complete, pressed, CD-ROM can be made for around $1 to $2 in quantity. Contrast that to floppies, which are anywhere from $.59 to $1 *per single floppy* (and typically you need many in order to contain a software program), and you can see the attraction. Instead of packaging $3 or more worth of floppies, you can put in a single CD-ROM for only a dollar or two and have plenty of room left to not only put in a lot of extras but also to put in your complete set of manuals.

In many cases you can also release both a Macintosh and Windows version of the software on the same disc. Thus, not only are production costs decreased, but the trouble of maintaining two separate SKUs is eliminated.

Couple all this with the fact that there are hardly ever any media errors with a CD-ROM, meaning few if any defective discs, and it's difficult to be unhappy with a media format that provides a ton more storage space at a fraction of the production cost, shipping weight, piracy risk, and defective-unit return rate, and which enables you to maintain just one SKU for two platforms. Thus it's not very difficult to see why the CD-ROM has become the darling of the software publishing industry.

There are Some Drawbacks...

But is the CD-ROM the answer to all our prayers? No, actually, it is not. To begin with, the media is not overwritable. This means that you can't save the current state of the program on it, the list of players, or even (for security purposes) a count of the number of times it's been played, or a password, serial number, or anything else. If you're going to ask the user for the serial number off the package, it's got to be stored on the hard disk. There's no writing it back to a CD-ROM.

This is a minor drawback, however, and there are ways to do things differently. The big problem, though, which has no easy workaround, is the tremendous *slowness* of the media. It drags. You *can* get fast performance off a CD-ROM, but you have to design your program with this in mind (and that's what this chapter is about). Left alone, CD-ROM performance is, quite frankly, awful. There's not a lot the user can do about the slow speed, short of just caching the hell out of the drive (and even that only helps a little).

The access times on hard-disk drives nowadays run anywhere from 8 milliseconds (ms) to 15 ms. Compare that to a CD-ROM drive, which has access times that may run from 150ms to 220ms. That's right—it's anywhere from 10 to 30 times slower. Not 10 to 30 *milliseconds* slower—10 to 30 *times* slower. That's why most programmers are in for a rude shock when they run their game from a CD-ROM for the first time.

Many people burn their CD-ROM as one of the last steps in the development process. Mistake, mistake, *mistake!* The last step in the process is not the time when you want to discover that your program will load data off the disc up to 30 times slower than you planned for.

Such carelessness leaves the developer with no time to make any appreciable changes, and the product (which ran great off a hard disk) has terrible performance when run from its distribution media. This practice certainly hasn't done anything to alleviate the public perception that the CD-ROM is a slow medium.

Do the benefits of CD-ROM outweigh the drawbacks? Yes. The ability to put a ton of stuff on the disc is a multimedia godsend. Video clips, wave files, animation—all these things take lots of room. Given that a single video clip can occupy some 5MB to 50MB of space, it's not hard to see why video clips for computers didn't get a lot of distribution before the advent of CD-ROMs.

The tremendous amount of space on a CD-ROM opens up the opportunity to incorporate a lot more—and different—material into a software product than ever before.

For instance, the national telephone-directory disks that you can now buy weren't practical with a floppy disk. Likewise, it is now possible to ascribe voice to many game characters. Previously, the only way one could get a voice was by speech synthesis, since using real voice would take a prohibitive amount of space in the form of wave files. With CD-ROM, this is no longer a barrier, and adding voice to products is now a possibility.

The read-only attribute of the CD-ROM can be either a benefit or a drawback. On the benefit side, it is not possible for a CD-ROM to have a virus on it that was introduced after the disc was created. As opposed to a floppy, if a CD-ROM was returned to the store or rented (a practice being considered in some places), there's no chance that anything on it wasn't put there by the original publisher.

The cost benefits, though, are the biggest draw. Some compiler manufacturers are foregoing printed manuals altogether in an effort to keep the cost down, and shipping CD-ROMs with just electronic versions of the manuals on them. This keeps the per-unit production cost down tremendously—not to mention the shipping weight. On top of that, the replacement of floppies with a less-expensive and more reliable medium has further served to bring the cost down. On the other hand, with the retail price not changing (or even getting higher), the profit margin increases.

CD-ROM software products have a high profit margin. Having very few media errors helps to maintain this profit margin. Whereas floppies were susceptible to a variety of ills (magnetism not being the least of them), CD-ROMs are relatively impervious to corruption and have a very long shelf life. Not having 3 percent of your inventory returned because of disk defects improves profitablity.

Testing, however, is not quite as cheap as with floppies, because the making of limited-run CD-ROMs is not cheap, at least in the pre-production phase. Unlike a floppy, which is easily duplicated, to make your own CD-ROMs requires a CD-ROM burner (currently costing anywhere from $2,500 to $6,000 for a dedicated machine), and blank CD-ROMs costing $10 to $20 a pop. The difference in cost between the burned CD and the type you get when you buy a shipping product is in the method of manufacture. The home one is "burned" and is typically gold in color, while the silver-colored mass-produced one is "pressed," not unlike a vinyl record pressed from a master. The pressing process enables you to produce final disks for only a $1 or $2 each, in quantity, not including setup costs.

If you are a developer of CD-ROMs, the lack of overwrite capability is something you will have to address. Shareware developers, or others who look to put some sort of "usage count" into the program, will have to rig up a way to do this on their hard disk. No matter how clever you are, though, your methods will be vulnerable, because you simply cannot write to the CD-ROM.

For those developers who want to register the program upon first use and have the user enter a name and a serial number to be permanently recorded, the registration would only be workable for that machine (assuming you store it on the hard disk). Put the CD-ROM in another machine, and it's like a brand-new install.

> You simply cannot write to the CD-ROM, which poses a problem for those who want to "register" the copy upon installation or perform some other install-time function. An alternative is to ship a floppy "installation" diskette with the CD-ROM, which would be required in order to install the software each time and to which the user *can* write. Of course, once you start including floppies, you leave yourself open to problems related to greater cost, potentially bad media, and so forth. However, these drawbacks may be worth undertaking if you simply must have a restricted install.

A CD-ROM's lack of overwrite capability will present other considerations for you. To begin with, it's common to execute a program and then write files to the default directory or to the directory the program was launched from. If you launch from the CD, that technique's not going to work, since the launch or default directory cannot be written to.

The typical solution (usually at install time) is to create a directory on the user's hard disk (with their permission, preferably), which you can use as a storage area or even a home base. Just creating a directory and making sure you write to it (and not the CD) might be enough. Sometimes, though, for reasons of convenience and speed, the executable program itself is installed on the hard disk, leaving the data and resource files on the CD-ROM. This has the following advantages: launching from the hard disk, which is typically faster; making your program/launch/default directory a writable directory on a hard disk as opposed to being on a non-writable CD-ROM; and enabling you to modify the installed executable, so as to display the serial number, or whatever you want, at startup.

But the biggest drawback of the CD-ROM is unquestionably its lack of speed. This is where we're going to focus our attention in this chapter.

What sort of applications are most likely to be affected by the CD-ROM speed bottleneck? Any application that needs to open and access a file on the CD-ROM drive. Be aware that such a file could be the application itself. It is for this reason that many applications install their executable into a directory on the computer's hard drive. Any data, music, image, video, or other file that the application has to open and access on the CD-ROM drive can cause a significant slowdown. If the application is always going to the CD-ROM, then slowdowns will be everywhere.

Speeding Up Your CD-ROM Application

Obviously, then, the first and easiest way to resolve the problem is to eliminate it. This means the application should install as many files as possible on the hard disk at setup time. Unfortunately, this won't win you many fans among the users, so you need to be very judicious and put the most common and reasonably-sized files on the hard drive. By most common, I mean the ones you're going to have to access the most and those which would benefit best by not being on the CD-ROM. But be respectful of the user. Nowadays it's not unusual to install 1MB or 2MB on the drive, and you can probably get away with installing as much as 4MB or even 6MB, which users will sometimes tolerate if you have a truly worthy game.

In any case, though, it's not going to be possible to put the whole CD-ROM on the local drive if there's a significant amount of data on the CD-ROM. In that case, you need to switch to Plan B.

Plan B says you should put as much on the hard drive as you can possibly get away with, while the game is running. When the game is over, get rid of it all.

> Putting as much on the hard drive as you can possible can—and then getting rid of it after the game is over—is a key strategy. The idea is to transfer critical files from the CD-ROM to the hard disk either as you need them or as you expect to need them. What constitutes a critical file? Well, it obviously depends on the application, but I tend to consider the audio files (voice in particular) to be critical, because their delay is most noticeable, along with the animation files.

This means creating a transfer buffer system. The implementation can vary from app to app, so I'll just outline the idea of it.

The appropriate place to put a buffer system on the hard disk is typically the current working directory, but as the implementation is up to you, you can get as fancy as you want. You may want to simply work within the limits of the current working directory, or you may want to make a temporary directory yourself, and you may want to search for the drive with the most available space.

What constitutes a critical file? Well, it obviously depends on the application. You're the best judge of your own program, so you will have to judge what's critical and what's not. Where do you perceive a delay when running your program? What's the program doing at that point? Is it reading something from a file? If so, there's a critical file. (It's critical *if it slows you down.*)

When a critical file is requested for use, or requested for preload, you copy it to that directory. For best results, give it a special extension, one that indicates it is a temporary file. (Use the extension .$$$ if possible, or if you need to differentiate by extension, you might be better off making a separate directory.) The point behind making special extensions or special directories is to make it easy to clean up after ourselves later.

During this process, you need to keep a record of what files you transferred over and, preferably, when you last accessed it. A simple way would be to add the file to a purge list, time stamped, when the file is no longer needed (that is, when you close it). If it is needed again, then you look to see if it's in the purge list, and make it available again (while removing it from the list). If you tie this to some in-house open and close routines, it becomes fairly automatic, in keeping with the natural use of the files.

When you start up the system and determine your transfer directory, you should at that point determine how much of the drive space you're going to enable your transfer buffer to take up. If you find yourself on a drive with very little space available, you might opt to not allow transfers at all, or find another, larger drive. Otherwise, you might elect to take as much as possible, leaving only 1MB or 2MB, or you might choose to take up to half of the available space.

When you go to copy the file, you should first check at that time whether there's enough space to accommodate the file. If there isn't, then you need to start purging. You can go through the purge list looking for the oldest time stamps. This means that the file hasn't been accessed in a long time and, one would assume, won't be needed again for a while. You can then delete that file from the disk (thus freeing up the space) and remove it from the purge list, and continue this process until enough space is free to accommodate the file you want to copy in. This is called the Least Recently Used method, or LRU.

If you're ambitious, you can devise an elaborate purge-priority system, whereby certain files can never get purged, some can get purged at any time, and so on. You can also have some intelligent analysis of the purge list where you ignore lots of little files in favor of perhaps one file, similarly old, that will get you the space you want. It's up to you.

Should you just not be able to copy the file, you probably want to remember it somehow so you don't make the same effort twice. Repeating a failed effort, unless you have reason to suspect it could succeed, will just cause the system to drag. You might want to keep a running tally of the total byte count on the purge list so that you don't even bother purging files if the byte count wouldn't free up enough space.

> When you do try to copy a file, you can add it to a copy list, which is a list of all files you had copied, or tried to copy, to the hard disk. That way, if you get a file that fails the copy, perhaps because its size exceeds the available space (purges and all), you can mark it so that you don't try to copy it again. This will keep you from wasting time in the future.

Should a file copy fail totally for some other reason (protection error, hard disk error, and so on), you probably want to disable all future transfers so you don't attempt future copies that are most likely to fail and thus waste time in the process.

> When you are ready to exit, you should delete all files with the special extension or in the special directory—that is, not just the ones on your copy list, but all the files that are the temp files. The reason for this is that if your program crashed previously, or the machine lost power while playing, you would have a bunch of temp files left behind that never got cleaned up. By cleaning up all qualified files regardless, you ensure that after at least one successful play, the program has cleaned up after itself.

For this reason, it's very important to have either a special directory or a unique extension (such as ._$_) that you're pretty sure no one else will have. Having something like .TMP or .$$$ is pretty well recognized as representing a temp file, but having your own unique one, such as ._$_, helps ensure you don't get mixed in with someone else's temp files.

Since the copying takes time, it's best to try and be a little smart about it and preload the files during a quiet time. One way to do so is to expand on the transfer function previously described, so that it allows preloading before actual usage and so that it can start a preload and then transfer the file in small increments (say somewhere between 4KB and 32KB) when requested, such as when you're idle. Thus you can ensure that the file works its way over without requiring everything else to stop and wait for it. Then, when you're ready to use it, it should be there. If you need to use it before it's finished transferring, have it set up so that upon an open request, the file automatically completes its transfer right then and there.

But It's Still Slow!

You try and you try, but it's still not getting faster. Well, there's one thing left to try: Reduce the amount of stuff you're transferring—not so much the number of files, but the *size* of those files. Make them smaller.

Ever since people began releasing software on floppies, they've been compressing the hell out of them just to make everything fit. Once CD-ROMs became available, everyone breathed a collective sigh. No more compression necessary, right? These things hold well over 600MB of data.

Think again.

Ironically, with a 600MB capacity, it is actually as important as ever to compress your data. It used to be necessary because of the limited space of the floppies, but now it's necessary because of the awful speed of the CD-ROM drives. For the sake of this discussion, let's pretend that a 400KB file takes 1 second to either load or transfer from the CD-ROM drive. If you can compress this file to only half it's size, then it will only take a half second. If you can get it down to 100KB, you're down to a quarter second, and if you can get it down to 50KB (which is possible, if it's text), then your delay time is a mere 1/8 second.

So just when we thought we were done with compression once and for all, we find it's back—big, ugly, and ready to ruin our day.

There are lots of compression techniques, and an analysis of the different kinds could be a book unto itself. You will probably find yourself using one or more of these techniques. Which one you use will depend on a lot of things: whether you need quick decode, or you need it integrated, or you need to decrypt at the same time you compress, or you want a program that's royalty-free, along with what kind of data you'll be using it on.

Text happens to compress very well, particularly with most of the popular general compressors. There are compressors tailored to certain kinds of data (say, images), and there are lossy and lossless compression techniques. A lossy technique is one that doesn't expand back to its original size and quality, having dropped non-critical information along the way in an effort to make things smaller. These methods are used for video, imaging, and sometimes audio. For things such as text, or executable code (.DLL's, and so on), you would want to use a lossless method—one that expands back to being a byte-for-byte duplicate of the original. The one drawback with these methods is that they don't typically achieve the same ratios of compression that a lossy method might. On the other hand, you might want to use them for things where you can't afford to lose information or quality. (The lossy ones take a toll on quality, sometimes).

Audio, unfortunately, is not an easy thing to compress, particularly if you want to retain the original quality via a lossless technique. There is one way to improve your results (I've managed up to a 40 percent compression with this method), but you'll need to make changes to the decompression software's source code. You can do this technique without changing the decompression source code, but then you effectively turn decompression into a two-step process, negating any time savings.

Delta Pre-Compression

To get a little extra compression out of your audio, first you need to understand a little about how wave files carry their data. Following the file header is the waveform data. Wave files work on a center line of 0x80 (midway between 0 and 0xFF). Wave file data composed of nothing but 0x80's is nothing but silence.

Unlike images, which vary their entries widely (0x14 one moment, 0xC0 the next), most audio tends to move up and down gradually. Delta pre-compression works particularly well with audio because of this gradual movement characteristic.

For example, the entries may run (in hex): 82 84 84 87 8A 88 8B 8D 8A 8C 8D. This, of course, represents a tiny sample, since waveform data consumes at a minimum some 11,000 bytes per second of single-channel sound. You will notice, though, that although the numbers differ widely (there are only three duplicates), the differences *between* the numbers does not vary so much. That is, if you were to map out the differences, you would see the following: 82 +2 +0 +3 +3 −2 +3 +2 −3 +2 +1. What we are charting here is not so much the data itself as the *movement* of the data. And the data tends to move in small increments, so instead of seeing 8As and 9Cs and E0s, we just see a whole bunch of +2s and +3s, and so on. With so much duplicate data it becomes much easier to compress to a smaller size.

Unfortunately, even with the set of compressible numbers reduced to a range most likely between −5 and +5, the total compression isn't tremendous. This is because the data still tends to change very often; that is, we don't typically have long runs of the same number, which would compress very well. Still, by using this technique (which I call Delta Pre-Compression), you can realize up to 40 percent compression, whereas you might have achieved only 15 percent or 20 percent before. Note, though, that it varies greatly with the audio samples, and it might not make much of an improvement on your compression at all.

I used to create precompressed files (using this technique) and then compress *those*. At decompression time, though, I'd do it all in one pass (both decompressing and recreating the data) within the decompression section of the program.

You could precompress just the wave-file data (skipping the header), but the header's so small, typically, that there's no reason. So, to precompress is very simple. Here's some pseudocode:

```
signed char difference

lastByte =0                                    // Assume we're starting from zero
while (not end of file)                        // Do the whole file
  thisByte =read(from file, single byte) // Read a single byte
  difference =thisByte - lastByte         // How does it differ?
  write(to output file, difference)       // Write out the difference
  lastByte =thisByte                            // This becomes the new last
byte for next time.
end {while}
```

Obviously you'd want to jazz it up and perhaps work from a memory buffer (instead of direct-to-file), but that's the essence of it.

To un-precompress is just the reverse—although, as mentioned, I tend to weave this in with the standard decompression code itself, so I don't find myself making a time-consuming second pass through the file. I want that file to decompress faster than I can snap my fingers.

```
Pseudocode to un-pre-compress:
  lastByte =0                                    // This is our starting point
  while (not end of file)                        // Do the whole file
    difference =read(from file, single byte) // See what the new difference is
    thisByte =lastByte + difference          // Combine it to get the current value
    write(to output file, thisByte)          // Write it out
    lastByte =thisByte                          // This becomes the starting point
                                                    for next time.

  end {while}
```

The moral of this example is that when playing your game from CD-ROM, every little bit counts (literally).

Speaking of every little bit, one easy target for speed-up is the wave files themselves. We were just talking about precompressing them, but if they're smaller to begin with, they move a lot faster. A seductive aspect of CD-ROMs is their storage capacity, and you might be tempted to think that with effectively unlimited storage capacity (as far as your game is concerned), you can use 44kHz, dual-channel audio wave files. Ha! Put this temptation aside.

When it comes to creating .WAV files for your CD-ROM game, you can no more afford 44kHz stereo now than you could before. 44kHz stereo is a pig. Try 11kHz mono. It's *eight times* smaller. That's eight times *fewer bytes* and eight times *faster* to transfer.

If you want to put 44kHz stereo direct on the CD-ROM and play directly from there, you can; but it means you can't have any other disk activity going on at the same time. However, if you can take a 44kHz master (or preferably, a DAT master) and reduce it to a decent-quality 11kHz mono, you'll be better off. This works particularly well with voice.

Not to impede the march of progress or anything, but CD-ROM stereo quality may not be something you can afford to put into your game, if you find it slowing down your application. Most users will be hard-pressed to appreciate the difference. Most assuredly, they will appreciate speed and performance before they will appreciate the difference between 11kHz and 44kHz.

> An alternative to waveform music is MIDI. Its benefits are its small size and, thus, quick transferability. When playing MIDI in Windows, however, it is necessary to keep up with the MIDI messages. I've fixed a number of apps that played fine on the hard disk only to suddenly experience "hung notes" when the apps are run from a CD-ROM.

"Hung notes" are notes that pause, playing for seconds on end until finally the music continues. Invariably the pause occurs at a time that the program goes to load something from CD-ROM. Thus, it's important that while transferring files or decompressing, you make sure you keep up with the MIDI messages so as to refresh when necessary.

Pirates, Ahoy!

Just because your program is on CD-ROM, is it safe from piracy? Wouldn't you like some measure of protection? Sometimes a game may have only 5MB or 10MB worth of data, but it is released on CD-ROM mainly because it's cheaper (not to mention more convenient for the user). In such cases, releasing a game on CD-ROM is not strictly necessary, since it could probably fit onto a few floppies.

There are a couple of ways to discourage pirating a CD-ROM title. The first is to insist that the drive it executes from, or references, is a true CD-ROM drive. Listing 2.1 is one way to do it.

Listing 2.1. Testing if a drive is a CD-ROM drive.

```
#include <windows.h>
#include <dos.h>

BOOL isCDROM(char whichDrive)
// Identifies whether or not a particular drive is a CD-ROM drive. Takes the drive
letter as a parameter.
```

continues

Listing 2.1. continued

```
{
     union REGS regs;

     whichDrive =whichDrive - 'A';
     regs.x.ax =0x1500;
     regx.x.bx =0;
     int86( 0x2F, &regs, &regs );
     if (!regs.x.bx)
        return (FALSE)
     ;
     regs.x.ax =0x150B;
     regs.x.cx =whichDrive;
     int86( 0x2F, &regs, &regs );
     if (!regs.x.ax)
         return(FALSE)
     ;
             return(TRUE);
} /* is cdrom */
```

```
Example:    if (isCDROM('D') )              // Then it's a CD-ROM drive!
```

This makes a call to MSCDEX, the CD-ROM driver. It'll work if the CD-ROM driver supports MSCDEX calls (which it should). It'll also work to the extent that no one is trying to bypass the system. It wouldn't be too hard to write a TSR that intercepted int 2Fh function 15h and lied that a particular drive (a hard drive) was a CD-ROM.

The second method, admirable in intent, but a failure in practice, is to test whether the drive has removable media and is write-protected. This would describe a CD-ROM, but it could also describe certain properly set-up removable systems such as SyQuest or Bernoulli.

The third method would be to create a certain volume label on the CD-ROM disk and require that it be there, but too many pirates are knowledgeable about that sort of thing nowadays, making it hard to keep people from copying your program to, say, a removable SyQuest.

The fourth and final method, which to my mind is the only alternative to the first, and probably the safest, is to simply require a certain file of a certain name and size to be present. That is, the program will only play if a particular 80MB file is present. This is a simple but effective barrier to piracy, and my personal feeling is that if someone wants to sacrifice upwards of a 100MB of disk space just to have the program, then they're welcome to it. Nothing says the file needs be 80MB, either—it could be 200MB. I'm just trying to find a size small enough to work with but large enough to be discouraging.

In summation, the four methods to discourage piracy are:

- Make sure the original CD-ROM is present, and in an actual CD-ROM drive. You run the risk, however, of being on some CD-ROM drive that—for some reason—isn't recognized, and refuses to play.

- Make sure the drive is write-protected and removable. This has a lot of workarounds, though, and isn't very secure.

- Require a certain volume label on the CD-ROM. This isn't as secret a technique as it used to be, and is easily defeated, however.

- Simply require a certain huge file (80MB to 200MB) to be present. Chances are that nobody is going to want to waste that much of their own space to pirate your work. This method works pretty well and is totally save from "false negatives" (that is, refusing to play when it should).

For testing on the hard disk, though, you could have an override (a command-line option, an environment variable, a secret file) that enables you to skip the check for the required file. This way, you won't find *your* hard disk unduly occupied by unwanted extra bytes during your period of program development.

Summary

When all is said and done, the CD-ROM game developer must test, test, and test again on a CD-ROM. CD-ROM has a lot to offer, in terms of its affordability, compact size, and huge capacity, but it is a loser in the speed department. At the time of this writing, quad-speed drives were starting to become more commonplace, but there's still a tremendous base of double-speed drives out there (and probably a few singles, too). Since we're typically obligated to target the least common denominator in machine capability, this means learning to write for a double-speed drive. If your development machine is a souped-up, quad-speeder, make sure you have access to a slower, less capable machine to test on.

Also, make sure you keep all files as small as possible, and always design your program with an awareness of when it'll need to go to the CD-ROM and how you can minimize the impact of that transfer.

Coding Your Game

P A **2** R T

SuperVGA

by Wayne Russell

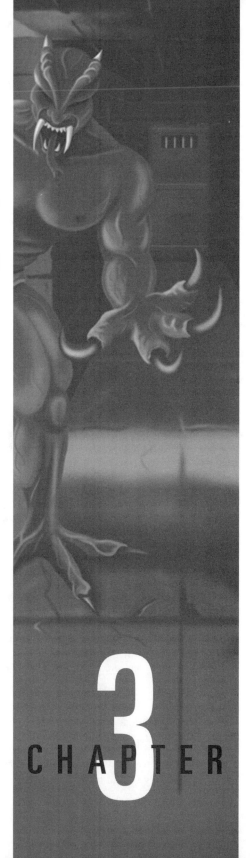

3

CHAPTER

Until recently, almost all games developed for PC hardware were written to use one of the low-resolution, 256-color, VGA modes—usually mode 13h, but sometimes the more exotic Mode X (DOOM, for instance).

In the last year or so, game developers have begun to take advantage of SVGA (SuperVGA) cards for certain types of games. We now see games with 256-color graphics at resolutions of 640×480, and few would dispute the fact that this is a good thing.

This chapter introduces the subject of SuperVGA, and covers its use in the specific context of game development. SVGA is a *big* topic, and most readers of this book will have neither the time nor the inclination to survey every aspect, even if that were possible (which it isn't, unless I were to take over the entire book). I have concentrated on those SVGA modes and facilities that are currently viable for mass-market leisure software—practically speaking, this means the 640×480 and 800×600 256-color modes that are available with most modern SVGA cards. On the same principle, I have steered away from "extra" facilities that are only available on newer or high-end cards (such as separate read and write banks, and finer granularity than 64KB).

This coverage of SVGA is practical rather than exhaustive. The aim is to enable you to write a game that utilizes a common SVGA mode, *not* to tell you everything there is to know about every SuperVGA card.

Working with Off-Screen Buffers

The technique of double-buffering by using a buffer in main memory is fairly widespread, even with ordinary VGA display systems. The principle is simple enough—you allocate a block of memory and direct all your screen update code into that block of memory. Then, when everything is ready, you copy the whole lot to the screen in one go.

With SVGA, the use of buffers in main memory is pretty much mandatory, because you don't know whether your user's SVGA card will support multiple video pages. The main problem with this is the sheer amount of memory required for the buffer—for the examples in this chapter, using 640×480 resolution, a 300KB buffer is required. If you are using a 16-bit real-mode compiler, that's more than half of the total memory you are likely to have available!

For this reason, the 16-bit examples in this chapter (which were written using Turbo C version 3.0) utilize MS memory for storing the screen buffer. The XMS utilities are included on the CD, and they work. Beyond that, I don't propose to go into the hows and whys of XMS—the interface to a C program is just about as simple as it could be, and the example code demonstrates this. The only thing to be aware of is that you must load HIMEM.SYS (or an equivalent), and you must have more than 1MB of memory.

For the 32-bit examples (which were written with Watcom C version 10.0), the location of the buffer is obviously not an issue—we just allocate the memory with an ordinary `malloc()` and copy to and from it using the ordinary techniques.

SuperVGA in Principle

This section provides an overview of the tenets of 256-color SVGA. It assumes a basic understanding of how ordinary mode 13h VGA (320×200) works for mode selection and direct memory access.

For all their differences and individual peculiarities, all SVGA cards behave similarly for most operations, and they all have a standard *modus operandi*. To start with, the good news is that you program SVGA in much the same way that you program low-resolution VGA, as follows:

1. The mode is selected with BIOS interrupt 10h

2. Video memory can be directly manipulated by writing to the 64KB page at address A000h

3. Color palettes work the same way that they do in VGA mode 13h

The only real difference between a 256-color SVGA mode and VGA mode 13h is one of memory requirement. With a resolution of only 320×200, the whole screen fits nicely into one 64KB segment, ideal for a DOS-based machine. At 640×480, though, you need 300KB; at 800×600, you need about 470KB; at 1024×768, heaven forbid, you need 768KB.

This, incidentally, is the main reason so few games, even today, use SuperVGA—at 640×480, you are dealing with nearly five times the amount of data required for VGA mode 13h. Updating this memory takes something in the order of five times the amount of time required for VGA mode 13h. So, on a 486/25 with a Trident 8900 SVGA card, the whole screen can only be refreshed about six times per second—and that's when the machine is doing nothing but refreshing the screen. This problem immediately rules out those game genres that involve a lot of on-screen activity—or rather, those games that require the entire screen to be refreshed on a frequent basis. The games that work well under SVGA are those that have only small animations going on. A good example is Sim City 2000, where only the occasional train or airplane is moving. A game such as Populous would also translate well to SVGA, because the moving characters are all tiny, and so the amount of actual screen updating required is fairly small.

So, there's a lot of memory to be moved around. Sadly, on top of this operational difficulty, there's a programming complication as well. As you have probably come to understand, programming the PC often seems to be more difficult than it need be, and here we have a case in point.

Under DOS, you only have a 64KB window on your video memory—this is the page that starts at A000h. It doesn't matter that you've got the latest accelerated video card with 2MB on-board—under DOS (even 32-bit Extended DOS), you've got a 64KB window, and it starts at A000h. The SVGA card manufacturers get around this by enabling you to update your screen in 64KB *pages*. (The terms *bank* and *window* are also used.) So, writing a full SVGA screen works like this:

1. Set the mode
2. Write the first 64KB, by hitting the memory at A000h directly
3. Program the SVGA card to move onto the next page
4. Move to the next 64KB chunk
5. Repeat steps 2 through 4 until the entire screen is refreshed

Updating the entire screen, therefore, is pretty simple.

It gets more tricky when you need to update part of the screen, however. As an example, let's imagine we are working with a 640×480 resolution SVGA screen. You don't need to be a mathematician to realize that 65536 (64KB) does not divide evenly by 640; what this means is that page changes usually occur *in the middle of a line*. This doesn't sound too terrible at first, but it makes the task of keeping screen pointers and buffer pointers aligned rather complicated. It's a terribly messy way of doing things, to be quite frank, but it's something you must live with if you want to program SuperVGA.

Other than that one complexity, processing an SVGA screen directly is similar to processing a VGA screen directly. The perception that SuperVGA is complicated comes from the fact that no two cards use the same technique for mode selection or swapping pages. This aspect of SuperVGA programming is undoubtedly a real pain, but it is rapidly becoming yesterday's problem—most SVGA cards are now compliant with the VESA VBE standard. The bulk of this chapter deals with VESA, but first we cover the specifics of programming SVGA directly, simply to demonstrate how similarly the cards behave (for the most part).

Selecting an SVGA Mode

Selecting an SVGA mode is extremely easy; it is no more difficult than selecting any other mode. The only catch is that the identifier for the mode you want differs from card to card. This is more an inconvenience than a real difficulty.

The video mode is set with a call to BIOS interrupt 10h, specifying a service of 0 in register AH and the desired mode number in register AL. This is true regardless of whether you are setting a text mode, an ordinary graphics mode or an SVGA mode. The following C functions will set a Trident SuperVGA card into 640×480×256 mode:

```
void SetTridentSVGA16(void)        /* 16 bit function - Turbo C */
{

union REGS r;

r.h.ah = 0;                /* AH=0, Set Video Mode */
r.h.al = 0x5d;             /* AL=5Dh, 640x480x256, for a Trident card */
```

```
int86(0x10, &r, &r);        /* Interrupt 10h, Video Services */

}


void SetTridentSVGA32(void)      /* 32 bit function - Watcom C */
{

union REGS r;

r.w.ax = 0x005d;      /* AH=0, Set Video Mode,
        AL=5Dh, 640x480x256, for a Trident card */
int386(0x10, &r, &r);       /* Interrupt 10h, Video Services */

}
```

Changing these functions to set different cards or different modes is as simple as changing the value we place into the AL register. Information about which modes your specific card supports, and what numbers you need to specify, is readily available from the manufacturer. Alternatively, there is a wealth of this kind of information floating about on BBSs, CompuServe and all over the Internet.

One such reference source is included on the CD which accompanies this book. VGADOC3, which is copyrighted Freeware from Finn Thoegersen, is extremely comprehensive, and covers cards that you've never even heard of. However, be warned—it is extremely technical, and useful only as a reference.

Vendor Contact Information

ATI Technologies Incorporated	1-905-882-2626
Diamond Computer Systems Inc.	1-408-736-2000
Orchid Technologies	1-510-683-0300
Trident Microsystems Incorporated	1-415-691-9211
Tseng Laboratories Incorporated	1-215-968-0502

Switching Pages

The differences between SVGA cards for mode selection are pretty trivial and only cause us a problem in that we might not have the documentation for every SVGA card out there. The page-switching techniques adopted by the different cards are, however, more of a problem.

The code required to switch pages is always a bit weird, regardless of the card involved. In fact, if you are a C programmer and never venture into Assembler, the code might make no sense at all. This shouldn't put you off, though—the code only needs to be written once, then you can put it in a standard library and forget about it forever.

These C functions switch a Trident SVGA card to a specific page:

```
void SetTridentPage16(char page)  /* 16-bit function - Turbo C */
{
int j, k;

k = page;

disable();
outp(0x03ce, 0x06);
j = inp(0x03cf);
outport(0x03ce, ((j ¦ 0x04) << 8) ¦ 0x0006);
outp(0x03c4, 0x0b);
j = inp(0x03c5);
outport(0x03c4, ((k ^ 0x02) << 8) ¦ 0x000e);
enable();

return(0);
}



void SetTridentPage32(char page)  /* 32-bit function - Watcom C */
{
short int j, k;

k = page;

_disable();
outp(0x03ce, 0x06);
j = inp(0x03cf);
outpw(0x03ce, ((j ¦ 0x04) << 8) ¦ 0x0006);
outp(0x03c4, 0x0b);
j = inp(0x03c5);
outpw(0x03c4, ((k ^ 0x02) << 8) ¦ 0x000e);
_enable();
}
```

Now, *why* you are required to involve yourself with such arcane code to switch a page on a Trident card, I don't know. Some cards are easier to program, some harder, some very similar. The thing to remember is that you only need to write this stuff once—then, you just use it and forget about it.

Most current games that utilize SVGA will attempt to "guess" at the particular card in your machine, and ask you for confirmation. Auto-detecting a SuperVGA card is, at best, an inexact science—if you intend providing direct support for SVGA cards in your game, you should at least enable the user to override any auto-detection you may have implemented.

You will need to contact the manufacturer for details of the page switching strategy used by your card, or hunt around online for it as described previously. One word of warning: This kind of information is often barely decipherable as English, and Assembler skills are pretty much needed just to understand what's being said.

The VESA Video BIOS Extension

As we have established, SVGA programming is often a pain in the technical backside; moreover, no matter how much effort you go to, you can never guarantee that your program supports *every* SVGA card. And, let's face it, *you* wouldn't be too happy if you bought a game that specified "SVGA, 512KB required" which then sullenly refused to work on your computer because you happen to own a non-standard 512KB SVGA card.

What we need is a standard SVGA card, and the good news is that somebody recognized this a long time ago. VESA is the Video Electronics Standards Association, a consortium of hardware manufacturers that exists to promote standards amongst its members. As long ago as 1989, it proposed a standard programmers' interface to SuperVGA. Now, six years later, we are at a point where almost all new computers are supplied with VESA-compliant SVGA cards. In another year or so, you'll be able to forget about the SVGA incompatibilities altogether.

The point of the Video BIOS Extension (the VESA VBE, as it is often known, or more commonly just *VESA*) is to give people like you and me a single, standard way to write programs that use SuperVGA modes. If you write a program that uses the VESA standard, you can confidently predict that your game will work on *any* VESA-compliant SVGA system with sufficient memory, much as you can guarantee that your mode 13h game will work on any VGA system.

VESA provides for a standard way to select a mode, and—more importantly—a standard way to switch pages. It allows for a ton of other stuff as well, but for our purposes these two are enough.

Mode selection under VESA is accomplished in a very similar way to mode selection in native modes. You use interrupt 10h, service 4F02h, passing the required mode number in BX. A list of common VESA modes is given in the section titled "A Simple PCX Viewer," later in this chapter.

Page switching under VESA—I'm sorry to report—is no simpler than it is for the various cards' "native" modes. The process is as follows:

1. You call a VESA interrupt to establish the available modes
2. You call another VESA interrupt to query/set up one of those modes
3. VESA provides you with a pointer to a function that will handle the page switching
4. When you want to switch pages, you call that function

This is easy enough, but there are two pitfalls: You need to get involved with Assembler, and converting to 32-bit protected mode is difficult. This is discussed in more detail in the section titled "A 32-Bit PCX Viewer," later in this chapter.

VESA cards differ from other SVGA cards in that they are able to provide the programmer with information about themselves. Much of the information available is of no direct use to us, because we are not too bothered here about all the fancy things that the latest cards can do. However, it is useful to know what information VESA cards provide about themselves. Listing 3.1 is a small program that derives and displays some basic VESA information. Tables 3.1 and 3.2 show sample output from this program on my two computers—one has a rather slow, old-fashioned Trident card, and the other is magnificently equipped with the latest Diamond Stealth card. As you can see, the VESA information returned is in the same format, underlining the fact that these two very different cards can be treated as identical, for programming purposes. Long live standards, say I.

Listing 3.1. A program to display information about your VESA card.

```
/************************
 *   VESAINFO.C  -  Display basic VESA information
 *
 *   This program has been tested with Borland Turbo C and
 *   16-bit Watcom C - it should compile without change under
 *   most 16-bit compilers.
 ************************/

/*   Basic VESA structures   */

typedef struct {
    char Signature[4];
    unsigned short int Version;
    char *OEMName;/* This is a FAR pointer - use Large model! */
    unsigned char Capabilities[4];
    unsigned short int *VideoMode;
    short int VideoMem;
    char dummy[238];                        /*Pad to 256 bytes */
    } VESAINFO;

typedef struct {
    unsigned short int ModeAttr;
    unsigned char WinAAttr;
    unsigned char WinBAttr;
    unsigned short int Granularity;
    unsigned short int WinSize;
    unsigned short int WinASegment;
    unsigned short int WinBSegment;
    unsigned short int (*PageSwitchFunction)();
    unsigned short int BytesPerScanLine;

    /*  The following info is optional - generally only provided for "weird" modes   */
```

```
       unsigned int XResolution;
       unsigned int YResolution;
       unsigned char XCharSize;
       unsigned char YCharSize;
       unsigned char NumberOfPlanes;
       unsigned char BitsPerPixel;
       unsigned char NumberOfBanks;
       unsigned char MemoryModel;
       unsigned char BankSize;
       char dummy[227];                  /*Pad to 256 bytes */
       } VESAMODEINFO;


int VESA_GetInfo(VESAINFO *);
int VESA_GetModeInfo(int, VESAMODEINFO *);

#include <stdio.h>

#ifdef __WATCOMC__
   #include <i86.h>
#else
   #include <dos.h>
#endif

main()
{

int j;

VESAINFO VESAInfo;
VESAMODEINFO VESAModeInfo;

VESA_GetInfo( &VESAInfo );

printf("Signature:       ");
for (j=0; j<4; j++)
   printf("%c", VESAInfo.Signature[j]);

printf("\nVESA Version:  %4X\n", VESAInfo.Version);
printf("Manufacturer:   %s\n", VESAInfo.OEMName);

printf("Capabilities:    ");
for (j=0; j<4; j++)
   printf("%c", VESAInfo.Capabilities[j]);

printf("\nVideo Memory:  %4dK", VESAInfo.VideoMem * 64);

printf("\nSupported Modes:\n");

while (*VESAInfo.VideoMode != 0xFFFF)
   {
   printf("%4X      ", *VESAInfo.VideoMode);
   VESA_GetModeInfo( *VESAInfo.VideoMode++, &VESAModeInfo);
   printf("Granularity: %2d    ", VESAModeInfo.Granularity);
   printf("Window Size: %3d    ", VESAModeInfo.WinSize);
   printf("Bytes Per Line:  %4d\n", VESAModeInfo.BytesPerScanLine);
   }
```

continues

Listing 3.1. continued

```
return;
}


int VESA_GetInfo(VESAINFO *Buffer)
{

union REGS r;
struct SREGS sr;

r.x.ax = 0x4F00;
sr.es = FP_SEG(Buffer);
r.x.di = FP_OFF(Buffer);

int86x(0x10, &r, &r, &sr);

if (r.h.al == 0x4F)
   return(0);
else
   return(-1);

}


int VESA_GetModeInfo( int Mode, VESAMODEINFO *Buffer )
{

union REGS r;
struct SREGS sr;

r.x.ax = 0x4F01;
r.x.cx = Mode;
sr.es = FP_SEG(Buffer);
r.x.di = FP_OFF(Buffer);

int86x(0x10, &r, &r, &sr);

if (r.h.al == 0x4F)
   return(0);
else
   return(1);

}
```

Table 3.1. Sample output from VESAINFO—Trident card.

C:\GURUS>vesainfo

Signature: VESA

VESA Version: 102

Manufacturer: Copyright 1988-1991 TRIDENT MICROSYSTEMS INC.

Capabilities:

Video Memory: 512KB

Supported Modes:

170	Granularity: 64	Window Size: 64	Bytes Per Line: 1024
171	Granularity: 64	Window Size: 64	Bytes Per Line: 1024
100	Granularity: 64	Window Size: 64	Bytes Per Line: 640
101	Granularity: 64	Window Size: 64	Bytes Per Line: 640
103	Granularity: 64	Window Size: 64	Bytes Per Line: 800
104	Granularity: 64	Window Size: 64	Bytes Per Line: 128
102	Granularity: 64	Window Size: 64	Bytes Per Line: 100
6A	Granularity: 64	Window Size: 64	Bytes Per Line: 100
108	Granularity: 64	Window Size: 64	Bytes Per Line: 160
109	Granularity: 64	Window Size: 64	Bytes Per Line: 264
10A	Granularity: 64	Window Size: 64	Bytes Per Line: 264
10B	Granularity: 64	Window Size: 64	Bytes Per Line: 264
10C	Granularity: 64	Window Size: 64	Bytes Per Line: 264

C:\GURUS>

Table 3.2. Sample output from VESAINFO—Diamond Stealth card.

D:\GURUS>vesainfo

Signature: VESA

VESA Version: 102

Manufacturer: S3 Incorporated. Vision864

Capabilities:

Video Memory: 1024KB

Supported Modes:

101	Granularity: 64	Window Size: 64	Bytes Per Line: 640
102	Granularity: 64	Window Size: 64	Bytes Per Line: 100
103	Granularity: 64	Window Size: 64	Bytes Per Line: 800
104	Granularity: 64	Window Size: 64	Bytes Per Line: 128
105	Granularity: 64	Window Size: 64	Bytes Per Line: 1024
106	Granularity: 64	Window Size: 64	Bytes Per Line: 160

continues

Table 3.2. continued

107	Granularity: 64	Window Size: 64	Bytes Per Line: 1280
109	Granularity: 32	Window Size: 32	Bytes Per Line: 264
10A	Granularity: 32	Window Size: 32	Bytes Per Line: 264
110	Granularity: 64	Window Size: 64	Bytes Per Line: 1280
111	Granularity: 64	Window Size: 64	Bytes Per Line: 1280
112	Granularity: 64	Window Size: 64	Bytes Per Line: 2560
113	Granularity: 64	Window Size: 64	Bytes Per Line: 1600
114	Granularity: 64	Window Size: 64	Bytes Per Line: 1600
115	Granularity: 64	Window Size: 64	Bytes Per Line: 3200
D:\GURUS>			

Other than for mode selection and page switching, *all* SVGA cards—VESA or otherwise—can be programmed identically, as long as you stick to the features and facilities common to all of them. Speaking of which…

Granularity

As we have already discussed, it isn't possible to address a random single byte of SVGA display memory directly—first, you have to select the appropriate display page, then offset into that page by an appropriate amount.

This inconvenience has many parallels with the Segment:Offset memory arrangement of a real-mode program—before you can address a byte in "far" memory, you must first set the segment appropriately (though your C compiler usually handles much of this messing about on your behalf). And, you'll be horrified to learn, the similarities go still deeper.

When memory of any sort is directly byte-addressable, it is said to be *linear*, or *flat*. When memory is only addressable via a Chunk:Offset arrangement, it is said to be *granular*, and the size of the "chunk" is called the *granularity*. The main memory in real mode is paragraph-granular (one paragraph being 16 bytes). This means that it is impossible to address a given byte directly; you need a nearby paragraph number as well. The combination of the paragraph number and the offset value point to the actual byte, just as the combination of an SVGA page and an offset into that page point to the actual pixel.

You have probably guessed where this is leading us: While SVGA pages are always 64KB long, they are *not necessarily* 64KB granular. Some cards (Paradise is a manufacturer that springs to mind) provide SVGA modes that are 4KB granular; there are undoubtedly other manufacturers providing other cards that use other granularities. Now, it would be marvelous if every card offered, for instance, a 16-byte granularity—this would make our lives a lot easier in terms of arranging for page changing. As it is, smaller granularities than 64KB simply cause us a problem, because it's just one more inconsistency that we don't need.

As you will have noted from the output of the VESAINFO program, the standard VESA modes that interest us are 64KB granular (or, at least, they are on every VESA-compliant card I've seen—the official documentation does not state that this must be the case, but then official documentation is often pretty useless when it comes to real-life usage). The examples later in this chapter show you how to directly program non-VESA cards, but they assume 64KB granularity, so be wary—you will get some rather strange results with other granularities.

A Simple PCX Viewer

Listing 3.2 is a complete, self-contained program to view 256-color PCX images at the three normal SVGA resolutions (640×480, 800×600, and 1024×768). In the interests of limiting the code length, the program assumes that the file passed to it will be a valid PCX image, so you would be unwise to try "tricking" it. Clearly, this program is not going to win any awards for innovation, but it does demonstrate most of the VESA basics, and provides a set of interface functions to the VESA VBE that can be re-used in your own programs. Note that this program makes use of XMS memory, so if you want to change and recompile it, you will need to link in XMS.OBJ—this file is provided on the CD.

Listing 3.2. A 16-bit PCX viewer.

```
/*  VESA.C  -  Example 16-bit program to directly update VESA-
               compliant video systems. */

/********************************************************************
    This program will compile under Watcom and Turbo/Borland C, and (probably)
    under others (eg, MS) as well.  You MUST use Large Model.

    Turbo/Borland C users:
      You **MUST** use the '-r-' compile switch, or switch off Register
      Variables in the IDE.  The program will not run correctly with this
      optimisation in place.

    Watcom C users:
      You **MUST** switch off the "Expand functions in-line" optimisation if
      you are using the IDE (it is a default in the IDE, but not on the
      command-line compiler).  The program will not compile with this
      optimisation in place.
********************************************************************/

#include <stdlib.h>
#include <dos.h>
#include <stdio.h>
```

continues

Listing 3.2. continued

```c
#include <conio.h>
#include <string.h>

#ifdef __WATCOMC__
    #include <i86.h>
    #include <malloc.h>
#else
    #include <alloc.h>
#endif

 /*   Basic VESA structures  */

typedef struct {
    char Signature[4];
    unsigned short int Version;
    char *OEMName;/* This is a FAR pointer - use Large model! */
    unsigned char Capabilities[4];
    unsigned short int *VideoMode;
    short int VideoMem;
    char dummy[238];                         /*Pad to 256 bytes */
    } VESAINFO;

typedef struct {
    unsigned short int ModeAttr;
    unsigned char WinAAttr;
    unsigned char WinBAttr;
    unsigned short int Granularity;
    unsigned short int WinSize;
    unsigned short int WinASegment;
    unsigned short int WinBSegment;
    unsigned short int (*PageSwitchFunction)();
    unsigned short int BytesPerScanLine;

        /*  Not all VESA cards provide the following optional information  */
    unsigned int XResolution;
    unsigned int YResolution;
    unsigned char XCharSize;
    unsigned char YCharSize;
    unsigned char NumberOfPlanes;
    unsigned char BitsPerPixel;
    unsigned char NumberOfBanks;
    unsigned char MemoryModel;
    unsigned char BankSize;
    char dummy[227];                         /*Pad to 256 bytes */
    } VESAMODEINFO;


/*  Information block for XMS memory copies */

typedef struct {
        unsigned long int len;
        unsigned short int  src;
        unsigned long int soff;
        unsigned short int  dh;
```

```
            unsigned long int doff;
            } XMSBLOCK;


/* Function protoypes */


int cdecl XMS_Initialize(void);
int cdecl XMS_Allocate(int);
int cdecl XMS_Dealloc(int);
int cdecl XMS_Copy(void *);
void XMS_CopyToDos(char *, unsigned int, unsigned long, unsigned long);
void XMS_CopyFromDos(char *, unsigned int, unsigned long, unsigned long);

long int cdecl XMS_ConvertPtr(char far *ptr);

#ifdef __WATCOMC__
    #pragma aux XMS_CopyToDos   modify [si];
    #pragma aux XMS_CopyFromDos modify [si];
#endif


int VESA_SetMode(int);
int VESA_GetInfo(VESAINFO *);
int VESA_GetModeInfo(int, VESAMODEINFO *);
void VESA_SetPage(int, void *);

void SetVGAPalette(char *);
void RestoreTextMode(void);

typedef struct {
        char manufacturer;
        char version;
        char encoding;
        char BitsPerPixel;
        int x1, y1;
        int x2, y2;
        int hres;
        int vres;
        char palette[48];
        char reserved;
        char color_planes;
        int BytesPerLine;
        int PaletteType;
        char filler[58];
} PCXHEADER;

PCXHEADER Header;

int DWidth, DHeight;        // Displayed Height & Width

char palette[768];

main(int argc, char *argv[])
```

continues

Listing 3.2. continued

```
{

FILE *fh;
unsigned int Width, Height, ScreenMode, j;
int hXMS;                       // The handle on our block of XMS memory
char res, *Clr;

VESAINFO VESAInfo;
VESAMODEINFO VESAModeInfo;

if (argc != 2)
{
printf("\nUsage:  VESA16 {PCX file name}\n\n");
exit(0);
}

if ( (fh = fopen(argv[1], "rb")) == NULL)
{
printf("\nFile %s not found\n\n", argv[1]);
exit(0);
}

printf("Enter screen mode: (1=640x480, 2=800x600, 3=1024x768, 4=Exit)\n");
res = 0;
while (res < '1' || res >'4')
   res = getch();

switch (res)
   {
   case '1':
   ScreenMode = 0x0101;
   DHeight = 480;
   DWidth = 640;
   break;

   case '2':
   ScreenMode = 0x0103;
   DHeight = 600;
   DWidth = 800;
   break;

   case '3':
   ScreenMode = 0x0105;
   DHeight = 768;
   DWidth = 1024;
   break;

   case '4':
   exit(0);
   }


fread(&Header, sizeof(PCXHEADER), 1, fh);

Width = (Header.x2 - Header.x1) + 1;
Height = (Header.y2 - Header.y1) + 1;
```

```
/* Although we COULD unpack direct to the screen in this example, in real life
   we will need to use a buffer in main memory.  To allow large images, we'll
   use XMS memory in the 16-bit implementation - so let's make sure there's
   enough available!  */

if (XMS_Initialise() == -1)
{
printf("\nNo XMS driver found - is HIMEM.SYS loaded?\n\n");
exit(0);
}

hXMS = XMS_Allocate( (int) ( ( (long)DWidth * DHeight) / 1024) );

if (hXMS == 0 || hXMS == -1)
{
printf("\nCould not allocate %3dK of XMS memory\n\n",
            (int) ( ( (long)Width * Height) / 1024) );
exit(0);
}

/* Clear the memory out, in case we're displaying, eg., a 640x480 picture
   at 1024x768 - this will stop garbage appearing on screen.  */

Clr = malloc(DWidth);
memset(Clr, 0, DWidth);
for (j=0; j<DHeight; j++)
    XMS_CopyFromDos(Clr, hXMS, (long)DWidth, (long)DWidth*(long)j);

/* OK, let's see if the card is capable of supporting this resolution */

if (VESA_SetMode(ScreenMode) != 0)
{
printf("\nYour display card is not VESA-compliant, or its VESA implementation\n");
printf("does not support a resolution of %4dx%3dx256 colors - try a lower
➥resolution\n\n",
DWidth, DHeight);
exit(0);
}


/* OK, we have a VESA card that can support the resolution */

VESA_GetInfo( &VESAInfo );
VESA_GetModeInfo( ScreenMode, &VESAModeInfo );


/*  OK, everything is in order - unpack the PCX image  */

UnpackPCX(fh, hXMS, Width, Height);

/*  Display the image  */

VESA_UpdateScreen(&VESAModeInfo, hXMS, DWidth, DHeight);
```

continues

Listing 3.2. continued

```
getch();
RestoreTextMode();
XMS_Dealloc(hXMS);      // This is very important!!

return(0);
}


UnpackPCX(FILE *fh, int hXMS, unsigned int Width,
                        unsigned int Height)
{

/*  Note that this is NOT a properly robust PCX reader - it's for the purposes of
this example only, and it makes a lot of assumptions, so it's easy to fool  */

char *wbuf, *wptr;
long int Off;
int j, k;
unsigned char c, l;
int WHeight;

/* Read and set the palette */
fseek(fh, -768L, SEEK_END);
fread(palette, 768, 1, fh);
SetVGAPalette(palette);

/* Reposition to the start of the image data, and continue */
fseek(fh, sizeof(PCXHEADER), SEEK_SET);

wbuf = malloc(Width);
Off = 0L;

if (DHeight > Height)
   WHeight = Height;
else
   WHeight = DHeight;

for (j=0; j<WHeight; j++)
{
wptr = wbuf;
for (k=0; k<Width;)
{
c = fgetc(fh);
if (c > 191)
{
l = c - 192;
c = fgetc(fh);
memset(wptr, c, l);
wptr += l;
k += l;
}
else
{
*wptr = c;
wptr++;   k++;
}
```

```
}
if (DWidth >= Width)
  XMS_CopyFromDos(wbuf, hXMS, (long)Width, Off);
else
   XMS_CopyFromDos(wbuf, hXMS, (long)DWidth, Off);

Off += DWidth;
}

/*  The above loop decompresses each scan line into a working buffer (wbuf),
    and copies it up into the XMS area after each line has been "un-crunched"
*/

free(wbuf);

return;
}

VESA_UpdateScreen(VESAMODEINFO *ModeInfo,
 int hXMS, int Width, int Height)
{

unsigned long int work1, work2, Off=0L;
unsigned int NoOfPages, LastPage;
int j;

/* Before we start, work out how many pages are required, and how many bytes
are needed in the last page.  */

work1 = (long)Width * Height;
NoOfPages = (int) (work1 / 65536L);

work2 = (long)NoOfPages * 65536L;
LastPage = (int) (work1 - work2);

/*  OK, now just update the screen  */
for (j = 0; j < NoOfPages; j++)
{
VESA_SetPage(j, ModeInfo->PageSwitchFunction);
XMS_CopyToDos( MK_FP(0xA000, 0), hXMS, 65536L, Off);
Off += 65536L;
}

if (LastPage != 0)
{
VESA_SetPage(j, ModeInfo->PageSwitchFunction);
XMS_CopyToDos( MK_FP(0xA000, 0), hXMS, (long)LastPage, Off);
}

return;
}

int VESA_SetMode(int Mode)
{

union REGS r;
```

continues

Listing 3.2. continued

```c
r.h.ah = 0x4F;
r.h.al = 2;
r.x.bx = Mode;

int86(0x10, &r, &r);


/*  Note - it's not possible to simply return AX (or AH), because AL will
    contain 4Fh after a successful call... */

if (r.h.ah == 0)
return(0);
else
return(1);

}

int VESA_GetInfo(VESAINFO *Buffer)
{

union REGS r;
struct SREGS sr;

r.x.ax = 0x4F00;
sr.es = FP_SEG(Buffer);
r.x.di = FP_OFF(Buffer);

int86x(0x10, &r, &r, &sr);

if (r.h.al == 0x4F)
return(0);
else
return(-1);

}


int VESA_GetModeInfo( int Mode, VESAMODEINFO *Buffer )
{

union REGS r;
struct SREGS sr;

r.x.ax = 0x4F01;
r.x.cx = Mode;
sr.es = FP_SEG(Buffer);
r.x.di = FP_OFF(Buffer);

int86x(0x10, &r, &r, &sr);

if (r.h.al == 0x4F)
return(0);
else
return(1);

}
```

```c
void VESA_SetPage(int Page, void *FunctionPointer)
{

/* Sorry - this function has to be in assembler...  */

#ifdef __WATCOMC__

    void AsmSetPage(void);

    #pragma aux AsmSetPage =     \
    "xor bx,bx"                  \
    "mov dx, Page"               \
    "call [FunctionPointer]";

    AsmSetPage();

#else

    asm {
        xor bx, bx;
        mov dx, Page;
        call [FunctionPointer];
        }

#endif

}

void XMS_CopyToDos(char *DosPtr, unsigned int hXMS, unsigned long Length,
                            unsigned long Off)
{

XMSBLOCK x;

x.len  = Length;
x.src  = hXMS;
x.soff = Off;
x.dh   = 0;                      //  An XMS handle of 0 means DOS memory
x.doff = XMS_ConvertPtr(DosPtr);

XMS_Copy(&x);

}

void XMS_CopyFromDos(char *DosPtr, unsigned int hXMS, unsigned long Length,
                            unsigned long Off)
{

XMSBLOCK x;

x.len  = Length;
x.src  = 0;                      //  An XMS handle of 0 means DOS memory
x.soff = XMS_ConvertPtr(DosPtr);
```

continues

Listing 3.2. continued

```
x.dh   = hXMS;
x.doff = Off;

XMS_Copy(&x);

}

void SetVGAPalette(char *Palette)
{

/* This function sets the palette (will work on any VGA or SVGA card) by
   programming the card directly.  There IS a BIOS function to do it, but
   doing it directly is both quicker and - for protected mode programs - more
   straightforward.  Note that Turbo C reports the outp() lines as having no
   effect - I don't know why it does this (you just try taking 'em away!)   */

short int i;
char far *p;

for (i=0; i<768; i++)
    Palette[i] = Palette[i] >> 2;

p = Palette;

outp(0x3c6, 0xff);
for (i=0; i<=255; i++)
    {
    outp(0x3c8, i);
    outp(0x3c9, *p++);
    outp(0x3c9, *p++);
    outp(0x3c9, *p++);
    }

return;

}


void RestoreTextMode()
{
    union REGS r;
    r.h.al = 0x03;                    /* 16-color VGA text mode */
    r.h.ah = 0x00;                    /* Set graphics mode */
    int86(0x10, &r, &r);

}
```

The bulk of this program is in "ancillary" code that probably tells you little you didn't already know. The interesting bits are those functions that start VESA_xxxx. The low-level interface functions—VESA_SetMode(), VESA_GetInfo(), VESA_GetModeInfo(), and VESA_SetPage()—make rather peculiar reading in C, because the interface would normally be in Assembler. I chose to implement it in C simply because many people are wary of Assembler, and not everyone has a separate Assembler in their toolkit. Anyway, the job can be equally well done in C (for the most part). If you have never directly generated interrupts by using int86() and a REGS block in C, most introductory books to the language cover it.

The first three interface functions look very similar, because they are all calling interrupt 10h. This is the Video Services BIOS interrupt, and you have doubtless used it in the past. The VESA VBE is accessed by requesting service 4Fh in AX, and the specific task you would like it to perform in AL. The AL values that we are interested in here are:

■ Get information about the card, into a block of type VESAINFO (see Table 3.3)

■ Get information about a mode, into a block of type VESAMODEINFO—most of this information is of no interest to us; the only value the examples use is the pointer to the page-switching function discussed later

■ Set a VESA mode (see Table 3.4)

Table 3.3. Structure of the VESAINFO block.

Field Name	Data Type	Comments
Signature	4 characters	Always "VESA"
Version	16-bit integer	High byte is major version, low byte is minor—in other words, 1.2 is returned as 0102h.
Manufacturer String	Pointer to null-terminated string	Usually the maker's name, but can be anything.
Capabilities	4 characters	This field is largely reserved for later VBE versions.
Video Mode List	Pointer to list of 16-bit integers	The end of the list is signified by a mode number of FFFFh.
Total memory	16-bit integer	Multiply by 64 to get the memory on the card.

Table 3.4. Common VESA modes.

Mode	Resolution and Color Depth
0101h	640 wide, 480 high, 256 colors
0102h	800 wide, 600 high, 16 colors
0103h	800 wide, 600 high, 256 colors
0104h	1024 wide, 768 high, 16 colors
0105h	1024 wide, 768 high, 256 colors

There are a number of other things you can ask the VBE to do, but none of them are particularly relevant to us; the only other service we will encounter is 4F05h, which is used in the 32-bit example.

The final interface function, VESA_SetPage(), is a bit more involved. As we discussed earlier, the main inconsistency between different SuperVGA cards is the way you tell them which *page* of their memory should appear at address A000h. Now then, the fact that two cards from different manufacturers both conform to the VESA standard does *not* mean that they both switch pages in the same way. Instead, each card will provide a little program in its BIOS that knows how to switch pages on that particular card. The "standard" part is our interface to that program—we are insulated from whatever mysterious process the card actually requires by a simple call that is the same from one VESA card to another.

The call to VESA service 4F01h—which is made for us by the VESA_GetModeInfo() function—places a pointer to this wonderful program into the VESAMODEINFO block. Unfortunately, this means that we need to do an explicit jump to that memory address, after directly setting some register values. This is not possible in C, so VESA_SetPage() is three statements of in-line Assembler. It simply sets BX to 0 (this means Set—rather than Get—the page), DX to the page number required, and then jumps to the page-switching code in the VESA BIOS. If this makes perfect sense to you, congratulations. If not, don't lose any sleep over it; just call the durned thing like any other C function.

Before we move on, a note if you intend to change and re-compile the 16-bit examples from this chapter. Both Turbo C and Watcom C—particularly the latter—have optimizing features which do not always work well in conjunction with in-line assembler. As noted in the program headers, you should switch off Register Variables if you are using Turbo C; and you should switch off the "Expand Functions In-line" feature if you are using Watcom C. It is important to be aware of these points, because very strange things will happen...

The UnpackPCX() function does just that, reading a PCX-compressed disk file and unpacking it into a buffer in XMS memory. I presume most readers will know how PCX works. XMS has been around for long enough that there's little point in me going into it here, but there are a couple of things to be aware of with these (indeed, *all*) XMS memory functions:

- You must call XMS_Initialize() before anything else.
- When you use XMS_Allocate() to grab a block of XMS memory, the block size you request is in kilobytes, not bytes.
- When using CopyFromDos() or CopyToDos(), remember that the Length and Offset parameters are of type long int. Also, don't try to copy an odd number of bytes—the XMS driver deals only in words, and it simply doesn't do anything if you ask for an odd number.
- Remember to use XMS_Dealloc() to free any blocks of XMS memory you have allocated. Unlike conventional memory, XMS memory remains allocated *after the program ends.* Only a re-boot will save you if you forget to do this.

OK, onto the function that actually does the work, VESA_UpdateScreen(). This function represents the simplest and most machine-efficient way to update the entire SVGA screen—a series of 64KB block copies. It first calculates the number of entire 64KB pages there will be for this resolution with 256 colors—this works out at four whole pages for 640×480, seven for 800×600 and 12 for 1024×768. It then calculates the remainder, so it knows how many bytes to copy to the last page. Note that nothing too terrible will happen if you copy too many bytes to the last page; as long as you don't copy more than 64KB, the garbage at the end will be copied into a non-displayed part of the memory, so the machine won't crash and you won't see anything wrong on-screen. However, you'll be spending time copying rubbish around, which is less than ideal.

The actual updating of the screen is simply a series of calls to VESA_SetPage(), followed by a memory copy to address A000h, the standard graphics memory area. As discussed earlier, we set page zero and write the first 64KB; then set page one and write the second 64KB; and so on, until the last whole page has been written. Finally, we write whatever's left into the last page. And that's that—your PCX graphic is displayed.

Although this program is fairly sizeable, the properly VESA-specific bits amount to around 50 lines of code, with hardly any Assembler needed at all—this SuperVGA business isn't so tricky…

A Simple 32-Bit PCX Viewer

Listing 3.3 is a 32-bit version of our Simple PCX Viewer, written for Watcom C and DOS/4GW. It is both shorter and simpler than the 16-bit version, mainly because we have direct, C-language access to as much memory as we're ever likely to want, so there's no need to mess about with kludges like XMS. Other than that, the two programs are very similar—except for one vital area.

Listing 3.3. A 32-bit PCX viewer.

```
/*  VESA32.C  -  Example 32-bit program to directly update
                 VESA-compliant video systems. */

/* Requires Watcom C ver. 10 and DOS/4GW  */

#include <stdlib.h>
#include <dos.h>
#include <i86.h>
#include <malloc.h>
#include <stdio.h>
#include <conio.h>
#include <string.h>


int VESA_SetMode(int Mode);
```

continues

Listing 3.3. continued

```c
typedef struct {
        char manufacturer;
        char version;
        char encoding;
        char BitsPerPixel;
        short int x1, y1;
        short int x2, y2;
        short int hres;
        short int vres;
        char palette[48];
        char reserved;
        char color_planes;
        short int BytesPerLine;
        short int PaletteType;
        char dummy[58];
} PCXHEADER;

PCXHEADER Header;

int DWidth, DHeight;

main(int argc, char *argv[])
{

FILE *fh;
int Width, Height, ScreenMode = 0;
char *Buffer, res;


if (argc != 2)
{
printf("\nUsage:  VESA32 {PCX file name}\n\n");
exit(0);
}

if ( (fh = fopen(argv[1], "rb")) == NULL)
{
printf("\nFile %s not found\n\n", argv[1]);
exit(0);
}

printf("Enter screen mode: (1=640x480, 2=800x600, 3=1024x768, 4=Exit)\n");
res = 0;
while (res < '1' ¦¦ res >'4')
   res = getch();

switch (res)
   {
   case '1':
   ScreenMode = 0x0101;
   DHeight = 480;
   DWidth = 640;
   break;

   case '2':
   ScreenMode = 0x0103;
```

```
        DHeight = 600;
        DWidth = 800;
        break;

        case '3':
        ScreenMode = 0x0105;
        DHeight = 768;
        DWidth = 1024;
        break;

        case '4':
        exit(0);
        }

fread(&Header, sizeof(PCXHEADER), 1, fh);

Width = (Header.x2 - Header.x1) + 1;
Height = (Header.y2 - Header.y1) + 1;

/* OK, let's see if the card is capable of supporting this resolution */

if (VESA_SetMode(ScreenMode) != 0)
{
printf("\nYour display card is not VESA-compliant, or its VESA implementation\n");
printf("does not support a resolution of %4dx%3dx256 colors - try a lower
➥resolution\n\n",
DWidth, DHeight);
exit(0);
}

/*  OK, everything is in order - unpack the PCX image  */

Buffer = malloc(DWidth * DHeight);
if (Buffer != NULL)
    {
    memset(Buffer, 0, DWidth * DHeight);
    UnpackPCX(fh, Buffer, Width, Height);

    /*  Display the image  */

    VESA_UpdateScreen(Buffer, DWidth, DHeight);

    getch();
    }

RestoreTextMode();

return(0);
}


UnpackPCX(FILE *fh, char *Buffer, int Width, int Height)
{

/*  Note that this is NOT a properly robust PCX reader - it's for the purposes of
this example only, and it makes a lot of assumptions, so it's easy to fool  */
```

continues

Listing 3.3. continued

```c
char palette[768];
char *wbuf, *wptr, c, l;
int j, k, WHeight;

/* Read and set the palette */
fseek(fh, -768L, SEEK_END);
fread(palette, 768, 1, fh);
SetVGAPalette(palette);

/* Reposition to the start of the image data, and continue */
fseek(fh, sizeof(PCXHEADER), SEEK_SET);
wptr=wbuf=malloc(Width);

if (DHeight > Height)
   WHeight = Height;
else
   WHeight = DHeight;

for (j=0; j<WHeight; j++)
   {
   for (k=0; k<Width;)
      {
      c = fgetc(fh);
      if (c > 191)
         {
         l = c - 192;
         c = fgetc(fh);
         memset(wptr, c, l);
         wptr += l;
         k += l;
         }
      else
         {
         *wptr = c;
         wptr++;   k++;
         }
      }
   if (DWidth >= Width)
      memcpy(Buffer+(j*DWidth), wbuf, Width);
   else
      memcpy(Buffer+(j*DWidth), wbuf, DWidth);

   wptr = wbuf;
   }

return;
}

VESA_UpdateScreen(char *Buffer, int Width, int Height)
{

int j;
unsigned int NoOfPages, LastPage;

/* Before we start, work out how many pages are required, and how many bytes
are needed in the last page.  */
```

```
NoOfPages = (Width * Height) / 65536;

LastPage = (Width * Height) - (NoOfPages * 65536);

/*  OK, now just update the screen  */
for (j = 0; j < NoOfPages; j++)
{
VESA_SetPage(j);
memcpy(0xA0000, (const void *)Buffer, 65536);
Buffer += 65536;
}

if (LastPage != 0)
{
VESA_SetPage(j);
memcpy(0xA0000, (const void *)Buffer, LastPage);
}

return;
}

int VESA_SetMode(int Mode)
{

union REGS r;

r.h.ah = 0x4F;
r.h.al = 2;
r.w.bx = Mode;

int386(0x10, &r, &r);


/*  Note - it's not possible to simply return AX (or AH), because AL will contain
➥4Fh after a
    successful call... */

if (r.h.ah == 0)
return(0);
else
return(1);

}



void VESA_SetPage(short int Page)
{


union REGS r;

r.h.ah = 0x4F;
r.h.al = 5;
r.w.bx = 0;
r.w.dx = Page;
```

continues

Listing 3.3. continued

```
int386(0x10, &r, &r);

}


void SetVGAPalette(char *Palette)
{

/* This function sets the palette (will work on any VGA or SVGA card) by program
➥ming the card
directly.  There IS a BIOS function to do it, but doing it directly is both quicker
➥and - for protected
mode programs - more straightforward    */

short int i;
char far *p;

for (i=0; i<768; i++)
    Palette[i] = Palette[i] >> 2;

p = Palette;

outp(0x3c6, 0xff);
for (i=0; i<=255; i++)
    {
    outp(0x3c8, i);
    outp(0x3c9, *p++);
    outp(0x3c9, *p++);
    outp(0x3c9, *p++);
    }

return;

}


void RestoreTextMode()
{
    union REGS r;
    r.h.al = 0x03;                      /* 16-color VGA text mode */
    r.h.ah = 0x00;                      /* Set graphics mode */
    int386(0x10, &r, &r);

}
```

Remember the way we needed to use assembly language in the 16-bit version, to implement a direct call to a VESA function? Remember how your heart either sank or sang, depending on your viewpoint? Well, prepare for it to do the opposite—the 32-bit program is 100 percent C, no Assembler required.

The VESA VBE provides an interrupt-based way to switch pages—you simply set up BX and DX as we did in the 16-bit example, and then generate interrupt 10h, service 4F05h. This can be implemented like any other interrupt in C, with an int86()/int386() and a REGS block. It's as simple as that.

Now, before you start sharpening knives and making effigies of me, let me explain. The reason VESA provides a direct call facility to its page-switching function is simple—it's quicker. As we have already found, you need every bit of performance you can get when dealing with SVGA, so the—albeit tiny—extra speed of the direct call is a blessing. After all, it's not that difficult to implement.

In Protected Mode, we're in a whole different world. Obtaining the pointer to the direct function is complicated, and calling the direct function is even more complicated. We are obliged to start generating multiple interrupt 31h's to instruct the DPMI host, and the end result would be difficult code that was no faster than issuing the single real-mode interrupt with int386() and letting DOS/4GW handle it all.

One side effect of using the interrupt rather than the direct call is that we no longer need to call VESA_GetModeInfo()—the only vital bit of information that routine returns is a pointer to the page switching code, which we no longer need. We don't *need* the list of supported modes—because VESA_SetMode() will return an error code if you try to set an unsupported one—and we can assume 64KB granularity for all the normal VESA modes. So, VESA_GetInfo() and GetModeInfo() VESA_ are not part of the 32-bit program.

SVGA and the Mouse

Many games make use of a mouse, and programmers have become used to providing support for one. The mouse is pretty easy to program for, and the driver even provides an on-screen pointer so your program doesn't need to.

If you plan on using a mouse in an SVGA application, prepare for a shock—the reported screen coordinates are incorrect, and there is no built-in pointer (which means you have to code your own). Yes, I know—that's what I thought as well. Still, these problems are not insurmountable once you get over the initial trauma.

In a SuperVGA mode, the mouse driver continues to report horizontal coordinates of 0–639 and vertical coordinates of 0–199, as it would for VGA mode 13h. One solution to this is to scale the reported coordinates to match the actual screen resolution. For example, in 800×600 mode you could multiply the reported horizontal coordinate by 800, then divide it by 640. This would give you quite an accurate result, because 640 and 800 are not too dissimilar. However, you would not get truly pixel-accurate results—the driver only sees 640 horizontal positions when there are actually 800. The upshot is that your pointer would skip pixels arbitrarily, making it impossible for the user to click certain pixels. This is not a very good way to win the affection of your users.

So clearly there has to be another way to do it. And, you'll be relieved to hear, it's fairly straightforward. Instead of asking the mouse driver where on the screen the pointer is, you ask it how far the mouse has moved since the last time you asked, using mouse driver function 0Bh. As long as you know your start point, the position is then easily calculated. Mouse movement is measured in Mouse Motion Counters according to the official technical documentation, but most people use the term "mickeys"—a fabulous bit of silly jargon in the same league as "nybble." The actual size of a mickey varies depending on the resolution of the mouse (1 mickey = 1 unit of mouse movement, so moving a 200dpi mouse exactly one inch would cause the driver to report 200 mickeys), but it's a simple enough task to scale the reported value to make the pointer move less quickly. Note that it's *not* possible to scale the value up, to make the pointer move more quickly—or rather, it is *possible*, but it causes the same lack-of-accuracy problem mentioned above. Incidentally, the "ballistic" or "turbo" mode offered by some mouse drivers is an example of such scaling—if the mouse is moved quickly, the values are scaled up; if the mouse is moved slowly, the values are left alone, or even scaled down (this makes clicking a specific pixel at high resolution easier).

Listing 3.4 shows an example of a mouse routine that uses function 0Bh to provide mouse coordinates under SVGA. The routine updates a global structure that contains the basic information about the current mouse status that the main application might want to know about—all pretty standard fare. The only interesting thing is the way this routine works out the current x and y coordinates. Normally, you would use interrupt 33h, function 3 to get both button and x/y position data. This routine still uses function 3 to get the button press status, but it then calls function 11 (0Bh, of course) to find out how far, in mickeys, the mouse has moved. Function 0Bh returns negative values for mouse movement towards the left or top of the screen, so all we have to do is add the mickey movement counters to the current x and y values. Of course, we need to check that this does not move the mouse pointer entirely off the screen, but that's all there is to it.

Listing 3.4. A mouse-handling function that works with SVGA.

```
#define MAXX 639
#define MAXY 479

struct m {
char lmb, rmb;        /* Button press status  */
char lmr, rmr;        /* Button release status */
signed int mx, my;    /* screen coordinates */
 };

MouseCheck()
{

signed int horiz, vert;

union REGS mo;

mo.x.ax = 0x0003;                    /* Get current x/y position and */
int86(0x33, &mo, &mo);              /* button status */


m.lmb = mo.h.bl & 1;                 /* LMB currently down */
m.rmb = mo.h.bl & 2;                 /* RMB currently down */
```

```
/*  Current mouse position, using Mickeys...  */

mo.x.ax = 11;
int86(0x33, &mo, &mo);

horiz = mo.x.cx;                    /* Either of these values can be negative */
vert  = mo.x.dx;

m.mx += horiz;
m.my += vert;

if (m.mx > MAXX)
   m.mx = MAXX;

if (m.my > MAXY)
   m.my = MAXY;

if (m.mx < 1)
   m.mx = 1;

if (m.my < 1)
   m.my = 1;

mo.x.ax = 0x0006;                   /* Get left button release status */
mo.x.bx = 0;
int86(0x33, &mo, &mo);

m.lmr = mo.h.bl;

mo.x.ax = 0x0006;                   /* Get right button release status */
mo.x.bx = 1;
int86(0x33, &mo, &mo);

m.rmr = mo.h.bl;

}
```

This routine was tested with a no-name 200dpi mouse, and also with the most recent Microsoft mouse and driver (though I don't know the resolution), and it works just fine. However, you might find that directly applying the mickey count causes "over-sensitivity"—you twitch, and the mouse pointer jumps from one side of the screen to the other. Happily, the solution to this problem is an easy one, and it points out the extra control we have gained by going to a slightly lower level. If the mouse is too sensitive, simply reduce the adjustment you make to m.mx and m.my by an appropriate value. For instance, to slow the mouse by 20 percent, try this:

```
m.mx += (horiz * 80) / 100
m.my += (vert * 80) / 100
```

This is, of course, preferable to multiplying by 0.8—the mouse handling code is going to be called *very* often, so it should be as quick as possible. Avoiding floating-point arithmetic is pretty much essential, and even integer arithmetic should be kept to a minimum.

Displaying the Mouse Pointer

Solving the first SVGA/mouse problem was pretty easy. Solving the second is a bit more involved.

Every text and graphics mode available on the display cards up to VGA comes complete with a built-in mouse cursor ("pointer" is a more common term, but "cursor" is a description less open to confusion when talking about programming). All you have to do is ask the mouse driver to display it, and it appears. This is not true with SuperVGA. There *is* a VESA standard available— not the VESA VBE we've already talked about, a different one—that aims to fix this problem once and for all, but it is not currently in wide use. So, today, you are obliged to write your own routine for displaying the mouse cursor.

Many people will have already done this in a VGA mode, because the system-provided mouse cursor is not very attractive, and using it causes problems when you are updating the display memory directly, as all games do. The principle is simple enough: write a function to draw an image (any image, your choice) at the current x and y mouse coordinates; when the mouse moves, erase the image and re-draw it at the new position. Easy.

> Although the example program shown here presents a traditional kind of mouse pointer, there is nothing to prevent you from using a more interesting image. As long as you keep the image fairly small—say, less than 40 pixels high—you can use anything you can draw in a paint package as a mouse cursor. You could easily arrange for several different cursors, just by loading several images. Even an animating cursor—a clock with moving hands, perhaps, or an arrow with moving "lights" on it—would be possible with only a small amount of work. You would simply arrange for the displayed image to change at regular intervals—this is easier to do with the code-driven approach presented in this chapter than with the more usual interrupt-driven approach.

All right, it's not *that* easy. There are a number of nasties. First, you need to be able to support transparent areas in your image, so that your heart-shaped mouse pointer isn't surrounded by a horrible black square. Secondly, you need to arrange for the background to remain intact as you move your mouse pointer around. Finally, with all of this, remember that your image might well be half in one SVGA display page, and half in another.

Clearly, we're in Animation Territory here. As you may or may not know, there are any number of workable techniques for sprite-type animation (although they are all based around the same couple of principles). The technique I've used here works like this:

1. Erase the mouse pointer from its old location by copying the saved background over the top of the pointer

2. Save the background "behind" the new location of the mouse pointer (from the buffer, not the screen)

3. Display the mouse pointer into the buffer

4. Copy the changed part of the buffer to screen memory

All the animation is done into the off-screen buffer, and the changed portions are then copied to the screen. Actually, for something as simple as a mouse pointer it is probably more appropriate to hit the screen memory directly. The problem with this approach is that you then have a mouse cursor which displays the same problems as the system-supplied cursors—you have to switch it off before you update the screen, or it'll muck up the display. An example that works via a buffer instead is more useful, because you'll almost certainly end up having to integrate your mouse pointer with your other screen updates as soon as you start doing anything serious with SVGA.

One note before we get into an explanation of the code: This example is code-driven—you *must* call function LoopCheck() regularly to have the mouse pointer properly refreshed. A more satisfactory method is to use the interrupt hook provided by the mouse driver, so that every time the mouse moves the LoopCheck() function (or some equivalent) is called automatically. I haven't done this because the 32-bit example would have been more complicated; there simply isn't the space here to start getting into the mechanics of Protected Mode. In any case, a code-driven approach is perfectly viable—in some ways it is even *preferable*—and it only requires a small amount of extra work.

Listing 3.5 shows the full 16-bit example program—remember to link in XMS.OBJ, and don't forget the provisos about optimization features. I make no claim that this is the only or best way to implement an SVGA mouse cursor—it demonstrates just one of the possible animation techniques, and it is written entirely in C (whereas a "real world" system would probably implement at least the draw and erase functions in Assembler). This example is hard-coded for a 640×480 resolution, but it would be a simple enough matter to change it to support a higher resolution. The interesting functions are in two groups: those that display and erase the cursor, and those that refresh the screen.

Listing 3.5. Implementing an SVGA mouse cursor.

```
/*  SVGAMOUS.C - 16-bit example implementing a mouse pointer at 640x480x256
                 resolution.  Includes example of direct support for non-VESA
                 card.   */

/*****************************************************************************
    This program will compile under Watcom and Turbo/Borland C, and (probably)
    under others (eg, MS) as well.  You MUST use Large Model.

    Turbo/Borland C users:
      You **MUST** use the '-r-' compile switch, or switch off Register
      Variables in the IDE.  The program will not run correctly with this
      optimisation in place.
```

continues

Listing 3.5. continued

```
    Watcom C users:
       You **MUST** switch off the "Expand functions in-line" optimisation if
       you are using the IDE (it is a default in the IDE, but not on the
       command-line compiler).  The program will not compile with this
       optimisation in place.
    ****************************************************************************/

#include <stdio.h>
#include <stdlib.h>
#include <string.h>
#include <conio.h>

#ifdef __WATCOMC__
    #include <i86.h>
    #include <malloc.h>
    #define enable _enable
    #define disable _disable
#else
    #include <dos.h>
    #include <alloc.h>
#endif


 /*    Basic VESA structures  */

typedef struct {
    char Signature[4];
    unsigned short int Version;
    char *OEMName;/* This is a FAR pointer - use Large model! */
    unsigned char Capabilities[4];
    unsigned short int *VideoMode;
    short int VideoMem;
    char dummy[238];                            /*Pad to 256 bytes */
    } VESAINFO;

typedef struct {
    unsigned short int ModeAttr;
    unsigned char WinAAttr;
    unsigned char WinBAttr;
    unsigned short int Granularity;
    unsigned short int WinSize;
    unsigned short int WinASegment;
    unsigned short int WinBSegment;
    unsigned short int (*PageSwitchFunction)();
    unsigned short int BytesPerScanLine;

        /*  Not all VESA cards provide the following optional information  */
    unsigned int XResolution;
    unsigned int YResolution;
    unsigned char XCharSize;
    unsigned char YCharSize;
    unsigned char NumberOfPlanes;
    unsigned char BitsPerPixel;
    unsigned char NumberOfBanks;
```

```
                unsigned char MemoryModel;
                unsigned char BankSize;
                char dummy[227];                          /*Pad to 256 bytes */
                } VESAMODEINFO;


        /*  Information block for XMS memory copies */

        typedef struct {
                unsigned long int len;
                unsigned short int  src;
                unsigned long int soff;
                unsigned short int  dh;
                unsigned long int doff;
                } XMSBLOCK;


        /* Function protoypes */


        int cdecl XMS_Initialise(void);
        int cdecl XMS_Allocate(int);
        int cdecl XMS_Dealloc(int);
        int cdecl XMS_Copy(void *);
        void XMS_CopyToDos(char *, unsigned int, unsigned long, unsigned long);
        void XMS_CopyFromDos(char *, unsigned int, unsigned long, unsigned long);

        long int cdecl XMS_ConvertPtr(char far *ptr);

        #ifdef __WATCOMC__
           #pragma aux XMS_CopyToDos   modify [si];
           #pragma aux XMS_CopyFromDos modify [si];
        #endif


        int VESA_SetMode(int);
        int VESA_GetInfo(VESAINFO *);
        int VESA_GetModeInfo(int, VESAMODEINFO *);
        void VESA_SetPage(int, void *);

        void SetVGAPalette(char *);
        void RestoreTextMode(void);


        #define TRIDENT 1
        #define VESA    2
        #define HUALON  3

        struct {                      //  Mouse info block
           signed int mx, my;         //  Current x/y position
           signed int px, py;         //  Previous x/y position
           char lmb, rmb;             //  Button press status, left and right
           char lmr, rmr;             //  Button release status, left & right
           int h, w;                  //  Height and width of pointer image
           char *image;               //  Pointer to image data
           char *background;          //  Pointer to saved background
           } m;
```

continues

Listing 3.5. continued

```
long stx[480];
char *sts[480];
char stb[480];
char stp[480];

char lastp = 0;

char SVGAcard;
unsigned short int (* VESApointer)();

VESAINFO VESAInfo;
VESAMODEINFO VESAModeInfo;

#define B 14                    //  Mouse border color
#define I 1                     //  Mouse "inside" color

/*  Define an image for our mouse pointer... */

char image[160] = { B,B,0,0,0,0,0,0,0,0,
                    B,I,B,0,0,0,0,0,0,0,
                    B,I,I,B,0,0,0,0,0,0,
                    B,I,I,I,B,0,0,0,0,0,
                    B,I,I,I,I,B,0,0,0,0,
                    B,I,I,I,I,I,B,0,0,0,
                    B,I,I,I,I,I,I,B,0,0,
                    B,I,I,I,I,I,I,I,B,0,
                    B,I,I,I,I,I,I,B,0,B,
                    B,I,I,I,I,I,B,0,0,0,
                    B,I,B,B,I,I,B,0,0,0,
                    B,B,0,0,B,I,I,B,0,0,
                    B,0,0,0,0,B,I,B,0,0,
                    0,0,0,0,0,B,I,I,B,0,
                    0,0,0,0,0,0,B,I,B,0,
                    0,0,0,0,0,0,B,B,0,0    };


void SVGA_InitTables(void);
void SVGA_SetMode(void);
void SVGA_DisplayBlock(unsigned int, int, int);
void SVGA_DisplayLine(unsigned int, unsigned int);
void SVGA_DisplayScreen(unsigned int);
void DisplayMouse(unsigned int, int, int);
void UnDisplayMouse(unsigned int, int, int);
void MouseImageInit(void);
void LoopCheck(unsigned int);

#ifdef __WATCOMC__
   #pragma aux XMS_CopyToDos   modify [si];
   #pragma aux XMS_CopyFromDos modify [si];
#endif

main(int argc, char *argv[])
{
unsigned int hXMS, j;
```

```
char clr[640];

SVGAcard = VESA;          // A sensible default!

if (argc == 2)
   {
   if (strcmp(argv[1], "TRIDENT") == NULL)
      SVGAcard = TRIDENT;
   if (strcmp(argv[1], "HUALON") == NULL)
      SVGAcard = HUALON;
   }

XMS_Initialize();

if ((hXMS = XMS_Allocate(300)) == NULL)
   exit(0);

for (j=0;j<480;j++)
   {
   memset(clr, (unsigned char)j, 640);
   XMS_CopyFromDos(clr, hXMS, 640L, (long)j*640L);
   }

MouseImageInit();
MouseInit();

SVGA_InitTables();

SVGA_SetMode();        // For this example, 640x480 only

for (j=0; j<480; j++)
   SVGA_DisplayLine(hXMS, j);

m.mx = 0;  m.my = 0;      // Start at the top-left of the screen...
m.px = 0;  m.py = 0;

DisplayMouse(hXMS, m.mx, m.my);

while(!m.lmr)
   {
   LoopCheck(hXMS);
   }

XMS_Dealloc(hXMS);

RestoreTextMode();
}


void SVGA_InitTables(void)
{

unsigned int j;
char page=0;
long runner=0L;
```

continues

Listing 3.5. continued

```c
for (j=0;  j<480;  j++)
    {
    stx[j] = (long)j * 640;
    sts[j] = MK_FP(0xa000, (unsigned int)runner);
    if (runner+640L > 65535L)
        {
        stb[j] = 1;
        runner -= 65536L;
        }
    else
        stb[j] = 0;

    if (j != 0 && stb[j-1] == 1)
        page++;

    stp[j] = page;
    runner += 640L;
    }
}

/***   MODE SELECTION AND PAGE-SWITCHING FUNCTIONS   ***/

void SVGA_SetMode(void)
{

union REGS r;

switch(SVGAcard)
    {
    case TRIDENT:
        r.x.ax = 0x005d;
        int86(0x10, &r, &r);
        break;

    case VESA:
        VESA_SetMode(0x0101);
        VESA_GetInfo(&VESAInfo);
        VESA_GetModeInfo(0x0103, &VESAModeInfo);
        VESApointer = VESAModeInfo.PageSwitchFunction;
        break;

    case HUALON:
        r.x.ax = 0x002d;
        int86(0x10, &r, &r);
        break;

    }
}


void SVGA_SetPage(char page)
{
int i, n;

lastp = page;
```

```
n = page;

switch(SVGAcard)
   {
   case TRIDENT:
      disable();
      outp(0x03ce, 0x06);
      i = inp(0x03cf);
      outpw(0x03ce, (( i ¦ 0x04) << 8) ¦ 0x0006);
      outp(0x03c4, 0x0b);
      i=inp(0x03c5);
      outpw(0x03c4, ((n ^ 0x02) << 8) ¦ 0x000e);
      enable();
      break;

   case VESA:
      VESA_SetPage(n, VESApointer);
      break;

   case HUALON:
      n = (n << 12) ¦ 0x00ee;
      outpw(0x03c4, n);
      break;

   }

}


int VESA_SetMode(int Mode)
{

union REGS r;

r.h.ah = 0x4F;
r.h.al = 2;
r.x.bx = Mode;

int86(0x10, &r, &r);

if (r.h.ah == 0)
   return(0);
else
   return(1);
}

int VESA_GetInfo(VESAINFO *Buffer)
{

union REGS r;
struct SREGS sr;

r.x.ax = 0x4F00;
sr.es = FP_SEG(Buffer);
r.x.di = FP_OFF(Buffer);

int86x(0x10, &r, &r, &sr);
```

continues

Listing 3.5. continued

```c
if (r.h.al == 0x4F)
   return(0);
else
   return(-1);
}


int VESA_GetModeInfo( int Mode, VESAMODEINFO *Buffer )
{

union REGS r;
struct SREGS sr;

r.x.ax = 0x4F01;
r.x.cx = Mode;
sr.es = FP_SEG(Buffer);
r.x.di = FP_OFF(Buffer);

int86x(0x10, &r, &r, &sr);

if (r.h.al == 0x4F)
   return(0);
else
   return(1);
}


void VESA_SetPage(int Page, void *FunctionPointer)
{

#ifdef __WATCOMC__

   void AsmSetPage(void);

   #pragma aux AsmSetPage = \
      "xor bx, bx"          \
      "mov dx, Page"        \
      "call [FunctionPointer]";

   AsmSetPage();

#else

   asm {
      xor bx, bx;
      mov dx, Page;
      call [FunctionPointer];
      }

#endif
}


/***   XMS FUNCTIONS   ***/
```

```
void XMS_CopyToDos(char *DosPtr, unsigned int hXMS, unsigned long Length,
                              unsigned long Offset)
{

XMSBLOCK x;

x.len  = Length;
x.src  = hXMS;
x.soff = Offset;
x.dh   = 0;                        //  An XMS handle of 0 means DOS memory
x.doff = XMS_ConvertPtr(DosPtr);

XMS_Copy(&x);
}

void XMS_CopyFromDos(char *DosPtr, unsigned int hXMS, unsigned long Length,
                               unsigned long Offset)
{

XMSBLOCK x;

x.len  = Length;
x.src  = 0;                        //  An XMS handle of 0 means DOS memory
x.soff = XMS_ConvertPtr(DosPtr);
x.dh   = hXMS;
x.doff = Offset;

XMS_Copy(&x);
}


/***  SCREEN UPDATING FUNCTIONS  ***/

void SVGA_DisplayBlock(unsigned int hXMS, int start, int end)
{
long wrk1;
char far *ScrPtr;
unsigned int Lngth, wrki;
long lgth;

if (start < 0) start = 0;     // Just to protect us from ourselves!
if (end > 479) end = 479;

if (lastp != stp[start])
   SVGA_SetPage(stp[start]);

/*  1.  The entire block is in one page - great!  */
if (stp[start] == stp[end])
   {
   ScrPtr = sts[start];
   Lngth = (int)((stx[end] - stx[start]) + 640L);
   XMS_CopyToDos(ScrPtr, hXMS, (long)Lngth, stx[start]);
   }

else

/*  2.  The block straddles a page boundary - not so great!  */
```

continues

Listing 3.5. continued

```
  {
  if (stp[end] - stp[start] == 1)
    {
    /*  OK, do the start page first... */
    ScrPtr = sts[start];
    Lngth = (int)((65536L * (stp[start]+1L)) - stx[start]);

    XMS_CopyToDos(ScrPtr, hXMS, (long)Lngth, stx[start]);

    /*  Right - swap pages and do the next one...  */

    SVGA_SetPage(stp[start]+1);

    lgth = ((stx[end]-stx[start]) + 640L) - (long)Lngth;
    wrk1 = stx[start] + (long)Lngth;
    Lngth = (int)lgth;

    ScrPtr = MK_FP(0xa000, 0);

    XMS_CopyToDos(ScrPtr, hXMS, (long)Lngth, wrk1);
    }
  else

/* 3.  This is a large block, and multiple page switches are required.
       Update it line-by-line, or the whole screen */
    {
    if (end - start > 150)
       SVGA_DisplayScreen(hXMS);
    else
       for (wrki=start; wrki<= end; wrki++)
          SVGA_DisplayLine(hXMS, wrki);
    }
  }
}


void SVGA_DisplayLine(unsigned int hXMS, unsigned int line)
{

char page, *ScrPointer;
long XMSOffset;
long lgth;

page = stp[line];
if (page != lastp)
   SVGA_SetPage(page);

XMSOffset = stx[line];
ScrPointer = sts[line];

if (stb[line] == 0)
   XMS_CopyToDos(ScrPointer, hXMS, 640L, XMSOffset);

else
```

```
    {
    lgth = (65536L * ((long)page+1L)) - XMSOffset;
    XMS_CopyToDos(ScrPointer, hXMS, lgth, XMSOffset);
    SVGA_SetPage(page+1);
    XMSOffset += lgth;
    ScrPointer = MK_FP(0xa000, 0);
    lgth = 640 - lgth;

    XMS_CopyToDos(ScrPointer, hXMS, lgth, XMSOffset);
    }
}


void SVGA_DisplayScreen(unsigned int hXMS)
{

/*  This function is hard-wired to update an entire 640x480 screen  */

char *ptr;

ptr = MK_FP(0xa000, 0);

SVGA_SetPage(0);
XMS_CopyToDos(ptr, hXMS, 65536L, 0L);
SVGA_SetPage(1);
XMS_CopyToDos(ptr, hXMS, 65536L, 65536L);
SVGA_SetPage(2);
XMS_CopyToDos(ptr, hXMS, 65536L, 131072L);
SVGA_SetPage(3);
XMS_CopyToDos(ptr, hXMS, 65536L, 196608L);
SVGA_SetPage(4);
XMS_CopyToDos(ptr, hXMS, 45056L, 262144L);
}

/*** MOUSE CURSOR DISPLAYING FUNCTIONS ***/

void DisplayMouse(unsigned int hXMS, int x, int y)
{
int j, k, c=0, bb, rb;
char *wrk;

wrk = malloc(640);

rb = x+m.w;
if (rb > 639)
   rb = 639;

bb = y+m.h;
if (bb > 479)
   bb = 479;

for (j=y; j<bb; j++)
   {
   XMS_CopyToDos(wrk, hXMS, 640L, stx[j]);
   c = (j-y) * m.w;
   for (k=x; k<rb; k++)
```

continues

Listing 3.5. continued

```
            {
            m.background[c] = wrk[k];
            if (m.image[c] != 0)
                wrk[k] = m.image[c];
            c++;
            }
        XMS_CopyFromDos(wrk, hXMS, 640L, stx[j]);
        }

SVGA_DisplayBlock(hXMS, y, y+m.h);

free(wrk);

}

void UnDisplayMouse(unsigned int hXMS, int x, int y)
{
int j, k, c=0, bb, rb;
char *wrk;

wrk = malloc(640);

rb = x+m.w;
if (rb > 639)
    rb = 639;

bb = y+m.h;
if (bb > 479)
    bb = 479;

for (j=y; j<bb; j++)
    {
    XMS_CopyToDos(wrk, hXMS, 640L, stx[j]);
    c = (j-y) * m.w;
    for (k=x; k<rb; k++)
        wrk[k] = m.background[c];

    XMS_CopyFromDos(wrk, hXMS, 640L, stx[j]);
    }

free(wrk);

}

/***  MISCELLANEOUS FUNCTIONS  ***/

void SetVGAPalette(char *Palette)
{

short int i;
char far *p;

for (i=0; i<768; i++)
    Palette[i] = Palette[i] >> 2;

p = Palette;
```

```
outp(0x3c6, 0xff);
for (i=0; i<255; i++)
    {
    outp(0x3c8, i);
    outp(0x3c9, *p++);
    outp(0x3c9, *p++);
    outp(0x3c9, *p++);
    }

return;
}


void RestoreTextMode()
{
    union REGS r;
    r.h.al = 0x03;                      /* 16-color VGA text mode */
    r.h.ah = 0x00;                      /* Set graphics mode */
    int86(0x10, &r, &r);

}

int MouseInit(void)
{

union REGS r;

r.x.ax = 0x0000;

int86(0x33, &r, &r);

return(r.h.ah);
}

MouseCheck()
{

union REGS r;

m.px = m.mx;
m.py = m.my;

r.x.ax = 0x0003;                    /* Get current x/y position and */
int86(0x33, &r, &r);               /* button status */

m.lmb = r.h.bl & 1;                /* LMB currently down */
m.rmb = r.h.bl & 2;                /* RMB currently down */

/*  Current mouse position in SVGA modes is worked out by applying the
    movement value, in Mickeys, from the last position.  */

r.x.ax = 11;
int86(0x33, &r, &r);

m.mx += r.x.cx;          // For a high-resolution mouse, try reducing CX and
m.my += r.x.dx;          // DX before applying them - eg, halve them.
```

continues

Listing 3.5. continued

```c
if (m.mx > 639)
   m.mx = 639;

if (m.my > 479)
   m.my = 479;

if (m.mx < 0)
   m.mx = 0;

if (m.my < 0)
   m.my = 0;

r.x.ax = 0x0006;                /* Get left button release status */
r.x.bx = 0;
int86(0x33, &r, &r);

m.lmr = r.h.bl;

r.x.ax = 0x0006;                /* Get right button release status */
r.x.bx = 1;
int86(0x33, &r, &r);

m.rmr = r.h.bl;

}

void MouseImageInit(void)
{

/* This function just provides an image for the mouse cursor.  Obviously, it
   would be better to create this image with a paint package and read it in,
   but this will serve as an example */

m.image = image;     // This assigns the pointer to the data block set up at
                     // the top of the program.
m.w = 10;
m.h = 16;
m.background = malloc(160);

}

void LoopCheck(unsigned int hXMS)
{
int dh;

MouseCheck();

if (m.mx != m.px || m.my != m.py)
   {
   UnDisplayMouse(hXMS, m.px, m.py);

   if (m.py > m.my)
      {
      dh = m.py - m.my;
      if (dh > m.h)
         dh = m.h;
```

```
            SVGA_DisplayBlock(hXMS, m.py+(m.h-dh), m.py+m.h);
            }

    if (m.py < m.my)
        {
        dh = m.my - m.py;
        if (dh > m.h)
            dh = m.h;
        SVGA_DisplayBlock(hXMS, m.py, m.py+dh);
        }

    DisplayMouse(hXMS, m.mx, m.my);
    }
}
```

Function InitSVGATables() sets up a number of arrays that are used throughout the program. The main problem associated with SVGA is updating the screen quickly enough—if we simply refreshed the entire screen every time the mouse moved, the visual effect would be very slow and jerky. Therefore, we need some way of refreshing just a small part of the screen, that part which has actually changed. This is rather trickier than it sounds, because we need to work out what SVGA page to switch to and how far into the A000h memory area we are on that page—and this is before we start thinking about the sobering fact that the page might well change in the middle of our update. The upshot is that some rather involved calculations are required; in the interests of speed, this program performs some of these calculations in advance, so we don't need to carry them out in the main code. The precalculated values are:

■ An offset into the XMS buffer for the start of each scan line (row)

■ A pointer to the start of each scan line in video memory (remember that this needs to wrap back to 0 every time we hit 64KB)

■ An SVGA page number for each scan line

■ A flag to indicate those scan lines that have a page change halfway through

These arrays make life a lot easier later on. For every line, we know where to copy from, where to copy to, and whether or not there are complications (for instance, a page change halfway through the line).

Function DisplayMouse() does just that. It copies the image data defined at the top of the program into the display buffer, trimming as required at the left edge and bottom, using the current x and y mouse coordinates. While it is doing so, it saves whatever was previously there into the Background memory area. The condition

```
if (m.image[c] != 0)
  wrk[k] = m.image[c];
```

is there to allow transparent areas in the image. It simply ignores the color 0 altogether, allowing the background to "show through." Note how the precalculated array values mentioned above are used to find the correct offsets into the XMS buffer, one line at a time.

Function `UnDisplayMouse()` is very similar. As you would imagine, it goes through exactly the same process, but copying the saved background data rather than the image data. So much for the mouse display functions.

The tricky bits of this program are functions `SVGA_DisplayLine()` and `SVGA_DisplayBlock()`. The first of these displays a single line on screen, by copying the appropriate data from the buffer. Since we already know the source address, the destination address and the length, this is a trivial operation—*except* when there's a page change halfway through the line. When we come across one of these awkward lines, the corresponding flag in the `stb[]` array will be set to 1. Then, it's a simple matter of working out how many bytes should be displayed prior to changing page, setting the video pointer back to A000h, and copying the remainder of the line. The line

```
lgth = (65536L * ((long)page + 1L)) - XMSOffset;
```

carries out this calculation. It is simply working out how many bytes there are between the start of the current line (as held in `XMSOffset`) and the end of this 64KB page. Because we know that the end of the page occurs on this line, it follows that the result is the number of bytes to display on this line, before switching pages and continuing. Easy.

`SVGA_DisplayBlock()` goes one step further, enabling us to copy a number of scan lines from the buffer to the screen. It is not strictly necessary—we now have the power to update individual lines, so we could just call `SVGA_DisplayLine()` several times. However, it is more efficient—and therefore quicker—to copy as much of the block as possible in one go. `SVGA_DisplayBlock()` does just this, and will generally out-perform repeated calls to `SVGA_DisplayLine()`. The meat of this routine is in the code that gets executed if the last line to update is not in the same page as the first line. The arithmetic to work out lengths and offsets should look familiar—it is pretty much exactly the same as the math used in the `SVGA_DisplayLine()` function. The only real difference is in the way the size of the second half of the block is calculated—in this routine, the size of the first half is subtracted from the overall size of the entire block.

As you will have noticed, `SVGA_DisplayBlock()` will display a block of any size, but is really intended for blocks that reside entirely in one or two pages—more than this, and the function simply makes use of `SVGA_DisplayLine()` for blocks less than half the screen in size, and `SVGA_DisplayScreen()` for blocks bigger than half the screen. `SVGA_DisplayScreen()` refreshes the entire screen in 64KB blocks—it is the same routine we used to do the simple VESA example earlier in the chapter.

The `LoopCheck()` function is partly straightforward and partly mysterious. Clearly, the calls to display and "undisplay" the mouse are pretty self-explanatory, but the code in between is a bit more opaque. The purpose of the two conditions is to ensure that only the portion of the screen which is no longer occupied by the mouse is "blanked" by redisplaying the background. The background is still restored entirely in the off-screen buffer—this code only affects what happens in the physical display memory.

The reason for doing this is that the redisplay of the background is—necessarily—handled before the next display of the mouse, and so there is a short delay between erasing the cursor and re-drawing it at its new position. If we simply erased and re-drew the cursor, there would regularly be short periods of time when the mouse pointer was not on the screen at all. Now, whether this causes you a problem or not depends largely on how much your computer cost you; but most will suffer from some degree of flicker in the mouse image.

> When you come to experiment with SVGA, you will soon find that it is impractical to refresh the entire screen frequently. Extensive use of the "dirty rectangle" technique shown here for the mouse cursor—whereby you only update those areas of the screen that have actually changed—makes Sprite-type animations much more effective.

This technique—which is an elementary example of a screen-updating method sometimes called *dirty rectangle*—gets around this artificial flickering by only refreshing those scan-lines which are actually different. So, if the mouse moves upwards one pixel, the program only redraws one line; if the mouse moves downwards 80 pixels in one go, the program refreshes every line; and if the mouse does not move up *or* down, the program doesn't refresh any lines at all. This works because the re-display of the mouse cursor itself refreshes entire lines—if you move the mouse sideways only, the necessary re-drawing of the background will be performed by the DisplayMouse() function as a side-effect.

Finally, this program gives you an idea of how to go about providing direct support for a non-VESA SuperVGA card. The functions SVGA_SetMode() and SVGA_SetPage() are the only areas of the program where extra code is needed—as long as the proprietary mode you are using has a granularity of 64KB (this is discussed in the section, "Granularity"). The program provides direct support for two cards—Trident and Hualon—at 640×480 resolution, and shows just how different the page switching code can be.

The 32-Bit Mouse Example

Listing 3.6 is the 32-bit Watcom C version of our mouse-displaying program. It works in exactly the same way, but is rather shorter and simpler because memory access is via ordinary memcpy() calls, not convoluted XMS bridges. The only thing to note is that direct access to interrupt 33h from Protected Mode is being generously provided to us by DOS/4GW—access to real mode interrupts is not, by default, this easy. If you are planning on converting the code to another 32-bit compiler, generating the interrupt may well involve the issuing of DPMI calls—it all depends on the particular DOS extender you are using.

Listing 3.6. 32-bit mouse cursor example.

```c
/*  SVMOUS32.C - 32-bit example implementing a mouse pointer at 640x480x256
                 resolution.  Includes example of direct support for non-VESA
                 cards.    */

/*  Requires Watcom C version 10.0 and DOS/4GW */

#include <stdio.h>
#include <conio.h>
#include <stdlib.h>
#include <i86.h>
#include <malloc.h>
#include <string.h>

#define TRIDENT 1
#define VESA    2
#define HUALON  3

struct {                        //  Mouse info block
    short int mx, my;           //  Current x/y position
    short int px, py;           //  Previous x/y position
    char lmb, rmb;              //  Button press status, left and right
    char lmr, rmr;              //  Button release status, left & right
    short int h, w;             //  Height and width of pointer image
    char *image;                //  Pointer to image data
    char *background;           //  Pointer to saved background
    } m;

long stx[480];
unsigned short sts[480];
char stb[480];
char stp[480];

char lastp = 0;

char SVGAcard;

#define B 14                    //  Mouse border color
#define I 1                     //  Mouse "inside" color

/*  Define an image for our mouse pointer... */

char image[160] = { B,B,0,0,0,0,0,0,0,0,
                    B,I,B,0,0,0,0,0,0,0,
                    B,I,I,B,0,0,0,0,0,0,
                    B,I,I,I,B,0,0,0,0,0,
                    B,I,I,I,I,B,0,0,0,0,
                    B,I,I,I,I,I,B,0,0,0,
                    B,I,I,I,I,I,I,B,0,0,
                    B,I,I,I,I,I,I,I,B,0,
                    B,I,I,I,I,I,I,I,I,B,
                    B,I,I,I,I,I,I,I,B,0,B,
                    B,I,I,I,I,I,B,0,0,0,
                    B,I,B,B,I,I,B,0,0,0,
                    B,B,0,0,B,I,I,B,0,0,
```

```
                           B,0,0,0,0,B,I,B,0,0,
                           0,0,0,0,0,B,I,I,B,0,
                           0,0,0,0,0,0,B,I,B,0,
                           0,0,0,0,0,0,B,B,0,0    };


        void SVGA_InitTables(void);
        void SVGA_SetMode(void);
        void SVGA_DisplayBlock(char *, int, int);
        void SVGA_DisplayLine(char *, unsigned int);
        void SVGA_DisplayScreen(char *);
        void DisplayMouse(char *, int, int);
        void UnDisplayMouse(char *, int, int);
        void MouseImageInit(void);
        void LoopCheck(char *);
        short int VESA_SetMode(short int);
        void VESA_SetPage(char);


    main(int argc, char *argv[])
    {
    unsigned int j;
    char  *Buffer;

    SVGAcard = VESA;            // A sensible default!

    if (argc == 2)
        {
        if (strcmp(argv[1], "TRIDENT") == NULL)
            SVGAcard = TRIDENT;
        if (strcmp(argv[1], "HUALON") == NULL)
            SVGAcard = HUALON;
        }

    if ( (Buffer = malloc(307200)) == NULL)
        exit(0);

    for (j=0;j<480;j++)
        memset(Buffer+(j*640), (unsigned char)j, 640);

    MouseImageInit();
    MouseInit();

    SVGA_InitTables();

    SVGA_SetMode();        // For this example, 640x480 only

    for (j=0; j<480; j++)
        SVGA_DisplayLine(Buffer, j);

    m.mx = 0;  m.my = 0;     // Start at the top-left of the screen...
    m.px = 0;  m.py = 0;

    DisplayMouse(Buffer, m.mx, m.my);

    while(!m.lmr)
```

continues

Listing 3.6. continued

```
    {
    LoopCheck(Buffer);
    }

RestoreTextMode();
}


void SVGA_InitTables(void)
{

unsigned int j;
char page=0;
long runner=0L;

for (j=0; j<480; j++)
    {
    stx[j] = j * 640;
    sts[j] = (short int)runner;
    if (runner+640 > 65535)
        {
        stb[j] = 1;
        runner -= 65536;
        }
    else
        stb[j] = 0;

    if (j != 0 && stb[j-1] == 1)
        page++;

    stp[j] = page;
    runner += 640;
    }
}

/***   MODE SELECTION AND PAGE-SWITCHING FUNCTIONS   ***/

void SVGA_SetMode(void)
{

union REGS r;

switch(SVGAcard)
    {
    case TRIDENT:
        r.w.ax = 0x005d;
        int386(0x10, &r, &r);
        break;

    case VESA:
        VESA_SetMode(0x0101);
        break;

    case HUALON:
        r.w.ax = 0x002d;
```

```
        int386(0x10, &r, &r);
        break;

    }
}


void SVGA_SetPage(char page)
{
int i, n;

lastp = page;

n = page;

switch(SVGAcard)
    {
    case TRIDENT:
        _disable();
        outp(0x03ce, 0x06);
        i = inp(0x03cf);
        outpw(0x03ce, (( i ¦ 0x04) << 8) ¦ 0x0006);
        outp(0x03c4, 0x0b);
        i=inp(0x03c5);
        outpw(0x03c4, ((n ^ 0x02) << 8) ¦ 0x000e);
        _enable();
        break;

    case VESA:
        VESA_SetPage(n);
        break;

    case HUALON:
        n = (n << 12) ¦ 0x00ee;
        outpw(0x03c4, n);
        break;

    }

}


short int VESA_SetMode(short int Mode)
{

union REGS r;

r.h.ah = 0x4F;
r.h.al = 2;
r.w.bx = Mode;

int386(0x10, &r, &r);

if (r.h.ah == 0)
    return(0);
```

continues

Listing 3.6. continued

```c
else
   return(1);
}


void VESA_SetPage(char Page)
{

union REGS r;

r.h.ah = 0x4F;
r.h.al = 5;
r.w.bx = 0;
r.w.dx = Page;

int386(0x10, &r, &r);

}


/***   SCREEN UPDATING FUNCTIONS   ***/

void SVGA_DisplayBlock(char *Buffer, int start, int end)
{
char *ScrPtr;
unsigned short int Lngth, wrki;
long lgth;

if (start < 0) start = 0;     // Just to protect us from ourselves!
if (end > 479) end = 479;

if (lastp != stp[start])
   SVGA_SetPage(stp[start]);

/*  1.  The entire block is in one page - great!  */
if (stp[start] == stp[end])
   {
   ScrPtr = 0xA0000;
   Lngth = (stx[end] - stx[start]) + 640;
   memcpy(ScrPtr+sts[start], Buffer+stx[start], Lngth);
   }

else

/*  2.  The block straddles a page boundary - not so great!  */
   {
   if (stp[end] - stp[start] == 1)
      {
      /*  OK, do the start page first... */
      ScrPtr = 0xA0000 + sts[start];
      Lngth = (65536 * (stp[start] + 1)) - stx[start];
      memcpy(ScrPtr, Buffer+stx[start], Lngth);

      /*  Right - swap pages and do the next one...  */
```

```
            SVGA_SetPage(stp[start]+1);

            ScrPtr = 0xA0000;
            lgth = (stx[end] - stx[start] - Lngth) + 640;
            memcpy(ScrPtr, Buffer+stx[start]+Lngth, lgth);
            }
        else

/*  3.  This is a large block, and multiple page switches are required.
        Update it line-by-line, or the whole screen */
            {
            if (end - start > 150)
                SVGA_DisplayScreen(Buffer);
            else
                for (wrki=start; wrki<= end; wrki++)
                    SVGA_DisplayLine(Buffer, wrki);
            }
        }
}


void SVGA_DisplayLine(char *Buffer, unsigned int line)
{

char page, *ScrPtr;
long lgth;

page = stp[line];
if (page != lastp)
    SVGA_SetPage(page);

ScrPtr = 0xA0000 + sts[line];

if (stb[line] == 0)
    memcpy(ScrPtr, Buffer+stx[line], 640);

else
    {
    lgth = (65536 * (page+1)) - stx[line];
    memcpy(ScrPtr, Buffer+stx[line], lgth);

    SVGA_SetPage(++page);
    ScrPtr = 0xA0000;
    memcpy(ScrPtr, Buffer+stx[line]+lgth, 640-lgth);
    }
}


void SVGA_DisplayScreen(char *Buffer)
{

/*  This function is hard-wired to update an entire 640x480 screen  */

SVGA_SetPage(0);
memcpy(0xA0000, Buffer, 65536);
```

continues

Listing 3.6. continued

```
SVGA_SetPage(1);
memcpy(0xA0000, Buffer+65536, 65536);
SVGA_SetPage(2);
memcpy(0xA0000, Buffer+131072, 65536);
SVGA_SetPage(3);
memcpy(0xA0000, Buffer+196608, 65536);
SVGA_SetPage(4);
memcpy(0xA0000, Buffer+262144, 45056);
}

/***   MOUSE CURSOR DISPLAYING FUNCTIONS   ***/

void DisplayMouse(char *Buffer, int x, int y)
{
int j, k, c=0, bb, rb;
char *wrk;

rb = x+m.w;
if (rb > 639)
   rb = 639;

bb = y+m.h;
if (bb > 479)
   bb = 479;

for (j=y; j<bb; j++)
   {
   wrk = Buffer + stx[j];
   c = (j-y) * m.w;
   for (k=x; k<rb; k++)
      {
      m.background[c] = wrk[k];
      if (m.image[c] != 0)
         wrk[k] = m.image[c];
      c++;
      }
   }

SVGA_DisplayBlock(Buffer , y, y+m.h);

}

void UnDisplayMouse(char *Buffer, int x, int y)
{
int j, k, c=0, bb, rb;
char *wrk;

rb = x+m.w;
if (rb > 639)
   rb = 639;

bb = y+m.h;
if (bb > 479)
   bb = 479;

for (j=y; j<bb; j++)
```

```
        {
        wrk = Buffer+stx[j];
        c = (j-y) * m.w;
        for (k=x; k<rb; k++)
            wrk[k] = m.background[c];

        }

}

/***  MISCELLANEOUS FUNCTIONS  ***/

void SetVGAPalette(char *Palette)
{

short int i;
char far *p;

for (i=0; i<768; i++)
    Palette[i] = Palette[i] >> 2;

p = Palette;

outp(0x3c6, 0xff);
for (i=0; i<255; i++)
    {
    outp(0x3c8, i);
    outp(0x3c9, *p++);
    outp(0x3c9, *p++);
    outp(0x3c9, *p++);
    }

return;
}


void RestoreTextMode()
{
    union REGS r;
    r.h.al = 0x03;                    /* 16-color VGA text mode */
    r.h.ah = 0x00;                    /* Set graphics mode */
    int386(0x10, &r, &r);

}

int MouseInit(void)
{

union REGS r;

r.w.ax = 0x0000;

int386(0x33, &r, &r);

return(r.h.ah);
}
```

continues

Listing 3.6. continued

```
MouseCheck()
{

union REGS r;

m.px = m.mx;
m.py = m.my;

r.w.ax = 0x0003;                    /* Get current x/y position and */
int386(0x33, &r, &r);               /* button status */

m.lmb = r.h.bl & 1;                 /* LMB currently down */
m.rmb = r.h.bl & 2;                 /* RMB currently down */

/*  Current mouse position in SVGA modes is worked out by applying the
    movement value, in Mickeys, from the last position.  */

r.w.ax = 11;
int386(0x33, &r, &r);

m.mx += r.w.cx;         // For a high-resolution mouse, try reducing CX and
m.my += r.w.dx;         // DX before applying them - eg, halve them.

if (m.mx > 639)
   m.mx = 639;

if (m.my > 479)
   m.my = 479;

if (m.mx < 0)
   m.mx = 0;

if (m.my < 0)
   m.my = 0;

r.w.ax = 0x0006;                    /* Get left button release status */
r.w.bx = 0;
int386(0x33, &r, &r);

m.lmr = r.h.bl;

r.w.ax = 0x0006;                    /* Get right button release status */
r.w.bx = 1;
int386(0x33, &r, &r);

m.rmr = r.h.bl;

}

void MouseImageInit(void)
{

/* This function just provides an image for the mouse cursor.  Obviously, it
   would be better to create this image with a paint package and read it in,
   but this will serve as an example */
```

```
m.image = image;      // This assigns the pointer to the data block set up at
                      // the top of the program.
m.w = 10;
m.h = 16;
m.background = malloc(160);

}

void LoopCheck(char *Buffer)
{
int dh;

MouseCheck();

if (m.mx != m.px  ||  m.my != m.py)
    {
    UnDisplayMouse(Buffer, m.px, m.py);

    if (m.py > m.my)
        {
        dh = m.py - m.my;
        if (dh > m.h)
            dh = m.h;
        SVGA_DisplayBlock(Buffer, m.py+(m.h-dh), m.py+m.h);
        }

    if (m.py < m.my)
        {
        dh = m.my - m.py;
        if (dh > m.h)
            dh = m.h;
        SVGA_DisplayBlock(Buffer, m.py, m.py+dh);
        }

    DisplayMouse(Buffer, m.mx, m.my);
    }
}
```

It is interesting to note that there is not a lot of difference in performance between the 16- and 32-bit code. I had expected the 32-bit programs to be significantly faster, because lots of memory is being shunted around, and 32-bit memory copies are rather faster than their 16-bit equivalents. However, an example program I wrote that simply refreshes the screen memory from the buffer 100 times in succession, using the fastest possible method, shows a performance advantage of only about 4 percent for the 32-bit program. This suggests to me that the bottleneck is the SVGA card itself. It further suggests to me that DOOM at 1024×768 resolution is not something you should be looking to write this year.

Summary

This chapter has only really scratched the surface of SuperVGA. There are all kinds of fabulous things that I haven't even mentioned: 24-bit color modes, super-high resolution, even an "unchained" 640×400 mode that behaves very similarly to our old friend Mode X. However, I hope it has been a useful, practical coverage of how you can drive a SuperVGA card directly, and quickly enough to be viable for a game.

Right now, the only workable SVGA resolution for a game is 640×480, and even then you will need to harshly restrict the amount of on-screen activity if you are not to appall your users with lumpy animations. That said, you can provide photo-quality graphics at 640×480 with 256 colors, and a number of successful games (Sim City 2000, Theme Park) have already succeeded in working around the speed problems. It undoubtedly represents the future.

In a couple of years, when a Pentium 90 is an entry-level machine and 2MB, true-color VESA cards are the norm, *all* games will be written for SVGA. Whether or not low-level knowledge of SVGA hardware will actually be required by then is a more difficult question. With the release of WinG—a set of Windows APIs specifically for games programmers—Microsoft has made Windows game development a much more viable proposition, both now and in the future. All WinG does is allow the programmer direct access to the "drawable" portion of a window, in much the same way as you have direct access to an off-screen buffer under DOS. Windows is managing all the screen updating, so you do not need to involve yourself with any of the tricky stuff presented in this chapter. And, of course, if your program is running under Windows you have access to all the nice things that Windows provides—display device independence, sound, automatic mouse support and multitasking, to name but a few.

So, it may well be the case that SVGA games development is set to become easier over the next few years, as Win 95 takes a hold and hardware capable of rapid, windowed animation becomes more generally available. Today, however, even DOS-based SVGA action games are quite rare—it seems clear that knowledge of the workings of SuperVGA cards will remain worthwhile for some time yet.

Binary Space Partitioned Trees

by Steve Larsen

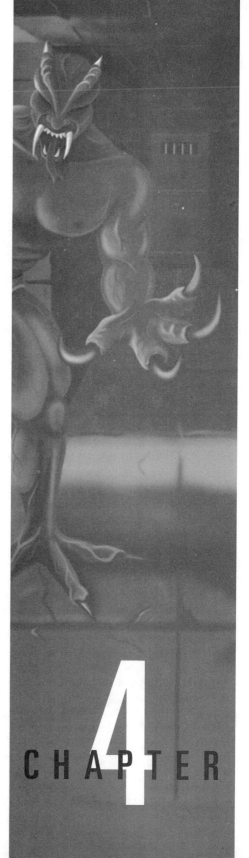

CHAPTER 4

Binary Space Partitioned (BSP) trees are frequently employed in many of today's rendering engines. They have many advantages that make them suitable for this type of application. Typical uses are flight simulators, ray-tracers, and other applications that frequently employ mostly static worlds.

In this chapter we will talk about BSP trees as they are used in games. BSP trees have been put to good use in many applications. In gaming, the most notable example is in DOOM, which employs BSP trees to allow quick rendering of its worlds. This speed does come with a price though, as we will see.

The BSP tree algorithm was originally meant to be used in 3-space. (3-Space is a notation to indicate three dimensional space. Similar notation will be used for other space orders.) However, it is applicable to other dimensions, including 2-space. In this chapter we will discuss the use of BSP trees in 2-space because it is easier to illustrate. Specifically, I have chosen to discuss BSP trees as they apply to rendering 2-D worlds in a pseudo-3-D manner, as in DOOM. I chose this approach for a couple of reasons:

- A lot of people seem to be interested in knowing how BSP trees are used in DOOM
- This type of geometry is easy to use in examples because it is simple to understand

Every element of the BSP-tree process that is discussed here can easily be extended to 3-space (and beyond). We will discuss 3-D BSP trees toward the end of this chapter.

When I am learning an algorithm/data structure or evaluating its suitability to a task, I like to ask myself three questions:

- What problem am I trying to solve?
- What is the algorithm/data structure, and how does it work?
- Does it solve the problem, and if so, how?

Let's start by answering these questions.

What Problem are We Trying to Solve?

We want to render 3-D scenes quickly on the PC. Our goal for this type of rendering is to fool the human eye into believing that it is viewing a "real-world" scene that is dynamic. We would like to achieve this illusion with as few CPU cycles as possible, in order to leave us some processing power to handle all the other duties of our game (such as monster AI, collision detection, and so on).

The human eye is very capable of extrapolating missing information from given data. This is how we can get a believable animation sequence from a discrete set of images. What the animation sequence does not supply, the Human Vision System (HVS) "guesses." The end effect is that we perceive a continuous analog image from a discrete set of digital ones. The cartoon we all watch Saturday morning is probably the best example of how discrete frames are displayed in quick succession to fool us into believing we are seeing a smoothly changing image. However, to maintain this illusion, we need to make the transition between frames as frequently as possible.

Unfortunately, the PC architecture does nothing to help us achieve this coveted speed. The PC's video sub-system was certainly not designed to facilitate this type of operation. We cannot rely on it to do the work for us as is the case with some of the high-end graphics workstations. While the graphics hardware is not geared toward this type of operation, we might as well wring as much performance out of it as we can. This topic, however, is beyond the scope of this chapter. To get information on doing this, I recommend you read the first *Tricks of the Game-Programming Gurus* book as well as the many definitive works by Michael Abrash.

The good thing about the hardware's inability to supply the performance we need is that we can exploit another thing the human mind is good at doing: improvising. If the hardware is not up to the task, then we need to devise software that is faster. Then, as hardware gets faster, we will have even faster implementations.

So, what do we need to do to make our rendering as fast as possible? Well, let's try to improve the performance of one of the most time-critical portions of the rendering pipeline: Hidden Surface Removal (HSR). Usually, HSR is actually composed of two parts. First we need a depth-sorted list of the objects we need to draw. Then we can decide which of these objects can be removed based on this depth sort and other knowledge we may have of the world. Consider the case where you are sitting in your livingroom watching TV. You can probably see a bunch of walls around the room; but, barring windows, you cannot see what is behind those walls. The wall on your neighbor's house, for example, might be completely occluded from your view. This wall is considered a hidden surface. It is a hidden surface since it is behind one of the walls in your living room.

What is a BSP Tree?

First, I need to elaborate on the term "BSP tree." A BSP tree is formally a data structure. However, a connotative meaning has been attached to the term. Basically it is used to describe either the data structure or the algorithm that is used to employ it. It is usually the case that the intended meaning can be inferred from context.

The BSP tree is a member of a group of algorithms known as "divide and conquer." These algorithms take problems that are impossible to solve as-is and break them down into components that can be handled. An example of the divide-and-conquer methodology is the way we add more than two numbers using a calculator. If we were handed a calculator and asked to add five numbers, we could not do it all at once. What we would do is add the first two numbers together, add the third number to that sum, add the fourth number to this sum, and so on. We have taken a problem that is not possible on the surface and divided it into components that we could handle.

The BSP tree performs this same simplification on the walls that we want to render for our game. After the BSP tree has been initialized, we can quickly render the walls in correctly depth-sorted order. It does not tell us which walls are visible, just how the walls relate to one another (which ones are in front of others). We will still have to decide which walls we can see, based on the direction we are looking.

As mentioned earlier, I will be mostly covering 2-D BSP trees here. It should be noted that the BSP-tree concept can easily be extended to any N-space. (N-space is a term used to encapsulate all possible dimensional spaces. We have a hard time imagining anything over 3-space since that is what we live in; however, the mathematics and algorithms of N-space are usually trivial extensions to the ones we are used to seeing.) What to do with a BSP tree in N-space is up to you.

How Do BSP Trees Solve Our Problem?

We decided that somehow we wanted to determine which walls were visible and how they should be drawn relative to each other. I have claimed that BSP trees can be used to help solve this problem, and now I shall put some proof where my mouth is.

Before I begin explaining BSP trees, I should elaborate a little about my claim. The BSP tree alone is not enough to solve this problem. It must be combined with other HSR algorithms to solve the problem. Most commonly, the so-called "painter's algorithm" is used in conjunction with BSP trees to completely solve the problem. What BSP trees will give you is a correctly depth-sorted list of the walls that are to be drawn. What the painter's algorithm tells us is that if we draw the walls starting with the farthest away and proceed, based on distance from our viewpoint, until we reach the wall that is closest, we will obtain correct results. Think of it like coats of paint on your house. Each time you add a coat, it covers up the one before it. You cannot see that layer of paint anymore.

Suppose we are writing a first-person maze game like DOOM. At this particular moment in the game, we happen to be in a simple square room with four walls. (See Figure 4.1.) We need to draw the walls for this room, and we would like it to appear just as it would if we were there ourselves. The question is, in which order should we draw the walls so that they will appear correctly? Well, since this room is basically just a square, the answer is simple—we can draw the walls in any sequence we want. No matter what position and orientation we have in this room, no wall will over occlude another. Therefore, it is irrelevant in which sequence we draw the walls. Think about this very carefully and make sure you understand what I have said, as it will be important to your total understanding.

Unfortunately for our renderer, it is rarely the case that the geometry of the rooms we would like · to see are this simple. Consider the room depicted in Figure 4.2. This isn't quite so trivial. The order in which we draw the walls is now important. If we were located in the position marked by the circle looking in the direction of the arrow, I would have to draw Wall B before Wall A.

(Wall C would not be drawn at all from this position because it is backfaced.) If I drew Wall A before Wall B, Wall B would cover up part of Wall A. This is not what we would like to have happen, since Wall B is behind Wall A from this position. This illustrates the problem; now let's look at the solution.

Figure 4.1.
A simple room with four walls.

Suppose we divide the room into two parts, as shown by the dotted line in Figure 4.3. Now what can we say about the different sides of the room based on that line that we have drawn? We know that every wall that is on the same side of the dotted line as us could never be obscured by a wall that is on the other side of the dotted line. So, what if I drew all the walls that are on the other side of the dotted line from me, then drew all the walls that are on the same side of the dotted line as I am? This would give us the correct results. From the position illustrated, part of Wall B is covered up by Wall A. That part of Wall B will not be visible to us. However, we need not worry about that, because when we draw Wall A (which will be after we have drawn Wall B), it will cover up this part of Wall B. This is the painter's algorithm in effect. So, by using this method we have correctly drawn the walls in this room. This illustrates the fundamental concept of Binary Space Partitioning.

Figure 4.2.
A not-so-simple room.

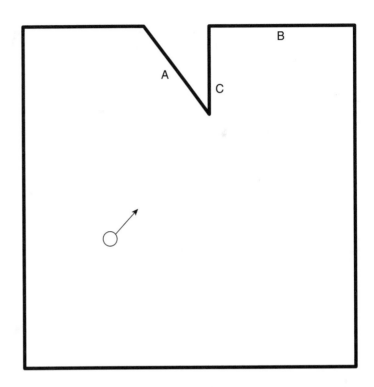

Before we go further, let's define some terms. An "area" will be defined as a space that contains one or more walls. An area will be called "atomic" if it contains only walls that cannot (from any position and orientation) occlude another wall in that same space. Figure 4.1 was an example of an atomic space, Figure 4.2 was not.

A BSP tree divides a space into atomic areas that are then extracted from the BSP tree in such a way as to give us the correct depth-sorted information. By dividing the space up into areas that are "atomic," we can just traverse the tree until we reach an atomic space and then draw all the walls in that space in any order we like. We just need to know in which order to draw the areas. Fortunately for us, the BSP tree traversal will give us exactly that information.

So now we have a correct depth-sort of the walls to be drawn. This was one of the problems we needed to solve. The companion requirement was that this would be fast. Well, we are in luck. One of the greatest things about BSP trees is that they are fast! This is because all the depth-sorting information is actually contained in the datastructure which is created *a priori* (in advance). So we are actually not doing any sorts during the game itself, merely traversing the tree.

We have met both of our requirements. We have employed BSP trees and the painter's algorithm to facilitate fast, correct rendering of a scene. Life is good.

Figure 4.3.
Dividing the room.

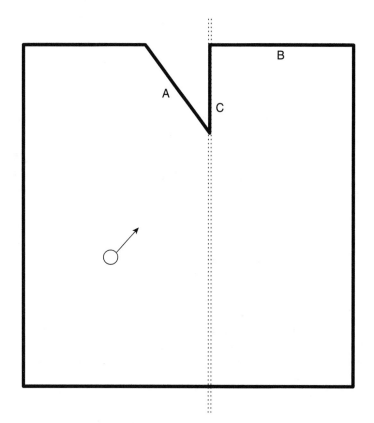

Advantages and Disadvantages of Binary Space Partitioning

As with any algorithm, BSP trees have advantages and disadvantages. Understanding these makes it possible for you to make an informed decision about its suitability to a given problem.

First, we will cover the advantages.

■ **BSP trees are fast.** The main reason for the inception of BSP trees was the need for speed. Fortunately they fit the bill nicely, but not without penalties. Many of the disadvantages that we will cover are directly a result of the attempt to make the process fast.

■ **The BSP tree only needs to be created once.** The main reason that rendering is so fast when using BSP trees is that the BSP-tree data structure only needs to be created once for each world that we are going to render. This can be done before the program even executes, since it will always be the same for a given world. Much of the functionality that traditional depth-sorting algorithms employ is built into the BSP-tree data structure, so, once this structure is created, time need not be wasted doing this during rendering.

Of course, nothing comes for free. We must make sacrifices to gain these advantages. Sometimes these sacrifices are too great to offset the advantages. It just depends on the requirements of our problem. The disadvantages are as follows:

- **The world must be static.** Probably the biggest liability associated with BSP trees is that we cannot change the world dynamically. Since we have constructed the data structure *a priori*, the relationship between members of this world must remain constant. If we change this relationship, we lose all confidence that our data structure is still correct. Certain types of applications are not really hindered by this restriction, because it is implicit in the task. For example, flight simulators are not really bothered by this, since the relationships between objects (mountains, rivers, buildings, and so on) in that world almost never change. Therefore this is not really an issue for this application.

- **Data structure required for tree.** As already mentioned, to implement BSP trees we must have a data structure. This means not only do we have to reserve space for this data structure somewhere, but we must also devise some way to extract the wanted information (depth-sorted walls) from it. The BSP-tree data structure can grow to considerable size depending on the complexity and size of the world to be rendered.

- **Caching considerations.** Closely related to the preceding concern is the impact that this data structure can have on cache coherency. If the data structure is not properly constructed, its traversal can have devastating effects on the PC's caching algorithms. If the data structure is well thought out, this problem can be minimized.

BSP-Tree Data Structure

This section describes the BSP-tree data structure in detail. Efficiency of rendering is directly related to the way that the data structure is created and used. Some of the cache-coherency concerns can be reduced to near negligible effects if this part of the process is handled correctly.

As per its name, a BSP tree is a binary tree. A binary tree is a data structure that is a subset of the group of tree data structures. If you are not familiar with tree data structures, I recommend you make yourself so. A good explanation of many types of tree structures can be found in *Algorithms in C* by Princeton Professor Robert Sedgewick.

A binary tree differs from the general tree class in one important way: a binary tree can have either zero or two children from any node. A node that has no children is called a *leaf.* From any node, the group of nodes containing its children, its children's children, and so on all the way to the bottom of the tree, are called *descendants.* Figure 4.4 shows an example of a binary tree and the names of the different components.

Figure 4.4.
Components of a binary tree.

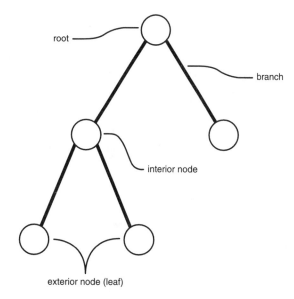

root

branch

interior node

exterior node (leaf)

The reason for using a binary tree (besides the fact that the name matches) is clear. At each step in the creation process, we will either need to divide the space into two parts, or we will have an atomic space. If the space is to be divided, each space resulting from the division can be represented by a branch leaving the current node.

In the last section, we discussed how the BSP tree works in a simplified world. There was a space that we wanted to render, and we used the BSP-tree algorithm to help us correctly draw the walls. In that example, we only needed to divide the space once, and in each of the remaining spaces, we knew that no wall could occlude another. It is not usually the case that our world is this simple and only one division is necessary. Usually we will have many more, so we must figure out some way to keep track of these divisions in some meaningful way.

If we are at an interior node in the tree, we know this space needs to be split into two more groups to (eventually) get us to atomic spaces. This tells us that there is a space division associated with each interior node. From this it follows that each leaf of the tree is associated with an atomic space, since no further divisions (no children) are required.

Now I think I need to explain in detail what a divider is. Simply put, it is whatever is necessary to divide the space we are working on into the two parts that we need. It so happens that there is a construct with exactly this quality: a hyper-plane. A hyper-plane is a plane from dimension N-1 that exists in dimension N. For 2-space (the dimension we will mostly be using), this is a line. For 3-space, it is a plane. A hyper-plane has the quality that it divides any space it lies in into two parts. That is exactly what we want.

It should be obvious that there are an infinite number of hyper-planes in 2-space and beyond. Somehow, we have to decide which of these will be used for our divider. I will discuss this at length in the section on BSP-tree construction.

The rest of this section will discuss the actual implementation of the BSP-tree data structure. Data structure implementation is a very important part of performance that is often overlooked by programmers. We should look for ways to improve our representation over traditional methods to allow for more efficient implementations.

Most tree data structures are implemented with a traditional linked-list approach. Basically, each interior node structure needs two pointers to other nodes of the same type (the children of this node), as well as any other information needed for that node. So, using this and other information supplied in this section, we know we need at least the following fields in the data structure:

- Divider for this space
- Pointer to "left" child
- Pointer to "right" child

For exterior nodes (leaves) of the tree, we do not really need all of this information, just the list of walls or other objects to render for the space this node represents. Somewhere in this tree, we are going to have to have interior nodes that have exterior nodes (leaves) as children. The problem is that we just said that each interior node was going to have two pointers to other nodes of its type. We said nothing about having pointers to another type of node (the leaf). There are a couple of different ways to solve this problem. The first method involves having four other fields for each interior node. Two of the fields are pointers to a node of the exterior type. The other two fields are flags that tell us whether each child is an interior or exterior node. If the node is an interior node, use the field outlined previously. If the child is a leaf, use the corresponding field for an exterior node.

This certainly solves the problem; however, it is not the most elegant way to handle this situation. We now have two different node types with which to deal. Let's try to figure out a way to only have to deal with one. If we are only going to have one node type, this type needs to contain fields for all the information required for both fields. Basically, that is just the previous list with an extra field to contain a list of the walls to render for the exterior nodes. If we are at an interior node, we will just leave this field as NULL. Similarly, the child pointer and divider fields are not used for an exterior node and can be set to NULL. What we will end up with might be declared something like this:

```
typedef struct Node NodePtr;
struct Node {
   DividorType *dividor;
   WallList *walls;
   NodePtr *leftChild;
   NodePtr *rightChild;
};
```

Note that DividorType and WallList have not been declared here. That is because we have not discussed exactly what the two are in detail. DividorType is a type that describes whatever divider we decide to use. What a divider is will be discussed in the section about BSP-tree construction.

`WallList` is a type for a linked-list of walls to render. The exact details of this type are unimportant to this topic.

I mentioned that a linked-list implementation is usually used for tree structures. Each node contains pointers to its (two) children. We get to one of the children using its pointer much the same way that we get to the next node in a linked-list using its `next` pointer. However, now we must choose between two pointers depending on the child we would like to visit. Once we have decided and made our traversal, the child node is treated just as its parent was for further descent. The ease of traversal between parent and child makes this a pragmatically pleasing solution.

While this is the most obvious and commonly adopted method, it has a problem. Each node of a linked-list (and hence, a BSP tree) is allocated as it is needed. When this allocation request is sent to the operating system, it is free to return any appropriately sized memory segment to the solicitor. Often times this segment of memory will be right next to the previous allocation, but not necessarily. Things such as fragmented memory and other interspersed memory allocations can cause it to be virtually anywhere. This does not affect the algorithm, but in our quest for speed, it can have repercussions. If just one of the nodes of the BSP tree is a large relative distance away from the others, we will get far more frequent cache-misses than if they were all very close together. Therefore it would be good if we could somehow group them together.

One possible solution to this problem starts with the prerequisite that you must know how many nodes will be in the tree before its allocation. This is not really a problem, since usually the tree will be constructed earlier and stored in a file. It would be a simple matter to include the number of nodes the tree contains in that file. Knowing the number of nodes, we start by allocating a block of memory that is large enough to hold all of the entries (number of nodes×size of node), and keep a pointer to this memory address in some variable. Each node is then assigned a number (beginning with 0) and all nodes are loaded into this newly allocated memory sequentially based on these newly assigned numbers. For each node, we will still keep track of both of its children; however, instead of keeping a pointer to the child, we will just keep the number we assigned to that child. When we want to go to a particular node, we take the variable that points to this allocated memory buffer (recall that we saved it), and add the number of the node we want to get to multiplied by the size (in bytes) of each node in order to get a memory address. This address is the child we wish to visit. See Figure 4.5 for an example layout to illustrate this method.

Now, the good thing about this method is that the nodes of the tree are guaranteed to be contiguous. We have allocated a contiguous block of memory to hold them, and since we decided that the BSP tree is static, it will never change. Therefore, these nodes will always be contiguous. This guarantees us the best possible configuration as far as caching is concerned. This achievement does not come without a price, however. One of the nice things about our first participant was that the traversal from parent to child was easy and fast. We have lost both of these qualities now. Not only do we have to do calculations to get the child, but this calculation contains multiplies. Multiplies are bad and should be avoided at all costs.

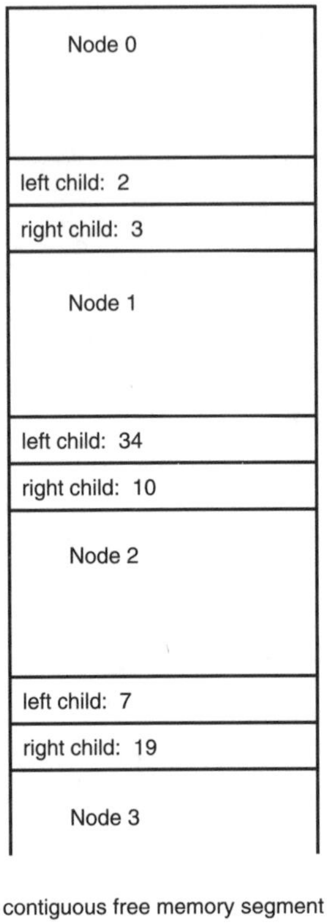

Figure 4.5.
Child is stored as index into contiguous memory area.

Node 0
left child: 2
right child: 3
Node 1
left child: 34
right child: 10
Node 2
left child: 7
right child: 19
Node 3

contiguous free memory segment

To this end, I propose a final solution. This solution is basically a hybrid of the two previous attempts. It starts off with the same prerequisite and setup as our second method. Start by allocating a buffer of contiguous memory and put each of the nodes in that memory. However, now, in each field, instead of having a number to represent a child node, create a pointer to that node. This pointer is calculated exactly the same way that the locations of nodes were calculated in the previous method; it is done one time only, when the BSP tree is loaded from the file. Now what we have is the best of both worlds. We have a simple traversal from parent to child with guaranteed contiguous node allocation. For a graphic example, see Figure 4.6.

All of this may seem to be picking at threads, but cache coherency should be a big consideration for any programmer who is trying to push the envelope of performance. It does not matter how great your algorithms are; if they are thrashing all over the cache, your performance will not be inspiring. However, if you pay attention to small details such as this throughout, you will be pleasantly surprised at the wonderful things you can do.

Figure 4.6.
*Child is stored as pointer
to the appropriate region.*

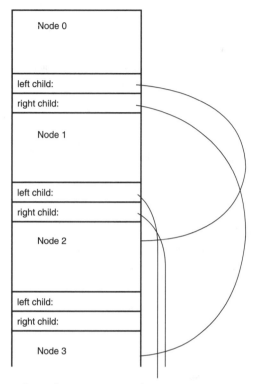

contiguous free memory segment

BSP Tree Creation

So far we have discussed a lot of things about BSP trees; now let's explore the creation of the tree itself. As mentioned earlier, one of the truly nice things about BSP trees is that much of the work is done *a priori*. Anything that can be done before the program starts (or at startup) is just one less thing we have to do while rendering. With BSP trees, we create a tree that describes how different elements (walls) of our world are positioned relative to one another. This information is used to good end—but how do we create it? Read on!

There are actually two different approaches to the creation of the BSP tree, as follows:

■ Create the tree once, and keep the information contained in the tree, as well as the structure of the tree, in a file. This file is loaded at runtime, and the BSP tree is extracted from it. As stated, the layout of the tree (that is, which nodes are children to which other nodes) is somehow stored in this file along with the actual node information. This means the BSP tree is only created one time and need not be created again.

■ Create the tree at runtime. The information for the world is stored in the file, and the BSP tree is created when the program is run. This uses less space in said file, but it causes the BSP tree to be re-made each time the program is run. This method would only be really useful if hard-drive space was at an absolute premium or if some runtime parameter could change the way the BSP tree is constructed.

Since neither of the possible advantages of the second method are very recurrent, I will discuss the creation from the point of view of the first method. The second method is not all that much different from a programming perspective, just place the tree building code in the application itself instead of in an external program.

Because we are constructing the BSP tree one time only, the speed of the creation process is not really a consideration. Rather, we should spend our time trying to create the tree in whatever way will make its use easier and faster. There are an infinite number of BSP trees possible for any world (of interest). We need to decide which of these trees is easiest and fastest to use. Let's discuss some of the qualities of a BSP tree that make this happen.

■ **Tree balance.** A balanced tree is one such that at any given node, the number of walls "below" one child for that node is equal to the number of walls "below" the other child for that same node. By "below" I mean that a wall is contained in some descendant of that child. Basically this means that each time you select a divider for some space in the creation process, you try to select it so that there are approximately the same number of walls on each side of that divider. If you imagined that each wall in every leaf had (equal) mass, then the tree would "balance" if a fulcrum was placed under the root node (or any node). To fully understand why BSP trees (and all binary trees, actually) strive to be balanced is a bit complex and not really necessary. We just need to know that a more balanced tree is more efficient for the renderer. Obviously, a fully balanced tree is not possible. Consider the world that has an odd number of walls. Obviously, these walls cannot be evenly divided in half.

■ **Fewest splits.** Suppose we have chosen a divider for a given space. Each wall in that space will be in one of three categories: on one side of the divider, on the other side of the divider, or crossing (intersecting with) the divider. A wall cannot be included in both subspaces of a divided space, so something else must occur. What happens is that the wall gets split into two walls, one on each side of the divider. This is not a good thing for a couple of reasons. First, we have essentially added an additional wall to render. While it is true that we have also decreased the size of another of the walls we are rendering, it is still a loss for us. Every time we render a wall, we must do some setup to get everything primed to render that wall. This setup code is usually not trivial. What we have essentially done is made it necessary to do setup code twice for each wall that gets split. Obviously, this is not desirable. The other reason that splits are not favored is discussed later.

■ **Divider is orthogonal to one of the principle axes.** It is of benefit if the divider for a space is orthogonal to one of the principle axes. The reason behind this lies behind the splitting process for walls that cross the divider. If a wall crosses a divider that is not orthogonal to a principle axis, the resulting point of intersection will not, in general, contain integral coordinates. On the other hand, if you had chosen a divider that was orthogonal to one of the principle axes, it is more likely that the intersection will occur at an integral coordinate. Since integer math is usually much faster than floating-point math, most games like to try to use integer representations whenever possible. Therefore, you should try to avoid dividers that are not orthogonal to one of the principle axes.

One interesting note related to this last issue. If you have played DOOM for any length of time, you have probably noticed a bug on map E1M1. To find it, proceed from the starting point of this level to the room with the zigzag floor. Just as you enter the room, you can see an Imp on a platform slightly to your left. If you position yourself correctly, you will also notice a section of the floor at the bottom of your screen that appears to be overrun by the texture on the more distant adjoining floor. There is a one- or two-pixel-wide "slime-stream" that runs from that adjoining floor (the floor that causes damage to you) down toward the bottom of the screen. It is kind of hard to get positioned correctly to see it, but it is usually right between you and the Imp. This anomaly is caused by precisely the phenomenon described herein. The divider for one of the spaces in the BSP tree intersects a wall at a non-integral point. Since the wall endpoints are integers in DOOM, the endpoint is just rounded to the nearest integral value. This causes a discrepancy that manifests itself as explained here. I, for one, sleep better at night knowing that even John Carmack (lead programmer at id Software) has made one or two mistakes in his life. Maybe he is human after all!

OK, so now we know what qualities we would like our BSP tree to possess; however, in practice it is not usually possible to fully realize these goals. Often times the tree-balancing and minimal-split goals are mutually exclusive, so a compromise must be struck. If a choice has to be made between splits and balance, I would lean towards minimizing splits. Splits seem to cause no end to problems and should be avoided if possible.

I have covered the concept behind space partitioning from a high-level point of view. Here is a more linear representation:

■ Start by dividing the given space (and all walls) into two parts with a divider

■ Take each subspace created by the division and repeat this process on it

■ Continue to do this until all subspaces are "atomic"

In the preceding instructions, the words "repeat this process" phrase should speak volumes to you about the nature of the construction algorithm. You will be using recursion. This instance of recursion is pretty straightforward and actually lends itself perfectly to our understanding of the partitioning process.

Notice the final step. You are asked to continue this process until all subspaces are "atomic." What stops the BSP-tree sub-division process depends greatly on the application. For the instance used predominantly throughout this chapter (pseudo-3-D rendering using 2-D BSP trees), we are only interested in the condition that any wall within a given subspace is unable to occlude another wall in that same subspace. This happens to be the case for my examples, but is by no means the definitive ending condition. This condition must be determined based on the problem to be solved.

The first bullet asks us to divide some space with a divider. What it does not say is how to select that divider. As we mentioned earlier, the divider will be a hyper-plane for the dimension of space we are considering. A hyper-plane for the example we are using (2-space) is a line. Generally, we would like to pick this dividing line to be coincident with one of the walls. This is not a hard-and-fast rule, but it is almost always the case. The reasons for this approach include the following, which focus on minimizing splits:

- All walls will intersect other walls at vertices. If the divider for this space is co-linear with a wall in this space, this divider cannot split any of the walls that this wall intersects. Basically, there are fewer possibilities for splits occurring.
- The wall we are coincident with cannot be split by this divider.
- Projections of walls beyond endpoints will often intersect other walls at vertices. This is not always the case, but it happens frequently enough that you might as well take advantage of it. Also, this effect can be maximized by advantageous arrangement of the walls in our world.

Some BSP tree renderers enforce the restriction that the partitioning lines (dividers) for the BSP tree are orthogonal to one of the principle axes. This solves certain problems both in the creation and rendering of the BSP tree. However, this procedure usually results in an inordinate amount of splits, which I feel makes it a poor overall choice for generic BSP-tree implementations.

We know we probably want to use one of the walls in our space as the partitioning line for the space—but which one? Yes, that is the million-dollar question, and probably the most complex issue in the creation process. The selection of a divider will have direct effects on the overall efficiency of the tree. Suppose we have a wall in mind for the division, but we would like to know if it is a "good" choice. Well, first you need to decide what "good" is. The most obvious answer is that it satisfies all your goals for the BSP-tree creation list. Unfortunately, we have already decided that it is virtually impossible to 100 percent satisfy these goals. So, what you need to do is determine how to satisfy the goals as much as possible. To this end, I propose that you attempt to assign some "rating" to this selection based on the qualifications outlined previously. This rating will mean nothing by itself, but it can be used to compare this selection with others to decide which is better than another. How you construct the rating will depend on which of the listed goals is most important to you. For general use, I give splits approximately 10 to 20 times the weight of each unbalanced wall, and non-orthogonal dividers about five times the weight. These are just figures that have worked well for me. Each application may require different values. Start with a value of zero. For each split, add 15. If the divider is not orthogonal to a principle axis, add five, then add the absolute value of the difference between the number of walls on each side of this node. This will give you a total. You can use this total to decide how good a divider this wall is compared to others. The lower the rating, the better choice this wall is.

Somewhere out there, for any given world, there is an optimal BSP tree. Now all we have to do is find it. A first pass at that goal might lead us to believe that if, at each level in the division process, we find the wall that is the best selection for our divider, we will end up with the optimal tree. Unfortunately, this is not the case. The reason is that although a certain wall might be a good choice at this level, choosing it may have unforeseen negative effects on subsequent sub-divisions. This implies that choosing a wall that is not as "good" at the current level might, overall, produce a better end result. The upshot of this is that the only way to determine the absolute optimal tree is to use the brute-force method. That is, try every possible combination of every wall at each level of sub-division and evaluate the final tree as compared to combinations. You do not need a degree in discrete mathematics to figure out that this could take a very long time!

This realization might be enough to leave you despairing. You want the optimal tree, but you do not want to spend days waiting for its completion. Fortunately, there is an alternative. At each level of sub-division, you can consider all of the walls as candidates for selection as the divider for that space. Pick approximately 1 percent (but not less than about 10) of these walls at random. Evaluate each wall in turn and decide which of them produces the best selection based on the discussed criterion. Use this wall as the divider for this space. Experimentation has shown that this will create a tree that is quite close to the optimal tree—in a fraction of the creation time.

Once you have decided which wall to use as a divider, you can allocate space for the two children's nodes. After you create these nodes, you step through all the walls. You assign each wall to one of the children based on that wall's position relative to the divider we have selected. Which side is associated with which child is not important, as long as it is constant throughout the entire build process. If one or more of the walls intersect the divider, you must split it. You do this by creating two walls out of the original wall by splitting it at the point it intersected with the divider. After the split is complete, we can put each one in its correct child's wall list. We may put the wall that is coincident with the divider in either of the children's wall lists that we would like. Once this classification is complete, we call this same function recursively on both of the children.

Traversing the BSP Tree

Now that we have discussed at length the process of creating the BSP tree, I will discuss how to use it to render our images and then cover an example traversal. To begin, we need to know where we are currently located in our world. This will be used by the BSP tree to make decisions that will give us a correctly depth-sorted list of walls to render. Also, it should be noted that the direction that we are looking is not important. We are looking for a depth-sort here, and the direction of our view does not effect that relative positioning. Later in the rendering cycle we will have to consider our field of view when determining which walls are visible, but not at this stage.

This is the process used to traverse the BSP tree:

1. Start at the root node for each scene to be rendered.

2. If this node is a leaf, render all the walls for this node (in any order).

3. Determine which side of the divider we are on for this node.

4. Using this information, determine which child node represents the sub-space that you are not currently in (in other words, the child whose space you are not in). If you are exactly on the divider, you can choose either child.

5. Traverse the pointer to that child and go to step 2. After that returns, go to the other child, and repeat from step 2.

The code to accomplish this task is surprisingly simple (which is one of the reasons it can be fast). The code is as follows:

```
void TraverseBSP(BSPNODE *BSPnode)
{
 if(!BSPnode->leftChild && !BSPnode->rightChild)
{
 RenderWalls(BSPnode);
 return;
}
 if (WhichSide(BSPnode) > 0)
{
TraverseBSP(BSPnode->leftChild);
 TraverseBSP(BSPnode->rightChild);
}
else
{
TraverseBSP(BSPnode->rightChild);
TraverseBSP(BSPnode->leftChild);
}
}
```

A few things are assumed here:

■ The first time this function is called, it will be passed to the root of the BSP tree as an argument

■ BSPNODE type is defined

■ There exists a RenderWalls function that will render all walls for a given node

■ There exists a WhichSide function that will return an appropriate value based on the player's current position relative to the divider for this node

That is really all there is to the traversal of the tree. Most of the work for the actual rendering is done in the RenderWalls function (and the functions it calls).

An Example

In this section I will work through an example. This example will illustrate the construction as well as the traversal of the BSP tree. This should tie everything together.

Let's start with some space that we are interested in rendering. The space that we will be dealing with contains some semi-complex geometry. A few divisions will be necessary to completely resolve the depth-sorting issues. First, let's look at each division graphically. Then we will construct the BSP tree from there. The geometry of the room is shown in Figure 4.7.

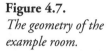

Figure 4.7.
The geometry of the example room.

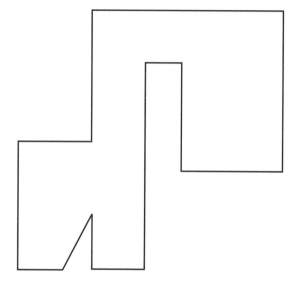

This is by far the most complex room we have dealt with yet, but it is still pretty reasonable. Now let's see each individual division that occurs to divide this room up into the atomic sub-spaces that we would like. Figure 4.8 shows the first division.

The dotted line represents the division that has taken place. The numeral 1 by it just means that this is the first division. This labeling will become important when we start constructing the tree itself. I chose this division rather arbitrarily. It may not be the best choice when using the criteria that we have described. The goal for this example is not an efficient tree, just a step-by-step understanding of the creation and use of the BSP tree. Figure 4.9 shows the first divisions in place.

Figure 4.8.
The first division.

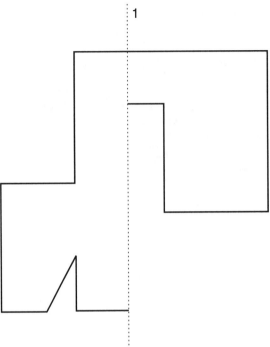

Figure 4.9.
*The first two divisions
in place.*

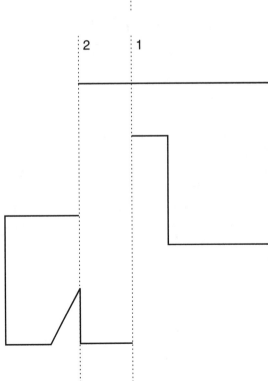

Now that the first two divisions are in place, we can see that the space to the left of the first divider has been successfully sub-divided into atomic regions. No wall in the region either left or right of divider 2 can occlude another wall in that same region, no matter what my view position. Now let's see the third and final partition, shown in Figure 4.10.

Figure 4.10.
The last partition.

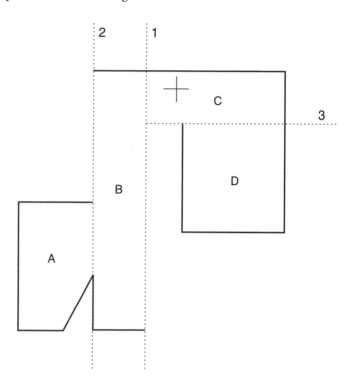

Now we see all the divisions that will be necessary. I took the liberty of labeling each atomic area for reference. There are four of them, and each follows our prerequisite for an atomic area. Now that we have graphically and conceptually created the BSP tree, let's look at the BSP tree. It is shown in Figure 4.11.

This is a very tidy looking tree. Notice that each interior node has been assigned to a divider, and each exterior node has been assigned to an atomic space as we have discussed. Another thing to notice is the order in which the nodes are labeled. It may seem as if I just labeled them left to right, but actually I put them in the tree based on their relationship to their parents. If you look at Figure 4.10, you will see that divider 3 is on the "right" side of divider 1. Therefore, I chose to place node 3 as the "right" child to node 1 in the tree. This decision is up to me, but once I make that decision, I have to conform throughout the creation of the tree. Atomic space D is on the "right" side of divider 3, so it occupies the "right" child of the interior node for divider 3. This is true throughout.

Figure 4.11.
The BSP tree.

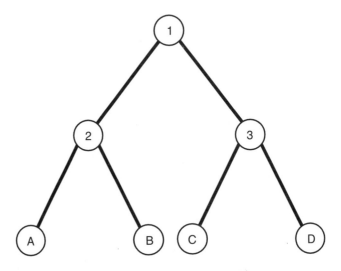

You may have noticed a "+" mark inside area C in Figure 4.10. Imagine that we are standing at this point in this room and would like to get a BSP-tree traversal so we can decide which order to render the walls in. OK, let's look at the BSP tree we've created and do the traversal by hand.

1. We start out at the root node. The divider for this node is Divider 1.
2. We are on the right side of Divider 1, so next we visit Node 2 (which corresponds to Divider 2).
3. We are also on the right side of Divider 2, so we first visit this node's left child, or exterior Node A.
4. Now that we are at a leaf, we draw all the walls from this atomic space.
5. Go back up to Node 2.
6. We now visit the remaining child of Node 2, which is node B.
7. This is atomic, so we render the walls in Leaf B.
8. Again, go back to Node 2.
9. We have visited all the children for Node 2, so we go back to its parent, Node 1.
10. We have visited Node 2 from here, so now let's go to Node 3. This is the first visit here, so we find out that we are on the left side of its divider.
11. Because we are on the left side of the divider, we visit the right child, Node D.
12. Node D is an atomic node, so we render all walls for Node D.
13. When we are done, we go back up to Node 3.
14. We visited the right child, so now we go to the left, Node C.
15. Node C is atomic, so render all walls for this node.

16. Go back to our parent, Node 3.

17. We have visited all the children for this node, so we go back to its parent, Node 1.

18. We have visited all of this nodes child, and since this is the root node, that means we are done with the traversal.

This traversal caused us to render the atomic areas in the following order: A, B, D, C. If we look back at Figure 4.10, I think we can agree that this is the correct way to draw the walls based on our position. Note: we may or may not actually draw all of the walls in each of these atomic spaces, depending on what happens below us in the rendering pipeline. For the purposes of this algorithm, we need not concern ourselves with this. We just need to pass all possible walls to the renderer and let it decide which ones to actually draw.

Figure 4.12 shows the BSP tree again, only this time the flow of the traversal is described by labeling the steps we took. These labeled numbers correspond to the number list created previously.

Figure 4.12.
The traversal-labeled BSP tree.

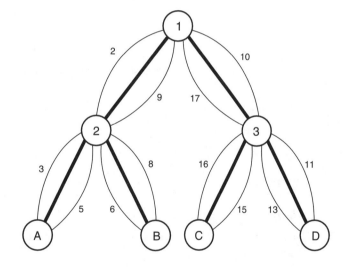

We have successfully divided the space up, created a BSP tree, and traversed that BSP tree. While this geometry was fairly simplistic, I think it serves to at least show the process. Geometries far more complex than this can be handled—and handled in exactly the same way. Everything will just be a little bigger.

Optimizations/Extensions to BSP Trees

This section discusses optimizations and extensions to the BSP-tree process.

One optimization involves the traversal of the BSP tree. In the examples, and in most practice, recursion is used. This is almost autonomic, since the algorithm lends itself to recursion so well.

Unfortunately, recursion has some drawbacks: a lot of stack space is used, and performance takes a hit because of the large number of function calls. Because we are looking for top performance, we should at least consider our alternatives. The following is just such an alternative to consider.

Suppose that we decided to eliminate recursion from the solution. We would need some way to keep track of the correct order of child traversal that we achieved by using recursion. Actually, this turns out to be pretty easy if we just fall back on some of the data structures we have used in the past. A stack will help us here.

We start out with an infinite loop. We only break out of this loop when there is nothing left on the stack to process. Instead of making successive recursive calls at each node, we just push both child pointers on the stack. Then, before the next iteration of the loop, we pop a pointer off the stack and use that as our current node.

Here is the code:

```
CurrentNode = BSPTree; // root of BSP tree
for (;;)
{
if (!currentNode)
break;
if (!currentNode->leftChild && !currentNode->rightChild) // leaf
RenderWalls(currentNode);
else if (WhichSide(currentNode->divider) > 0) // we are on "left" side
{
Push(currentNode->leftChild);
Push(currentNode->rightChild);
}
else // we are on "right" side
{
Push(currentNode->rightChild);
Push(currentNode->leftChild);
}
Pop(currentNode);
```

As before, some things are assumed:

- BSPTree is initialized to point to the root of the BSP tree
- currentNode is a declared NodePointer
- There is a RenderWalls function that will render all walls for a given node
- There is a WhichSide function that will return a value based on the player's current position relative to the divider for a given node
- Push and Pop stack functions have been implemented for pointers

Of course, this is not the most efficient form of this code, but it is pretty good. You would probably want to go over the code and optimize it quite a bit, since the whole reason for using stacks is performance.

Does this really make a difference? Well, yes; I have timed code like this against the recursive version and there is definitely a speed increase. However, it was only a matter of micro-seconds for approximately 1,000 polygons, so I am not sure it is really worth worrying about. But if you are looking for that last ounce of performance, or system stack space is tight, this is a possible answer.

Front-to-Back Traversal of the BSP Tree

Throughout this chapter, I have discussed what is known as a back-to-front traversal of the BSP tree. This is because it is simpler to understand and maintain than the alternative. However, if we are willing to embrace that encumbrance, we can do some good things.

A front-to-back traversal is simply a traversal of the tree in exactly the reverse order from the way we have seen so far. It routes us through the nodes in a way that will expose us to the closest walls first, followed by the next closest set of walls, all the way down to the most distant walls. You might wonder why we would want to do such a thing. On the surface it seems ridiculous. If we render walls closest-to-farther using the painter's algorithm, we will not get the results we are looking for. True enough. One of the effects of using this method is that we can no longer use the painter's algorithm. We must look for something different.

Basically what we would like to do is force ourselves to only draw each pixel one time per frame of animation. Therefore, once we have drawn a wall, nothing could draw over that wall. This would prevent a wall that is occluded by another wall from being drawn, and we have successfully removed all hidden surfaces.

What kind of data structure could we use to keep track of this? Well, we could declare a two-dimensional array the same size as the screen to which we are rendering. The array would contain Boolean elements, and as each pixel on the screen is drawn, the corresponding element in the array is set to True. Before any pixels may be drawn, the correct index must be tested to see if we are able to draw there. This certainly solves our problem, but it is grossly inefficient. Not only do we have a huge data structure for even the smallest screens ($320 \times 200 = 64,000$), but we also have to set each element in this array to false before each frame. This aspect alone makes this solution totally unusable.

We need something a little easier to manage. One such solution employs the always helpful linked-list. Suppose we create an array of size equal to the height of the screen to which we are rendering that contains pointers to a linked list. These linked lists will keep information about which horizontal spans of pixels have been drawn. Each node in the list will have a starting value and ending value for its span, and a pointer to the next span. In Figure 4.13. you see a box that you have drawn on the screen. Also, you see one of the elements of this array for scan-line 50.

Figure 4.13.
The box.

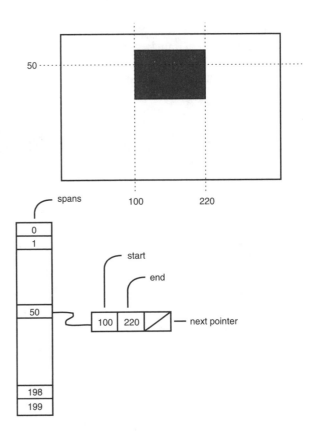

So, index 50 in our spans array has a node that corresponds to the row of pixels that have been drawn on the screen on that scan-line. Now, each time we need to set a pixel, we step down the linked list. If the X-coordinate of the pixel we want to set is between the start and end field for any node in that list, we cannot draw it. Otherwise, we can draw it, but we must also update this data structure to reflect that we have now set that pixel so that no other object could over-write it.

Maintaining these linked-lists require a fair amount of processing time, but there are quite a few advantages:

■ Each pixel is only set one time. This is in contrast to the painter's algorithm, which can set a pixel multiple times. On architectures where VRAM writes are slow (such as the PC), the overhead of the list management is nothing compared to the time required to make multiple writes to almost every pixel on the screen. This effect, of course, can be lessened to a serious degree by keeping an off-screen buffer so the multiple writes are done to DRAM; however, this solution has problems also, which is a topic for another chapter.

- Initializing this data structure merely entails setting all of the pointers to NULL. This is quite a bit faster than clearing a huge array.

- Entire lines of spans can be eliminated at once. In the previous example, if I tried to draw a line that ran from (150,50) to (170,50), I could disallow this entire line with one check.

Again, this doesn't come without a cost. There are a couple of problems. First, we must also free each of these nodes between each frame. This can take some time. Second, allocating and de-allocating memory like this can seriously fragment it, causing poor performance and sometimes program failures.

This is just a single example of a type of data structure that we can use to allow front-to-back traversals. It is often the case that even more efficient ones exist for a particular application. The key is realizing exactly what you can say about the geometry and to take maximum advantage of that knowledge.

So now that we can correctly display a BSP tree by traversing front-to-back, let's discuss other advantages that come with this method. One thing we can do is stop traversing the tree if every pixel on the screen has been set. Obviously, when every pixel has been set, nothing else can be drawn. It may be the case, however, that at this point we are still not done traversing the BSP tree. Well, that does not matter. We can abort the traversal at this point, since we know nothing else can be drawn.

Another advantage of front-to-back traversal is that it can give huge increases in performance. Earlier, I told you that the direction you are looking would never play any part in the traversal of the BSP tree. While that is correct for traditional traversals, we can implement an extension to the front-to-back traversal that will change this. Here is the idea: we eliminate parts of the BSP tree that we know cannot be seen from our current position and Line of Sight (LOS). Figure 4.14 illustrates this.

The circle represents our position. The two dotted lines emanating from the circle describe our field of view. The larger vertical dotted line is a BSP node divider. From this picture, it is obvious that we could never see anything on the other side of the divider, so we need not even consider the walls that are over there. For certain situations, this can save huge amounts of traversal overhead.

The example given previously is rather simplistic, mainly because we are looking straight west. We need a more general way to decide if what we are traversing is at all possible to see. Suppose that for each node of the BSP tree, we create two more fields. These fields will keep a bounding rectangle for each of the two children. We know that if we are to be able to see anything contained in the space described by that child, at least part of that bounding rectangle must be contained in our field of view. In other words, we need to intersect two lines (the edges of our field of view) with a rectangle (the bounding rectangle). This can be done very fast using traditional methods. If either line intersects the rectangle, at least part of the area could possibly be visible (if it is not occluded by other walls). If neither line intersects the rectangle, it could still be the case that the entire rectangle lies between these two lines. We must check for this possibility. If that is also not the case, then this sub-space could not be visible, and we may disregard that entire branch of the tree! This can result in massive speed increases.

Figure 4.14.
The line of sight.

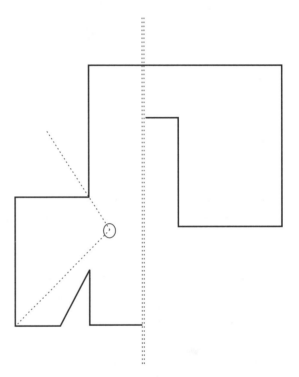

Dynamic Modification of the BSP Tree

I have told you that one of the disadvantages of using BSP trees is that the scene must stay static. Well, I lied. (Please don't hold it against me. I promise not to do it again, at least in this chapter.) The static nature of BSP trees is probably their greatest liability. It would be nice if we could lift this restriction. Well, as you have probably surmised, that is the topic of this section.

One of the reasons that BSP trees are so fast is that the scene cannot change, so information about the relative positions of objects in the world can be created in advance and do not have to be recalculated during the rendering process. However, sometimes we would like to make modifications to the tree.

> If you are rendering a scene that is frequently changing, then BSP trees are not the approach to take. Investigate one of the other methods of depth-sorting. The extension to BSP trees described here is really only useful for infrequent changes to the world and should not be used too often, as it will degrade performance.

Suppose that we want to change just one part of the world. Maybe it is just one room out of a hundred. What we can do is modify the BSP tree to accommodate that desire. For instance, we could just modify the world and regenerate the BSP tree for the entire world. I'm sure you can imagine just how fast that would be. No, we need something a little better than that. We know regenerating the entire tree is too cumbersome—but maybe we could regenerate a part of it. That is what we will do.

First, we would like to minimize the build process, so it behooves us to find the smallest area to change. Basically we need to find the node that has the least area that still encompasses all of the changes we would like to make. This is not really too hard. Just traverse the BSP tree front-to-back using one of the changing walls at the "current position." At each node in the traversal, decide if its bounding-box still describes the desired area (that is, all of the changing walls). When this is not true, we know that the parent is the node we would like to start rebuilding from. One thing that would help this process would be to create pointers in each node that point to that node's parent. Then once we have decided that a current node's bounding rectangle does not encapsulate the necessary space, we can just follow that pointer to get to the node we want.

Now that we know where to start the build process, we build a new BSP tree, given the walls contained in the area of the node we have found. Once this tree is finished, we want to attach it in place of our newly found node. Again, we need to go to the parent and make the appropriate child pointer point to the new BSP tree that we have created. Voila! We have changed our world. (Do not forget to free the space for that old sub-tree.)

Of course, this is not a panacea. We would not want to do this very often, or on large areas of space, lest we incur a performance hit. Also, all this allocation and freeing of memory has defeated our best efforts to help cache coherency. However, if you would like to change small parts of the tree on an infrequent basis, this will certainly work.

Another extension involves much the same process, but it applies to well-known changes. Considering the previous example, what if the room in question changed to one of, say, four well-defined states? If this is the case, we could pre-compute four separate BSP trees for this room. Then as the room changed, we could just replace that branch of the world BSP tree with the correct version of the changing room. This would be very fast and allow for a fairly dynamic world.

Modeling Solids

To this point, I have talked about using BSP trees for rendering worlds with walls. There is no inherent reason to restrict their use in this way—I just chose this example to illustrate how to use them. Another promising use for BSP trees is in modeling 3-D solids. Many of the games today use flat bitmaps for Sprites. While this provides a fairly realistic interpretation, it leaves a little to be desired. Often the Sprite will appear identical, no matter which direction you look at it from. This is a memory-versus-speed consideration that was necessary because PCs had limited computing power. Now, as PCs get more powerful, we can move on to more realistic renderings.

BSP trees can be used to model a solid that is approximated by some planar geometric forms (triangle, planar polygon, and so on). The construction and use are really no different from the examples we have discussed. The only difference is that we will never be "inside" the space described by the BSP tree. We are now viewing the object from the outside. This will change our back-facing determination, but for purposes of BSP trees, the traversal and creation are identical.

One interesting related idea concerns using 3-D BSP trees to model objects, as described previously. What if this object is in a world that is rendered using BSP trees? It would be nice if we could connect them somehow. Well, it so happens that we are in luck. We can just add the BSP tree for the object as a child to the one for the world. By merging the BSP tree for this object with the BSP tree for the world, we can render the two very quickly. Also, the object BSP tree benefits from all of the optimizations that have been set up for the world BSP tree (such as the bounding-area check).

3-D BSP Trees

Throughout this chapter we have been using 2-D BSP trees as our examples. This is because 2-D space is conceptually easier to understand. But I think this chapter would be useful to anyone planning to use BSP trees, regardless of which dimensionality they plan to use. The ideas are identical for other spatial configurations, with only semantic differences between the examples I showed and the similar concepts for 3-space. Here are a few of the differences for 3-D BSP trees:

- Node divider is a plane instead of a line.
- The math for calculating which side of the divider you are on is more complex in general.
- A bounding rectangle becomes one of many 3-D constructs. (Choose the one that is best suited to the types of worlds to be rendered.)
- Splits are even more grotesque. We have to split a plane with another plane. All manners of singularities can result from this. We may want to increase the penalty for splits in the creation process.

Though the process is quite a bit more mathematically intense than the 2-D version, it is still an extremely good way to render 3-D worlds.

Summary

BSP trees are an exciting new approach to a traditional rendering problem. By using them, we can attain new levels of performance. They are not without fault, and they are certainly not the end-all for depth-sorting. However, if you can live with the seemingly incidental disadvantages, they offer a lot. All of this praise notwithstanding, I would like to make one final point: no algorithm or data structure is a suitable replacement for thought. Perhaps for the application you are building, there is a simpler approach that will solve all your problems. Maybe by making minute changes to an existing approach you can get what you need. Always consider your alternatives.

Designing the
User Interface

by Eagle Jones

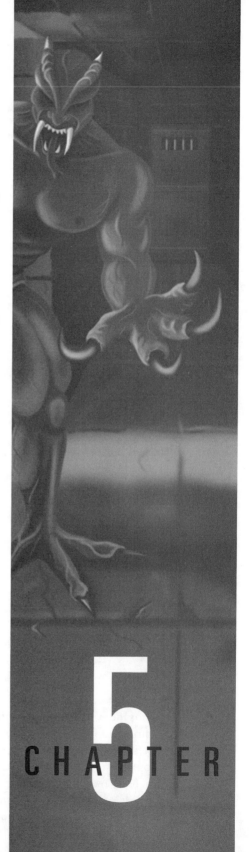

CHAPTER **5**

The user interface, of course, is the part of your game that connects the audience with your program. You must establish a comfortable feeling from the start. Remember, you want people to be afraid of the monster around that next corner, not afraid that their computers will crash. In programming a game, what you are seeking to do is control the user's emotions. The interface is the most important element of that process.

In this chapter, you will learn some of the most vital aspects of game programming. The entire point of a game is to create a fun experience. The most impressive technical achievements in three-dimensional rendering or virtual reality are worthless without a good connection to the user. The first part of this chapter will primarily discuss psychology, which can help us to understand what we need to do to promote the responses that we want from the user. Then we will see how to specifically apply this to certain aspects of game programming. We'll cover the following topics:

- Basic psychology
- The awareness center
- The intellectual center
- The emotional center
- The action center
- The psychology of color
- Implementing pyschology in the game environment
- The game start-up
- Menus and options
- Game play
- The keyboard
- Exit
- Errors

Psychology

For our purposes, we can think of the human mind as working in four fundamental sections: the awareness, intellectual, emotional, and action centers. These parts of the mind work in concert, allowing us to operate effectively within our environment.

The first, the awareness center, provides input. It makes no evaluations or decisions but simply reports the existence of something through one of our senses. The intellectual center stores and evaluates information that is passed to it by the awareness center, also relating it to previous experiences in the form of memories. The intellectual center, however, is limited to factual information. Therefore we need the emotional center in order to make value judgments. Rather than using memories to store its previous information, the emotional center has a set of values to help it make decisions. Once the intellectual and emotional centers have made their decisions, they pass information to the fourth part of the mind, the action center. As you might have guessed, this causes some sort of action to take place, usually through physical movement. This four-part model thus provides us with an object-oriented approach to the mind.

The interface to the computer must be a natural extension of these processes. When the player sees something on the screen, it must be easily recognizable so that the awareness center can quickly classify it and make sure the rest of the mind gets the information necessary to process it correctly. Once a decision has been made, the input from the user must be a natural extension of the action process.

For example, a monster appears on the screen. The awareness center immediately recognizes it as a demon. The emotional center quickly responds with feelings of fear and hatred. The intellectual center evaluates the information and decides that since the player is only at 10 percent health and the demon is a tough monster, the logical response is to run. In this case, the "flee" response is sent to the action center. The action center takes this impulse and connects it with the idea that pressing the down arrow will cause the player to go backwards.

The next few pages look at how interface design relates to each of these psychological centers.

The Awareness Center

Because the awareness center makes no judgments, it's fairly easy to satisfy this part of the mind. All you need to do is give it something that it can recognize and classify. Good artwork and presentation are the keys to this. In other words, make sure your monsters really look mean, that it's easy to tell the difference between different objects (unless you are trying to create a certain amount of confusion to make the game harder), and that your sounds really sound like what they're supposed to be. Text should be easy to read, with a recognizable character set.

The Intellectual Center

The intellectual center wants information. Because it is not unbiased (memories from outside of the game can affect its decisions) and it does make evaluations, it's a little more difficult to please this part of the mind than the awareness center. Strive for efficient, accurate presentation of relevant information. One of the best ways to do this is to implement a status bar at the bottom of the screen that contains all the information you are trying to give to the user. More on the status bar will come later in this chapter.

The Emotional Center

In designing a game, it is perhaps most important that you appeal to the emotional center. Ultimately it is the emotional center that will evaluate the game itself. In the case of shareware, the emotional center will decide whether or not to register, and in the case of commercial software, it will decide whether or not to buy more titles from the same company. The intellectual center does evaluate certain facts, such as the price, reviews from other sources, and other information, but the emotional center is key. Therefore the programmer must carefully manipulate it.

When someone plays your game, many feelings and emotions will be crowding his or her mind. These sensations will come on basically three levels. The first level reflects how the person was feeling before he played your game. We cannot really control this directly, but a good game can make a person feel better when he or she plays it. Likewise, a poor game can make somebody feel worse. The feelings on the other two levels can spill over into real life. These two levels contain emotions directed at the world that you create within your game and feelings directed at the program itself.

Negative emotions should not be generated by the user interface or the program itself. Far too often, the lack of a good interface creates feelings of frustration and anger for users. That's why you must be so careful about creating a good interface. But there are also many other things in the game design that can, and should, contribute to emotions.

The full range of feelings should be brought out within the world of your game. Graphics, sound, and the general atmosphere and story line of your game will contribute to this. Within the game, it is often desirable to generate negative emotions, such as fear and anger, which add to the experience of playing the game. When creating all of these aspects, however, it is important to keep in mind the mood of the game and the target audience for which you are aiming. It's generally not a good idea to create too much anger and fear in a children's educational game.

Some of the most important aspects of generating emotions come from color and sound. Consider the games you have played. Wouldn't the entire experience of DOOM be different if the walls were in pastels and the soundtrack was pure disco? Color is discussed in more detail later in this chapter.

The Action Center

The action center is the part of the mind that finally does something. As game programmers, we need to figure out what the action center wants to do and make the game respond to it. Since I haven't figured out how to read the minds of users yet (watch for source code in a forthcoming book!), we have to settle for some other way of naturally affecting an action. There are three basic approaches to setting up user input; only one of them truly follows this paradigm.

The completely intuitive user interface is our goal. It's also probably an unattainable one in a complex game with multiple levels, weapons, and actions. Every control should make as much sense as using the up-arrow key to move up or forward. Unfortunately, the arrow keys are about the only intuitive part of the keyboard, and the mouse and joystick only provide equivalents to these, along with perhaps an intuitive button to fire the weapons. Thus, the limitations of the system in which we must work—mainly the lack of an intuitive device that provides many control options—make it quite difficult for us to create the perfect interface.

The least effective interface is a reverse-intuitive system that the user will never become accustomed to. Unfortunately, this is more common than you might think. An exaggerated example of a reverse-intuitive design would be to have the up arrow move the character down. This obviously makes no sense, and players will probably never get the idea. At this point, you might say, "No problem—I'm not going to make a non-intuitive interface. I don't think I've ever even seen one." Think again. How many times have you played a game in which Ctrl+F7 loaded your missiles or double-clicking with the right mouse button made you jump? While most users will eventually be able to memorize such commands, they will not be nearly as effective as commands that are a little more intuitive to the users.

You need to make sure that the key assignments make some sense. To get the idea of this, imagine a situation in which you bought a game and found that the documentation wasn't in the box. If you can just start the game and play it, then you have an interface that works. Try buying a game and playing it without reading any of the documentation, online help, or keyboard reference cards. Evaluate the interface and see what makes sense and what doesn't.

Also, if you foresee that your game is destined for international distribution, remember that customs in other countries can be entirely different from your own. Just as people drive on the left side of the road in England, certain controls might make more sense to certain users if the controls were placed in a different configuration. If you plan on distribution in other countries, make sure that you first get input from testers in those places.

Unfortunately, most games cannot be made completely intuitive. Therefore, we must combine aspects of a fully intuitive system with a neutrally intuitive system. A neutrally intuitive system is just what it sounds like—the controls are not automatically obvious, but they also don't contradict the player's natural instincts. Most newer games are getting better at this. The best way to make it really work for your game is to enable the user to configure the controls. The defaults should be chosen wisely, however, since many users will still never change them.

Now that we have seen how each part of the mind works when playing a game, we'll look at one of the design elements that has a big impact effect on this process: color.

Color Psychology

When designing your game, it's important to keep in mind how color will affect the emotions of the players. Most artists will do this somewhat automatically as they create art, but a little conscious manipulation of colors can allow you to strengthen your control over the emotions that people should be feeling as they play your game. Table 5.1 shows common reactions to specific colors.

Table 5.1. Colors and their associations.

Color	Appearance and Associations	Impressions
Red	Brilliant, heat, fire, blood	Danger, excitement, rage
Orange	Glowing, warm	Force, energy
Yellow	Sunny, radiant	Cautious, cheerful
Green	Moist, clear, cool, nature	Refreshing, peace, ghastliness

continues

Table 5.1. continued

Color	Appearance and Associations	Impressions
Blue	Transparent, cold, water, sky, ice	Subduing, fear
Purple	Deep, darkness, shadow	Dignified, loneliness
White	Light	Clean, pure, normal
Black	Darkness	Mourning, ominous, death

Note that many colors are associated with contradictory feelings. The green of grass, for example, gives people a positive, comforting feeling—they're in nature, and it's a good thing. If a person's skin looks greenish, however, it is a sign of sickness. Green light shining on human skin is even stronger in its negative effects. A green toxic-waste pool is quite fearful. Thus you must remember: The color associations have much to do with the context in which the colors are seen.

In general, colors can be divided into "warm" and "cool" colors. Warm colors are those that we associate with heat and fire: reds, oranges, and yellows. Cool colors are greens and blues, associated with water and nature. Warm colors have an intense, exciting effect, while cool colors have a calming, relaxing effect. This is more than just a mental abstraction. Studies have shown that people working under red lights have higher blood pressure, accelerated heart beats, and tenser muscles, actually raising their body temperature. On the other hand, under blue lights, people really do cool off, experiencing lower heart rates and blood pressure, leading to a more relaxed feeling. If you're playing DOOM sometime and feel as if the experience is very intense, think about the colors and you'll see what their effect is.

There are also warm and cool variations of individual color families. Pastels, even of reds and oranges, are cooler, especially when placed in the same scene as warmer versions of the colors. A small band of light pink placed in a hot red scene can seem comparatively frigid. Also, "hot" or "neon" versions of colors can turn a cool color into an intense hot color. A toxic-waste pool might use a hot green or blue. If some artwork in your game has something about it that makes it look wrong, but you can't quite place the problem, the warmth of the colors might be the problem. Consider the purpose of the artwork. If it is meant to be a violent, intense scene, try warming it up with more reds and oranges, or just intensify the colors you already have by adding warmer hues to them. If the scene is supposed to be calm and natural, but it comes off as somewhat awkward, cool it down.

Along with considering the psychological and physiological effects of colors, we need to keep in mind that people simply like some colors more than others. A number of scientific studies, including one that tabulated preferences for over 21,000 individuals, have determined a generalized universal color preference for adults, in this order: blue, red, green, violet, orange, yellow. Children generally prefer colors of light with longer wavelength; the general order is: red, blue, green, violet, orange, yellow. These orders have been confirmed for many different ethnic groups and for both sexes. Of course, you shouldn't therefore go and use shades of blue for every part of your program. People much prefer a variety of colors at the same time; combining colors in certain ways can create different reactions.

When placing colors within the same scene, whether in artwork or in the color scheme for menus and displays, we need to keep in mind which colors will fit together and which will clash. Just as in a combination of musical notes can produce either a chord or a dischord, multiple colors can produce either pleasant or unpleasant sensations. Of course, unpleasant combinations of color can be useful if the intent is to arouse the associations that they bring up. In general, people like color combinations that are based on closely related or complementary colors. Stated another way, people prefer combinations of colors that are either very similar to or very different from each other. Warm and cool colors generally do not go together very well. They fight for dominance of the scene, and the colors that are in greatest abundance in the scene generally win. The other colors then make a nuisance of themselves.

Also, colors placed together can affect the way the other colors in the scene appear. Our eyes enhance the contrast between two colors, so that darker colors placed on lighter backgrounds will seem darker, and vice versa. Figure 5.1 illustrates this phenomenon. The background of Figure 5.1 is a gradient fill, getting lighter from left to right. The band in the foreground is actually one solid color, but our eyes contrast it with the background to make it appear darker against the lighter background and lighter against the darker background. Optical tricks such as this can either spoil parts of your game or be used to your advantage.

Figure 5.1.
An optical trick in two colors.

Implementation

Now that you understand some of the psychological theory behind interface design, we'll look at specific aspects of the game-playing process.

Start-Up

No matter how sick you get of hearing people say that the first impression is the most important, it's still true. Your start-up screens must look professional and establish the mood for the rest of your game. You will want a graphic that fits in with your game, but don't use a screen shot; some hand-drawn art will be valuable here. Many games also include a brief cinematic opening that helps create the story behind the game. Be sure to include a way to bypass it; even the most impressive sequence can get dull after watching it five times.

Be sure to tell the user what you're doing. If you have a long start-up with many files to load, the simple message `Initializing...`, or something to that effect, can be very comforting. However, more detailed messages as you load can provide two things. They give the user something to watch, some movement that confirms the program is running. Just as a week in Hawaii feels like a day and a day at work feels like a week, 30 seconds spent staring at a blank screen with a churning hard drive feels a lot longer than 30 seconds watching interesting messages go by. These messages can also provide you with helpful information when debugging your software and when providing technical support to somebody trying to run your game. If the last message displayed before the game crashed was `Starting the sound system...`, then you know where you might need to look.

Don't include any shareware delays (screens which freeze for a few seconds with a message encouraging registration) in your start-up, your exit, or anywhere else in the software. Delays generally make users feel frustrated, giving them a feeling that they do not have control. In general, the shareware games that have sold the most copies don't have shareware delays; most users who will purchase the software evaluate it for the quality of the product, and will register if they think the game is worth it. Additional incentive to buy the registered version of the software can be provided by including additional levels, additional modes of play, or a printed manual with cheat codes and hints.

Menus and Options

Once all your files are loaded and you're ready to go, a simple menu should be presented, with a graphical background of some type; if you have a start-up graphic, that should work here. Choose a color for the menu that reflects the theme of the game. Blue or red would probably be your first two choices if you keep in mind the color preferences of most people.

All menus should be navigable with any of the input devices available in your game. You should keep a consistent design to the menus, the ESC key should always back out or exit, arrow keys should navigate and change selections, the Spacebar and Enter should select options. To change options such as sound volume, screen brightness, or detail level, horizontal sliders should be used, with the arrow keys controlling the settings. The best way to keep a consistent interface is to use one routine to display all of your menus. It needs to carry out the following steps:

1. Accept as input the information that should be displayed on the menu
2. Display each of these options and allow them to be changed
3. Return to the main program, changing what has been selected

Because we want to have a variety of options and submenus in our system, we need a variety of controls. The menu routine needs to handle each differently, within the parameters of the preceding Step 2. It should be able to handle the following:

- On/off switches
- Horizontal sliders
- Options that cause an event to occur (submenu displayed, game started, joystick calibrated, and so forth)

While we will also want to be able to accept other types of input, such as configuring controls or enabling the user to type their name, these are too specialized to include in the actual menu routine. If you feel that you need one of these things within the menu, you could add it to the routine. Listing 5.1 addresses the main possibilities outlined previously. To enhance understanding, I wrote the routine in pseudocode. The actual drawing of the text and controls in the menu is going to be very different in various games, so it's easier just to get the idea with this skeleton.

Listing 5.1. A generalized pseudocode menu routine.

```
menu_def is a structure which contains:
    type:integer;               //The type of control to display

    text:string;                //The text to display

    value:integer;              //The current value for the option. Could be:
                                //Zero or One for on/off switch
                                //A number for a slider
                                //Undefined for event-causer

    max:integer;                //Maximum value. It assumes that 0 is minimum.
                                //One for on/off switch
                                //A number for a slider
                                //Undefined for event-causer

menu_array is an array type that contains as many elements as you could
possibly need for one level of the menu. Each element is of type menu_def.

//The following two routines assume that there are other routines to draw the
//actual graphics. In this form it passes them no parameters but the values to
//display; in a real program, they would need to know where on the screen to
//draw. This would be determined from the current menu option—there could be a
//look-up table that declares where to draw each option.
```

continues

Listing 5.1. continued

```
procedure draw_menu(cur_menu:menu_array, cur_option:integer);
        //This procedure redraws one option of the menu. It assumes that the
        //screen is already clear, or that the background is taken into
        //account in the actual drawing routines.

        select based on cur_menu(cur_option).type from

                1:if cur_menu(cur_option).value=1 then         //On/off switch
                        set_style(bold);                //ON
                else
                        set_style(normal);              //OFF
                draw_text(cur_menu(cur_option).text);           //Display it.

                2:set_style(bold);                              //A slider
                draw_text(cur_menu(cur_option).text);
                draw_slider(cur_menu(cur_option).value);

                3:set_style(bold);                              //Event
                draw_text(cur_menu(cur_option).text);

end of procedure;

function do_menu(var cur_menu:menu_array, num_options:integer) returns integer;
        //This procedure is the one that is called from the main program.
        //It calls draw_menu for each option. The parameter cur_menu, which
        //would be a var in Pascal or a pointer in C, is changed. The main
        //routine must update its records based on that parameter after this
        //function is done.

        temporary variables:

                cur_option:integer;       //What is currently selected?

                //This holds input from mouse, keyboard, or joystick.
                result:type which is returned from input routines;

                done:boolean;             //Tells us when to quit

                return:integer;           //This returns 0 if aborted, or
                                          //the item number if an event causer
                                          //was selected.

        //Display the entire menu.
        for cur_option from 1 to num_options, draw_menu(cur_menu,cur_option);

        done=false;
        cur_option=1;

        while not done, do:

                draw_menu(cur_menu,cur_option); //Refreshes current selection

                highlight(cur_option);            //Could use bullet, highlight
                                                  //bar, or other indication.

                result=get_next_control;          //Wait for next movement.
```

```
        remove_highlight(cur_option);

        select based on result from

                abort:done=true;            //Was escape key-no selection.
                return=0;

                up:dec(cur_option);        //Go up one, wrapping around.
                if cur_option=0 then cur_option=num_options;

                down:inc(cur_option);
                if cur_option=num_options+1 then cur_option=1;

                //Note that the following procedures will work for
                //On/Off switches or sliders. Since right/left should
                //not change event-causers, and event causers are
                //undefined, it works just fine as well.

                left:dec(cur_menu(cur_option).value);
                if cur_menu(cur_option).value=-1
                    then inc(cur_menu(cur_option).value);

                right:inc(cur_menu(cur_option).value);
                if cur_menu(cur_option).value>cur_menu(cur_option).max
                        then dec(cur_menu(cur_option).value);

                //Button click, space, or enter:
                //For this, we must handle each type separately.
                selector:select based on cur_menu(cur_option).type from

                        //Toggle on/off switch
                        1:logical_not(cur_menu(cur_option).value);

                        //Do nothing to a slider.
                        2:;   //This could increment instead.

                        //Return to main for an event.
                        3:done=true;
                        return=cur_option;

        end of while;

        return(return);

end of function;
```

The preceding code should be a good basis for your menu-display routine. In addition to the menu routines, you will also want to have code for things such as dialog boxes, input forms, and other parts of the interface that you need. Ideally, you should be able to build up an interface library, which can be included in any game with little modification to take care of these aspects in a consistent and polished manner. That's why Windows is so popular—it provides a consistent and clean interface, freeing programmers to develop the heart of the software. Note that the procedures shown in the preceding code can be created relatively independently of the actual graphics-display routines. All the routines in your interface library should keep that in mind, so they will work in any situation.

When actually setting up your menus, the most frequently used options in each menu should be listed first. Remember to keep them simple and clear. Every game command should be configurable and help should be available to describe all functions that are not directly obvious. A quick reference chart of commands can also be useful. The following should give you a brief idea of how you might configure your menus:

- Start Game
  - Level
  - Difficulty
- Options
  - Sound Volume
  - Music Volume
  - Controls
    - Select Device
    - Configure/Calibrate
  - Graphics Detail
  - Brightness
- View Demo
- View High Scores
- Information and Help
- Credits
- Exit to DOS

Users should never have to exit the game to change any options, except for the actual hardware setup (sound card, video mode, installation directory, and so on). The keyboard and mouse-button assignments, joystick calibration, and sound volume should be accessible within the game. Also, if your game provides network or modem play, these should be started from within the game, and players should not have to quit to DOS to disconnect. This is especially important considering the start-up time required for many of today's games. Just a couple of minutes spent quitting, configuring, and restarting can be frustrating.

Game Play

The part of the user interface that is used the most is the game-play interface. This interface takes the information provided through the keyboard, mouse, joystick, or other input device, and modifies the state of the game in some way that the user intends. It also displays useful information for the user. All the controls should be configurable, and the defaults should be very intuitive. For example, in multi-player mode, the M key should be used to send messages to other players, not F7 or Alt+K. The number keys are frequently used to select weapons, and the function keys can be put to good use as user-definable macros.

The screen should follow a clear, logical layout. It should be dominated by the main view of the game world; if your game has to consider speed on different machines, the screen should be resizable to reduce drawing time. A status bar should be provided, either as a separate area on the screen, or integrated as a component of the world; a car-racing game might include the status bar as a dashboard. One glance should be sufficient to find any information that the user needs. Icons can be used to aid understanding, but make sure that they are understandable, not tiny hieroglyphs.

Feedback can be provided through text, graphics, or audio. All of these provide the brain more information to work with. For example, changing the weapon might cause the following events:

- The message `Big Gun Selected` appears on the screen
- A picture of the weapon appears on the status bar
- The sound of ammunition being loaded is played

Try to employ elements that will make it seem less like a computer game and more like a real experience. Careful selection and sampling of sounds can do a great deal to help this. The quiet growling of a far-off monster goes a lot further in producing the emotions that you are seeking than any visual cues that you can provide. Again, you are seeking to control the users' emotions and make them react in the way that you want. Remember that sound strongly affects emotions.

The Keyboard

The input device that will play the biggest role in most games is the keyboard. Unfortunately, in order to interface with the keyboard for a game, we cannot use the BIOS. This is not a speed constraint—the BIOS routines work fast enough for keyboard input—but what they provide us with is not what we want.

> You may still wish to use the BIOS keyboard routines for some purposes. (Note however that you'll have to disable and re-enable this handler each time you wish to use BIOS. That's not too hard—it just takes two calls.) For information on using these routines, as well as getting input via the mouse and joystick, see *Tricks of the Game Programming Gurus*.

The BIOS works in a buffered system, enabling us access to only one key press at a time. We can't tell whether keys are being held down or whether more than one key is being pressed. These limitations are no problem for a word processor or utility program. You'll probably want to use the BIOS routines for receiving typed input. However, they kill a game that must allow movement, firing, and other commands simultaneously, in a continuous manner. Thus, we must work with the keyboard directly. In order to do that, we need to have a good idea of how it works on the hardware level.

The keyboard is nothing but a big collection of on-off switches. When you press a key, a circuit is closed, and this sends a *make code* to a controller chip in the computer. When you release the key, breaking the circuit, a *break code* is sent to the computer. Both of these codes are bytes. They are the same code, except that break codes have the high bit set, and make codes don't. These codes are converted by the controller in the PC to *scan codes*. If you want to get deeper into the hardware, you can learn about the controller chip and the handshaking protocol, but those are not especially relevant to us. Once the controller chip does its job, it sends the scan codes to port 60h in the PC and calls interrupt 09h. There it becomes available to the BIOS, DOS, and software.

Normally, the BIOS handles calls to interrupt 09h. It stores key presses in a buffer, converts them to ASCII codes, repeats keys that are held down, and performs a few other manipulations. DOS and software programs can get the keypresses from BIOS via interrupt 16h. (The DOS input commands call the BIOS routine to get keystrokes.) Interrupt 09h is where we can cut in line and swipe the keys before the BIOS can get them. We need to write an interrupt handler that will do the following:

- Input the key code from port 60h
- Set some variables that can be accessed by the main program, telling us what keys are currently pressed

Before we can start on this code, we need to think of a strategy that will enable us to keep track of the key presses for the program. Since we will know when keys are pressed and released, we can have a set of flags in memory that will be set or cleared by the interrupt handler. Then, we can read these flags from our main program to decide how to move. You can use a look-up table in your program to allow each command to be configured. Each entry in your look-up table would refer you to an entry in the key-flag table. To reconfigure a command, just change the entry in the look-up table to the scan code of the key you want. Listing 5.2 implements this interrupt handler in assembly code.

Listing 5.2. Handling the keyboard interrupt. (KEYINTR.ASM)

```
_mydat          segment para public 'data'
extrn           _flagtable:byte
OldInt9         dw      0000,0000       ;Address of old interrupt 9 handler
_mydat          ends

_mycode         segment para public 'code'
public          SetKb,_ResetKb
assume          cs:_mycode,ds:_mydat

;This is the new interrupt 09h handler.
int9            proc
                cli                     ;Disable other interrupts
                push    cx              ;We've got to save all registers
                push    bx
                push    ax
                push    ds
                mov     ax,SEG _flagtable  ;Set up addressing
                mov     ds,ax           ;For the data.
```

```
WaitForIt:      in      al,64h          ;64h is status port-key done yet?
                test    al,02h          ;Check if controller is done
                loopnz  WaitForIt       ;Not ready-wait
                in      al,60h          ;It's ready-get the code.
```

;The make or break code is now in al. Remember that make and break codes are
;the same, except for the high bit. So, we can use some shifts to get the high
;bit out, and use it to set our flags.

```
                xor     ah,ah           ;Clear ah first
                shl     ax,1            ;ah contains the high bit
                shr     al,1            ;al contains just the low bits.
                xor     ah,1            ;Invert-Make code should be one.
                xor     bh,bh           ;Clear bh
                mov     bl,al           ;Load bx with scan code
                mov     _flagtable[bx],ah ;Send it to the table
```

;Need the following to make keyoard controller happy.

```
                in      al,61h          ;Get control status
                mov     ah,al           ;Copy it
                or      al,80h          ;Set KB enable bit
                out     61h,al          ;Write to control port
                xchg    ah,al           ;Send original value
                out     61h,al          ;Back again
```

;Clean up and exit the interrupt.

```
                mov     al,20h          ;Tell interrupt chip
                out     20h,al          ;That we're done.

                pop     ds              ;That's it.
                pop     ax
                pop     bx
                pop     cx
                sti                     ;Reenable interrupts.
                iret
int9    endp
```

;Install the Keyboard interrupt handler-call this at startup
```
_SetKb          proc    far
                push    ds              ;Save registers
                push    es
                push    ax
                push    dx
                mov     al,9h           ;Request keyboard interrupt
                mov     ah,35h          ;DOS get interrupt vector
                int     21h             ;DOS call
                mov     ax,seg OldInt9  ;Get the address to save it at.
                mov     ds,ax
                mov     OldInt9[0],bx   ;Save offset
                mov     OldInt9[2],es   ;Save segment
                mov     ax,seg int9     ;Get new segment
                mov     ds,ax
                mov     dx,offset int9  ;Get new offset
                mov     al,9h           ;Change keyboard interrupt
                mov     ah,25h          ;DOS change interrupt vector
                int     21h             ;DOS call
                pop     dx
                pop     ax
                pop     es
```

continues

Listing 5.2. continued

```
            pop    ds
            retf
_SetKb      endp

;Remove the Keyboard interrupt handler-call this at shutdown
_ResetKb    proc   far
            push   ds                    ;Save registers
            push   ax
            push   dx
            mov    ax,seg OldInt9        ;Get the address to restore from.
            mov    ds,ax
            mov    dx,OldInt9[0]         ;Restore offset
            mov    ax,OldInt9[2]         ;Restore segment
            mov    ds,ax
            mov    al,9h                 ;Change keyboard interrupt
            mov    ah,25h                ;DOS change interrupt vector
            int    21h                   ;DOS call
            pop    dx
            pop    ax
            pop    ds
            retf
_ResetKb    endp
_mycode     ends
ends
end
```

This is not a stand-alone executable file. Note the external references and the public declarations. This should be compiled as an object file, then linked with your main program. It's easy to add this code to a C program. All you have to do is:

1. Declare the keyflags variable as an array of 128 unsigned chars
2. Declare the SetKb and ResetKb as extern procedures
3. Call SetKb and ResetKb at the beginning and end of your program
4. Simply access the keyflags array as you would any other, and the values will all be set automatically by the interrupt handler

Listing 5.3 is an example program to demonstrate the use of these routines.

Listing 5.3. A C program to demonstrate the keyboard handler. (TESTKEY.C)

```
unsigned char flagtable[128];                //Table to contain key flags

extern void SetKb();                         //Declare external procedures
extern void ResetKb();

void main()
{
      SetKb();                               //Set up new handler
      do
      {
            printf("%d",flagtable[72]);      //Print status of up arrow
```

```
    }
    while (flagtable[28]!=1);              //Until Enter is pressed
    ResetKb();                             //Restore normal BIOS interrupt
    exit();
}
```

When this program starts, a bunch of zeros should scroll by. Press the up-arrow key. The zeros will change to ones until you release the key. It's that easy. Press Enter to quit when you've had enough. The interrupt handler is reset, and you're back in DOS.

These routines should definitely be in your user-interface library. This is the lowest possible level on which to program your keyboard, unless you want to open the case and do some circuit-board etching. It's fast and it gives you full control over everything you need.

Exit

Always confirm the user's choice to exit; it's very frustrating to have to re-play an entire level because you accidentally pressed the ESC key. Use a simple dialog box that pops up with a question such as Are you sure you want to quit? (You don't have to limit yourself to that question of course. DOOM and many other games have several interesting and humorous queries from which one is selected at random.)

Make sure to return the computer to the state that it was in when you started. Remove temporary files and restore the video mode to mode 3 via the BIOS set-video-mode routine. Restore any interrupt handlers that you may have changed.

The exit screen, like the start-up screen, is very important. It provides the final view of your game, and the emotions that the user feels when seeing it will strongly affect the feelings that are attached to the entire game itself. As always, keep it simple. Don't try to sell 30 other games to the players as they quit, and don't include a shareware delay. However, a message that will keep the users interested and make them want to come back for more should be included. For shareware games, pricing information and phone numbers can be put in the exit screen.

Generally, the closing screen will be in text mode and can be enhanced by using carefully selected colors. Remember to think about color combinations and associations when putting together the closing screen. Also, the extended ASCII character set provides characters for drawing lines and boxes, which can add a professional look to the screen.

When you change the colors of the screen, make sure you change only the attributes for parts that you use. When you release control back to DOS, the attributes for all characters below the bottom of your exit screen should be set to white on black (attribute 7), and the cursor should be moved to the left side of the screen, one line below the bottom of your text. If you do not make sure this happens, the DOS prompt could pop up anywhere on the screen, or not at all, and possibly in strange colors. At the very least this could seem unprofessional or give the users the impression that the exit was not clean. They might think the game, and possibly the computer, has crashed.

There are many programs available to use for making a text-mode screen. One of the best is called The Draw. It is available as shareware and enables you to create screens using a variety of tools. It can export the finished products into formats for Pascal, C, and many other programs. Once you create a screen with The Draw and export it for inclusion in your program, it only takes a few commands to display it; you don't need to worry about any of the details of directly writing the screen to text-mode memory. For your convenience, The Draw has been included on the CD-ROM accompanying this book.

Errors

Unfortunately, problems occur all too frequently when dealing with modern games. The user may try to run your game with inadequate hardware, insufficient memory, or incorrectly configured settings. Also, other programs on the computer can cause a great number of conflicts. When problems do occur, the game must handle them smoothly and quietly.

If at all possible, the game should not be aborted. There's no reason to crash out of the program just because the sound card didn't respond. Just display a message saying what happened and asking the user to provide the correct parameters.

Frequently, for errors involving such things as memory allocation or corrupt files, aborting to DOS is the best and possibly the only option. If you must exit to DOS, include a message describing as much as possible of what happened. This may enable the user to fix the problem and will help in providing technical support. Just as in the clean exit, try to return the computer to its original state, removing temporary files and freeing allocated memory and interrupt handlers.

Summary

This chapter covered a variety of topics that will augment your programming skills for a successful game design. Remember to keep the interface simple and intuitive. Think of the emotions that are brought out by the situations in the game, and make sure you invoke the response that you want. Too many programmers get caught up in the "exciting" parts of programming, giving their games a great basic engine but neglecting the user interface. With the information provided here, you can put the icing on the cake of your code and make people want to play your game.

Scaling and Rotating Bitmaps

by Peter Freese

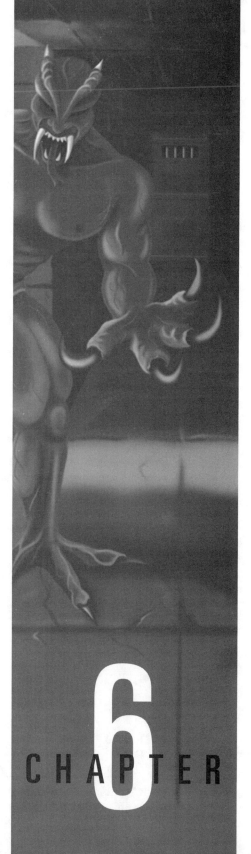

6
CHAPTER

A Drakhi fighter screams past your starboard wing, firing a volley of green plasma as it passes. You curse under your breath, tap your turbo thrusters and pull back on your joystick, climbing away from the deadly green fire.

You hear Paladin's voice over your radio. "Laddie, watch your tail!" Sure enough, another Drakhi is coming up from underneath, getting a lock on your exhaust. You pull back on the thrusters and lean hard to the left and then to the right. The sudden maneuver catches the Drakhi off guard, and you curve around behind him.

You wait until his semicircular wings are just about to enter your targeting crosshairs, and then you thumb your fire button. A blast of searing laser hits the Kilrathi fighter, and it explodes in a fireball of flame and debris. A strange piece of hosepipe goes spiraling past your cockpit window.

From the other Kilrathi fighter, you hear the echoing scream: "You cannot defeat the Drakhi!"

Yeah, right buddy...

The year was 1990, and the game was Wing Commander, one of the most engaging and exciting space-combat simulators ever seen. Realistic looking spaceships dove in and out of laser fire in a hitherto unseen display of graphics wizardry. Countless game players upgraded their computers, buying sound cards, VGA adapters and monitors, and more memory, just to play this game, which pushed the technical limits of computer gaming to a new plateau. Wing Commander was, to put it mildly, a stunning success.

One of Wing Commander's technical achievements was the way in which it rendered the spacecraft and other objects onto the display. Rather than rendering objects as collections of polygons, each object was stored as several bitmaps representing different three-dimensional views. These bitmaps were then rotated and scaled to the display, giving the impression of complex and highly detailed spacecraft.

In this chapter you're going to learn how to scale and rotate bitmaps, and you're going to learn how to do it *fast*. After all, if it can't be done quickly, it's not worth doing in a game.

This chapter covers the following:

- Bitmap scaling
- Bitmap rotation
- Fixed-point math
- Incremental calculations
- Affine transformations

What Good is Scaling and Rotation?

The most obvious use for scaling and rotation is in representing objects in a game where the size of the Sprite is determined by its distance from the viewer/player. Besides the obvious examples such as in Wing Commander, there are many other applications for scaling and rotation.

Imagine a small iconized picture expanding to fill the whole screen when the player selects it. Or imagine a strategy simulation that presents an overhead view of a battlefield but enables the player to zoom in and out to see various levels of detail. Imagine rotating the entire screen to simulate a roll in a driving simulation.

The uses for scaling and rotation are nearly limitless. There's probably a whole new type of game that hasn't been invented yet that will make use of dynamic scaling and rotation. (Perhaps you'll be the one to create it!)

The concepts you'll learn in this chapter go far beyond just scaling and rotation. The theory and math behind these techniques form the basis for fast texture mapping of polygons, drawing floor and ceiling textures for games like DOOM, and terrain rendering of voxel landscapes.

To Be or Not to Be Dynamic

Now that I've extolled the virtues of dynamic scaling and rotation, I should point out that there are times when you shouldn't use these techniques. In these cases, you'll want to pre-render your bitmaps at the appropriate size or rotation beforehand.

Why would you want to pre-render? One potential reason is *aliasing*. Aliasing is the result of *point sampling*, which is when an algorithm selects a value for a pixel from only a single point in the source bitmap. Because only a finite set of points are sampled, important pixels from the source may be missed. To make matters worse, as the object is scaled or rotated, important pixels may pop in and out of existence in the destination, leading to a sparkling effect. Straight lines can also become jagged and look like stairsteps.

Techniques to minimize or reduce aliasing are referred to as *antialiasing*, and images produced using these techniques are said to be *antialiased*. The simplest way of achieiving antialiased bitmap rotation and scaling is to use *area sampling*. In area sampling, the value for each pixel is determined by averaging together several pixels from the source image, sometimes using a weighting function.

Area sampling works great. However, area sampling can be hundreds of times slower than point sampling. The fast techniques we discuss in this chapter all use point sampling. Therefore, you have a choice between smooth area sampling beforehand and fast, dynamic point sampling at run-time.

Figure 6.1 illustrates the difference between point sampling and area sampling. The image on the left is the original image of a white pawn. The center image was created by rotating the pawn 45° clockwise with point sampling. This is how the bitmap would look using the dynamic-rotation techniques you will learn in this chapter. The image on the right was created by rotating the pawn 45° using area sampling. Notice the smoothness of the edges of the area-sampled pawn versus the jagged edges of the point-sampled pawn.

Figure 6.1.
Point-sampled and area-sampled rotations.

Pre-Rendering

To generate the best pre-rendered rotated or scaled bitmaps, you'll need an art program capable of doing area sampling. Some programs will call this antialiasing; some won't call it anything at all. I have found that the best way to do this is to work with 24-bit color images. Most programs do point sampling in paletted (256-color) mode, and area sampling in 16-bit (high color) or 24-bit (true color) modes. After you've generated your scaled or rotated versions, color-reduce them back down to your game palette. The resulting images will look a lot smoother than they would had you done point sampling.

If your program can do antialiased scaling (some programs call this *resampling)* but not antialiased rotation, one trick I've come up with is this:

1. Scale the image up by a factor of two and double the size of the image.

2. Rotate the image to the angle you need.

3. Scale the image down to its proper size.

How Fast is Enough?

Wing Commander ran well even on 80286 machines. The average machine today has far greater processing power and speed. Obviously it is possible to do bitmap transformations fast enough to produce a high-quality game. But one question you may be asking yourself is, "Should I pre-scale/pre-rotate my bitmaps for speed?" My answer is a definitive "Maybe not." The techniques we'll learn in this chapter are very fast, but certainly not as fast as straight blitting. However, it is senseless to evaluate the speed of a particular algorithm or approach out of context. What I mean by that is that you really should experiment to find the best approach.

There are many factors that affect performance, and one that is often overlooked is the effect of moving large amounts of data around, not just to and from the disk, but in memory. We'll go into this more later, but for now, think about how much memory it will take to store all the necessary rotated or scaled versions of your bitmaps versus a single bitmap. Those extra bitmaps will increase the size of your working set, and if you use any sort of virtual memory scheme, it is going to cause a lot of thrashing of your cache.

The Scaling Algorithm

Now that we've talked about the uses and considerations for scaling, let's get right down and find out how to actually do it.

The basic concept in scaling is a simple one: Take one range of values, and stretch or shrink it to fit a second range of values. In the case of bitmap scaling, we're doing a two-dimensional scaling process. Both the width and the height are scaled to fit a new width and height.

The next equation is a generalized equation for scaling. We could use it to convert a measurement in inches to centimeters, or a temperature from Celsius to Fahrenheit. Here we're going to use it to convert source pixels to destination pixels.

$$n_1 = \min_1 + (\max_1 - \min_1) \frac{n_0 + \min_0}{\max_0 - \min_0}$$

The values $\min_0$ and $\max_0$ in the equation represent the source range, and $\min_1$ and $\max_1$ represent the corresponding destination range. For example, to scale a value in the range of zero to 100 into the range 32 to 212, we would use the equation:

$$n_1 = 32 + (212 - 32) \frac{n_0 + 0}{100 - 0}$$

This simplifies to:

$$n_1 = 32 + 1.8 \times n_0$$

You probably noticed that 32 and 212 are the freezing and boiling points of water in degrees Fahrenheit. And since zero and 100 are the freezing and boiling points of water in degrees Celsius, our equation will convert from Celsius to Fahrenheit. (See, I told you we could use it to convert temperature!)

Now that we've seen that the general scaling equation works, let's apply it to pixel coordinates. Since the upper left coordinates of our source bitmap are always 0,0 regardless of its size, $\min_0$ will be equal to zero, and $\max_0$ will be equal to the width or height of the bitmap. The values for $\max_0$ and $\max_1$ will be equal to the left and right or the top and bottom coordinates.

Here's how we might scale the bitmap coordinates (i, j) into a destination specified by the rectangle (x0, y0, x1, y1):

```
x = x0 + (x1 - x0) * i / width;
y = y0 + (y1 - y0) * j / height;
```

Naive Scaling

Let's use this to write our first routine for scaling bitmaps. We'll write it in two halves. The first half will be a test scaffold, and the second half will be the actual routine to scale a bitmap. I chose to do it this way because it lets us concentrate on how to actually scale the bitmap, without repeating all the support code needed for loading the bitmap, entering graphics mode, and timing the routine. Listing 6.1 shows our scaffold program.

Listing 6.1. SMAIN.C.

```c
#include <stdio.h>
#include <stdlib.h>
#include <mem.h>
#include <conio.h>
#include <palette.h>
#include <pcx.h>
#include <dostime.h>

/****************************************************************
 * Type definitions
 ****************************************************************/
typedef unsigned char UBYTE;
typedef unsigned short UWORD;
typedef signed short WORD;
typedef unsigned long ULONG;

/****************************************************************
 * Global variables
 ****************************************************************/
PALETTE palette;
int width, height;

/****************************************************************
 * External Functions
 ****************************************************************/
void cdecl ScaleBlit( UBYTE *bitmap, int x0, int y0,
    int x1, int y1);

/****************************************************************
 * Functions
 ****************************************************************/
int getvmode( void );
#pragma aux getvmode =\
    "mov    ah,0x0F",\
    "int    0x10,"\
    "and    eax,0xFF",\

int setvmode(int);
#pragma aux setvmode =\
    "int 0x10",\
    parm [eax]\

void main()
{
```

```
        char *fname = "ROCKET.PCX";
        UBYTE *rocketBitmap = NULL;
        int nOldMode;
        int nResult;
        int width2, height2;
        ULONG startTime, stopTime;
        int fps, frames = 0;

        nResult = ReadPCX256(fname, &palette, &width, &height,
            &rocketBitmap);
        if ( nResult != pcxOkay )
        {
            printf("Error reading %s\n", fname);
            exit(1);
        }

        width2 = width;
        height2 = height;

        nOldMode = getvmode();
        setvmode(0x13);
        gSetDACRange(0, 256, palette);

        startTime = GetDosTicks();

        while ( 1 )
        {
            if ( kbhit() )
                break;

            width2 = 2;
            height2 = 2;

            while (height2 < 200 && width2 < 320)
            {
                ScaleBlit(
                    rocketBitmap,        // bitmap
                    160 - width2 / 2,    // x0
                    100 - height2 / 2,   // y0
                    160 + width2 / 2,    // x1
                    100 + height2 / 2    // y1
                );

                height2 += 2;
                width2 += 2;

                frames++;
            }
        }

        stopTime = GetDosTicks();

        setvmode(nOldMode);

        fps = frames * 182 / (stopTime-startTime);
        printf("Average frame rate: %i.%i fps\n", fps / 10, fps % 10);
}
```

This code program was written to compile under Watcom C 10.0. I chose to use Watcom for these examples because it offers one of the few 32-bit flat-model programming environments for the PC. It also has one of the best optimizers that I've seen on a C compiler. The flat 32-bit address space and optimizer combined with register parameter passing and a non-standard stack frame make it easy to produce faster code than any other compiler. If you are serious about high-performance game development (and I assume you are, or you wouldn't be reading this book), then Watcom is the compiler of choice. And I don't get paid to say that, either.

This program loads a bitmap of a rocket ship from the file ROCKET.PCX, shown in Figure 6.2. I've insulated you somewhat from the mundane aspects of decoding the .PCX file, setting the palette registers, reading the clock, and so forth, by putting those routines in a separate library. I want us to concentrate on bitmap scaling and rotation, and putting those sorts of routines in a library is a good idea in general, because it makes it easy to reuse them in other programs.

Figure 6.2.
Here is our test bitmap,
the Sams rocket.

The lines with the #pragma aux directives are inline assembler functions. This is a bit different from the way other compilers implement inline assembler, but it is fairly straightforward once you get used to it, and powerful as well. The two inline functions are used to get and set the current video mode.

I'm a polite guy. I believe that when you use things, you should put them back the way you found them, and this is as true in programming as it is anywhere else. That's why the scaffold program gets the current video mode before entering graphics mode 0x13. This enables us to restore the display to the mode it was in before our program ran. I urge you to do this sort of thing in your programs as well. Few things are as annoying as exiting a program and having it leave your screen in some weird color set or in a different resolution than you are used to. Your goal should be to entertain your users, not annoy them. End of lecture.

One additional thing that the scaffold program will do for us is to measure the speed of our scaling code. The program will scale the bitmap in size from 2×2 all the way up to 200×200. It will continue drawing the scaled bitmap until a key is pressed, at which point it will report the results as the average number of blits per second. We're going to go through several iterations of the scaling routine, and it will be useful to see how far we've come. But first, we have to start; so without further ado, Listing 6.2 is our first implementation of scaling.

Listing 6.2. SCALE1.C.

```c
/******************************************************************
 * Type definitions
 ******************************************************************/
typedef unsigned char UBYTE;
typedef unsigned short UWORD;
typedef signed short WORD;
typedef unsigned long ULONG;

/******************************************************************
 * Global variables
 ******************************************************************/
UBYTE *screen = 0xA0000;
extern int width, height;

/******************************************************************
 * ScaleBlit()
 ******************************************************************/
void cdecl ScaleBlit(UBYTE *bitmap, int x0, int y0,
    int x1, int y1)
{
    int i, j, x, y;

    for ( i = 0; i < width; i++ )
    {
        for ( j = 0; j < height; j++ )
        {
            x = x0 + (x1 - x0) * i / width;
            y = y0 + (y1 - y0) * j / height;
            screen[x + y * 320] = bitmap[i + j * width];
        }
    }
}
```

The function ScaleBlit() will iterate through each pixel in the source bitmap, calculate the scaled screen coordinates for that pixel, and write it to the screen at the calculated position.

I've declared ScaleBlit() as a cdecl function, which means that it uses standard C calling convention. For Watcom, this means that it will pass parameters on the stack and use standard C name mangling. Later, when we try our hand at an assembly language version of ScaleBlit() this will make mixing C and assembly language relatively painless. Writing assembly language routines that adhere to Watcom's register-parameter passing scheme is not for the faint of heart!

Because our program consists of more than one file, we'll need a make file to put it all together. Listing 6.3 is the make file for building SCALE1.EXE.

Listing 6.3. SCALE1.MAK.

```
.c.obj:
        wcc386 -w4 -4r -mf -oneatx $[*

scale1.exe : smain.obj scale1.obj
    wlink n scale1 f smain f scale1

smain.obj : smain.c

scale1.obj : scale1.c
```

The function ScaleBlit() in Listing 6.2, looks like a straightforward implementation of the scaling equation we discussed earlier, but there's one small problem with it: It is fundamentally flawed. Build the program and run it. You'll notice right away that something is wrong. The screen will look something like Figure 6.3.

Figure 6.3.
The display from
SCALE1.EXE.

It looks vaguely enough like the rocket ship to let us know that it partially working, but it is difficult to see exactly what is going wrong. Let's clear the screen between blits, and pause after each one so we can see exactly what is happening. Listing 6.4 shows a new version of ScaleBlit() with these changes.

Listing 6.4. SCALE2.C.

```
#include <mem.h>

/****************************************************************
 * Type definitions
 ****************************************************************/
typedef unsigned char UBYTE;
typedef unsigned short UWORD;
typedef signed short WORD;
typedef unsigned long ULONG;

/****************************************************************
 * Global variables
 ****************************************************************/
UBYTE *screen = 0xA0000;
extern int width, height;

/****************************************************************
```

```
 * ScaleBlit()
 ********************************************************************/
void cdecl ScaleBlit(UBYTE *bitmap, int x0, int y0,
    int x1, int y1)
{
    int i, j, x, y;

    memset(screen, 0, 64000);

    for ( i = 0; i < width; i++ )
    {
        for ( j = 0; j < height; j++ )
        {
            x = x0 + (x1 - x0) * i / width;
            y = y0 + (y1 - y0) * j / height;
            screen[x + y * 320] = bitmap[i + j * width];
        }
    }

    while ( !kbhit() );
    getch();
}
```

Listing 6.5 is the make file for building SCALE2.EXE.

Listing 6.5. SCALE2.MAK.

```
.c.obj:
      wcc386 -w4 -4r -mf -oneatx $[*

scale2.exe : smain.obj scale2.obj
    wlink n scale2 f smain f scale2

smain.obj : smain.c

scale2.obj : scale2.c
```

Now when you run the program, you should be able see each frame independently. Build and run SCALE2. You'll see that when the bitmap is being scaled down, it looks fine; but when it is being scaled up, the pixels get drawn in the right locations, but gaps become visible between them, as shown in Figure 6.4.

Figure 6.4.
The display from
SCALE2.EXE.

The problem is that we are scaling the coordinates of the source pixels, not the pixels themselves. How do we scale the source pixels? Before we go too far in our discussion of this, I want to point out ahead of time that the solution is exceedingly simple, but it takes a leap of logic.

Inversion

In brainstorming sessions, *inversion* is a useful tool for solving problems when everyone is stumped for ideas. Essentially what you do is ask the opposite of the question you are trying to answer. For example, if you are trying to figure out ways to improve the efficiency of automobile engines, you would ask, "What techniques decrease the efficiency of the engine?" The answers to this question can give you insight into your original problem.

We can use a slight variation of inversion to solve our scaling problem. Our original problem was, "Where do source pixels go in the destination?" To invert this problem, we stand it on its head and ask, "Where do destination pixels come from in the source?"

Just as we can use a scaling equation to convert from Fahrenheit to Celsius as easily as Celsius to Fahrenheit, we can convert destination coordinates to source coordinates to find our where each pixel comes from. Here's how we can scale the destination coordinates (x, y) into a source pixel location (u, v) in the bitmap:

```
u = width * (x - x0) / (x1 - x0);
v = height * ( y - y0) / (y1 - y0);
```

I use the variables u and v to refer to coordinates within the source bitmap. This is somewhat a matter of convention when describing locations within images or bitmaps, just as x and y are traditionally used for screen coordinates. Following these sorts of conventions is a good idea because it enables programmers to communicate ideas readily without explaining every term. It helps when everyone speaks the same language. You're almost certain to see the terms u and v used extensively in discussions of texture mapping and image transformation.

Let's modify the ScaleBlit() function to work in terms of destination coordinates. Listing 6.6 shows the new function.

Listing 6.6. SCALE3.C.

```
/****************************************************************
 * Type definitions
 ****************************************************************/
typedef unsigned char UBYTE;
typedef unsigned short UWORD;
typedef signed short WORD;
typedef unsigned long ULONG;


/****************************************************************
 * Global variables
 ****************************************************************/
UBYTE *screen = 0xA0000;
extern int width, height;
```

```
/*****************************************************************
 * ScaleBlit()
 *****************************************************************/
void cdecl ScaleBlit(UBYTE *bitmap, int x0, int y0,
    int x1, int y1)
{
    int u, v, x, y;

    for ( x = x0; x < x1; x++ )
    {
        for ( y = y0; y < y1; y++ )
        {
            u = width * (x - x0) / (x1 - x0);
            v = height * (y - y0) / (y1 - y0);
            screen[x + y * 320] = bitmap[u + v * width];
        }
    }
}
```

Listing 6.7 is the make file for building SCALE3.EXE.

Listing 6.7. SCALE3.MAK.

```
.c.obj:
        wcc386 -w4 -4r -mf -oneatx $[*

scale3.exe : smain.obj scale3.obj
    wlink n scale3 f smain f scale3

smain.obj : smain.c

scale3.obj : scale3.c
```

Now when you build and run SCALE3.EXE, you should see a working bitmap-scaling routine. Congratulations! After exiting the program, you should have your first useful benchmark result as well. On my test machine, a 486DX2 66MHz with a VLB ET4000W32 video card, SCALE3 clocks in at about 30.5 scaled blits per second. That's pretty darned slow! The primary explanation is that we are doing too much math in the proverbial inner loop. Two multiplications and two divisions per pixel do not make a fast algorithm. Don't worry; by the time we're done we'll have it working at more than 20 times that speed—plenty fast enough for a high-performance game.

Incremental Algorithms

In the domain of computer-graphics primitives, there exists a wide class of algorithms that falls under the category of *incremental algorithms*. These algorithms solve certain equations rapidly by using information from a previous quantity rather than calculating everything at each iteration. Bresenham's line-drawing algorithm determines where to place each successive pixel by using the location of the previous pixel and several state variables.

As an example of how an incremental algorithm works, imagine writing a program that would print all the multiples of five up to 1,000. The brute force method might be

```
i = 1;
do {
    n = 5 * i;
    printf("%i\n", n);
    i++;
} while ( n < 1000);
```

The incremental approach to solving the same problem would be

```
n = 0;
do {
    n += 5;
    printf("%i\n", n);
} while ( n < 1000);
```

The incremental will beat the pants off the brute force approach in speed any day of the week. It does less work, and with simpler operations. We can solve our coordinate scaling calculation incrementally by determining the difference, or *delta*, shown by the Greek symbol, Δ, between each successive scaled value.

If we know how to determine any point u_i from x in our scaling equation

$$u_i = width \ \frac{x - x_0}{x_1 - x_0}$$

then we can determine u_{i+1} from x+1

$$u_{i+1} = width \ \frac{x + 1 - x_0}{x_1 - x_0} = width \ \frac{x - x_0}{x_1 - x_0} + width \ \frac{1}{x_1 - x_0}$$

This simplifies down to:

$$u_{i+1} = u_i + width \ \frac{1}{x_1 - x_0}$$

which tells us how to calculate any value for *u* from the previous one. The difference between each successive value is

$$\Delta u = \frac{width}{x_1 - x_0}$$

Calculating the delta for *v* is a similar process and yields the following equation:

$$\Delta v = \frac{height}{y_1 - y_0}$$

If you understood the math, good for you! If not, I suggest you reread it until it makes sense. The concept of incremental algorithms goes a long way in computer graphics and is an extremely powerful optimization tool.

Now that I've shown you how to calculate the deltas for the u and v coordinates, how do we put it into practice? I wish I had an easy answer for you at this point, but I don't. There's one more thing I need to show. You see, up to this point our algorithm has worked with integer values. However, the delta values can't be adequately expressed as integers. Does this mean we need to use floating-point numbers? Using floating-point numbers in the inner loop of a drawing algorithm is generally regarded as a very bad idea, simply because CPUs are much faster at integer math than floating-point math. Fortunately, there's another way.

Fixed-Point Math

Floating-point numbers are named as such because the decimal point, or more generally speaking, the *radix point*, can "float" to express very large or very small numbers. This is accomplished by storing the number in two parts: a mantissa and an exponent. The *mantissa* is the number normalized so that the radix point appears at the beginning, and the *exponent* indicates how far to the left or right to shift the radix point. This scheme allows floating-point numbers to encompass a wide range of values, but it also increases the complexity of manipulating those numbers.

It is possible to represent numbers containing whole and fractional parts within a single integer without using floating point. By default, the integers that the CPU manipulates have an implicit radix point that is all the way to the right of the last binary digit. If we want, we can treat integers as having a radix point at a different location if we want. There's no special trick to this; it's all in how we interpret the numbers.

For example, we could treat each 32-bit number as if there were a radix point right in the middle. This would give 16 bits to the left of the radix point, and 16 bits to the right of the radix point. This is referred to as 16:16 or 16.16 fixed-point format.

Converting to and from Fixed Point

In general, all we need to do to convert integers to fixed-point numbers is change the location of the radix point. This is as easy as using the shift operator. For example, to convert the value 12 into 16:16 format, all we need to do is shift left by 16:

```
n = 12 << 16;
```

This makes sense when you consider that the original value is actually in an implied 32:0 fixed-point format. To move the radix point to the left, shift left. To move the radix point to the right, shift right. What could be simpler?

Addition and Subtraction

Before adding or subtracting fixed-point numbers, you need to put them in the same format. If the radix points aren't in the same location, you won't get meaningful results. Just as you need to line up the decimal points when adding decimal numbers by hand, you need to shift the radix points to a common position when adding or subtracting fixed-point numbers. The resulting sum will be in the same format as the operands.

Multiplication

When multiplying two fixed-point numbers together, they do not need to be in the same format. To determine the format of the result, add together the number of bits to the left of the radix point for each operand, and add together the number of bits to the right of the radix point for each operand. This will give you the format of the result. For example, a 24:8 number multiplied by a 24:8 number will yield a 48:16 result. A 16:16 number multiplied by a 16:16 number will similarly have a 32:32 result. Notice that the result of multiplying two 32-bit values together is a 64-bit result. Most compilers throw the upper 32 bits away, but in assembly language you can access full 64-bit results.

Division

Division works the same way as multiplication, except instead of adding together the number of bits to the left and right of the radix point, you subtract them. For example, a 32:32 number divided by a 8:24 number yields a 24:8 result. A 48:16 number divided by a 32:0 number will have a 16:16 result. You'll notice that the dividend examples I gave are 64-bit numbers. Before dividing a 32-bit value by another 32-bit value, the compiler must sign-extend the dividend to a 64-bit number.

One bit of warning when doing fixed-point math in C: If you multiply two 32-bit values together to get a 64-bit number, and then divide by a 32-bit value to get a 32-bit result, you may not get the right answer. The reason is that, as I mention previously, most compilers (Watcom included) throw away the upper 32 bits resulting from multiplying, even if they are needed for the very next dividend. This is one reason why fixed-point math is best done as assembly language, inline or otherwise.

Also, don't get the idea that you're going to be able to write a fixed-point math library and get great performance. Although fixed-point math is generally faster than floating-point math, the function-call overhead will eat you alive. The same principle applies to creating a fixed-point class wrapper in C++. Compilers just aren't as good at optimization as you and I are.

Fixed-Point Scaling

Now that you've gotten a grasp on incremental algorithms and fixed-point math, let's put them together in a new version of ScaleBlit() and see what they can do for us. Listing 6.8 shows ScaleBlit() rewritten using these techniques.

Listing 6.8. SCALE4.C.

```c
/*******************************************************************
 * Type definitions
 *******************************************************************/
typedef unsigned char UBYTE;
typedef unsigned short UWORD;
typedef signed short WORD;
typedef unsigned long ULONG;


/*******************************************************************
 * Global variables
 *******************************************************************/
UBYTE *screen = 0xA0000;
extern int width, height;


/*******************************************************************
 * ScaleBlit()
 *******************************************************************/
void cdecl ScaleBlit(UBYTE *bitmap, int x0, int y0,
    int x1, int y1)
{
    int x, y, u, v, du, dv;
    UBYTE *destRow, *dest, *sourceRow;

    du = (width << 16) / (x1 - x0);
    dv = (height << 16) / (y1 - y0);

    v = 0;
    destRow = screen + 320 * y0 + x0;

    for ( y = y0; y < y1; y++ )
    {
        u = 0;
        sourceRow = bitmap + (v >> 16) * width;
        dest = destRow;

        for ( x = x0; x < x1; x++ )
        {
            *dest++ = sourceRow[u >> 16];
            u += du;
        }
        v += dv;
        destRow += 320;
    }
}
```

The delta values for *u* and *v* (*du* and *dv*) are stored in 16:16 fixed-point format to give us a balance of precision between the whole and fractional parts. This works well for scaling where the range of scale factors is centered on 1. If we were always scaling up, the deltas would be smaller, and we might choose an 8:24 format. Conversely, if we were always scaling down, the deltas would be larger, and we might choose a format favoring a larger number of bits to the left of the radix point.

You'll notice that the inner loop is extremely compact, with no multiplications or divisions—only two additions and a shift. This is because both the source- and destination-pixel address calculations are done incrementally. At the beginning of each horizontal row of pixels, we calculate the vertical location in the source bitmap using the *v* value and store it in sourceRow. Then, in the inner loop, all the pixels from the source come from that location offset by the value in *u*. In the same way, we add 320 to the destination pointer at the end of every scan line rather than recalculate the screen address at the start of each row.

Listing 6.9 is the make file for building SCALE4.EXE.

Listing 6.9. SCALE4.MAK.

```
.c.obj:
      wcc386 -w4 -4r -mf -oneatx $[*

scale4.exe : smain.obj scale4.obj
   wlink n scale4 f smain f scale4

smain.obj : smain.c

scale4.obj : scale4.c
```

You might have noticed the function ScaleBlit() is a little longer than the previous incarnation. Does this mean it is more complex? No, not really. The major difference is that we're doing the work instead of the compiler. The size of the object files code for Listing 6.6 and Listing 6.8, shown previously, are nearly identical.

How does the incremental fixed-point approach stack up to the previous version? My test machine reports an average rate of 368.5 blits per second. If you're not convinced that incremental algorithms and fixed-point math are cool, read those numbers again. That's *more than 12 times faster* than the previous version. At this point, you might call it a day and be satisfied with our scaling function. But if you do, you'll be missing the show. If you want to learn how to scale bitmaps even faster yet, read on!

Scaling in Assembly Language

There are a few tweaks we could do to the code in Listing 6.8, but none are likely to yield any dramatic improvements. In fact, some things that might seem to be intuitive improvements will actually slow down the routine. I know, I've tried it. Optimization is a somewhat arcane art, and it certainly doesn't help us understand what's happening when the compiler is writing the machine code for us. To get any significant improvement at this point, we need to switch to assembly language.

Listing 6.10 is a fairly straightforward port of ScaleBlit() into assembly language. I've added one small optimization in the translation. Up to this point, the size of our source bitmap hasn't changed. This is a ripe opportunity for optimization. Since the width of our rocket-ship bitmap is 32, rather than multiplying the integer part of v each time by the width, we can shift left by 5. Shifting is extremely fast on the 80×86 CPU, and it is always preferable to multiplying.

We can even multiply y0×320 to figure out the initial destination address by using a combination of shifts and adds:

```
320 * y = y * 5 * 64 = (y * 4 + y) * 64 = ((y << 2) + y) << 6
```

Is this actually faster than multiplying? Absolutely, and it's one of the oldest tricks in the trade.

Listing 6.10. SCALE5.ASM.

```
                IDEAL
                P386

DEST_WIDTH      EQU     320
DEST_HEIGHT     EQU     200
SOURCE_WIDTH    EQU     32
SOURCE_WBITS    EQU     5
SOURCE_HEIGHT   EQU     32
SCREEN          EQU     0A0000h

        MODEL   FLAT, C

        DATASEG

        CODESEG

PROC    C ScaleBlit
        ARG bitmap:PTR BYTE, x0:DWORD, y0:DWORD, x1:DWORD, y1:DWORD

        LOCAL   du:DWORD, dv:DWORD, rowCount:DWORD
        LOCAL   destWidth:DWORD, destHeight:DWORD

        PUBLIC ScaleBlit

        USES    esi,edi

        ; du = (width << 16) / (x1 - x0)
        mov     eax,SOURCE_WIDTH SHL 16
        mov     ebx,[x1]
        sub     ebx,[x0]
        mov     [destWidth],ebx
        sub     edx,edx
        idiv    ebx
        mov     [du],eax
```

continues

Listing 6.10. continued

```
        ; dv = (height << 16) / (y1 - y0)
        mov     eax,SOURCE_HEIGHT SHL 16
        mov     ebx,[y1]
        sub     ebx,[y0]
        mov     [destHeight],ebx
        sub     edx,edx
        idiv    ebx
        mov     [dv],eax

        mov     esi,[bitmap]

        ; v = 0
        sub     edx,edx

        mov     eax,[destHeight]
        mov     [rowCount],eax

        ; destRow = screen + 320 * y0 + x0
        mov     edi,[y0]
        shl     edi,2
        add     edi,[y0]
        shl     edi,6
        add     edi,[x0]
        add     edi,SCREEN

@@rowLoop:

        ; u = 0
        sub     ecx,ecx

        ; sourceRow = bitmap + (v >> 16) * width;
        mov     esi,edx
        shr     esi,16
        shl     esi,SOURCE_WBITS
        add     esi,[bitmap]

        mov     ebx,[destWidth]
        push    edi

@@colLoop:

        ; *destRow++ = sourceRow[u >> 16];
        mov     eax,ecx
        shr     eax,16
        mov     al,[esi+eax]
        mov     [edi],al
        inc     edi

        ; u += du
        add     ecx,[du]

        dec     ebx
        jnz     @@colLoop

        pop     edi
```

```
        ; v += dv
        add     edx,[dv]

        ; destRow += 320
        add     edi,320

        dec     [rowCount]
        jnz     @@rowLoop

        ret
ENDP

ENDS

END
```

Listing 6.11 is the make file for building SCALE5.EXE. Notice the changes from the previous make files.

Listing 6.11. SCALE5.MAK.

```
.c.obj:
        wcc386 -w4 -4r -mf -oneatx $[*

.asm.obj:
        tasm $[* -mx -m2 -q

scale5.exe : smain.obj scale5.obj
    wlink n scale5 f smain f scale5

smain.obj : smain.c

scale5.obj : scale5.asm
```

How does our assembly language version of ScaleBlit() stack up against the C version? Not too well, I'm afraid. My test machine reports a speed of 346.9 blits per second. That's about 10 percent slower than the C version. Slower? How can the assembly language version be slower than the C version? What's wrong?

The problem is that we wrote an assembly language version of the C function. We're competing against the compiler's optimizer and losing. There's a valuable lesson here. Assembly language isn't magic, and it doesn't guarantee faster code any more than using hexadecimal constants guarantees faster performance than decimals. If we're going to get any improvements at all, we have to think more in terms of the machine.

In each iteration of the inner loop, we need to shift u (stored in ecx) right by 16 to get to the whole part. What if there were a way to store u so that we could access the whole and fractional parts separately? We can do this if we split u into two registers and treat them as a 32:32 fixed-point number. Then, to access the whole part of u, we don't have to shift; we just use the register containing the upper 32-bits. And since that value is added to esi every time to calculate the address of the source pixel, we don't actually need an additional register, we can use esi, as follows:

```
        mov     al,[esi]
        mov     [edi],al
        inc     edi

        ; u += du
        add     ecx,[duFract]
        adc     esi,[duWhole]
```

That tightens up the inner loop considerably, but now we're referencing two stack-based variables, [duFract] and [duWhole] each time through the loop. Is there any way to speed this up? Putting those values into registers would help, but unfortunately we've run out of registers. We could try moving some of the other values out of registers, but all we're doing at that point is juggling with too many balls in the air. If only the 80×86 had more general purpose registers…

Making Registers Out of Thin Air

It turns out that there is a way of getting the *effect* of having extra registers without actually using registers. The technique is hardly documented in any other books that I've seen on graphics or assembly language programming, yet it's positively necessary if you're interested in writing the absolutely fastest code. The technique is *self-modifying code*, sometimes called *code patching*.

The 80×86 processor is about as fast at accessing immediate values as it is at accessing register values. That is,

```
mov     eax,12345678h
```

takes about as long to execute as:

```
mov     eax,ebx
```

I'm not going to count cycles at you, because there's a myriad of processes that affect execution time. This bit of trivia is useful because immediate values are stored in memory as part of the instruction and are accessible elsewhere in our programs. That means we can change an immediate value on the fly, and voilá—instant register.

For example, we can write:

```
        mov     eax,[someValue]
        mov     [DWORD PTR @@fixup+2],eax
        .
        .
        .
@@fixup:
        add     ecx,12345678h
```

When the add instruction at the label @@fixup gets executed, the immediate value actually added to ecx will have been modified to equal [someValue]. To alter the immediate value, we need to add an offset of 2 to the label @@fixup to address the immediate value. The first two bytes form the instruction opcode.

Self-Modifying Code Caveats

Using self-modifying code can yield important "down to the metal" performance improvements, but there are a couple of hazards and traps you can fall into.

First, self-modifying code won't work easily under a protected segmented operating system. You need to be able to easily write to the place in memory where the executable code is stored. This is simple under a flat-model memory such as that provided by Watcom and DOS4GW, since CS and DS both map to the same physical address space. Under Windows or other protected-mode DOS extenders, you must create an alias to the code segment before you can write to it. This is another reason why Watcom is the compiler of choice for high-performance game development.

Second, immediate values are only fast when they are used as immediate values. When you access them as memory addresses, there's no benefit. If you need to alter a value in an inner loop, it's not a good candidate for a self-modifying code fixup, and better off left in a register.

Third, when creating assembly-code instructions which have immediate values that are referenced elsewhere, don't use values less that 10000h as dummy values, or the assembler will generate an optimized opcode that zero-extends the value from an 8- or 16-bit number. I recommend that you use the value 12345678h as I have here, since it assembles to the right size value and it's obviously a contrived number. Better yet, create an EQUATE for the dummy value called FIXUP so it's clear to anyone else reading your code.

Fourth, keep in mind that instructions have varying opcode sizes, so calculating the fixup location from the start address of the instruction can become tricky. A better way to address the immediate value is to place a label *after* the instruction and reference the label minus the size of the immediate operand. Since immediate operands always form the last bytes of the instruction sequence, this will work no matter what the length of the opcode.

Here's an example using these tips:

```
FIXUP   equ     12345678h
        mov     eax,[someValue]
        mov     [DWORD PTR @@fix-4],eax
        .
        .
        .
        add     ecx,FIXUP
@@fix:
```

Unrolling the Loop

One additional bit of optimization that will speed up our routine is to unroll the inner loop slightly. Every bit of knowledge about how the routine will be used is an optimization opportunity. The more specific your code is, the faster it can be. The more generic it is, the more you are limited in how you can optimize. Our scaffold program always scales the bitmap to a width that is an even value. Knowing this, it is an easy task to divide the width by two for the loop count, and change the inner loop to write two pixels at a time.

All Together Now

Listing 6.12 is the assembly language version of `ScaleBlit()` modified to use the three new techniques discussed. Study the code carefully. There are a lot of changes, but they pay off handsomely, as we'll see.

Listing 6.12. SCALE6.ASM.

```
                IDEAL
                P386

DEST_WIDTH      EQU     320
DEST_HEIGHT     EQU     200
SOURCE_WIDTH    EQU     32
SOURCE_WBITS    EQU     5
SOURCE_HEIGHT   EQU     32
SCREEN          EQU     0A0000h
FIXUP           EQU     12345678h

        MODEL   FLAT, C

        DATASEG

        CODESEG

PROC    C ScaleBlit
        ARG bitmap:PTR BYTE, x0:DWORD, y0:DWORD, x1:DWORD, y1:DWORD

        LOCAL   dv:DWORD, y:DWORD, v:DWORD
        LOCAL   destWidth:DWORD, destHeight:DWORD

        PUBLIC ScaleBlit

        USES    esi,edi

        mov     eax,SOURCE_WIDTH SHL 16
        mov     ebx,[x1]
        sub     ebx,[x0]
        sub     edx,edx
        idiv    ebx

        sub     edx,edx
        shld    edx,eax,16
        shl     eax,16
        mov     [DWORD PTR @@fduWhole1-4],edx
        mov     [DWORD PTR @@fduFract1-4],eax
        mov     [DWORD PTR @@fduWhole2-4],edx
        mov     [DWORD PTR @@fduFract2-4],eax
        shr     ebx,1
        mov     [destWidth],ebx
```

```
            ; dv = (height << 16) / (y1 - y0)
            mov     eax,SOURCE_HEIGHT SHL 16
            mov     ebx,[y1]
            sub     ebx,[y0]
            sub     edx,edx
            idiv    ebx
            mov     [dv],eax
            mov     [destHeight],ebx

            mov     esi,[bitmap]

            sub     eax,eax
            mov     [v],eax

            ; destRow = screen + 320 * y0 + x0
            mov     edi,[y0]
            shl     edi,2
            add     edi,[y0]
            shl     edi,6
            add     edi,[x0]
            add     edi,SCREEN

            mov     edx,[destHeight]

@@rowLoop:

            mov     esi,[v]
            shr     esi,16
            shl     esi,SOURCE_WBITS
            add     esi,[bitmap]

            mov     ebx,[destWidth]

            push    edi

            sub     ecx,ecx

@@colLoop:

            mov     al,[esi]

            add     ecx,FIXUP
@@fduFract1:
            adc     esi,FIXUP
@@fduWhole1:

            mov     ah,[esi]

            add     ecx,FIXUP
@@fduFract2:
            adc     esi,FIXUP
@@fduWhole2:

            mov     [edi],ax
            add     edi,2

            dec     ebx
            jnz     @@colLoop
```

continues

Listing 6.12. continued

```
        pop     edi

        ; v += dv
        mov     eax,[dv]
        add     [v],eax

        ; destRow += 320
        add     edi,320

        dec     edx
        jnz     @@rowLoop

        ret
ENDP

ENDS

END
```

Listing 6.13 is the make file for building SCALE6.EXE.

Listing 6.13. SCALE6.MAK.

```
.c.obj:
        wcc386 -w4 -4r -mf -oneatx $[*

.asm.obj:
        tasm $[* -mx -m2 -q

scale6.exe : smain.obj scale6.obj
    wlink n scale6 f smain f scale6

smain.obj : smain.c

scale6.obj : scale6.asm
```

How does Listing 6.12 fair? My test machine reports a blit rate of a screaming 609.5 scaled blits per second. That's more than twice as fast as our previous assembly language effort and *more than 20 times faster* than our original (working) algorithm in C.

Here's a wrap-up of my benchmarks of the various incarnations of the scaling routine:

Version	Blits/Second
Scale3—First C version	30.5
Scale4—Incremental C version	368.5
Scale5—Incremental Assembly version	346.9
Scale6—Optimized Assembly version	609.5

Is the final version as fast as it can be? No, certainly not. I'm sure that there are a few optimizations left to be done; but if I were to do them all, what would be left for *you* to do? Consider them exercises.

I didn't discuss how to do clipping of the scaled bitmaps, but that's also something you should try to figure out on your own. I'm a firm believer in the adage, "Give a man a fish, and he'll eat for a day; teach him to fish, and he'll eat for a lifetime." To really assimilate this material, you need to experiment with these routines and learn by doing.

Bitmap Rotation

If you can visualize how the point specified by the *u* and *v* coordinates changes as the scaled bitmap is being drawn, you'll see that it moves through the source bitmap in discrete increments. In the inner loop of the algorithm, each increment is one step to the right of a distance specified by *du*. In the outer loop, it moves down by the distance *dv* for every row. By changing *u*, we moving horizontally through the bitmap. By changing *v*, we move vertically.

Suppose we changed both u *and* v in the inner loop of the routine. Then, instead of iterating horizontally through the bitmap, we'd actually be moving through the bitmap at an angle determined by *du* and *dv*. That, in essence, is the key to fast bitmap rotation.

The question then is, "How do we determine what values to use for *du* and *dv*?" The answer requires a little bit of trigonometry. Together, *du* and *dv* are Cartesian components of a vector, which is a value that has both a magnitude and a direction. To convert a vector into its Cartesian components, we use the following equations:

$$u = n \times \cos\Theta$$

$$v = n \times \sin\Theta$$

where *n* is the magnitude of the vector, and Θ is the angle. Take a look at Figure 6.5. You'll see that we actually need two vectors, one for columns, and one for rows. This means that we'll need two sets of values for *du* and *dv*.

Figure 6.5.
Determining the rotation vectors.

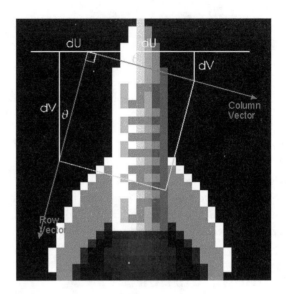

You'll notice that the two vectors form equal triangles, which means that we can determine the column deltas from the angle and the magnitude, and then get the row deltas from the column values in the following fashion:

```
duRow = -dvCol;
dvRow = duCol;
```

Combining Scaling and Rotation

It's fairly obvious that the angle of the column vector represents the rotation of the bitmap, but where do we get the magnitude? The magnitude determines the *scale* of the transformation. If we are simply rotating, then the magnitude of the vector is 1. To double the size of the bitmap, we would use a magnitude of 0.5. To halve the size of the bitmap, we would use a magnitude of 2.0. The reason for the inverse relationship is that the magnitude describes the increment for moving through the *source* bitmap. Clearly if you move in steps of 0.5, it takes twice as many steps to traverse the bitmap, and therefore twice as many destination pixels.

Let's create a program to do bitmap rotation. However, instead of merely rotating a single bitmap, let's also look at how to tile the rotated bitmap onto the screen. The program will fill the screen with adjoining bitmaps, creating the impression of a continuous pattern of rocket ships.

We'll use the same approach as in the scaling examples of separating a test shell from the actual rotation routine. Listing 6.14 shows the scaffold program for rotating bitmaps.

Listing 6.14. RMAIN.C.

```c
#include <stdio.h>
#include <stdlib.h>
#include <mem.h>
#include <conio.h>
#include <math.h>
#include <palette.h>
#include <pcx.h>
#include <dostime.h>


/******************************************************************
 * Defines
 ******************************************************************/
#define kAngle360       256
#define kAngleMask      (kAngle360 - 1)
#define kAngle180       (kAngle360 / 2)
#define kAngle90        (kAngle360 / 4)
#define kPi             3.141592654


/******************************************************************
 * Type definitions
 ******************************************************************/
typedef unsigned char UBYTE;
typedef unsigned short UWORD;
typedef signed short WORD;
typedef unsigned long ULONG;


/******************************************************************
 * Global variables
 ******************************************************************/
PALETTE palette;
int width, height;
long sinTable[kAngle360];


/******************************************************************
 * External Functions
 ******************************************************************/
void cdecl RotateBlit(UBYTE *bitmap, int angle, long scale);


/******************************************************************
 * Functions
 ******************************************************************/
int getvmode( void );
#pragma aux getvmode =\
    "mov    ah,0x0F",\
    "int    0x10,"\
    "and    eax,0xFF",\

int setvmode(int);
#pragma aux setvmode =\
    "int 0x10",\
    parm [eax]\

void InitSinTable()
{
    int i;
```

continues

Listing 6.14. continued

```c
    for (i = 0; i < kAngle180; i++)
        sinTable[i] = sin((double)i * kPi / kAngle180) * 0x10000L;

    for (i = kAngle180; i < kAngle360; i++)
        sinTable[i] = -sinTable[i - kAngle180];
}

void main()
{
    char *fname = "ROCKET.PCX";
    UBYTE *rocketBitmap = NULL;
    int nOldMode;
    int nResult;
    int angle;
    ULONG startTime, stopTime;
    int fps, frames = 0;

    InitSinTable();

    nResult = ReadPCX256(fname, &palette, &width, &height,
        &rocketBitmap);
    if ( nResult != pcxOkay )
    {
        printf("Error reading %s\n", fname);
        exit(1);
    }

    nOldMode = getvmode();
    setvmode(0x13);
    gSetDACRange(0, 256, palette);

    startTime = GetDosTicks();

    while ( 1 )
    {
        if ( kbhit() )
            break;

        for (angle = 0; angle < kAngle360; angle++)
        {
            RotateBlit(rocketBitmap, angle,
                sinTable[angle] / 2 + 0x9000);
            frames++;
        }
    }

    stopTime = GetDosTicks();

    setvmode(nOldMode);

    getch();

    fps = frames * 182 / (stopTime-startTime);
    printf("Average frame rate: %i.%i fps\n", fps / 10, fps % 10);
}
```

Fast Trigonometry

The scaffold program does some additional setup that involves creating a table of sine values. Why not just use trigonometry functions? The main consideration is speed. Library trigonometry functions are notoriously slow, certainly not something we want to call thousands of times per second. Another reason is that trigonometry functions return floating-point values. Since our inner loops use fixed point, that means we have to convert from floating point to fixed point. Again, this eats up a lot of processor time.

Finally, if you are writing for 386-class computers, the lack of a processor floating-point unit (FPU) means that trigonometry functions are implemented through FPU emulator code, which is horribly slow. Trigonometry tables can be built ahead of time and loaded during your program's initialization. For our example, we'll just create the sine table dynamically.

The sine table in RMAIN.C contains 256 entries, but this can be changed easily by modifying the kAngle360 constant. You'll notice that several other angle constants are based on this value. The constant kAngleMask is a bit mask that is used for preventing overflow of angle values and is determined by kAngle360 - 1. For this to work properly, kAngle360 must be a power of 2. I did it this way because evaluating the expression

```
sinTable[angle & kAngleMask]
```

is much faster than the functionally equivalent

```
sinTable[angle % kAngle360]
```

How large should the sine table be? This is really a matter of how much angular precision you need, balanced with the memory requirements of the table. Although you could potentially create a sine table for only a single quadrant and use symmetry to determine values for the other three quadrants, the benefit of this is minimal compared to memory requirements for the full arc. If you are going to load a sine table from disk, however, storing only the first quadrant makes sense in order to reduce your disk storage.

Rotation in C

Let's move right ahead with a rotation function in C that uses the incremental techniques we learning in scaling. We'll use the optimization tricks we learned as well. Listing 6.15 shows the rotation function in C.

Listing 6.15. ROTATE1.C.

```
/*****************************************************************
 * Defines
 *****************************************************************/
#define kBitmapWidth    32
#define kScreenWidth    320
#define kScreenHeight   200
```

continues

Listing 6.15. continued

```
#define kScreenCenterX  (kScreenWidth / 2)
#define kScreenCenterY  (kScreenHeight / 2)
#define kAngle360       256
#define kAngleMask      (kAngle360 - 1)
#define kAngle180       (kAngle360 / 2)
#define kAngle90        (kAngle360 / 4)

/*****************************************************************
 * Type definitions
 *****************************************************************/
typedef unsigned char UBYTE;
typedef unsigned short UWORD;
typedef signed short WORD;
typedef unsigned long ULONG;

/*****************************************************************
 * Global variables
 *****************************************************************/
UBYTE *screen = 0xA0000;
long aspectAdjust = (6 << 16) / 5;
extern long sinTable[kAngle360];

/*****************************************************************
 * Inline Functions
 *****************************************************************/
long Mul16_16( long a, long b );
#pragma aux Mul16_16 =\
    "imul    edx",\
    "shrd    eax,edx,16"\
    parm [eax] [edx]

/*****************************************************************
 * RotateBlit()
 *****************************************************************/
void cdecl RotateBlit(UBYTE *bitmap, int angle, long scale)
{
    UBYTE *dest;
    long u, v, rowU, rowV, startingU, startingV;
    long duCol, dvCol, duRow, dvRow;
    int x, y;

    // center of 32x32-bitmap
    startingU = 16 << 16;
    startingV = 16 << 16;

    // calculate deltas
    duCol = sinTable[(angle + kAngle90) & kAngleMask];
    dvCol = sinTable[angle];

    duCol = Mul16_16(duCol, scale);
    dvCol = Mul16_16(dvCol, scale);

    duRow = Mul16_16(-dvCol, aspectAdjust);
    dvRow = Mul16_16(duCol, aspectAdjust);
```

```
        startingU -= kScreenCenterX * duCol + kScreenCenterY * duRow;
        startingV -= kScreenCenterX * dvCol + kScreenCenterY * dvRow;

        rowU = startingU;
        rowV = startingV;
        dest = screen;

        for ( y = 0; y < 200; y++)
        {
            u = rowU;
            v = rowV;

            for ( x = 0; x < 320; x++)
            {
                *dest++ = bitmap[((u >> 16) & 31) +
                    ((v >> 16) & 31) * 32];
                u += duCol;
                v += dvCol;
            }

            rowU += duRow;
            rowV += dvRow;
        }
    }
```

Aspect-Ratio Correction

All the examples in this chapter use the PC's graphics mode 13h. This is a simple and fast graphics mode to use because of the linear addressing of pixels. One of the disadvantages, however, is the slightly odd pixel shape. Instead of being square, the pixels are stretched somewhat vertically. PC color monitors have a 4:3 aspect ratio, which means that the display area is 33 percent wider than it is tall. Graphics modes such as 320×240, 640×480, and 1024×768 all share the same aspect ratio, which gives them nice square pixels.

The non-square pixels of mode 13h become a concern when rotating your bitmaps, because if the pixel shape is not taken into consideration, the bitmap will stretch and distort as it rotates. The constant aspectRatio corrects for the irregularity of the pixels by modifying the row *du* and *dv* values.

Fixed Point Revisited

Earlier, I mentioned that one of the difficulties of using fixed point in C is that compilers aren't very smart about what to do with the results of multiplication. This problem rears its head in our rotation function wherein we need to multiply the sine of the angle by the scale factor. Both these values are 16:16 fixed-point numbers, and we want a 16:16 result.

You might wonder what would happen if we simply used the following:

```
dvCol = (sinTable[angle] * scale) >> 16;
```

This certainly *seems* as if it should work, and it does—most of the time. The problem is overflow. Let's suppose the value for the sine is 00010000h (1.0), and the scale is 00018000h (1.5). Multiplying these two values together gives 180000000h, which becomes truncated to 8000000h to fit into 32 bits. After shifting, our result would be 00008000h, which isn't right at all.

To get the proper result, we need to do a quick bit of inline assembly language, which is what the `#pragma Mul16_16` function does. This inline function multiplies two 16:16 values together and shifts the full 64-bit result to get the proper 16:16 answer.

Wrapping the Bitmap

Deep in the innermost loop of the rotation function is a line that reads:

```
*dest++ = bitmap[((u >> 16) & 31) + ((v >> 16) & 31) * 32];
```

This long-winded expression is the *source-pixel address calculation*. This expression is hard coded for a 32×32-bitmap. This provides an opportunity for the compiler's optimizer to produce some very fast code, much faster than had we tried to create a routine that would rotate any size bitmap. After the *u* and *v* coordinates are shifted to get the whole values, they are ANDed with 31. This mask clears the upper bits of the coordinate and allows the values to "wrap," which results in the tiling effect.

Listing 6.16 is the make file for building ROTATE1.EXE.

Listing 6.16. ROTATE1.MAK.

```
.c.obj:
        wcc386 -w4 -4r -mf -oneatx $[*

rotate1.exe : rmain.obj rotate1.obj
    wlink n rotate1 f rmain f rotate1

rmain.obj : rmain.c

rotate1.obj : rotate1.c
```

The output from ROTATE1.EXE is shown in Figure 6.6. Listing 6.15, shown previously, performs admirably well for a rotation function in C. It contains a good deal of high-level optimization that integrates well with the compiler's optimizer. On my test machine, it clocks in at about 40 frames per second. It's not likely you'll be able to speed up this algorithm much in C, so let's go forward with an optimized assembly language implementation.

Figure 6.6.
*The display from
ROTATE1.EXE.*

Listing 6.17 contains an assembly language version of the RotateBlit() function. It contains many optimizations over the C version, but the most significant is the pixel-address calculation for the source bitmap. It consists of these three instructions:

```
mov     ebx,edx
shr     ebx,32 - SOURCE_SBITS
shld    ebx,ecx,SOURCE_SBITS
```

Rather than use 16:16 values and masking off the upper bits to wrap the coordinate values, I stored the coordinates in 5:27 (as determined by the constant SOURCE_SBITS) format. Overflow of the register eliminates the need to mask off unused bits.

It also means that to calculate the source-pixel address, I can combine the upper five bits of v with the upper five bits of u to form the 10-bit pixel address by using the shld operator. This is an extremely useful instruction for calculating addresses within bitmaps, and it enables our whole address calculation to take place in just five cycles.

Listing 6.17 also unrolls the inner loop to do four pixels at a time. The four pixels are combined into a 32-bit register and then written to the destination in a single write. This can make quite a difference when writing directly to the display, because every access to video memory can incur wait states, whether the access is for 8-bits, 16-bits, or 32-bits.

Listing 6.17. ROTATE2.ASM.

```
                IDEAL
                P386

ANGLE360        EQU     256
ANGLEMASK       EQU     (ANGLE360 - 1)
ANGLE180        EQU     (ANGLE360 / 2)
ANGLE90         EQU     (ANGLE360 / 4)
SCREEN_WIDTH    EQU     320
SCREEN_HEIGHT   EQU     200
SCREEN_CENTERX  EQU     (SCREEN_WIDTH / 2)
SCREEN_CENTERY  EQU     (SCREEN_HEIGHT / 2)
SOURCE_SIZE     EQU     32
SOURCE_SBITS    EQU     5
SCREEN          EQU     0A0000h
FIXUP           EQU     12345678h
```

continues

Listing 6.17. continued

```
        MODEL    FLAT, C

        DATASEG

        EXTRN    C sinTable:PTR DWORD

aspectAdjust    dd       (6 SHL 16) / 5

        CODESEG

PROC    C RotateBlit
        ARG bitmap:PTR BYTE, angle:DWORD, scale:DWORD

        PUBLIC RotateBlit

        LOCAL startingU:DWORD, startingV:DWORD
        LOCAL dUCol:DWORD, dVCol:DWORD, dURow:DWORD, dVRow:DWORD
        LOCAL rowCount:DWORD

        USES     esi,edi,ebx,ecx

; calculate horizontal deltas

        mov      eax,[angle]
        add      eax,ANGLE90
        and      eax,ANGLEMASK
        mov      eax,[sinTable + eax * 4]
        shl      eax,16 - SOURCE_SBITS
        imul     [scale]
        shrd     eax,edx,16
        mov      [dUCol],eax
        mov      [DWORD PTR @@fdUCol1-4],eax
        mov      [DWORD PTR @@fdUCol2-4],eax
        mov      [DWORD PTR @@fdUCol3-4],eax
        mov      [DWORD PTR @@fdUCol4-4],eax

        mov      eax,[angle]
        and      eax,ANGLEMASK
        mov      eax,[sinTable + eax * 4]
        shl      eax,16 - SOURCE_SBITS
        imul     [scale]
        shrd     eax,edx,16
        mov      [dVCol],eax
        mov      [DWORD PTR @@fdVCol1-4],eax
        mov      [DWORD PTR @@fdVCol2-4],eax
        mov      [DWORD PTR @@fdVCol3-4],eax
        mov      [DWORD PTR @@fdVCol4-4],eax

; calculate vertical deltas

        mov      eax,[dVCol]
        neg      eax
        imul     [aspectAdjust]
        shrd     eax,edx,16
        mov      [dURow],eax
```

```
        mov     eax,[dUCol]
        imul    [aspectAdjust]
        shrd    eax,edx,16
        mov     [dVRow],eax

        mov     eax,80000000h
        mov     [startingU],eax
        mov     [startingV],eax

; move up by yOrg

        mov     eax,[dUCol]
        imul    eax,SCREEN_CENTERX
        sub     [startingU],eax

        mov     eax,[dURow]
        imul    eax,SCREEN_CENTERY
        sub     [startingU],eax

        mov     eax,[dVCol]
        imul    eax,SCREEN_CENTERX
        sub     [startingV],eax

        mov     eax,[dVRow]
        imul    eax,SCREEN_CENTERY
        sub     [startingV],eax

; fixup end of row deltas

        mov     eax,[dUCol]
        imul    eax,SCREEN_WIDTH
        neg     eax
        add     eax,[dURow]
        mov     [DWORD PTR @@fdURow-4],eax

        mov     eax,[dVCol]
        imul    eax,SCREEN_WIDTH
        neg     eax
        add     eax,[dVRow]
        mov     [DWORD PTR @@fdVRow-4],eax

        mov     esi,[bitmap]
        mov     edi,SCREEN

        mov     ecx,[startingU]
        mov     edx,[startingV]

        mov     eax,SCREEN_HEIGHT           ; initialize row count
        mov     [rowCount],eax

@@rowloop:
        push    ebp
        mov     ebp,SCREEN_WIDTH / 4        ; initialize column count

@@colloop:
        mov     ebx,edx
        shr     ebx,32 - SOURCE_SBITS
        shld    ebx,ecx,SOURCE_SBITS
```

continues

Listing 6.17. continued

```
        add     edx,01234567h
@@fdVCol1:
        add     ecx,01234567h
@@fdUCol1:
        mov     al,[esi+ebx]

        mov     ebx,edx
        shr     ebx,32 - SOURCE_SBITS
        shld    ebx,ecx,SOURCE_SBITS
        add     edx,01234567h
@@fdVCol2:
        add     ecx,01234567h
@@fdUCol2:
        mov     ah,[esi+ebx]

        shl     eax,16

        mov     ebx,edx
        shr     ebx,32 - SOURCE_SBITS
        shld    ebx,ecx,SOURCE_SBITS
        add     edx,01234567h
@@fdVCol3:
        add     ecx,01234567h
@@fdUCol3:
        mov     al,[esi+ebx]

        mov     ebx,edx
        shr     ebx,32 - SOURCE_SBITS
        shld    ebx,ecx,SOURCE_SBITS
        add     edx,01234567h
@@fdVCol4:
        add     ecx,01234567h
@@fdUCol4:
        mov     ah,[esi+ebx]

        rol     eax,16

        mov     [edi],eax
        add     edi,4
        dec     ebp
        jnz     @@colloop

        add     ecx,01234567h
@@fdURow:
        add     edx,01234567h
@@fdVRow:

        pop     ebp
        dec     [rowCount]
        jnz     @@rowloop

        ret

ENDP

ENDS

END
```

Listing 6.18 is the make file for building ROTATE2.EXE.

Listing 6.18. ROTATE2.MAK.

```
.c.obj:
        wcc386 -w4 -4r -mf -oneatx $[*

.asm.obj:
        tasm $[* -mx -m2 -q

rotate2.exe : rmain.obj rotate2.obj
    wlink n rotate2 f rmain f rotate2

rmain.obj : rmain.c

rotate2.obj : rotate2.asm
```

ROTATE2.EXE clocks in at just under 90 frames per second on my test machine. That's over twice as fast as the C version, so the assembly language optimization certainly paid off. At 90 FPS, the routine is rotating and scaling at a rate of 5.5 million pixels per second. That's darn close to the video bandwidth, which means that there aren't a lot of wasted cycles in Listing 6.17. Nevertheless, I never assert that code is fully optimized, so I encourage you to try your hand at improving its performance. (If you do, let me know!)

The Processor Cache Effect

If you experiment with rotating tiled bitmaps of various sizes, you'll observe a very curious phenomenon. The larger the source bitmap is, the slower the performance of the code. Here are some results to illustrate:

Size	FPS
32×32	90
64×64	90
128×128	75
256×256	60
512×512	45
1024×1024	20

Even stranger is that the frame rate only slows down for the larger bitmaps at certain angles. When the bitmap is rotated to 0° or 180°, there is no significant slowdown. When the bitmap is rotated to 90° to 270°, the frame rate drops incredibly. The above values are *averages* for the full 360°. Just what the heck is going on, here? Is there some obscure bug in the rotation code?

I must admit, when I first encountered this I was stumped. Whatever was happening certainly was significant and couldn't be ignored. Why did it only kick in for bitmaps 128×128 and larger? Then it occurred to me: a 128×128 bitmap takes 16384 bytes, but a 64×64 bitmap is 4096 bytes, and the 32×32-bitmap is only 1024 bytes. Why is this significant? The 486 DX2 processor has an 8KB internal cache. When the bitmap wasn't large enough to fit in the cache, the frame rate dropped.

Why only the slowdown at certain angles? It has to do with the way the bitmap is laid out in memory. Adjacent horizontal pixels are at neighboring addresses. When the bitmap is drawn at its normal orientation, only pixels in a small address range are used in the course of drawing a scan line. When the bitmap is sideways, however, pixels from the entire address span of the bitmap are used, resulting in the internal CPU cache becoming frequently invalidated.

What can you do about the effect of the internal cache? Absolutely nothing. You should definitely be aware of it, however, and you should design your code to minimize its effects.

Affine and Other Transformations

The scaling and rotation algorithms we've discussed in this chapter fall under a much larger category of processes known as *affine (pronounced uh-FYN) transformations*. The transformations have the property of preserving the parallelism of lines, but not lengths and angles. One outcome of this is that we can render the transformations by using constant values for *du* and *dv* throughout the routine. They are, in effect, linear processes. It is easy to see how we could modify the examples from this chapter to skew bitmaps, which is another affine transformation.

Summary

We've covered the essential elements of scaling and rotating in the chapter, and picked up some useful optimization tricks as well. Even if you don't use the scaling or rotation techniques, you will definitely be able to write faster low-level code with the knowledge you've obtained. We've learned that we can't always beat the compiler just by switching to assembly language; sometimes we require a new way of thinking about the problem!

Hopefully, you'll find yourself working with fixed-point math as easily and as casually as if you were born with a radix point between your thumbs. It's a skill that you won't soon outgrow, because even the floating-point speed improvements of the latest generation of processors aren't much benefit when it comes to conversion to integers.

The algorithms for rotating bitmaps should give you some insight into many other graphics techniques, such as texture mapping and raycasting. I encourage you to experiment and explore—there's a virtually unlimited range of bitmap effects that you can achieve with just some basic incremental algorithm knowledge.

Real-Time Voxel Graphics

by Peter Freese

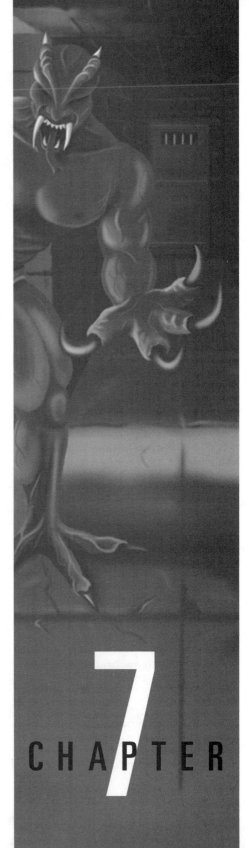

CHAPTER 7

When I was 10 years old, I had a vivid series of dreams about flying. In each dream, I would stand on a rocky ledge, spread my arms out to my side, and transform into a great white swan as I fell forward from the ledge. I'd dive down within inches of the rocks below, then swoop up into a stall. Beating my wings, I'd rise above the earth, higher and higher, until my vista included all the landscape of my childhood experience. I could see the center of town, far off to the east, and the pond where I went fishing to the south. As I flew over vaguely familiar landmarks, I'd see them from a view never observed by those who stayed on the safety of the ground. I noticed how the shape of the pond resembled a face of a gnome; how one of the cows in the neighboring farm had wandered off to a barren field, and how far away my friend's house seemed. The sky was unlimited, and so too was my freedom in the air. I remember resolving at that age that I would become a pilot. I reasoned that my dreams were surely a subconscious expression of my desire to fly.

I never did become a pilot (at least not yet, anyway). However, I've logged countless hours flying the world's fastest and most heavily armed fighter jets, spacecraft, and helicopters—right here at my desk. Until fairly recently, though, these experiences lacked the visual realism of the flight sequences in my dreams. The biggest problem facing designers of flight simulations is the display of the ground, a process called *terrain visualization*. While buildings and other aircraft can be made up of a handful of polygons, the surface of the earth (or any planet, for that matter) just isn't that simple to model. If you want things to look interesting, you *need* rolling hills and valleys.

In this chapter, we're going to learn a technique for terrain visualization called *height mapping*. This technique is sometimes also called *voxel graphics*, although technically, that term is incorrect.

This chapter covers the following:

- Generating terrain
- Height mapping
- Ray casting

What Are Voxels?

Before we get too far into height mapping, I want to give a brief discussion of voxels, because the terms height-mapping and voxel graphics are often used interchangeably, and you should know what voxels are and what they aren't.

The term "voxel" comes from "volumetric pixel." A voxel volume is produced either by a mathematical model, or the voxels are collected from the real world, such as in medical imaging. Voxels can be stored in a hierarchical data structure, such as an octree, or a large three-dimensional array. Medical imaging has turned out to be one of the most popular applications of voxels. Data collected from tomographic (solid-body) systems can be viewed as a three-dimensional object and rotated about to suit the needs of the clinician. The basic idea in rendering voxels is that the viewer should be able to perceive a *volume* from a rendered projection.

There are two major approaches to rendering voxels: ray casting (backward mapping) and plane compositing (forward mapping). The ray-casting approach shoots a ray for each pixel on the screen and determines what voxel it hits. The plane compositing technique projects each pixel onto the frame buffer, moving from back to front through the volume data.

Each voxel can be rendered as a cube or approximated as a single upright rectangle. The important distinction to make about voxels as that they are used to represent a *volume*. They can be viewed at any angle, since they are a true three dimensional data representation.

There's a very good reason not to use voxels to model terrain, and that's storage. A typical dataset from a CT scanner, for example, might be 64×256×256 = 4.2 million voxels. That's a large dataset and not a lot of spatial resolution. A voxel database contains more information than is necessary to model terrain because of its three-dimensional freedom.

A far better method of storage comes to mind when you realize that due to the force of gravity, landscape is much more two-dimensional than three-dimensional. In chaos theory, the fractal dimension of the earth's surface is indeed closer to two than three. Except for the occasional twisted desert rock formations, the earth's surface never overlaps itself. At any given location, the ground has only one height.

It would be very efficient to create an array that contained the height of the terrain within a rectangular grid. Rendering that array is what height mapping is all about.

Generating Terrain

Before you can render terrain data, you've got to have some. If you are going for total realism, you can obtain genuine height data of the earth's surface. The U.S. government has detailed survey data of the United States and North America; other governments also maintain extensive geographic databases of their respective countries.

If you don't need to display terrain for a particular region, you can do just as well or better by algorithmically generating terrain. One way that this can be better than using authentic data is that you can choose what sort of geographical features you want in your world. If you want mountains with a river flowing down a deep draw, you don't have to search for a suitable location—you simply create it. Another way is that you can combine generation of the terrain height map with the terrain color map. Geographical survey data includes only height information, and not data about what the ground actually *looks* like. In order to render terrain quickly, you'll want to create two databases: a height map containing the elevation at each grid point; and a color map containing the ground color at each grid point.

Ideally, the color map should be a view of the terrain from directly above, with lighting from the side to enhance the relief features of the terrain. By making the shading information part of the color map, you'll save yourself some expensive calculations at rendering time.

Fractal Subdivision

Fractal geometry provides an elegant, efficient way to model the detail and irregularity found in natural terrain. Fractal subdivision starts with a triangle. The algorithm finds the midpoint of each of the triangle's sides, then displaces each midpoint a random distance. Joining the displaced midpoints generates a new triangle and divides the original figure into four smaller triangles. The same procedure is applied in turn to each of the four new triangles, generating 16 triangles, to each of which the procedure is recursively applied again. The process continues until the triangles are sufficiently small. The resulting mesh is a complex polygonal surface.

The component triangles do not necessarily need to be identical or even equilateral. In fact, for creating height maps within a rectangular grid, they *can't* be equilateral. Figure 7.1 illustrates the process of subdividing a rectangle into a triangle mesh. The rectangle is original divided into two triangles, which are then recursively subdivided. The midpoint of each triangle side occurs on a square grid point.

Figure 7.1.
Fractally subdividing a grid.

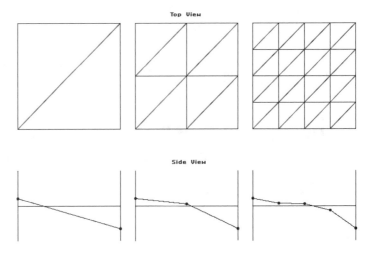

At each level of recursion, the length of the sides of the triangles are halved, and so too is the range of random displacement. The linear relationship between the size of the triangle and the range of displacement gives the entire mesh a uniform "fractalness."

Fractal subdivision offers some unique benefits in terrain generation. The designer can set the initial altitudes for the control points at any given level of mesh—specifying the locations of mountain peaks and valleys—and have the algorithm fill in the terrain detail. The roughness of the terrain, determined by the displacement range, is consistent through the surface.

Fault Generation

Fault generation is a method of creating terrain that attempts to simulate the geological processes of nature. To understand how fault generation works, first imagine the height map containing all constant values representing flat terrain. Next create a fault line through the height field. The line can be at any angle and location, provided it passes through the data set. Raise all the points on one side of the line, and lower all the points on the other size. Repeated applications of this procedure can produce highly detailed and realistic looking landscapes.

The fault displacement can be consistent through each iteration, or it can vary. One technique of fault generation is to use a function of the form $f(i) = k/i$, where i is the iteration and k is a constant represent the amount of the first fault. This produces one large initial fault, and then successively smaller faults with each iteration.

Digital Filtering

One problem that both fractal subdivision and fault generation suffer from is that they can produce terrain that is *too rough*. The surface of the earth has been subject to millions of years of erosive forces such as wind and rain that have tempered the jagged formations of earth into smooth rolling hills and valleys. You can simulate these effects as well in your terrain generation. Digital filtering algorithms are a method of image manipulation that can smooth or enhance the detail in an image, as well as turn your steep cliffs into gentle slopes.

The essential element in a digital filter is a filter matrix, or *convolution kernel*. This matrix determines how to calculate the value of a pixel from its neighbors. It does this by assigning a weight, or multiplier, to each value in the matrix. The pixel of concern is located at the center of the matrix. For example, a simple smoothing function might look like the following:

```
1   2   1
2   4   2
1   2   1
```

The output value of the filter for a given pixel is determined by summing the product of each factor in the matrix and with its relative pixel in the source. The sum of all the factors in the matrix is 16, which means that we'll have to divide by 16 to normalize the result. Sums that are powers of two can speed up the filtering process, because instead of dividing, we can simply shift right.

In the preceding example, to determine the output pixel at location x,y, we would take the sum of:

```
i[x-1,y-1] + 2×i[x,y-1] + i[x+1,y-1]
+ 2×i[x-1,y] + 4×i[x,y] + 2×i[x+1,y]
+ i[x-1,y+1] + 2×i[x,y+1] + i[x+1,y+1]
```

and divide by 16.

Digital filters can do much more than smoothing. By changing a few values in the matrix, you can have a filter which enhances edges:

$$\begin{array}{rrr} 1 & -2 & 1 \\ -2 & 5 & -2 \\ 1 & -2 & 1 \end{array}$$

The sum of the values in this filter is 1, so no divide is necessary.

There is no rule that states convolution kernels must be symmetrical. You can easily create a filter which emulates the constant erosion from wind and water flowing a certain direction. Experiment with convolution kernels and the terrain generation techniques described previously and you're sure to discover new ways of creating realistic landscapes.

Vista Pro

If you are more interested in creating great landscapes than the technical aspects of doing so, you're in luck. Vista Pro, published by Virtual Reality Laboratories, is described as being a "3-D landscape generator and projector capable of accurately displaying real-world and fractal landscapes." What Vista Pro is, for the landscape designed, nothing short of marvelous.

The program is supplied with geographical survey data for various scenic sites in the United States, but you can also create your own terrain using its fractal terrain generator. This program has controls for many aspect of generating terrain, including scaling, adjusting the fractal dimension, automatically creating rivers and lakes, and smoothing. Figure 7.2 shows a landscape in progress in Vista Pro.

Figure 7.2.

Creating a landscape in Vista Pro.

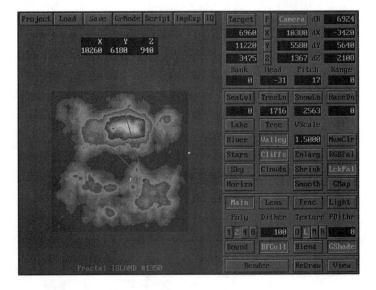

Besides enabling you to create and edit landscapes, Vista Pro can render them in beautiful detail, complete with fractal clouds and trees, shading and shadows, atmospheric hazing, and bump-mapped textures.

I used Vista Pro to create the height maps and color maps for the demo in this chapter. (See Figure 7.3.) In doing so, I discovered one small difficulty in using Vista Pro for this purpose: There is no way to directly generate the color map. Vista Pro always renders terrain in a perspective fashion from a specified camera position. The trick around this is to place the camera extremely high above the terrain and zoom in as far as is necessary to generate a near square color map.

Figure 7.3.
The terrain as rendered by Vista Pro.

The Floating Horizon

In the summer of 1993 I was working at an educational software company in the Northwest, rewriting their aging EGA graphics library. Almost anything is more fun than writing 16-color planer graphics code, so I spent a lot of time talking to my fellow engineers about *real* graphics programming—things like 256-color modes, polygons, and texture mapping. One day the conversation turned to flight sims and frame rates, and someone asked me if I had seen Commanche. "Commanche?" I replied. "What's that?"

The next day he brought in Commanche: Maximum Overkill by NovaLogic. This helicopter simulation went on to be one of the year's most influential games in terms of its engine and the technology used to create it. Commanche was the first game of any type to employ real-time height mapping. My first reaction to seeing Commanche was a literal jaw-dropping. "How are they doing that," I wondered. More importantly, "how are they doing that so *fast*?"

I spent more than a few hours staring at the pixels on the screen, and at the strange rectangular patterns that formed when you flew close to the terrain. After a few days, I thought I had figured out what the ingenious programmers at NovaLogic had accomplished. The approach I came up with is called the "floating-horizon" algorithm, and in hindsight I'm fairly certain that this *isn't* the technique that NovaLogic used in Commanche. Nevertheless, the algorithm works, and it is worth taking a look at.

The floating-horizon algorithm divides the height field into a series of slices taken at various distances from the viewer. These slices are within the triangle of the view cone, as seen from above in the right side of Figure 7.4. The algorithm then traverses these slices (usually left to right) and draws pixels at the projected height, almost the same way an artist draws a skyline. Each slice into the height field is a horizon line, and successive slices "float" off into the distance.

Figure 7.4.
The floating-horizon algorithm.

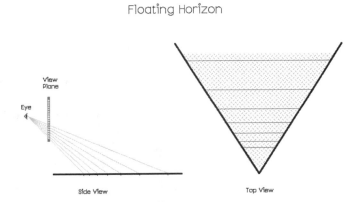

Floating Horizon

Slices can be drawn back-to-front, in which case each horizon can partially occlude the ones behind it, or they can be drawn front-to-back, in which case the algorithm must keep track of the height pixel drawn for each column. Rendering back-to-front allows objects to easily be drawn in the world, but causes a great many pixels to be rendered multiple times.

Viewing Systems

Before we go any further into our description of the floating-horizon algorithm, we need to establish some definitions and descriptions of viewing systems. Computer graphics displays are inherently two-dimensional, and the transformation of a three-dimensional world to the screen involves a viewing transformation. Implementation of a view system requires a firm grasp of the way in which various parameters affect the nature of the projection on the screen.

The most basic of concepts is the *viewpoint*. This is the location of the imaginary observer from which the world is seen. The viewpoint is considered to be the position of the viewer's eye or the position at which a virtual camera is placed. By changing the location of the viewpoint, we change the location from which the world is observed.

Projected a distance away from the viewpoint is an imaginary plane called the *view plane*. Three-dimensional points within the world are projected onto the view plane to form the image that camera sees. If you are sitting in your chair in front of your computer, your eye (just one!) is the viewpoint, and the surface of your monitor lies on the view plane.

Since your monitor is of a finite size, it makes up a subset of the view plane called the *view plane window*. If you imagine the viewpoint (your eye) as being the tip of a pyramid, and the view plane window (your monitor) being the base of a pyramid, then you are visualizing the tip of the *view cone*. The view cone extends outward infinitely from the viewpoint. Everything within this cone is the *view volume*.

A convenient method of mathematically describing a viewing system is with the following:

- View angle
- View cone angle
- View plane distance

The view angle is simply the direction in which the camera is pointed. The height mapping techniques we discuss in the chapter are not true 3-D viewing transformations. They are 2-1/2-dimensional systems which make use of tricks and limitations in order to render very quickly. The view angle, therefore, is only a compass direction, and does not enable the viewer to look up or down.

The view cone angle describes how wide the observer's field of vision is. Very small angles will give the effect of tunnel vision, and large angles can give a fish-eye lens effect. A good choice for a view cone angle is in the 60° to 90° range. Smaller values make the view seem claustrophobic, and larger values can produce excessive distortions.

The view plane distance is simply to distance from the eye to the screen in world coordinates.

Projecting the View Cone

The left and right edges of each depth slice can be determined by projecting a ray out along the left and right edges of the view cone. These rays shoot out at angles of Θ–viewConeAngle/2 and Θ+viewConeAngle/2.

Okay, now we know where the depth slices are, but how do we transform the altitude in the height map into a pixel height on the screen? The answer comes from some simple geometry and knowledge of similar triangles. Similar triangles are triangles that have the same shape, that is, all the same angles.

Figure 7.5 shows a side view of the way our view system works. Similar triangles are formed by the eye position, the view plane, and an imaginary line going through each point in the height map.

Figure 7.5.
View projections can be solved by using similar triangles.

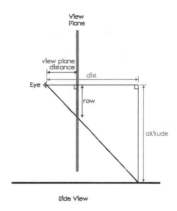

The useful geometric property of similar triangles is that the ratios between the lengths of their sides are equal. This means that for our view projection, the following relationship is true:

$$\frac{pixelHeight}{viewPlaneDistance} = \frac{altitude}{distance}$$

Solving for `pixelHeight` gives us:

$$pixelHeight = viewPlaneDistance\ \frac{altitude}{distance}$$

The inverse relationship of size to distance is the basic element in any perspective transformation.

The only issue that remains to complete our description of the floating-horizon technique is determining at what distance to traverse the depth slices.

One approach would be to render depth slices at unit distances into the height field, up to some predetermined distance. While this approach is sort of a leave-no-stone-unturned method, it's obviously going to involve checking far more height points than we need. Going back to our similar triangles, we can project view distances for each row on the screen by using the same ratios and solving for distance.

$$distance = altitude\ \frac{viewPlaneDistance}{pixelHeight}$$

Trouble in Paradise

I'm going to save a lot of trouble at this point and tell you that the floating-horizon algorithm suffers from two major problems.

The first problem is that of performance. For every value in the height field that the algorithm visits, it must do a transformation to get the projected height in the view plane. Whether it draws pixels or not, it still needs to do the math.

The second problem is related to projecting through each screen row to get the depth slice distance. If you refer to Figure 7.4, shown previously, you'll see that as the slices move away from the viewer, the distance between each becomes progressively greater. Visually, what happens is that you can see the steps taken between each depth slice. Hills in the distance will appear as cross sections, and as the viewpoint moves, the cross sections undulate horribly. This problem is a thorny one, because the simplest cure—stepping at finer intervals—dramatically increases the rendering time.

Ray Casting to the Rescue

If we processed our floating horizons in front-to-back order, we would need to keep track of the highest pixel we had drawn for every column on the screen. Whenever we encountered a height point that projected above the highest value, we would draw the necessary number of pixels, and update the array for that column.

This technique works, but it is math-bound because every height point must be multiplied by a scale factor. Multiplication and division are the bane of fast graphics, and these processes should be avoided whenever possible. What if, instead of comparing the projected height value to the height pixel drawn, we inverted the test? By projecting the highest pixel drawn to the height field distance, we can simply compare it against the value in the height field.

The problem with this is that projecting the highest pixel involves just as much math as projecting the value in the height field. Fortunately, this is a problem that can be solved with an incremental algorithm and a 90° rotation in our thinking.

The floating horizon works by traversing each depth slice left to right across the view volume. Ray casting works by stepping through the height map away from the viewpoint, shooting a ray out once for each column, and seeing what it hits along the way.

Figure 7.6 shows how ray casting through a height map works from the side. First, a ray is shot out from the viewpoint at a downward slope so that it passes through the bottom of the view plane window. As the ray moves outward, it has an x,y location and a height z. We move the ray in unit steps determined by dx, dy, and dz.

Figure 7.6.
A ray is shot out from the viewpoint until it intersects the ground.

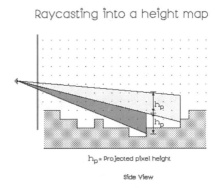

Eventually, at some point, the *z* value of the ray will be below the height of the height field at location *x,y*. That point is the intersection of the ray with the ground.

A pixel can be drawn at the current screen height by looking up the color value from the color map at location *x,y*. I've create a color map, shown in Figure 7.7, and a height map, shown in Figure 7.8, using Vista Pro. The height map, although shown in color, needs no palette, and is stored in PCX format for convenience. I've chosen to create the maps at a resolution of 512×512.

Figure 7.7.
The color map for the demonstration program.

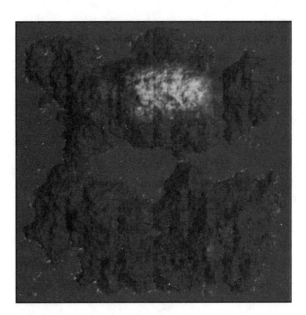

At every ray intersection, we need to draw one or more pixels representing the difference between the ray *z* and the terrain height, and we need to adjust the slope of the ray.

In order to determine how many pixels to draw, we need to know the projected pixel height (shown as h_p in Figure 7.6). Fortunately, we can calculate the projected pixel height in an incremental fashion. This means at each step, all we need to do is add a constant to the previous pixel height.

Figure 7.8.
The height map for the demonstration program. The gradient palette makes it look like a contour map.

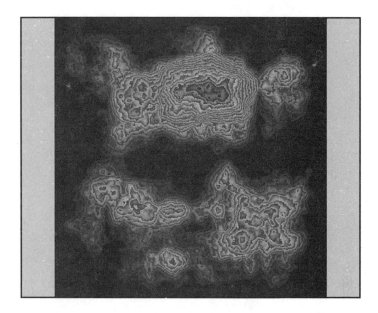

Adjusting the slope is just as easy, since it turns out that the change in slope is the same as the change in pixel height for each step.

Listing 7.1 is the complete source for a ray-casting program. The program initializes a fixed-point sine table, reads in the height map and color map from two .PCX files, installs a low-level keyboard handler, and then enters the main rendering loop.

The rendering all happens in one function, CastRay(), which is called for each column on the screen.

Listing 7.1. HEIGHT1.C.

```c
#include <stdarg.h>
#include <conio.h>
#include <stdio.h>
#include <stdlib.h>
#include <string.h>
#include <mem.h>
#include <dos.h>
#include <math.h>
#include <fcntl.h>
#include <io.h>
```

continues

Listing 7.1. continued

```
#include "palette.h"
#include "dostime.h"
#include "key.h"
#include "pcx.h"

/****************************************************************
 * Defines
 ****************************************************************/
#define kPi             3.141592654

#define kFieldBits      9
#define kFieldSize      (1 << kFieldBits)
#define kFieldBytes     (kFieldSize * kFieldSize)

#define kRendHeight     200
#define kRendWidth      320

#define kMaxSpeed       (100 << 8)
#define kAccel          16
#define kMaxAltitude    1000

#define kAngle360       0x1000
#define kAngleMask      (kAngle360 - 1)
#define kAngle180       (kAngle360 / 2)
#define kAngle90        (kAngle360 / 4)
#define kAngle60        (kAngle360 / 6)
#define kAngle45        (kAngle360 / 8)
#define kAngle30        (kAngle360 / 12)
#define kViewAngle      (kAngle60/2)     // half view cone angle

#define SIN(x)          sinTable[(x) & kAngleMask]
#define COS(x)          sinTable[((x) + kAngle90) & kAngleMask]

#define kDefaultPitch   (kRendHeight / 2)
#define kYawAccel       (kAngle360 / 256)


/****************************************************************
 * Type definitions
 ****************************************************************/
typedef unsigned char UBYTE;
typedef unsigned short UWORD;
typedef signed short WORD;
typedef unsigned long ULONG;


/****************************************************************
 * Global variables
 ****************************************************************/
long        sinTable[kAngle360];
UBYTE       gHeightMap[kFieldBytes];
UBYTE       gColorMap[kFieldBytes];
int         xOrg = 128L << 16;
int         yOrg = 128L << 16;
char        gRendBuffer[kRendWidth * kRendHeight];
long        gAltitude = 220;               // arbitrary start height
```

```
int        gYaw = kAngle90;
int        gPitch = kDefaultPitch;      // horizon line
PALETTE    palette;


/******************************************************************
 * Inline functions to get and set video mode
 ******************************************************************/
int getvmode( void );
#pragma aux getvmode =\
    "mov    ah,0x0F",\
    "int    0x10,"\
    "and    eax,0xFF",\

int setvmode(int);
#pragma aux setvmode =\
    "int 0x10",\
    parm [eax]\


/******************************************************************
 * Quit the program with a variable arg message.
 ******************************************************************/
void QuitMessage(char * fmt, ...)
{
    char msg[80];
    va_list argptr;
    va_start( argptr, fmt );
    vsprintf( msg, fmt, argptr );
    va_end(argptr);
    setvmode(0x3);
    printf(msg);
    exit(1);
}


/******************************************************************
 * Initialize the sin table.  Values are 16:16 fixed point.
 ******************************************************************/
void InitMathTables()
{
    int i;
    for (i = 0; i < kAngle180; i++)
        sinTable[i] = sin((double)i * kPi / kAngle180) * 0x10000L;

    for (i = kAngle180; i < kAngle360; i++)
        sinTable[i] = -sinTable[i - kAngle180];
}


/******************************************************************
 * Load in the height and color fields.
 ******************************************************************/
void InitHeightField()
{
    UBYTE *heightMap = gHeightMap;
    UBYTE *colorMap = gColorMap;
```

continues

Listing 7.1. continued

```
    int width, height;
    int r;

    width = height = kFieldSize;
    r = ReadPCX256("demoh.pcx", NULL, &width, &height,
        &heightMap);
    if (r != pcxOkay)
        QuitMessage("Error reading height map");

    width = height = kFieldSize;
    r = ReadPCX256("democ.pcx", palette, &width, &height,
        &colorMap);
    if (r != pcxOkay)
        QuitMessage("Unable to read height map");
}


/******************************************************************
 * Calculate a texel address from u,v coordinates.
 ******************************************************************/
int CalcOffset(int u, int v);
#pragma aux CalcOffset = \
    "mov     ebx,edx" \
    "shr     ebx,32-9" \
    "shld    ebx,ecx,9" \
    parm [ECX][EDX] \
    value [EBX];


#define kVScale        0x600
#define kDepthClip     (256 * kVScale)


/******************************************************************
 * Main rendering loop.  Shoots a ray from the origin along the
 * specified vector.
 ******************************************************************/
void CastRay(int col, int horiz, int dx, int dy)
{
    int x, y, z, dz, h, ph;
    int pixel, offset;
    UBYTE c;

    dz = (horiz - (kRendHeight - 1)) * kVScale;

    // point to bottom of the column
    pixel = col + (kRendHeight - 1) * kRendWidth;

    // initial projected pixel height
    ph = 0;

    // initial ray height
    z = gAltitude << 16;

    // initial coordinates
    x = xOrg << (16 - kFieldBits);
    y = yOrg << (16 - kFieldBits);
```

```
    while (ph < kDepthClip)
    {
        y += dy;
        x += dx;
        z += dz;
        ph += kVScale;

        // calculate the offset in the height field
        offset = CalcOffset(x, y);

        h = gHeightMap[offset] << 16;

        // an intersection occured
        if (h > z)
        {
            c = gColorMap[offset];
            do
            {
                // increment slope
                dz += kVScale;
                gRendBuffer[pixel] = c; // draw the pixel
                z += ph;
                pixel -= kRendWidth;    // move up one line
                if (pixel < 0)
                    return;
            } while ( h > z);
        }
    }
}


#define RADIX (32 - kFieldBits)

/******************************************************************
 * Render the view.  RADIX defines the radix point for coordinates
 * in the height and color fields.  Once the view is rendered, it
 * is directly copied to the screen.
 ******************************************************************/
void UpdateScreen()
{
    long dx, dy;
    int col, angle;
    int i;
    int skyHoriz = gPitch + 20; // overlap clipping of terrain
    UBYTE *d;

    // draw the gradient sky
    d = gRendBuffer;
    for ( i = 0; i < skyHoriz && i < kRendHeight; i++)
    {
        memset(d, 0xC2 + (skyHoriz - i) / 4, kRendWidth);
        d += kRendWidth;
    }

    for ( col = 0; col < kRendWidth; col++ )
    {
        angle = (kViewAngle * (kRendWidth - col * 2)) / kRendWidth;
```

continues

Listing 7.1. continued

```
        dx = COS(gYaw + angle) << (RADIX - 16);
        dy = SIN(gYaw + angle) << (RADIX - 16);

        // the -40 forces the view down to see more of the terrain
        CastRay(col, gPitch - 40, dx, dy);
    }

    // copy the buffer to the screen
    memcpy((char *)0xA0000, gRendBuffer, kRendWidth * kRendHeight);
}


/******************************************************************
 * Process keystrokes.  This is a pretty poor flight model, but
 * does manage to show off the abilities of the rendering code.
 ******************************************************************/
int CheckKeys()
{
    static speed = 0x200;

    if ( keyGet(KEY_ESC) )
        return -1;

    if (keyTest(KEY_PLUS))
        speed += kAccel;

    if (keyTest(KEY_MINUS))
        speed -= kAccel;

    if (speed < -kMaxSpeed) speed = -kMaxSpeed;
    if (speed > kMaxSpeed) speed = kMaxSpeed;

    if ( keyTest(KEY_UP) ¦¦ keyTest(KEY_DOWN) )
    {
        if (keyTest(KEY_UP))
            gPitch -= 4;

        if (keyTest(KEY_DOWN))
            gPitch += 4;
    }
    else
    {
        if ( gPitch < kDefaultPitch )
            gPitch++;
        else if ( gPitch > kDefaultPitch )
            gPitch——;
    }

    if (keyTest(KEY_LEFT))
        gYaw = (gYaw + kYawAccel) & kAngleMask;
    if (keyTest(KEY_RIGHT))
        gYaw = (gYaw - kYawAccel) & kAngleMask;

    gAltitude += (speed * (gPitch - kDefaultPitch)) >> 14;
    gAltitude = min(gAltitude, kMaxAltitude);
```

```
    xOrg += speed * COS(gYaw) >> 8;
    yOrg += speed * SIN(gYaw) >> 8;

    return 0;
}

/*****************************************************************
 * Main program.  This shell loads the terrain, calls the main
 * rendering loop, and does some quick and dirty benchmarking.
 *****************************************************************/
void main(void)
{
    ULONG startTime, stopTime;
    int fps10, frames = 0;
    int nOldMode;

    printf("Initializing math tables...\n");
    InitMathTables();

    printf("Loading terrain...\n");
    InitHeightField();

    keyInstall();        // install low-level keyboard handler

    nOldMode = getvmode();
    setvmode(0x13);
    gSetDACRange(0, 256, palette);

    startTime = GetDosTicks();
    while ( CheckKeys() != -1 ) {
        UpdateScreen();
        frames++;
    }
    stopTime = GetDosTicks();

    setvmode(nOldMode);

    keyRemove();         // remove low-level keyboard handler

    fps10 = frames * 182 / (stopTime - startTime);
    printf("Height Mapping Demo ");
    printf("Copyright (c) 1995 Peter M. Freese\n");
    printf("Average frame rate: %i.%i fps\n", fps10/10, fps10%10);
}
```

The first part of CastRay() sets up the initial values for the ray and then enters the rendering loop beginning with the line:

```
    while (ph < kDepthClip)
```

The variable ph contains the projected pixel height, and since it increases the further we get from the view point, we can compare it with a precalculated threshold to determine when to bail out of the rendering loop. We could also keep track of distance as a separate variable, but the code has already been optimized somewhat to reduce the working set of registers.

The first part of the loop steps the ray one unit distance forward. This involves adding the ray deltas to the *x,y* variables, adding the slope to the *z* variable, and adding a constant to the projected pixel height.

```
y += dy;
x += dx;
z += dz;
ph += kVScale;
```

The constant kVScale is related to the vertical view cone angle. It is a fixed-point number representing the difference in slope between a line from the viewpoint to two vertically adjacent pixels on the screen. If we were to graph projected pixel height against distance from the view point, kVScale would be the slope of the graph. Adjusting this value is a quick way of changing the vertical scale of the height map. Smaller values will exaggerate mountains, and large values will flatten out the height field.

I've used an in-line assembly function to convert the *x,y* locations into offsets in the height map and color map arrays. The *x* and *y* variables contain the locations in 9:22 fixed-point format. The reason for this apparently odd format is to accommodate the height field size of 512×512 while taking advantage of the maximum precision possible. If you decide to change the size of the height field by modifying the defines at the beginning of the code, you'll need to change the CalcOffset assembly code as well. I've been unable to figure out a way to make Watcom's compiler use manifest constants in in-line assembly pragmas.

Once an intersection with the ground is determined, we enter this drawing loop:

```
do
{
    // increment slope
    dz += kVScale;
    gRendBuffer[pixel] = c; // draw the pixel
    z += ph;
    pixel -= kRendWidth;      // move up one line
    if (pixel < 0)
        return;
} while ( h > z);
```

We need to test the pixel offset going off the top of the screen, and if so, we can bail out early for the column. Otherwise, the ray casting continues until the projected pixel height reaches our clipping threshold. This test produces a clipping distance, which is absolutely necessary, otherwise the ray could continue out infinitely, which would take a very long time indeed!

Figure 7.9 shows the results of running HEIGHT1.EXE. The program enables you to maneuver around in the height mapped world using the left and right arrow keys. You can adjust the speed of the virtual camera using the minus and plus keys.

Figure 7.9.
The display produced by HEIGHT1.EXE.

Previously, I said that the height-mapping techniques in this chapter were not fully 3-D and that you could not look up and down. That doesn't mean we can't fake things a little. One of the parameters of our viewing system is the horizon line, represented by gPitch in the program. By changing the value of gPitch and thus the horizon, we can get *the effect* of looking up and down.

If you press the down-arrow key (sort of like pulling back on an airplane yoke), the view will shift upward, and the altitude of the camera will increase. If you move high enough, you'll reach a point where the terrain does not get drawn sufficiently far to cover the sky. You'll see bits and pieces of the previous frame left uncovered. In your programs you'll want to limit the range of camera movement to avoid problems like this. Often it's easier (and faster) to simply limit what the player can do, rather than trying to create a graphics engine that can handle every possible viewpoint.

If you're like me, you can't help but think of how neat it would be to actually roll in a turn while flying around the terrain. How can we roll the view in our ray-casting engine? The answer to that is simpler than you might think.

Because we are rendering into a buffer, we can translate that buffer to the screen however we want. We learned in a previous chapter how to do bitmap rotation; why not apply some of that knowledge to rotate the buffer as it is copied to the screen?

Let's snazz up the view as well. Instead of drawing a gradient for the sky, we'll use a bitmap of some clouds, shown in Figure 7.10.

Figure 7.10.
A texture mapped sky sure would look nice!

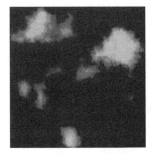

We could just use the clouds as a flat background, but it would look much better if we texture mapped them onto the sky.

If you remember how we determined the depth-slice distance in the floating-horizon technique, we can apply the same calculation to project texture coordinates onto a flat sky plane at some fixed z height. This is the same technique that is used to draw floors and ceilings in 3-D games such as DOOM.

Finally, since we're adding all these new features, we might as well optimize and recode the inner ray-casting loop in assembly. Listing 7.2 is the updated C code (HEIGHT2.C) for the height mapper, and Listing 7.3 is the assembly source (HEIGHT2A.ASM) for the ray-casting loop, sky texture mapping, and view rotation code.

When you build and run HEIGHT2.EXE, you'll see a screen like that shown in Figure 7.11. Now when you use the left and right arrow keys to turn your aircraft, the entire view will roll appropriately. I should point out that this isn't a very realistic flight model, but it's certainly enough to give you the idea of flying. You can roll through a full 360°, and even fly upside down if you like.

The sky is projected as a plane a relative distance above the viewer. No matter how high or how low you fly, it will always appear the same height above you. This gives the illusion of the sky being incredibly high and large. You can change the relative sky height by using the Page Up and Page Down keys.

Figure 7.11.
*Here's the height mapper
with all the bells and
whistles.*

Listing 7.2. HEIGHT2.C.

```c
#include <stdarg.h>
#include <conio.h>
#include <stdio.h>
#include <stdlib.h>
#include <string.h>
#include <mem.h>
#include <dos.h>
#include <math.h>
#include <fcntl.h>
#include <io.h>

#include "palette.h"
#include "dostime.h"
```

```c
#include "key.h"
#include "pcx.h"

/*****************************************************************
 * Defines
 *****************************************************************/
#define kPi             3.141592654

#define kFieldBits      9
#define kFieldSize      (1 << kFieldBits)
#define kFieldBytes     (kFieldSize * kFieldSize)

#define kRendBits       8
#define kRendSize       (1 << kRendBits)

#define kMaxSpeed       (100 << 8)
#define kAccel          16
#define kMaxAltitude    1000

#define kAngle360       0x1000
#define kAngleMask      (kAngle360 - 1)
#define kAngle180       (kAngle360 / 2)
#define kAngle90        (kAngle360 / 4)
#define kAngle60        (kAngle360 / 6)
#define kAngle45        (kAngle360 / 8)
#define kAngle30        (kAngle360 / 12)
#define kViewAngle      (kAngle60/2)     // half view cone angle

#define SIN(x)          sinTable[(x) & kAngleMask]
#define COS(x)          sinTable[((x) + kAngle90) & kAngleMask]

#define kDefaultPitch   (kRendSize / 2)
#define kRollAccel      32
#define kSkyHeight      60                // scale sky height

/*****************************************************************
 * Type definitions
 *****************************************************************/
typedef unsigned char UBYTE;
typedef unsigned short UWORD;
typedef signed short WORD;
typedef unsigned long ULONG;


/*****************************************************************
 * Global variables
 *****************************************************************/
long        sinTable[kAngle360];
UBYTE       gHeightMap[kFieldBytes];
UBYTE       gColorMap[kFieldBytes];
int         xOrg = 128L << 16;
int         yOrg = 128L << 16;
char        gRendBuffer[kRendSize * kRendSize];
long        gAltitude = 220;             // arbitrary start height
int         gYaw = kAngle90;
int         gRollAngle = 0;
int         gPitch = kDefaultPitch;      // horizon line
```

continues

Listing 7.2. continued

```
char        *cloudMap = NULL;
int         gSkyHeight = kSkyHeight;
PALETTE     palette;


/************************************************************************
 * External declarations
 ***********************************************************************/
void cdecl CastRay(int col, int horiz, int dx, int dy);
void cdecl CopyRotate(void);
void cdecl RipHoriz8(int y, int u0, int v0, int u1, int v1, char *texture);


/************************************************************************
 * Inline functions to get and set video mode
 ***********************************************************************/
int getvmode( void );
#pragma aux getvmode =\
    "mov    ah,0x0F",\
    "int    0x10,"\
    "and    eax,0xFF",\

int setvmode(int);
#pragma aux setvmode =\
    "int 0x10",\
    parm [eax]\


/************************************************************************
 * Quit the program with a variable arg message.
 ***********************************************************************/
void QuitMessage(char * fmt, ...)
{
    char msg[80];
    va_list argptr;
    va_start( argptr, fmt );
    vsprintf( msg, fmt, argptr );
    va_end(argptr);
    setvmode(0x3);
    printf(msg);
    exit(1);
}


/************************************************************************
 * Initialize the sin table.  Values are 16:16 fixed point.
 ***********************************************************************/
void InitMathTables()
{
    int i;    for (i = 0; i < kAngle180; i++)
        sinTable[i] = sin((double)i * kPi / kAngle180) * 0x10000L;

    for (i = kAngle180; i < kAngle360; i++)
        sinTable[i] = -sinTable[i - kAngle180];
}
```

```c
/******************************************************************
 * Load in the height and color fields.
 ******************************************************************/
void InitHeightField()
{
    UBYTE *heightMap = gHeightMap;
    UBYTE *colorMap = gColorMap;
    int width, height;
    int r;

    width = height = kFieldSize;
    r = ReadPCX256("demoh.pcx", NULL, &width, &height,
        &heightMap);
    if (r != pcxOkay)
        QuitMessage("Error reading height map");

    width = height = kFieldSize;
    r = ReadPCX256("democ.pcx", palette, &width, &height,
        &colorMap);
    if (r != pcxOkay)
        QuitMessage("Unable to read height map");
}


int CalcOffset(int x, int y);
#pragma aux CalcOffset = \
    "mov    ebx,edx" \
    "shr    ebx,32-9" \
    "shld   ebx,ecx,9" \
    parm [ECX][EDX] \
    value [EBX];


#define RADIX (32 - kFieldBits)

/******************************************************************
 * Render the view.  RADIX defines the radix point for coordinates
 * in the height and color fields.  Once the view is rendered, it
 * is translated affinely to the screen with CopyRotate().
 ******************************************************************/
void UpdateScreen()
{
    long dx, dy;
    int col, angle;
    int i;
    long dist,lsin,lcos,rsin,rcos;
    long u0,v0,u1,v1;
    int skyHoriz = gPitch + 20; // overlap clipping of terrain

    // draw the texture mapped sky
    lsin = sinTable[(gYaw + kViewAngle) & kAngleMask];
    lcos = sinTable[(gYaw + kViewAngle + kAngle90) & kAngleMask];
    rsin = sinTable[(gYaw - kViewAngle) & kAngleMask];
    rcos = sinTable[(gYaw - kViewAngle + kAngle90) & kAngleMask];

    for ( i = 0; i < skyHoriz && i < kRendSize; i++)
    {
```

continues

Listing 7.2. continued

```
        dist = (gSkyHeight << 8) / (skyHoriz - i);
        u0 = (lcos >> 8) * dist + (xOrg >> 10);
        v0 = (lsin >> 8) * dist + (yOrg >> 10);
        u1 = (rcos >> 8) * dist + (xOrg >> 10);
        v1 = (rsin >> 8) * dist + (yOrg >> 10);

        RipHoriz8(i, u0, v0, u1, v1, cloudMap);
    }

    for ( col = 0; col < kRendSize; col++ )
    {
        angle = (kViewAngle * (kRendSize - col * 2)) >> kRendBits;
        dx = COS(gYaw + angle) << (RADIX - 16);
        dy = SIN(gYaw + angle) << (RADIX - 16);

        // the -40 on the pitch forces the view down to see more of the terrain
        CastRay(col, gPitch - 40, dx, dy);
    }

    CopyRotate();
}


/****************************************************************
 * Process keystrokes.  This is a pretty poor flight model, but
 * does manage to show off the abilities of the rendering code.
 ****************************************************************/
int CheckKeys()
{
    static speed = 0x200;

    if ( keyGet(KEY_ESC) )
        return -1;

    if (keyTest(KEY_PAGEUP))
        gSkyHeight++;

    if (keyTest(KEY_PAGEDN))
        gSkyHeight—;

    if (keyTest(KEY_PLUS))
        speed += kAccel;

    if (keyTest(KEY_MINUS))
        speed -= kAccel;

    if (speed < -kMaxSpeed) speed = -kMaxSpeed;
    if (speed > kMaxSpeed) speed = kMaxSpeed;

    if ( keyTest(KEY_UP) ¦¦ keyTest(KEY_DOWN) )
    {
        if (keyTest(KEY_UP))
            gPitch -= 4;
```

```
            if (keyTest(KEY_DOWN))
                gPitch += 4;
        }
        else
        {
            if ( gPitch < kDefaultPitch )
                gPitch++;
            else if ( gPitch > kDefaultPitch )
                gPitch——;
        }

        if (keyTest(KEY_LEFT) ¦¦ keyTest(KEY_RIGHT))
        {
            if (keyTest(KEY_LEFT))
                gRollAngle = (gRollAngle - kRollAccel) & kAngleMask;
            if (keyTest(KEY_RIGHT))
                gRollAngle = (gRollAngle + kRollAccel) & kAngleMask;
        }
        else
        {
            if ( gRollAngle > 0 && gRollAngle < kAngle180 )
                gRollAngle = (gRollAngle - kRollAccel / 2) & kAngleMask;
            else if ( gRollAngle > kAngle180 && gRollAngle < kAngle360 )
                gRollAngle = (gRollAngle + kRollAccel / 2) & kAngleMask;
        }

        gYaw  = (gYaw - (SIN(gRollAngle) >> 11)) & kAngleMask;
        gAltitude += (speed * (gPitch - kDefaultPitch)) >> 14;
        gAltitude = min(gAltitude, kMaxAltitude);
        xOrg += speed * COS(gYaw) >> 8;
        yOrg += speed * SIN(gYaw) >> 8;

        return 0;
}


/******************************************************************
 * Main program.  This shell loads the terrain, calls the main
 * rendering loop, and does some quick and dirty benchmarking.
 ******************************************************************/
void main(void)
{
    int width = 0, height = 0;
    UBYTE *background = NULL;
    ULONG startTime, stopTime;
    int fps10, frames = 0;
    int nOldMode;
    int r;

    printf("Initializing math tables...\n");
    InitMathTables();

    printf("Loading terrain...\n");
    InitHeightField();

    printf("Loading cloud map...\n");
    r = ReadPCX256("clouds.pcx", NULL, &width, &height, &cloudMap);
    if (r != pcxOkay)
        QuitMessage("Unable to load cloud map.");
```

continues

Listing 7.2. continued

```
width = 320;
height = 200;

r = ReadPCX256("backgrnd.pcx", NULL, &width, &height,
    &background);
if (r != pcxOkay)
    QuitMessage("Unable to load background.");

keyInstall();        // install low-level keyboard handler

nOldMode = getvmode();
setvmode(0x13);

gSetDACRange(0, 256, palette);

memcpy((UBYTE *)0xA0000, background, 320 * 200);

startTime = GetDosTicks();
while ( CheckKeys() != -1 ) {
    UpdateScreen();
    frames++;
}
stopTime = GetDosTicks();

setvmode(nOldMode);

keyRemove();         // remove low-level keyboard handler

fps10 = frames * 182 / (stopTime - startTime);
printf("Height Mapping Demo ");
printf("Copyright (c) 1995 Peter M. Freese\n");
printf("Average frame rate: %i.%i fps\n", fps10/10, fps10%10);
}
```

Listing 7.3. HEIGHT2A.ASM.

```
            IDEAL
            P486

; these equates must match their counterparts in the C file

; # bits to represent size of render buffer
REND_SIZEBITS   EQU     8
REND_SIZE       EQU     (1 SHL REND_SIZEBITS)

SCREEN_WIDTH    EQU     240
SCREEN_HEIGHT   EQU     200
SCREEN_PITCH    EQU     320
SCREEN_XCENTER  EQU     120
SCREEN_YCENTER  EQU     100
VIDEO_MEMORY    EQU     0A0000h

; offset at which to copy rotated screen
COPY_OFFSET     EQU     40
```

```
                ; # bits to represent height field coord
                FIELD_BITS      EQU     9

                ; quick triangle calc for view dist
                VSCALE          EQU     600h

                ; clipping distance for rendering
                DEPTH_CLIP      EQU     (256 * VSCALE)

                FIXUP           EQU     01234567h
                ANGLE_360       EQU     1000h
                ANGLE_MASK      EQU     (ANGLE_360 - 1)
                ANGLE_90        EQU     (ANGLE_360 / 4)

                        MODEL   FLAT, C

                        DATASEG

                        EXTRN C gHeightMap:BYTE
                        EXTRN C gColorMap:BYTE
                        EXTRN C gAltitude:DWORD
                        EXTRN C xOrg:DWORD              ; 16:16
                        EXTRN C yOrg:DWORD              ; 16:16
                        EXTRN C gRendBuffer:BYTE
                        EXTRN C sinTable:PTR DWORD
                        EXTRN C gRollAngle:DWORD

                        CODESEG

aspectAdjust    DD      13333h  ; (1.2 << 16), adjust for mode 13h

; factor to scale render buffer (256x256) to screen
copyScale       DD      0C400h

dXTemp          DD      ?
dYTemp          DD      ?
slopeTemp       DD      ?
pixel           DD      ?


;******************************************************************
;* void cdecl CastRay(int col, int horiz, int deltaX, int deltaY)
;*
;* This is the core rendering code for the height mapping (voxel)
;* engine.  It casts a ray out from the observer, moving at an
;* angle specified by (deltaX, deltaY) through the height field,
;* and at an initial slope determined by gAltitude.  Once an
;* intersection with the height field occurs, a column of pixels
;* is drawn to represent the difference between the ray intersect
;* height and the height of the voxel.  The slope of the ray is
;* then adjusted so that it is tangent to the top of the voxel,
;* and the process repeated.  The function bails out after the
;* projected pixel height reaches DEPTH_CLIP.
;*
;* Whenever you see a label of the form @@f____, it's a self-mod
;* fixup location.
;******************************************************************
```

continues

Listing 7.3. continued

```
PROC C CastRay col:DWORD, horiz:DWORD, deltaX:DWORD, deltaY:DWORD
                PUBLIC  CastRay

                USES    esi,edi,ebp

                mov     eax,[deltaX]
                mov     [dXtemp],eax

                mov     eax,[deltaY]
                mov     [dYtemp],eax

                mov     eax,[horiz]
                sub     eax,(REND_SIZE - 1)
                imul    eax,VSCALE
                mov     [slopeTemp],eax

; point to bottom of the column
                mov     eax,[col]
                add     eax,(REND_SIZE - 1) * REND_SIZE
                mov     [pixel],eax

; initial ray height
                mov     edx,[gAltitude]
                shl     edx,16

; initial coordinates
                mov     esi,[xOrg]
                shl     esi,16 - FIELD_BITS
                mov     edi,[yOrg]
                shl     edi,16 - FIELD_BITS

; do fixups for vector deltas
                mov     eax,[dXtemp]
                mov     [DWORD PTR @@fdX-4],eax

                mov     eax,[dYtemp]
                mov     [DWORD PTR @@fdY-4],eax

                mov     ebp,[slopeTemp]
                xor     eax,eax

; initial projected pixel height offset by DEPTH_CLIP
                mov     ecx,-DEPTH_CLIP
                jmp     $+2                 ; clear prefetch queue

@@scanLoop:

                add     edi,FIXUP           ; next y coordinate
@@fdY:
                add     esi,FIXUP           ; next x coordinate
@@fdX:
                add     edx,ebp             ; next z coordinate

; calculate the offset in the height field

                mov     ebx,edi
                shr     ebx,32-FIELD_BITS
```

```
            shld    ebx,esi,FIELD_BITS
            mov     al,[gHeightMap+ebx]     ; get the height

            add     ecx,VSCALE              ; next pixel height
            jc      @@done

            shl     eax,16
            cmp     eax,edx                 ; below ray z?
            jl      @@scanLoop

            ; an intersection occured
            mov     al,[gColorMap+ebx]      ; get the color
            mov     ebx,[pixel]

@@drawLoop:
            add     ebp,VSCALE              ; increment slope
            lea     edx,[edx + ecx + DEPTH_CLIP];   ; z += ph
            mov     [gRendBuffer+ebx],al    ; draw the pixel
            sub     ebx,REND_SIZE           ; move up one line
            jb      @@done
            cmp     edx,eax                 ; z < h[u,v]?
            jl      @@drawLoop
            mov     [pixel],ebx
            jmp     @@scanLoop

@@done:
            ret
ENDP


;********************************************************************
;* void cdecl CopyRotate(void)
;*
;* This function copies the render buffer to the screen, and
;* rotates and scales it in the process.  This is an adaptation of
;* my spin code.
;*
;* The render buffer must be sized to a power of two, specified in
;* REND_SIZEBITS.  Theoretically, the buffer doesn't have to be
;* square, but it makes things a bit simpler.  The transformation
;* uses a constant specified in the DWORD copyScale, which is tuned
;* to give the best resolution without overflow, i.e., no matter
;* what angle the buffer is rotated, you won't see the edges.
;*
;* The rotation occurs around the center of the screen and the
;* center of the buffer
;********************************************************************
PROC C CopyRotate
            PUBLIC  CopyRotate

            LOCAL startX:DWORD, startY:DWORD
            LOCAL dXCol:DWORD, dYCol:DWORD
            LOCAL dXRow:DWORD, dYRow:DWORD

            USES    esi,edi,ebp

; calculate horizontal deltas
```

continues

Listing 7.3. continued

```
                mov     eax,[gRollAngle]
                and     eax,ANGLE_MASK
                mov     eax,[sinTable + eax * 4]
                imul    [copyScale]
                shrd    eax,edx,REND_SIZEBITS
                mov     [dYCol],eax

                mov     eax,[gRollAngle]
                add     eax,ANGLE_90
                and     eax,ANGLE_MASK
                mov     eax,[sinTable + eax * 4]
                imul    [copyScale]
                shrd    eax,edx,REND_SIZEBITS
                mov     [dXCol],eax

; calculate vertical deltas

                mov     eax,[dYCol]
                neg     eax
                imul    [aspectAdjust]
                shrd    eax,edx,16
                mov     [dXRow],eax

                mov     eax,[dXCol]
                imul    [aspectAdjust]
                shrd    eax,edx,16
                mov     [dYRow],eax

                mov     eax,1 SHL 31
                mov     [startX],eax
                mov     eax,1 SHL 31
                mov     [startY],eax

; move up to top from center

                mov     eax,[dXRow]
                imul    eax,(SCREEN_YCENTER)
                sub     [startX],eax
                mov     eax,[dYRow]
                imul    eax,(SCREEN_YCENTER)
                sub     [startY],eax

; move to left edge from center and fixup column deltas

                mov     eax,[dXCol]
                mov     [DWORD PTR @@fdXCol1-4],eax
                mov     [DWORD PTR @@fdXCol2-4],eax
                mov     [DWORD PTR @@fdXCol3-4],eax
                mov     [DWORD PTR @@fdXCol4-4],eax
                imul    eax,(SCREEN_XCENTER)
                sub     [startX],eax

                mov     eax,[dYCol]
                mov     [DWORD PTR @@fdYCol1-4],eax
                mov     [DWORD PTR @@fdYCol2-4],eax
                mov     [DWORD PTR @@fdYCol3-4],eax
                mov     [DWORD PTR @@fdYCol4-4],eax
```

```
                imul    eax,(SCREEN_XCENTER)
                sub     [startY],eax

; fixup end of row deltas

                mov     eax,[dXCol]
                imul    eax,SCREEN_WIDTH
                neg     eax
                add     eax,[dXRow]
                mov     [DWORD PTR @@fdXRow-4],eax

                mov     eax,[dYCol]
                imul    eax,SCREEN_WIDTH
                neg     eax
                add     eax,[dYRow]
                mov     [DWORD PTR @@fdYRow-4],eax

                mov     edi,VIDEO_MEMORY + COPY_OFFSET

                mov     ecx,[startX]
                mov     edx,[startY]

; initialize row count
                mov     esi,SCREEN_HEIGHT

; clear prefetch queue
                jmp     $+2

@@rowloop:
; initialize column count
                mov     ebp,SCREEN_WIDTH / 4

@@colloop:
                mov     ebx,edx
                shr     ebx,32 - REND_SIZEBITS
                shld    ebx,ecx,REND_SIZEBITS
                add     edx,FIXUP
@@fdYCol1:
                add     ecx,FIXUP
@@fdXCol1:
                mov     al,[gRendBuffer+ebx]

                mov     ebx,edx
                shr     ebx,32 - REND_SIZEBITS
                shld    ebx,ecx,REND_SIZEBITS
                add     edx,FIXUP
@@fdYCol2:
                add     ecx,FIXUP
@@fdXCol2:
                mov     ah,[gRendBuffer+ebx]
                bswap   eax

                mov     ebx,edx
                shr     ebx,32 - REND_SIZEBITS
                shld    ebx,ecx,REND_SIZEBITS
                add     edx,FIXUP
@@fdYCol3:
                add     ecx,FIXUP
```

continues

Listing 7.3. continued

```
@@fdXCol3:
                mov     ah,[gRendBuffer+ebx]

                mov     ebx,edx
                shr     ebx,32 - REND_SIZEBITS
                shld    ebx,ecx,REND_SIZEBITS
                add     edx,FIXUP
@@fdYCol4:
                add     ecx,FIXUP
@@fdXCol4:
                mov     al,[gRendBuffer+ebx]

                bswap   eax

                mov     [edi],eax
                add     edi,4
                dec     ebp
                jnz     @@colloop

                add     ecx,FIXUP
@@fdXRow:
                add     edx,FIXUP
@@fdYRow:

; address start of next row
                add     edi,SCREEN_PITCH - SCREEN_WIDTH

; decrement row count
                dec     esi
                jnz     @@rowloop

                ret

ENDP            CopyRotate



PROC C RipHoriz8 y:DWORD, u0:DWORD, v0:DWORD, u1:DWORD, v1:DWORD, texture:PTR BY
                PUBLIC  RipHoriz8

                USES    esi,edi,ebp

                mov     eax,[u1]              ; 24:8
                sub     eax,[u0]              ; 24:8
                shl     eax,16 - REND_SIZEBITS ; 8:24
                mov     [DWORD PTR @@fdu1-4],eax
                mov     [DWORD PTR @@fdu2-4],eax
                mov     [DWORD PTR @@fdu3-4],eax
                mov     [DWORD PTR @@fdu4-4],eax

                mov     eax,[v1]
                sub     eax,[v0]
                shl     eax,16 - REND_SIZEBITS ; 8:24
                mov     [DWORD PTR @@fdv1-4],eax
                mov     [DWORD PTR @@fdv2-4],eax
                mov     [DWORD PTR @@fdv3-4],eax
```

```
                mov     [DWORD PTR @@fdv4-4],eax

                mov     edi,OFFSET gRendBuffer
                mov     ebx,[y]
                shl     ebx,REND_SIZEBITS
                add     edi,ebx

                mov     esi,[texture]

                mov     ecx,[u0]            ; 24:8
                shl     ecx,16              ; 8:24
                mov     edx,[v0]            ; 24:8
                shl     edx,16              ; 8:24

                mov     ebp,REND_SIZE / 4

; clear prefetch queue
                jmp     $+2

@@colLoop:
                mov     ebx,edx
                shr     ebx,32 - 8
                shld    ebx,ecx,8
                add     edx,FIXUP
@@fdv1:
                add     ecx,FIXUP
@@fdu1:
                mov     al,[esi+ebx]

                mov     ebx,edx
                shr     ebx,32 - 8
                shld    ebx,ecx,8
                add     edx,FIXUP
@@fdv2:
                add     ecx,FIXUP
@@fdu2:
                mov     ah,[esi+ebx]

                bswap   eax

                mov     ebx,edx
                shr     ebx,32 - 8
                shld    ebx,ecx,8
                add     edx,FIXUP
@@fdv3:
                add     ecx,FIXUP
@@fdu3:
                mov     ah,[esi+ebx]

                mov     ebx,edx
                shr     ebx,32 - 8
                shld    ebx,ecx,8
                add     edx,FIXUP
@@fdv4:
                add     ecx,FIXUP@@fdu4:
                mov     al,[esi+ebx]
```

continues

Listing 7.3. continued

```
            bswap   eax

            mov     [edi],eax
            add     edi,4
            dec     ebp
            jnz     @@colLoop

            ret
ENDP

ENDS

END
```

Outward and Onward

In the two years that have passed since Commanche: Maximum Overkill was released, there have been very few games that have employed height mapping. In late 1994, NovaLogic released Armored Fist, a tank simulation game, which was heavily criticized for its blocky graphics. A common lament was, "what worked at 100 feet above the ground looks pixelated and ugly from 10 feet away." One might speculate that the success of Commanche was a fluke and that height mapping has limited potential for use in game play. Or possibly companies are wary of NovaLogic's pending patent for their "Voxel-Space" technology.

Whatever the reason, height-mapping techniques can go far beyond Commanche, Armored Fist, or what I've presented here. By using a hybrid between height mapping and a 3-D polygon engine, it is possible to render smooth terrains of immense size. Instead of *drawing pixels*, an engine might use height mapping to add polygons to a list of visible objects.

Summary

Height mapping, if done *fast*, can certainly win your game "coolness" points. Big, flat, shaded polygons can't hold a candle to the smooth rolling hills and valleys obtained from a well-rendered height map. In this chapter I discussed several methods of generating terrain, digital filtering techniques, and presented two algorithms for terrain visualization:

- Floating horizon
- Ray casting

I'm certain that there is a whole new generation of "killer" graphics games that will build upon techniques such as these to create huge virtual worlds for players to explore and discover. So what are you waiting for? Get started!

Virtual Screens

by Lee Taylor

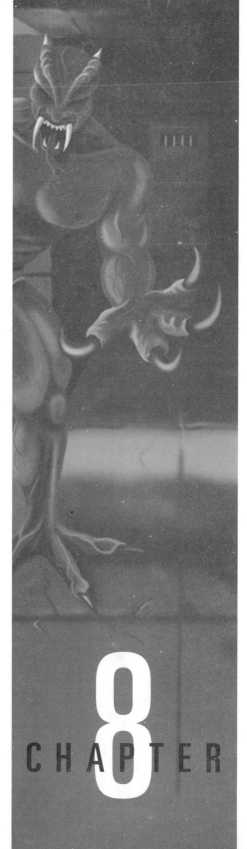

8

CHAPTER

This chapter discusses one of the easiest methods to enhance the quality of your game and to give it a professional appearance. Virtual screens eliminate the need for the player of your game to see each individual screen or image drawn.

All source code in this chapter is included on the companion CD-ROM.

What is Covered in this Chapter

In this chapter, you learn how to use virtual screens effectively and efficiently. The following topics are covered:

- What is a virtual screen?
- Advantages of using a virtual screen
- Disadvantages of using a virtual screen
- Allocating memory for a virtual screen
- Writing graphics functions that use the virtual screen
- Copying the virtual screen to video RAM
- High-speed, assembly, language functions
- Compiled Sprites
- Avoiding Sprite clipping

This chapter assumes you have a basic knowledge of the workings of video mode 13h and how basic graphics functions are written. The chapter also assumes you have a knowledge of C and assembly language.

What is a Virtual Screen?

A *virtual screen* is an imaginary screen, an area of memory that mimics real video memory. A graphical image, scene, or frame of animation is drawn on this virtual screen, and after the whole image is complete, it is quickly transferred from the virtual screen to real video memory and the real screen.

Imagine two monitors, one of which is hidden from view. This hidden monitor is the virtual screen. Graphics are drawn on this monitor piece by piece. After the whole image is drawn, it is copied to the visible monitor. Then the hidden monitor is cleared and the next image is drawn on it, while the visible monitor still displays a completed image. This process is then repeated. (See Figure 8.1.)

Figure 8.1.
Virtual screen visualization.

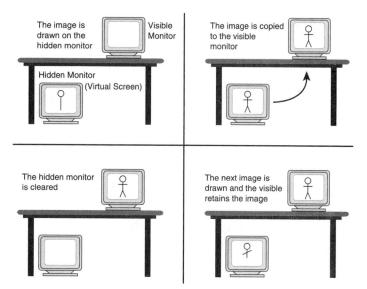

A similar but different technique is called *page flipping.* When page flipping is used, the virtual screen is not copied to video memory with each frame. Instead, you tell the video card to switch between two different memory locations. The active memory location, or page, is then used by the video card to construct the screen image. You alternate drawing on each of the pages. When one image is complete, you then tell the video card to make the page with the newly completed image active and you can then draw the next image on the inactive page. The process is then repeated. (See Figure 8.2.) Unfortunately, this technique is not supported by many video modes (such as the one we will be using, video mode 13h), so I will not discuss it further.

Figure 8.2.
Page-flipping visualization.

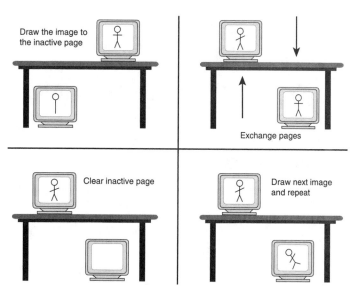

Advantages of Using a Virtual Screen

Your games can be improved in many ways through the use of virtual screens. Some of these ways are as follows:

- The current image on the screen is not changed during the drawing of the next image and stays on the screen until the new image from the virtual screen replaces it.
- Players of your game do not see the images being drawn because they are drawn to the hidden virtual screen.
- Animations do not flicker as new images are drawn because the visible screen is not being cleared and redrawn with each frame.
- Drawing to virtual screens is usually faster than drawing directly to video memory, which is often slow because the processor must share the memory with the video card, which constantly reads it to construct an image.
- Special tricks can be used to prevent such things as Sprite-clipping and thus remove the need for lengthy calculations.
- Virtual screens are not video-mode dependent. Unlike page flipping, they can be used with any video mode.

Disadvantages of Using a Virtual Screen

Virtual screens do have a few disadvantages, as follows:

- Virtual screens consume relatively large amounts of memory, often at least 64KB.
- Occasionally, the use of virtual screens will be slower than directly writing to video RAM, because of the extra copying from the virtual screen to video memory. This only happens if there is a very small amount of data being drawn with each frame, and it is dependent upon the speed of your graphics card, memory, and processor.

Allocating Memory for a Virtual Screen

Virtual screens require proper handling of memory. The number of bytes of memory required for any given video mode can be determined by a simple formula:

```
X_resolution * Y_resolution * bytes_per_pixel
```

The values $X\_resolution$ and $Y\_resolution$ are the dimensions of the screen, in pixels. $bytes\_per\_pixel$ is the number of bytes (for most video modes this value is usually 1 or less) required to describe the color of one pixel. If you are only working with 16 colors, this value would be one-half, since only four bits are required to describe each pixel, which can be one of 16 possible colors. With mode 13h (320×200 in 256 colors), this value is 1 because each pixel in this mode can be one of 256 possible colors and one byte can store a number between 0 and

255. Video mode 13h is the mode that I will deal with throughout this chapter since it is the most popular mode and the easiest to use. In this mode, the above formula would be

```
320   *   200   *   1   =   64,000 bytes
```

This shows us that 64,000 bytes are required for each virtual screen. In order to avoid the possible corruption of other data that the compiler may place in the segment with the virtual screen if invalid coordinates are fed to a drawing function, I suggest you allocate the whole 64KB segment and just ignore the extra 1,536 bytes at the tail end of the page for now. Later, we will learn another way to make use of this extra space and avoid the clipping of Sprites in the process. Another advantage is the guarantee you will get an offset of 0 within the segment for the start of the virtual screen, which makes drawing functions easier to write and faster.

The next step is to actually allocate the memory so the program can use the virtual screen. This can be done in one of two ways in C. The first method is to define an array of 64KB chars:

```
far char virtual_page[65535];
```

This can be referred to as an array or the pointer virtual_page. The second method is to define a pointer called virtual_page and dynamically allocate 64KB for it to point to, as follows:

```
far char *virtual_page;
virtual_page = farmalloc(65535);
```

The first method makes things little bit easier to use if you are writing functions in C, but if you use assembly language, it doesn't matter. Since we will be using assembly language for most of the functions in this chapter, we will use the second method.

It's important to remember that the virtual screen must always be declared as far, in the screen's definition, function prototype that use the virtual screen as a parameter, and anywhere else the screen is referenced. If you remember to do this, you can save yourself many hours of debugging trying to find out why your program locks up while drawing to the virtual screen because it was using a local address and writing over areas of code. (Trust me on this one—I know from personal experience.) Another point is you need to use a memory model that enables you to have more than 64KB of data. I recommend the large memory model; it supplies you with more than enough space for code and data.

Writing Graphics Functions that Use Virtual Screens

Graphics functions written for virtual screens operate the same way that regular graphics functions do. They are still given x,y coordinates, they translate them into an offset into memory, and they change the values of those memory locations. The basic functioning of graphics functions should be understood. I will only detail the changes that have to be made in order for the function to work with a virtual screen, which are few.

An example of a standard putpixel function for video mode 13h is given in Listing 8.1.

Listing 8.1. A standard `putpixel` **function.**

```
void putpixel(int x, int y, char color)
{
  asm {
    push es
    mov ax,[y]
    mov bx,320
    mul bx
    add ax,[x]
    mov di,ax
    mov ax,0xa000
    mov ds,ax
    mov al,color
    stosb
    pop es
  }
}
```

You may have noticed that I use inline assembly language. I do this because you don't have to worry about the various interfacing concerns when working with standard .ASM files that are then linked with C code. This is only my choice; you can work with .ASM files that are assembled separately and then linked with the proper C code.

The operation of the function is fairly straightforward. First it calculates the offset of the pixel. Then it changes the color of the pixel by writing the color value to that offset from the beginning of video memory.

The change required to use a virtual screen is very simple, as shown in Listing 8.2.

Listing 8.2. A virtual screen `putpixel` **function.**

```
void vputpixel(int x, int y, char color, char far *vscreen)
{
  asm {
    push es
    mov ax,[y]
    mov bx,320
    mul bx
    add ax,[x]
    les di,[vscreen]
    mov di,ax
    mov al,color
    stosb
    pop es
  }
}
```

A fourth parameter is added, which is the address of the virtual screen. This parameter is used to determine what area of memory will be written to. This way, instead of writing to video RAM all the time, you can write to a virtual screen located anywhere in memory. You can also use this function to write to actual video RAM directly, by passing a pointer to segment a000h, offset zero, which is the address of video RAM. Here one of the reasons for allocating a full segment should become apparent as well. Since whole segments start at offset zero, we do not have to add the offset at which the virtual screen begins to the offset at which we want to draw the pixel within the virtual screen. Instead, we can just move the offset of the pixel, contained in AL to the destination offset register, DL.

Any graphics function can easily be altered in this way to operate with a virtual screen.

Copying the Virtual Screen to Video RAM

In order to do the copy as quickly as possibly, we will use assembly language. A function that does this is shown in Listing 8.3.

Listing 8.3. Copying the virtual screen to video RAM.

```
void copy_vscreen(char far *vscreen)
{
  asm {
    push es         /* save the segment registers */
    push ds
    lds si,[vscreen]   /* get the address of the virtual screen */
    mov ax,0xa000    /* load the address of video ram into the destination */
    mov ds,ax
    xor di,di     /* zero the destination offset */
    mov cx,32000   /* we need to copy 32000 words */
    rep movsw     /* perform the copy */
    pop ds        /* restore the segment registers */
    pop es
  }
}
```

The first thing the function does is save the registers that will be used to perform the copy. We only have to worry about ES and DS because the compiler takes care of the others for you. Next, the address of the virtual screen is loaded into the source address registers, DS:SI. Then the address of video RAM, A000:0000h, is placed in the destination registers ES:DI. Then a count value is loaded into CX. We only have to perform 32,000 copies because we will move two bytes each time with the REP MOVSW function. Lastly, we return the saved registers to their original conditions.

This function can be modified to work more efficiently if it completes the copy during the vertical retrace of the monitor. The vertical retrace is the time during which the electron beam in the monitor moves from the bottom-right corner to the top-left corner in order to refresh the screen once again. During this time, the video memory is not accessed by the video card and therefore can be worked with at a faster rate. In order to copy during this time, we must modify the function as shown in Listing 8.4.

Listing 8.4. Copying the virtual screen to video memory during vertical retrace.

```
void copy_vscreen(char far *vscreen)
{
  asm {
    push es          /* save the segment registers */
    push ds
    lds si,[vscreen]   /* get the address of the virtual screen */
    mov ax,0xa000      /* load the address of video ram into the destination
    mov ds,ax
    xor di,di    /* zero the destination offset */
    mov cx,32000 /* we need to copy 32000 words */

    mov dx,0x03da /* Status register one of the VGA card */
  }
  wait_for_retrace:
  asm {
    in al,dx  /* get the value of status reg 1 */
    test al,0x08  /* test to see if retrace is in progress */
    jnz wait_for_retrace /* if not, keep waiting */

    rep movsw     /* perform the copy */
    pop ds        /* restore the segment registers */
    pop es
  }
}
```

The change lies in the loop that constantly tests bit 3 of the video card's first status register, located at port 0x3da, until it is set, which means the vertical retrace has begun and the copy can be made. Even though the code looks as if it should operate slower because of this loop, it is much faster because the video card will not insert wait states into the memory accesses that change the video memory during the retrace. Another benefit is that this helps to prevent shearing during scrolling. If your game screen looks cracked in half as it scrolls, it is not waiting for the retrace. What is happening is the video card is reading the memory at the same time it is changed, and half of the screen will show the previous image, and the other half of the screen displays the new image, which has moved.

High-Speed, Assembly-Language Functions

Now that you know the basics of using a virtual screen, we can get into some high-speed routines. These routines will basically deal with putting Sprites on the virtual screen in a quick and efficient manner.

The first thing that must be determined is a standard method of storing the Sprites in memory. We will use a standard method taken from the way the video mode itself is organized. The Sprites will be scanned horizontally for each Y row in turn. Unless all our Sprites will be the same size, we also need to also come up with a standard for telling the putsprite function the dimensions. There are two ways that we can do this. The first is to pass the dimensions into the function as parameters. The problem with this method is that it is not very reliable, as you may forget the dimensions and wind up with an improperly drawn Sprite. This method is also awkward if you use arrays to store your Sprites since you will need two extra arrays for the X and Y dimensions. A better method is to store the dimensions in the first two bytes of the Sprite data. The one limitation of this is that your Sprites have a maximum size of 256×256, but the bytes can easily be turned into integers, although, that size should be large enough. This is the method we shall use.

Given the above standards, we can develop a putsprite function as shown in Listing 8.5.

Listing 8.5. A putsprite **function.**

```
void vputsprite(int x, int y, char far *sprite, char far *vscreen)
{
  asm {
    push es      /* Save the segment registers */
    push ds
    mov ax,[y]   /* calculate the offset of the sprite into video memory */
    mov bx,320
    mul bx
    add ax,[x]
    lds si,[sprite]  /* load the address of the sprite into the source register
    les di,[vscreen] /* Load the address of the virtual screen into the dest. */
    mov di,ax        /* put the offset into the destination */
    mov dx,ds:[si]   /* get the x size of the sprite */
    mov cx,ds:[si+1] /* get the y size of the sprite */
    inc si     /* move the source to the beginning of the sprite data */
    inc si
    sub bx,dx  /* create a constant to add to the offset after each x row */
  }              /* is drawn */
  yloop:
  asm {
    push cx    /* save the height left to draw */
    mov cx,dx  /* load the sprite width to use for a loop */
  }
  xloop:
  asm {
    lodsb      /* get the pixel's color */
    cmp al,0     /* is it zero? */
    jz skip_pixel /* if so, skip it, it is transparent */
    stosb        /* if not zero, draw the pixel */
    loop xloop   /* go to next pixel */
    jmp endx     /* when done with x's for this y coord, jump to end of loop *
  }
  skip_pixel:
  asm {
    inc di    /* if color of pixel was zero, move to next offset */
    loop xloop /* and go to next pixel */
  }
  endx:
  asm {
    add di,bx  /* add constant to offset to start at next y position */
    pop cx     /* restore the height left to draw */
```

continues

Listing 8.5. continued

```
    loop yloop  /* go to next y positon */
    pop ds      /* restore segments */
    pop es
  }
}
```

After first saving the segment registers, the function calculates the offset of the Sprite into the virtual page. Then it loads the addresses of the Sprite and the virtual page into the source and destination register pairs. Next, the X and Y sizes are loaded into the DX and CX registers. The X size of the Sprite is then subtracted from 320 to find the value that will be added to the offset into the virtual page of the current pixel of the Sprite when the entire width of the Sprite has been drawn and we are ready to move to the next line below. The non-zero pixel data is then copied to the virtual screen in the proper locations. Finally, the function terminates after restoring the segment registers.

Another necessary function is one that will clear the virtual screen. A function that will do this is shown in Listing 8.6.

Listing 8.6. Clearing the virtual screen.

```
void clear_vscreen(char far *vscreen)
{
  asm {
    push es  /* save segment register */
    les di,[vscreen]  /* load the address of the virtual screen */
    mov cx,32000  /* we need to clear 32000 words */
    xor ax,ax  /* clear to zero */
    rep movsw  /* do the clear */
    pop es /* restore segment register */
  }
}
```

The function loads the address of the virtual screen and fills it with zeros.

Compiled Sprites

If you think that the last function was fast, wait till I tell you about compiled Sprites. Think about the last function—what were the slowest parts of it? If you said "The tests for zero," you were correct. What else was slow? The loops, the multiple memory-to-memory transfers, and working with only one byte at a time. So, if we do away with all of those slow operations, our Sprites can be blitted lightning fast. Better yet, what if we do away with the blitter itself, and tell the Sprites to draw themselves. Impossible? Let's see.

In order to make each Sprite capable of drawing itself, we need to make each Sprite into a function. To do this, we compile each Sprite. An example of a compiled Sprite is shown in Listing 8.7. The whole function is not listed, because it is quite long, but it follows an apparent pattern.

Listing 8.7. Example of compiled Sprite.

```
void  brick(int x,int y, char far *vscreen)
{
asm {
push es
mov ax,[y]
mov bx,320
mul bx
add ax,[x]
les di,[vscreen]
mov di,ax

mov word ptr[es:di+0], 0xDEDD
mov word ptr[es:di+2], 0xDEDD
mov word ptr[es:di+4], 0xDBDD
mov word ptr[es:di+6], 0xDEDD
mov word ptr[es:di+8], 0xDED7
mov word ptr[es:di+10], 0xD4D5
mov word ptr[es:di+12], 0xD9DB
mov word ptr[es:di+14], 0xDDDD
mov word ptr[es:di+320], 0xD9D9
...
pop es
}
}
```

The compiled Sprite starts off by finding the offset in the virtual screen to which it will be drawn. Once that is found, it uses indexed addressing to copy the proper colors into the proper locations of memory. With this method, all the tests for transparent pixels are gone, there are no loops, and no memory-to-memory copies. The one problem that should become apparent is this: How do you create these compiled Sprites? I know you don't want to code them by hand. Therefore we will use a program to create them.

Listing 8.8 is a Sprite compiler. It will take a Sprite file in our standard format and convert it into a C file that is ready to compile and link into our games. The program works by processing each byte of the Sprite in turn, ignoring any zero-colored pixels. It then translates the bytes into the associated MOV instruction based on their location.

Listing 8.8. Sprite compiler.

```
#include <stdio.h>
#include <stdlib.h>
#include <conio.h>
```

continues

Listing 8.8. continued

```c
void main(void)
{
  char infilename[80],outfilename[80],spritename[40];
  FILE *infile,*outfile;
  char xsize,ysize;
  unsigned int offset;
  unsigned char byte1,byte2,x,y;

  printf("\nEnter input file name (sprite file) :");  /* get filenames */
  scanf("%s",infilename);
  printf("\nEnter output file name :");
  scanf("%s",outfilename);
  printf("Enter sprite name (function name) :");
  scanf("%s",spritename);
  printf("\n\n");
                                       /*—————Open files————*/
  if((infile = fopen(infilename,"rb")) == NULL)
  {
    printf("Could not open input file\n");
    exit(1);
  }
  if((outfile = fopen(outfilename,"wt")) == NULL)
  {
    printf("Could not open output file\n");
    exit(1);
  }
      /*——Output standard data to output file——*/
  fprintf(outfile,"void  %s(int x,int y, char far *vscreen)\n{\n",spritename);
  fprintf(outfile,"asm {\npush es\nmov ax,[y]\nmov bx,320\n");
  fprintf(outfile,"mul bx\nadd ax,[x]\nles di,[vscreen]\n");
  fprintf(outfile,"mov di,ax\n\n");

  printf("compiling...\n\n");

  xsize=fgetc(infile);
  ysize=fgetc(infile);
  offset=0;
  for (y=0;y<ysize;y++)
  {
    for(x=0;x<xsize;x+=2)
    {
      byte1=fgetc(infile);  /* get the next two bytes */
      byte2=fgetc(infile);
      if(!byte1 && !byte2)      /* if they are both zero, do nothing */
      {
      }
      if(byte1 && !byte2)    /* if one is not zero, it will be copied */
      {
        fprintf(outfile,"\nmov byte ptr[es:di+%i], 0x%X", offset, byte1);
      }
      if(!byte1 && byte2)   /* dido */
      {
        fprintf(outfile,"\nmov byte ptr[es:di+%i], 0x%X", offset+1, byte2);
      }
```

```
      if(byte1 && byte2)  /* neither zero- both copied */
      {
        fprintf(outfile,"\nmov word ptr[es:di+%i], 0x%X%X", offset, byte1, byte2);
      }
      offset+=2;  /*increment offset*/
    }
    offset+=(320-xsize);  /* move to next line below in offset */
  }

  fprintf(outfile,"\npop es\n}\n}\n");

  fclose(infile);  /* clean up and exit */
  fclose(outfile);

  exit(0);
}
```

The compiler first asks for the names of the appropriate files and opens them. Then the standard header is written to the output file, and we start processing the Sprite. Two bytes are read at a time. If one of them is zero, only the other byte will be translated into a MOV instruction. If both are non-zero, they will both be translated into a MOV instruction. If both are zero, they will be ignored. When the compiler is finished with one X row, it increments the offset by 320 less the width of the Sprite and moves to the next row. When all is complete, the ending is written to the output file and both files are then closed.

One important note should be made. Since this compiler works with two bytes at a time, only Sprites with an even width can be processed by it.

Avoiding Sprite Clipping

One problem that you may have noticed with compiled Sprites is that, although they are very fast, they do not allow for clipping when one is drawn near the edge of the screen. Therefore we must think of a way to overcome this problem. It seems that the problem exists with the edges of the screen. So, if we take away the edges of the screen, our problems are over. Unfortunately, we cannot take away the edges altogether, but we can widen them somewhat. We can widen the edges of the screen by 16 pixels on either side, letting us use Sprites up to 16 pixels in width. Then, when we copy the virtual screen to real video RAM, we just ignore the extra pixels to either side. So instead of clipping every individual Sprite by a different amount each time they are drawn, we clip the entire screen by a constant amount every time it is copied. Our new virtual screen will work as shown in Figure 8.3.

The one problem with this technique is that we need some creative problem solving in order to stay within one segment. If we use the formula from earlier in this chapter, we will see that we now need over 64KB of memory:

```
352  *  200  *  1  =  70400
```

Figure 8.3.
*Widening the
virtual screen.*

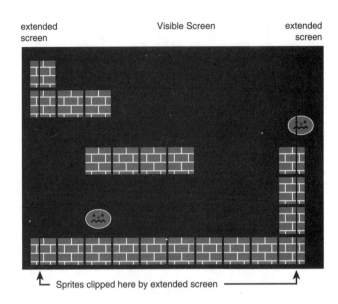

Figure 8.4.
Widening only one side.

Therefore, unless we want to rewrite all our functions to work with multiple segments, we need to modify our method. If you think about it, you may realize that we do not need to widen our screen by 16 pixels on both sides, because the end of one line of the screen will wrap around to the beginning of the next lower line of the screen. So, if we only widen the left side of the screen, any Sprites that would be clipped against the left side of the screen just wrap around to the extended portion of the screen on the left side, as shown in Figure 8.4.

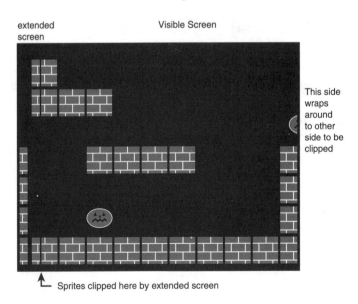

Now, when we plug numbers into our formula, we will see the following:

```
336 * 200 * 1 = 67200
```

Thus we are still over the 64KB limit. Now what? you may ask. Another simple calculation is required. How many 16-pixel-high Sprites can fit within the 200-pixel vertical dimension? The answer: 12.5. So, if we get rid of the half Sprite, we reduce our Y dimension to only 192, which, when plugged into the formula gives us the following:

```
336 * 192 * 1 = 64512
```

We have finally reduced our solution to a usable amount of memory, without any great loss. The small portion of visible screen that is lost on the bottom (or top) can be used as a status area, showing player health, weapons, etc.

In order to use this method, all that is required are simple changes in our offset calculations. Instead of multiplying the Y dimension by 320, will now multiply it by 336. The function that copies the virtual screen to video RAM must also be altered to ignore the extra space, as shown in Listing 8.9.

Listing 8.9. Copying the virtual screen to video RAM with Sprite-clipping modifications.

```
void copy_vscreen(char far *vscreen)
{
  asm {
    push es          /* save the segment registers */
    push ds
    lds si,[vscreen]   /* get the address of the virtual screen */
    mov ax,0xa000    /* load the address of video ram into the destination */
    mov ds,ax
    xor di,di      /* zero the destination offset */
    mov si,16      /* start 1 pisels from the side */
    mov cx,192     /* we need to copy 192 rows */

    mov dx,0x03da /* Status register one of the VGA card */
  }
  wait_for_retrace:
  asm {
    in al,dx   /* get the value of status reg 1 */
    test al,0x08  /* test to see if retrace is in progress */
    jnz wait_for_retrace /* if not, keep waiting */
  }
  yloop:
  asm {
    push cx        /* save the row count */
    mov cx,320     /* 320 columns per row */
    rep movsw      /* perform the copy */
    add si,16      /* skip the 16 pixel edge */
    pop cx         /* restore row count */
    loop yloop     /* repeat until finished */
    pop ds         /* restore the segment registers */
    pop es
  }
}
```

Of course, this technique can be modified to work with up/down clipping instead of left/right; or, with a little more loss of the viewing area for more memory, it can be used to work in both directions.

Summary

There is an example program, EXAMPLE.C, included on the CD-ROM that accompanies this book. EXAMPLE.C shows all the techniques discussed in this chapter. The example program shows different operations being performed with and without virtual screens.

In this chapter you have learned many techniques that can be used to give your game a professional look and feel. You learned how to work with virtual screens, compiled Sprites, and a technique that enables you to skip the clipping of Sprites when you draw them near the edges of the screen. Virtual screens are one of the most common techniques used by pros such as id Software (the creators of DOOM) and Epic Megagames (the authors of Jazz Jackrabbit). If you use these techniques, you too can hit the big time and make money in the process.

Memory Management in Real and Protected Modes

by Michael J. Norton

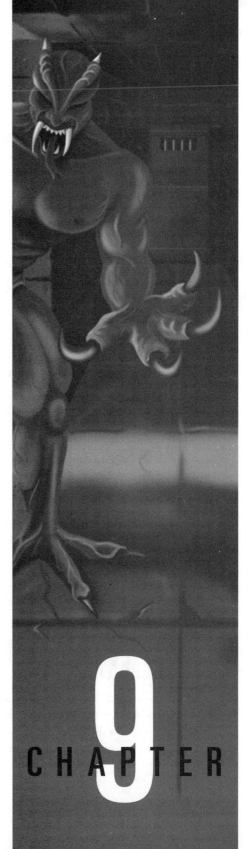

I remember the first time I fired up the video game DOOM. With the impatience of a 4-year-old on Christmas morning, I pulled up DOOM and feverishly hacked my way past the instructions screen. (It was in the way; I had to see what lay in store in this new game.) Selecting a moderately unfair skill level to satisfy the bloodthirsty audience looking over my shoulder, I took off down the textured corridor, killing anything that moved, exploring this virtual playland that id Software had created.

When the newness of DOOM wore off, I started to wonder how the game had been programmed, and I played it for purely analytical reasons. (At least that's what I told my wife for three straight months.) The most notable feature during initialization of the game is the Watcom DOS/4GW banner. At that time, I had only vaguely heard of Watcom. Watcom was most noted for developing Fortran compilers somewhere up in Canada. With so many questions in my mind, it was time to consult the all-knowing Internet. Surprisingly, hundreds of forums and newsgroups devoted to DOOM had already sprouted up, all asking the same questions.

My most important revelation from DOOM was that really cool things could be done with games written in Protected Mode. The rest is history, and Watcom is no longer known exclusively for its Fortran compilers. In this chapter, you will learn about:

- Real mode architecture
- Protected mode architecture
- Object oriented design
- Pixel buffer class
- C++ Memory Allocation
- C++ operator overloading
- Real mode blitting
- Phar Lap 286 | DOS-Extender
- Blink*inc* Blinker linker
- Phar Lap TNT 7.0 DOS-Extender
- Watcom DOS4/GW
- Watcom WASM and DOS4/GW

Real Mode and the 80x86 Processor

The Intel 286, 386, 486, and Pentium family of processors have two execution modes: 8086 Real Address Mode (commonly referred to as Real Mode) and Protected Virtual Address Mode (which is commonly referred to as Protected Mode). The 286 (technically known as the 80286) processor was the first in the Intel family to introduce separate operating modes. The architectural features of Protected Mode included larger physical memory, better memory management, and hardware support for multi-tasking and task-switching operations.

When the 80286 was unveiled, its predecessor, the 8086, was already extremely popular in the microcomputer market and it also drove a rapidly growing software market centered around the 8086 architecture for the IBM PC and its clones. Intel realized early on it would have to provide upward compatibility for its line of processors. The result of this endeavor was what is now called Real Mode. In Real Mode operation, iAPX 8086 (iAPX, Intel Advance Processor X) code can be executed on newer processors without the need for recompiling or assembling and linking.

Real Mode operations are the same across the suite of processors. The processor, whether it's a 286 or a Pentium, behaves just as if it were an iAPX 8086 executing 8086 code. In fact, when any of the processors come up or have been reset, they initialize in 8086 Real Mode.

Programs executing in Real Mode on the newer processors are essentially using privilege level 0, the inner most privileged level. The newer processors have supersets of instructions and registers that supersede the original 8086 architecture. The most notable differences are in the bit sizes of the general purpose registers and in the base architecture. (See Figure 9.1.)

Figure 9.1.

The 8086 and 80386 general purpose registers.

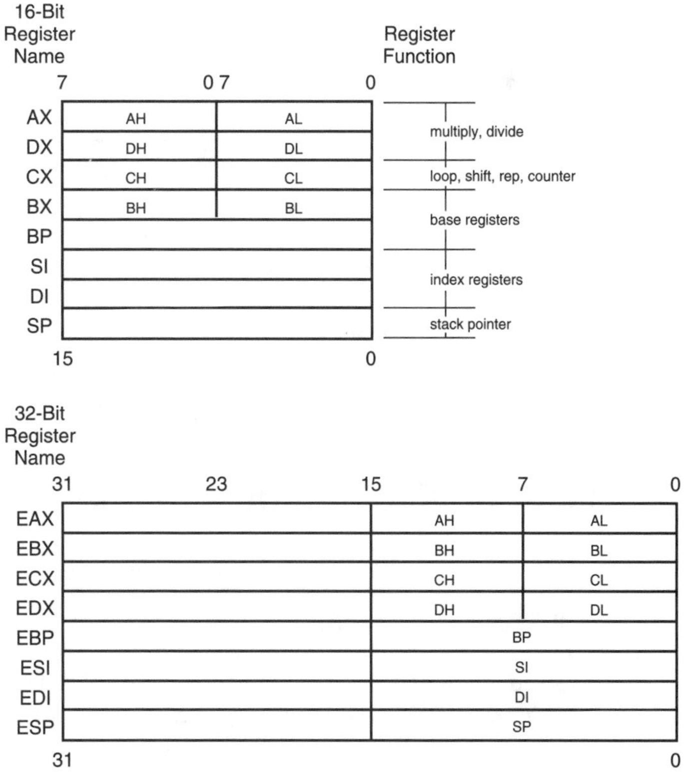

Memory Architecture in Real Mode

Memory in the 8086 architecture is a linear storage sequence of up to 1 million (1,048,576) bytes. The fundamental unit of storage is a byte, which is 8 bits. Real Mode memory is accessed with 16-bit pointers in a segmented memory scheme. Segments are linear sequences of memory of up to 64KB. A 16-bit pointer can reference up to 2^{16} bytes, or 64KB.

The 8086 processor has special-purpose registers reserved for segmented memory operations. Segment registers are considered special purpose because they can't be used in the same way a general-purpose register is used. For example, segment registers can't be used for the basic operations of adding and subtracting. In 8086 assembly-language programming, an immediate value may not be directly moved into a segment register. The 8086 architecture has defined four 16-bit segment registers to handle this addressing scheme: CS, DS, SS, and ES. (See Figure 9.2.)

CS: Code segment register; points to the segment of the code currently executing.

DS: Data segment register; contains the segment of the effective address for program variables and tables.

ES: Extra segment register; points to external data such as video memory.

SS: Stack segment register; points to the base of the stack.

Figure 9.2.
Diagram of the 8086 processor's segment registers.

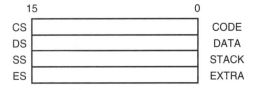

The primary function of the segment registers is address computation. Although the addresses are stored as 16-bit, they are actually 20-bit. The 20-bit physical address is calculated by shifting the value in the segment register left four bits. Adding a logical address to this value, called an offset, is how 1 million bytes of memory can be accessed in Real Mode.

Using Segments and Offsets

In Real Mode, the 80×86 processor can access up to 1,024KB of memory using segments and offsets. An offset is a 16-bit logical address used to reference bytes within a segment. The first byte in a segment is at offset 0000, the second byte at 0001, and the last byte is at offset FFFF, assuming a 64KB segment. In the segment offset notation, the first byte of VGA memory is referenced by A000:0000. The segment is A000, and the offset to the first byte is 0000. The offset simply represents the distance in bytes from the base address of the segment. The segment base value combined with the offset value is also commonly referred to as a logical addressing scheme. Such architecture is extremely useful for relocatable code. This implies that a program may be moved to different areas in memory and only have to update the segment registers to the base of the new memory areas.

```
mov    ax, 0a000h      ; put video segment into ax
mov    es,ax           ; move into segment register es
mov    ax,0            ; set index to first byte
mov    di,ax           ;    in vga segment

mov    ax,12ch         ; set byte value (arbitrary value)
mov    cx,64000        ; vga segment is 64k bytes long
vLoop:
mov    es:[di],al      ; write byte at location seg:off
inc    di              ; increment offset to next location
loop   vLoop           ; loop to write all 64k bytes
```

*Source snippet from vtest.asm using segment:offset technique to write to VGA memory

Physical Address Resolution

Programmers are primarily concerned with how code will behave in a logical-segment offset environment. The CPU, on the other hand, requires knowledge of the full 20-bit address when it is accessing memory. This 20-bit address is called the physical address and is used to uniquely reference a byte in memory. A physical address may have any value in the range of 00000–FFFFFh (0 to 1,048,575).

The processor computes the 20-bit address by taking the 16-bit value in one of its four segment registers. The contents of the register are first shifted left four times, which is equivalent to multiplying by 10h (16).

The offset value is then added to this result to produce the physical address. Note the importance of the shift-left operations. Shifts are used to emulate a multiplication by 10h. Shifting bits in a processor is faster than multiplying, because one shift left is equivalent to multiplying by 2. Shifting left four times is then equivalent to multiplying $2 \times 2 \times 2 \times 2 = 16$.

The base-16 number 10h (which is 16 in base 10) is also significant. In the conventional base-10 numbering scheme that we use every day, any number multiplied by 10 picks up an extra digit. The same is true in base 16 when multiplying by 10h. For example, arbitrarily assume the extra segment register, ES, has the value A000h. The offset value of 001Fh is stored in the destination index register, DI, for this particular operation.

```
ES:DI  A000:001F
ES contains segment: A000
DI contains offset: 001F
```

The processor first performs the shift-left operation four times on the contents of ES. Therefore, the address in the ES register is A0000h (A000h * 10h). Computing the physical address is done as follows:

```
ES:DI     A000:001F

    ES contains address:      A0000   segment * 10h
+   DI contains offset:       001F    add offset
    20-bit physical address:  A001F
```

Multiplying by 10h enables the 16-bit segment registers to hold a 20-bit address. The operation of multiplying by 10h always results in the rightmost four bits holding the value of zero. Therefore, the 8086/8088 processors store the segment in the segment register as a four-digit hex, A000, with the rightmost digit implied as being a zero. This clever design enables the processor to store an implied 20-bit value in a 16-bit register. Without an implied hex digit, the maximum base address that could fit into the segment register would be FFF0h (65520), compared to the 20-bit address with value FFFF0h (1048560). This is how, in Real Mode operation, an 80×86 can address 1MB of memory.

A key attribute of a segment boundary is that its physical address is in multiples of 16 bytes. These 16-byte units of memory are referred to as *paragraphs*.

Concurrent Programming

One of the best features of developing under the Microsoft NT operating system is the flexibility and ease of switching between GUI development tools and a DOS-emulated window. Multiple programs can execute at once. One window may be accessing information off a Microsoft Developer's CD-ROM. Another window may have a Watcom Integrated Developer's Environment running and a DOS window minimized in the background. Using operating system terminology, each one of these programs is defined as a *task*. This term is also used in Windows and Windows NT where executing programs are defined as tasks. A simple experiment is to click the mouse pointer on the upper left corner of an active form. A menu will appear. One of the options on the menu is Switch To (Ctrl+Esc). Select this option and a Task List window will appear on the screen.

Concurrent programming is the study of how a computer or set of computers utilizes resources for program execution. A fundamental unit in concurrent programming is a task or process. A task is defined as a program consisting of code and data. In processors such as the 80286 and the 80386, multiple tasks can execute on a computer simultaneously. The tasks must share the processor in a manner that makes all the tasks appear to be running simultaneously. A task may not consume the processor or deny other tasks access. This is defined as processor starvation. The processor etiquette is to allow one task to execute its critical code and then suspend its operation for another task to execute. For instance, if a CD-ROM drive is being accessed, this task may be suspended until the access is completed. During this time, another task may use the processor. When the CD-ROM has completed the access, an interrupt signals the processor and the current task is suspended.

The complexity of isolation and delegation of memory resources are beyond the scope of the application developer. It is the operating system that allocates task memory and resources. The 80386 processor provides hardware for memory-management and protection. The operating system uses these protection mechanisms to ensure tasks don't violate or corrupt each other's resources or the operating system itself.

Task Isolation

A task is isolated if its code and data cannot corrupt the operating system's code and data and an executing external task cannot interfere or use the current task's code and data. Isolation is provided by assigning a task a layer in which to operate. There are four layers in the Intel model. (See Figure 9.3.) This layering system is called Privilege Level Protection.

Figure 9.3.
A graphical representa-
tion of the Intel four-
layer model.

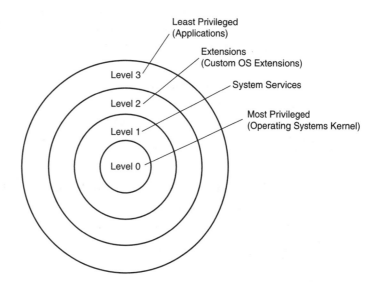

A privilege level is a physical attribute that is assigned to a task. Levels are numbered sequentially, 0–3, to accommodate four protection levels. The assignment of privileges is hierarchical. Level 0, denoted PL0 (Protection Level 0), is the most privileged. Level 3, denoted PL3, is the least privileged. The mechanism operates along the guidelines that the operating system is the most privileged task and can access resources and tasks operating at lesser privilege levels. Tasks running at lesser privilege levels, such as PL2 and PL3, cannot interfere with resources operating at the higher privilege levels, PL0 and PL1. The operating system is protected from the applications. MS-DOS, on the other hand, is not protected, and an application may improperly access operating-system resources and cause devastating effects.

MS-DOS is a Real Mode operating system. On the 80286 and 80386, the operating system and applications execute with a privilege level of PL0.

The operating system is defined as the highest-privilege task, operating at PL0. Level 0 is also referred to in Intel documentation as the Kernel Level. A kernel is an abstraction in which multiple tasks executing on one processor behave as though they each had their own processor. The role of the kernel at level 0 is very fundamental, and executes atomic actions (very simple instructions). These actions may include memory management, interrupts, and basic task management.

System services at PL1 is the next *inner* most-privileged layer. This level handles more complex tasks, such as scheduling, file descriptors, and complex data communications. System-services level is protected from the two outermost levels, PL2 and PL3. The kernel of the operating system is operating at privilege level 0 and the rest of the operating system is at level 1. Therefore, the kernel has access to all segments in the task and the rest of the operating system can access all segments except ones used by the kernel at PL0.

The OS extensions level PL2 is an intermediate level suited for system software customization. This level is not to be confused with the privilege level of DOS extenders, which are mini-operating systems and are PL0 tasks. The OS extensions level may be more suited to developers of advanced applications, such as Oracle, who require advance handling of file descriptors.

The Applications level PL3 can access code and data only its own segments.

Segment Descriptors

In the Real Mode environment, code and data reside in segmented memory and are accessed by using byte offsets. In a Protected Mode environment, memory tables are maintained by the processor to keep track of segmentation for each task. These tables contain *segment descriptors*, which provide data for translating logically mapped memory into linear addresses. (See Figure 9.4.) When a task allocates a new segment, the task is assigned a new descriptor. Each descriptor is essentially an 8-byte entry that contains three fields: segment base address, segment size limit, and specific segment attributes.

Figure 9.4.
A diagram of the 80286 and 80386 segment descriptor formats.

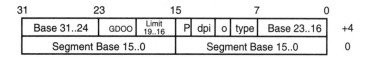

The 80286 segment descriptor formats

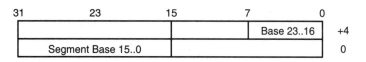

The 80386 segment descriptor formats

Segment Descriptor's Base Field

The base field in the descriptor is a 24-bit field, in bytes 2–4, on the 286 and higher processors. (See Figure 9.5.) This field contains the physical address of the segment within the 16MB of address space. An interesting feature of the base field is that it is stored in bytes 2–3, and part of byte 4 of the descriptor. This non-sequential method of storing data is called *fragmentation*. In the 386 processor and higher, the base field is not only fragmented across bytes 2–4, but also in byte 7 to compose a 32-bit address value. The processor is responsible for *defragmenting* (putting back in order) these values when it references them.

Figure 9.5.
The 24-bit 80286 and 32-bit 80386 base fields of the segment descriptor.

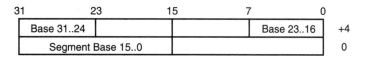

The 80286 24-Bit Segment Base Address

The 80386 32-Bit Segment Base Address

The Intel 80286 Programmer's Reference mentions that values in bytes 6 and 7 must be set to zero for forward compatibility with the 80386. It was Intel's intention to squeeze as much as it could into the first six bytes for 24-bit addressing and fragment the rest of the data in the last two bytes for the 80368's 32-bit addressing capabilities.

Segment Descriptor's Limit Field

The limit field on the 286 is a 16-bit field composed of bytes 0 and 1 in a segment descriptor and contains an integer value for segment size. (See Figure 9.6.) This form of protection prevents accessing data from beyond the specified size limit. Therefore, a segment can be anywhere from 1 byte to 64KB ($2^{16}-1$ = 65535 bytes) in size. Even though the 80286 can address up to 16MB of memory, it can only do so in 64KB units.

Figure 9.6.

The limit fields of the 80286 and 80386 segment descriptor.

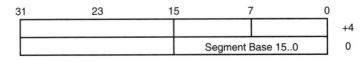

The 80286 16-Bit Limit Field

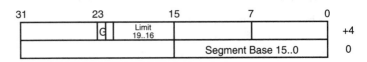

The 80386 32-Bit Limit Field

On the 386, the limit field is fragmented across bytes 0, 1, and 4 bits of byte 6. Defragmenting these bits results in a 20-bit value. The processor then interprets this value depending on how the last bit of the sixth byte is set. This bit is defined as the granularity bit. When the granularity bit is not set (G=0), the segmentation will be in units of 1 byte, with an upper limit of 1MB. This is a substantial gain over the 16-bit segmentation limit of 64KB on the 286. Setting the granularity bit (G=1) delivers even more impressive results with segmentation in 4KB units up to 4GB in length.

For example:

```
(G=0)
segment base = 54230000h
limit = fff0h
granularity = 0
```

This describes a segment base at linear address 54230000h with valid offsets of 0 up to 64KB. The granularity bit is not set, so units of memory will be 1 byte.

Example:

```
(G=1)
segment base = 00000000h
limit = 0FFFFFh
granularity = 1
```

The granularity bit is set, so the example is in 4KB units of segmentation. The math gets a bit tricky, especially when hand-held calculators don't handle the "giga" digits. The computations is as follows:

```
Segment Limit = limit << 12 + 0FFFh = limit * 1000h + 0FFFh = 0FFFFFh * 1000h +
0FFFh
                        = 0FFFFFFFFh = 4G
```

The segment address is at linear address 0, and the segment maps a 4GB address. Using granularity on the 386, it is now possible to have a segment size ranging from 1 byte to 4 gigabytes.

Segment Descriptor Attributes

The *Type* field is a 4-bit field located in byte 5 of the descriptor. (See Figure 9.7.) This field is used to define the type of segment this descriptor references, such as stack, data, or code segment. The four bits allow for 16 different defined-descriptor segment-type values. These values determine whether code, data, or stack segments are read only, executable, or have other special purposes.

Figure 9.7.
A diagram of the segment descriptor attributes in byte 5 of the segment descriptor.

Segment Descriptor Attributes

The *Descriptor Privilege Level* (DPL) bit field is also located in byte 5. It is two bits in size and holds a value from 0 to 3. Level 0 is the most privileged level, and level 3 is the least privileged.

Maintenance of Descriptors

The segment descriptor contains information to map a logical address into a linear address. Segment descriptors are maintained by operating systems, DOS extenders, advance compilers, and linkers.

Descriptor Tables

The segment descriptor defines a segment's location in memory and its attributes. The segment descriptor defines only one segment. To define multiple segments, the operating system must maintain memory-resident arrays, called *descriptor tables*. Since these tables maintain memory for the operating system, they are said to be *dynamic* tables, meaning they can vary in size from

8 bytes to 64KB. These tables are referenced by another data structure called a selector. A selector is 16 bits in size and reserves the latter 13 bits for indexing the descriptor table. This 13-bit index sets the upper limit on how big a descriptor table can grow. Doing a quick calculation on the back of an envelope reveals that a table can hold up to 8192 (2^{13}) 8-byte segment descriptors.

Three different classes of descriptor tables exist in the Protected Mode environment; a Global Descriptor Table (GDT), Local Descriptor Tables (LDTs), and the Interrupt Descriptor Table (IDT). These descriptor tables are accessible only by the operating system in order to prevent applications from accessing these segments.

The GDT holds descriptors that are available to nearly all tasks in the system. Unlike LDTs, there is only one GDT and it is used by the Protected Mode operating system to manage code and data segments. The descriptors for tasks' LDTs also reside in the GDT. The GDT allows global data to be shared among individual tasks.

The first descriptor entry in the GDT is not used by the processor. The index into this field of the GDT is called a *null selector.* The processor will generate a general-protection-fault error if an attempt is made to access memory using this descriptor. (See Figure 9.8.)

Figure 9.8.
A diagram of a Global and Local descriptor table referencing physical memory.

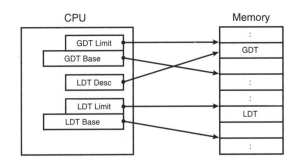

The LDT contains descriptors that are owned by a task. The operating system is responsible for assigning each task an LDT. The LDT isolates the applications code and data from the rest of the system. Descriptors, belonging to a task, are maintained by the LDT. (See Figure 9.9.)

Figure 9.9.
A diagram of a LDT descriptor referencing a segment of memory.

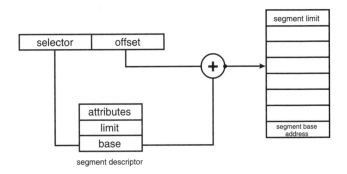

The third descriptor table, the IDT which is used in Protected Mode, services interrupts instead of the interrupt vector table at Real Mode address 0000:0000. The IDT is capable of holding up to 8192 descriptors. However, only 256 service interrupts are actually available.

> Address 0000:0000 in Real Mode is the start of the Vector Interrupt Table. In Protected Mode, address 0000:0000 represents a null selector.

Segment Selectors

In 8086 Real Mode addressing, the physical memory is contiguous up to an address of 1MB. This memory is accessed with a 16-bit value to represent a 20-bit segment address. The *selector*, in Protected Mode, is a logical address of a descriptor in a descriptor table. This is the primary difference between Real Mode and Protected Mode addressing: the method in which the address is calculated. The selector specifies an index into an operating-system-maintained table. A 32-bit segment base address is referenced from the table and a physical address is formed by adding the offset.

The selector must store three variables in order to provide the operating system with enough information to access the correct descriptor table and descriptor. All this information is neatly packed into 16 bits. Therefore, the information isn't fragmented like a segment descriptor. (See Figure 9.10.)

Figure 9.10.

Examples of an LDT, GDT, and a null selector.

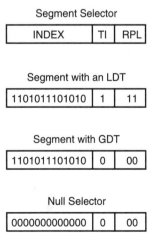

The two low-order bits of the selector represent the selector privilege level. This field is denoted as the Requested Privilege Level (RPL). A 2-bit field can accommodate binary values 0b–11b (0–3), which are precisely the values used to determine protection levels. When a pointer is passed to the operating system, its privilege level is checked, using the RPL field, to ensure it doesn't access higher-privileged memory.

A selector uses the Table Indicator (TI) bit, in bit 2, to identify the descriptor table. A value of TI = 0 identifies the descriptor to be in the GDT. Setting the bit TI = 1 identifies the descriptor to be in the current LDT. The TI field preceding the 13-bit index field gives a mathematical significance to the size of the virtual address space. A selector uniquely identifies a segment by comprising both the TI and index fields. This 14-bit combination results in a possible 2^{14} (16,384) unique segments. If TI = 0, then there are 2^{13} (8192) possible segments. That is to say, if the TI bit is set (TI = 1), the task's virtual address space can be subdivided into two separate halves. These halves are labeled *global address space* and *local address space*.

General Protection Faults

A Protected Mode environment uses selectors and descriptor tables to determine whether a pointer is valid. For example, a 16-bit selector points to a 32-bit base address in a descriptor table. Any attempt to submit a 16-bit segment base address will surely generate a *general protection fault* (GP fault). The processor will issue an INT 0Dh exception, indicating a protection violation. The Protected Mode handler, intrinsic to the operating system, will terminate the task and display a register dump. This is what is meant by a Protected Mode environment. Thus a buggy application can no longer be fatal in the event of a invalid pointer.

To the programmer, this means a familiar video-segment base address, such as 0xA000, cannot be written to as in the Real Mode environment. The segment address is no longer valid, because in Protected Mode it is a selector.

Decoding the selector:

```
A000 = 1010 0000 0000 0000
index = 1010 0000 0000 0        (1400h)
TI = 0                                        ( GDT )
RPL = 00                              (ring 0)
```

As a selector, value 0xA000 is indexing a descriptor (index = 1400h), in a global descriptor table (TI = 0), and has a privilege of 0. These values are all attributes of a privileged task belonging to the operating system. Listing 9.1 attempts to write a byte to video segment 0xA000. The mistakes here are perfectly valid as far as the compiler is concerned. It won't be until the code is executed that the protection violation will be caught and a GP fault handler will terminate the bad code.

Listing 9.1. An example of generating a GP fault using the Phar Lap 286 | DOS-Extender SDK.

```c
/* badsel.c */
/* bad selector to generate a GP fault */
void main(void)
{
  char far *vidPtr = (char far *) A0000000L;
  *vidPtr = 0x1c;                           /* write a byte to bogus location */
}


C:\286>badsel
Fatal error 286.3330: General protection fault detected.
PID=0001  TID=0001  SID=0001  ErrorCode=a000
AX=80D3  BX=A000  CX=7FDE  DX=80D3  SI=0174  DI=0174  BP=0000
CS:IP=033F:0003    DS=034F  ES=0317  SS:SP=034F:1702    FLAGS=3246

C:\286>
```

The GP fault register dump in this particular example gives CS=033F and DS=034F. These are not the segment addresses for the code and data segments; these are selectors. Carrying out the calculations on the back of a cocktail napkin yields the following information:

```
CS = 033F = 0000 0011 0011 1111
index field = 0000 0011 0011 1          (67h)
TI field = 1                                    (LDT)
RPL field = 11                            (Ring 3)
```

The application BADSEL.C had its code segment referenced by descriptor 67h in a LDT (TI = 1) and was executing at ring level 3 (RPL = 3) before it was abruptly terminated by the operating system. The address arithmetic displayed here is only useful for analyzing GP faults. It is unlikely that the programmer will sit down and do calculations of which selectors reference what in a descriptor table. The tedious chore of memory management has already been taken care of by the operating-system designers.

Coding Conventions

Portability is a concern for software publishers, especially those who distribute titles among several platforms. Placing an emphasis on multiple platforms early in the design will pay off in the long run. Industry professionals are all too aware of the mad rush in July to push a code release for a product that needs to be on the shelves by Christmas.

A simple coding convention that assists in portability is to exclude inline assembly calls from the code. That is, calls to video usually require assembly functions, so put the functions in a library outside of the code. Software professionals should consider inline assembly as a programming faux pas.

Memory allocation should be handled through standard means, such as a `malloc` in ANSI C or through a `new` operator in C++. Pointers to services should be as platform-independent as possible. For instance, in 8086 Real Mode, segments and offsets can easily be accessed directly with the following C struct:

```
union sgptr {
  char _far *p;
  struct {
      unsigned int offset;
      unsigned int segment;
  } wrd;
};

typedef sgptr SegPtr;
SegPtr vgaMem;
vgaMem.wrd.segment = 0xA000;
vgaMem.wrd.offset = 0x0000;
```

If this code is to be ported over to a DOS extender SDK, it will have to be re-written. A cleaner, more readable, and more portable approach is the following:

```
char _far pVideoMem = (char _far *) MK_FP(0xA000,0);
```

The common library function, `MK_FP()`, is available on DOS platforms and is upwardly compatible to Protected Mode environments. DOS extender vendors such as Phar Lap and Watcom use `MK_FP()` as a mechanism for accessing protected memory. Explicit calls using far pointers will cause program termination through GP fault handlers.

The downside to using DOS extenders is that commercial applications may require a royalty fee. Some illustrious programmers have gone as far as to code their own extenders. A word of advice is to pay the royalty fee. Ray Duncan may have made protected-mode coding sound easy in his book, *Extending DOS*, but the truth is that it is an operating system. Computer environments have become as unique as each user and his/her own installations. Only large companies with deep pockets have the resources for complete software testing of an operating system on such a broad scale.

Technical support is another factor to keep in mind. DOS-extender developers have experience and professional expertise with their own products. Some commercial-product suppport, such as Phar Lap's, is free for a limited time and provides quick, same-day response over e-mail. At the other end of the spectrum, one vendor sent a customer an automated e-mail response and never replied to the particular query.

A Simple Pixel Buffer Class

The following exercise will discuss basic object-modeling techniques for designing a simple pixel-buffer class. Several methodologies are broadly accepted in the industry for object modelling. The two most prominent techniques are those of Grady Booch and James

Rumbaugh. This discussion will focus on using Rumbaugh's Object Modelling techniques and will use his notation.

An *object*, as defined by Rumbaugh, is a decomposition of a clearly defined problem. This decomposition is a model or a behavior of a real-world problem that can be implemented by a computer. A decomposition in computer science is referred to as an *abstraction*. Data abstraction is strongly linked to top-down structured design, as in C programming. A structured approach decomposes steps of an overall process using an algorithmic analysis. Many trade-journal articles have erroneously referred to *object oriented design* (OOD) as a new means of data abstraction. The key difference is that data abstraction is concerned with data flow, and OOD is focused on object behavior. Algorithmic decomposition uses functional elements to solve a problem. Objects, on the other hand, may collaborate to solve the same problem.

Objects with similar behaviors and attributes are said to belong to the same *class*. Pixel bytes are typically always blitted or masked in one form or another. Sprites require blitting and masking, as do screen updates. These operations are common to both the Sprite object and screen object. Rather than writing individual operations for the screen buffer and the Sprite buffer, these objects can be members of the same class. Operations and attributes can now be written once for the class, and all objects in the class can use the code.

Object Diagrams

Just as structured design uses flow diagrams for functional analysis, OOD uses *object diagrams* for modelling concepts. There are two types of object diagrams: a *class diagram* and an *object instance* diagram. (See Figure 9.11.) A class diagram describes the object class; it is represented by a box with the name of the class typed in bold font. The object instance diagram is represented as a box with round edges with the name of the class enclosed in parantheses in boldface and the name of the object instance is beneath it in standard face. The object-instance diagram is used to show object similarity.

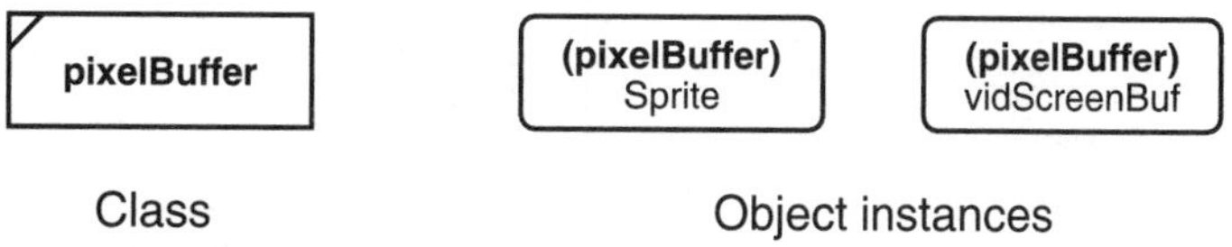

Figure 9.11.
A `pixelBuffer` *class diagram and two object-instance diagrams using Rumbaugh modelling.*

pixelBuffer

Class

(pixelBuffer)
Sprite

(pixelBuffer)
vidScreenBuf

Object instances

The pixel buffer class contains "data values," examples include a buffer, buffer size, row offset, logical height, and width. These values are said to be *attributes* of the class. The attributes are the data values necessary to adequately describe the pixels in memory, in both a logical format (screen coordinates) and a physical format (buffer in memory). These attributes are placed in the lower part of the class diagram. A line is drawn between the class name and the attributes.

A class box doesn't necessarily have to be drawn with attributes; this is just for providing a level of detail. The attributes are shown in the box with their attribute name and colon separating the data type. Object-instance diagrams can also show their attributes; typically they display actual values that differentiate themselves from other objects. These values could include unique Sprite height, width, and buffer size. (See Figure 9.12.)

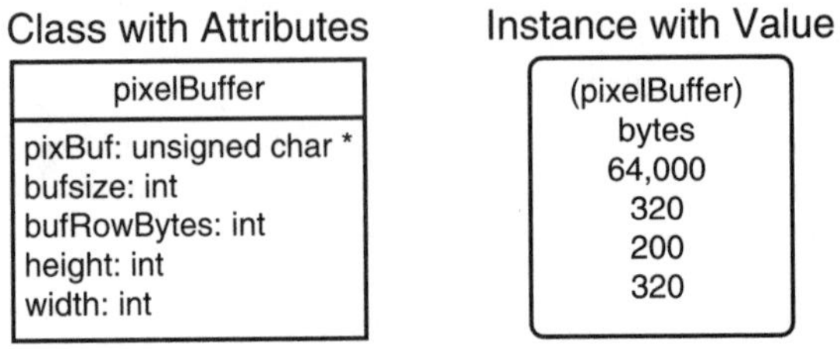

Figure 9.12.

A Rumbaugh diagram of a pixelBuffer *class with attributes and an object instance with values.*

Class with Attributes

pixelBuffer
pixBuf: unsigned char *
bufsize: int
bufRowBytes: int
height: int
width: int

Instance with Value

(pixelBuffer)
bytes
64,000
320
200
320

An *operation* is a function shared by all members of a class. Operations would include copying pixels, masking pixels, and transparent pixel copying. A purist may raise an eyebrow at distinguishing between two different operations for masking. This distinction between masking and transparent pixel copying merely exists for operating-system portability. The Macintosh and X Windows environments sometime requires a mask bitmap or pixmap in order to perform masking. It is for this reason that the distinction is made.

In the object diagram, operations are listed beneath the attributes with a line separating the two. (See Figure 9.13.) Operations are typically listed with their arguments and return types. The operations' arguments are listed in parantheses, and are separated by commas. Operations with no arguments are said to be empty and require no listing. The return type field follows the argument list and is separated by a colon.

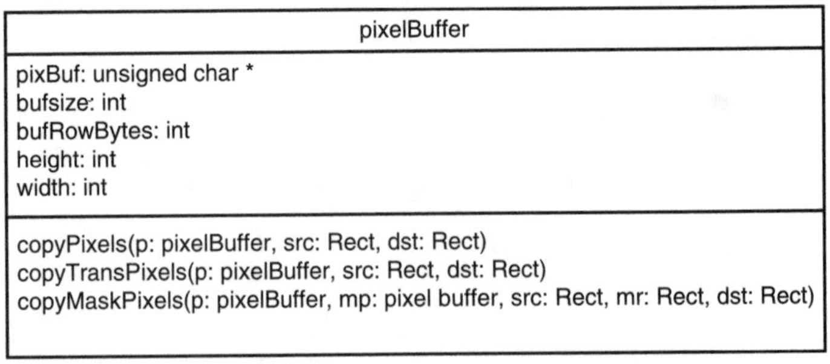

Figure 9.13.

A Rumbaugh class diagram depicting the pixelBuffer *class with attributes and operations.*

pixelBuffer
pixBuf: unsigned char *
bufsize: int
bufRowBytes: int
height: int
width: int
copyPixels(p: pixelBuffer, src: Rect, dst: Rect)
copyTransPixels(p: pixelBuffer, src: Rect, dst: Rect)
copyMaskPixels(p: pixelBuffer, mp: pixel buffer, src: Rect, mr: Rect, dst: Rect)

One of the true beauties of object modelling is that a well-designed model and its diagrams reveal the architecture of the class header file. In this case, taking the class diagram of pixelBuffer, with its attributes and operations, provides the header-file template, called the class body, detailed in Listing 9.2. Header files in C++ typically have the extension of .HPP to distinguish them from their H file cousins in the C language. Similarly, C++ source-code files have the .CPP extension.

Listing 9.2. A simple class body definition.

```
#ifndef PIXBUF_HPP
#define PIXBUF_HPP
class pixelBuffer{          // class declaration

  friend class Rect         // external class used for describing logical coordi-
nates

  // attributes
  private:                  // private: can be accessed by only members of this class
    unsigned int bufSize;         // BYTE size of buffer
    unsigned int bufRowBytes;     // # BYTE's of pixels in each row
    unsigned int width, height;    // logical width and height

  public:                 // public: can be accessed by non-class members
    unsigned char *pixBuf;        // buffer for pixels

// operations (member functions)
// copy pixel BYTEs
    void copyPixels( const pixelBuffer&,const Rect&, const Rect& );
    void copyTransPixels( const pixelBuffer&,const Rect&, const Rect& );
};
#endif
```

The header file isn't complete; it lacks C++ conventions and declarations necessary to implement it. What is important is that the object diagrams provide a template for the header file itself and will serve as a road map throughout the implementation process.

Memory Management and C++

Programs written in C++ have an unallocated pool of memory called a *free store*. The free store is said to be *dynamic memory allocation* because it is called upon at runtime of the program. Memory in the free store is uninitialized and only accessible through pointers. Allocation of memory occurs by invoking a call to the new operator with a type or class specifier. The operator will return a pointer to a single object or an array of objects.

```
pixBuf = new char[bufSize];               // allocate memory for a buffer
assert( pixBuf != 0);                     // is free store exhausted?
pixelBuffer *ptrPixBufArray = new pixelBuffer[20];    // allocate an array of
pixelBuffer objects
```

The objects allocated in the free store have a *dynamic extent*. This means that the object's memory can be bound for the life of the program or it can be explicitly deallocated by the programmer. Memory in C++ is deallocated by calling the delete operator. For example:

```
delete pixBuf;                  // delete the buffer
delete ptrPixBufArray[];              // delete the array of objects
```

The program knows at runtime how much memory it will need for any one object. In C++, pointers to objects are said to be *statically* allocated—that is, the compiler does the work of determining how much memory will be required for the pointer. The compiler gets this information from the class declaration in the header file.

The class body now needs a mechanism to assist the compiler in object initialization. This is achieved through a special-class member function called a *constructor*. The constructor is a member function, whose name is the same as the name of the object class declaration. This function does not allocate storage; it initializes the newly allocated object. Constructors are usually supplied by the programmer, but one will be supplied by the compiler if the programmer so chooses. A constructor can take an argument, but never does it return a value. The constructor for initializing the `pixelBuffer` object looks like the following:

```
#ifndef PIXBUF_HPP
#define PIXBUF_HPP
class pixelBuffer{          // class declaration

    :
    :

  public:                   // public: can be accessed by non-class members
    unsigned char *pixBuf;        // buffer for pixels

 // constructor
pixelBuffer();              // default constructor
pixelBuffer( int size );          // overloaded constructor
pixelBuffer( const pixelBuffer &p);    // copy constructor

};
#endif
```

The *default constructor* is provided by the programmer and requires no arguments. This is considered to be the default initialization of an object. The code for the defualt constructor is located in the source-code file (pixbuf.cpp). In some cases, if the code is short, the default constructor may be declared *inline* and its source included in the header file. The code for the default constructor looks like that shown in Listing 9.3.

Listing 9.3. A default constructor for the `pixelBuffer` class.

```
/////////////////////////////////////////////////////////////////////////

pixelBuffer::pixelBuffer()
{
    printf("default pixelBuffer constructor\n");
    bufSize = 0;
    bufRowBytes = 0;
    width = height = 0;
    pixBuf = NULL;  // reserve a place on that stack!

    // set default bounds
    bounds.right = 0; bounds.top = 0;
    bounds.left = 0; bounds.bottom = 0;
    printf("default contructor pixelBuffer done\n");
}

/////////////////////////////////////////////////////////////////////////
```

The double-colon (::) operator in the code (pixelBuffer::pixelBuffer()) is referred to as the scope operator. It tells the compiler the function being defined is a member of the pixelBuffer class. If the class name with double colon is not present before the function name, the compiler will definitely return an error about an undefined function in the source-code file.

An important memory-management consideration in the default constructor is the fact that the buffer pixBuf is not automatically initialized to NULL. A common error that is frequently made is to forget to initialize an empty buffer in the default constructor. This error will not be caught by the compiler, and most likely the code will execute. However, a runtime error will generate, and a disasterous message of Cannot find command.com may result. The only means of recovery is the shameful three-finger salute to the keyboard (Ctrl+Alt+Del).

More than one constructor may be present in the class body. Defining multiple constructors is known as constructor overloading. It is illegal to declare two member functions with the same name and same arguments, such as pixelBuffer(int) and pixelBuffer(int). The compiler would complain that this is ambiguous and break from its compilation. The ambiguity is removed by providing different types of calling arguments to each overloaded constructor. The purpose of overloading constructors is to explicitly provide flexibility in initialization schemes.

```
pixelBuffer sprite;         // object initialization with default constructor
pixelBuffer vidScreenBuf(64000);    // object initialization with overloaded
constructor
```

The first example of initialization, the pixelBuffer object Sprite, invokes the default constructor, pixelBuffer(), for its initialization. The second example of initialization, vidScreenBuf(64000) object, invokes the overload constructor pixelBuffer(int size), because the compiler resolved that a data type of integer was passed as a calling argument. More than one overloaded constructor may be provided, as long as the ambiguity can be resolved by the compiler. The source code for some useful overloaded constructors looks like that shown in Listing 9.4.

Listing 9.4. An example of an overloaded constructor using size as an initialization argument.

```
/////////////////////////////////////////////////////////////////////////////

pixelBuffer::pixelBuffer( unsigned int n )
{
    bufSize = n;
    pixBuf = new char[bufSize];
    assert( pixBuf != 0 );
    width = height = 0;

    // set default bounds
    bounds.right = 0; bounds.top = 0;
    bounds.left = 0; bounds.bottom = 0;
}

/////////////////////////////////////////////////////////////////////////////
```

In this example, the constructor takes an argument of bufSize and allocates the memory for the buffer using the new operator. If the allocation is successful, the object is then initialized with default values. (See Listing 9.5.)

Listing 9.5. An example of an overloaded constructor using a Rect object for initialization.

```
/////////////////////////////////////////////////////////////////////////

pixelBuffer::pixelBuffer( const Rect& r )
{
    // determine buffer size
    bufRowBytes = r.right-r.left;  // calculate the # BYTES per row
    width = bufRowBytes;           // logical width = bufRowBytes
    height = r.bottom - r.top;     // calculate logical height
    bufSize = bufRowBytes * height;// calculate buffer size needed

    // set up buffer bounds
    bounds.left = r.left;
    bounds.top = r.top;
    bounds.right = r.right;
    bounds.bottom = r.bottom;

    // allocate the buffer
    pixBuf = new unsigned char _far[bufSize];
    assert( pixBuf != 0);
}

/////////////////////////////////////////////////////////////////////////
```

In this example, an object Rect, is passed as an argument to the constructor. This provides the flexibility of initializing an object in terms of logical coordinates. In game design, Sprites are always referred to as an entity of geometric shape (such as a 64×64 pixel object). This constructor enables the programmer to define object initialization in terms of logical graphic coordinates.

A special member function called a *copy constructor*, is present in the sample header file. This constructor takes an argument of pixelBuffer, and inititializes the calling object as a copy of the supplied object.

```
pixelBuffer offScreenBuf( vidScreenBuf);      // example of initializing with copy
constructor
```

This example takes a new unitialized object, offScreenBuf, and initializes it to the contents of of an already initialized object, videScreenBuf. A copy constructor should be supplied by the programmer to explicitly define memberwise initialization of the particuliar object. If one is not supplied, the compiler will most likely provide one at its discretion. It's a good programming practice to supply one; the results may be more predictable. Listing 9.6 is an example of a copy constructor.

Listing 9.6. An example of a copy constructor for the `pixelBuffer` **class.**

```
////////////////////////////////////////////////////////////////////////////

pixelBuffer::pixelBuffer( const pixelBuffer& p )
{

    bufSize = p.bufSize;            // get bufSize of object
    bufRowBytes = p.bufRowBytes;    // get bufRowBytes of object
    if (!pixBuf)
    {
      pixBuf = new unsigned char _far[bufSize]; // new buffer
      assert( pixBuf != 0 );         // check allocation
     }
    bounds = p.bounds;              // new bounds = old
    width = p.bounds.right - p.bounds.left;
    height = p.bounds.bottom - p.bounds.top;
    memcpy(pixBuf, p.pixBuf, bufSize);
}

////////////////////////////////////////////////////////////////////////////
```

Just as the class designers are responsible for initializing an object, they are responsible for the un-initialization of an object. This is where the programmer is responsible for cleaning up before the termination of an object. A *destructor* is a member function that handles this deinitialization. Similar to the constructor naming convention, the destructor has the name of the class as its function name. The distinction is made with a ~ preceding the class name for a destructor. However, a destructor may not be overloaded, nor will it return a value. The destructor is the mechanism a programmmer uses to clean up with. If any memory was allocated with the new operator in a constructor, it should be explicitly deleted in this section of code.

```
#ifndef PIXBUF_HPP
#define PIXBUF_HPP
class pixelBuffer{          // class declaration

    :

 // constructor
pixelBuffer();              // default constructor
pixelBuffer( int size );        // overloaded constructor
pixelBuffer( const pixelBuffer &p);     // copy constructor

    :

 // destructor
~pixelBuffer() { if (!pixBuf) delete pixBuf; };
};
#endif
```

Operator Overloading

The constructors and destructor provide invaluable tools for object initialization. However, before deeming the header file complete, it would be nice to provide `pixelBuffer` specific operators. One of the powerful advantages of C++ over ANSI C is the ability to overload the functionality of predefined operators and use them to provide custom operators to work with a class object.

An overloaded operator declaration in C++ is defined in the same way as a member function in a class. In this case, it would be useful to have an assignment operator that is functional in the `pixelBuffer` class. Overloading the assignment operator would allow for the following declaration in the source code:

```
spriteA = spriteB;
```

What distinguishes the operator from a member function is the keyword operator preceding a C++ provided operator. This would appear in the class header file in the following manner:

```
// overloaded operator '='
pixelBuffer& operator=(const pixelBuffer &p);
```

This is similar to the functionality of the copy constructor but is not the same. The copy constructor provided a means to copy an object during an object's initialization. The assignment operator copies the content of one object to an already initalized object. The code that does this looks like that shown in Listing 9.7.

Listing 9.7. The assignment operator.

```
///////////////////////////////////////////////////////////////////////////

pixelBuffer&    pixelBuffer::operator=(const pixelBuffer &p)
{
   bufSize = p.bufSize;
   bufRowBytes = p.bufRowBytes;
   height = p.height;
   width = p.width;
   if (!pixBuf)
     pixBuf = new char[bufSize];
   memcpy(pixBuf, p.pixBuf, bufSize);

return *this;
}

///////////////////////////////////////////////////////////////////////////
```

The `return *this;` statement in the operator function has a special meaning. The operator explicitly requires a source object (`pixelBuffer p`) as a calling argument. In the `operator=` code, the `pixelBuffer` object `p` is the source object. The object currently being manipulated is the object referenced by the *this pointer. Its useage in functions is typically implicit; that is, data members are referenced as rowBytes and height, rather than this->rowBytes, and this->height. However, on a return call, the keyword, *this, is required in order to tell the compiler that a pointer to the current object is being returned.

The header file now has the fundamental members for describing the pixelBuffer class. The header file includes the default constructor, overloaded constructors, and a copy constructor (for object initialization), and a destructor (for object de-initialization). For programming convenience, an overloaded assignment operator was also included. With these functions in mind, the header file has the format shown in Listing 9.8.

Listing 9.8. The class body of pixelBuffer.

```
/////////////////////////////////////////////////////////////////////////

class pixelBuffer{
    friend class Rect;
  private:
    unsigned int bufSize;          // BYTE size of buffer
    unsigned int bufRowBytes;      // # BYTE's of pixels in each row
    unsigned int width, height;    // logical width and height
    Rect bounds;                   // logical rectangular boundaries

  public:
    unsigned char _far *pixBuf;         // buffer for pixels

    // default constructor
    pixelBuffer();
    // constructor based on buffer size
    pixelBuffer( unsigned int n );
    // constructor based on rect
    pixelBuffer( const Rect& r);
    // copy constructor
    pixelBuffer( const pixelBuffer& );

    // over loaded assignment operator
    pixelBuffer& operator=(const pixelBuffer&);

    // member functions
    void copyPixels( const pixelBuffer&,const Rect&, const Rect& );
    void copyTransPixels( const pixelBuffer&,const Rect&, const Rect& );
    void copyMaskPixels( const pixelBuffer&, const pixelBuffer&,
                                      const Rect&, const Rect&, constRect&);
     // default destructor
    ~pixelBuffer(){};
};

/////////////////////////////////////////////////////////////////////////
```

Designing the Member Functions

The overall goal of the `pixelBuffer` class is to perform byte-level operations on a buffer with graphical content. A set of operations will be required to move pixels from one buffer to another. These operations should include a means of manipulating the contents of the buffers. Operations of this nature are declared in the class body and are called *member functions*.

Member functions are considered to be privileged over ordinary external functions. Ordinary functions have access to only data members declared *public* in the class body.

```
private:
    unsigned int bufSize;           // BYTE size of buffer
    unsigned int bufRowBytes;       // # BYTE's of pixels in each row
    unsigned int width, height;     // logical width and height
    Rect bounds;                    // logical rectangular boundaries

  public:
    unsigned char _far *pixBuf;        // buffer for pixels
```

In this case, only the buffer, `*pixBuf`, is accessible to outside functions. The five other data variables, `bufSize`, `bufRowBytes`, `width`, `height`, and `bounds`, are not accessible. The data members declared *private* are accessible by the class member functions. This form of restricting access is known as *information hiding*. Implementing information hiding in software development is beneficial. For instance, if a bug was found in the `pixelBuffer` class just prior to code release only the member functions of the class itself would have to be rewritten and compiled. The external code would most likely only have to be relinked with the new object code.

The class `pixelBuffer` is designed to handle Sprites in geometrical terms. The underlying functions must accept logical coordinates and internally translate this information into physical locations in the buffers. The programming interface into the member functions will accept these coordinates in terms of an external class, `Rect`.

The `Rect` class is declared in the class body `pixelBuffer` as a *friend*. This technique in C++ gives a nonmember of a class access to its nonpublic members. By making class `Rect` a friend, the members and member functions of class `Rect` are given access to the nonpublic members of class `pixelBuffer`. The class body of `pixelBuffer` has declared `Rect bounds` as a private data member. In order for class `Rect` to access the private `Rect bounds` data members, class `Rect` must be declared a friend to class `pixelBuffer`. Some compilers will not be so strict on this rule and will allow class `Rect` to access the data members of object `bounds`. If this rule is enforced, the compiler will generate an error about accessing a privileged data member not belonging to the class.

A fundamental operation that should exist is one that enables a buffer to copy bytes from one to another. The first operation that comes to mind is the function `memcpy`. The disadvantage to `memcpy` is that its functionality requires linear copies. It would be more beneficial to the graphics programmer to copy in units of rectangles, which are more native to Sprites and bitmaps. This functionality is achieved through the member function `copyPixels()`. The calling arguments to this function are listed here.

```
void copyPixels(const PixelBuffer& srcPixels, const Rect& srcRect, const Rect&
dstRect);
```

The key feature of this member function is that no destination buffer has been included in the calling arguments. The reason for this is that member functions explicitly reference the object that invoked them. This means the destination buffer is a data member of the object that called `copyPixels()`.

The second and third arguments passed to `copyPixels()` are objects of class Rect. This is the interface to the programmer to allow for describing buffers in terms of logical coordinates. For example, a source `pixelBuffer` object called nastyAlien contains a Sprite. The bounds of nastyAlien are 32,32,64,64, as determined from a paint program. The destination object is the `vidScreenBuf` which contains the screen background, VGA mode 13h, 320×200.

The code must translate the logical coordinates into units that the computer can understand. Memory is linear, so a mechanism must be in place to describe rectangular coordinates as chunks of linear memory. The following code converts the srcRect coordinates into units that are meaningful for memory access and pointer arithmetic.

```
    unsigned int srcRowHeight, srcRowBytes;


    srcRowHeight = srcRect.bottom - srcRect.top;    // physical row height of src
    srcRowBytes = srcRect.right - srcRect.left;     // physical row width of src
```

The measurement srcRowHeight contains the physical number of consecutive memory chunks to be copied. The calculation of srcRowBytes has the physical length of each memory chunk. To give copyPixels() some flexibility it must be assumed that the top row of a Sprite could be a non-zero value. In the case of the nasty Alien object, the Sprite is located in a buffer at the following coordinates:

```
srcRect.left = 32
srcRect.top = 32
srcRect.right = 64
srcRect.bottom = 64
```

This means that the function doesn't want to copy any bytes for the first 32 rows of pixels. So the following calculation must represent the starting row of source pixels to copy:

```
srcRowOffset = srcRect.top * srcPixels.bufRowbytes;    // logical top * number of
bytes per row
```

This value will allow copyPixels() to ignore the first n (=srcRowOffset) linear chunks of memory and reference the first row to be copied. Likewise, the destination row offset must be computed. The assumption needs to be made that the source and destination logical coordinates are identical in size but reference the same or different locations. For this example, the destination coordinates of vidScreenBuf have the following values:

```
dstRect.left = 64
dstRect.top = 64
```

```
dstRect.right = 128
dstRect.bottom = 128
```

A similar computation is made for the linear offset in memory of the starting row for the destination buffer.

```
rowOffset = dstRect.top * bufRowBytes;    // destination logical top * destination
bytes per row
```

It is important to note that the srcRowOffset and rowOffset use their own bufRowByte values. This flexibility enables buffers of different sizes to be copied to one another. Simple bounds checking can be enforced by checking the sizes of srcRect and dstRect. In other words, check to make sure the srcRect is less than or equal to the dstRect.

```
if (srcRowHeight != dstRowHeight)
   {
     printf("ERROR: copyPixels() h bounds mismatch\n");
     printf("srcRowHeight[%d]\n", srcRowHeight);
     printf("dstRowHeight[%d]\n", dstRowHeight);
     exit(1);
   }

   if (srcRowBytes != dstRowBytes)
   {
     printf("ERROR: copyPixels() w bounds mismatch\n");
     printf("srcRowBytes[%d]\n", srcRowBytes);
     printf("dstRowBytes[%d]\n", dstRowBytes);
     exit(1);
   }
```

With these values computed, copyPixels() now has enough information to exchange pixels from the source pixelBuffer and destination pixelBuffer objects. The remaining code looks like this:

```
// index for row bytes loop
   for (rowIndex=0; rowIndex < srcRowHeight; rowIndex++) // row index
   {
       _fmemcpy(pixBuf + rowOffset + dstRect.left,
                   srcPixels.pixBuf + srcRowOffset + srcRect.left, bufRowBytes);
       rowOffset += bufRowBytes;         // increment dest row bytes index
       srcRowOffset += srcPixels.bufRowBytes; // increment src row bytes index
   }
```

The source code for copyTransPixels() is nearly identical to copyPixels(). The arguments passed to this function are even identical. The major difference is that copyTransPixels() uses a simple masking technique called transparent pixel copying. This means that certain pixel values are not copied over into the destination buffer. Thus, certain discretionary values in the destination buffer are left unchanged. This operation is significant in copying Sprites to their respective backgrounds.

Where the code differs is in the actual pixel-copying process. Since the copying over to the destination buffer is done selectively, byte by byte, the memcpy() function is no longer useful. In fact, a nested loop is required to walk the linear segments of the source and destination rows for the copy. This is achieved in the following code:

```
for (rowIndex=0; rowIndex < srcRowHeight; rowIndex++) // row index
    {
        // rowbytes index
        for (rowBytesIndex=0; rowBytesIndex < srcRowBytes; rowBytesIndex++)
        {
            pixelByte = srcPixels.pixBuf[srcRowOffset + rowBytesIndex +
srcRect.left];
            if(pixelByte != 0)
                pixBuf[rowOffset + rowBytesIndex + dstRect.left] = pixelByte;

        }
        rowOffset += bufRowBytes;        // increment dest row bytes index
        srcRowOffset += srcPixels.bufRowBytes; // increment src row bytes index
    }
```

The inner loop walks the row in byte increments and examines each byte. If the byte is zero (the transparent byte value), then it is not copied into the destination buffer. This selective copying is a quick and resourceful way to do masking.

A slower and more memory-consuming operation for masking is the `copyMaskPixels()` function. This operation requires three buffers, and three sets of logical coordinates. The operation involves aligning the three buffers and examinng each pixel in the buffer. All pixels are compared against the mask pixel; if the mask pixel is black, the source pixel is drawn to the destination buffer. If the mask pixel is white, the source pixel is skipped, and the destination buffer pixel is left unchanged. This technique is commonly used in graphical environments such as color QuickDraw using pointers to `CGrafPort`, `PixMaps`, or `GWorlds` on the Macintosh, and in a similar fashion to pixmaps on X Window. The masks in these environments are considered to be pixmaps of 1 bit in depth, called bitmaps. A comparable masking scheme is included in the `pixelBuffer` class for operating-system portability.

The functionality of `copyMaskPixels()` is very similar to `copyPixels()`. However, additional computations must be made to align the mask buffer.

```
maskRowOffset = maskRect.top * maskPixels.bufRowBytes;
```

In a similar fashion, bounds checking must be made to ensure that all buffers are attempting to use regions of the same size. When this criteria is met, the function can invoke the masking operation. The masking involved is byte by byte, so `memcpy()` cannot be used. Just as `copyTransPixels()` uses an inner loop for each row, so does `copyMaskPixels()`. The code itself is not so easy to follow, especially with the nested pointer arithmetic involved. The pseudocode looks like this:

```
        for (rowBytesIndex=0; rowBytesIndex<srcRowBytes; rowBytesIndex++) //
rowbytes index
        {
            pixBuf =  ( maskPixels.pixBuf & pixBuf ) ¦ srcPixels.pixBuf;
        }
```

The actual code, with the pointer indexes in place, is as follows:

```
for (rowIndex=0; rowIndex < srcRowHeight; rowIndex++) // row index
   {

     for (rowBytesIndex=0; rowBytesIndex<srcRowBytes; rowBytesIndex++) //
rowbytes index
       {
         pixBuf[dstRowOffset+dstRect.left+rowBytesIndex] =
              ( maskPixels.pixBuf[maskRowOffset + rowBytesIndex + maskRect.left]
            & pixBuf[dstRowOffset+dstRect.left+rowBytesIndex] )
                ¦ srcPixels.pixBuf[srcRowOffset + rowBytesIndex + srcRect.left];
       }
       dstRowOffset += bufRowBytes;       // increment src row bytes index
       srcRowOffset += srcPixels.bufRowBytes;
       maskRowOffset += maskPixels.bufRowBytes;
   }
```

The operations provided by class `pixelBuffer` are simple; the critical reasoning is machine-independent code. Hobbyists rarely have the luxury of developing code on platforms other than what is available at home. Industry professionals, on the other hand, are often employed on a contractual basis for one project only. A large game publisher may have deep pockets and offer Silicon Graphics Iris systems with software emulators as the game-design platform. At the other extreme (which is all too common in the industry) is the small game-development shop that is hanging on by a thread, using Apple Quadras with MPW as its development platform. If the nomadic professional is prepared for these situations, his or her focus can shift from rewriting old code for the new platform to developing video and keyboard I/O as part of an evolving portable software library.

Building a Real Mode `pixelBuffer` Class Driver

The `pixelBuffer` class is simple and offers no mechanism to write an object's buffer, `pixBuf`, to the screen. Writing to devices, such as the screen, is *machine dependent*, and for this reason it is not included in the `pixelBuffer` class. C++ offers the flexibility for external functions to access data members of an object. (Recall the earlier discussion on information hiding.) The data member, `pixBuf`, is declared *public* so that functions which are not members of the `pixelBuffer` class may access the pixels in memory. This can be achieved in the following fashion:

```
#include "pixbuf.hpp"

    :
void foo( const pixelBuffer &p)         // external function foo with a pixelBuffer
argument
```

To write the pixels to the video screen in Real Mode, a few tools are necessary. For instance, the pixels in the `pixelBuffer` object require 320×200 256-color display (VGA mode 13h). The default DOS video mode is 03h, an 80×25 text display. A software tool is required to change video modes in order to display the pixels. Simply writing the pixels to video memory will not display them on the screen.

The Intel processors operating in Real Mode use INT (interrupt) services to perform input and output. Services that require displaying information on the screen use INT 10h. The video mode can be switched in assembly language by setting register AH to 00h, which is the interrupt function for set mode. The desired video mode is placed in register AL. The following example sets the video mode to 320×200 pixels, VGA mode 13h:

```
mov    ah,00    ; function set video mode
mov    al,13h   ; request 320 x 200, VGA mode 13h
int    10h      ; call interrupt
```

The three major DOS compiler vendors—Borland, Microsoft, and Watcom—provide access to interrupts via an int86() function call. (Check manual or online help for function name and specifics.) This is the preferred method of calling interrupts from ANSI C or C++ rather than using inline assembly calls. Various structures are provided for the corresponding register sizes.

```
union REGS
    struct WORDREGS x;  // ax - dx registers
    struct BYTEREGS h; // al,ah - dl,dh registers
};

struct WORDREGS
{
    unsigned int AX, BX, CX, DX, SI, DI, CFLAG;
};

struct BYTEREGS
{
    unsigned char AL, AH, BL, BH, CL, CH, DL, DH;
};
```

Using the int86() style function call, the change video-mode function can be written as shown in Listing 9.9.

Listing 9.9. Changing the video mode in 8086 Mode.

```
///////////////////////////////////////////////////////////////////////

void setVideoMode( int xmode)
{   union REGS regs;

  regs.x.ax = xmode;
  int86( 0x10, &regs, &regs);
}

///////////////////////////////////////////////////////////////////////
```

Function setVideoMode() requires a video-mode setting as its calling argument. The usage of the compiler's built-in register structs provides code readability with no loss of performance. This simple function enables the program to toggle video modes. All that is required now is a function to write the pixelBuffer object contents to the video screen.

Memory in Real Mode is accessed by segments and offsets. The memory for VGA mode 13h starts at segment A000, with a maximum offset at 64,000 bytes (320 pixels per row × 200 rows). In assembly language, the entire screen can be filled with byte value 12ch, with the following code:

```
mov     ax, 0a000h   ; request segment A000
    mov     es,ax        ;       es = A000
    mov     ax,0         ; start at offset 0000
    mov     di,ax        ;   di = 0000

    mov     ax,12ch      ; byte value to write
    mov     cx,64000     ; loop all 64000 byte locations
vLoop:
    mov     es:[di],al   ;  write the byte value
    inc     di           ;     ; increment to next offset
    loop    vLoop        ; loop if < 64000
```

Novice programmers with experience in assembly tend to drop into inline assembly in order to code video drivers. This is okay for testing and experimenting, but rarely does inline assembly code provide any kind of optimization benefits. In some cases, inline assembly calls may be inferior to using ANSI C and C++ pointers to video memory.

The contents of a `pixelBuffer` object can be easily written to the screen using pointers. MS-DOS compilers provide mechanisms for accessing segmented memory, a common function that is used is `MK_FP()` (MaKe Far Pointer).

```
void far * MK_FP( unsigned segment, unsigned offset );
```

This function accepts the segment and offset of the location in memory that is to be referenced. A pointer can be initialized to VGA memory using this function call. Particular attention should be paid to the fact that far pointers are used in Real Mode to access video memory. Far pointers indicate that code and data segments are separate. This means that the compiler must be instructed to use a LARGE memory model. Compilers don't always check pointer usage against memory models, the code will compile and link, but it will execute with unexpected results.

A simple function, called `writeVideo()`, takes a `pixelBuffer` object (320×200) as its argument and writes it to the screen. This is what will be used in Real Mode for screen updates. The function loops through all 200 rows of the offscreen object and writes it to the corresponding video memory. In Listing 9.10, note the usage of `MK_FP()` to assign the pointer `pVideoMem` the segment and offset of VGA memory.

Listing 9.10. Writing an off-screen buffer to VGA memory using 8086 Real Mode.

```
/////////////////////////////////////////////////////////////////////////////

void writeVideo( pixelBuffer &p)
{
    unsigned char _far *pVideoMem;
    unsigned int rowIndex,  offset;
```

```
        rowIndex = offset = 0;

        // use MK_FP macro to form far pointer to video
        pVideoMem = (unsigned char _far*)MK_FP(0xA000,0);

        // loop 200 rows of video mode 13h
        for (rowIndex=0;rowIndex<200;rowIndex++)
        {
            // copy the pixel buffer to the logical row
            _fmemcpy(pVideoMem + offset, p.pixBuf + offset, 320);

            // increment to the next row, 320 pixels per row
            offset += 320;
        }
}

/////////////////////////////////////////////////////////////////////////////
```

The basic functionality is now in place to start playing with some pixel objects. The only operation that is really missing is a means to read pixels in from a file. There is a broad spectrum of file formats to choose from. To keep the pixelBuffer class as simple and portable as possible, a design decision was made to make file-format reading external to the pixelBuffer class. Since the data member pixBuf is public, external functions can write to the pixelBuffer object as well. Included with this source is a tool to read Deluxe Paint .LBM and .BBM files. Computer artists for video games are fond of the Amiga, and having a tool available to read Deluxe Paint files is very handy. The lbm class utility was put together with assistance from Electronic Arts and from invaluable information provided by a contributing author to the shareware ACK3D library, Jaimi McEntire. Listing 9.11 is the complete driver for the pixelBuffer class in Real Mode operation.

Listing 9.11. The 8086 Real Mode pixelBuffer class driver (PBDRVR.CPP).

```
// I N C L U D E S ///////////////////////////////////////////////////////////

#include <stdio.h>
#include <conio.h>
#include <string.h>

#include "gks.hpp"
#include "iff.hpp"
#include "pixbuf.hpp"
#include "vtools.hpp"

#ifdef __WATCOMC__
#define _getch getch
#endif

// MAIN ///////////////////////////////////////////////////////////////////////

void main()
{
```

continues

Listing 9.11. continued

```
// Rect objects
Rect offScreenRect;      // Rect describing the offscreen pixelBuffer object
Rect rUman7;             // Rect for the sprite
Rect dstRect;            // Rect for destination of sprite

// Rect objects initializations
offScreenRect.setRect(0,0,320,200);    // initialize bounds of offscreen object
rUman7.setRect(0,0,82,100);            // initialize bounds of sprite object
dstRect.setRect(108,50,190,150);

// pixelBuffer obects
pixelBuffer offScreenPix( offScreenRect );// offscreen pixelBuffer object
pixelBuffer uman7Pix( rUman7 );           // sprite pixelBuffer object

// lbm objects
lbm offScreenLBM;        // lbm object for background lbm file
lbm uman7BBM;            // lbm object for sprite bbm file

// lbm object IFF file reader
offScreenLBM.unPacker("scene.lbm", offScreenPix);  // unpack offscreen pixels
uman7BBM.unPacker("uman7.bbm", uman7Pix);   // unpack sprite pixels

uman7BBM.freePalette();

// blit sprite object pixels to offscreen object pixels
offScreenPix.copyTransPixels(uman7Pix, rUman7, dstRect);


setVideoMode( 0x13 );    // set video mode to VGA mode 13h

setVGAPalette((char *)offScreenLBM.palette);  // set 256 color palette from lbm

waitRetrace();                    // wait for a retrace

writeVideo( offScreenPix );  // write the objects to video

_getch();
setVideoMode( 0x03 );    // set the video mode to text

printf("done\n");        // done
}
```

Using the `pixelBuffer` Class with Phar Lap's 286 | DOS-Extender

The implementation of the `pixelBuffer` class in Real Mode was relatively simple. Porting the code over to Phar Lap's 286 | DOS-Extender SDK (Software Development Kit) will be equally as simple because the `pixelBuffer` class was designed to be machine independent. In fact, the same source files used in the Real Mode example will be used for this example, excluding the class-driver source file itself and the video tools source. Remember a point made earlier, that all machine-dependent services, such as video, should be kept external of the class. This is true here, where video services rely upon calls to Phar Lap's SDK for handling interrupts and video memory in 286 Protected Mode.

A new vtools source file is required for using the pixelBuffer class in 286 Protected Mode. The Real Mode vtools source will not work, because the Phar Lap 286 | DOS-Extender is an operating system executing under DOS. The new pixelBuffer class driver will be executing in Protected Mode and requesting services from the Phar Lap 286 | DOS-Extender. Phar Lap's SDK provides an API (Application Programming Interface) to access these services.

To change the video mode, a request must be made via the DOS extender, which in turn knows how to handle the interrupt. (See Listing 9.12.) Changing video modes on the PC, using INT 10h, is a very common task, and it is supported by Phar Lap's API. The code in 286 Protected Mode has the same look and feel as its Real Mode counterpart, with a few subtle differences.

Listing 9.12. Changing the video mode using the Phar Lap 286 | DOS-Extender SDK.

```
/////////////////////////////////////////////////////////////////////////////
void setVideoMode( unsigned int videoMode )
{
   REGS16 regs;

   memset( &regs, 0, sizeof regs );
   regs.ax = videoMode;
   DosRealIntr(0x10,&regs,0,0);
}

/////////////////////////////////////////////////////////////////////////////
```

The 286 | DOS-Extender obviously uses its own struct for passing arguments to and from registers. This structure is provided by the 286 | DOS-Extender SDK and looks like the following:

```
struct REGS16
{
    unsigned short es, ds;
    unsigned short di, si, bp, sp, bx, dx, cx, ax;
    unsigned short ip, cs, flags;
};
```

The memset() call is important, and if it is not supplied, the code definitely will produce unexpected results and possibly a GP fault. The only register that is set is the AX, which supplies function and mode to the INT 10h request. The Real Mode int86() function is replaced by the SDKs call, DosRealIntr(), which is the Protected Mode function to handle Real Mode interrupts.

Memory usage in Protected Mode is different then that of Real Mode. Using the Real Mode segment and offset scheme, location A000:0000 is video memory. In Protected Mode, recall the following:

```
A000 = 1010 0000 0000 0000
index = 1010 0000 0000 0        (1400h)
TI = 0                                ( GDT )
RPL = 00                          (ring 0)
```

The pointer A000:0000 is a selector indexing a descriptor, 1400h, in a global descriptor table, and it has a privilege of 0. Any attempt by an application to write to the protected location in the GDT would generate a GP fault and terminate the program.

The DOS Extender API provides access to absolute video addresses through the function call DosMapRealSeg(). In order to use the absolute location A0000h as video memory a function must be provided in the vtools source to allow addressing to this location. This looks like the code shown in Listing 9.13.

Listing 9.13. Initializing a selector to access video using the Phar Lap 286 Protected Mode SDK.

```
///////////////////////////////////////////////////////////////////////////

char _far *getVideoBuffer( unsigned short videoSegment, SEL selector )
{
  REGS16 regs;

  regs.es = videoSegment;
  regs.di = 0;
  regs.ax = 0x13;
  if(DosMapRealSeg(regs.es, (long) regs.di + 64400, &selector)!=0)
  {
    printf("Error: DosMapRealSeg\n");
    exit(0);
  }
  return (char _far *) MAKEP(selector, regs.di);
}

///////////////////////////////////////////////////////////////////////////
```

The function getVideoBuffer() requires a segment address, A000, and a selector, initialized to zero, as its calling arguments. The function uses Phar Lap's REGS16 structure for assigning the registers their corresponding values. The value in regs.es is set to the video segment desired. The offset index, in regs.di, is set to 0. The value set in regs.ax is the video mode (this is strictly informative and does not set the video mode). After the respective fields in the REGS16 structure are supplied, they are passed as arguments to DosMapRealSeg(). The second argument passed to DosMapRealSeg is the size of memory to be mapped. In this case, VGA mode 13h is 320×200 pixels, so 64,000 bytes are required (regs.di + 64,000). The final argument is a pointer to the selector that is returned. The selector is then passed to a macro function provided by the SDK,

MAKEP(). Macro function MAKEP() is complementary to MK_FP(), except it constructs a far pointer from a selector and an offset. For more details on this function, examine the PHAPI.H file.

The completion of the vtools function getVideoBuffer() returns a pointer to the mapped video segment. This is all the information that is required in order to write to the video memory. The function write286PVideo() is very close to the Real Mode function writeVideo(), except for the additional argument for the mapped video-segment pointer. (See Listing 9.14.)

Listing 9.14. Writing a `pixelBuffer` object to 286 Protect Mode video memory.

```
////////////////////////////////////////////////////////////////////////

void write286PVideo( pixelBuffer &p, char *pVideoBuf )
{
  unsigned int rowIndex, pixelIndex, offset;

  rowIndex = pixelIndex = offset = 0;  // initialize indices

  // loop the 200 rows of video mode 13h
  for (rowIndex = 0; rowIndex < 200; rowIndex++)
  {
    // walk the rows and copy byte by byte
    for (pixelIndex = 0; pixelIndex < 320; pixelIndex++)
      pVideoBuf[offset + pixelIndex] = p.pixBuf[offset + pixelIndex];

        // go to the next row
    offset += 320;
  }
}


////////////////////////////////////////////////////////////////////////
```

The implementation of the 286 | DOS-Extender pixelBuffer class driver is rather similar to the Real Mode driver source code. The source code for the .LBM reader is unaltered as well. This is because the work of managing memory is being handled by the compiler, the linker, and the DOS extender. All memory allocations and deallocations were achieved through the C++ new and delete operators. This allowed the code to port over without alteration. The listing for PB286DVR.CPP is shown in Listing 9.15.

Listing 9.15. The `pixelBuffer` class driver using the 286 DOS | Extender SDK (PB286DVR.CPP).

```
// I N C L U D E S ///////////////////////////////////////////////////////

#include <stdio.h>
#include <conio.h>
#include <string.h>

#include "gks.hpp"
#include "iff.hpp"
#include "pixbuf.hpp"
#include "vtools.hpp"
```

continues

Listing 9.15. continued

```
#ifdef __WATCOMC __
#define _getch getch
#endif

// MAIN ////////////////////////////////////////////////////////////////////

void main()
{
    char _far *videoBuffer;         // pointer to mapped video buffer segment
    SEL vidSegMapSelector = 0;      // selector indexing mapped video segment


    // Rect objects
    Rect offScreenRect;     // Rect describing the offscreen pixelBuffer object
    Rect rUman7, rDst7;

    // Rect objects initializations
    offScreenRect.setRect(0,0,320,200);   // initialize bounds of offscreen object
    rUman7.setRect(0,0,82,100);
    rDst7.setRect(108,50,190,150);

    // pixelBuffer obects
    pixelBuffer offScreenPix( offScreenRect );// offscreen pixelBuffer object
    pixelBuffer uman7Pix( rUman7 );

    // lbm objects
    lbm offScreenLBM;       // lbm object for background lbm file
    lbm uman7BBM;

    // lbm object IFF file reader
    offScreenLBM.unPacker("scene.lbm", offScreenPix);   // unpack offscreen pixels
    uman7BBM.unPacker("uman7.bbm", uman7Pix);   // unpack sprite pixels
    uman7BBM.freePalette();

    printf("done reading IFFs\n");


    // blit sprite object pixels to offscreen object pixels
    offScreenPix.copyTransPixels(uman7Pix, rUman7, rDst7);

    // request pointer to real mode mapped video segment
    videoBuffer = getVideoBuffer(0xA000,vidSegMapSelector);

    setVideoMode( 0x13 );   // set video mode to VGA mode 13h

    setVGAPalette((char *)offScreenLBM.palette);   // set 256 color palette from lbm
    waitRetrace();              // wait for a retrace

    // write pixel buffer to real mode mapped segment
    write286PVideo( offScreenPix, videoBuffer );

    _getch();
    setVideoMode( 0x03 );   // set the video mode to text
```

```
    printf("done\n");       // done
}
```

//

Using Phar Lap's SDK with Windows Development Tools

In recent years, the major software development vendors have moved away from tedious command-line compiling and linking to a rich, user-friendly Microsoft Windows environment. Phar Lap's SDK is a very nice "bolt-on" to the Windows compilers. The following discussion covers configuring the Microsoft Visual Workbench to compile and link 286 | DOS-Extender executables. The configuration of other Windows-based environments is similar, but this is covered to clarify any confusion that may arise.

To build the pixelBuffer class and its driver, a new project must be created. This is accomplished in Visual Workbench by selecting New from the Project menu. A New Project dialog box will appear on the screen. (See Figure 9.14.)

Figure 9.14.
Creating a New Project in Visual C++ 1.51.

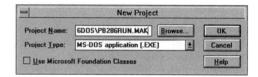

1. Select the Browse button to locate the drive and the directory where the project will be built
2. Type the project name, PB286RUN.MAK, into the Project Name box
3. Select the Project Type box, use the pull-down list and select MS-DOS application (.EXE)
4. Click OK to close the New Project dialog box

When the New Project Dialog box closes, the Edit dialog box shown in Figure 9.15 appears:

1. Use the Add button to add the required source code
2. Select the List of File Type pull-down list, and scroll down to the selection, Definition (*.DEF)

   Add the file PB286RUN.DEF
3. Close the Edit dialog box

Figure 9.15.
The project Edit window in Visual C++.

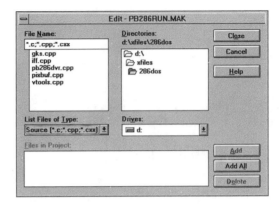

The .DEF file, PB286RUN.DEF (shown in Listing 9.16), needs to be included as a source file in the project for users compiling from Visual Workbench:

Listing 9.16. The definition file for compiling the class driver (PB286DVR.DEF).

```
name 'pb286dvr'
protmode
exetype os2
stub 'gorun286'
```

A similar file is required for Borland compilers. (Consult the 286 | DOS-Extender SDK manual for Borland C++ users.)

The compiler must be configured to handle large memory models. This is primarily because far pointers are used in the body of the code. The compiler can be configured in the following manner from Visual Workbench for Visual C++. (See Figure 9.16.)

Figure 9.16.
An example of selected compiler options for the Phar Lap 286 |DOS-Extender SDK in Visual C++.

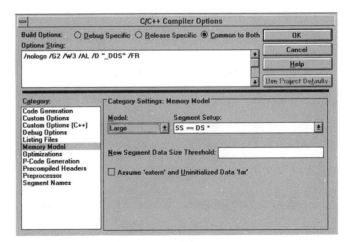

1. Pull down the Options menu from the Visual Workbench menu bar and select Project. The Project Options dialog box will appear.

2. Select the Release Specific radio button.

3. Select the Compiler button for the C/C++ Compiler Options dialog to appear.

4. Select Memory Model from the Category Options box. Category Settings For Memory Model will become active.

5. Pull down the Model Options in Category Settings For Memory Model. Select the Large memory model for the compiler.

6. Select the OK button to close the C/C++ Compiler Options dialog.

The linker must now be configured to use the Phar Lap linker and options for the 286 | DOS-Extender SDK. (See Figure 9.17.) This can be edited in the following manner:

Figure 9.17.
The Linker Options window showing the additions required for the 286 | DOS-Extender SDK.

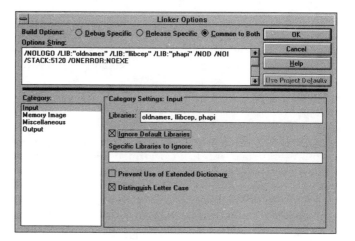

1. Select the Linker from the Project Options menu dialog box

2. Edit the libraries to `oldnames`, `llibcep`, `phapi`

3. Select the Ignore Default Libraries box

The compiler and linker are now configured for the Phar Lap SDK. A final step is required to tell the compiler where the libraries and include files are located. (See Figure 9.18.)

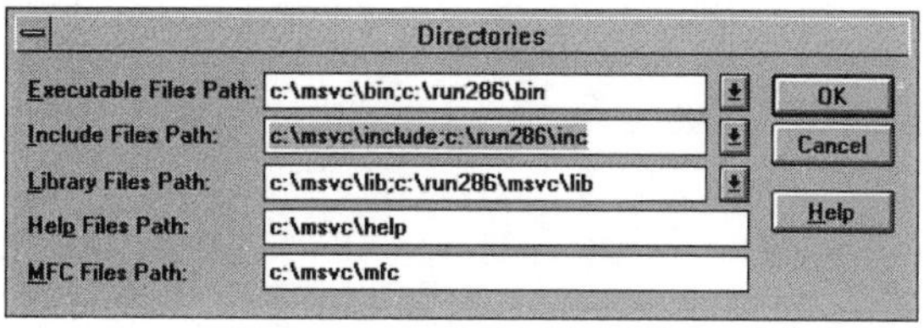

Figure 9.18.
Setting the paths for Phar Lap's binaries, includes, and libraries using the Directories window.

A little effort is required up front before using the 286 | DOS-Extender SDK. After the SDK install disks are loaded, the compiler-specific libraries must be loaded out. Some time should be spent flipping through the compiler guides and playing with the examples to get a feel for using the SDK. Once it is properly installed, it is rather easy to use and fun to play with. Programmers with access to Internet e-mail will find Phar Lap's tech support indispensable and quick to respond.

The Blinker Linker for 286 DOS Protected Mode Programming

The Blinker overlay and Protected Mode linker is another product for 286 | DOS-Extender development. Like Phar Lap, Blink*inc* has had a foothold in this market for some time as well. Their trademark poster depicts the skeletal remains of a programmer who died waiting for his linker to finish. In the late 1980s, it was common for programmers in the Silicon Valley to have this pinned up in their cubicles. For those youngsters who haven't the foggiest idea of what I'm talking about, don't worry. Us old timers always tend to drift off and reminisce about the good old days.

The Blinker linker is an advance linker that's capable of generating overlays and DOS extender executables. An overlay is a technique used in Real Mode programming wherein a small core program executes within the 640KB memory and stays resident, while it swaps memory out for other executables in extended memory. This code swapping is really complex, and DOS extenders provide a better solution to the problem.

The preparations of the `pixelBuffer` class are just as simple as with the Phar Lap 286 | DOS-Extender SDK. Since all the memory allocation calls for the buffers are handled by C++, nothing needs to be modified in class source code. However, the vtools must be rewritten to use the Blinker libraries for servicing interrupts and handling the video buffers.

As in the previous 286 Protected Mode example, a method must be provided in a library to generate Real Mode interrupts. The Blinker include file, BLX286.H, provides a structure, REGS16, for modifying individual registers. This structure must be initialized with zero values using the `memset()` routine. The library call to generate an interrupt is `DosRealIntr()`. The routine parameters are also identical to the previous 286 Protected Mode example using the Phar Lap 286 | DOS-Extender SDK. The source code for vtools come as no surprise, and it looks identical to the previous `setVideoMode()` used. (See Listing 9.17.)

Listing 9.17. Setting the video mode using the Blinker 3.0 286 Protected Mode Libraries.

```
////////////////////////////////////////////////////////////////////////////
void setVideoMode( unsigned int videoMode )
{
   REGS16 regs;
```

```
    memset(&regs,0,sizeof(REGS16));
    regs.ax = videoMode;
    DosRealIntr(0x10, &regs, 0L, 0);
}
```

///

The setVideoMode() routine provides a mechanism to toggle between video modes in 286 Protected Mode. The vtools routine now needs a function to address Real Mode video memory from Protected Mode. The library call, DosMapRealSeg(), is provided by the Blinker to convert a Real Mode pointer into a Protected Mode selector. A routine needs to be added to vtools to construct such a pointer for referencing video memory. This function is called getVideoBuffer() and looks like that which is shown in Listing 9.18.

Listing 9.18. Initializng a selector to reference video memory using the Blinker 3.0 libraries.

///

```
unsigned char *getVideoBuffer()
{
  USHORT pVidMem;    // selector to video memory

  DosMapRealSeg(vidBaseAddr, 64000, &pVidMem);
  return (unsigned char *)MK_FP(pVidMem,0);
}
```

///

The Blinker library routine DosMapRealSeg takes as its arguments the Real Mode video-memory base-segment address, the buffer size of video memory, and a selector. Upon completion of the call, the selector to the video memory will be in the variable pVidMem. This value is then returned as far pointer at the completion of the getVideoBuffer() routine.

Writing to video memory is just as simple as in the Real Mode example. The source code is strikingly familiar, with the exception of the routine name being changed. (See Listing 9.19.)

Listing 9.19. The Blinker 3.0 version of writing the pixelBuffer class to 286 protected memory.

///

```
void writeBlinkerVideo( pixelBuffer &p, unsigned char *pVideoBuf )
{
  unsigned int row, offset;

  row = offset = 0;  // initialize indices

  // loop the 200 rows of video mode 13h
  offset = 0;
```

continues

Listing 9.19. continued

```
for (row=0; row<200; row++)
{
  memcpy(pVideoBuf + offset, p.pixBuf + offset, 320);
  offset += 320;
}
}
```

///

The source code for the `pixelBuffer` class driver using the Blinker linker and libraries is also astonishingly similar to the Real Mode example. Here, the exceptions are the calls to convert a pointer to reference Protected Mode video memory. The call to `writeBlinkerVideo()` is different too, because the video pointer must be passed to this routine to reference video memory. The selector initialization could have easily appeared in the `writeBlinkerVideo()` routine, but this would require initializing the selector each time the call to `writeBinkerVideo()` is made. This is senseless and only needs to be initialized once.

The source code for the Blinker 286 Protected Mode `pixelBuffer` driver looks like that which is shown in Listing 9.20.

Listing 9.20. The `pixelBuffer` class driver using the Blinker 3.0 libraries (PBBLNKR.CPP).

```
// I N C L U D E S /////////////////////////////////////////////////////////

#include <stdio.h>
#include <conio.h>
#include <string.h>

#include "gks.hpp"
#include "iff.hpp"
#include "pixbuf.hpp"
#include "vtools.hpp"

// MAIN //////////////////////////////////////////////////////////////////////

void main()
{
    unsigned char *pv;      // video memory pointer

    // Rect objects
    Rect offScreenRect;     // Rect describing the offscreen pixelBuffer object
    Rect rUman7;            // Rect for the sprite
    Rect dstRect;           // Rect for destination of sprite

    // Rect objects initializations
    offScreenRect.setRect(0,0,320,200);   // initialize bounds of offscreen object
    rUman7.setRect(0,0,82,100);           // initialize bounds of sprite object
    dstRect.setRect(108,50,190,150);

    // pixelBuffer obects
    pixelBuffer offScreenPix( offScreenRect );// offscreen pixelBuffer object
    pixelBuffer uman7Pix( rUman7 );           // sprite pixelBuffer object
```

```
    // lbm objects
    lbm offScreenLBM;          // lbm object for background lbm file
    lbm uman7BBM;              // lbm object for sprite bbm file

    // lbm object IFF file reader
    offScreenLBM.unPacker("scene.lbm", offScreenPix);  // unpack offscreen pixels
    uman7BBM.unPacker("uman7.bbm", uman7Pix);    // unpack sprite pixels

    // blit sprite object pixels to offscreen object pixels
    offScreenPix.copyTransPixels(uman7Pix, rUman7, dstRect);

    pv = getVideoBuffer();  // initialize pointer to video memory

    setVideoMode( 0x13 );   // set video mode to VGA mode 13h

    setVGAPalette(offScreenLBM.palette);  // set 256 color palette from lbm

    waitRetrace();

    writeBlinkerVideo( offScreenPix, pv );  // write the objects to video

    _getch();
    setVideoMode( 0x03 );   // set the video mode to text

    printf("done\n");       // done
}
```

The Blinker linker is primarily a command-line style linker and requires simple scripts to build executables. An example of a make file for this project is listed here:

```
cl -c -AL test.cpp gks.cpp pixbuf.cpp iff.cpp vtools.cpp
blinker @pbblnk
```

The *cl* command is the command-line compiler for Microsoft Visual C++ 1.5. The -c option tells the compiler to compile only and not to link. The program linking is handled by invoking blinker.exe, which requires a script file as its calling argument. The Blinker linker expects a script file PBBLNK.LNK. Note the @test definition. (See Listing 9.21.)

> The name of the file containing the link script is the name of the executable followed by the file extension .LNK.

Listing 9.21. The script file for linking using the Blinker 3.0 linker.

```
# PBBLNK.LNK             script for linking pixelBuffer class driver
BLINKER EXECUTABLE EXTENDED  # build a 286 protected mode program
FILE test                                          # source files
FILE gks
FILE pixbuf
FILE iff
```

continues

Listing 9.21. continued

```
FILE vtools
SEARCH BLXMVC10                            # search blinker directories for
Microsoft Visual C++ library
LIB LLIBCE                                            # use Microsoft Visual C++
Library llibce
```

The script file states BLINKER EXECUTABLE EXTENDED. The program undergoing the build is a 286 DOS Protected Mode program. Notice that source files are added to the linkage process by using a reserved word, FILE, followed by the object filename. The library files used by the Blinker linker are compiler-specific. The proper library to be used by the Blinker is requested by SEARCH BLXMVC10 if the Microsoft Visual C++ compiler is being used. The setting LIB LLIBCE tells the Blinker linker to use the Microsoft Visual C++ library routines. This library is needed for the non-Blinker routines, such as _outp().

The Blinker linker and libraries are fairly easy to use. Developers writing games for a network might want to take this package into consideration. The overlays and extended memory enable code to execute out above the 640KB limit. This lower memory area is commonly used up by network drivers and protocol stacks.

Technical support for the 286 Blinker is expensive after the first 90 days of free support. $100 per hour is a fairly large chunk of change for the average home hobbyist. But as a helpful hint, Blink*inc* never enforced this fee when tech support calls were placed to them. Programmers take note that software developed with the Blinker linker is royalty free!

Phar Lap's TNT DOS-Extender SDK

Phar Lap's TNT 7.0 DOS-Extender SDK is a really nice compiler bolt-on to complement any DOS or NT development environment. Phar Lap requires at least a 386 to develop code, but to utilize this package to its fullest, a 486 running NT is recommended. The TNT SDK provides a suite of tools to access DOS calls and BIOS interrupts, as well as NT Win 32 API functionality. To become moderately proficient in the SDK and its usage requires several evenings of reading (removal of manual shrink wrap is required) and playing. A night or two alone may be required just to configure the compiler and linker properly. This is not a downfall; in fact, the TNT SDK package snaps rather nicely into the Visual C++ 2.0 and Watcom 10.0 development environments.

Using TNT DOS-Extender allows segments up to 4GB in size. The DOS-Extender maintains the LDT and GDT. The GDT is used by the extender to map its own segments and the LDT maps the application segments. Using the privilege mechanism, all applications are unprivileged by default.

Porting code to the 32-bit environment requires a few considerations. For instance, in Real Mode, the large memory model is used for compiling and linking. This means that the size of the code is allowed to exceed the size of the segment. In Real Mode, code typically exceeds the 64KB segment size; however, in Protected Mode, a segment can be as large as 4GB.

> The TNT SDK links Protected Mode applications with the code, data, and stack segments in a single program segment.

To enable the `pixbuf` code to run under the TNT DOS-Extender, a few minor changes must be made to the buffer declarations and allocation calls. Since the SDK fully supports the common C library function calls, the `malloc` and `new` operators may be used. Under the Real Mode version of `pixbuf` code, the following declaration is made in the class body:

```
public:
    unsigned char _far *pixBuf;          // buffer for pixels
```

The keyword `_far` indicates the pointer is a 32-bit address that can reference data in any segment. This is quite useful in Real Mode; however, in Protected Mode, code and data are in the same segment.

```
public:
    unsigned char *pixBuf;           // buffer for pixels
```

Similar modifications should be made to the `new` operator calls. Recall that in Real Mode, the `_far` keyword was required in the `new` operator call.

```
pixBuf = new unsigned char _far[bufSize]; // new buffer
```

The `new` operator call in the 32-bit environment produces the same result.

```
pixBuf = new unsigned char[bufSize]; // new buffer
```

The contrast in near pointer for Real Mode and Protected Mode is interesting. The near pointer in Real Mode only enables a pointer to reference data within a 64KB segment. Under Protected Mode, the pointer (32-bit pointer) may reference data anywhere within a segment up to 4GB in size. This allows several graphics buffers of 64KB (VGA mode 13h) to be allocated in a single Protected Mode segment. The limitation would actually be based on the physical limitations of the machine memory itself.

Access to BIOS interrupts is interesting as well. Remember that most interrupt services for DOS are provided by INT 21h. The TNT DOS-Extender is compatible with DOS, Windows, and Windows NT. Considerations for development environments must be made up front for the choice of interrupt-service access. For instance, the Visual C++ 1.51 and Watcom 10.0 compilers running under Windows provide libraries for DOS interrupts in header files DOS.H and INT86.H respectively.

The standard DOS method for accessing interrupts from TNT is

```
#include <dos.h>
#include <pldos32.h>    // union _REGS

union _REGS regs;

  regs.x.ax = 0;   // select function 00h, program terminate
  _int86( 0x21, &regs, &regs);  // C library function to call DOS interrupt
```

Using interrupts from the Visual C++ 2.0 environment running under Windows NT provides no libraries for DOS interrupt access. In fact, an MS-DOS executable is not an available selection for setting up the project. The application is considered to be a Win32 console application, and DOS interrupt access is only provided by the TNT SDK. Since the include file DOS.H is not available in Visual C++ 2.0, the C library call _int86() is not available. The TNT SDK provides a C library call for both DOS (DosStyle) and NT (NtStyle) console applications.

```
#include <pldos32.h> // structure SWI_REGS and function _dx_real_int()

SWI_REGS regs;

  memset(&regs, 0, sizeof(regs));  // initialize struct with zeros
  regs.eax = 0; // select function 00h, program terminate
  _dx_real_int(0x21, &regs);
```

This solution provides full functionality for both DosStyle and NtStyle applications. For programmers who are strictly command-line or Windows-environment developers, this isn't a big issue. However, 32-bit DOS applications developed from Windows NT using Visual C++ 2.0 need to employ this mechanism. The Watcom 10.0 development system running under NT does provide full DOS capabilities, and the union _REGS scheme will work. However, employing the SWI_REGS structure will provide cross-compiler compatibility in the NT environment. It is important to distinguish that the union REGS structure is compatible only with TNT DosStyle applications, while the structure SWI_REGS is compatible on both DosStyle and NtStyle applications. Visual C++ 2.0 does not support any DOS functionality in its libraries. Access to registers and interrupts is achieved through calls to the Phar Lap TNT SDK. The SWI REGS structure allows an NtStyle application to make interrupt and register calls. This application can then be ported over as a 32-bit DOS application by rebinding the NtStyle application into a DosStyle application.

With a mechanism available to issue interrupts, a Protected Mode tool can be written to set the video mode. Using the TNT SDK function call, _dx_real_int(), the code looks like that which is shown in Listing 9.22.

Listing 9.22. Setting video modes in 386 Protected Mode using Phar Lap's TNT 7.0 SDK.

```
//////////////////////////////////////////////////////////////////////

void setVideoMode( int xmode)
{
 SWI_REGS regs;
```

```
    memset(&regs, 0, sizeof(regs));
    regs.eax = xmode;
    _dx_real_int(0x10, &regs);
}
```

//

Since toggling the video mode is not native to NtStyle applications, this mode of operation is referred to as *hybrid* in the Phar Lap TNT DOS-Extender Reference Manual. Applications developed in the NT environment must use the Phar Lap TNT rebind utility.

After our discussion of near memory pointers, it's time to introduce the FAR pointer. Video memory in Protected Mode is not located in the flat memory segment of the application. Recall that the application contains only the code, data, and stack in its segment. Video memory can be accessed via segment 0034h. Since this segment is external to the application segment, it will require a far pointer. The Visual C++ 32-bit suite does not provide support for far pointers because data can be accessed from within the program by a near 32-bit pointer. In Protected Mode programming, accessing any code or data segment outside of the program segment requires a far pointer. Phar Lap does provide a special data structure, called the FARPTR, to overcome this minor dilemma. FARPTR is compatible with Watcom C++ 10.0, but it is not needed because Watcom's 32-bit compiler supports far pointers. Its declaration looks like this:

```
FARPTR pVideoMem, vgaBaseAddr;
```

These far pointers can be used in a similar manner as their Real Mode counterparts. Phar Lap provides library calls that even appear similar to the Real Mode MK_FP() style routines but operate on selectors. For instance, to set up a selector to reference video memory, the following code would be used:

```
FP_SET(vgaBaseAddr, 0xA0000, SS_DOSMEM);
```

This library call constructs a far pointer, vgaBaseAddr, to reference VGA memory using selector 0x34h, defined in header file PHAR LAP.H as SS_DOSMEM. A selector exists in this same file labeled SS_SCREEN, selector 0x1Ch, but it is only intended for character-mode graphics.

> Watcom users, the first megabyte of memory is mapped as a shared linear address. This means video memory can be accessed by using its linear address of A0000h. Since video memory is accessible by the application, the pointer to video memory is of the near type.

Phar Lap provides routines to read and write FARPTR type memory. These are PeekFarByte(), and PokeFarByte(). These calls would be useful for examining and writing individual bytes of video memory. For illustrative purposes, a pixelBuffer could be written to the video screen as shown in Listing 9.23.

Listing 9.23. Using FARPTR to write to video memory in 386 Protected Mode.

```
//////////////////////////////////////////////////////////////////////////

void writeVideo( pixelBuffer &p)
{

  FARPTR pVideoMem, vgaBaseAddr;
  unsigned int rowIndex, pixelIndex, offset;
  unsigned char *pixelBytes;


  rowIndex = pixelIndex = offset = 0;
  FP_SET(vgaBaseAddr, 0xA0000, SS_DOSMEM);        //0x34

  for(rowIndex=0; rowIndex<200;rowIndex++)
  {

    FP_SET(pVideoMem, FP_OFF(vgaBaseAddr) + offset, FP_SEL(vgaBaseAddr));
    pixelBytes = p.pixBuf;
    pixelBytes += offset;
    WriteFarMem(pVideoMem, pixelBytes, 320);
    offset += 320;
  }
}

//////////////////////////////////////////////////////////////////////////
```

The Watcom compiler using DOS4GW maps the first linear megabyte of memory. So don't use FARPTR if you are developing with the Watcom compiler.

Analogous to the MK_FP(), FP_SEG(), and FP_OFF() calls in Real Mode programming, Phar Lap provides FP_SET(), FP_SEL(), and FP_OFF(). These are the Protected Mode counterparts for accessing and manipulating Protected Mode memory using the FARPTR datatype. The FP_SET() call from the PokeFarByte() demo code constructs the FARPTR to video memory.

For throwing a buffer out to the screen, like a .PCX or .LBM viewer, the PokeFarByte() calls would be adequate. But for animation-quality performance, writing individual pixels is time-consuming. It would speed things up if entire buffers could be written to VGA memory rather than individual bytes. The C library function memcpy() does not know how to handle data type FARPTR. The SDK provides routines for shuffling around FARPTR bytes. However, the problem still remains that the pixelBuffer class keeps its data in unsigned char buffers. Phar Lap provides a routine to write conventional C-style buffers to its data type FARPTR. This is accomplished through the SDK library call WriteFarMem(). Making some minor changes to the writeVideo() call using PokeFarByte(), the following code snippet illustrates how to write buffers to video memory:

```
unsigned char *pixelBytes;

  for(rowIndex=0; rowIndex<200;rowIndex++)
  {
    FP_SET(pVideoMem, FP_OFF(vgaBaseAddr) + offset, FP_SEL(vgaBaseAddr));
    pixelBytes = p.pixBuf;
    pixelBytes += offset;
    WriteFarMem(pVideoMem, pixelBytes, 320);
    offset += 320;
  }
```

Not only is this code easier to read, it's also faster. The nested inner loop required to transverse the bytes on each row is gone. One loop walks the 200 rows of VGA memory, and the WriteFarMem() routine writes each row with the pixelBuffer contents.

The routines in vtools now provide the functionality of setting video modes and writing video buffers. A discussion of the driver for viewing buffers is rather anticlimatic at this point, since it's nearly identical to the last drivers for the pixelBuffer class. The source listing for the pixelBuffer class running under Phar Lap TNT DOS-Extender is shown in Listing 9.24.

Listing 9.24. The simple pixelBuffer class driver using Phar Lap's TNT 7.0 SDK (PBTNTDVR.CPP).

```cpp
// I N C L U D E S //////////////////////////////////////////////////////////
#include <stdio.h>
#include <conio.h>
#include <dos.h>

#include "gks.hpp"
#include "vtools.hpp"
#include "pixbuf.hpp"
#include "iff.hpp"

#ifdef __WATCOMC__
#define _getch getch
#endif

// MAIN //////////////////////////////////////////////////////////////////////

void main()
{
  // Rect objects
  Rect offScreenRect;     // Rect describing the offscreen pixelBuffer object
  Rect spriteRect;        // Rect describing the sprite pixelBuffer object
  Rect dstRect;

  // Rect objects initializations
  offScreenRect.setRect(0,0,320,200);  // initialize bounds of offscreen object
  spriteRect.setRect(0,0,82,100);            // initialize bounds of sprite object
  dstRect.setRect(108,50,190,150);

  // pixelBuffer obects
  pixelBuffer offScreenPix( offScreenRect );// offscreen pixelBuffer object
  pixelBuffer spritePix( spriteRect );  // sprite pixelBuffer object
```

continues

Listing 9.24. continued

```
    // lbm objects
    lbm offScreenLBM;        // lbm object for offscreen pixel file
    lbm spriteBBM;      // lbm object for sprite pixel file

    // lbm object IFF file reader
    offScreenLBM.unPacker("scene.lbm", offScreenPix);  // unpack offscreen pixels
    spriteBBM.unPacker("uman7.bbm", spritePix);    // unpack sprite pixels

    // blit sprite object pixels to offscreen object pixels
    offScreenPix.copyTransPixels(spritePix, spriteRect, dstRect);

    // set the video to mode 13h VGA 320 x 200
    setVideoMode( 0x13 );

    setVGAPalette((char*)offScreenLBM.palette);
    // write the pixel buffer to the screen
    writeVideo(offScreenPix);

    // pause
    _getch();

    // return to standard text video mode 03h
    setVideoMode( 0x03 );

    printf("done\n");
}
```

///

A driver for static Sprites and backgrounds is adequate for testing video drivers or testing new ideas, but the overall goal in video games is to provide action. It would be more interesting to have dynamic Sprites and backgrounds. Scrolling backgrounds in Real Mode may be more difficult, because multiple buffers must be used for offscreen backgrounds. (See Figure 9.19.) In Protected Mode, an offscreen buffer can be allocated twice the width of a 320×200 byte VGA mode 13h screen—that's a 128KB buffer.

The pixelBuffer class can be used in such a way that a logical buffer, the viewPortBuf, 320×200 pixels, can slide across the large offscreen buffer and update the screen with its current contents. Using only the routines discussed so far and introducing no new techniques, a simple horizontal screen animation can be accomplished with the code shown in Listing 9.25.

Figure 9.19.
A graphical representation of a scrolling viewport.

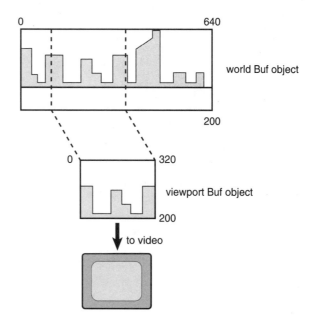

Listing 9.25. The `pixelBuffer` **class driver using Phar Lap's TNT 7.0 SDK (PB386DVR.CPP).**

```
// I N C L U D E S ////////////////////////////////////////////////////////////

#include <stdio.h>
#include <conio.h>
#ifdef __WATCOMC__
#else
#include <Phar Lap.h>
#endif

#include "gks.hpp"
#include "vtools.hpp"
#include "iff.hpp"
#include "pixbuf.hpp"

// MAIN ////////////////////////////////////////////////////////////////////////

void main()
{

    Rect viewPortBounds, worldBounds;
    Rect frame1, frame2, copyBounds;

    Rect rUman1, rUman2, rUman3, rUman4, rUman5, rUman6, rUman7, rUman8;
    Rect rDst1, rDst2, rDst3, rDst4, rDst5, rDst6, rDst7, rDst8;

    rUman1.setRect(0,0,68,106);
    rUman2.setRect(0,1,74,101);
    rUman3.setRect(0,0,68,103);
    rUman4.setRect(0,0,44,104);
```

continues

Listing 9.25. continued

```
rUman5.setRect(0,0,50,102);
rUman6.setRect(0,0,84,102);
rUman7.setRect(0,0,82,100);
rUman8.setRect(0,0,58,104);

rDst1.setRect(108,50,176,156);
rDst2.setRect(108,51,182,151);
rDst3.setRect(108,50,176,153);
rDst4.setRect(108,50,152,154);
rDst5.setRect(108,50,158,152);
rDst6.setRect(108,50,192,152);
rDst7.setRect(108,50,190,150);
rDst8.setRect(108,50,158,154);


pixelBuffer uman1Pix( rUman1 );
pixelBuffer uman2Pix( rUman2 );
pixelBuffer uman3Pix( rUman3 );
pixelBuffer uman4Pix( rUman4 );
pixelBuffer uman5Pix( rUman5 );
pixelBuffer uman6Pix( rUman6 );
pixelBuffer uman7Pix( rUman7 );
pixelBuffer uman8Pix( rUman8 );


worldBounds.setRect(0,0,640,200);   // worlds
frame1.setRect(0,0,320,200);
frame2.setRect(320,0,640,200);
viewPortBounds.setRect(0,0,320,200);

pixelBuffer worldBuf(worldBounds);
pixelBuffer viewPortBuf(viewPortBounds);

lbm uman1BBM;
lbm uman2BBM;
lbm uman3BBM;
lbm uman4BBM;
lbm uman5BBM;
lbm uman6BBM;
lbm uman7BBM;

lbm uman8BBM;


lbm lbmTest;

lbmTest.unPacker("scene.lbm", viewPortBuf);
uman1BBM.unPacker("uman1.bbm", uman1Pix);   // unpack sprite pixels

uman2BBM.unPacker("uman2.bbm", uman2Pix);   // unpack sprite pixels

uman3BBM.unPacker("uman3.bbm", uman3Pix);   // unpack sprite pixels

uman4BBM.unPacker("uman4.bbm", uman4Pix);   // unpack sprite pixels
```

```
uman5BBM.unPacker("uman5.bbm", uman5Pix);    // unpack sprite pixels

uman6BBM.unPacker("uman6.bbm", uman6Pix);    // unpack sprite pixels

uman7BBM.unPacker("uman7.bbm", uman7Pix);    // unpack sprite pixels

uman8BBM.unPacker("uman8.bbm", uman8Pix);    // unpack sprite pixels

printf("unPacker() done\n");

// load offscreen wolrd
worldBuf.copyPixels(viewPortBuf, viewPortBounds, frame1);  // cell 1
worldBuf.copyPixels(viewPortBuf, viewPortBounds, frame2);  // cell 2

viewPortBuf.copyPixels(worldBuf, frame2, viewPortBounds);
viewPortBuf.copyTransPixels(uman1Pix, rUman1, rDst1);
getch();


setVideoMode( 0x13 );

setVGAPalette((char*)lbmTest.palette);

unsigned int cell=1;
unsigned int ticks=0;  // delay count
unsigned int i;
unsigned int l,t,r,b;
t = 0; b=200;

for (i=0;i<320;i++)
{
  l=i; r=l+320;
  copyBounds.setRect(l,t,r,b);
  viewPortBuf.copyPixels(worldBuf,copyBounds,viewPortBounds);

      switch(cell)
      {
        case 1:
        viewPortBuf.copyTransPixels(uman1Pix, rUman1, rDst1);
          break;
        case 2:
        viewPortBuf.copyTransPixels(uman2Pix, rUman2, rDst2);
          break;
        case 3:
        viewPortBuf.copyTransPixels(uman3Pix, rUman3, rDst3);
          break;
        case 4:
        viewPortBuf.copyTransPixels(uman4Pix, rUman4, rDst4);
          break;
        case 5:
        viewPortBuf.copyTransPixels(uman5Pix, rUman5, rDst5);
          break;
        case 6:
        viewPortBuf.copyTransPixels(uman6Pix, rUman6, rDst6);
          break;
        case 7:
        viewPortBuf.copyTransPixels(uman7Pix, rUman7, rDst7);
          break;
```

continues

Listing 9.25. continued

```
            case 8:
            viewPortBuf.copyTransPixels(uman8Pix, rUman8, rDst8);
                    break;
            }

            waitRetrace();

            writeVideo(viewPortBuf);
            if (ticks > 4)
            {
            if (cell > 6)
              cell = 1;
            else
              cell++;
            ticks = 0;
            }
            ticks++;
    }
  getch();
  setVideoMode( 0x03 );
  printf("done\n");
}
```

///

The code looks relatively similar to the code for the static Sprite and background driver, with the exception of a few added objects to assist in creating the object worldBuf, the offscreen 640×200 byte buffer. Note that the 320×200 .LBM picture was copied into the buffer twice using member function copyPixels(), and logical coordinates provided by Rect objects frame1, and frame2.

The main workhorse of the animation is performed in the for loop, as follows:

```
unsigned int i;
unsigned int l,t,r,b;
t = 0; b=200;

    for (i=0;i<320;i++)
    {
      l=i;  r=l+320;
      copyBounds.setRect(l,t,r,b);
      viewPortBuf.copyPixels(worldBuf,copyBounds,viewPortBounds);
      viewPortBuf.copyTransPixels(pixBBM, bbmRect, bbmRect);
      writeVideo(viewPortBuf);
    }
```

The illusion of the sliding window is provided by the Rect member function setRect(). The variables, l,t,r, and b, are left, top, right, and bottom coordinates, respectively, of the sliding window. The new coordinates of the Rect object copyBounds are updated with each iteration of the loop. These coordinates are passed to the copyPixels() member function for object viewPortBuf. The contents of viewPortBuf buffer are updated and then written to the screen with the vtools routine writeVideo().

Phar Lap's TNT DOS-Extender and Visual C++ 2.0 for Windows NT

The installation and operation of the Phar Lap SDK is well documented in the manuals that accompany the development kit. However, Visual C++ 2.0, the latest 32-bit compiler release from Microsoft, isn't covered in the documentation. The Visual workbench environment has changed from the last release, and configuration can be a bit tricky.

Configuring a New Project Using Visual C++ 2.0 and TNT SDK

The first order of operation is to set up a new project. To configure a new project, pull down the File menu and select the option New. A New dialog box will appear on the screen with a listbox. Highlight the word Project in the listbox. This specifies that a new project is being created. (See Figure 9.20.)

Figure 9.20.
Select Project from the New dialog box.

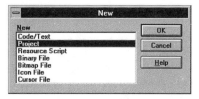

Double-click the OK button to enable the selection. The New dialog box will close and a New Project dialog box appears on the screen (See Figure 9.21.)

Figure 9.21.
Configure application as a Console Application in the New Project dialog box.

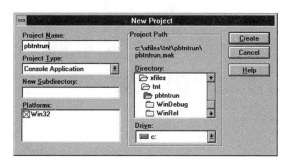

1. Type the project name in the Project Name box

2. From the Project Type box, use the drop-down list to choose Console Application

3. Select the working directory for the project in the Directory box

4. Click the Create button to complete the project setup

The New Project dialog will close, and the Project Files dialog box will appear on the screen. (See Figure 9.22.)

Figure 9.22.
Select the desired source files from the Project Files dialog.

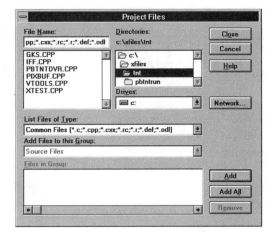

1. Highlight the desired source files from the File Name box, and use the Add button to add them to the project

2. Click the Close button when all the desired source files have been added to the project

This concludes the initial setup of the project in NT. However, the working directories must now be configured to use the TNT SDK.

Configuring the Directories Options for Visual C++ 2.0 and TNT SDK

1. From the Tools menu, select Options. The Options dialog box will appear on the screen with a selection scheme that resembles tabs on a file folder. These tabs are called Message map tabs. Select the map tab for Directories. (See Figure 9.23.)

Figure 9.23.

Use the Options dialog to configure the bin, include, and library directories.

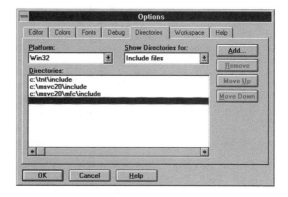

2. The Show Directories drop-down box has options for executable files, include files, and library files. The following three must be configured:

   Include files: `c:\tnt\include`
   Library files: `c:\tnt\cofflib`
   Executable files: `c:\tnt\bin`

3. When all three file types have been added to the Show Directories dialog, click the OK button.

Configuring the Linker for Visual C++ 2.0 and TNT SDK

1. From the Project menu, select Settings. The Project Settings window will appear on the screen. (See Figure 9.24.)

2. Select the message tab labeled Link.

Figure 9.24.

Configure the linker for the TNT libraries using the Project Settings dialog box.

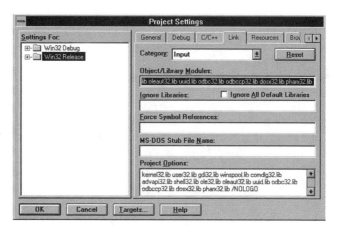

3. From the Category box, select Input from the drop-down list.

4. To the Object/Library Modules box add the two Phar Lap libraries DOSX32.LIB and PHARX32.LB.

5. Select the Targets button, and a Targets window will overlap the Project Settings window.

6. Select the Target type, Win32 Release, in the Target box. (See Figure 9.25.)

Figure 9.25.
Configure the Target settings for Win32 Release.

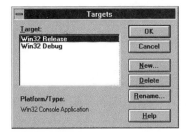

7. Select the OK button to close the Targets window.

8. Select the OK button on the Projects Settings window to close this window.

pixelBuffers and Watcom DOS/4GW

One of the simplest ways to get started with Protected Mode programming is with the Watcom 10.0 DOS/4GW development system. The environment is identical for both Windows and Windows NT. Furthermore, the NT platform enables development of DOS and Protected Mode DOS apps natively. This feature may be important if NT is the chosen development platform. However, most game designers still choose to develop from DOS command lines, using make and batch files.

Implementing the pixelBuffer class and its driver will be quite a bit simpler than with the Phar Lap TNT SDK. For instance, with just a few minor modifications, the Real Mode vtools code can be modified to run under DOS/4GW. The changes reflect the C library calls for the Watcom compiler and are not really all that specific to DOS/4GW.

The developers of the Watcom compiler went to great effort to make the Protected Mode memory and interrupt access look similar to the Real Mode methodology. The same structure (union REGS) used in Real Mode can be used in Protected Mode to request and service interrupts. The differentiation between Real and Protected Mode calls is determined by which C library routine is called. The int86() call is used in Real Mode. The routine int386() is used in both Real Mode and Protected Mode. The call for a processor interrupt using Watcom's Protected Mode 386 C library looks like the following:

```
#include <i86.h>   // structure union REGS and int386() routine
#include <dos.h>

union REGS regs;

  regs.w.ax = 0;   // select function 00h, program terminate
  int386( 0x21, &regs, &regs );
```

The solution to modifying the Real Mode vtools routine `setVideoMode()` is straightforward. Using the wonders of modern cut-and-paste technology, the code for setting the video mode is revealed as shown in Listing 9.26.

Listing 9.26. Changing the video modes using DOS/4GW.

```
///////////////////////////////////////////////////////////////////////////

void setVideoMode( unsigned int xmode )
{
   union REGS regs;

  regs.w.ax = xmode;
  int386( 0x10, &regs, &regs );
}

///////////////////////////////////////////////////////////////////////////
```

Modifying the vtools routine `writeVideo()` is just as simple using Watcom's environment. The first megabyte of memory in DOS/4GW is mapped as a shared linear address. This means video memory can be accessed by using its linear address of A0000h. Since video memory is accessible by the application, the pointer to video memory is of the near type. A pointer to VGA memory looks like the following:

```
char *vgaBaseAddr = (char*) 0xA0000;
```

This scheme of addressing allows simplistic modifications to the Real Mode `writeVideo()` function. Replacing the Real Mode `_far` keywords and the far type function `fmemcpy()`, the DOS/4GW `writeVideo()` function is shown in Listing 9.27.

Listing 9.27. Writing to video memory using DOS/4GW.

```
///////////////////////////////////////////////////////////////////////////

void writeVideo( pixelBuffer &p)
{
    char *pVideoMem;
    unsigned int rowIndex, pixelIndex, offset;

    pixelIndex = rowIndex = offset = 0;
    pVideoMem = (char*)0xA0000;

    for (rowIndex=0;rowIndex<200;rowIndex++)
```

continues

Listing 9.27. continued

```
    {
        memcpy(pVideoMem + offset, p.pixBuf + offset, 320);
        offset += 320;
    }
}
```

///

The uneventful process of porting vtools from Real Mode to Protected Mode is completed. The code for the scrolling screen driver from the Phar Lap example, SCROLL.CPP, can be used explicitly with no modifications. Watcom has taken much of the burden out of learning or looking up proprietary calls for their libraries.

The Watcom development environment also comes with an assembler, WASM. Very little information is provided about WASM in the online documentation. The beauty of WASM is that assembly source files can be included in a Watcom project with C or C++ files, and during the build process, the WASM assembler is invoked. This convience assists in adhering to the coding conventions where inline assembly should be avoided and all assembly routines should be kept in assembly libraries.

The WASM assembler and its integration to the Watcom compiler couldn't be any simpler. A C++ function calling a WASM routine passes arguments, in Protected Mode, on the 80386 registers. The idea is to write the assembly procedure as if all calling arguments are currently loaded into the proper registers. By default, Watcom passes the parameters to eax, ebx, ecx, and edx.

There is no hassle or computation of what pointer or data type is where on the stack. These methodologies can be demonstrated by writing vtools routines using WASM.

The simplest routine to code is setVideoMode(). Since the function has only one calling argument, it will be passed to the assembly procedure on register eax. Using the default parameter-passing scheme, the value to change the video mode to is already in the proper register for the INT 10h call. The assembly routine merely has to call the interrupt and return. (See Listing 9.28.)

Listing 9.28. Changing the video mode using Watcom's Assembler (WASM).

```
public  setVideoMode_

; setVideoMode_ sets the desired video mode
;   according to the value passed in register eax
setVideoMode_   PROC    NEAR
                int     10h                 ; call BIOS (video)
                ret
setVideoMode_   ENDP
```

WASM has a special naming convention for procedures—it is the procedure name followed by an underscore (for example, myWASMProc_). This is used in the public setVideoMode_ declaration. Procedure names may not have an underscore (_) prefix; this is reserved for segment definitions, such as _TEXT, and _DATA.

The C++ driver for calling the assembly procedure setVideoMode_ looks like the following:

```
extern "C" void setVideoMode(int);

void main()
{
    setVideoMode( 0x13);
}
```

The *linkage specification* extern "C" void setVideoMode(int) declares a function defined with C-type language parameters. The function setVideoMode(0x13) is the call to the assembly-language routine.

The setVideoMode() call is identical to the Real Mode call, except that the actual source itself is in 386 Protected Mode assembly.

The routine writeVideo() is also a simple routine in assembly. From a C++ perspective, it is non-trivial to port the code verbatim into assembly. But that's not the idea. Coding conventions demand thinking in terms of the language that is being used. To code in assembly language requires thinking in assembly language. The goal is to write an assembly-language procedure to move the contents of one buffer into another. It just so happens that the 386 has an instruction for such an operation, movsd. The instruction movsd, moves a doubleword (4 bytes = 32 bits) from a buffer referenced by esi into a buffer referenced by edi. Since the viewPortBuf object has a buffer of 320×200 bytes (64,000 bytes), the instruction movsd will have to be called in a loop 16,000 (64,000 bytes / 4 byte moves) times. Repetitive string moves are so common on the 386 that there is a special prefix, rep, so looping will not be necessary. The rep prefix needs a counter initialized in ecx. This counter is the number of times the movsd operation needs to be performed. The assembly code for writeVideo_ is shown in Listing 9.29.

Listing 9.29. A procedure to write the entire contents of 320×200 pixelBuffer object to the screen.

```
public   writeVideo_

; writeVideo_  writes the entire 320 x 200 offsreen buffer to
;  VGA mode 13h memory
writeVideo_            PROC NEAR
            mov     edi, 0a0000h       ; write buffer [esi] to video memory
[edi]
            mov     ecx, 16000         ;  repeat 16000 (64000 bytes / 4 bytes
per movsd) times
            rep     movsd              ;  perform 32-bit move string operation
            ret
writeVideo_           ENDP
```

The interesting catch to procedure `writeVideo_` is that it expects the pointer to the source buffer to be passed as an argument in esi. Watcom by default passes arguments on registers eax, ebx, ecx, edx, and then uses the stack. The C++ code needs to be given information on how to override the default argument-passing convention. This is achieved with the auxiliary pragma, which defines an auxiliary function. This looks like the following:

```
extern "C" void near writeVideo(char *buffer);

#pragma aux writeVideo "*_" parm caller [esi];

void main()
{
    pixelBuffer viewPortBuf;
        :
    writeVideo ( viewPortBuf);
}
```

The declaration *#pragma aux* writeVideo declares the auxiliary pragma function. The funky notation *_ is a symbol-name placeholder. Notice that the C++ function calls writeVideo() and the assembly-language procedure is writeVideo_. The symbol placeholder *_ merely retains this information to resolve the ambiguity. The *parm caller* declaration provides the mapping of how the arguments are to be passed. In this case the register esi will be used for passing an argument to the assembly routine.

> The linkage specifications must preclude the #pragma aux declarations or else the compiler will terminate with errors.

The examples of setVideoMode() and writeVideo() aren't really illustrative examples of assembly-language programming. It just so happens that their solutions are trivial in assembly. To emphasize the complexity of assembly, suppose the viewport was allowed to be non-static. That is, the viewport is a resizable window of up to 320×200 pixels in size. An example would be the DOOM and DOOM II resizable play window. The assembly routine takes a buffer 320×200 pixels in size and only writes the logical rectangular region to the screen.

The calling parameters from C++ would look like this:

```
extern "C" void near viewPort(char *buffer, int,int,int,int);

#pragma aux viewPort "*_" parm caller [esi] [eax] [ebx] [ecx] [edx];

void main()
{
  setVideoMode(0x13);

  viewPort((char*)viewPortBuf.pixBuf, 64, 64, 128,128);

  setVideoMode(0x03);
}
```

In the example, only the pixels bounded by the rectangular coordinates 64,64,128,128, would be drawn to the video screen. The standard conventions are present for calling the assembly routine. Notice the linkage specification extern precedes the auxiliary pragma declaration. The argument mapping provided by parm caller indicates that the pointer to the buffer will be passed on register esi, and the rectangular coordinates will be passed on registers eax through edx respectively.

An assembly-language code snippet for retrieving the coordinates of the rectangle looks like this:

```
_DATA
left        dd    ?
top         dd    ?
right       dd    ?
bottom  dd     ?
_DATA    ENDS

_TEXT
public viewPort_

viewPort_    PROC NEAR
    mov    left,eax;                  ; left coordinate is passed in on eax
    mov    top,ebx;                   ; top coordinate is passed in on ebx
    mov    right,ecx;                 ; right coordinate is passed in on ecx
    mov    bottom,edx;                ; left coordinate is passed in on edx
     :
viewPort_    ENDP
```

A few preliminary computations must be made by the routine to determine the width and height of the viewport. Since the logical coordinates are passed as left, top, right, and bottom, simple relationships can be used to equate the height and width of the port. A fundamental relationship of the VGA screen is that its coordinates become increasingly larger to the right. Similarly, the VGA screen coordinates increase towards the bottom of the screen.

With this relationship, established the height and width can be determined as follows:

```
width = right - left
height = bottom - top
```

The value computed in the width represents width in bytes. The 386 register is capable of handling four bytes of screen data on any one operation. Since the width value will be used to control loop iterations for drawing pixels, it needs to be adjusted to reflect that 32 bits of data will be drawn to the screen instead of eight bits. This adjustment can be made by dividing the width by four.

The height value is left alone, because the 386 doesn't improve on how many rows are drawn. That is, if the viewPort_ procedure is drawing the entire screen (320/4×200), it will still have to process all 200 rows. The code to compute the height and width for viewPort_ is as follows:

```
_DATA
bufferWidth    dd    ?
rowHeight        dd    ?
    :
```

```
_DATA

_TEXT
     :
; compute view port width
     sub    ecx, eax                  ; ecx (width ) = ecx (right) - eax (left)
     shr    ecx,2                         ; width = width / 4
     mov    bufferWidth, ecx      ; save computed width

; compute view port height
     sub    edx, ebx                  ; edx (height) = edx (bottom) - ebx (top)
     mov    rowHeight, edx       ;  save computed height
     :
_TEXT
```

> Use shl and shr whereever possible instead of mul and div instructions. It's faster!

The viewing port is assumed to be an arbitrary rectangle up to 320×200 pixels in size. This means that the viewer won't always start displaying from the logical coordinate 0,0. As in the C++ example, the starting coordinate is 64,64 (left, top), so the top of the first row must be computed in the physical starting offset plus its left-coordinate offset. The starting physical byte offset value is:

```
starting physical byte offset = top * rowBytes (320 pixels)  + left
                              = 64 * rowBytes + 64
```

This may seem confusing since the value rowBytes (320) wasn't divided by four. This is because it is a pointer referencing a buffer of 64,000 bytes in size. The pointer arithmetic needs to reflect this. Only the byte operations are handled as double words (four bytes). The code snippet to compute the starting row offset in the source buffer is:

```
rowBytes  dd    320
     :
     mov    eax,ebx                         ; get logical top row
     imul   eax,rowBytes                 ; compute starting physical offset
     mov    ebx,eax
     add    ebx, left                        ; ebx contains the physical offset
```

These are the only values necessary to construct the resizable view port. With the easy stuff out of the way, now it's time to write nested loops to walk the rows and rows bytes of the viewing region. It would be illogical to walk all 200 rows of a source buffer if only data from 64 consecutive rows is to be drawn to the screen. This is also an optimization enhancement—the smaller the viewport, the faster the code executes. From this monumental decision, the outermost loop will be initialized to walk a maximum of rowHeight rows. The pseudocode looks like this:

```
     mov    edi, 0a0000h                   ;  initialize edi to reference VGA memory
     mov    ecx, rowHeight                ; maximum rows to walk
rowLoop:
     :
     **   nested loop: copy the desired bytes
     :
```

```
    pop     ecx                         ; restore rowLoop counter
    add     ebx, rowBytes           ; increment the offset to reference the
next row
    sub     ebx, right                  ; arithmetically compensate for right
coordinate offset
    add     ebx, left                   ; add left offset at the start of
new row
    loop rowLoop
```

The nested loop does the actual double-word copying. The contents of the source buffer, referenced by ds:[esi] are copied into the 32-bit register eax. The contents of eax are then loaded to video memory referenced by es:[edi]. The copying is a 32-bit operation; therefore, the segment index must be incremented by four to maintain coherence with double-word operations. The code for copying the bytes is as follows:

```
    push    ecx             ; save rowLoop counter
    mov     ecx, bufferWidth  ; copy only bufferWidth amount of pixels
bltLoop:
    mov     eax, ds:[esi+ebx]  ; transfer buffer contents to eax
    mov     es:[edi+ebx], eax  ; copy eax to video memory
    add     edi,4                       ; update edi index
    add     esi,4                       ; update esi index
loop    bltLoop
```

The resizable viewport is now ready for testing. The entire source listing for assembly procedure viewPort_ is shown in Listing 9.30.

Listing 9.30. The WASM code to complement the vtools C++ routines (vidtools.asm).

```
;////////////////////////////////////////////////////////////////////
;
;   vtools graphics routines for WASM
;
;////////////////////////////////////////////////////////////////////

; _DATA SEGMENT
; define data and variables to be used by vtools routines
_DATA           SEGMENT 'DATA'  USE32
rowBytes        dd      320     ; 320 bytes/row
left            dd      ?       ; left coordinate of rectangle
top             dd      ?       ; top coordinate of rectangle
right           dd      ?       ; right coordinate of rectangle
bottom          dd      ?       ; bottom coordinate of rectangle
bufferWidth     dd      ?       ; calculated buffer width
rowHeight       dd      ?       ; calculated buffer height
_DATA           ENDS

; _TEXT SEGMENT
; code for vtools routines
_TEXT   SEGMENT PUBLIC  'CODE'  USE32

        public  setVideoMode_, viewPort_, writeVideo_, setVGApalette_, waitRetrace_

; setVideoMode_ sets the desired video mode
;   according to the value passed in register eax
```

continues

Listing 9.30. continued

```
setVideoMode_   PROC    NEAR
                int     10h             ; call BIOS (video)
                ret
setVideoMode_   ENDP

; viewPort_ displays a regional content of a 320 x 200 pixel
;   buffer to the VGA mode 13h memory
viewPort_       PROC NEAR
                mov     left, eax    ; get bounding rectangle
                mov     top,ebx
                mov     right,ecx
                mov     bottom,edx

                sub     ecx, eax     ; compute logical width
                shr     ecx, 2       ; divide by 4
                mov     bufferWidth,ecx ; save buffer width

                sub     edx, ebx     ; compute logical row height
                mov     rowHeight, edx ; save row height

                mov     eax,ebx      ; get logical top row
                imul    eax,rowBytes ; compute physical row offset
                mov     ebx,eax      ;
                add     ebx, left

                mov     edi,0a0000h  ; initialize edi to video memory

                mov     ecx, rowHeight    ; maximum rows to walk
        rowLoop:
                push    ecx               ; save row loop counter
                mov     ecx, bufferWidth  ; copy only bufferWidth amount of pixels
        bltLoop:
                mov     eax, ds:[esi+ebx] ;transfer buffer contents to eax
                mov     es:[edi+ebx], eax ; copy eax to video memory
                add     edi,4             ; update edi index
                add     esi,4             ; update esi index
                loop    bltLoop
                pop     ecx               ; restore rowLoop counter
                add     ebx, rowBytes     ; increment the offset to reference the
next row
                sub     ebx, right        ; arithmetically compensate for right
coordinate offset
                add     ebx, left         ; add left offset at the start of new row
                loop    rowLoop
                ret
viewPort_       ENDP

; writeVideo_  writes the entire 320 x 200 offsreen buffer to
;   VGA mode 13h memory
writeVideo_             PROC NEAR
                mov     edi, 0a0000h      ; write buffer [esi] to video memory
[edi]
                mov     ecx, 16000        ;  repeat 16000 (64000 bytes / 4 bytes
per movsd) times
                rep     movsd             ;  perform 32-bit move string operation
                ret
```

```
writeVideo_              ENDP

; write the DAC registers with a VGA a palette
setVGApalette_   PROC NEAR
                 cli
                 mov   edi, eax
                 dec   edi
                 mov   ecx, eax
                 add   ecx, 767d

                 mov   dx, 3c8h               ; write port
                 xor   al, al
                 out   dx, al

                 mov   dx, 3c9h               ; data port

         loopPal:
                 inc   edi
                 mov   ax, ds:[edi]
                 out   dx, al
                 inc   edi
                 mov   ax, ds:[edi]
                 out   dx, al
                 inc   edi
                 mov   ax, ds:[edi]
                 out   dx, al

                 cmp   edi, ecx
                 jne   loopPal
                 sti

                 ret
setVGApalette_   ENDP

; wait for the vertical retrace to complete
waitRetrace_     PROC NEAR
                 mov   dx, 3dah
         vrtOff:
                 in    al, dx
                 test  al, 8h
                 jnz   vrtOff
         vrtResume:
                 in    al, dx
                 test  al, 8h
                 jnz   vrtResume
                 ret
waitRetrace_     ENDP

_TEXT            ENDS
                 END
```

By now your heads should be sufficiently full, and you are hereby dismissed for a 10-minute neurological break. However, there are some martyrs in the audience, so I'll add a few closing words about Watcom. The integrated development environment itself is really nice to code and play in. The major drawbacks to Watcom are its automated e-mail tech-support system and its online documentation. Getting any form of technical support from Watcom is difficult for the average noncommercial user. E-mail has always been a work-around to this problem. However, e-mail sent to Watcom is automatically responded to with a UNIX SMTP reply. From there it is queued up on the Watcom event horizon, never to been heard from again. Luckily Watcom has a strong user following and technical user forums can usually be found on the Internet and online services such as CompuServe and AOL.

The online documentation that ships with Watcom 10.0 can be described in one word: aggravating. All the documentation for the compiler is somewhere on that 650MB CD-ROM. Finding the particular information you want it is the hard part.

On the flipside of the coin—customer support—Watcom graciously distributed CD-ROM upgrades (version 10.0a) absolutely free to the registered owners of version 10.0, as long as the 10.0 compiler was purchased within a four-month period of the 10.0a release.

Summary

A lot of information has been dumped here, kind of like a *Reader's Digest* version of three semesters at Stanford. Many key topics were covered to enable you to start dabbling in Protected Mode programming. The information on interrupts, such as setting video modes, was deliberately kept simple. However, enough examples were provided to enable you to go off in a corner and come up with a joystick or keyboard driver using these same techniques.

In this chapter you learned the following:

- Memory in Real Mode is accessed using segments and offsets
- How to calculate a physical address in Real Mode
- The basics of Protected Mode memory architecture, selectors, descriptors, and descriptor tables
- How to generate an interrupt in Protected Mode
- How to use selectors to access memory in Protected Mode
- Why C++ interfaces to the SDKs are better than using the low-level languages

I began this chapter with a comment regarding DOOM, so it's appropriate to close with one. The majority of the code for DOOM was developed on a NeXT workstation using C++ and object-oriented techniques. The code for DOOM could be ported over to the PC because the code was designed with portable coding conventions. This game was quickly ported to almost every computing environment, and it is now available on the PC (DOS and Linux), Sega, Sun, SGI, and other platforms. It is rumored that the port from DOS to Linux was carried out in one week because the code was so portable. (Keep in mind that a typical game developer requires approximately nine months to port Donkey Kong 13 from Nintendo to Sega.)

Go forth into the world and program fun games.

Being Heard

P A **3** R T

Integrating Music and MIDI into Your Game

by Tim Melton

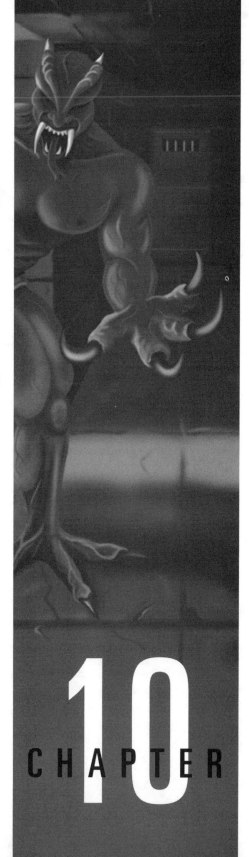

CHAPTER 10

This chapter will focus on MIDI, music, and digital recording in the realm of computer-game software from the perspective of the computer musician. The business of computer music is a highly specialized field, and unless your organization is lucky enough to have a staff composer, you will probably need to work with a composer by means of telephone, fax, and modem. Often, just knowing what term to use in discussing the music for a project can help the programmer and composer communicate more effectively and save time and money.

Music is, and has been, an important part of most visual media since the days of the first motion pictures. Even before "talkies," films were screened with a continuous accompaniment of music. Live performances, such as opera, drama, and dance, have always relied heavily on music for support. It would be difficult to imagine a popular film, video production, Broadway show, or ballet without music.

The world of personal computers is no exception. Today, computers with sound cards capable of music production are a mass-market staple. In the past few years, sound cards for computers have gone from cheap FM-based synthesizers to sophisticated wave-table and sample-based devices. Sales of sound cards continue to increase, while prices fall. And as technology continues to advance, so will the need for capable composers and computer musicians.

Music, as used in the digital domain of personal computers, is stored in two forms: MIDI and digital recordings. Each form will be discussed here based on their uses by computer musicians. Technical specifications of each form will not be discussed in detail, but they will be referred to. Some sources for obtaining complete technical data are listed at the end of the chapter.

Music

Music is one of the oldest forms of human expression. From its early days of primitive percussion and horns made of wood and bone, music has developed into highly complex forms and many different styles. Though the stylistic differences are extreme, most kinds of music share a common bond: emotion. It is this common thread that allows music to be the universal language.

Humans are emotional beings and have a need to express themselves in an emotional way. Music allows both the performer and the listener to express or experience emotions that might be otherwise difficult to share (hence the development of music therapy).

When used in conjunction with the visual arts, music can convey a mood and yet allow the visuals and dialogue to be unobstructed. A good film composer knows how to construct a score that will support the images on screen without drawing attention away from them. The same should be true for a composer of music for games.

Music Terms

To facilitate this discussion, it is important to become familiar with some of the terminology of music. Though the definitions of some of these terms may be obvious, others may not. What follows is a quick glossary of musical terms.

Bar (measure): A unit of division within a printed music score. A measure of music may be somewhat analogous to a paragraph in writing.

Clef: The symbols on the music staff indicating the pitch. The treble clef references the G above middle C. The bass clef indicates the F below middle C. Although there are several clefs, these are the two most common.

Dynamics: The volume or intensity at which a passage of music is played is indicated in the score by a script *p* or *f*. *p* indicates *piano*, or soft. *f* indicates *forte*, or loud. The more *p*s or *f*s, the softer or louder the music should be played.

Key: The pitch and scale a piece is written in. The scale is a series of notes that determine whether a key is major or minor. The key is the pitch that the scale is based around. There are 12 major and 12 minor keys. A major key is a characteristically bright sounding key, while a minor key is somewhat somber, sad, or ominous.

Meter: This refers to the rhythmic feel of a piece of music. Meter is usually indicated in printed music by two numbers at the beginning of the score. The top number indicates how many beats there are in each bar. The bottom number indicates what type of note is held for the length of one beat. An example would be 4/4 (called "four-four," not "four-fourths") time. There would be four beats in each bar, and a quarter note would receive one beat.

Note: The basic building block of music. A note can have pitch, as in a piano or flute, or be a sound that does not have a discernible tonal center, such as a drumbeat. The lengths of notes range from whole notes (and double whole notes) to sixty-fourth notes. Note lengths work like fractions—that is, the time given to two half notes would equal the time given to one whole note.

Rest: A period of silence in a piece of music. Rests are divided into time units, just as notes are.

Tempo: The speed at which a piece of music is played. It is often expressed in terms of beats per minute. A metronome uses this unit. An example metronome marking would be "MM=120," meaning the tempo is 120 beats per minute.

This is by no means a complete glossary of musical terms. It is meant to familiarize the games programmer with enough terms to communicate with the composer. An image of a typical musical score is shown in Figure 10.1.

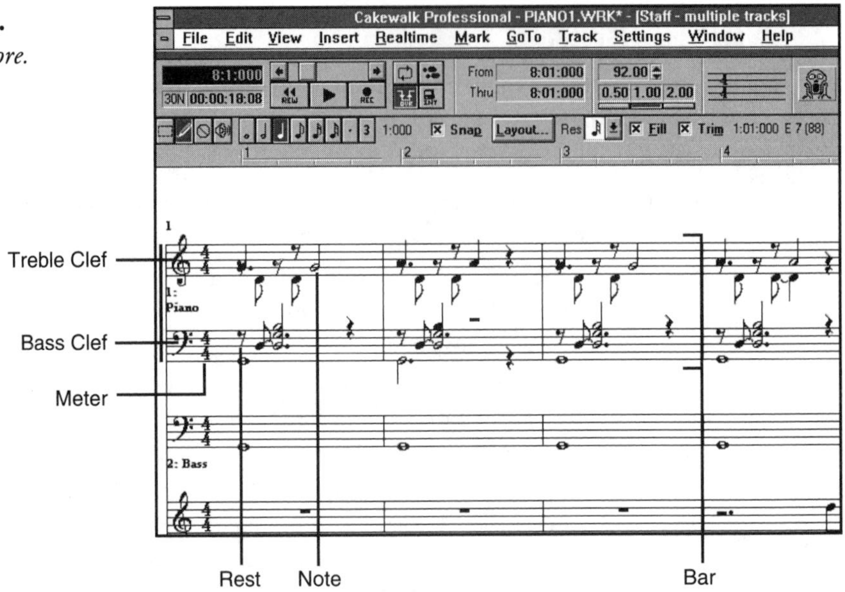

Figure 10.1.
A musical score.

MIDI

MIDI is an abbreviation for Musical Instrument Digital Interface. MIDI was invented in the early 1980s as a means for data exchange between musical synthesizers. MIDI is based on a serial protocol with a baud rate of 31.25KB/second. The original design envisioned applications in the realm of electronic musical instruments, but more recently MIDI has been adopted by manufacturers and users of lighting and professional audio. A new subset of the MIDI specification, MIDI Show Control, uses MIDI data to control equipment in recording studios and live productions. For instance, the Mackie 1604 mixing console, a popular mixer in project studios and video post production facilities, uses an optional module to control audio level changes in real time by the use of MIDI commands. Many new lighting consoles for theater and concert production come equipped with MIDI capabilities which allow the lighting console to be controlled from a master MIDI controller, such as a PC.

MIDI Terms

What follows is a basic glossary of MIDI terms. As with the music terms, this should help the game programmer understand what certain terms mean and help communications with your composer.

> **Bank:** A group of patches constitute a patch bank. (A *patch* is a set of electronic tonal parameters that produce a specific instrument sound. See the definition of patch,

which follows.) There are a maximum of 128 patches in a patch bank. MIDI standards, such as General MIDI, specify what type of instrument sound will be found in each patch bank slot. For instance, patch 1 in General MIDI is an acoustic grand piano sound; patch 68 is an oboe sound.

Channel: Similar to channels used in television, MIDI channels are discrete lines of data flow. Devices in the MIDI data path will respond only to data sent on channels that they are set to receive from.

General MIDI specifies channels 1–9 and 11–16 as melodic instrument channels. That is, instrument sounds that have pitch will be used on these channels. Channel 10 is used for percussion. Each note on channel 10 has a specific percussion-instrument sound assigned to it.

Controller: This term can have several meanings. In the context of MIDI software, it refers to a MIDI event that will set a parameter in the MIDI hardware. MIDI controllers are used to control modulation (vibrato), volume, sustain (like holding down a damper pedal on a piano), reverb, chorus (another modulation effect), and pan. In the MIDI specification, there are 128 controller numbers. Only a portion of these numbers have been assigned for use with musical-instrument applications. The rest are now being used in a new area for MIDI Show Control (MSC). MSC is used in theater and live performances for staging purposes.

Duration: The length of a note. Each note in MIDI is represented by a "note on" command and a "note off." Duration would be the length between these two commands.

General MIDI: A subset of the original MIDI specification, General MIDI standardizes patch assignments, patch sounds, minimum polyphony, and percussion assignments. This standardization allows files produced on one General MIDI compliant device to be correctly played on other General MIDI devices. Although instrument sounds are defined, they are flexible enough to allow new synthesis technologies to "improve" the sound quality of the instruments. General MIDI is the standard used by most multimedia and game developers today.

MIDI Mapper: Microsoft Windows uses a software interface to route MIDI data flow. The software included with most sound cards includes a MIDI Mapper specific to that card. The MIDI Mapper often has several setups, which route MIDI data to different channels. Most OEM MIDI Mappers will have a Basic MIDI setup and an Extended MIDI setup.

Operator: In FM synthesis, an operator is a digital circuit consisting of an oscillator, an envelope generator, and inputs and outputs to connect to each other and to a D/A converter. The way operators are arranged is called an algorithm. An operator whose output feeds the input of another operator is called a modulator. An operator whose output goes to a D/A converter is called a carrier.

Pan: Short for panorama. This indicates placement of the sound in the stereo field from left to right. MIDI controller 10 sets pan position.

Patch: This term is a holdover from the early days of synthesizers when all the components in an electronic instrument were connected by means of patch cables. Today a "patch" means a setting of the parameters of a synthesizer to produce a specific sound. Some makers of electronic instruments use the term "voice" to refer to a patch. General MIDI specifies what instrument sound is assigned to each of the 128 available patch numbers.

Polyphony: In the context of MIDI and electronic instruments, this term refers to the maximum number of notes that can be sounded at any given time. All electronic synthesis devices have a maximum number of notes that can sound at once.

PPQ: The resolution of a MIDI file. PPQ is an abbreviation for Pulses Per Quarter (note). That is, for each quarter note that occurs in the file, a clock pulse subdivides the basic musical beat. The higher the PPQ, the finer the resolution.

Quantization: A process used in MIDI sequencing software to correct timing errors for note data. Most sequencing software will offer different resolutions to round to. Heavily quantized music tends to sound "stiff" and machine-like, while music that is less quantized tends to retain its "personality" (since humans usually don't play exactly on the beat).

Sequencer: A software program used to create, edit, play, and save MIDI information. (See Figure 10.2.)

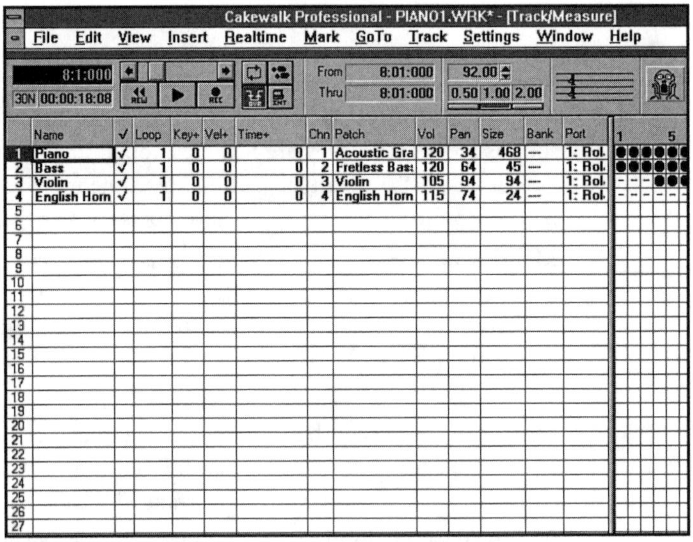

Figure 10.2.

Track/Measure screen of Cakewalk Pro for Windows.

Sys-ex: This is an abbreviation for System Exclusive. This is a type of MIDI message used to send information to a specific device while other MIDI devices in the MIDI data path ignore it. The second byte in a MIDI sys-ex transmission is a manufacturer's ID number, which will get the attention of the intended device.

Track: In a sequencer, a track is similar to a tape track. It contains MIDI data assigned to one MIDI channel. More than one track can be assigned to the same MIDI channel. A track should contain data to indicate a patch and a volume level as well as pan information.

Velocity: This term refers to how hard (loud) a note is played. In MIDI terms, this number is from 0-127, with 127 being the loudest. Please refer to the example MIDI file, VELOCITY.MID. The first note has a velocity of 20, the second note has a velocity of 64, and the third note has a velocity of 127. Different MIDI devices respond differently to velocity information.

Before MIDI, most electronic instruments were stand-alone devices with audio as their only output. A few synthesizers had jacks for input or output of control voltage, which could be used to adjust another instrument's oscillator or filter. Many of the pre-MIDI synths that had access to control-voltage circuits also had gate inputs and outputs which would be used to trigger another synth's envelope generator(s). This was about the extent of the interfacing between instruments. The one exception to this was the big modular systems made by Moog, ARP, and others.

The main problem in trying to connect two or more instruments with analog connections was that there was no standard for all instruments. One manufacturer might use 1-volt-per-octave as the standard for keyboard scaling, while another might use 1.1-volt-per-octave. This could create some very incompatible musical scales.

Because MIDI is a digital form of communication, computers became a natural part of the formation of MIDI setups. Computers made it possible to store and edit instrument settings (also known as patches) and to play, edit, and store music performances in the form of Standard MIDI files.

Today it is common to see solo or duo musical acts making use of a notebook computer to play accompaniment parts. This allows the musician to have the sound of a full band—without all the headaches of getting a band together for practice, arguing about arrangements, and all the other things that go along with performing with a group of live players.

MIDI has also become a part of computer-game development. Many game developers prefer using MIDI for music playback to using digital recordings because of the small size of music files stored in MIDI form. MIDI files are not really recordings, but rather sets of instructions for a MIDI device to play back. This form of music storage also makes music much more interactive, since the user can change many parameters of the music without altering other aspects. For instance, the tempo of a piece of music stored in MIDI form can easily by changed without raising or lowering the pitch. This is difficult to do in the world of recorded sound.

The first MIDI devices used in computer games were FM-based cards. FM technology was developed by Yamaha Corporation of Japan during the late 1970s and early 1980s. Their DX7 synthesizer used this technology to produce some very complex sounds, and it became the best selling synthesizer to date. The FM devices used now in computer sound cards are not as versatile as the DX7, and therefore they are very limited in the range of sounds they can produce. Nevertheless, they have been widely used for several years as the basis for music playback in computer games.

Authoring MIDI for game use requires a few simple conventions. First, the music should be recorded on individual tracks according to the natural structure of the music. For instance, place the melody on track 1, a counter-melody second melody on track 2, a harmony part on track 3, a bass part on track 4, and percussion on track 5. To make mixing the parts easier, percussion could be placed so that each instrument, such as kick drum, snare drum, and cymbals, could occupy individual tracks. After the music is recorded onto separate tracks, patch, volume, and pan settings should be entered for each track. If separate tracks are used for each percussion instrument, each track should be set for MIDI channel 10, and volume, pan, and patch settings need only be entered for one track assigned to channel 10. Patch 0 should be used as a default setting for channel 10 in all files authored for FM cards with Midpak, as well as wavetable and sample-based devices. MIDI files authored for WORX should use patch 126 for channel 10.

At this point, MIDI default controllers should be added to each track. This process can be made easier by cut-and-paste functions found in most sequencing software. Please refer to Table 10.1 for MIDI default controllers and their values. These authoring steps apply to all MIDI hardware, however, since the sound quality and response of MIDI hardware varies a great deal, each type of hardware will need to be dealt with. FM-based sound cards used in DOS products will use drivers chosen by the game developer. FM cards used in Windows products will most likely use the driver included with the user's card.

When setting patches and volume levels, it is best to play the music on several different brands of FM cards, and find several patches that will sound acceptable on all cards. You will find that some patches that sound good on one or two cards may sound terrible on another card. Note velocities for FM devices need to be set to a level of 100 to 120, with volume levels set by MIDI controller 7 events. MIDI for FM cards is not very responsive to dynamic changes.

Wavetable and sample-based cards are usually easier to author for. When setting patches and volume levels for these devices, always use the Roland Sound Canvas as a reference. Note velocities for wavetable and sample-based devices can be more dynamic, allowing for more expression.

When interfacing game software with MIDI, most game developers use software tools that are already available rather than creating their own. Two of the most popular software tools for DOS are Midpak and WORX. Midpak was developed by John Ratcliff and John Miles. WORX is a software package developed by Mystic Software. No matter what software tools you use to integrate MIDI into your game, you should make sure that a play utility is available in order to give your composer the ability to author the music properly. A play utility is any small executable program that will play the MIDI files as they will sound in the game software.

Midpak uses its own form of MIDI information. An Extended MIDI file, or XMID (.XMI), is usually smaller than its Standard MIDI counterpart. The Midpak/Digpak development kit includes a utility, MIDIFORM.EXE, to convert Standard MIDI files into .XMI files. Since there are no editors on the market for .XMI files, music stored in this format is relatively immune from alteration. One other handy feature of the MIDIFORM utility is its ability to take a group of Standard MIDI files and convert them into one .XMI file that will play in the order specified in the text file used to compile the .XMI.

Midpak also uses a proprietary form of patch bank for FM-based cards. These banks determine what instrument sounds are played when a .XMI file is played. Midpak includes patch banks with both Roland MT-32 and General MIDI emulation. Both the MT-32 and General MIDI banks were programmed by The Fat Man, George Sanger, and are about as good as FM patches get. Most MIDI files authored on the Sound Canvas will need little, if any, editing in order to sound good with the GM emulation bank in Midpak.

WORX is available from Mystic Software. Unlike Midpak, WORX uses Type 1 Standard MIDI files, so no conversion is necessary. WORX also uses the .IBK patch bank format. .IBK patch banks can be programmed using any of several software-authoring programs, such as SB Timbre (pronounced TAM-ber). .IBK banks can also be found on several of the on-line services as well as many music- or MIDI-oriented BBSs.

Beware of patch banks of unknown origin, however, since they might be part of a copyrighted software package and would therefore be illegal to use without the owner's permission.

There are some basic file conventions to use when constructing MIDI files for game use. All MIDI files should not exceed the maximum polyphony of the device it is intended to be used with. FM-based cards can produce a maximum of 20 notes in two-operator mode or 11 notes in four-operator mode. Since FM cards are widely used, it is usually best to keep musical arrangements to a reasonable number of instrumental parts.

FM cards do not respond well to dynamic changes, so don't expect a very expressive, tender, quiet passage to be followed by a crashing double or triple forte. Wavetable devices can handle dynamics much better, for the most part, but you should still not expect the full range of a live symphony orchestra with any PC sound card.

One guideline that is important for developers of DOS games, especially those that will be used on machines with older 386 processors—or games that will require extreme amounts of graphics processing—is to keep the resolution of the MIDI files to a reasonable level. While MIDI files with a resolution of 480 PPQ allow for great flexibility in musical "feel," the higher the resolution, the more attention from the CPU will be needed for MIDI playback.

> 120 PPQ is a good compromise between musical feel and CPU usage.

Another general rule for MIDI files in games is the use of default MIDI controllers at the very beginning of each MIDI file. This is very important, because music used in games is often interrupted during play for new music to start. Suppose a MIDI file that has been playing has changed a parameter in the hardware for a musical effect and not changed it back when it is stopped. A screen change occurs and new music begins to play. The resulting effect on playback of the new file can sound terrible. Table 10.1 lists some basic default settings. These are intended as a starting point, as more may be needed for specific hardware. MIDI hardware varies from one device to another in terms of which MIDI commands it responds to.

Table 10.1. MIDI controller default settings.

MIDI Controller	Setting (Value)
Wheel (Bender)	0
1 Modulation	0
11 Expression	127
64 Sustain (damper) pedal	0
91 Reverb	0–127 (depending on its use by a device)
93 Chorus	0–127 (depending on its use by a device)

These default controllers should be placed at the very beginning of a track, before any note data. The controllers for each channel should not all occur at the same time. The MIDI protocol is a serial protocol, and "stacking" too many controllers to occur at the same time (clock pulse) could mean the hardware may not respond properly. Generally, the defaults should be placed one clock pulse apart. Settings for volume (controller 7), beginning patch commands, and pan information (controller 10) should be the only data to precede default controllers. Note data should then immediately follow the default controllers.

> A MIDI sequencer can be useful for checking presence and placement of default controllers. Select a sequencer that enables you to see individual MIDI events.

Quite often music used in computer games is written to loop—that is, it is written so that at the end of the MIDI file, a loop command can return playback to a specified point earlier in the file. This should be done seamlessly. Midpak makes use of two controllers that have no specified function in the original MIDI specification. Controller number 116 with a value of 0 is placed at the precise point where playback would begin again. Controller 117 with a value of 127 would be placed at the point where the file would return to the beginning. It is important that any default controller or note data not occur at the same clock pulse (or tick) as these two events.

The need for MIDI default controllers is the same when authoring MIDI files for use in Windows' applications. What is different about using MIDI in Windows is the wide variety of sound drivers. Each driver will emulate General MIDI instrument sounds differently, so one instrument sound on one card may sound quite different on another card and driver. Since Midpak and most other sound toolkits for DOS use drivers that will ship with the product, authoring MIDI files for these drivers results in predictable results during music playback. In the Windows environment, there are at least as many drivers, each containing sound banks, as there are sound cards. Manufacturers of many sound cards update drivers occasionally, which adds to the confusion. It is difficult, at best, for a composer to have access to all sound cards and all those drivers.

There are several steps you can take to minimize unpredictable playback problems with end users. Your composer should have at least two or three sound cards to play back files on. One of these cards should be a Sound Blaster, since this is the most common sound card today. Also, make sure that your composer has the latest driver updates from the cards' manufacturers. Many are available from the commercial on-line services and from the individual manufacturer's own BBSs.

The biggest potential for problems with MIDI implementation is the Windows MIDI Mapper. The MIDI Mapper can have many different configurations, each dependent on the sound-card manufacturer, the computer builder, and whether or not a user has altered it. MIDI Mappers can be set up for Basic MIDI, Extended MIDI, or use of all MIDI channels.

The idea of Basic and Extended MIDI originated in the Multi Media Extensions of Windows 3.0. Basic MIDI uses only MIDI channels 13–16. Channel 13–15 are used for melodic instrument sounds, and channel 16 is used for percussion only. Extended MIDI uses MIDI channels 1–10, with channels 1–9 used for melodic instruments and channel 10 used for percussion.

Extended and Basic MIDI setups also limit polyphony. A Basic MIDI setup limits polyphony to six notes for melodic instruments and five notes for percussion instruments. Extended MIDI limits melodic instruments to a maximum of 16 notes and percussion to eight notes. You will notice that Basic MIDI limits the available number of instrument sounds that can be employed at once to three, since melodic instruments can only use channels 13–15. Extended MIDI limits the maximum number of instrument sounds to nine at any one time.

> The easiest way to ensure compatibility with most MIDI Mapper setups is to use the Microsoft guideline for channel assignment when authoring MIDI files. This will require the composer to include a dual arrangement in the MIDI file. The entire piece will be on channels 1–10, following the limits of polyphony and instrumentation, and also on channels 13–16, again following the limits of polyphony and instrumentation. As you can see, the musical arrangement used in channels 13–16 may have to be condensed, since there are fewer instrument assignments and fewer notes to work with.

Most FM cards that use the OPL 3 chip can easily conform to the limitations of Extended and Basic MIDI. The MIDI Mappers that come with these cards usually include options for either Basic, Extended, or All MIDI channel setups. Earlier cards, such as the original Sound Blaster and Adlib cards, are Basic MIDI-only devices. It quickly becomes apparent how difficult it can be to integrate MIDI with all those different sound cards out there. With a little planning and sufficient notice and documentation for your end users, compatibility problems can be kept to a minimum. The bottom line is to have your MIDI files authored according to Microsoft guidelines, with Basic and Extended versions side by side within the same file, and let your end users know that they must use either Basic or Extended. Playback of a file through both Basic and Extended channels with a MIDI Mapper set for All MIDI channels will probably result in many note dropouts.

Sample-based devices, such as the Roland Sound Canvas, do not have the driver problems that FM cards do. That is because FM cards must use a driver to set its patches. The Sound Canvas uses samples stored in ROM to produce sound. Wavetable cards use drivers to load patchbanks, but generally have a capacity for higher polyphony than FM cards do.

Digital Recordings

Many developers of multimedia CD-ROM applications prefer digital recordings to MIDI. Digital recordings are stored in a variety of formats, most of which are variations of PCM (Pulse Code Modulation) encoding. Some of the more common formats are .WAV (Microsoft Windows), .VOC (Creative Labs format), and the AIFF format used in Macintosh computers.

The advantage is that the sound of the music will be the same for all users. Differences in playback quality will vary from one sound card to another, but the basic mix and tonality will be the same.

The downside to digital recording is the file size. Even short clips recorded at higher resolutions can take up more disc space than may be practical for distribution diskettes. Table 10.2 shows file sizes for some of the more common recording rates and resolutions.

Table 10.2. Common recording rates and resolutions.

Sampling Rate	Resolution	File size (per minute of recording time)
44100 Hz stereo	16-bit	10.5MB
44100 Hz mono	16-bit	5.25MB
44100 Hz stereo	8-bit	5.25MB
44100 Hz mono	8-bit	2.125MB
22050 Hz stereo	16-bit	5.25MB
22050 Hz mono	16-bit	2.125MB
22050 Hz stereo	8-bit	1.06MB
22050 Hz mono	8-bit	530KB

The sampling rate for standard audio CDs is 44100 Hz (stereo) at 16-bit resolution. As is apparent from this chart, digitally recorded music for most software distributed on diskette has limited use. Even with software compression, size only decreases by one quarter, and compression is not widely used, so digital audio is likely to remain a space hog for the near future.

As with music and MIDI, a quick glossary is included to familiarize you with some of the terms of digital audio:

A/D, D/A: These terms stand for *analog-to-digital* and *digital-to-analog*. They refer to the circuits that convert analog signals to digital and back again. This is usually the weakest link in the digital-audio chain.

Dynamic Range: The distance between the noise floor and the loudest sound that a circuit can reproduce without distorting. It is often represented in terms of dB. The higher the number, the wider the range and the better the sound.

Normalize: A process of maximizing the volume of a selected portion or the entire digital file. A good editing program will have a normalize function. The term "maximize" should not be used for this function, as the Windows environment uses the term "maximize" to refer to the sizing of a window.

Resolution: This number represents how many levels of loudness (volume) will be used to store an incoming sound. Eight-bit resolution allows for a maximum of 256 levels of volume (256 = two to the eighth power). Sixteen-bit resolution allows for a maximum of 65,536 levels of volume (two to the sixteenth power).

Sampling Rate: This is a number representing how often the incoming analog signal is "looked at" by the A/D converters. At each sampling cycle, a number is assigned to that portion of the sound wave so it can be stored in binary form. The sampling rate is measured in Hertz (or Hz, cycles per second).

The average range of human hearing is 20Hz to 20,000Hz. A sampling rate of 44,100 Hz allows for an upper range in a recording equal to the upper average range of humans. Every time you divide the sampling rate in half, you also lower the upper range of frequencies that can be recorded. In the interest of space, even with CD-ROM applications, oftentimes sampling frequencies are limited to 22,050 Hz.

Recording in 16-bit resolution yields good results, with enough dynamic range to record and reproduce music with the loudest and softest passages intact. Eight-bit recording is roughly equivalent to AM radio. It is adequate for speech, but music suffers. Almost every consumer-grade sound card can play eight-bit files, but there are still a sizable number that cannot use 16-bit files. One solution to this problem is to use only 8-bit files. The down side to this is that 8-bit audio is noisy, compared to 16-bit audio. Another solution is to offer 8-bit and 16-bit files and use your install or setup program to use one or the other. The down side to this is the amount of disc space required.

Most Windows-based digital sound editors have the ability to read and write 16-bit and 8-bit files, as well as to convert from one to the other. Common features also include cut-and-paste functions, digital signal processing (echo, reverb, equalization, etc.), zoom in and out controls to view the waveform, volume controls (fade in, fade out, normalize, mute, etc.), and the ability to import and export file formats like .WAV, .VOC, and many other common file formats.

Correctly edited digital files will have a short (.02 seconds or so) silence at the beginning of the file. This allows sound cards which might have a relatively slow D/C reaction time to go to full volume. The end of the file should have any unnecessary silence cut. Care should be taken that the end of the music doesn't sound chopped off. All files should be normalized as well, to minimize background noise. A digital editor will allow you to check the files to ensure they are edited correctly. Most good digital editing programs for the PC are Windows-based, and include Sound Forge, Wave for Windows from Turtle Beach, and Cool Edit, which is a shareware program.

Hiring a Composer

Before hiring a composer, give the music portion of your project some thought. What kind of mood do you want to create in each part of the story? Some of these ideas will flow from the graphics. It often helps the music along if you can provide your composer with some visuals from the project. These can include stills, but moving graphics in the form of a working demo can be a greater help.

If you are not sure where to find a composer, sources are close at hand if you have an account on one or more of the commercial on-line services or an Internet connection. Look for areas or forums that specialize in MIDI, multimedia, and game development. Browse around and see what kind of messages are posted to be sure you are in the right area. When posting a message, be concise and ask for private e-mail replies. It is OK to ask for samples or a demo cassette.

Consider several things when hiring a composer to provide music for your project. Obviously, one of the first things to consider is his or her compositional style and abilities. Does the composer have a demo tape or disc that contains examples in a variety of styles? As you are well aware, music for games has gone way beyond the days of the Pac Man era. A composer with a broad range of demo music has a better chance of providing the music you want.

Another consideration when hiring a composer is experience. The number of musicians who own a PC with MIDI capabilities is rapidly growing. Many of these musicians are talented players and composers, but they are unaware of how to author MIDI files for software use. MIDI use in Windows is especially demanding, so experience goes a long way when working in Windows. This is not to say that someone new to this field should be ruled out automatically. Don't pass up a talented composer just because he or she might be relatively new to this aspect of MIDI. With a little work and research, many newcomers can learn the ropes and provide you with excellent work.

When hiring a composer or musician, also consider whether your candidate has the proper tools. This may seem like a given, but never assume anything. Don't be afraid to question your prospects about their tools. Most musicians are happy to discuss their setups. Here is a basic list of tools a composer should have:

- PC with MIDI interface
- Professional-level sequencing software (such as Cakewalk Pro or standard, Voyetra SP Gold, Master Tracks Pro, and Cubase)
- MIDI Keyboard
- Sound Blaster (if FM cards are part of your intended market)
- Sound Canvas (any of the SC series)
- A pair of good monitor speakers
- A pair of cheesy PC speakers
- A good, quiet mixer (if he or she will be recording to digital)
- A modem (unless you live close enough in order to shuttle discs)

When doing business with any professional, a solid agreement, in writing, is necessary. Many composers have standard contract forms already prepared. Some will not, so it may be necessary for you to come up with a contract that is workable for you and your composer. This is the time to consult competent legal counsel. It is important to find an attorney who is versed in contract law and is knowledgeable in the computer-software business. One thing to remember is that laws vary from one state to another, so it is important to have a document written that will be valid in your area as well as the state your composer lives in.

It used to be common for game and multimedia developers to demand total legal ownership of the music used in their software. This is changing as the software industry matures and adopts methods used in other entertainment industries. Licensing certain (limited) rights can guarantee that the music you paid to use in your product will not appear in a product from your competitor. It also enables the composer to retain ownership of his or her creation.

The creative process, whether visual or musical, is sometimes hard to put into words. It is important to communicate as clearly and precisely as possible what you want to hear in the music for your project. Familiarizing yourself with the terms used in MIDI and music will go a long way in helping you and your composer understand each other. Don't be afraid to ask "dumb" questions.

After getting all your business and technical ducks in a row, you can start to enjoy the process of integrating music into your project. You will find that good music can bring a screen to life—especially music that was written just for you.

Royalty-Free Music Collections

There are many sources available today for royalty-free collections of music which can be used in game software. These collections offer an alternative to original music written just for your production. Be aware, however, that if you use music from this type of music source, you will probably hear the same music in other products at some point.

When using royalty-free music, be sure to read and understand any and all restrictions placed on the use of the music. What may appear to be a bargain may not be if there are limitations placed on how many clips or how the music may be used.

Summary

By learning how MIDI and digital audio files are constructed and used, you will be better prepared to find and use music that will enhance your software. The following checklist will help you integrate MIDI and digital audio into your program:

- Determine what format the music will be stored in, based on how the software will be distributed. Games that will be marketed on diskettes will probably need to use MIDI for music playback. Software that will be marketed on CD-ROM will probably have the storage space to use digital audio for the music.

- Select musical styles that will support and enhance the action or lack of action on the screen. Often, contrasting the music used for a title or opening screen used during play will add variety and work well together. This step will obviously come after story development has begun.

- Determine a budget for music and decide whether you would prefer to have exclusive use of the music. Exclusive use of the music will cost more than if you use it on a non-exclusive basis. If the budget is low, less than $100, your choices are limited to royalty-free music clips. Depending on who you choose to provide original music, expect to pay from $50 to $500 for a one minute piece of music. The more experienced and better known composers command the highest prices. You should also expect to pay for a portion of the composer's services upon signing a contract, with the remainder paid upon completion of the work.

- Solicit a music provider and discuss your project. Don't be afraid to ask about experience and equipment he or she has at their disposal. Ask for samples of his or her work. Ask if deadlines for completion of work are attainable, and how work will be sent.

- When you have chosen a composer, provide visual aids the composer might need. These could be a few stills in .GIF or .PCX format, or a working model of the game.

- It is helpful to keep in touch with your composer, once work has begun, to occasionally check on progress. E-mail will often work well, since you and your composer can respond at your convenience. E-mail can also come in handy if you wish to communicate often and minimize your long distance calls.

- Always "quality check" the work before it goes into final production. Make sure that the music plays properly every time. Beta test on systems with a variety of sound cards.

- When the work is completed, send the composer a copy of the product. This is an extra "thanks."

Sources for Information

The MIDI specification document is a copyrighted publication. It is available for a nominal fee from the two organizations listed here. They can also provide complete information about General MIDI.

MIDI Manufacturers Association
P.O. Box 3173
La Habra, CA 90632
(310) 947-4569

International MIDI Association
23634 Emelita St.
Woodland Hills, CA 91367
(818) 598-0088 voice
(818) 346-8578 fax

Midpak/Digpak development kit is available on Compuserve in library 14 of the Game Developers' Forum (GO GAMDEV). The filename is DMKIT.ZIP.

WORX is available from:

Mystic Software
434 Haight Street
Alameda, CA 94501
BBS (510) 865-3856

General MIDI Patch Assignments

Pianos/Keyboards

001-Acoustic Grand Piano
002-Bright Acoustic Piano
003-Electric Grand Piano
004-Honky Tonk Piano
005-Rhodes Piano
006-Chorused Piano
007-Harpsichord
008-Clavinette

Chromatic Percussion

009-Celeste
010-Glockenspeil
011-Music Box
012-Vibraphone
013-Marimba
014-Xylophone
015-Tubular Bells
016-Dulcimer

Organs

017-Hammond Organ
018-Percussive Electronic Organ
019-Rock Organ
020-Church (pipe) Organ
021-Reed Organ

022-French Accordion
023-Harmonica
024-Tango Accordion

Guitars

025-Nylon String Guitar
026-Steel String Acoustic Guitar
027-Jazz Guitar
028-Clean Electric Guitar
029-Muted Guitar
030-Overdrive Electric Guitar
031-Distortion Electric Guitar
032-Guitar Harmonics

Basses

033-Acoustic Bass
034-Fingered Bass
035-Picked Bass
036-Fretless Bass
037-Slap Bass 1
038-Slap Bass 2
039-Synth Bass 1
040-Synth Bass 2

Strings and Orchestra

041-Violin
042-Viola
043-Cello
044-Contrabass
045-Tremolo String Section
046-Pizzacato String Section
047-Orchestral Harp
048-Tympani

Ensemble

049-String Section
050-String Section with slow attack
051-Synthesized Strings 1

052-Synthesized Strings 2
053-Choir Aahs
054-Choir Oohs
055-Synthesized Voice
056-Orchestra Hit

Brass

057-Trumpet
058-Trombone
059-Tuba
060-Muted Trumpet
061-French Horn
062-Brass Section
063-Synthesized Brass 1
064-Synthesized Brass 2

Reed

065-Soprano Saxophone
066-Alto Saxophone
067-Tenor Saxophone
068-Baritone Saxophone
069-Oboe
070-English Horn
071-Bassoon
072-Clarinet

Pipe

073-Piccolo
074-Flute
075-Recorder
076-Pan Flute
077-Bottle Blow
078-Shakuhachi
079-Whistle
080-Ocarina

Synthesizer Lead

081-Square Wave
082-Sawtooth Wave
083-Synthesized Calliope
084-Chiffer Lead
085-Charang
086-Solo Voice
087-Sawtooth Wave in Fifths
088-Bass and Lead

Synth Pad

089-Fantasia
090-Warm Pad
091-Polysynth
092-Space Voice
093-Bowed Glass
094-Metal Pad
095-Halo Pad
096-Sweep Pad

Synth Effects

097-Ice Rain
098-Soundtrack
099-Crystal
100-Atmosphere
101-Brightness
102-Goblin
103-Echo Drops
104-Star Theme

Ethnic Miscellaneous

105-Sitar
106-Banjo
107-Shamisen
108-Koto

109-Kalimba
110-Bag Pipe
111-Fiddle
112-Shannai

Percussive

113-Tinkle Bell
114-Agogo
115-Steel Drums
116-Woodblock
117-Taiko
118-Melodic Drum
119-Synth Drum
120-Reverse Cymbal

Special Effects

121-Guitar Fret Noise
122-Breath Noise
123-Seashore
124-Bird Chirps
125-Telephone (warble)
126-Helicopter
127-Applause
128-Gun Shot

Percussion Assignments

Please note that many General MIDI devices have additional percussion sets available by inserting patch numbers for channel 10. These are not part of the General MIDI specification and should not be used to avoid problems with incompatible devices. (See Table 10.3.)

Table 10.3. Additional percussion sets.

MIDI Note Number	Sound
1–26	(none)
27	High Q (filter Q)
28	Slap
29	Scratch Push
30	Scratch Pull

MIDI Note Number	Sound
31	Sticks
32	Square Wave Click
33	Metronome Click
34	Metronome Bell
35	Kick Drum 2
36 C2*	Kick Drum 1
37	Side Stick
38	Snare Drum 1
39	Hand Clap
40	Snare Drum 2
41	Low Tom 2
42	Closed High Hat
43	Low Tom 1
44	Pedal High Hat
45	Mid Tom 2
46	Open High Hat
47	Mid Tom 1
48 C3*	High Tom 2
49	Crash Cymbal 1
50	High Tom 1
51	Ride Cymbal 1
52	Chinese Cymbal
53	Ride Cymbal (bell strike)
54	Tambourine
55	Splash Cymbal
56	Cowbell
57	Crash Cymbal 2
58	Vibra-Slap
59	Ride Cymbal 2
60 (middle C) C4*	High Bongo
61	Low Bongo
62	Mute High Conga

continues

Table 10.3. continued

MIDI Note Number	Sound
63	Open High Conga
64	Low Conga
65	High Timbale
66	Low Timbale
67	High Agogo
68	Low Agogo
69	Cabasa
70	Maracas
71	Short High Whistle
72 C5*	Long Low Whistle
73	Short Guiro
74	Long Guiro
75	Claves
76	High Wood Block
77	Low Wood Block
78	Mute Cuica
79	Open Cuica
80	Mute Triangle
81	Open Triangle
82	Shaker
83	Jingle Bell
84 C6*	(none)
85	Castanets
86	Mute Surdo
87	Open Surdo
88-127	(none)

* indicates position on standard musical keyboard

Advanced Sound Programming

by Keith Weiner and Erik Lorenzen

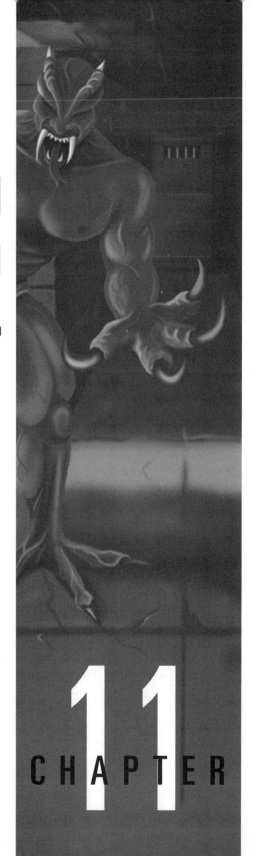

11

CHAPTER

In this chapter we're going to discuss the Sound Blaster family of hardware. We're going to cover, at the low level, how you can make a SB sing, scream, and generate lots of interesting noise.

Our goal is to present an understanding of the hardware which was gleaned from numerous technical specifications, reference manuals, and countless hours in front of the debugger.

> The authors have developed a sound toolkit for DOS games, called DiamondWare's Sound ToolKit (a fully-functional demo of which is included on the CD-ROM in the back of the book). They may be reached at: `keith@dw.com` or `erik@dw.com`.

Some History

In the beginning, microcomputers were silent. Computers such as the Commodore Pet and the TSR-80 had no ability to make noise. To overcome this, game programmers had to be inventive. For example, the developer of a UFO shoot-em-up game for the TSR-80 told players to put an AM radio next to the computer, tuned to 770 (as I recall). The interference generated by the computer made "alien" sounds. Needless to say, the TSR-80 and Commodore Pet were not good for games.

Next came the Apple II with a built-in speaker, which you could program to move in/out at will. The clever programmer could even produce 1-bit speech on it. The super-genius programmer could even do this while animating graphics. But the hardware was weak, the sound was poor, and the CPU was slow.

Until 1987, the PC had only an internal speaker for sound. It could be manipulated manually, just like on the Apple II. If you wanted to devote lots of CPU attention to it, the sound quality could almost be called acceptable, although it could never play loudly. The speaker could also be hooked up to a programmable hardware timer. Used like this, it could play square waves. The music and sound effects thereby generated were not satisfactory at all.

But then the Adlib sound card was released. Its FM (Frequency Modulation) synthesizer was capable of clear music, with 9- or 11-note polyphony (sounds played at the same time), parameterized instrument sounds, rich timbre, decent dynamics, and so on. This card could also be used for sound effects, but that was never its forte.

In 1989, Creative Labs released the Sound Blaster card. It was fully Adlib-compatible (it had the same Yamaha OPL2 FM chip on it), and it offered one additional thing: a DSP (Digital Signal Processor). While this chip isn't powerful at manipulating digital signals, it offers the ability to play and record digital sounds.

We're going to discuss programming the FM section of the Sound Blaster to make music, and programming the DSP for sound effects. It's possible to get sound effects using FM synthesis, but you'll spend more effort to get less consistent, less predictable, and lower-quality sound. It's also possible to produce music using the DSP, but this consumes more memory and directly trades off with your ability to play effects.

FM Synthesis

What is FM?

Before we discuss FM synthesis, let's define our terms. In modulation synthesis, a modulator (sine) wave alters a carrier (sine) wave. The resulting output of the carrier is not sinusoidal.

Because it's less complicated than FM, let's take a brief look at AM (Amplitude Modulation) synthesis. This method uses the voltage output by the modulator to alter the amplitude of the carrier. (See Figure 11.1.) Notice how the amplitude of both the modulator and the carrier have an effect on the amplitude of the output.

The problem with AM is that it doesn't really sound very interesting.

In FM, the voltage output by the modulator is used to alter the frequency of the carrier. Using just two sine waves, it's possible to produce an infinite variety of very rich sounds. (See Figure 11.2.) Unlike in AM, the amplitude of the modulator has no effect on the amplitude of the output.

FM synthesis produces sounds that are more exciting, because the output waveform is much more harmonically rich.

Note that the OPL2 chip is entirely digital. The output is actually a 13-bit floating-point number, which is converted to analog by a separate DAC (Digital-to-Analog Converter), in 16 bits of precision.

Figure 11.1.
*The carrier, the
modulator, and
the AM output.*

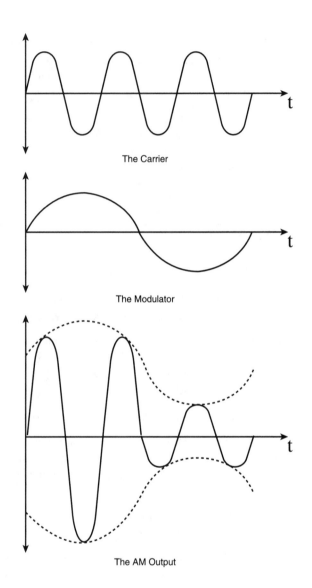

The Carrier

The Modulator

The AM Output

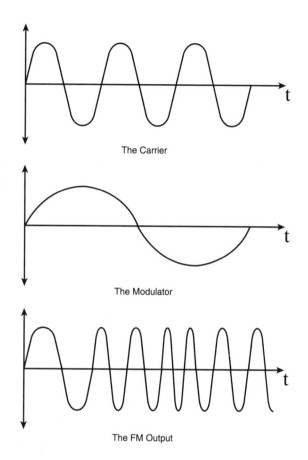

Figure 11.2.
The carrier, the modulator, and the FM output.

The Carrier

The Modulator

The FM Output

The Basics of Music Synthesis

Before we get into the details of programming the OPL2 chip, let's go over the basic theory of operation in music synthesis.

We have a waveform. Simply switching it on when a note is hit, and switching it off when the note is done doesn't sound very musical. It's not natural. Notes played on real instruments don't instantly hit full volume when they're first struck, and they don't instantly shut down to 0 when they're released.

Instead, the characteristics of a realistic note be defined by an *envelope* (a set of parameters to apply to the output waveform). The four parameters are *attack* (how fast the output level rises when the note is first hit), *decay* (how fast it falls after the initial attack), *sustain* (the level it holds for a while), and *release* (how fast it falls to 0 when it's finished). (See Figure 11.3.)

Figure 11.3.

The two envelope types.

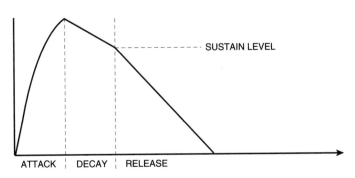

Envelope for a Diminishing sound

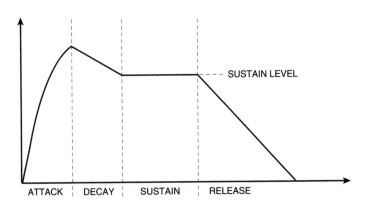

Envelope for a Continuing sound

With proper envelopes applied, notes will sound much better. The FM chip is capable of approximating the sound made by real accoustic instruments, although it's obviously better at electronic sounds.

The sound card gives you only two ports with which to access the OPL2. For this discussion, we'll call them X and Y. On the Adlib, these are hard-wired to X=388h and Y=389h. The Sound Blaster supports these addresses for compatibility purposes but it also makes X=BASE+8, and Y=BASE+9. For example, if BASE=220h (the most common address by far), then X=228h and Y=229h.

The OPL2 chip has many registers. Except for the status register, they're all write-only (when will hardware designers wake up?), and they're multiplexed into ports X and Y.

Port X is read/write. Reading from it returns the status register. Writing to it selects the address of an internal register and latches it. Port Y is write only. Writing to port Y writes to the currently selected register.

> You must wait 3.3 microseconds after writing to port X before any other access is valid. You must wait at least 23 microseconds after writing to port Y. This allows the slow, asynchronous hardware to complete your request.

In addition to its nine voices, the OPL2 also includes two timers. Timer 1 ticks at 12,500 Hz (ticks are 80 microseconds apart). Timer 2 ticks at 3125 Hz (ticks are 320 microseconds apart).

Yamaha intended these timers to be able to generate interrupts when they timed out. On the Adlib and Sound Blaster, however, they're not connected to the interrupt controller, but they do set readable flags when they timeout.

We are going to describe, in detail, the registers of the OPL2 synthesizer. For each, we'll first present a table. It will show you where we're going, and later it will be a useful reference. Following the table, we'll discuss each bit, if necessary, in text.

The top three bits in the status register correspond to the "IRQ" state, the first timer, and the second timer, respectively. (See Table 11.1.)

Table 11.1. The read/write status register.

D7	D6	D5	D4	D3	D2	D1	D0
IRQ	T1	T2	-	-	-	-	-

All other registers are write-only. Table 11.2 gives an overview of them. Note that there are three types. Some contol the entire chip, some control one voice, and some control only one operator. We'll cover this last point in more detail in later sections.

Don't be afraid of our heavy use of acronyms. Read on for the full exposition.

Table 11.2. Write-only registers.

Address	Description
01h	Wave select, Test
02h	T1 (Timer 1)
03h	T2 (Timer 2)
04h	IRQ Reset, Timer controls
08h	Composite Speech Mode, Keyboard Split Point
*20h–35h	AM, VIB, Envelope type, KSR, Multiple
*40h–55h	KSL, Total level
*60h–75h	Attack, Decay

continues

Table 11.2. continued

Address	Description
*80h–95h	Sustain, Release
+a0h–a8h	Low F-Number
+b0h–b8h	Key on, Block, High F-Number
bdh	AM depth, VIB depth, Rhythm enable, Drum keys on
+coh–c8h	Feedback, Connection
*e0h–f5h Wave select	

* There is one of these registers for each operator.
\+ There is one of these registers for each voice.

Some registers apply to the entire OPL2 chip; there is only one of each of these. Other registers apply to one voice; there are nine of each of these.

Some registers apply to each operator; there are 18 of each of these. Table 11.3 is a chart showing the offset of each, the number of the operator it controls, the number of the voice, and whether the operator is the (M)odulator or the (C)arrier:

Table 11.3. Details of register offsets.

Offset	00	01	02	03	04	05	08	09		
	0a	0b	0c	0d	10	11	12	13	14	15
Operator	1	2	3	4	5	6	7	8		
	9	10	11	12	13	14	15	16	17	18
Voice	1	2	3	1	2	3	4	5		
	6	4	5	6	7	8	9	7	8	9
Function	M	M	M	C	C	C	M	M		
	M	C	C	C	M	M	M	C	C	C

The Nitty Gritty

This section will cover all the registers of the OPL2 synthesizer chip. We'll cover them in numerical order.

Wave Select (Register 01h)

Set/reset bit 5 to enable/disable wave-selection mode for each operator. Reset all other bits.

Timer 1 (Register 02h)

Writing to this register controls the duration of Timer 1. The countdown time is given as

```
T = (256 - N) * (80 microseconds)
```

When Timer 1 times out, the IRQ and Timer 1 flags are set in the status register, and the Timer begins again with the same value.

Timer 2 (Register 03h)

This is the same as Timer 1, except that the resolution is 320 microseconds.

IRQ Reset, Timer controls (Register 04h)

This register controls the two timers provided on the OPL2 synthesizer chip. See Table 11.4 for a bit-by-bit description.

Table 11.4. Register 04h.

D7	D6	D5	D4	D3	D2	D1	D0
IRQ	Reset	T1 Mask	T2 Mask	-	-	T2 enable	T1 enable

Set bit 7 to reset all flags in the status register.

Each mask bit prevents the status register from showing the corresponding timer as "timed out."

Each enable bit starts and stops the corresponding timer.

Composite Speech Mode, Keyboard Split Point (Register 08h)

Register 08h controls the mode of the chip (composite speech mode, or FM music synthesis). It also specifies the keyboard split point. (See Table 11.5.)

Table 11.5. Register 08h.

D7	D6	D5	D4	D3	D2	D1	D0
CSM	Kbd split	-	-	-	-	-	-

Composite speech mode was never popular, and it probably hasn't been used in years (since the advent of the Sound Blaster DAC).

The "keyboard split point" effects when the OPL2 thinks a note is "high." With KSR (Keyboard Setting of Rate), set in register 20h–35h, high notes' envelopes are shortened (as in real life). We've never heard any difference resulting from how this bit is set; outside Yamaha documentation, nothing really explains it. Reset both bits.

Tremolo, Vibrato, Envelope, KSR, Multiple (Register 20h–35h)

This register specifies some parameters for how a note will sound. (See Table 11.6.)

Table 11.6. Register 20h–35h.

D7	D6	D5	D4	D3	D2	D1	D0
AM	VIB	ET	KSR	Mult3	Mult2	Mult1	Mult0

Setting AM to 1 enables Amplitude Modulation of 3.7 Hz (tremolo). The depth of the tremolo is determined by the AM depth field of register bdh.

Setting VIB to 1 enables a 6.4 Hz vibrato effect. The depth of vibrato is determined by the VIB depth field of register bdh.

Setting ET to 1 makes the operator continuing. Resetting it makes the operator diminishing.

Setting the KSR to 1 enables shortening of high notes' envelopes.

The 4-bit Multiple is used as a table look-up. The result is literally multiplied times the frequency of the operator. (See Table 11.7.)

Table 11.7. The KSR 4-bit multiple.

Multiple	Frequency factor
0	0.5
1	1
2	2
3	3

Multiple	Frequency factor
4	4
5	5
6	6
7	7
8	8
9	9
0a	10
0bh	10
0ch	12
0dh	12
0eh	15
0fh	15

KSL, Total Level (Register 40h–55h)

Bits 6–7 of this register are the KSL (Key Scaling Level). This parameter cuts the volume of high-frequency notes as show in Table 11.8.

Table 11.8. The volume of high-frequency notes.

KSL	Attenuation
00	-
10	1.5 db/oct
01	3 db/oct
11	6 db/oct

Total level would be better named "Attenuation." The output of the operator will be attenuated by 0.75 total level.

Attack, Decay (Register 60h–75h)

The Attack rate and Decay rate are four bits each; together, they specify the first half of the envelope for a sound.

Sustain, Release (Register 80h—95h)

Sustain level and Release rate are four bits each. For sustaining sounds, Sustain is the level held by the sound until the note is released. For diminishing sounds, Sustain is the level where the decay part of the envelope transitions to the release part of the envelope.

Low F-Number (Register a0h—a8h)

This register holds the bottom eight bits of F-Num.

Key on, Block, High F-Number (Register b0—b8)

This register controls the "key on" bit and the octave for a note. (See Table 11.9.)

Table 11.9. Register b0—b8h.

D7	D6	D5	D4	D3	D2	D1	D0
-	-	Key on	BL2	BL1	BL0	F-Num9	F-Num 8

F-Number is a 10-bit number formed from the 8 bits of Low F-Number and High F-Number. Block is a 3-bit number which is essentially the octave. Set the Key On bit to play the note. Reset Key On to stop it.

The actual frequency of the operator is given as:

```
F = 50000 * F-Number * 2^(Block - 20)
```

AM depth, VIB depth, Rhythm Enable, Drum Keys On (Register bdh)

This register controls some miscellaneous global sound parameters, plus the percussion section of the chip. (See Table 11.10.) Doesn't hardware penny-pinching make the programmer's life easy and simple?

Table 11.10. Register bdh.

D7	D6	D5	D4	D3	D2	D1	D0
AM depth	VIB depth	Rhythm	Bass	Snare	Tom	Cym	Hi-hat

AM stands for Amplitude Modulation, which is tremolo. If AM depth is 1, tremolo depth is 4.8db; if it's 0, tremolo depth is 1db.

VIB stands for vibrato. If VIB depth is 1, vibrato is 14 percent; if it's 0, vibrato depth is 7 percent.

Rhythm Enable puts the OPL2 into percussion mode. In this mode, there are only six melody instruments, plus five drums: bass, snare, tom, top cymbal, and hi hat.

In percussion mode, the remaining bits key these drums on/off.

Feedback, Connection (Register c0h—c8h)

This register controls the setup of the two operators of a sound. (See Table 11.11.)

Table 11.11. Register c0h—c8h.

D7	D6	D5	D4	D3	D2	D1	D0
-	-	-	-	FB2	FB1	FB0	Connection

Feedback is a three-bit quantity. Use it as a lookup into Table 11.12 to determine feedback FM modulation of the modulator operator:

Table 11.12. Feedback FM modulation of modulator.

Feedback	000	001	010	011	100	101	110	111
Modulation	0	P/16	P/8	P/4	P/2	P	2 P	4 P

If the Connection bit is reset, then the two operators for this voice are connected for frequency modulation. If it's set to 1, then they're connected in parallel. (They're both carriers.)

Wave Select (Register e0h-f5h)

The bottom 2 bits of this register determine the waveform used to synthesize the sound. See Figure 11.4.

This register is ignored, unless bit 5 of register 1 is set.

The OPL FM synthesizer chips are surprisingly powerful, and also complex little beasts. We presented each register in this section, giving you everything you need to write drivers for FM music.

Figure 11.4.
Wave types.

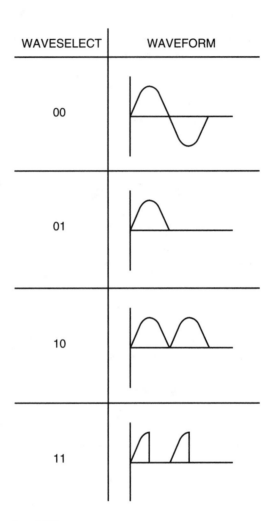

WAVESELECT	WAVEFORM
00	
01	
10	
11	

Storing Instruments in Files

You can store everything required to program a sound in 11 bytes (although it's padded out to 16), which we'll call an *instrument patch*. Table 11.13 describes each byte and indicates which register should be programmed with this parameter.

Table 11.13. The instrument patch.

Byte	Description	Register
00	Modulator Sound Characteristic	20h–35h
01	Carrier Sound Characteristic	20h–35h

Byte	Description	Register
02	Modulator Scaling/Output Level	40h–55h
03	Carrier Scaling/Output Level	40h–55h
04	Modulator Attack/Decay	60h–75h
05	Carrier Attack/Decay	60h–75h
06	Modulator Sustain/Release	80h–95h
07	Carrier Sustain/Release	80h–95h
08	Modulator Wave Select	e0h–f5h
09	Carrier Wave Select	e0h–f5h
10	Feedback/Connection	c0h–c8h
11–15	Padding	-

The .IBK file consists of a header, which is IBK\1a; 128 instruments of 16 bytes each; and 128 instrument names of nine characters apiece.

The AT-101 Keyboard

We'll briefly discuss the AT-101 keyboard (since we're using it in the accompanying program).

The keyboard controller generates an interrupt on IRQ 1 (Interrupt 9 to the CPU) for each *key make* (when a key is hit), for each *key break* (whenever it lets up), and whenever it wants to auto-repeat a key that is being held down.

For a synthesizer (or a game), you want to know what keys are being held down right now. You probably want to deal with auto-repeat yourself, if at all. So, we'll bypass the DOS/BIOS keyboard handler and services.

The key (slight play on words intended) is to write an interrupt handler for the keyboard interrupt. That way, we can intercept all these messages. We'll create an array to store the state of each key. When we get an interrupt for a key make, we'll set the byte corresponding to that key. When we get a key break, we'll reset the corresponding byte. Auto-repeats just come in as key makes, so there will be no harm done.

Since we're going to cut the DOS and/or BIOS keyboard handlers out of the chain (for the duration of our execution), it's important to ensure that our program can terminate. If it doesn't, not even the Vulcan Nerve Pinch (Ctrl+Alt+Del) will work.

In C, it's important to declare the array with the volatile type qualifier. This tells the C compiler that the values therein could change at any time (literally), and so it won't cache them in registers.

Make sure that you disable stack checking in any interrupt handler! And do not call any standard library or DOS functions from an interrupt handler. They're not designed to be re-entrant— you'll cause intermittant crashes.

We're dealing with scan codes and not ASCII. We've provided a table of many useful scancodes in KEY.H.

Key makes are raw scan codes. Key breaks are also scan codes but with the high-bit set.

KEY.C shows you what you need to do to trap the keyboard interrupt in your own programs.

The OPLKBD Program

OPLKBD is provided as an example program that uses the OPL2.

It loads an .IBK file (128 instruments) into memory. It determines if there's an OPL2 in the system. It performs a RESET operation on it. It goes into a hot-loop watching for keypresses. It enables you to raise or lower the octave. It enables you to change the instrument. It also enables you to play several notes simultaneously. It terminates when you hit ESC.

To play a note, it looks in a shadow array for an unused voice in the OPL2 chip and marks it as used. It programs the voice with the parameters for the current instrument and sounds the voice. When you let up on the key for that note, it keys off the OPL2 voice, and marks it as unused.

The code itself is straightforward and self-documenting.

To run the program, you'll need an .IBK file. (GM1.IBK, included with DiamondWare's Sound ToolKit on the bundled CD-ROM, will work fine.)

Make sure you compile for large model!

Try hitting several keys at the same time. Based on what you hear, you can modify the .IBK file to improve it.

Tab stops are set to 2.

Digitized Sounds

How Does Digitized Sound Work?

In digitized sound, you start with an analog wave and digitize it (periodically measure its voltage). Until it's digitized, it's analog. It can be distorted or filtered either deliberately or accidentally.

Figure 11.5 shows a continuous (analog) and a discrete (digitized) wave. Digitized sounds are discretely quantized. This means they have a finite value for a finite number of instants in time.

Figure 11.5.
Comparing continuous and discrete waves.

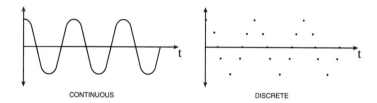

The range of values for each sample is finite. Let's take the case of an eight-bit system, which allows values from −128 to +127. Any sound softer than +/−1 is lost. Any sound louder than +127/−128 will be clipped (distorted badly). This applies to each sound individually and to the total if we're mixing several sounds together.

Just as the range of samples is not infinite, neither is the domain. We call digitized sounds "discretely quantized" because they are not contiguous in the time domain. They're sampled at T=1 and T=2, but not at T=1.5. There's obviously sound at every moment, even during those moments in-between the sample points. This is a non-trivial problem.

Let's briefly look at analog waveforms. Digital signal theory asserts that every possible analog waveform can be represented by the sum of a series of pure sine waves. Any finite waveform, such as those produced in the real world, is the sum of a finite series of sine waves. The highest frequency sine wave in this series is no higher than the highest frequency in the original wave.

In this model, the waveform is the time domain, as would be shown on an oscilliscope. The vertical axis indicates amplitude (voltage), and the horizontal indicates (increasing) time. The coefficients of the sine waves could be said to be the frequency domain. The horizontal axis of a plot of this would represent (increasing) frequency. (See figures 11.6 and 11.7.)

Figure 11.6.
A wave in the time domain.

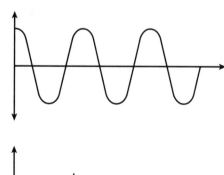

Figure 11.7.
The same wave in the frequency domain.

It's been determined that, *in order to capture a waveform containing frequencies up to F, you need to sample it at a rate of at least 2F.* This is called the Nyquist rate.

Lower sampling rates will cause aliasing problems, where high-frequency sounds are aliased as one or more lower frequencies. This sounds like a harsh, metallic overtone added to the original sound. To visualize this better, think of the infamous problem of drawing a diagonal line on a low-resolution screen, or of watching a spinning propeller seem to turn slowly backwards. The frequency (resolution) of the screen is too low to display the line. The sampling rate of the human eye is too low to see a 15,000 RPM propeller.

Figures 11.8, 11.9, and 11.10 show an analog wave and its frequency spectrum. If it's sampled above the Nyquist rate, as shown in Figure 11.9, it can be reconstructed correctly. Otherwise, as shown in Figure 11.10, alaising occurs.

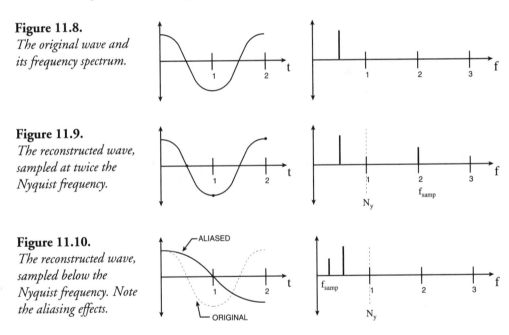

Figure 11.8.
The original wave and its frequency spectrum.

Figure 11.9.
The reconstructed wave, sampled at twice the Nyquist frequency.

Figure 11.10.
The reconstructed wave, sampled below the Nyquist frequency. Note the aliasing effects.

You might wonder how we can reconstruct a sine wave from only two points per cycle. It's possible because we know, *a priori,* that it is a sine wave. Only one frequency will fit both points.

As shown in Figure 11.11, the reconstructed wave looks quite square. Those sharp edges are built from a large number of very high frequencies (which are all above the Nyquist rate). This is an artifact of the quantization and reconstruction process; it sounds like a harsh metallic overtone added to the original sound. Fortunately, we can simply low-pass filter the output analog wave, as shown in Figure 11.12.

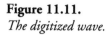

Figure 11.11.
The digitized wave.

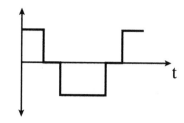

Figure 11.12.
The filtered wave.

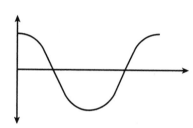

Although the following doesn't really relate to game-sound playback, I'll mention it because it's used in every CD player. Analog filters distort the sound. The steeper the cutoff, the worse they sound. So instead of the manufacturers trying to build a filter that passes everything below 20 KHz and cuts everything above 20.001 KHz, they use oversampling. If you take the sample data in the frequency domain, add extra zeroes for all the frequencies above your actual sound data, and convert back to the time domain, you'll have a smoother interpolation of the original sound. And the harmonic overtones will be at a higher frequency and thus easier to filter. So don't let that cocky salesman tell you "This player reads the disc eight times, so it doesn't make as many errors."

The Sound Blaster Family

Creative Labs has produced 10 distinct models in its Sound Blaster series of sound cards. The most popular are the SB16, SB Pro2, and SB2.1, which are all still selling in 1995.

They are all built on a common architecture, which was first used in the Sound Blaster 1.5. Table 11.14 shows the complete model line.

Table 11.14. The Sound Blaster model line.

Model	DSP* Version	Type (as used in BLASTER variable)
SB 1.5	1.*xx*	1
SB 1.5 MCV+	1.*xx*	1

continues

Table 11.14. continued

Model	DSP* Version	Type (as used in BLASTER variable)
SB 2.0	2.00	2
SB 2.1	2.01	2
SB 2 CD	2.??	2
SB Pro 1	3.*xx*	3
SB Pro 2	3.*xx*	4
SB Pro MCV+	3.*xx*	5
SB 16	4.*xx*	6
SB AWE32	4.*xx*	6

* Digital Signal Processor (Creative Labs' term for the SB's brain)
+ Micro Channel version

We'll discuss the SB 2.01 because it's the least common denominator still available today. The higher models are all backwardly compatible to it.

Finding the Sound Blaster

You can ask the user for the parameters to his sound card. But, for the mass market, this solution is unworkable. The average user often doesn't know the answers.

One way to find the SB is to parse the BLASTER environment variable. It's the easiest method, and it's recommended by Creative Labs and other manufacturers. Parsing environment variables can't cause a system crash—but running sound code configured with the wrong parameters can.

A typical BLASTER variable might look like this:

```
BLASTER=A220 I5 D1 H5 P330 T6
```

A is the base port address. Values from 210h to 280h are valid.

I is the IRQ level. Values may be 2, 3, 5, 7, or 10.

D is the 8-bit DMA channel. Values may be 0, 1, or 3.

H (if present) is the 16-bit DMA channel: 5, 6, or 7.

P (if present) is the port for MPU401: 300h or 330h.

T is the type. (See Table 11.14.)

Programming the Sound Blaster

In this section, we'll present the DSP section of the Sound Blaster board, plus the other PC hardware you'll need. The DSP, interrupt controller, and DMA controller work together to play sound while the CPU does other work.

There are 15 steps to programming the SB:

1. Reset the SB DSP, and put it into a known state
2. Setup your Interrupt Service Routine (ISR)
3. Enable the IRQ used by the SB
4. Program the DAC speaker
5. Program the DMA controller for single transfer auto-init mode
6. Program the playback rate (Time Constant)
7. Program the DSP Output for auto-init single-transfer mode

Sound transfer (playback) begins immediately after Step 7. Now the sound code operates in the background (during interrupts). When the current DMA buffer is done playing, the SB generates an interrupt. This will transfer control to the ISR. The ISR must:

8. Mix sounds into DMA buffer
9. Acknowlwdge the SB DSP
10. Send the Programmable Interrupt Controller (PIC) an End Of Interrupt (EOI)

Before the program terminates, we need to:

11. Disable the DAC speaker
12. Disable our IRQ
13. Disable our DMA channel
14. Unhook our ISR
15. Reset the SB DSP (leave it in a good state for other apps)

Before we get into the details, we need to cover the ports used by the SB. Table 11.15 shows the addresses used by the SB DSP. Note that reading and writing are not complementary! Also note that one port behaves differently during an interrupt than at other times. If this seems complex, it's typical of mass-market hardware where saving 30 cents per unit might mean $3 million to $5 million!

Table 11.15. The SB DSP.

Port	Write	Read	During IRQ
2X6h	sb_RESET	none	normal
2XAh	none	sb_READ_DATA	normal
2XCh	sb_WRITE_COMMAND	sb_WRITE_STATUS	normal
2XEh	none	sb_READ_STATUS	sb_ACKIRQ (read-only)

X denotes base address. For a base address of 220h, ports are 226h, 22Ah, 22Ch, and 22Eh.

Look Before You Leap

We don't want to accept the BLASTER variable's word on faith, not if we can verify some of it on our own. We can check to see if a SB DSP is really in the system at the expected port address. Incidentally, this will reset it, which is required anyway. Here's what you do:

1. Write a 1 to sb_RESET port.
2. Wait three microseconds.
3. Write a 0 to sb_RESET.
4. Read sb_READ_STATUS (up to 65,535 times) waiting for the msb to be set.
5. If it never gets set, there is no SB.
6. Read sb_READ_DATA. If the return value is AAh there is a SB present.
7. If not, repeat steps 4 to 6 until the count runs out or SB is found.

Reading and Writing

To read data from the DSP we must read from sb_READ_STATUS until the MSB is set. Then read from sb_READ_DATA.

To write to the DSP, read from sb_COMMAND_STATUS until the MSB is reset. Then write the desired command (or command data) to sb_WRITE_COMMAND.

DMA Transfer

The DSP and DMA controller will play sound for a while without CPU attention. When the buffer has been emptied, the SB DSP generates an interrupt. Our ISR will catch this signal and set up the next buffer.

Using DSP Commands

There are dozens of DSP commands supported by the Sound Blaster family. In the included code, we use five of them. (See Table 11.16.)

Table 11.16. Some SB DSP commands.

Number	Description
40h	Set time constant.
48h	Set block transfer size.
1ch	Start eight-bit auto-init DMA output.
D1h	Enable DAC speaker.
D3h	Disable DAC speaker.

The function `sb_WriteDSP`, from the included source code, is used to send DSP commands.

The DAC speaker setting determines if we can hear the SB (for playing), or if it can hear us (for recording). With the speaker on, we can hear the digitized playback, but the SB can't hear us (record), and vice versa.

To turn on the speaker, send `sb_DACSPKRON` to the DSP. After this, you have to wait at least 112 microseconds before touching the SB DSP again:

```
sb_WriteDSP(baseport, sb_DACSPKRON);
```

To turn off the speaker, send `sb_DACSPKROFF` to the DSP, and then wait 220 microseconds:

```
sb_WriteDSP(baseport, sb_DACSPKROFF);
```

Do not program the speaker while DMA transfer is in progress; this can have undesired (and unpredictable) results.

The `sb_SETTIMECONST` command controls the transfer rate of playback or recording (and hence the sampling rate). You have to convert the frequency to SB Time Constant, and then send this to the SB. The TC is an unsigned byte. Use the following code to program the rate:

```
rate = 256 - (1000000 / (num_channels * sampling_rate));
sb_WriteDSP(baseport, sb_SETTIMECONST);
sb_WriteDSP(baseport, rate);
```

In order to play a sound, you have to tell the DSP to start. There are many different commands for this, depending on the desired mode. We'll use 1ch (start eight-bit auto-init DMA output). Here's how you do it:

```
sb_WriteDSP(baseport, sb_SETBLOCKTRANSIZE);
sb_WriteDSP(baseport, (BYTE)(buffsize - 1));       //low byte
sb_WriteDSP(baseport, (BYTE)((buffsize - 1) >> 8)); //high byte
sb_WriteDSP(baseport, sb_PLAY8BITMONO);
```

In this mode, the SB samples at rates from 4000Hz to 23,000Hz.

The Programmable Interrupt Controller (PIC)

As we mentioned previously, the SB DSP generates an interrupt when it wants another buffer. Let's go over the details of this process involved in an Interrupt ReQuest (IRQ).

Building an IRQ

Here's a blow-by-blow description of what occurs during the process of creating an IRQ inside the hardware:

- The SB DSP pulls an Interrupt Request Line (IRL) high, signaling that it wants CPU attention
- The PIC sets the corresponding bit in the Interrupt Request Register (IRR)
- The PIC looks at the Interrupt Mask Register (IMR) to see if this is allowed
- No: The PIC waits until it's unmasked
- The PIC checks the In Service Register (ISR) for higher-priority IRQ's
- Yes: The PIC waits until all have sent an End of Interrupt (EOI)
- The PIC sends an INT signal to the CPU
- The CPU checks the Interrupt Flag
- Reset: Wait until the flag is set
- The CPU sends an INTerrupt Acknowledge (INTA) to the PIC
- The PIC checks the corresponding bit in IRR
- Reset: IRQ level is 7 (spurious)
- Set: IRQ level is determined from which line was pulled
- The PIC sets the corresponding bit in the ISR (unless IRQ is spurious)
- The PIC resets the corresponding bit in the IRR
- The CPU sends a second INTA
- The PIC puts the 8-bit IRQ level on the data bus
- The CPU pushes the flags, CS, and IP registers, respectively, on the current stack
- The CPU sets CS:IP to the address specified in the vector table for this IRQ
- Execution begins in the ISR

Handling the IRQ

These are steps you must take to handle an IRQ in your code:

1. Acknowledge the hardware (SB DSP), which makes it stop pulling the IRL
2. Send an EOI to the PIC
3. Optionally set a global variable (flag) for use by the main program loop
4. Prepare the next sound buffer
5. Return from interrupt (IRET instruction)

See the included sample code for an example on how to do all this.

The DMA Controller

The DMA controller can transfer data between memory and the I/O bus without CPU involvement. This is how sound is played in the background.

> Although the DMA controller transfers data without using the CPU, it must impose wait-states on the processor because they share the same bus.

AT-compatibles have two DMA controllers, one for eight-bit transfers and one for 16-bit transfers. We'll look at the eight-bit channels, because most Sound Blasters are 8-bit boards. Possible channels are 0, 1, and 3. 2 is for the floppy drives, and 4 through 7 are 16-bit channels.

We're using single transfer mode. In this mode, one byte is transferred by the DMA controller for each Data REQuest (DREQ) it receives from the SB DSP.

Setting Up

The following listing shows the steps involved in initializing the DMA controller:

1. Disable interrupts
2. Disable our DMA channel*
3. Reset the flip-flop*
4. Set our channel's mode+
5. Program the address register+
6. Program the page register+

7. Program the count register (with 1 less than the actual transfer count)+

8. Enable the DMA channel*

9. Enable interrupts

---

* This is a shared register; it's used for all channels.

\+ This is a channel-specific register.

You program the DMA controller with physical addresses, not with *segment:offset* addresses or selectors. In real mode, it's easy to translate from *segment:offset* to physical address.

The page number is calculated from a physical address by dividing by 65,536. The DMA controller cannot cross page boundaries when transferring data, so you must ensure that your DMA buffer does not cross a 64KB boundary—even in protected-mode. Within the page, the DMA controller increments a simple index.

To translate from *segment:offset* to page:

```
off = (*((unsigned _far *)&(buffer)));
seg = (*((unsigned _far *)&(buffer) + 1));
seg <<= 4;
padd = seg + off;                       // calc physical address
page = padd >> 16;                      // calc page number
```

Don't be put off by our ugly-looking method to get the segment and offset of a pointer. We're simply taking a pointer to buffer. Then, we're taking a pointer to this. The first word at this address is the offset of our buffer, and the second is the segment.

In the last few sections, we covered the SB DSP, PIC, and DMA controller. These different pieces of hardware work together to provide background playback of digitized sound.

The SFXMIX Program

SFXMIX is provided on the bundled CD-ROM as an example program that programs the Sound Blaster DSP.

It reads in several .WAV files (specified on the command line) and enables you to trigger them in real-time using the keyboard. It sets up the DMA controller, interrupt controller, and SB DSP for auto-init DMA transfer. Whenever you hit a key corresponding to a .WAV file, it mixes it into the DMA buffer. It clips the output if it exceeds eight bits.

You'll need several .WAV files. (Some are included with the source code for this chapter.)

The code that accompanies this chapter was tested with Microsoft C/C++ 7, Borland C/C++ 3, Borland C/C++ 4 (with some warnings), Turbo C/C++ 3 (with some warnings), and Watcom C/C++ 10 (real-mode). It should port easily to other DOS C environments. We used the large memory model when we compiled it. We tested it with a Sound Blaster 2.1, Pro 2, 16, and AWE32. Make sure you compile for large model!

Tab stops are set to 2.

If This Isn't Enough

For further information, we refer you to two good books that provide in-depth explanations of PC sound engineering:

Developer Kit for Sound Blaster Series, 2nd Edition, Creative Labs, 1993.

Hans-Peter Messmer, *The Indispensible PC Hardware Book*, Addison-Wesley, 1993.

Summary

The Sound Blaster card is really two totally different pieces of hardware in one physical package. The FM synthesizer chip does a decent job producing music, though programming it is far from straightforward. The DSP chip enables you to reproduce any sound which can be recorded— what else can you ask for?

This chapter provides a basic introduction to these two chips. The astute reader has probably noticed that we haven't covered how to play MIDI music on the FM chip. This would involve reprogramming the timer chip, parsing the MIDI file format, and mapping its events to OPL2 programming. Each of these steps is non-trivial.

Similarly, we didn't cover digital polyphony. Most games today can play more than one sound simultaneously. The SB DSP cannot. It's possible to mix digital sounds in software.

To be fair, however, we covered the hardware in enough detail so that you can program it. Once you know how to talk to the machine at the lowest level, you can build structures as high as you wish.

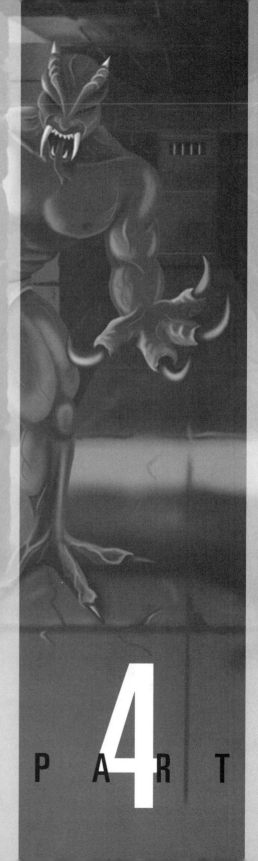

Fine Tuning

P A R T 4

Debugging Games

by Mark Seminatore

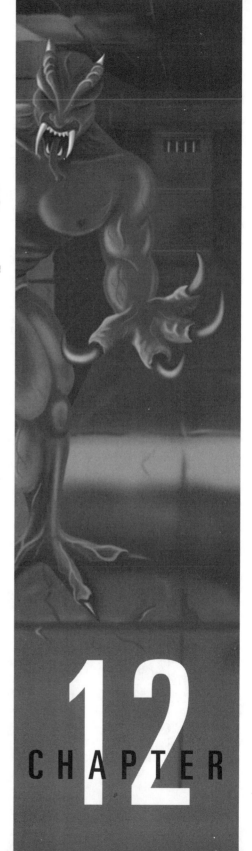

CHAPTER 12

Already this book has covered a great deal of information on developing computer games. There have been chapters on high-performance graphics, realistic digital sound effects, and advanced topics such as code optimization. You may have also read the predecessor to this book, entitled *Tricks of the Game Programming Gurus*. The first book also covered many facets of game development. So perhaps now you are ready to tackle a game development project of your own. Before you do, however, it might be worth taking a few minutes to read this chapter; it discusses a very important aspect of game development—debugging your code.

Introduction to Debugging

Do you remember the last time you developed a large and complicated application? It doesn't matter how large or how complicated it was; just remember your most difficult project. Now, which part of the development process did you find to be the most frustrating (that is, other than meeting your deadlines)? I will bet that your answer was tracking down and eliminating the last few bugs before release. I will also wager that you found this phase of the development process to be the most time-consuming. In fact, it is quite possible that you spent several weeks tracking down subtle bugs in your code. The errors may have been in your code, in the code generator of your compiler, in the compiler runtime library, or perhaps in third-party libraries that were used.

Debugging is a critical part of development and is therefore a necessary evil. If a bug slips through the development process and gets caught by the beta-testers, it can be embarrassing to the developers. Even worse, if the bug shows up after the program is commercially released, it can be costly. Thanks to the online gaming community, you can be sure that news of a bug in your game will spread. If you don't respond quickly and the bug affects game playability, you may find that your sales are significantly reduced. The cost of providing bug patches and technical support can be overwhelming, especially for small development teams. This has to be one of the worst nightmares of a game programmer—it is also the main reason why software undergoes rigorous beta-testing before final release. No, beta-testing won't eliminate every bug in your application. A good beta-test process should, however, catch bugs your endusers are most likely to encounter. (We won't discuss beta-testing here since the subject is covered in detail in Chapter 15, "Beta-Testing Your First Game.")

> Of all the phases of game development, debugging is by far the most critical. Nobody wants to play a game which is full of annoying bugs. Unfortunately, debugging is often the largest source of lost productivity in game development. Remember that time spent tracking down persistent bugs wastes precious development money and resources and adds little value to the finished game.

For the purposes of this discussion, it is convenient to divide debugging into two subcategories. These are bug prevention and bug detection/elimination. Sounds easy enough, but mastering these processes is one of the more difficult aspects of programming. The first part of this chapter will focus primarily on bug prevention. The remaining portion will cover bug detection and other debugging topics.

> This chapter was written with C/C++ development in mind, and this is reflected in the code examples. However, the techniques presented in this chapter should transfer to other programming environments as well. All code was written and tested under the Borland C++ 3.1 IDE. Every effort has been made to avoid Borland-specific dependencies when possible. The code was also tested with Watcom's C32 or DOS compiler, version 9.5b. In any case, the general debugging ideas presented in this chapter are not tied to a particular debugging product. Feel free to compile the example programs and load them into your debugger as the chapter moves along.
>
> The following command lines may be used to compile the examples:
>
> ```
> BCC -ms -w
>
>
> WCL386 /l=386 /w3
> ```

Which Debugger Should I Use?

A logical question at this point might be: "Which debugger should I use?" Or perhaps you might ask, "Should I simply use the debugger that came with my compiler?" The answer to both of these questions is basically the same. As when choosing a programming language, the choice of a debugger is most often a matter of personal preference. The bottom line is, pick the debugger with which you are the most comfortable. After all, you are likely to use it for hours on end. If you find a debugger that meets your needs, whether it came with your compiler or not, then by all means use it.

Actually, most compilers today come bundled with excellent debugging applications. Some compiler vendors even produce programming environments that integrate the compiler, editor, and debugger into a single application. I personally prefer the Borland IDE integrated debugger. Be aware, however, that the integrated debuggers, as they are called, may only support a subset of the features included in a stand-alone debugger. For serious application development, a stand-alone debugger is essential. There are many good stand-alone debuggers available. The Turbo Debugger from Borland has long been a favorite of many game developers. In my opinion, Turbo Debugger was, and in many ways still is, way ahead of the competition. In fairness, some of the popularity of Turbo Debugger is due to the fact that it comes bundled with the Borland Pascal and Borland C/C++ programming languages.

Why do you need a stand-alone debugger? Probably the most important reason is that the memory requirements for debugging large executable files typically exceed the abilities of most integrated debuggers. For example, when developing a large application, it is not uncommon to encounter symbol-table sizes of a megabyte or more. The C++ language is particularly notorious in this respect. Even modest C programs can have very significant symbol-table sizes. The debugger will typically attempt to load a significant portion, if not all, of this symbol table into memory. The debugger needs to access the symbol table to map memory references to variable names. For this reason, most stand-alone debuggers attempt to use expanded or extended memory for storing the symbol table. Some debuggers even use DOS Extenders to run in 286 or 386 protected mode. The primary objective is to provide as much memory as possible to both the debugger and the application being debugged.

Some third-party debugging tools are well worth examining. Depending on your needs, and if your budget allows, you may wish to add these tools to your arsenal.

A Quick Debugging Review

Before we delve into a discussion of more advanced debugging techniques, it is probably worthwhile to briefly review some debugging basics. If you are an experienced programmer, you will probably want to skip ahead to the next section. However, if you are a beginner, or if you have not programmed in a while, you may find this section to be a useful refresher. This is not intended to be a complete tutorial—just an introduction to some basic debugging skills.

Single-Stepping Through Your Code

In order to locate the line(s) containing bugs, you must use a feature of your debugger called single-stepping. This enables you to execute your code one line at a time. Each execution is called a "step." In between each step, you would typically use other features of your debugger to examine the state of your program. For example, after each step, it is often useful to "examine" or "watch" the contents of certain critical variables. (These terms are explained forthwith.) When debugging, it is important to step through all your code.

Single-stepping through your code is very useful for tracing the flow of your program. This shows you which branches were taken on conditional statements such as *if* and *switch*. As you single-step through your code, keep checking to see that the correct branches are taken. You may find, on occasion, that a different branch was taken than you expected. Examine your algorithm carefully and see if this behavior is expected. You may have just located a bug in your code.

Let's walk through a very simple program to illustrate the use of the single-step feature. Take a look at the code in Listing 12.1. In this example, we have a function, `EventLoop()`, that simulates some event-processing code which might typically be used in a game. The function is passed an integer parameter, `Message`, that represents the type of event that has occurred. The function uses a simple switch statement to decide how to process each event it receives.

Listing 12.1. Step (STEP.C).

```c
//
// Standard include files
//
#include <stdio.h>
#include <stdlib.h>

//
// Define some useful constants
//
#define MOVE_UP     0x01
#define MOVE_DOWN   0x02
#define MOVE_LEFT   0x03
#define MOVE_RIGHT  0x04

//
// Simple function with a switch statement.  Simulates an
// event processing loop in a game.
//
void EventLoop(int Message)
{
  switch(Message)
  {
  case MOVE_UP:
    printf("Moving up\n");
    break;
  case MOVE_DOWN:
    printf("Moving down\n");
    break;
  case MOVE_LEFT:
    printf("Moving left\n");
    break;
  case MOVE_RIGHT:
    printf("Moving right\n");
  default:
    printf("Unknown message: %d\n",Message);
  }
}

//
//  Main program entry point
//
void main(void)
{
  EventLoop(MOVE_RIGHT);
}
```

If you want to try it yourself, compile the program and load it into the debugger. Otherwise you may trace through the code in the listing. Single-step through the code until the switch statement is executed. Did the debugging cursor move to the MOVE_RIGHT block of code as you would expect? If it did, good. Next, single-step to the end of the function. Did you notice what happened? Instead of exiting the switch statement after completing the MOVE_RIGHT block, the execution fell through to the default block. This is definitely an error in the code.

Sure, this was an artificial example, and the code contained what many of you would consider to be a very obvious mistake. It is not uncommon for novice C programmers to forget a break within a switch statement, but most programmers learn to avoid this mistake very early in their programming careers. An experienced programmer would never make a silly mistake like this, right? Wrong. And in a large project, encompassing dozens of code modules, it can be very difficult to spot a mistake as obvious as this one.

I should mention that single-stepping through code can be very difficult at times. This is particularly true if your compiler performs sophisticated code optimization. In an effort to optimize the performance of your code, the code generator often rearranges your code. The result of all this code shuffling is that as you single-step through highly optimized code, the debugging cursor may leap around unpredictably. Generally, it is best to disable most code optimizations when you plan to single-step through your code. Save the optimizations for your beta-test builds when performance is more important than ease of debugging.

What Is a Watch?

When debugging, it is often useful to periodically *watch, examine,* or *inspect* the contents of certain program variables. You typically set a watch variable by entering a command such as examine, or print, followed by a variable name. In some cases, you may fill in a dialog box activated by a menu selection. There is a difference between *watching* and *examining* a variable. When you *examine* the contents of a variable, you look at a single variable at a single point in time. Typically, when using a *watch,* several variables can be viewed simultaneously, and the display is continually updated as the program executes.

Let's take a look at an example of a variable watch. Suppose that we are debugging the short program shown in Listing 12.2. This program contains a simple function, Factorial(), that calculates the factorial of the number passed as an argument. In case you have forgotten, the factorial of a number, say 5, is defined as follows:

```
5! = 5 * 4 * 3 * 2 * 1 = 120
```

For now, let's assume that the program passes the number 5 to the function Factorial(). Let us further assume that we have already single-stepped our way to the first line of the function Factorial(). Note that, when debugging C programs, the first executable line of a function is located after all local variable declarations. This is not true in C++, where variables may be declared at any point within a function. In our example, the first executable line of the function should read as follows:

```
theResult = —val;  // initialize theResult
```

The debugging cursor should now be pointing to this line. Single-step to the next line and examine the contents of the variable theResult. The contents of the variable should be 5, the first number in the factorial equation. The debugger will show you that the variable theResult actually contains 4, not 5. If you are sharp, you may have already spotted the error in the code. The problem is that in the very first line of the function, the code used the pre-decrement operator, --val, instead of the post-decrement operator, val--.

Listing 12.2. Watch (WATCH.C).

```
//
//   Standard include files
//
    #include <stdio.h>
    #include <stdlib.h>

//
// Simple function for calculating the factorial of a given number
//
unsigned long Factorial(unsigned val)
{
  unsigned long theResult;

  theResult= --val;     // initialize theResult to first number
  for(; val; val--)        // loop till val = 0
    theResult*=val;     // accumulate results of multiplies
  return theResult;     // return factorial of 'val'
}

//
//   Main program entry point
//
#pragma argsused
void main(int argc,char *argv[])
{
  unsigned factor;

// get the first command-line parameter
  factor=(unsigned)atoi(argv[1]);

// show the results
  printf("result of %u! = %lu\n",factor,Factorial(factor));
}
```

This type of bug can be difficult to spot when you are staring at pages of code. The real problem is that the code is perfectly legal; it just doesn't correctly implement the algorithm we are using to calculate factorials. The only sure-fire way to locate this type of bug is to single-step through your code and carefully examine the variables at each step.

It helps if you include comments that state explicitly your intent to pre- or post-decrement a variable within an expression. For example, the first line of code could have been written as follows:

```
theResult = —val;  // put val in theResult and _then_ decrement val
```

In this case, the comment makes it clear that the intent of the code is to post-decrement val. A quick scan of the code would probably have flushed out this bug. Using a combination of single-stepping and variable watches, you should be able to isolate the majority of the bugs in your code. If you are thinking that this approach could take a long time, you are right. Nonetheless, it is always a good idea to step through new code.

As you might imagine, the ability to examine a set of variables as you single-step through your code is a very useful feature. Once you have become accustomed to this feature, you will find that it is nearly impossible to do without it. Most debuggers will also enable you to alter the contents of a variable while it is being examined. I will discuss this later. These days I would expect every debugger to support the variable-watch feature. If yours doesn't, you may want to consider purchasing a better debugger right away!

What Is a Breakpoint?

The ability to single-step through code is certainly a nice feature, but what happens if the bug is in the last line of code? Do you have to step through all the other code first? Of course not, fortunately most debuggers support a feature called an *execution breakpoint* or simply a *breakpoint*. A breakpoint is a flag, set by you, which tells your debugger to "stop execution right here." This enables you to effectively "jump" to a function suspected of containing a bug without single-stepping your way through all the intermediate code. Now that you are in the region of the suspected bug you can continue by single-stepping through the function.

Let's look at a typical use for a breakpoint. In the previous example, Listing 12.2, we could have set a breakpoint at the start of our function Factorial() and then simply run the program. The program would have executed normally, under control of the debugger. However, when the program reached the breakpoint, the debugger would have interrupted the execution. The debugger typically updates the display to show the source code near the current breakpoint. Any variable watches that were active would be updated at this point, showing their current contents.

Is there such a thing as a debugger that does not support execution breakpoints? I sure hope not! There are some debuggers that extend the idea of a breakpoint in interesting ways. For example, Borland's Turbo Debugger supports breakpoints that can conditionally interrupt program execution based upon accesses to I/O ports, global memory, or even based on the value of a user-entered expression.

An Ounce of Prevention...

In an ideal world, programmers would write code without any errors. In the real world, this never happens. Fatigue, stress, and Murphy's law all work against the programmer in this regard. There are, however, a number of steps that can be taken to reduce the occurrence of many bugs in new code. This section discusses a number of techniques for preventing different types of common bugs from entering your code. I emphasize prevention here because that is exactly what we want to do whenever possible.

The premise is that it takes much less effort to prevent a bug during the programming process than it takes to find one later during the testing phase. Despite all the fancy tools out there, the basic debugging tool is still the dreaded step/watch cycle. Because it is so time-consuming, we want to try to minimize the amount of time spent stepping through code looking for bugs.

We will not eliminate every bug using these techniques, but that is OK. Just remember that each and every bug avoided when code is first written is a bug that will not show up later. Something else to consider is that the bugs that do show up later tend to do so when your boss is looking over your shoulder.

Enable All Compiler Warnings

You may already know this, but one of the simplest ways to improve your code is to enable each and every warning that your compiler supports. If your compiler is worth its code generator, there should be plenty of them. The more warnings, the better. Typically, compilers enable the user to allow support for several different classes of warnings. One of these classes should definitely include ANSI C compatibility violations.

So why does enabling all compiler warnings help to eliminate bugs? To better understand the answer to this question, let's briefly examine what a compiler really does. By definition it parses source code and generates object code. Functionally, parsing and code generation are two separate processes that are called the front-end and back-end of the compiler. In the process of parsing your code, a compiler usually identifies and reports any syntax errors that are present in your code. The error reporting is, however, largely a by-product of the parsing process. Any violation of the language definition trips up the parsing code, and the result is an error message.

While it is parsing your code, the compiler also gathers information on the various data types, structure definitions, function parameters, and variable declarations in your code. It does this primarily to generate proper object code and to enforce the typing rules imposed by the language definition. At this point, the compiler has gathered a great deal of information about the structure of your program. Compiler vendors have found that it is not very difficult to use all this information to generate warnings that point out dangerous or questionable code. Using a compiler with all warnings enabled is like running your code through a sophisticated code analyzer—but in this case, it's free!

Why aren't all these warnings enabled by default? I'm sure that some compilers do enable all errors by default. There are several common reasons why your compiler might not. One reason has to do with support for pre-ANSI C code. Before ANSI C existed, the official specification of the C language was the K&R definition. The K&R definition was written by Brian Kernighan and Dennis Ritchie, the original authors of the C programming language. The specification was a little loose when it came to some definitions of the language. This was done intentionally to provide compiler vendors with the flexibility to take advantage of different hardware architectures. Unfortunately, this flexibility led to many subtle incompatibilities between different C implementations, especially between different hardware platforms. The ANSI C specification strengthened many of these definitions.

For an example of a K&R-style program, take a look at the code in Listing 12.3. This code is the same as the last code example shown in Listing 12.2. The main difference is in the way that functions are defined. If you've never seen this before, it may look very strange. Don't worry, I won't spend any more time discussing the arcane differences between ANSI-C and K&R C. I just wanted to give you a little background.

Listing 12.3. PreAnsi (PREANSI.C).

```
/*
Standard include files
*/
#include <stdio.h>
#include <stdlib.h>

/*
Define some useful constants
*/
#define MOVE_UP     0x01
#define MOVE_DOWN   0x02
#define MOVE_LEFT   0x03
#define MOVE_RIGHT  0x04

/*
 Simple function with a switch statement, using K&R style.  Simulates
an event-processing loop in a game.
*/
EventLoop(Message)
int Message;
{
  switch(Message)
  {
  case MOVE_UP:
    printf("Moving up\n");
    break;
  case MOVE_DOWN:
    printf("Moving down\n");
    break;
  case MOVE_LEFT:
    printf("Moving left\n");
    break;
  case MOVE_RIGHT:
    printf("Moving right\n");
  default:
    printf("Unknown message: %d\n",Message);
  }
}
```

```
/*
  Main program entry point
*/
int main()
{
  EventLoop(MOVE_RIGHT);
  return 0;
}
```

If you take a "bug-free" application written in pre-ANSI C and recompile it under an ANSI C compiler, you may be overwhelmed by a flood of warnings and possibly even some error messages. Sure, most of these warnings are harmless—after all, the code worked before. That is why compiler vendors give you the option of disabling them.

Why not just ignore all those ANSI C warnings? The problem here is that some of the warnings may be due to mistakes in your code. It can be very tedious to wade through all the ANSI violations to look for legitimate warning messages. The other alternative is to rewrite the old code to conform to the ANSI C definition. I'll bet that not many of you would want to sign up for that job. In any event, the general result of this particular set of circumstances was that compiler vendors typically enable, by default, only a subset of their supported warnings.

> Pay attention to every compiler warning. The compiler is trying to tell you something very important. Find out what the problem is and fix your code. If you get tired of seeing a particular warning message, change your programming habits, don't disable the warning message.

The other reason for disabled compiler warnings has to do with the common habits of C programmers. As you might expect, there is a great deal of debate among programmers regarding matters of programming style. Some typical programming habits, while legal according to the ANSI C language definition, are not recommended due to the potential for introducing errors. What are some of these warnings? Take a look at the following list, which shows a few common warnings.

- Using constant values greater than 65535 without an explicit L defining the constant as type long
- Implicit type conversions from long to int in an assignment, which result in a loss of significant digits
- Mixing pointers to types unsigned char and signed char
- Use of a variable before it is explicitly initialized and declared
- Calling a function without an explicit prototype

The flexibility of the C programming language is certainly one of its great strengths. The drawback to all this flexibility is that much of the responsibility for checking code for errors is shifted from the compiler to the programmer. There are many occasions when the programmer fully intends for a piece of code to do unconventional things. The use of extensive compiler warnings provides a safety net for the programmer—helping to pinpoint questionable code for those instances when it is not intentional.

Preventing Portability Bugs

I would like to see more support for 32-bit code-migration warnings—even if you are still writing 16-bit DOS-only code, you might as well prepare for the future. Without a doubt, the future of game development lies in 32-bit code. Already many games are written using 32-bit DOS extenders. Examples include DOOM, SimCity 2000, Rise of the Triad, and Descent. As a side note, these titles were all written using the Rational Systems 32-bit DOS extender, due to its generous run-time distribution license. The advantages in terms of speed and resources are just too great to ignore. So brace yourself, you may very soon be faced with the task of porting 16-bit graphics or sound code to a 32-bit environment.

The subject of 32-bit game development could easily occupy an entire chapter of its own, so I won't pretend to present a complete discussion of the subject. For now, let's just take a quick look at an example of the type of 16-bit/32-bit compatibility warnings I would like to see. Take a moment and scan the small piece of code in Listing 12.4. How many compilers would issue even a single warning message for this code?

Listing 12.4. Jiffy (JIFFY.C).

```
//
// Standard include files
//
    #include <stdio.h>

//
// Declare a typical disk file data structure
//
typedef struct tagJiffyFile
{
    char signature[3];
    unsigned int length;
} JiffyFile;

//
// Create an instance of data type 'JiffyFile'
//
JiffyFile aJiffyFile;
```

```
//
// Main program entry point
//
void main(void)
{
  FILE *f;

  f=fopen("foo.dat","rb");
  fread(&aJiffyFile,sizeof(JiffyFile),1,f);
  fclose(f);
}
```

I am sure that we have all written code similar to this. The code looks pretty solid, so there shouldn't be any portability problems, right? Now, suppose that your compiler produced some warnings messages similar to the following example:

Compiler warning 1, line 3:
The field "signature" in structure "JiffyFile" was padded out to 4 bytes so that the remaining fields fall on double-word boundaries. The target platform you have selected requires memory accesses to occur on double-word boundaries.

Compiler warning 2, line 4:
The size of field "length" in structure "JiffyFile" will vary among different compilers and hardware. The selected target platform is a 32-bit application where the intrinsic data type int is 4 bytes long.

Compiler warning 3, line 10:
sizeof(JiffyFile) is compiler dependent and may vary between 16-bit and 32-bit environments.

Compiler warning 4, line 10:
The structure of "JiffyFile" may not match the contents of the disk file.

Compiler warning 5, line 10:
Variable "f" should be replaced with a more descriptive name. Variable names can be up to 32 characters in length.

Sure, some of these warnings may be a bit annoying or even blatantly obvious. The last warning is certainly just a matter of personal preference. On the other hand, if any of my compilers had these types of warnings when I was porting game code to a 32-bit compiler, I might have saved myself many hours of aggravation. The point is that during parsing, the compiler has all the information necessary to provide these types of warnings.

Listing 12.5 includes a header file that I use in all my development. The file defines some user data types that help to separate your code from the compiler implementation. If you are a Windows programmer, you may notice a similarity. Microsoft introduced many of these definitions to Windows programmers as a way to soften the transition to the 32-bit Windows API. The idea is that if you want to use a variable of a specific size—for example, a 16-bit signed integer value—you would use the compiler-independent data type INT instead of the standard-C type int. The reason being that the C language definition allows type int to be the natural size for the specified code target.

Listing 12.5. Compat32 (COMPAT32.H).

```
//
//  This header file defines some machine-independent data types to
//  simplify porting code between 16-bit and 32-bit compilers.
//

#ifndef __COMPAT32_H
#define __COMPAT32_H

  typedef char BYTE;
  typedef unsigned char UCHAR;


//
// Remember:
//        int can be 16- or 32-bit depending on compiler
//

#ifdef __386__                          // catch 32-bit DOS compilers
  typedef unsigned short WORD;          // 16-bit unsigned int
  typedef unsigned int   DWORD;         // 32-bit unsigned int
  typedef short INT;                    // 16-bit signed int
#else
  typedef unsigned int   WORD;          // also 16-bit unsigned int
  typedef unsigned long DWORD;          // also 32-bit unsigned int
  typedef int    INT;                   // also 16-bit signed int
#endif

#endif  // __COMPATH32_H
```

The code in Listing 12.6 shows the previous example to be compiler- and target-independent. Notice that there are only a few differences. The declaration for the structure type `JiffyFile` now includes explicit padding to account for differences in memory access requirements. The field length is now explicitly declared to be a 16-bit signed integer to allow for disk file compatibility between 16-bit and 32-bit versions of the application.

Listing 12.6. Jiffy 32–bit (JIFFY1.C).

```
//
// Standard include files
//
#include <stdio.h>

//
//  Include file for 32-bit code compatability
//
#include "compat32.h"

//
// Declare a typical disk file data structure
//
typedef struct tagJiffyFile
```

```
{
    char signature[3];
      char dummy1[1];     // pad to double-word boundary
    WORD length;          // use compiler-independant sizes
} JiffyFile;

//
// Create an instance of data type 'JiffyFile'
//
JiffyFile aJiffyFile;

//
// Main program entry point
//
void main(void)
{
  FILE *fptr;

  fptr=fopen("foo.dat","rb");
  fread(&aJiffyFile,sizeof(JiffyFile),1,fptr);
  fclose(fptr);
}
```

The Lint Utility

If you have a background in UNIX programming, you may be aware of the utility called *lint*. As mentioned in the last section, lint is a code analyzer. It is really a C compiler front-end that parses C code, gathering information on the structure of the code. Rather than having a code generator as a back-end, however, lint uses a set of rules to analyze your code. Instead of producing object code, lint produces warning messages—and usually it produces a lot of them. Lint was originally designed to produce warnings on code that might not be portable between different UNIX implementations.

When running lint against existing code you may be shocked by the number of warnings that are generated. Don't worry, as in the ANSI C example, most of these messages can probably be safely ignored for existing code. However, you might be surprised to find that lint picked up a subtle bug in your code. Even if lint doesn't locate any bugs, don't completely ignore the warnings. Like compiler warnings, they are trying to teach you something. As you revise your existing code modules, take a few extra minutes and explore the warnings that lint reported. When you add new code, make sure that lint doesn't produce any warnings.

> If you have access to *lint*, you should definitely use it. It is well worth the investment of time required to bring your code into lint-free shape.

Developing Good Programming Habits

As a game developer, you are nearly always in a race against the clock. Your financial well-being, and very often your personal sanity, depend on getting your game code developed, tested, and shrink-wrapped as quickly as possible. When faced with this kind of pressure, it is natural to want to churn out code as fast as you can. The problem with this approach is that, while it may appear that a lot of progress is being made, behind-the-scenes bugs may be scurrying all over the place. Remember, our goal is to prevent bugs from occurring whenever possible.

This section covers some suggested programming practices that will help to prevent bugs from crawling into your game code. Many of these suggestions may already be part of your standard bag of tricks. If so, then you are ahead of the game. It has taken me quite a while to train myself to adopt safe programming habits. I started out programming games in BASIC and Assembly language more than 17 years ago on machines with only 4KB of RAM. Such programming was very different, and old habits die hard, I guess.

Use Safe and Simple Code

Try to write code that is safe, simple, and easy to understand. Remember, someone else may have to decipher your code. Even if you aren't part of a programming team now, you may be in the future. Or perhaps you might decide to sell parts of your game, as code libraries, to fellow game developers. In such cases, other programmers will need to maintain and possibly extend your code. Sure, it is easy to understand the clever algorithms and performance tricks in a piece of code right after it is written; but what happens six months or a year later, when you or someone else looks at the code? Ask yourself the question: "Is the specific intent of the code clear?" If not, then consider rewriting the code.

Similarly—and I hope we all do this regularly—you should always include plenty of comments in your code. I have gotten myself into the habit of adding a lot of comments to my code, and I mean *a lot*. I even have keyboard macros defined to insert some standard ones automatically. This way, if I turn over the development of a code module to someone else, I don't necessarily have to spend a week reviewing the code with them. Some of the standard comments I use are shown here:

```
//
//  This function is a quick hack.  Needs a better algorithm.
//

//
//  Watch out, machine specific code below
//

//
//  Critical performance code - may need to be re-written in assembly
//
```

Some of you may argue that games are different—performance is the main objective, not maintainability. After all, games are conceived, developed, and marketed in a relatively short period of time; and after the popularity of the game has run its course, much of the code will get archived and shelved. While this may once have been true, most game developers are now favoring the development of core gaming engines. With a gaming engine, you could change the graphics and sound, and you've suddenly got a new title ready for packaging. With the level of technological sophistication required to create a game from scratch, it is too resource-intensive to develop entirely new code for each and every title.

For example, take the raycasting engine developed by id Software for Wolfenstein 3D. The raycasting engine was licensed, in various forms, to a number of other developers. Did the other titles compete with Wolfenstein? To some degree they might have, but who buys just one game a year? If you liked Wolfenstein, you probably bought one of the other titles, and vice versa.

Besides, id wasn't sitting back trying to squeeze the market for Wolfenstein 3D dry. Instead, they were busy working on newer technology for their next big title, DOOM. (The core engine of DOOM was also licensed to at least one other developer.) Through licensing agreements for their core gaming engines, id was able to leverage their development efforts to a greater extent (i.e., they made a lot more money). Of course, I haven't seen the source code for either game engine, but you can be reasonably sure that the code was clean and well written. Understandable code isn't necessarily slow, and likewise, obscure code isn't necessary fast or optimized.

Put Debugging Code in Your Game

One really good idea is to instrument your code with lots of assertions. This helps a great deal during initial development and also when debugging. The idea is to let your code tell you where bugs are lurking without any extra effort on your part. If you are not familiar with the `assert()` macro, try compiling the code shown in Listing 12.7.

Listing 12.7. `assert()` **macro (ASSERT.C).**

```
//
//   Standard C include files
//
#include <stdio.h>
#include <stdlib.h>

//
//   Pull in assert() macro
//
#include <assert.h>

//
//   Change these defines for different video modes or window sizes
//
#define SCREEN_MINX 0
```

continues

Listing 12.7. continued

```
#define SCREEN_MINY 0
#define SCREEN_MAXX 319
#define SCREEN_MAXY 199


//
//  This code uses constant sprite sizes
//
#define SPRITE_WIDTH  16
#define SPRITE_HEIGHT 16


//
//  Simple structure for holding sprite data
//
typedef struct
{
  int x,y;          // current sprite location
  char *bitmap;     // pointer to sprite bitmap
} Sprite;


//
//  Stub for BitBlt() function - might be in a third-party graphics
//  library or incustom code.
//
#pragma argsused
void BitBlt(char *bitmap,int x,int y,int w,int h)
{
  if(bitmap == NULL)
  {
    printf("This would have been a hidden bug!\n");
    exit(0);
  }
  else
    printf("BitBlt drew the sprite\n");
}


//
//  Simple sprite drawing function
//
void DrawSprite(Sprite *asprite)
{
//  Make sure a valid pointer was passed
  assert(asprite != NULL);

//  Make sure we point to a valid bitmap
  assert(asprite->bitmap != NULL);

//  Make sure bitmap location is reasonable
  assert(asprite->x >=SCREEN_MINX &&
    asprite->x <=SCREEN_MAXX &&
    asprite->y >=SCREEN_MINY &&
    asprite->y <=SCREEN_MAXY);

// Draw the sprite with clipping
  BitBlt(asprite->bitmap,
    asprite->x,
    asprite->y,
```

```
      SPRITE_WIDTH,
      SPRITE_HEIGHT);
}

//
//  Standard C program entry point
//
void main(void)
{
  Sprite theSprite;

  theSprite.bitmap=NULL;
  DrawSprite(&theSprite);
}
```

When you executed the code in Listing 12.7, what happened? The program should have aborted with an error message that the assertion failed. The assert() macro even told you the source code module and line number where the failure occurred. You should place assertions in your code to verify that reasonable and valid arguments have been passed to all of your functions. You may also want to verify that calls to functions in third-party libraries, including the compiler libraries, have not corrupted important data structures.

The best news about assertions is that they do not add overhead to the production version of your code. To disable the assertions, simply insert the following definition in your code before you include the assertion.h header file:

```
#define NDEBUG      // disable assertion tests
#include <assert.h>   // include assert() macro definition
```

When NDEBUG is defined in your code, all assertions are replaced with empty macro definitions, and therefore no overhead is added to your code. This means that all this error checking can be accomplished with a single body of source code. When NDEBUG is not defined, the assertions perform the test passed as an argument to the macro.

In general, you will want to maintain two executable versions of your program during development. One version will be the debugging version, which includes assertions and other debugging code. Use the debugging version at all times during game development. The assertions will help to quickly identify bugs in your code. You may also want to consider play-testing and even beta-testing with the debug version. In this way, you may be able to quickly locate and eliminate any bugs that show up during testing. (Be sure to inform your testers that the code is not yet optimized and that they should document and report any assertion failures.)

The other version will be your release version, which will be free of most debugging code. Notice that I said free of *most*, not *all*, debugging code. You may want to consider leaving in debugging code that does not affect the performance of your game. This could help you later, in the event that you need to track down a bug in the shipping version of your game.

To help you manage the release and debugging versions of your game, you may want to create different makefile targets. For example, look at the sample Makefile shown in Listing 12.8. This makefile has two different executable targets. The first target, debug, builds a hypothetical debugging version of a game called myappd.exe. The second target, nodebug, builds a hypothetical release version called myapp.exe. A third target, all, will make both versions. A final target, clean, will delete intermediate files such as map files (.MAP), object files (.OBJ), and so on.

Listing 12.8. Makefile (MAKEFILE).

```
#
#  Automatically check for file dependencies
#
.AUTODEPEND

#
#  Define a memory model - small by default
#
!if !$d(MODEL)
MODEL=s
!endif

#
# Set compiler flags
#
!if $d(DEBUG)
CFLAGS = -O2 -3 -DDEBUG
!else
CFLAGS = -3
!endif

CC = bcc
OBJS = main.obj foo1.obj foo2.obj

#
# Make the debug version, the default
#
debug:
    echo Making debug version...
    make -DDEBUG myappd

#
# Make the production version
#
nodebug:
    echo Making release version...
    make myapp

#
# Make em all
#
all:
    make clean
    touch *.c
    make debug
    touch *.c
    make nodebug
```

```
#
# Link the release version
#
myapp:      $(OBJS)
    $(CC) -m$(MODEL) $(CFLAGS) -e$@ $(OBJS)


#
# Link the debug version
#
myappd:     $(OBJS)
    $(CC) -m$(MODEL) $(CFLAGS) -e$@ $(OBJS)


#
# Clean up unneeded files
#
clean:
    del *.obj
    del *.map
    del *.bak
```

If you don't use make, you could just as easily set up a batch file to build each version. Or, if your programming environment supports application projects, you could set up a different project file for each version of your game. It doesn't matter how you do it; just remember to exercise the debugging version as much as possible.

Watch Out for Stolen Hardware Interrupts

When debugging games, one of the thornier problems that you will run into is the issue of hardware interrupts. For performance reasons, we will often want to intercept one or more hardware interrupts from the BIOS. The most common instance of this is the keyboard hardware interrupt 09h. Games install custom keyboard interrupt handlers for many reasons, but the main reason is to disable BIOS keystroke buffering.

This becomes a problem when setting execution breakpoints. When the debugger reaches a breakpoint, it interrupts the program execution and displays the source code near the breakpoint. However, since the keyboard interrupt vector no longer points to the BIOS handler, keypresses are still processed by the custom interrupt handler. The result is that the debugger is unable to respond to user keypresses. Obviously, this makes debugging very difficult.

One way to work around this problem is through the use of conditional compilation. In the debugging version of the game, some code is added that selectively enables/disables the custom keyboard handler based upon the state of a flag variable. When the flag variable is non-zero, the custom keyboard handler is installed. When the flag is zero, the keyboard handler is not installed. The flag variable is enabled by default, and it is set to zero using a command-line argument (-K, for example). The code in Listing 12.9 shows an example of how this might work in a game.

Listing 12.9. Keyboard (KEYBOARD.C).

```
//
// Pull in standard header files
//
    #include <stdio.h>
    #include <dos.h>


//
// Don't need flag in release version of program
//
#ifdef DEBUG
    int KeyboardFlag=1;  // set to true by default
#endif


//
// Last keypress scancode.  Updated by custom int handler
//
    int volatile ScanCode;


//
// Pointer to save BIOS interrupt vector
//
    void static interrupt (*OldInt09)(void);


//
// Acknowledge interrupt to 8259 PIC
//
    #define EOI() outp(0x20,0x20)


//
// Define constant for the keyboard hardware interrupt
//
    #define KEYBOARD_INT 0x09


//
// Scancode for Escape keypress
//
    #define ESC_PRESSED 129


//
// This is a stub for a hardware interrupt routine
//
    static void _interrupt NewInt09(void)
    {
      register int x;

      ScanCode=inp(0x60);        // read key code from keyboard
      x=inp(0x61);
      outp(0x61,(x|0x80));
      outp(0x61,x);
      EOI();                     // acknowledge interrupt
    }


//
// Install our custom keyboard handler
//
```

```
    void InstallKeyboardInt(void)
    {
      // Save the original BIOS interrupt vector
      OldInt09=_dos_getvect(KEYBOARD_INT);

      // Install our own custom interrupt handler
      _dos_setvect(KEYBOARD_INT,NewInt09);
    }

//
// Restore the BIOS keyboard handler
//
    void RestoreKeyboardInt(void)
    {
      _dos_setvect(KEYBOARD_INT,OldInt09);
    }

//
//  Perform required initialization
//
    void Initialize(void)
    {
#ifdef DEBUG
      if(KeyboardFlag)        // flag set from command line
#endif
        // install the custom interrupt handler.
        // note that this _always_ happens in the release version
        InstallKeyboardInt();
    }

//
//  Clean up before program exit
//
    void CleanUp(void)
    {
#ifdef DEBUG
      if(KeyboardFlag)        // flag set from command line
#endif
        // Restore the BIOS interrupt handler.
        // note that this _always_ happens in the release version
        RestoreKeyboardInt();
    }

//
//  Main game loop - processes all external events
//
    void EventLoop(void)
    {
      while(ScanCode != ESC_PRESSED)
        printf("Scan code is: %d.  ",ScanCode);
    }

//
//  Main C program entry point
//
    #pragma argsused
    void main(int argc, char *argv[])
```

continues

Listing 12.9. continued

```
    {
// Note that this code is not in release version
#ifdef DEBUG
    int index;

    // loop over all command-line parameters
    for(index=1; index < argc; index++)
    {
      // look at the _second_ character (first could be '-' or '/')
      switch(argv[index][1])
      {
      case 'k':
      case 'K':
        // do not install keyboard handler
        KeyboardFlag=0;
        break;
      }
    } // for()
#endif  // DEBUG
    Initialize();
    EventLoop();
    CleanUp();
  }
```

The example does not do anything significant; the main program loop simply displays the scan code of the last key pressed. When the Esc key is pressed, the program exits. If the program is compiled with DEBUG defined, the state of the keyboard handler can be controlled using command-line options. Also notice that when the release version of the code is compiled, without DEBUG defined, the keyboard handler is always installed. This makes sense; there is probably no good reason to disable the keyboard handler in the release version of the game.

Using this approach, however, we soon discover another problem. When the custom keyboard handler is disabled, the debugger is able to respond to keypresses; but now it is impossible to test the game because the game's keyboard handler is not installed. Fortunately, there are a couple of ways to work around this new difficulty. One solution is to write an alternate keyboard-input routine that uses the BIOS for keyboard input. Alternately, if your game supports mouse or joystick input, you should test your game using these alternate input devices. A third solution to this problem is to use remote debugging, which is discussed in more detail later in this chapter.

Bug Detection

We know that we can't prevent bugs in every case, so eventually we will have to track down and fix bugs in our game code. Let's discuss what happens when a bug shows up in our game code.

The first thing to do is find out where the bug is in the code. It is usually not difficult to determine whether a bug exists, especially when developing game code. In fact, much of the time the errors will be only too apparent. This is one of the advantages of developing graphically oriented applications, since there is a graphical representation of the state of the application and its data, and thus the existence of a bug is apparent.

The challenge is to isolate the source of the bug in the code. Unfortunately, this topic could easily fill up several book chapters, and we don't have that much space. Rather than just leave you hanging, however, let me try to offer you some suggestions. These may help to stimulate some of your own ideas:

- Use third-party debugging tools.
- Periodically log the values of critical variables to a file. Include filename and line number.
- Reimplement interfaces to third-party libraries to include assertions and argument checking.
- Reimplement interfaces to C library functions; use the source if it's available. Create a debugging version of the libraries.
- Include a hotkey in your game to dump contents of global variables to a log file when a bug is found during testing. (This is great for post-mortem diagnosis.)

Custom Debugging Tools

You may find at some point that your team needs more sophisticated debugging tools or libraries to aid in debugging. There are many excellent third-party tools available that are great aids in the debugging process. However, purchasing third-party debugging tools may prove prohibitively expensive for some developers. In this case, it might make sense to create some of your own debugging tools.

Let's examine how we could do this with one of the more difficult kinds of bugs to detect and isolate: memory-related bugs. This class of bug includes errors such as memory leaks, referencing freed memory, dangling pointers, and referencing outside of array bounds. The C programming language has earned quite a reputation for these types of bugs.

Again, because of space constraints, I cannot provide a complete discussion of this lengthy topic. I will, however, provide a few brief thoughts on the subject. It is quite possible to write function wrappers for the standard memory-allocation routines. There are a number of third-party tools that do this in order to aid in debugging memory bugs. Such wrapper functions would, in addition to allocating and freeing memory blocks, keep track of these transactions. This could be accomplished by maintaining a list of pointers to allocated memory blocks. The list could also keep track of other useful parameters, such as the size of the memory block and even the line number and module where the allocation took place. When an application using these functions failed to free allocated memory, an error could then be signaled. The wrapper for the `free()` function might also fill free memory blocks with a known value so that references to free memory could be recognized. Third-party debugging applications such as Bounds Checker by NuMega Software and HeapAgent by MicroQuill employ essentially this type of memory checking. These tools, of course, also add many additional features to your debugging arsenal.

Debugging Strategies

This next section discusses several different strategies for bug prevention and detection. Each of these systems has its own advantages and disadvantages. Because of the significant advantages some of these systems provide, they are often used by professional game developers. Unfortunately, the cost of these options can sometimes be prohibitive, especially for small teams with limited budgets.

Dual-Monitor Debugging

One relatively inexpensive debugging tool that every game programming guru should consider is a dual-monitor system. It should be possible to purchase an 8-bit monochrome video adapter for about $10 these days. A monochrome monitor is also required, but it should not cost more than about $80. You may even be able to find a used monochrome monitor at an even better price.

The monochrome adapter card gets installed on your system alongside your current VGA or SVGA adapter card. By default, DOS should consider the VGA card to be the primary video adapter and the monochrome card to be the secondary video adapter. All video output gets routed by the system to the primary video adapter.

Once the hardware is installed, you are ready to try out some dual-monitor debugging. To give the system a try, compile and link an application and load it into your debugger. Make sure to read the manual for your debugger to find out how to tell it to use your second monitor. If you are using Borland's Turbo Debugger, the command-line option is -do. When you execute the program, something really neat happens. The debugger displays the output from the game (text or graphics) on the VGA monitor and displays the source code on the monochrome monitor.

Basically, you now have a separate, dedicated video monitor for viewing source code, setting breakpoints, and watching variables. Figure 12.1 illustrates what a dual-monitor system looks like. With the dual-monitor system, your debugger doesn't have to attempt to save and restore the state of the graphics display each time you step through code.

Yes, most debuggers enable you to flip or swap to a "user-screen" for viewing graphics output. These debuggers, however, often fail to properly save and restore the state of the VGA registers between flips or swaps. Failure to properly preserve the state of the VGA registers during a debugging session can leave the video display in an unknown state. Not only can this be frustrating, it could also potentially damage your video monitor.

Figure 12.1.
Dual-monitor system example.

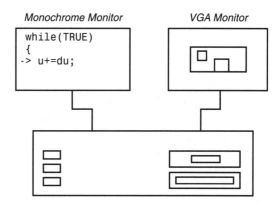

Debuggers most often have problems correctly saving the video state when the game uses a non-standard video mode, such as the popular mode X. Since many games rely on page flipping, off-screen memory, and other neat features of nonstandard video modes, this presents a significant problem. In most respects, debugging with two monitors is the same as with a single monitor. You have the ability to step through the code, set breakpoints, and watch variables as usual. However, because screen swapping is no longer required, you will probably find that dual-monitor debugging is much more efficient. Even better, when a bug does show up, you can simply glance over at the second monitor and see which line of code is to blame.

See Table 12.1 for a comparison of dual-monitor and regular debugging. Before deciding to use this system, you should make sure that your debugger supports dual-monitor systems. (Most debuggers do.) Otherwise you may find that you have to purchase a new debugger. In any event, considering the total cost, a dual-monitor system is an excellent investment.

Table 12.1. Dual-monitor system advantages and disadvantages.

Pros	Cons
Only one computer needed	Poor 8-bit video performance
Relatively inexpensive	Extra hardware needed
View code and output simultaneously	

There is one particularly nagging problem with dual-monitor systems, however. There are no 16-bit monochrome video adapters on the market. Why is this significant? Well, as soon as you install an 8-bit video adapter in your system, the entire bus behaves as if it is only an 8-bit bus. This effectively halves the video performance of your system. If you are wondering why there are no 16-bit monochrome video adapters out there, that's a good question. There is one simple reason: There isn't enough of a market to justify the cost of producing them commercially. That is too bad because it limits the usefulness of the system if you need to remove the 8-bit adapter when you want to test your game at full speed. The only other solution is to have another computer handy for performance testing. If you do happen to have another computer handy, then you will probably want to read on to the next section.

> Be aware that installing an 8-bit video card in your system will cause your 16-bit video card to drop into 8-bit mode. This effectively halves your video performance. Therefore, for conducting performance tests of your game, either use a different machine or remove the 8-bit video card.

Remote Debugging

An alternative to a dual-monitor system is the remote debugging system. What is remote debugging? Remote debugging is a debugging system wherein two computers are linked together. The debugger then runs on one computer, while the application being debugged runs on the other. The system that the debugger executes on is called the *local* system. The system on which the application runs is called the *remote* system. Typically, a small driver application must be executed on the remote system. The driver program manages the communication between the local and remote systems.

Not surprisingly, there is very little difference between remote debugging and dual monitor debugging. Breakpoints, variable watches, and single-steps should function as expected.

The main difference is that the debugger—and more significantly, the debugging symbol table—reside on a separate computer. The big advantage of this is that the game being debugged has access to nearly all of the system memory. Therefore, it is possible to debug much larger and more complex games without running out of system resources. Also, because the debugger does not intrude on the remote system, the system more closely resembles the end-user's execution environment.

The obvious disadvantage of remote debugging is that it requires two complete computer systems. In addition, when debugging, both computers are occupied with the same task. Dedicating two computers to a single task is certainly not a luxury that many small developers can afford. Notwithstanding, the advantages of remote debugging are very significant and may, in the end, outweigh the disadvantages. Table 12.2 lists some advantages and disadvantages of remote debugging.

Table 12.2. Remote-debugging comparison.

Pros	Cons
Maximum memory available	Requires two systems
Much less intrusive debugging	Both systems are dedicated

Pros	Cons
Cabling is relatively cheap	Typically slower debugging
All the advantages of dual-monitor system	

You may be wondering just how the two computers are linked together. There are actually a number of different methods, each with its own strengths. As with dual-monitor debugging, make sure that your debugger supports remote debugging. Most commercial debuggers do, but you should check anyway.

Connecting via the Serial Port

The easiest and least expensive connection method for remote debugging is to use an RS-232C serial link. All that is required is a free serial port on each machine. The only cabling required is a standard null-modem cable. You should be able to purchase a null-modem cable, or a null-modem adapter with a serial cable, at most computer stores.

The maximum data-transfer rate for an RS-232C serial connection is approximately 115,000 kbs (that's kilobits-per-second). That roughly translates to about 14 kbytes-per-second. In order to use the serial connection reliably at full speed, each machine should have a 16550 UART. The term UART stands for Universal Asynchronus Receiver-Transmitter. This chip manages the serial port communications. The 16550 UART was designed for reliable high-speed serial communications and therefore has an on-chip FIFO buffer for incoming data. Older serial adapters probably do not have this chip; but don't worry, a new 16550 UART chip costs only about $9 in most stores, and in most cases, the existing UART can simply be replaced with the 16550 chip. Without the 16550 UART, it is possible run the serial link at a slower data-transmission rate. Fortunately, the amount of data that the debugger must send across the connection is relatively low, so debugging performance is not greatly reduced.

Connecting via the Parallel Port

Some debuggers also support remote debugging using the parallel port. Using the parallel connection has many of the same advantages as serial debugging. The main difference is in the connection speed. The parallel port can handle much higher data-transfer rates than a serial connection. Given the choice of serial or parallel, it probably makes sense to go with the faster connection. Note that the cable required is a special cable, so check your manual for instructions. Many file transfer programs, such as LanLink and the DOS 6.x Interlink application, use similar cables.

Connecting via a Local-Area Network

Probably the most popular method of remote debugging uses a local-area network (LAN) as the connection medium. This type of system is popular with professional software developers for many reasons. Most development teams already have local-area networks installed for file- and printer-sharing. With the falling cost of Ethernet cards and peer-to-peer network operating systems, this option is probably within the means of even the smallest development teams. The most expensive item is still the cost of multiple computer systems.

Remote network debugging typically requires a NetWare IPX- or NetBios-compatible network. Most likely, even if your network runs over TCP/IP, it probably has drivers that can emulate a NetBios layer. If there are networks out there that don't support any of these protocols, they should probably be upgraded. A single-license peer-to-peer network operating system typically costs less than $100.

A back-of-the-envelope comparison between the various debugging systems discussed in this section is shown in Table 12.3. These estimates assume the developer currently has only a single computer system. Obviously, if multiple computer systems are already available, the costs will be quite different.

Table 12.3. Debugging-cost comparison.

Device	Cost
Dual-Monitor System	
8-bit monochrome video adapter	$ 8
Monochrome monitor	$80
	$88
Serial Remote Debugging	
Null-modem cable	$10
Second computer	$2,000
	$2,010
Network Remote Debugging	
Two network adapters	$200
Network Operating System (NOS)	$200
Second computer	$2,000
	$2,400

Using Another Operating System

This may sound like a crazy idea, but there are times when it makes sense to develop game code under another operating system. Whenever it's a practical option, it's really not that bad of an idea. The goal of this approach is to use whichever operating system offers the features and characteristics that make game development more efficient for you. A prime example of an operating-system feature to consider is stability. How much easier would game development be if the system didn't require a reboot after your game crashes? Another useful feature might be preemptive multi-tasking.

The choice of what operating system to use for development can be a difficult one. There are many developers using OS/2 for game development. I am not talking about native OS/2 games, but rather DOS-based games developed under OS/2. System stability during debugging is the reason given by many of these developers. I am not plugging OS/2 here by any means, and I cannot speak from direct experience regarding its stability relative to other operating systems. The point is that other developers do feel that there is an advantage. That alone makes the idea worth investigating. In game development, you must reach for every advantage you can get.

I currently develop much of my code, whether for games or otherwise, under Linux. This is a freeware ($0) UNIX clone with has an amazing number of features. Many vendors sell CD-ROM archives of Linux for around $25. These archives also are widely available via anonymous ftp. The home base for many of the Linux distributions is `sunsite.unc.edu`, but there are also dozens of mirror sites. If you have done any programming in a UNIX environment, you may be pleasantly surprised by all the programming tools that have been ported to Linux. If you haven't installed Linux yet, you may want to consider getting yourself a copy.

Make an extra effort to isolate all operating-system-specific code in separate code modules. Also create wrapper functions, or macros, to hide system specific function calls. These steps will help when porting the game to the target operating system.

Using Another Compiler

Do you think that you can't afford another compiler? How about getting the Gnu C++ compiler for the cost of a download or an anonymous ftp? The Gnu project has compilers available for nearly every combination of operating system and hardware platform. The Gnu C++ compiler has many features found only in higher-end development systems. Even more importantly, the compiler tends to incorporate new features and bug-fixes at a much faster rate than commercial systems.

Using another compiler provides several advantages. First of all, it forces your code to be more portable. The use of compiler-specific features is a bad idea because it ties your code to a single vendor. It is often very convenient to use a nifty compiler-language extension, but it hurts when code needs to be ported. Using two compilers tends to keep programmers honest.

Second, using two different compilers might smoke out bugs in the compiler run-time libraries or code generators. You can watch out for differences in behavior between the two different executables. Finally, if halfway through development, you find that a third compiler generates significantly better code, you will probably be able to move your code to it without changing a single line of source code.

Using Another Hardware Platform

Game development can also be greatly enhanced using higher-powered systems. This could mean using a 100 Mhz Pentium system for development even though the target platform is a 40 Mhz 386. It could also mean using a RISC-based UNIX workstation. (UNIX workstations can be networked to PC-based systems without too much trouble.) The advantages we are looking for are raw speed and rock-solid system stability. But whichever development platform you choose, you should not get too accustomed to the speed. Keep the target end-user system in mind. This should be obvious, but it bears mentioning: Always conduct performance testing on the target system.

Using All of the Above

I have used combinations of all the previous detailed approaches at times, and it has worked quite well. If you don't think that these ideas are worth the trouble, you should consider the following: DOOM was developed on a NeXT Cube using the Gnu Objective-C compiler and the NeXT Step operating system. The code was then ported to the PC and the Watcom compiler under the Rational Systems 32-bit DOS extender. That's a combination of a different compiler, a different operating system, and even a different hardware platform!

Developing on Different Hardware

During development, it is very important to test games on many different hardware systems. In the PC gaming market, there is a nearly infinite combination of hardware elements. This makes hardware and software compatibility a very big issue. Because of the tremendous demands placed on system resources, games tend to bring these incompatibilities to light more often than other applications.

Many development teams try to use as diverse a mix of hardware as possible. Each team member might have completely different tools. In some cases, this might present some compatibility problems. That is good—the development phase is precisely where we want these problems to surface! The goal is to detect and resolve hardware incompatibilities as early as possible in the development process.

Summary

I hope this chapter has provided you with some new ideas on how to debug games. Nobody knows everything about debugging, and it can be considered as much an art as it is a science. I am continually trying to improve the quality of the code I write, and I find that talking to other programmers about their experiences helps me a great deal. I also try to keep a log book next to me at all times. Whenever I track down a particularly nasty bug, I write down how I found it, what I did wrong, and how I might have prevented the bug from occurring in the first place. Then, the next time I am confronted with a troublesome bug, the first thing I do is grab my log book. Many times the answer is already in there.

Good luck, and remember to have fun—after all, that's what games are about.

Optimizing Your Code

by Bob Pendleton

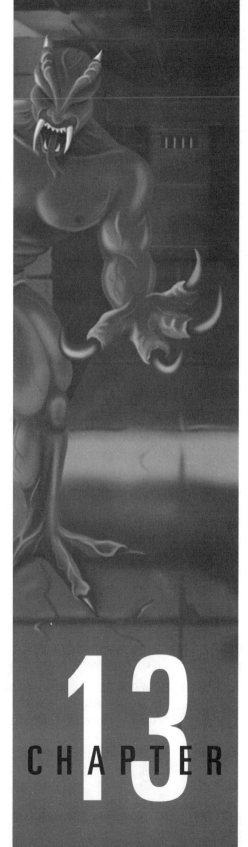

From the moment when I start a programming project until the day it is shipped, optimization is always on my mind. The basic conflict in every game-development project is the difference between what the computer can do and what the game designer wants to do. Optimization techniques bridge the gap between the limits of the computer and the imagination of the game designer.

In this chapter, I'm going to show you some of my favorite tricks of the trade. I'm going to tell you how I avoid wasting development time by making sure a project is actually do-able, and I'll give you hints on how to pick a compiler and how to get the most out of it. I'm going to spend a lot of time talking about how to optimize the kinds of loops you see in high-performance graphics programs and tell you where you can find more examples of commercial-quality, high-performance graphics code. This chapter also will touch briefly on the finer points of fast memory management and the neglected topic of fast file I/O. Finally, I'll tell you how to get more out of your CPU by showing you how to do fast integer divides, how to use assembly language code to get the most out of 32-bit integer and fixed-point arithmetic, and the advantages of using pure fractional fixed-point numbers.

Reality Check

The computer your game is designed to run on determines a lot of things for you. You don't design the same way for a 286 with 512KB of RAM as you would for a PowerMac with 16MB. The speed of the processor has an obvious effect on your plans. The number of registers in the CPU affects how you lay out loops. The size, layout, and the number of levels of cache memory you have force you to fit your code into concise chunks so you don't thrash the cache. Cache can also force you to lay out data structures in what may seem like odd ways. And the amount of RAM on your target machine makes a difference in the trade-off between space and speed. You don't use a lot of look-up tables on a machine with 512KB, but you will use table look-ups for speed-ups when you expect the target machine to have many megabytes to play with.

If you were only writing code for one machine, the job would be a lot easier. But in reality, even if you are only developing for PCs you are developing for a wise range of computers, computers that range in performance from ancient 286s to modern P5-based machines (not to mention clone processors from several different manufacturers and all the new machines, like the P6 and K5, that are coming soon). And, if your game is a success, it will be ported to a number of different platforms—no matter what platform it was originally developed for.

Successful PC games are ported to the Mac and PowerMac, 3DO, Sony PlayStation, Sega Saturn, and all the other new 32-bit game systems. Successful Mac games are ported to the PC. More and more titles are being developed on some or all of these platforms at the same time. This trend is dictated by economics. It costs less to develop versions of one game for several platforms than to develop several different games. And if you have a successful game, you want to sell it to as many customers as possible.

Optimize Your Time First

The first optimization you do is deciding which parts of the project are going to be portable and which parts are going to be machine- or architecture-specific. The idea is to put firewalls between portable code and machine-specific code. The goal is to optimize time involved in writing the game. Game development is a business, and you have to make a profit or you won't be in business for long. That means that you have to get the project done under budget and on time.

The next thing I do is a series of reality checks. Can the target platform support the game I want to write? The details vary from game to game and from platform to platform. For the following example, I'm going to use a full-screen, 3-D dungeon crawl, as in DOOM.

First off, can I do the graphics on the target machine? Table 13.1 lists common CPU clock speeds down the side and common screen resolutions across the top. The table shows the number of CPU cycles that are available for each screen pixel if you are updating the screen at 10 frames per second. Ten frames per second is not really fast enough for a 3-D game. At 10 frames per second, you can play the game but you don't really feel like you are "there." To get that feeling of reality, you need to run at as close to 30 frames per second as you can.

Table 13.1. Number of CPU cycles that are available for each screen pixel at 10 frames/second.

| CPU Speed | Screen Resolution | | |
	320×200	320×240	640×480
25Mhz	39	33	8
33Mhz	52	43	11
66Mhz	103	86	21
100Mhz	156	130	33

Table 13.1 can make a lot of decisions for you. When you see that one multiply instruction on a 486 can take longer than 39 cycles, you realize the limits you face and how good the competition is. Notice that Table 13.1 assumes that you are spending 100 percent of the CPU on graphics. In reality, you spend a lot of time on game-play code.

Plan Memory Usage, Will it Fit?

The second thing I do is lay out the memory map. Games suck up memory faster than almost anything else. Depending on the game, you may be trying to fit dungeon maps, sound effects, character-animation frames, wall graphics, item graphics, program code, and MIDI scripts all into memory at the same time. Considering that you can spend up to 22KB of memory for one second of sound and that one 64×64 pixel image can suck up 4KB, it is really easy for even a simple game to use up 4MB of memory.

One of the most important optimizations you will perform is to trim the proposed game design to fit the target machine. I've never seen a case where you could *expand* the design to fit the machine. Imagination always exceeds the hardware.

One rule you just have to live with: You can't optimize for a machine you don't have. If you decide that your game is going to run on a 486/25 with 4MB, you have to actually have such a machine in the developer's office. No matter how hard you try to avoid it, you wind up optimizing for the kind of machine you have on your desk.

Picking Your Tools

There is one lesson that every mechanic knows by heart but half the programmers I've met never understood: Good tools make the job easier, and the right tools make the job possible. I swear, the average mechanic spends more money on socket wrenches in a year than the average programmer spends on programming tools in a decade.

Pick your compiler with care. Just because everyone you know bought one kind of compiler doesn't mean it is the best one out there. Most commercial compilers these days are oriented toward building commercial database applications. The speed of commercial applications depends more on the speed of the database system than on the speed of the compiler. If the database engine is fast, a very bad compiler will still generate "fast" applications because the only time that is spent in compiler generated code is in what I call "human speed" code. "Human speed" code is code that only has to be fast enough not to annoy people. You have to find a compiler that was designed for systems programming work.

Compilers I've Used

Just because one compiler company has the edge this year doesn't mean a different one won't be better next year. On my bookshelf, I have compilers from five different companies (and more than one version from several of them—and that's just the PC compilers I've used in the last five years). I'm currently using Watcom's 10.0a compiler. Watcom is famous for the quality of their code generators. Their compilers are among the best I have ever used. The rest of their tools are also very good. But their integrated development system needs work and their customer support has slipped from very good to bad since the company was sold. I can't think of a commercial DOS game I've seen in the last two years that wasn't developed using the Watcom compiler. This is the compiler I've used for all the examples in this chapter.

Before I switched to Watcom I used the Zortech version 3.1 compiler. Zortech made a very good compiler. The code it generated isn't as good as the code the Watcom compiler generates but Zortech included a better DOS extender. I did a lot of work with the compiler and was quite pleased with it. I switched because the next release of the Zortech compiler, sold under the Symantec name, had so many bugs that it was unusable. I watched the Zortech support group on the Internet for several months after the "upgrade" release and based on the constant stream of bug reports and Symatec's inability to correct them I decided to look for another compiler company.

At one point I did a lot of recreational programming using DJGPP, the DOS version of Free Software Foundation's C and C++ compilers. I've used these compilers on UNIX machines for years and there is nothing bad that I can say about these compilers. They are simply great compilers. Better yet, you can get the source code. If you aren't used to working with UNIX style software you won't like these compilers. The last time I looked at DJGPP I wouldn't have recommended it for commercial game programming. That may have changed.

I have always had a lot of respect for Microsoft. So when I wanted a solid bug free compiler for doing Windows development I bought Microsoft's C version 7.0. You'd think that a company like Microsoft would have a good compiler. Based on my experience with their C compiler it will be a long time before I spend money on a programming tool from Microsoft again. The compiler had a lot of nice features but it's code optimizer not only doesn't do a very good job, as was noted in *Tricks of the Game-Programming Gurus*, it generates buggy code.

In the beginning there was Borland. I've used Borland's compilers since Turbo Pascal 2.0 for CP/M. That is, since before there were IBM compatible PCs and Macs. I was a very happy Borland customer for many years. The last version of Borland C/C++ that I bought was version 3.0 and I bought it just to get an updated version of TASM, Borland's wonderful assembler. When I bought my first 386 based computer I wanted to buy a 32-bit compiler to use with it. It seems absurd to develop 16-bit applications for a 32-bit computer. Borland didn't have a 32-bit compiler and it took them a very long time to finally develop one. Everyone who wanted to go on to 32-bit code had to leave Borland behind.

Picking a Compiler

When looking for a compiler, I first look at the quality of the code it generates. The code optimizer is your secret weapon. You only have so much time to spend on a game. A good code generator means that all the code in the program will be nearly as good (and usually better) than your best hand-coded assembly language.

I used to write compilers. I've seen good optimizers humble the best assembly-language programmers I've ever met. I've seen optimizers generate code that was faster than the hardware designers thought was possible. This all happens because the optimizer remembers everything it "knows" about the machine and every trick that has been programmed into it and applies this knowledge to every instruction it generates.

I can give you a lot of tips on how to get the most out of compilers, but to find your own tricks you need to have to know how compilers work. It would be a gross understatement to say there isn't room here to teach the basics of compiler construction. I can only recommend that you read a book such as *Compilers, Principle, Techniques, and Tools*, by Aho, Sethi, and Ullman on compiler construction and that you get the source code for the Free Software Foundation compilers and read it.

If you find yourself stuck with a buggy optimizer, complain to the compiler vendor until they either fix the problem or refund your money. If I buy a wrench and it turns out to be broken, the manufacturer will either replace it or refund my money, no questions asked. Yet compiler companies often expect us to buy broken tools and pay to repair them by buying upgrades. I don't think so.

Code Analysis Tools

You can't do low-level optimization without an accurate and easy-to-use sampler and profiler. The sampler is a tool that measures where your program actually spends its time. Samplers work in a lot of different ways, but a sampler that won't tell you what percentage of the time your program spends in library calls or in the operating system is nearly worthless. You need to know where your program is spending all its time. The profiler formats the information the sampler collected so you can get some use out of it.

You might think you know where your program is spending its time, and you'd even be right once in a while. But you'll be surprised often enough to make using a sampler and profiler worth the effort. Recently, one of my company's game programmers was stuck because graphics performance just wasn't acceptable. The game was in danger of being canceled because of the poor graphics performance. The graphics code, based on code I wrote, had been reworked several times. I was asked to take a look at the problem. I asked what the profiler said. It turns out that neither the programmer nor the manager had profiled the code. The profiler then told us that the game was spending a huge percentage of its time in system-storage allocation calls. That was easy to fix, and soon the graphics performance was right where it needed to be. Lesson: Don't waste time—use a good profiler.

 You can't fix it if you don't know it is broken. Use a sampler and profiler to find out where your program is spending it's time.

The profiler and sampler that come with the Watcom compilers are the best ones I've seen on PCs.

Disassembly, a Window on the Code

If you are going to try to improve the performance of a piece of code by rewriting it in assembly language, you have to know what the compiler is already doing for you (or to you). I've seen more that one programmer scratching his head upon finding out that his highly optimized, hand-coded assembly version of a subroutine was slower than the code the compiler was already generating. It was exactly that kind of experience that made me start looking very carefully at what code optimizers do.

I use the disassembler that comes with the Watcom compiler to disassemble object modules generated by the Watcom compiler. It does what I need it to do.

Optimizing Loops

All the games that I've worked on spend most of their time in graphics code. Graphics code is dominated by copy loops. So let's look at some of the things you can do to speed up loops.

Listing 13.1 shows a typical, straightforward, C-language copy loop. Because it's a typical and straightforward form of a loop, most compilers actually do a very good job of compiling this code. It would take a bit of work to write a loop that's faster.

Listing 13.1. Loop 1.

```
#define bSize (99999)

    int bufSize = bSize;

    char buf1[bSize];
    char buf2[bSize];

    int i;

    for (i = 0; i < bufSize; i++)
    {
        buf1[i] = buf2[i];
    }
```

There are three things about this loop that stand out as candidates for speed-up. Compilers aren't always very good about computing subscripts. This is particularly sad because techniques for generating good code for loops have been known since the first FORTRAN compiler was written in the late 1950s. Listing 13.2 shows the same loop written using pointer variables instead of using subscripts.

Listing 13.2. Loop 2.

```
int i;
    char *p1, *p2;

    p1 = &buf1[0];
    p2 = &buf2[0];
    for (i = 0; i < bufSize; i++)
    {
        *p1++ = *p2++;
    }
```

The next thing to worry about is the counter variable i. It serves no real purpose in the loop. It looks like it is needed to make sure the loop stops at the right time, but you can do the same job by computing the address of the end of the destination buffer and testing p1, the destination pointer, against the end address.

By getting rid of i, you get rid of at least one instruction from the inside of the loop—the instruction that increments i before it is tested. You also free up the CPU register that the value of i is being stored in. In these simple examples, freeing up a register is not that important. In real code you want to make sure that every value used inside a loop fits in a register. Otherwise you wind up paying to read values in from memory and to write values back to memory inside the loop. Saving one memory read/write pair inside a critical loop can have a dramatic effect on your overall performance.

Saving one register may not seem like much, but on $x86$ architecture machines, which are notoriously short on registers, it can mean the difference between a successful game and a dog. On newer RISC-based machines, such as the PowerPC, you have a lot more registers available, and saving one register is not as big a concern; but you can still run into the situation where adding one more assignment statement to the body of a loop slows the loop down dramatically. Listing 13.3 shows the same loop without i.

Listing 13.3. Loop 3.

```
    int i;
    char *p1, *p2;

    p2 = &buf2[0];
    for (p1 = &buf1[0]; p1 <= &buf1[bufSize - 1]; p1++)
    {
        *p1 = *p2++;
    }
```

The last thing to look at, and the most important, is the structure of the loop itself. The C for loop is a standard looping structure inspired by the discipline of structured programming, and it is perfect for expressing some kinds of iteration. But every looping structure can be expressed in terms of if and goto statements. Listing 13.4 shows a simple counter-controlled for loop and what it would look like if you had to code it using only if and goto statements.

Listing 13.4. Loop 4.

```
int i;

    for (i = 0; i < 10; i++)
    {
        do_something;
    }
```

becomes:

```
    int i;

    i = 0;
l1:;
    if (i >= 10) goto l2;
        do_something;
    i++;
    goto l1;
l2:;
```

The second version of the loop has two goto statements. Each of these statements becomes a machine-language jump instruction. The top goto becomes a conditional jump, and the bottom one becomes an unconditional jump. The unconditional jump is executed every time through the loop. Without it, there would be no loop. The conditional jump is also executed every time through the loop, using up memory space and some number of CPU cycles every time it is executed. But, the conditional jump only has any effect when it is time to exit the loop. The conditional loop spends most of its time doing nothing. Seems like a waste of scarce CPU cycles. This is a problem with all test-at-the-top loops, such as the C for and while loops.

Flip Loops for Speed

A standard compiler optimization is to "flip" test-at-the-top loops to convert them into test-at-the-bottom loops. Listing 13.5 shows two different ways to convert a for loop into an equivalent test-at-the-bottom loop. The first version uses only if and goto statements. The second version shown in Listing 13.5 uses the C do loop.

Listing 13.5. Loop 5.

```
int i;

    i = 0;
    goto l2;
l1:;
    do_something;
```

continues

Listing 13.5. continued

```
    i++
l2:;
    if (i < 10) goto l1;

or

    int i;

    i = 0;
    goto l1;
    do
    {
        do_something;
        i++;
l1:;
    } while (i < 10);
```

In both of the flipped loops, there is an unconditional jump—a goto statement that is executed once and only once at the beginning of the loop—and a conditional jump at the bottom of the loop that is executed every time through the loop. By flipping the loop, we've eliminated one more instruction that has to be executed every time through the loop.

Not only did we eliminate one more instruction, we eliminated a jump instruction that was usually not taken. Most modern processors have some kind of an instruction pipeline. This means that they are actually processing more than one instruction at a time. How many they are processing at once depends on the kind of processor we're talking about—the newer the processor, the smarter the pipeline. Jumps put a kink in the pipe. Normally the next instruction the processor is going to execute is the next one in memory. Instruction-prefetch hardware, along with any cache memories the system has, makes sure that the next instruction gets to the processor as fast as possible. When you hit a jump, the processor might already have grabbed several instructions after the jump and started processing them. When the processor hits the jump, it has to flush all the work it has already done on those instructions and start over. That's why early RISC processors always executed the instruction that followed a jump.

Unconditional jump instructions put a kink in the instruction pipeline, but conditional jumps are even worse. With an unconditional jump, at least the processor knows where to go for the next instruction. When the processor hits a conditional jump, the next instruction can come from two different places. What's a processor to do? In the past a number of different solutions have been tried. Modern processors use a branch prediction table that keeps track of which way the jump went last time. The processor bets that the branch will always go the same way it went last time. If you look at the branch at the bottom of a loop you can see that this is a good bet.

No matter how the processor handles conditional jumps, it is best to have as few of them as possible and to make sure they are placed so that they are usually taken. Loop flipping does exactly that.

Loop Flipping Without `goto` Statements

Listing 13.6 shows a version of a flipped `for` loop that doesn't use any `goto` statements. This is for programmers who, like me, have a religious aversion to the `goto` statements.

Listing 13.6. Loop 6.

```
int i;

    i = 0;
    if (i < 10)
    {
        do
        {
            do_something;
            i++;
        } while (i < 10);
    }
```

Although loop flipping is a very old optimization technique, I've worked with people doing academic research in compiler design who had never heard of it. I've also seen more compilers that *didn't* do loop flipping than compilers that *did* do loop flipping. Also, compilers tend to be conservative about which loops they will flip.

> Don't count on the compiler. Flip your own loops.

Getting back to our example, Listing 13.7 shows a version of our copy loop that is flipped, has the counter variable removed, and uses pointers instead of subscripting. I've left in the `goto` statement to show the general loop structure, even though it isn't needed for this loop.

Listing 13.7. Loop 7.

```
int i;
    char *p1, *p2, *lst;

    p1 = &buf1[0];
    lst = &buf1[bufSize - 1];
    p2 = &buf2[0];

    goto l1;
    do
    {
        *p1++ = *p2++;
l1:;
    } while (p1 <= lst);
```

Loop flipping is an important technique that will let you improve all your loops independent of the compiler you're using. But there is still quite a bit you can do to optimize a loop.

Duff's Device

This next technique is a version of Duff's device (described forthwith). I picked up this technique from reading the source code for the MIT X Server. The X server is a great source of techniques and source code for doing just about any kind of computer graphics.

Duff's device is a technique for generalizing unrolled loops. Loop unrolling simply makes several copies of the body of a loop. The idea is to spend more time doing work and less time processing jump instructions. If we naively unroll our copy loop, we get something like the code in Listing 13.8.

Listing 13.8. Naive loop unrolling.

```
int i;
    char *p1, *p2, *lst;

    p1 = &buf1[0];
    lst = &buf1[bufSize - 1];
    p2 = &buf2[0];

    if (p1 <= lst)
    {
        do
        {
            *p1++ = *p2++;
            *p1++ = *p2++;
            *p1++ = *p2++;
            *p1++ = *p2++;
        } while (p1 <= lst);
    }
```

The code in Listing 13.8 does four times as much work between conditional jumps as does the code in Listing 13.7. But we pay for the speed-up with a loss of flexibility. The loop in Listing 13.7 only works if the number of things we are copying is a multiple of four. This is not much good for general-purpose code where we may be working with any number of things.

Reading working programs is a great way to learn and the Internet is a great source of programs that are worth reading. Look for the X Server for highly optimized graphics code and for VOGLE (Very Ordinary Graphics Learning Environment) for very readable examples of three-dimensional graphics code.

Duff's device combines a `switch` statement with the loop in such a way that an unrolled loop can be used to process any number of items. The original version of Duff's device actually intertwined the `switch` loop with a `while` loop in a way that was legal C code but that many compilers had trouble with and which many programmers, including me, found confusing. Listing 13.9 shows a portable version of Duff's device.

Listing 13.9. Loop 8.

```c
int i;
    char *p1, *p2, *lst;

    p1 = &buf1[0];
    lst = &buf1[bufSize - 1];
    p2 = &buf2[0];

    switch(bufSize & 0x3)
    {
    case 3:
        *p1++ = *p2++;
    case 2:
        *p1++ = *p2++;
    case 1:
        *p1++ = *p2++;
    }

    if (p1 <= lst)
    {
        do
        {
            *p1++ = *p2++;
            *p1++ = *p2++;
            *p1++ = *p2++;
            *p1++ = *p2++;
        } while (p1 <= lst);
    }
```

The `switch` statement executes the body of the loop from zero to three times. This makes sure that the do loop has to be executed a multiple of four times. Duff's device let's you unroll a loop as many times as you like and still handle any number of items. Unrolling loops can give you a real speed-up, but if you unroll the loop too many times, it will overflow the machine's cache memory and cause a dramatic slowdown of execution.

Unrolling too far will slow you down!

Listing 13.10 shows the same loop unrolled eight times. The use of & (bitwise and) in the switch statement forces you to unroll the loop a number of times that is a power of two (2, 4, 8, 16, and so on). Using % (mod) instead of & lets you unroll the loop any number of times, but mod uses a divide operation that is very slow compared to an and.

Listing 13.10. Loop 9.

```
int i;
    char *p1, *p2, *lst;

    p1 = &buf1[0];
    lst = &buf1[bufSize - 1];
    p2 = &buf2[0];

    switch(bufSize & 0x7)
    {
    case 7:
        *p1++ = *p2++;
    case 6:
        *p1++ = *p2++;
    case 5:
        *p1++ = *p2++;
    case 4:
        *p1++ = *p2++;
    case 3:
        *p1++ = *p2++;
    case 2:
        *p1++ = *p2++;
    case 1:
        *p1++ = *p2++;
    }

    if (p1 <= lst)
    {
        do
        {
            *p1++ = *p2++;
            *p1++ = *p2++;
            *p1++ = *p2++;
            *p1++ = *p2++;
            *p1++ = *p2++;
            *p1++ = *p2++;
            *p1++ = *p2++;
            *p1++ = *p2++;
        } while (p1 <= lst);
    }
```

Talk is cheap. Tables 13.2 and 13.3 show the actual execution times of the six versions of the copy loop I've shown here. The tests were run on a 40Mhz AMD 386 and a 33Mhz Intel 486SX. The tests were compiled and run twice. Both times they were compiled with stack checking turned off. The first time, they were compiled with all compiler optimizations turned off. The second time, they were compiled with all optimizations turned on. Each loop was run 500 times with a buffer size of 99,999 bytes. The code was compiled with a 32-bit compiler and run under 386 protected mode using a 32-bit DOS extender. The times are rounded to the nearest tenth of a second.

Table 13.2. Unoptimized.

	386	486
Loop 1	81.1	35.3
Loop 2	94.7	38.7
Loop 3	93.2	43.0
Loop 4	61.8	26.6
Loop 5	42.9	22.8
Loop 6	39.9	22.9

Table 13.3. Optimized.

	386	486
Loop 1	44.5	13.0
Loop 2	29.0	14.3
Loop 3	32.5	18.8
Loop 4	26.4	14.3
Loop 5	17.1	10.2
Loop 6	15.9	9.5

The measured performance shows that loop flipping (Loop 4) and Duff's device (Loops 5 and 6) result in significant performance improvements. Looking at the data, you might come to the conclusion that getting rid of the counter loop and subscripting didn't help much; but I tried a version of Loop 4 with a counter variable and subscripting, and it was much slower than the version I've shown here. Try it.

Another thing to notice is the dramatic improvement that using the code generator made. The effect of the optimizer is most visible on the 486—where the slowest version of the loop that was run through the compiler's optimizer is faster than the fastest version of the loop that wasn't compiled using the code optimizer. A good code optimizer is worth a lot.

A Clean Loop is a Fast Loop

There are two more general rules I want to talk about for optimizing loops. One of them is very simple: Move anything that doesn't need to be inside a loop out of the loop. This is so obvious that I shouldn't have to say it—yet I see garbage in loops all the time. Again, a good code optimizer will find a lot of this stuff and move it out of the loop for you, but—as we have seen—the better the input code, the better the job the optimizer can do.

Strength Reduction

The other technique is called "strength reduction" and it's another old compiler optimization method. The basic idea is to convert expensive operations like multiplication into cheap operations like addition. On the Intel 486, a 32-bit ADD instruction costs one CPU cycle, and a 32-bit IMUL instruction costs between 13 and 42 cycles. Converting a multiply into an add is well worth the effort. Listing 13.11 shows two versions of a loop. The first version uses a multiply; in the second version the multiply has been converted to an add.

Listing 13.11. Strength reduction.

```
int i;
    char *screen = (char *) 0xa0000000;

    for (i = 0; i < 240; i++)
    {
        *(screen + (i * 320)) = color;
    }

becomes

    for (i = 0; i < 240; i++)
    {
        *screen = color;
        screen += 320;
    }
```

I'd provide you with timings for the difference in execution times of the two loops, but the compiler I'm using to test my examples converts the multiplication into a series of additions even when I explicitly turn off all optimizations.

Memory Optimization

Memory management presents game programmers with two conflicting problems. First, there is no such thing as "enough memory." It's a programmers' rule-of-thumb that games always expand to fill the available memory. If there is any memory left, someone will want to add one more cool feature, add a few pixels to the art work, or add one more sound effect. Secondly, computers are never fast enough, and when you want memory, you want it right now.

General-purpose memory-allocation routines such as malloc() and free() are designed around the assumption that they are called in random order. While this assumption is generally true, it is often not true in practice. Instead, you find that graphics routines and AI code allocate memory in distinct patterns. By making use of these patterns, you can make memory allocation much faster.

> Look at how your program uses memory and build a memory manager optimized for your program.

A Fast Memory Allocator

In graphics code, such as a concave-polygon drawing routine, you allocate lots of little chunks of memory while you're drawing the polygon. When you've finished drawing, you need to free all the chunks at once. In this case, all the calls to malloc() come before all the calls to free()—and all the calls to free() come at one time. This pattern fits perfectly with an array of the things you want to allocate and an index that points to the next free item in the array. The code in Listing 13.12 shows a generic allocator that handles this pattern very well.

Listing 13.12. Fast allocator.

```
#define itemHeapSize (1000)
int itemHeapIndex = 0;
item itemHeap[itemHeapSize];

item *
allocItem()
{
    item *addr = NULL;

    if (itemHeapIndex < itemHeapSize)
    {
        addr = &itemHeap[itemHeapIndex];
        itemHeapIndex++;
    }

    return addr;
}

void
initItemHeap()
{
    itemHeapIndex = 0;
}
```

Just fill in whatever type you need for an item, and you have a memory allocator. You do need to make sure that the array of items is as big as it will ever need to be. I've always been able to find the maximum size by analysis or testing. I've measured the performance of this kind of allocator and found that it is more than 10 times faster than malloc() and free(). That's enough to make using it well worth the effort.

Watch for Wasted Memory

Array-based allocators do have the disadvantage that they permanently tie up a large chunk of memory. Usually that isn't a problem, because you're using the memory all the time anyway. If you only need the memory once in a while, then instead of statistically allocating the memory in an array, you can use one call to malloc() to allocate the memory, do fast allocations out of it, and then free() the whole thing at once.

Fast Stack-Based Allocator

The other common allocation pattern fits a stack instead of a simple array. You see this pattern when you are manipulating trees. Of course, local variables and memory allocated with alloca() in procedures are allocated off of your program's stack, and you can usually make do with that. But, the program's stack is usually pretty small, and you might need memory that stays around after a subroutine exits. The code in Listing 13.13 implements a simple stack-like allocator.

Listing 13.13. Fast allocator.

```
#define itemHeapSize (1000)
item itemHeap[itemHeapSize];
item *itemHeapPtr = &itemHeap[0];
item *itemHeapEnd = &itemHeap[itemHeapSize];

item *
allocItem()
{
    item *addr = NULL;

    if (itemHeapPtr < itemHeapEnd)
    {
        addr = itemHeapPtr;
        itemHeapPtr++;
    }

    return addr;
}

void
freeItem(item *freePtr)
{
    if (freePtr >= &itemHeap[0] && freePtr < itemHeapPtr)
    {
        itemHeapPtr = freePtr;
    }
}

void
initItemHeap()
{
    itemHeapPtr = &itemHeap[0];
}
```

The `freeItem()` routine in Listing 13.13 "pops" the allocation point back to an earlier position, freeing anything that was allocated after that point. You only have to keep track of the points you want to free from.

I've used versions of both of these allocators in commercial products. The stack allocator was actually used as a replacement for `alloca()` when tests showed that it was quite a bit faster that the version of `alloca()` that came with the system I was using at the time.

The other problem with `malloc()` and `free()` comes from the fact that game programmers need to use every byte of available memory. As memory is allocated and freed over time, it gets broken up into lots of little chunks, with allocated chunks mixed in with free chunks. This condition is call fragmentation. When memory is fragmented, you can have megabytes of memory free, but no single free block will be bigger than a few thousand bytes. This means you can have megabytes of free memory and not be able to allocate a 100KB array.

The reasons that `malloc()` can't unfragment memory is pretty simple. `Malloc()` gives you the real address of each chunk of memory that it allocates. Because you have the real address of the memory, it can't be moved. To move it, `malloc()` would have to be able to find every place where you've saved the address and update the address to point to the chunk's new location. This process is called "garbage collection," and some languages, such as LISP and SCHEME, provide it. None of the languages commonly used for game programming support it.

The General Solution

The only general solution to the problem that I've found is to write my own storage manager. My manager does the same thing that the storage managers in Windows 3.x and the Mac storage manager do. My storage manager does not give you the address of a chunk of memory. It gives you the address of the address of the chunk. This "address of the address" is called a "handle." The only nice thing about handles is that since the storage manager only gives out handles it always knows where the one and only copy of a chunks address is. That means the storage manager can move chunks to unfragment memory if it has to.

The use of handles is confusing and error prone. Before you actually do something with a chunk of memory you have to get an actual pointer to the chunk and while you are using the pointer you have to make sure that you don't do anything that will cause the allocator to move chunks around. On the other hand we've never had any memory fragmentation problems when using this memory allocation scheme.

Disk I/O

When we're optimizing code, we're used to thinking about scraping a few nanoseconds off of a process that might be measured in microseconds. But when it comes to disk I/O, we're talking about real pieces of moving metal. Metal doesn't move at the speed of light. The disk spins around, and on average you have to wait for half a rotation for the part you want to pass under the read/write heads. The read/write heads have to be moved from track to track before you can even start waiting for what you want to pass by.

If the disk rotates at 3,600 RPM then you have to wait an average of 33 milliseconds for the data to come under the head, and moving the head from track to track (a seek operation) can take another 15+ milliseconds. And that's on hard drives. On a CD-ROM, a seek can take up to half a second (500 milliseconds) for the head to get to where you want it to be.

If the disk I/O is inefficient, users will walk away from your game. If it's really obnoxious, they will complain about it on the Internet. To make matters worse, a modern adventure game is likely to be put together from hundreds of files comprising megabytes of data.

> To make disk I/O as fast as possible, merge all your little files into one big file. This lets you open and close it once, and if you put all related files close together in the big file, you will minimize disk head movement and reduce your disk I/O greatly. Merging files is especially important if you are playing an animation sequence off of the disk.

The easiest way to merge your files is to write a simple program that reads a list of files and copies each file from the list onto the end of one big output file and then writes a directory containing the original filenames along with the files size and starting location in the merged file. The last thing you write to the merged file is the offset of the start of the directory and the size of the directory. Listing 13.14 shows the structure of a merged file.

Listing 13.14. Merged file format.

```
DATA
        file #1
        file #2

           .
           .
           .
        file #N
    directory
        file #1 name, start, length
        file #2 name, start, length

           .
           .
           .
        file #N name, start, length
    directory offset
    directory size.
```

This file structure lets you write the merged file in one pass and lets you read it with a minimum of seeks.

Reading the file is also pretty simple. Since you know the size of the directory offset and the size entries in the merged file, you can use `lseek()` or `fseek()` to get to that data. From there you can get to the first entry in the directory and read the directory. From there you can look up any file and read it in.

Arithmetic

There is more to say about computer arithmetic than I can cover in this chapter, so I'm just going to cover some of my favorite tricks of the trade. In several places you will be referred to *Tricks of the Game-Programming Gurus* for background explanations.

Fast Divide

Division is the slowest arithmetic operation on most machines. *Tricks of the Game-Programming Gurus* showed you how to do fast multiplication. It then went on to say that you can divide using a similar technique. Every time I've seen fast multiplies described, it always says you can divide, but it never shows you how. I decided to show you how.

Every C programmer knows that you can divide by two by shifting a number left by 1 bit, divide by four by shifting left 2 bits, and so on. Fast division is done by approximating the result as a sum of binary fractions. Table 13.4 lists a small number of both integer and fractional powers of two.

Table 13.4. Binary powers of 2.

Decimal	Binary
16	10000.000000
8	01000.000000
4	00100.000000
2	00010.000000
1	00001.000000
0.5	00000.100000
0.25	00000.010000
0.125	00000.001000
0.0625	00000.000100
0.03125	00000.000010
0.015625	00000.000001

For example, to divide by 3, we need to add up binary fractions to get as close to 0.333333... as we can get. The way to find out which fractions to add up is look at the bits in the fractional part of the fixed-point representation of 1/3. (The basics of fixed-point arithmetic were covered in *Tricks of the Game-Programming Gurus.*) In hexadecimal notation, fixed-point 1 with 16 bits of fraction is

```
1.0000
```

Dividing by 3, the fixed point result in hex is

```
0.5555
```

and in binary it's

```
0.0101010101010101
```

So a binary approximation of 1/3 is

```
0.01 + 0.0001 + 0.000001
```

or using decimal values from Table 13.4, we get

```
0.25 + 0.0625 + 0.015625 = 0.328125
```

which is accurate to within one decimal digit. If we add one more term, we get

```
0.25 + 0.0625 + 0.015625 + 0.0.00390625 = 0.332031
```

which approximates 1/3 accurate to within two decimal digits.

Using this technique, division by 3 in C is

```
(x >> 2) + (x >> 4) + (x >> 6) + (x >> 8)
```

The trouble with this technique is that for most divisors it gives you an approximate result. The result is always just a little bit too small. If you are doing fixed-point arithmetic, it is probably good enough. Listing 13.15 is a simple program that uses this technique to compute the 16-bit fixed-point inverse of any number.

Listing 13.15. Fast divide demo.

```c
#include <stdio.h>
#include <stdlib.h>

void
main()
{
    int i;

    long one;
    long divisor = 0;
    int leftShift;
    float v, d;
```

```
    scanf("%d", &divisor);
    one = 0x10000;

    while (divisor != 0)
    {
        d = 0;
        v = 0.5;
        leftShift = 1;
        one /= divisor;
        while (one)
        {
            if (one & 0x8000)
            {
                d += v;
                printf("leftShift=%4d d=%f v=%f\n", leftShift, d, v);
            }
            one <<= 1;
            one &= 0x0ffff;
            v /= 2.0;
            leftShift++;
        }

        scanf("%d", &divisor);
        one = 0x10000;
    }
}
```

mulDiv

If you take a look at the multiplication and division instructions built into modern CPUs, you'll find that if you multiply two 32-bit numbers, you get a 64-bit result. You'll also find that when you want to divide by a 32-bit number, you first have to extend the dividend to be a 64-bit number, and the result is a 32-bit quotient and a 32-bit remainder. This behavior is an example of a general rule of arithmetic that we learned grade school: If you have a number with N digits and you multiply it by a number with M digits you get a number with at most $N + M$ digits. This means that if you multiply two 32-bit numbers, you have to get a 64-bit result.

Now take a look at the * and / operations in high-level programming languages such as C and Pascal. In C, when you multiply two 32-bit numbers together, you get a 32-bit result. This looks pretty suspicious to me! Well, not really. The result has to fit in the variable you want to store it in, which means you have to force it back to 32 bits (or to whatever size values you're using). The problem is that if you multiply two large values together, you lose the top part of the result.

In graphics code, especially in line and polygon clipping code, you see code that looks like ((A * B) / C), where A and B are large enough that (A * B) is too large to fit in a 32-bit value but ((A * B) / C) fits very nicely in a 32-bit value. If you carry out this bit of arithmetic in a high-level language, the 64-bit value of (A * B) is computed. Then the top 32 bits of the value are thrown into the bit bucket. The truncated result is converted to an incorrect 64-bit value. The bogus 64-bit value is divided by the 32-bit value of C, and you get an incorrect result.

To demonstrate this problem in C, I tried (1111111 * 1111111) / 1111111, which should have given the result 1111111. The result I got was –4853. The difference between the answer I got and the correct answer is big enough to cause some serious problems. In line-clipping code, this would give you lines running off into Never Never Land.

This is one case where you have to go to assembly language on the target machine to get the correct answer. Listing 13.16 shows an implementation of mulDiv() as an inline 386 assembly-language function for use with the Watcom 10.0a C compiler.

Listing 13.16. mulDiv for Watcom C.

```
/
// Multiply to 32 bit numbers giving a 64 bit
// result then divide the 64 bit number by a 32
// bit value and return the result.
//

long
mulDiv(long value, long mulBy, long divBy);
#pragma aux mulDiv = \
    "imul    ecx" \
    "idiv    ebx" \
    parm [eax] [ecx] [ebx]\
    modify [edx] \
    value [eax];
```

The key parts of this version of mulDiv() are the IMUL and IDIV instructions. Those instruction do the work. The rest of the code is there to tell the compiler the name of the function and enough about what it does so that the optimizer and code generator can insert the code in the program to give the fastest possible execution time.

MulDiv() multiplies the first two numbers together, giving a 64-bit result, then divides that value by a 32-bit number and returns the final 32-bit result.

When I tried mulDiv(1111111, 1111111, 1111111) the result was 1111111—just what it is supposed to be.

One caution on the use of mulDiv(): If the final result doesn't fit in 32 bits, you will get a divide fault. Nothing is without risk.

When I started working with Windows, I was not surprised to find the win16 API supplies a 16-bit version of mulDiv(), called MulDiv(), and that the win32 API supplies a 32-bit version also called MulDiv(). You really need mulDiv() for graphics programming.

Extending Fixed Point

The same conflict between programming languages and computer hardware that forces the use of assembly language for implementing mulDiv() forces the use of assembly language for implementing multiplication and division for fixed-point arithmetic.

As described in *Tricks of the Game-Programming Gurus*, fixed-point arithmetic is performed using integer numbers with an assumed decimal point (or, more properly, "binary point," because this is binary arithmetic) breaking the numbers into two fixed-sized integer and fractional parts. A common format for fixed-point arithmetic is 16 bits of integer and 16 bits of fraction.

Fixed point number formats are described using *I.F* notation, where *I* is the number of bits of integer in the number and *F* is the number of bits of fraction. Listing 13.17 shows the definition of a 16.16 fixed-point data type and routines that do addition, subtraction, multiplication, and division with full 32-bit precision on that data type.

Listing 13.17. 32-bit, fixed-point arithmetic.

```
typedef long fp;

//
// Divide two 16.16 fixed point numbers giving
// a 16.16 fixed point result.
//

fp
fpDiv(fp d1, fp d2);
#pragma aux fpDiv = \
    "cdq" \
    "shld    edx, eax, 16" \
    "sal     eax,16" \
    "idiv    ebx" \
    parm [eax] [ebx]\
    modify [edx] \
    value [eax];

//
// Multiply two 16.16 fixed point numbers giving
// a 16.16 fixed point result.
//

fp
fpMul(fp m1, fp m2);
#pragma aux fpMul = \
    "imul    ebx" \
    "shrd    eax, edx, 16" \
    parm [eax] [ebx]\
    modify [edx]\
    Value [eax];
```

continues

Listing 13.17. continued

```
//
// Add and subtract fixed point numbers.
//

#define fpAdd(a1, a2) ((a1) + (a2))
#define fpSub(s1, s2) ((s1) - (s2))
```

The code in Listing 13.17 was developed for a project I did a few years ago and has since been used in several commercial projects. This version of the code is written as 386 assembly language in the form of inline assembly-language routines compatible with Watcom C. Versions of these routines have been used in commercials games on the PC and on 68KB-based Macintosh computers.

The arithmetic routines shown in Listing 13.17 can be changed to support any 32-bit fixed-point format by changing the 16 to give the number of fraction bits you want. In my current project, I use fixed point numbers in 18.14, 24.8, and 0.15 formats, depending on the range of numbers I need.

Both fpMul() and fpDiv depend on the use of 64-bit intermediate results to maintain precision. fpMul() multiplies two 16.16 fixed-point numbers, producing a 32.32 format number. It then gets rid of the top 16 bits and the bottom 16 bits to get back to a 16.16 format 32-bit, fixed-point number. FpDiv() first extends the divisor from a 16.16 format to a 32.32 format and then divides, giving a 16.16 format fixed-point number.

Even though fpMul() maintains 32 bits of precision, it still suffers from the kinds of truncation problems that we see when using integers. These are the same kinds of problems we used mulDiv() to get around.

Fractional Arithmetic

There is one form of fixed-point numbers that deserve special attention. This is the pure fraction format for fixed-point numbers. In this format, the decimal point is placed to the left of all the digits of the number.

Integer	101001010.
Fixed point	101001.010
Fraction	.101001010

The pure fraction form of fixed-point numbers is used so often in computer graphics that it's what many programmer think you're talking about when you say "fixed point."

Pure fractions are worth looking at for several reasons. From the programmer's point of view, one of the greatest advantages of fractions over other forms of fixed-point numbers is that a multiply cannot overflow. The product of two fractions is always a fraction. When you multiply two 32-bit fractions, you get a 64-bit result. You get back to a 32 value by throwing away the least significant 32 bits of the number. When working with integers and other kinds of fixed-point numbers, you always have to throw away some of the most significant bits of the product to get back to a 32-bit value.

You can get overflow on division, addition, and subtraction. But division is rare compared to multiplication, and you can check for divide overflow before doing the division. You can only get divide overflow if the fraction you are dividing by is less than or equal to the fraction being divided. Overflow of addition and subtraction can be detected by looking at the carry/borrow flag after the operation is complete.

Modern computers represent negative numbers using the "two's complement" of the number. You form the two's complement by inverting each bit of the number and adding 1 to the result. For example: 5 in binary is 0101 to compute –5 we first invert 0101 giving 1010. (If a bit is 0 then the inverse of the bit is 1 and vice versa.) We then add 1 giving 1011 which is the two's complement representation of –5. We can check the result by testing to see if –(–5) is 5. With –5 equal to 1011 the inverse is 0100. Adding 1 we get 0101 which is binary 5.

Two's complement numbers have the odd property of having one more negative value than positive value. To see this consider that the largest 4-bit positive binary number is 0111 and the largest negative 4-bit number is 1000. The two's complement of 0111 is 1001 and the two's complement of 1000 is 1000.

Two's complement is not the only way to represent negative binary numbers. One's complement numbers also work. The one's complement is formed by inverting the bits of the number. One's complement numbers have the odd property of having two different representations for 0. In four-bit binary, one's complement numbers 0000 is positive zero and 1111 is "negative" zero. Notice that negative zero is not equal to positive zero. I've worked on a one's complement machine and having to worry about two different values for zero is just not worth it.

Another way to represent negative binary numbers is to use signed magnitude representation. Signed magnitude representation dedicates the high order bit of every number for use as a sign bit. We normally write decimal numbers using a signed magnitude form but we use "+" and "–" signs to tell us that a number is positive or negative instead of using a bit. Computers don't use signed magnitude numbers because using them forces a computer to have hardware that both adds and subtracts. By using one's complement or two's complement numbers computers only need to have hardware for addition.

All the different ways of representing negative binary numbers have there problems. Of all of them, two's complement has the fewest problems. That extra negative number does cause problems. Usually the problem is caused by forgetting that the extra negative number exists.

Because modern computers use two's complement arithmetic, the values for fractional numbers range from –1 to slightly less than 1 because of the extra negative number you get from using two's complement numbers. If we're using 16-bit signed numbers, then the two's complement integer number range is –32768 to 32767. Converting to fractions by dividing by 32768 (the same as moving the decimal point from the left end to the right end of the word) gives us a fractional number range of –1 to approximately 0.99969 which is just 1/32768 less than 1. For 16-bit numbers, this gives just a bit more than four decimal digits of precision. If you go to 32-bit fractions you get better than nine decimal digits of precision.

Because the most significant bits of a fraction are always in the high order bits of a word, it's easy to use them as indexes into tables. If you have a sine table with 256 entries and you map the 0 to 359 degrees onto the range 0/256 to 255/256 (which is roughly 0 to .996), you can convert the fractional form of the angle to an index by simply grabbing the high-order 8 bits of the fraction. If you have a larger table, take more bits; for a smaller table, take fewer bits. Just make sure your tables are powers of two in size.

"But," you say, "my numbers aren't fractions." Well, they could be. Any integer or fixed-point number in a computer has an absolute upper and lower bound. Just divide by the absolute value of the lower bound, and you have mapped your numbers onto the range –1 to nearly 1. Or, you can add the absolute value of the lower bound to each number and then divide by the same value and map your numbers onto the range 0 to nearly 1.

Let's say you are doing a 3-D adventure game and your world is 20,000 units wide, high, and deep. The location of every point in your game world can be represented by using three numbers—the x, y, z coordinates—in the range 0 to 20,000. If you divide each of those numbers by 20,000 then the location of every point in your world can be represented by three fractional numbers in the range 0 to 1. If your world coordinates are in the range –20,000 to 20,000 then dividing each coordinate by 20,000 will map the coordinates onto the range –1 to 1. Or you could first add 20,000 to each coordinate moving them from the range –20,000 to 20,000 to the range 0 to 40,000. If you then divide each coordinate by 40,000 you've mapped all the coordinates from the range –20,000 to 20,000 to the range 0 to 1. Once the coordinates have been mapped to the range 0 to 1 you can use fractional arithmetic for all your 3-D transformations.

Summary

This chapter has looked at optimization from several different directions. We've looked at ways to optimize your time by making sure you don't waste time optimizing code that doesn't need to be optimized. We've shown the need for testing to verify that an optimization is really an optimization. You've seen what good programming tools can do for you. We've looked at ways to make sure that the computer is fast enough and has enough memory to run the game you want to write. We've presented general rules for optimizing loops and how to use a specific technique, Duff's Device, to write generalized unrolled loops. We've looked at ways to optimize memory allocation and file I/O. We've looked at the need to drop out down to assembly language age for doing arithmetic. This chapter also has presented you with a technique for doing fast divides and with the advantages of using fractional arithmetic.

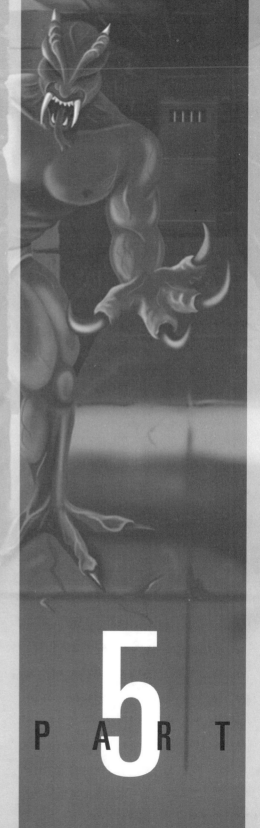

Wrapping It All Up

PART

5

Delivering Your Software to the End User

by Brad Whitlock

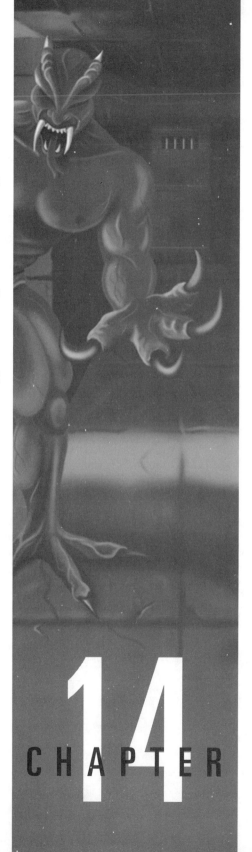

CHAPTER 14

Once you've created your game software, you are still not finished. You need to consider how you'll get your game installed to the user's computer. This is an important subject, even though some software architects consider it mundane. This chapter will show why it's important to give this issue consideration.

First Impressions Last

Your manuals, along with the installation program for your software, are your user's first introduction to your software. Since we all know that users typically don't read manuals, you're left with your installation routine as the first dance between you and the user. You don't want to step on your user's toes during this first dance. If you fail with this initial encounter, the quality of your actual software product becomes a moot point to the user—no matter how good or fancy it is, no matter what great things it does, the user will never find out about it if he can't get your software installed. The smoother and easier your software installation is accomplished, the better the impression your user will have of the software.

Not only is the installation of your software the first impression your user will get of your product, it can also be a very lasting one. How many times have you let a first impression control your feelings about a new service you were trying or a person you've just met? Does a sloppy ticket counter promote confidence in an airline? Does a person with bad breath leave a positive impression on you?

A software program without an adequate installation routine is like a person with bad breath—it leaves a bad impression regardless of how good a program you have created. Can you afford to overcome such a hurdle before your customer has even used your software? Probably not.

Figure 14.1 graphically illustrates a very simple notion regarding users' tolerance and frustration levels: Their tolerance level is inversely proportional to the difficulty encountered in using the software, while the frustration level is directly proportional.

Figure 14.1.
The user's frustration level in using software directly correlates to the ease of using that software.

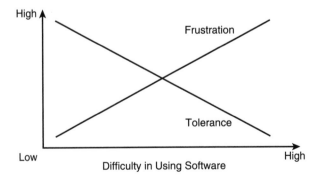

An individual with programming experience may be willing to persevere through a difficult software installation, but a novice end user is seldom willing to do so. Therefore it is imperative that you provide a clear-cut approach to installing your software.

Support Calls: Minimize Them

Another reason for concentrating on the installation aspect of your software is the support consequences of *not* doing so. Whatever you do, you must try to minimize the support effort involved with any software you write—unless you make money off support by charging for it! Generally, fee-for-support is not the case with game software, so the more you can reduce your support costs (in both time and money), the better off you will be.

One way to accomplish this is with an adequate installation program. Studies show that the initial installation of a software package is often one of the chief sources of calls to support hot lines. Indeed, if you can get the user through the installation process successfully, you may not hear from the user at all. This is particularly common with game software (unless there is some obvious program flaw that the user discovers.)

Making Your Software More Attractive

A third reason to exercise care over your installation process is self-interest.

Independent software architects and small software companies often find themselves looking for a publisher to acquire rights to their software for the obvious financial and resource benefits. With all the software being written these days, it's important that your product not only be nifty and work well but that your software installs easily and in a professional-looking manner. Missing the opportunity of a publisher acquiring rights to your product because they had trouble installing it is a needless disappointment that can be avoided by addressing the issue of software installation up front.

Users Do the Darnedest Things

It's always important to know your audience when delivering a product—be it a book, a magazine article, a speech, or software. As mentioned previously, most users have little tolerance for a software package that they can't install and use immediately. This is particularly true of game software. The anticipation of the users is just too great—they require *immediate gratification* to be happy. And unhappy users do the darnedest things.

Following is a brief User Aptitude Test for software architects to help you think about the software installation process from the user's point of view.

User Aptitude Test

Question #1: What will your user do if he cannot get your software installed to his computer properly the first time he tries? (Circle one answer only)

1. Call a computer-knowledgeable friend for help.

2. Read the manual for further assistance.

3. Lay the software aside until he has more time to deal with it.

4. Call the vendor (you) for help.

5. Return it for a refund.

Answer: If you answered Number 1, you're right about 10 percent of the time.

If you answered Number 2, you're dreaming.

If you answered Number 3, you're right about 10 percent of the time.

If you answered Number 4, you're right about 10 percent of the time (and you know what it's like to be tied up on the phone rather than getting software written!)

Unfortunately for you, Number 5 is what happens most of the time. This directly affects your pocketbook. Although you may be writing software for fun, you are also probably writing software to make money. It's important to eliminate things that *cost* you time and money. In this scenario, you not only lose the initial purchase price but the potential ongoing upgrade dollars that would have flowed from this user.

Question #2. Are the following installation instructions in your software manual adequate? (True or False).

1. At the DOS prompt (usually `C:\>`), type `MD GAME` and press Enter. This creates a new directory on your drive called Game. If you already have a directory with this name, or want to use another directory name, type `MD` followed by a space, then a directory name, and press Enter. A directory name can contain up to eight characters.

2. Insert the Game disk into a disk drive.

3. Type `COPY A:\*.* C:\Game` and press Enter. If the disk is in a drive other than A, type that drive letter in the command statement. Likewise, if you have stored the Game files in a different drive or directory, substitute the path to the Game files in the command statement and then press Enter. For example, you might type: `COPY B:\*.* D:\Game` and press Enter.

Answer: If you answered True, we'll send you a new answering machine, because your current one is going to wear out from all the support calls the users of your software are going to make to you. If you answered False, then you know that installation instructions, by their very definition, should be as short and sweet as possible and allow for virtually a 100-percent success rate on the user's part. (We know nothing is for sure in this business, but we're willing to bet that the software-installation problem can be reduced to one problem for every 100 users—maybe even less than that.)

Not only are the preceding instructions difficult for many users to understand, they are also woefully inadequate. For example, what if the user doesn't have enough hard-drive space? Simple, you say, they delete some files. Many users will not understand to do this or which files to delete. You cannot, (read *must not*), depend on the user to take all the appropriate and proper actions.

Note: The preceding instructions were taken from an actual software manual for a commercially available product—the software name was changed to protect the guilty. Boy, how would you like to be on their support phone-line staff?

Question #3. Are the following installation instructions too much work or impossible to accomplish? (True or False).

1. Insert your disk to the floppy drive.

2. Type INSTALL.

Answer: If you said False, you're right. Installation instructions do not have to be complicated and overly thorough; professional installation routines do not have to be difficult and time-consuming to produce. If you answered True have we got a surprise for you. Read on about how to easily achieve an installation routine for your software that allows your manual to simply state the preceding installation instructions.

Next we'll take a look at what makes a good install routine, then we'll look at a profile of end users today. We'll also discuss some of the available software installation tools that can save you time and money (and prevent your support-line answering machine from wearing out!)

What Makes a Good Installation Routine?

Because software products and applications are different, so too are individual installation requirements likely to be different for any particular software product or application. Given that, however, it is also safe to say that while the installation requirements may differ in their specifics, they are often similar from a general point of view. It is this general point of view I will address for a few moments so that we can approach the subject of developing an effective software installation routine with some structure.

Basic Considerations for Installation Routines

Some basic factors that need to be considered regarding installation include the following:

■ **Checking the system configuration:** This may be a simple matter of seeing whether the user has enough disk space for the software or if the user is operating from the correct drive. Or it could be much more involved. For example, does the user have enhanced graphics capability? Is the user running the correct operating-system version?

■ **Working with directories and files:** Checking the existing directories will help determine what directories need to be created. For instance, the user may have already created directories that we were planning to use. Appropriate action needs to be taken. The same applies to files. Are any files that are needed already present on the user's disk? Do they have the right date/time stamp? Are there existing files that we will need to overwrite?

■ **Interacting with the user:** At a minimum we need to let the user know what's going on during the installation process. Are things going OK? Was the install successful? Perhaps the user needs to answer some questions we pose so that appropriate action can be taken based on the answers. Any user interaction needs to be done in a clear, concise, consistent and friendly manner.

■ **Error handling:** Abnormal situations that occur during the installation should be handled smoothly by the install program without the user getting involved.

■ **Packaging the installation program with your software:** It's important to properly package the installation routine together with the software being distributed. This can involve, among other things, compressing and/or splitting application files across multiple diskettes (if necessary) and, of course, making sure the installation handles the merging and decompression properly during the install.

How Far Should You Go?

Normally, the less the user has to do to install your software, the better the installation process is. An ideal installation routine will check every possible aspect of the user's configuration that might have an impact on your software and will handle any error or special situation that occurs.

From a practical point of view, it's important that the areas mentioned in the previous section be handled in almost any installation program. The degree to which they are handled depends somewhat on the user of the software, the type of software being installed, and your time constraints.

If your intended user is a programmer, you can get away with a little less hand-holding during the installation than you can with a novice user. The novice user should be led each step of the way. On the other hand, even programmers like software that installs quickly and easily. This lets them start using your product much quicker.

It's not unusual to put off the writing of an installation program because of time constraints. But remember, it's probably worth investing a little extra time into the installation program to avoid the phone calls and problems later.

Installation-Routine Checklist

The following are some things to think about with regard to your installation process. This is far from an exhaustive list, but it may spark some ideas for you. Of course, all of these items are dependent on your specific software requirements.

System Configuration Considerations

Numerous aspects of the user's system configuration may need to be considered, including, but not limited to:

- Drives
- Machine type
- Parallel or serial port status
- FILES, BUFFERS, or other CONFIG.SYS settings
- PATH or other updates of the AUTOEXEC.BAT file
- Updates to .INI files
- Adequate disk space
- Adequate available memory
- Check for EGA or VGA board, color graphics, math co-processor
- Proper operating system version
- Check machine and processor type
- Environment variables that need to be set

Working with Directories and Files

There are several considerations regarding files and directory manipulation on the user's target machine, including:

- Does the user already have directories and/or files that you're about to move to his or her machine? If so, how should the conflict be handled?
- Do you want to set up directories and/or files for the user, or let him or her do it?
- If there are particular files or directories your software requires, are the right ones in place, and are they the right version? What's their time/date stamp? How old are they?
- Do any files need to be erased or renamed?
- Does a date/time stamp need to be set on a file?

User Interaction Issues

When interacting with the user, aim for simplicity and completeness. Some of the user inter-action issues include:

- Consistency of displays to the user. Displays should have consistent color and place-ment on the user's screen.
- Prompting the user for information and checking the user's answer to a prompt.
- Checking to see if the user has hit any extraneous keys on the keyboard.
- Pausing the installation program to display messages.
- Sounding tones to the user under special circumstances.
- Disabling the Break key during installation.
- Making your installation displays professional while not overshadowing your actual product.

Error Handling Considerations

Errors during installation must be handled cleanly. Most errors will confuse the user unless clearly handled and interpreted. Issues include:

- Error trapping—handling DOS/system errors versus program errors
- Proper actions to take on certain errors
- Suppressing some error messages to avoid confusion

Other Potential Issues

Of course, with any programming task, there are a host of other potential issues to address, such as the following:

- Other software that needs to be available or called
- Testing the routine completely prior to distributing
- Securing the installation routine—preventing end-user changes
- Running copy protection (if needed) reliably
- User disdain for copy protection (keeping it invisible)
- Any other items that could go wrong during the installation

Windows Considerations

If your software is written for Windows, you have even more to consider. At the top of the list of installation issues is updating the program manager—specifically group and icon installation.

This can be as exciting for you and the end user as manually modifying the AUTOEXEC.BAT or CONFIG.SYS files.

Imagine the following installation instructions for a Windows product:

1. Start Windows and switch to the Windows File Manager.

2. Insert the game disk into the disk drive.

3. From the File Menu, choose Create Directory. The Create Directory dialog box appears.

4. In the Directory text box, type C:\Game and click OK. If you already have a directory with this name, type a new directory name and click OK. A directory name can contain up to eight characters.

5. Click the drive icon at the top of the File Manager window containing the disk with the game files. The files appear in the File Manager window.

6. Select all the files on the disk. If you are short of disk space, you can copy only selected library files.

7. From the File Menu, choose Copy. The Copy dialog box appears.

8. Type C:\Game in the To text box and click OK. If you have stored the Game files in a different drive or directory, substitute the path to the Game files in the command statement and then click OK. For example, you might type D:\Game and click OK.

9. Exit File Manager by clicking File and then clicking Exit.

10. Create a program icon for the game by first opening the group window you want to add an item to.

11. From the File Menu, choose New.

12. In the New Program Object dialog box, select the Program Item option, then choose the OK button.

13. Fill in the Program Item properties dialog box as necessary, and choose the OK button.

Sounds like fun, eh? Certainly not for your user.

Let's visit for a moment the least predictable factor we are up against: the end user.

Users Do the Darnedest Things, Part II

End users are funny creatures. We'd be lost without them—after all, what good is software if no one uses it? But they can be very frustrating to deal with at times. We're not referring to a programmer or an experienced end user—they usually are willing to persevere if they encounter a problem or even read the manual to see if there was something they missed in the process!

But novice end users (who unfortunately are in the majority) don't react quite the same way. Believe it or not, today there are more novice users than ever. As discussed in a previous section, they can get frustrated quickly. And their perception of computers and computing is often slightly skewed. The Story of the Any Key comes to mind…

Once upon a time, a user was running the nifty software he had just purchased. At one point, not too far into the program, an informative message was displayed. The thinking software architect had placed a message at the bottom of the screen to let the user know how to continue after he had read the informative message. The message to continue was "Press Any Key to Continue." This seemingly harmless message caused the user to search and search his keyboard—and finally phone the software vendor's support line complaining that his keyboard did not have an ANY key and thus there was no way for him to continue processing!

End-user bloopers go back through the history of computers. In the days of mainframe timesharing, most of the customers of large timesharing firms linked up to the computer via acoustical modems (rather than the built-in modems we all enjoy in our personal computers today). These modems required the user to dial the connect number, then place the phone handset in the modem. One day, not long after an introductory training class had been held, a new user was attempting to access the mainframe system for the first time (using her acoustical coupler.) She carefully studied her notes that instructed her to turn the computer and modem on, dial the number, wait for the access tones, and place the receiver in the modem. As she proceeded through the steps, she waited for the access tones. Instead she heard "Good Morning, Thank you for calling ABC Timesharing." "My gosh, it talks!" she exclaimed. Unfortunately, the user had called the main office phone number instead of the computer access number and had connected to the receptionist instead of the computer.

Users often tend to take instructions and directions literally. They have found from experience that if they don't, things might not work right. (That's why *press* is always a better instruction than *hit*.) (See Figure 14.2.)

Figure 14.2.
Users often tend to interpret instructions literally.

Sometimes you can't prevent users from doing themselves in. For example, it's out of your control when the user puts the disk in upside down or backwards. However, you can give good, precise installation directions in addition to providing a comprehensive installation process. When possible, minimize your use of computer terms and jargon. Remember that even common computer terms can confuse a novice user. A list of computer terminology that may confuse the user includes such terms as

DOS
Windows
Enter
directory
file
path
memory
hard drive
RAM
video display
Escape

And, don't be fooled—users are not necessarily that much more knowledgeable than they were five years ago. Those who started using computers five year ago may be more knowledgeable today than they were then, but there is a whole set of new users every day, particularly now that personal computers are in such widespread use in areas no one ever imagined.

Documented Benefits

These days, a lot of software (unfortunately not all) comes with some type of installation routine.

Companies have learned that it just isn't worth it to skip this step. As much as we would all like to think that end users know what they are doing, it is usually a critical mistake to ignore the installation process for your software.

A company in California recently proved this when they did a software survey of their users. They were distributing their software applications internally to more than 300 end users. The survey showed that the users, more than half the time, had trouble using the software that had been sent to them. It turns out that the users never even used the actual applications that were sent to them because of problems they encountered installing the applications. When the company instituted a policy of standardized installation routines for each application that was sent out, the utilization rate went up to more than 80 percent of the recipients. (Apparently, there was no hope for about 20 percent of their users.)

Another company that markets a tax package claims the calls to their support line regarding installation of their software dropped to virtually nothing after replacing their "baling wire and chewing gum" batch install routine with a thorough, comprehensive routine.

Building Your Installation Routine

Hopefully, you've been convinced to package some form of installation routine with your software. Don't let your installation instructions be just a couple of pages in your manual. You're inviting extra support costs (both time and money) and your users will be less satisfied with your software.

Choices for Installation Routines

You have two basic choices for building an installation routine for your software: You can build the routine from scratch using DOS batch commands, C, or your favorite programming language; or you can obtain one of several software-installation toolkits that will automate the building process for you (or at least give you a big head start).

Checklist

Some of the issues you should examine when thinking about writing your own installation program versus using an installation toolkit are detailed forthwith.

Considerations: Writing Your Own Install versus Using a Toolkit

- Time (yours)
- Money (yours)
- Maintenance of the installation routine
- Completeness of the installation routine
- Testing the installation routine in a variety of machines/environments
- Future upgrades of hardware/software
- Conventions/standards
- Proper/logical defaults
- Reducing support time/costs

You can probably produce a pretty reasonable installation routine using C, Pascal, Basic, or even DOS batch commands. But the nice thing about the installation toolkits is that they are specifically geared toward handling installation issues and problems. And, for the money you would spend for one, you would probably have to write your own installation routine in three to four hours or less in order for it to be more cost-effective than using a toolkit.

Particularly useful is the fact that most of the installation toolkits will handle issues regarding installation that you're probably not going to want to bother with, including file compression, splitting large files across multiple distribution disks, tracking correct disk insertion during the installation, and so on.

Software vendors' highest costs are probably the people costs for doing support and programming. It is worth the investment in a software tool that will cut those support costs for you.

A Bulletproof Installation Routine in Minutes

To achieve a comprehensive, professional-looking, bulletproof installation routine in the least amount of time, software installation toolkits are the answer. With the right toolkit (such as one of those described forthwith), you can have a thorough, comprehensive installation routine that is every bit as good as what the "big guns" in the software arena put out. And it is not unusual to have your installation routine completed in an hour or less with these tools.

Sure, you can probably build something similar to what these packages produce. The issues are time and money. Many of the toolkits represent two to three years of development. They cover esoteric as well as mundane issues. They handle errors (even oddball ones) properly. They provide most if not all the ingredients of successful software-installation program. And, best of all, they don't cost a lot of money. If things are really tight, you can even try out shareware versions of installation toolkits (though you'll find the capabilities are usually reduced and, as with any shareware, support services for the software package may be lacking.)

Available Installation Tools

A variety of installation toolkits are available from vendors. Three or four commercial toolkits rise to the top because they have been available the longest and have the most features. Some acceptable shareware installation tools are also available. These, however, tend to suffer from lack of support, and are limited in features. Nevertheless if any cost to you is significant, you might search the bulletin boards for a shareware installer and try them out.

Foremost among the commercial products is EZ-INSTALL, a well-accepted, widely used utility that was released in 1986. I mention it first here because it has been available the longest and seems to have the most straightforward approach to developing an installation routine while at the same time being laden with features for controlling your installation. EZ-INSTALL provides a toolkit for installing with a DOS-based interface or a Windows-based interface. EZ-INSTALL is a comprehensive utility that handles virtually any installation consideration without requiring any programming on your part. One of EZ-INSTALL's principle features is its Installation Aid setup environment that literally automates the building of the installation routine for you. In this environment, you simply mark choices or fill in values for factors relating to your software's installation, and Installation Aid handles the rest for you. Once you have described your installation to EZ-INSTALL, you can even build your master distribution disks from within EZ-INSTALL's Installation Aid.

A demonstration of the EZ-INSTALL installation toolkit can be found on the CD-ROM included with this book. This will give you a good idea of how these tools can help you address the subject of software installation adequately, quickly, and cost-effectively.

HPI's Installit and Knowledge Dynamic's Install are also popular installation tools. They both offer DOS and Windows interfaces. Contrary to EZ-INSTALL's approach, Installit and Install provide you with a script language with numerous keywords for controlling your installation. You edit, or build, a script using the keywords. This determines how your installation proceeds, what occurs during the installation, and when the various steps occur. So, although there is no specific programming involved, there are script keywords to learn. Sample scripts are provided with both products to speed your learning process of the keywords.

If you have very extensive Windows installation requirements, Installshield, from Stirling Technologies, is worth looking into. Installshield also works on a script basis and has a plethora of keywords for controlling the installation. We found the product to be pricey and slightly bug-ridden but worth checking into if the other installation toolkits mentioned here don't have the features you need.

Vendor contacts for the products mentioned here are as follows:

> **EZ-INSTALL**: The Software Factory, Inc. (303) 674-9430 (e-mail address: WJMH77A@PRODIGY.COM)
> **Install**: Knowledge Dynamics, Inc. (210) 979-9424 (e-mail address: 71333.3444@COMPUSERVE.COM)
> **Installit**: HPI (205) 880-8782 (e-mail address: FTP.INSTALIT.COM)
> **Installshield**: Stirling Technologies (708) 240-9111 (e-mail address: INFO@INSTALLSHIELD.COM)

Packaging and Duplication

One more thing to consider when distributing your software is the area of diskette duplication and packaging.

An installation "gotcha" that crops up too frequently is the "bad disk." Disks received in unusable condition are often blamed on the post office, the delivery service, or the diskette manufacturer—when, in fact, these disks may have been fine had they been duplicated properly.

What is involved in producing diskettes? Unfortunately, a lot...

Disk Problems

End users that encounter the "Abort, Retry, Fail" message (or similar messages) when trying to run your installation routine may not understand that this isn't a problem with your software. Typically, these errors indicate a problem with the user's machine reading the disk that you have sent. These errors almost always result from a physical problem with a file or some form of physical diskette problem. Causes of this include, but are not limited to

- A file is "broken." It cannot be executed because the operating system views it, or a portion of it, as unreadable.

- The diskette has been corrupted in transit to the user (or by the user). This can happen in obvious ways, including damage by the mail service or the diskette being placed near a magnetic field such as a motor or stereo speaker. If the disk is damaged in this way, disk-management utilities (such as CHKDSK and/or SCANDISK) will usually show the disk has a problem.

- The diskette cannot be properly read by the user's floppy drive. Generally, this results from "track misalignment." Most typically, track misalignment occurs when a 5.25" low-density disk has been produced either by a disk duplicator or on a computer with a 5.25" floppy drive that reads both high-density and low density 5.25" disks. It is a well-documented problem that this can result in unreadable sector(s) by the target machine diskette drive due to "track misalignment." Basically, what happens here is that the drive alignment on one machine does not match the other, resulting in a *misread*.

  Occasionally, track misalignment will occur with other kinds of diskettes, but the 5.25" low-density disk is the most common troublemaker.

  For same of the same reasons, misreading can also occur if you use "preformatted" diskettes—for instance, if drive alignment between machines does not match.

What You Can Do

To minimize any "read" problems of the diskettes you distribute, follow these general rules:

- Do not use preformatted diskettes.

- Format and produce your master sets on the same floppy drive.

- Test your files and disks before and after the master sets are produced.

- Don't use the DOS DISKCOPY command to produce your distribution disks. If possible, use any of the popular software "duplicating" packages, such as EZ-Diskcopy PRO and Disk Dupe. These products turn a PC into a disk-duplicating machine without any extra hardware. They simultaneously format, copy, and verify your disks all in one step.

- To avoid shipment problems, sturdy mailers and good packaging are a must.

- If you have to use a duplicating machine, make sure it is a high-quality one.

- Always test your master disks before you start to duplicate from them.

Summary

In this chapter, I have tried to remind you of the obvious and discuss the not-so-obvious details regarding distributing your software to your ultimate end user. Not only do first impressions last, they can be a killer.

I've shown you some safe, reliable, yet inexpensive ways to make sure your user gets your software installed properly. I've also shown the types of issues you need to consider when addressing your software installation process.

Remember, there are lots of good reasons to spend time on your installation process—not the least of which are time and money. Time spent up front on this issue can save you many hours of grief down the road.

Beta-Testing Your First Game

by Andrew D. Lehrfeld

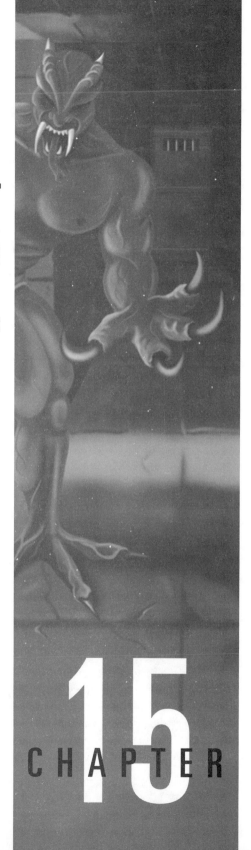

CHAPTER 15

You've spent a great deal of time and effort on your game. Before you release your work to the buying public, you should invest the additional time and effort required to properly beta test the software. A thorough beta-testing cycle can do more than just eliminate bugs in the program. Properly executed, it can introduce your program to a group of game enthusiasts who will share their comments, suggestions, and criticisms with you. And if you follow my advice and select beta testers carefully, you can elicit some high-quality, low-cost market research as well.

This chapter will discuss ways to build your own team of beta testers from scratch, and how to use their bug reports, comments, and suggestions to your benefit. The basic steps for beta testing your first game include organizing the beta team and gathering their comments and reports.

Organizing the Beta-Test Team

Unless you are fortunate enough to have your game published by a company with an established team, you must put together a team of beta testers on your own. In addition to simply organizing the team, you will also need to provide a BBS or private area on an existing online service that can serve as your home base of operations. You'll use this area to distribute files and to conduct messaging with the beta testers.

To begin with, a single-node BBS is sufficient. You can dedicate a machine to this task and run your BBS 24-hours-a-day, or if resources are limited, you can put your BBS up only at night, or during specified hours, making use of the computer you use for development during the day (assuming you work during the day, which many programmers do not!). Be sure your BBS is set up to provide adequate security for those who will have access to it. Also be certain to utilize some type of security feature within the game files themselves. Password-protect your files and distribute the password only to your beta testers, but be prepared for a leak. Since hackers, pirates, and other unscrupulous types would just love to get their hands on your work before it's released, put the words "Beta Test Version" across your title and opening screens, and anywhere else you can. This will make the beta version less desirable, and may help deter software pirates. It will also help to get the message across to unwary users who might otherwise think they own a legitimate copy of your game.

I have found that an excellent way to uncover potential candidates for a beta-test team is to frequent the places that avid computer gamers can be found, and then listen. Computer gamers congregate on bulletin boards and online services, such as CompuServe. They visit these places for a variety of reasons, but most importantly they visit to obtain the latest shareware releases and to exchange gameplay tips and techniques. Here, as an observer, you will see game enthusiasts post and respond to messages, often revealing clues about their technical expertise, their personality, and their willingness to help others. Since you will be relying heavily on your beta testers to provide you with meaningful reactions that you can put to real use, I suggest spending time to find the best available testers. Here are the qualities to look for:

■ **Look for someone who can write intelligibly.** This may surprise you, but my experience has been that written skills are valid indicators of academic and professional performance. Scanning messages left casually on BBSs and online services may expose you to a person's worst writing habits; nevertheless, this is an even playing field, and those who shine above the others will continue to shine, even if you judge their worst writing samples. I look for complete sentences, correct grammar and punctuation, and a professional style. I have found these qualities in candidates ranging in age from 12 to 65, and in persons from all walks of life. Steer clear of candidates who write the way *Beavis and Butt-head* talk.

■ **Look for a willingness to help others.** The successful beta-test candidate is someone who takes pride or pleasure out of helping others overcome an obstacle or solve a problem. Since your beta testers will likely be working for free, you need to find people who gain satisfaction internally from a job well done. Paying attention to the way people respond to others' problems will lend a clue in this regard. The game enthusiast who replies to a message on a BBS or online service and offers advice or help is likely to enjoy beta testing and find satisfaction in it.

■ **Look for technical expertise.** This is desirable, but it is not absolutely mandatory, since technical expertise can be taught (and, to a lesser degree, is even unnecessary, since beta testers will not be called upon to fix the bugs they find). I would like to caution here that technical expertise is desirable in moderation. A candidate who uses technical language too often in his or her writing, or who attempts to impress me with technical expertise, is not a good candidate. These people scare me. Their actions and language give me reason to think they may know even more than they are revealing, and this concerns me from a security standpoint. Also, persons with limited technical knowledge who think they have great technical expertise can be dangerous. A beta tester should know his or her limitations, and not try to be everything to everyone. Furthermore, good beta testers are constantly seeking added technical knowledge; they don't come into a situation purporting to know it all already. A good case-in-point happened to me recently. A tester with good technical knowledge—one who had often helped out on the boards answering tech-support questions—had a basic question concerning serial ports and their effect on gameplay with modems. The tester chose to post a question to the other members of the beta team to be sure she had the facts needed to make a proper decision.

With these three qualities in mind, you can set out to uncover some hidden beta-test talent in cyberspace. One of my favorite places to visit is the Gamer's Forum on CompuServe. Here, you will find game enthusiasts of every level, from novice computer users to skilled hackers. I have seen game designers post an "open call" for interested beta testers; this might generate a large number of responses, but not necessarily from qualified individuals. The method I prefer involves listening. I think of it as "trolling" for the talent I need. I read message threads, take notes, then return a few days later. Those participants who construct thoughtful messages, who display insight or good ideas, and those people who volunteer to solve someone else's technical problem are the ones I try to follow. After several visits to the forum or the particular BBS, if I see the same people demonstrating the same behavior and skills, I may take the next step, which is to contact them privately.

I have all potential beta testers fill-out an application which, among other things, enables me to study their system configurations and determine whether or not we have a need for such a system on our beta team. I build and maintain a database of all testers and solicit the testers' help in keeping the file current by having them report all system changes to me. The application also provides a consistent form to record an applicant's prior testing experience, reasons for wanting to join the team, and so forth.

> See Appendix A, "Beta-Testing Documents," for examples of the Epic MegaGames Beta Tester's Application, Non-Disclosure Agreement (NDA), a checklist that beta testers can follow, and rules for beta testers. The documents are also available on this book's accompanying CD-ROM.

With several dozen applications in-hand from prospective beta testers, you can elect to send a Non-Disclosure Agreement (NDA) to those you are interested in working with. (Epic's NDA, provided in Appendix A and on the CD-ROM, is an example.) The NDA is a legal document that binds the beta tester to certain terms and restrictions. If you distribute these and expect your beta testers to sign them, be prepared to protect your rights and your interests, and prosecute anyone who violates the agreement. Depending on the sensitivity of the project you will expose to your team of beta testers, you may want to have a lawyer review the NDA before you distribute it. Following the approach I've outlined here, I was able to develop a team of approximately 40 beta testers within the first three months of taking over the leadership of the beta team for Epic on CompuServe. Now, one year after its inception, the Epic Beta Team is made up of members who are all excellent, highly-motivated people.

Gathering Bug Reports and Comments and Suggestions

Each new member of the beta team should receive some introductory information, either in the form of a printed manual, or more often, as a file they can download and review as needed. We provide new beta testers with a Beta Testing Checklist and Beta Testing Rules. The checklist enables testers to follow a carefully-scripted check for hardware and system conflicts, which is helpful because it forces all the team members to start at the same place. From there, each can elaborate on conflicts or problems he or she discovers. The rules document outlines a code of conduct and a set of guidelines we expect all our beta testers to follow. (Both documents are included in Appendix A and on the accompanying CD-ROM.) Note that the rules include the number of times a beta tester must visit the forum at minimum, and so on.

I find that beta testers who are chosen according to the methods I've outlined are generally very enthusiastic, self-motivated people; therefore, soliciting their opinions, comments, and bug reports is not a difficult task. I try to make the beta-testing forum a congenial place, where members are encouraged to voice their comments and opinions freely. This elicits both creative criticism as well as the bug reports and technical problems you ordinarily associate with beta testing.

Your game is ready for the beta testers when you have it running reliably on your own machine. But be forewarned: The beginning of your beta-test cycle does not necessarily signal that the completion of your work is near. Post the game on your beta-test BBS or in your private online area, along with a text file or instructions that direct the testers to known problems or particular features you need to point out. Then, have your beta testers begin by systematically testing that the game runs reliably on their own computers, and marking the results on the Beta Test Checklist.

I expect beta testers not to simply report bugs they find, but to search for solutions too. For example, I frown on testers who simply say that such-and-such is not working on their system; what you really want is to have the testers discover for themselves why a particular part of the game isn't working. This can sometimes be accomplished through a process of trial-and-error, but even if it cannot, the tester needs to let you know what he has tried in an attempt to remedy the problem. When a tester reports that sound code is not working properly, he should also state whether or not he's tried different sound-card setups (if available in the game), whether he's tried from a clean boot, whether he's certain his required sound drivers are loading, and whether he has the most up-to-date drivers for his sound card. One advantage to having a large beta group is that there is almost always more than one tester with the same sound card or other piece of hardware, and this helps determine where a problem might lie. I often find that one tester is having problems with a video or sound card but another tester is using the same card with no problems. The fix is usually a simple one, and it may have nothing to do with the game you've written.

Your beta testers will expect feedback, too. Be certain that their reports, comments, and messages are responded to, if not individually, at least in a message in which you acknowledge the recent bug reports and describe what you are doing to address them. I find that beta testers whose comments and bug reports go unaddressed will lose interest in the project, and in the end, you are the one who will suffer as a result. I am always frustrated when good beta testers leave the team; fortunately it does not happen often.

This is a good opportunity to mention my philosophy that beta testing is a two-way relationship. I began work as a beta tester for a game company that did not foster this kind of feeling. Instead, the company made the beta testers feel as though they were doing the testers a favor by enabling them to contribute to a game's development. Many testers on the team resented this, and good ones, like myself, sought other opportunities. Remember that beta testers are volunteers who are helping you to develop a product from which you hope to earn some money. Treat them with the same respect you'd give any other partner, and you will reap the rewards of their skill and creative input.

I spoke previously about market research. This is an important time to listen carefully to what your beta testers are saying—as well as what they're not saying—about your game. This is likely the first opportunity you've had to expose the memebers of a wide audience to your game all at once. You may get some surprising comments; you could be very pleased, or you could be very, very disappointed. Never underestimate the value and importance of these first comments. Remember, you pulled your group of beta testers together from a universe of game enthusiasts. They're good people and they like computer games. They represent your target market. Take their comments, suggestions, and criticisms seriously, and don't fall into the trap of hearing only the good reports and not the bad ones. As I said, the beginning of the beta-test cycle doesn't mean you're nearing the end of your work.

There are many ways in which the beta testers can open your eyes to new ideas and improvements for your game. They have a tremendous advantage over you in critiquing the game and offering ways to better it. Simply stated, they haven't been staring at the game for hours on end, month after month, they way you may have been. They are fresh and without expectations, and they can view your game with a clear head. Suggestions may include enhancements to the game's storyline, changes in play speed or level of difficulty, changes in text font or screen colors to improve readability, changes in scoring and timing procedures, improvement of the online help system, user interfaces (including the logical construction of menus), and so on.

For example, during the beta testing of the game Traffic Department (released by Safari Software, an Epic division), the beta testers almost unanimously agreed that the game's movement controls were too difficult to master, much to the surprise of the game's designer. The decision was made to change the movement controls, something that no one expected would happen at this late stage of development.

It may be very easy to implement some of the suggestions the beta testers give you. For example, changes in font and color to improve clarity or re-arranging certain menu elements can all be relatively minor fixes that will go a long way in making your release version look that much more polished and professional. Other suggestions will be tougher to implement, and you'll need to weigh the value of the idea with the time and effort it would take to build-in the change. You may have to simply wait until next time to implement such beta-tester suggestions as "How about adding a 3-D perspective?", "Can you make them morph?", or "Are you sure you can't have digitized speech and still keep the game under 1 meg?"

Good luck with your first beta-test cycle, and I hope you produce some awesome games. Enjoy.

Summary

In this chapter, you have learned how to assemble a team of beta testers from available sources, such as BBS's and online services, and how to gather and use bug reports, comments, and criticisms to your advantage in developing your first game.

Writing
Documentation

by Eagle Jones

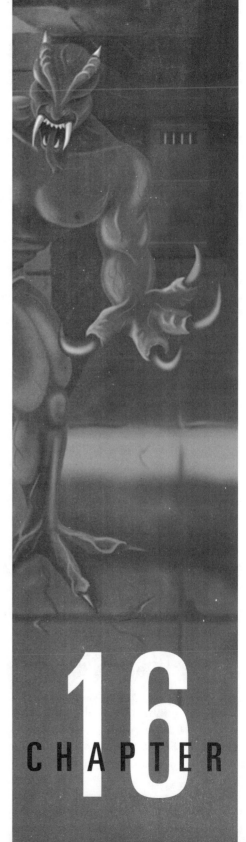

16

More than 30 percent of all problems that people have with software is due to inadequate documentation. As a game developer, your only real form of direct communication with the user is your documentation. Therefore, you need to be sure to present the information that the user needs to play your game, in a way that makes it easy—perhaps even enjoyable—to learn. In this chapter we'll look at the following aspects of documentation:

- Forms of documentation
- Online help
- Tutorials
- Text files
- Printed manuals
- Sections of your documentation
- An example documentation file
- Making an executable documentation file

Forms of Documentation

It's up to you how to present your particular documentation. Many approaches can be used effectively, depending on the complexity of your game and the audience at which it is aimed. For example, a simple game like Space Invaders might have a small text file accompanying the program, or one or two screens of online help. Complex strategy games like SimCity require extensive written documentation and online tutorials. Some games might not be too complex, but have additional features like modem play that require expanded explanations.

For shareware games, most use a text file that is installed in the same directory as the game, called README.TXT or something to that effect. You could also choose to have no external instruction file at all, and rely solely on online help. This is probably not the best way to go however, as some form of documentation is usually necessary for most people just to get the game started. If you are writing a commercial game, then you'll have a printed manual that is included in your box. Special concerns arise with each form of documentation; each is explored a little further in the following sections.

Online Help

Whatever form your main documentation takes, you will definitely want to have help and instructions available from within the game. While this can be a comprehensive manual, it does not have to be. If your main documentation is an external file or a printed manual, you need only a few short, to-the-point online help screens. You may want to simply provide a screen which displays all the control keys, along with its corresponding action.

If the game is complex, then context-sensitive help, or help which is different depending on what part of the game the user is in, should be provided. It is customary in most programs to access help with the F1 key. The amount of online help to provide is your decision. Some programs provide extensive context-sensitive help for every situation, while others only have one or two screens, meant to supplement the external documentation.

Tutorials

One main form of online help is the tutorial. The first time your game is run, you can create a sequence of events where the game will pause at key points and display a message describing important objects or actions. Tutorials are one of the most effective methods of documentation from the user's point of view, for several reasons. First of all, it allows immediate feedback, in an interactive show-and-tell type format. Thus, it's easy to see what exactly you mean. Also, a tutorial can be much, much more interesting than reading a long file—you actually get to play the game as you learn the controls.

If you want to include a tutorial in your game, you should keep that in mind when you are first developing the game. Keep a method open that will allow you to prompt users at certain steps along the way, then give full control back to the user once the tutorial is complete. There are many ways to implement this. For an adventure game, you could simply make the first few characters that are met in the game help you out by giving extra information about how to play. A mission-based battle game might have the first mission be a tutorial, in which the messsages would be caused by certain events such as killing a particular monster or picking up a gun.

Text Files

For almost all shareware games, and some commercial games, the main documentation is provided in the form of a text file. It's more convenient for the user if you make the documentation into an executable file with built-in controls to scroll through or print out the instructions. I develop a program to do this later in the chapter.

Careful attention should be paid to formatting your text file. Headings should be offset, so that separate sections are clearly discernible. You can use ASCII line and box-drawing characters to add emphasis and a polished look. Clear formatting will make the information easier and more interesting to read.

Printed Manuals

If you are developing a commercial game, you will probably work with your game publisher to create a printed manual. The considerations for this situation are mostly the same as for a shareware game with a text file, discussed above. However, you need to pay especially close attention to formatting and layout for a printed manual, as flaws in printed matter are much more apparent than in a text file. You will also most likely have advantages such as including diagrams and screen shots in a printed manual.

Sections of Your Documentation

Whatever form of documentation you select, your main documentation will be enhanced by beginning with a brief story, which sets the stage for the game. Make sure the player knows what's going on and what the object of the game is; or, if part of the game is finding these things out, build the atmosphere of suspense, mystery, or intrigue that you're looking for. It does not need to be a Pulitzer Prize candidate, but a well-written paragraph or two will work just fine. If your game does not have much of a story to tell, just describe the main idea of the game. For example, a flight simulator might simply start out with, "Super-Flight puts you in control of a single-engine aircraft and lets you fly over the city of San Francisco." Some games go far overboard with the story and set up the entire manual along some theme. When overdone, this can destroy the purpose of the story and be confusing and annoying to the reader.

Once the stage is set for your game, you should tell the user how to start. Mention the required and recommended system configurations, and say what additional hardware is supported. Describe how to install and configure the game and how to run it.

Next, describe the game play and controls. What is the user's role in the game? What should they expect to see and how do they interact with the environment? Remember that they probably have not run the game yet, so be sure to provide complete information that does not depend on having seen the game. If you find that some important aspect of the instructions is too difficult to describe completely, you might want to say something like, "At this point, go ahead and start the game and get a feel for playing it. Then continue reading the manual."

Next, many manuals, including the example I will develop later in this chapter, include a set of hints that can help a user to perform well in the game, especially as they get started. Including a section like this will help to build the confidence and comfort level of the user. If they start out knowing some useful strategies, then the initial learning curve is lessened and they feel more comfortable.

Additional sections can be added to describe major functions of the game that aren't covered in the other sections; in the case of the example at the end of this chapter, multi-player modes are discussed. This will not only make sure that every component of the game is well documented, it will also draw attention to unique features.

Finally, a section of the manual should be a trouble-shooting guide, addressing common problems that might arise. The vast majority of problems are shared by many users, so pay careful attention to the common problems that arise with beta testers, and address these in the trouble-shooting section. Marketing, legal information, disclaimers, and copyright information should come last in the manual.

Thus, we can see the main points which make up good documentation for a game:

- Include online help as well as an external documentation file
- Tell a story to grab the reader's attention
- Describe the hardware requirements and how to set up the game
- Provide information on the controls and game-play, giving the user an idea of what to expect once they start playing
- Reveal a few hints and tips
- Add sections which glorify and describe additional features
- Give fixes and troubleshooting information for common problems
- Make sure the file is formatted clearly and attractively

An Example Documentation File

The best way to get an idea of how to write your manual is to see what good documentation should look like. Listing 16.1 is an example documentation file. It's not actually from a real game, so it's briefer in some sections than a real manual might be. Of course, don't follow it to the letter, but adapt the idea to work for your particular game. It should help to provide a useful model to follow.

Listing 16.1. An example documentation file (README.TXT).

```
                        BattleMechs

                        by

                        Mega Software, Inc

Table of Contents
==================
            1. Getting Started
                    a. Story
                    b. Requirements
                    c. Installation & Setup
                    d. Starting & Command Line Options
                    e. Navigating the Menu
            2. Controlling and Playing the Game
            3. Tips for beginners
            4. Network & Modem Play
            5. Troubleshooting & Technical Support
            6. Registering


1. Getting Started
===================

a. Story
--------
```

continues

Listing 16.1. continued

"I remembered something today. I haven't always been like this. Once, I was real. I don't remember anything else, but I just remember that there was an accident. I remember horrible pain, but I don't feel pain anymore, so that must mean something was different before that accident happened. I must have been born, just like the little children which we have compassion training with. We've had less compassion training lately. XRK-51 thinks we're going to fight soon, but I think it's just because the guards saw some incidents. They don't realize that we're usually nicer than they are, so they must have been shocked when they saw us sharing food. It doesn't matter, though. Compassion training is a nice break, but now I've got something more important to think about. What was I? Or maybe it was just a dream? I need to find out."

That was your diary entry for July 17, 2132. You are XRK-52, a Battle-Oriented, Mechanically Advantaged Sentient, or BattleMech. You have no life before you woke up at the biological age of twenty. In the six years since then, you've been trained as a soldier. The things you wrote in your diary today gave you a new mission: you must get out of this prison, or training facility, as the people in charge call it, where you've lived all your life. You want to find out what you were and then...who knows? Somehow, you think that there's something better than rotting away here all of your life, preparing for the next war.

b. System Requirements
- -

To run BattleMechs, you'll need the following system:
*An IBM-compatible, 386 or better computer
*Four Megabytes of RAM
*A VGA monitor
*Hard Disk with seven Megabytes free

You'll have more fun with these recommended additions:
*Pentium processor
*Eight Megabytes of RAM
*16-bit soundcard with wavetable synthesizer
BattleMechs Supports the following sound cards
        *Gravis UltraSound
        *Sound Blaster (AWE32, 16, pro, and original, as well as
        compatibles)
        *Roland Sound Canvas and MT-32 (General MIDI)

c. Installation and Setup
- -

To get started with BattleMechs, do the following:
1. Insert Disk 1 in your floppy disk drive
2. Change to that drive and type: "INSTALL" and press Enter
3. Follow the directions on-screen to install and configure BattleMechs for your computer. If you want to change the sound setup at a later time, run the program "SETUP" in the directory where you installed BattleMechs.

d. Starting & Command Line Options

> To start the game, just change to the directory in which BattleMechs is
> installed, type "BM" and press Enter. There are several optional
> command line parameters which you can use by following "BM" on the
> command line with a space and as many of the following as you wish:
>> "-NOSOUND" turns the sound off.
>> "-MOUSE" will use the mouse to control the game.
>> "-KEY" will use the keyboard to control the game.
>> "-JOY" will use the joystick to control the game.
>> "-INFO" will display additional troubleshooting information at
>> the startup.
>
> Once you start the game with your parameters, the game will load, and
> you should see the opening screen. After a few seconds, the main menu
> will be displayed.

e. Navigating the Menus

> You can use the mouse, keyboard, or joystick to make a selection on the
> menus. Up and down will change the highlighted options, and Enter will
> change that option or bring up a sub-menu. Horizontal slider controls
> for the volume, brightness, and some other controls can be moved with
> the left and right controls. To start the game, just choose "New Game"
> from the main menu. Before doing this, however, you'll probably want to
> use the other menu options to configure the game to suit your computer.

2. Controlling and Playing the Game
===================================

> You can use the mouse, keyboard, or joystick to move yourself through
> the game. You can choose your input device from the main menu by
> choosing the "CONTROLS" option. This will also enable you to configure
> the keys and buttons to match your preferences. By default, the arrow
> keys or movement of the joystick and mouse will move your character,
> Space, the left mouse button, or joystick button one will shoot, and
> Alt, the right mouse button, or joystick button two will change
> weapons. You can bring up the map with Tab and the main menu with Esc.
> Doors will open automatically as you shoot them.
>
> BattleMechs have a surgically implanted computer which provides a
> variety of useful information. Messages from the computer are displayed
> on the top of your field of view. At the bottom is a display which
> tells you current ammunition amounts, weapons, health and armor damage,
> and items you are carrying. The computer also makes an automatic
> mapping of surrounding areas. Be sure to make use of the information
> the computer provides you with.

3. Tips for Beginners
=====================

> *Watch the messages from the computer. It knows a certain amount of
> information about most of the things you'll encounter. You can ask it
> for additional information by pressing D for a detailed status report.
>
> *Don't fight everything you see. Some things and creatures may be
> helpful in your mission. If you're not sure, ask the computer.

continues

Listing 16.1. continued

*Use the automatic mapper. You can mark spots on the map with M, so if you've found the exit door but don't have the key, or found food but have 100% health, you can come back later.

*Keep an eye on your health. If it gets too low, make a trip back to one of the spots you marked.

4. Network & Modem Play
========================

You can play with up to seven other players with a network game, or one other person in a modem or serial link game. You can choose to play cooperatively, or to play without monsters against each other. To start a network or modem game, just choose "Network/Modem Play" from the main menu. You'll be asked to provide the information about the network or modem you're using, and then the multiple player game will be ready to start on a network or serial link. On the modem, you will be asked for the phone number, or to wait for a call. Once the connection is established, the game will be ready to start. You can start a game immediately, or press C to chat with the other players and verify that you're ready to play. At any time during the game, you can press M to send a message to the other players.

5. Troubleshooting & Technical Support
==

If you have a problem, chances are you can fix it without needing to get help. Try the following:

*Never run BattleMechs under Windows or any other multi-tasking environment. This can cause problems in running the program, and can also make it run much more slowly.

*If the game says you have insufficient memory, or if it crashes, try rebooting without loading any TSR programs, such as your disk cache.

*If you don't get any sound, make sure the mixer settings of your soundcard are set correctly.

*If the screen is to dark to see, try turning up the brightness on your monitor.

*If you are unable to fix your problems, try calling technical support at 1-800-555-1212, or contacting us via electronic mail: tech@mega.com. Make sure you include your computer configuration and what you were trying to do when you encountered the problem. Also include any error messages that were displayed.

6. Registering
==============

This is the shareware version of BattleMechs. Share it with everyone you know! Buy the full commercial version of BattleMechs with 40 new levels and exciting new foes to battle by sending a check or money

```
    order for $49.95 to:

    Megasoft
    123 Easy St.
    Washington, DC 11111

    You'll also get a printed manual with hints, maps, cheat codes, and fun
    pictures to color. Order now!

BattleMechs is Copyright 1995 by MegaSoft, Inc.
All Rights Reserved.
```

Note the formatting of this listing. Main headings are double underlined, and sub-headings are single underlined. All paragraphs of text are indented, to make the headings stand out in the left column. By formatting your document, you not only add a more professional look to it, you make it easier to read and find information in.

Making an Executable Documentation File

Once you have your document written, you might want to present it as a program that can be run from DOS to automatically scroll through and print the documentation. This will be more convenient for the users, so they don't need an external viewing file. However, some people prefer to view it as a separate text file, so you want to have both options available. The best way to work with this is simply to load the text file into your viewing program at run-time. We start by developing the main viewer program, which we need to do the following:

- Display the text in the file
- Enable the user to scroll using the arrow keys, Page Up and Page Down, and the Home and End keys
- Enable the user to print the entire documentation
- Enable the user to print only parts of the documentation

Listing 16.2 is a Pascal program to do just that. For enhanced understanding, I've included the Pascal code here; however, a version in C is included on the CD.

Listing 16.2. A self-contained documentation program (README.PAS).

```pascal
program display_doc;
{This program displays a documentation file.}

{We need to do screen and printer output.}
uses crt,printer;

{Declare our filename.}
const filename='readme.txt';

{Use a margin of 79 characters to avoid wrapping.}
```

continues

Listing 16.2. continued

```
const rmargin=79;

{Remove automatic I/O error checking.}
{We want to handle printer errors ourselves.}
{$I-}

var quit,              {Tells us when we're done.}

    print,             {Flag to log text to the printer.}

    redraw,            {Tells us whether or not to redraw the screen.}

    bright,            {Tells us if the text is highlighted.}

    tbool:boolean;     {A temporary boolean, used to ignore results of}
                       {a boolean function, if we want.}

    tchar:char;        {Holds the input key.}

    head,              {Points to the first character of the current screen.}

    thead:word;        {Temporary head pointer if we want to move around.}

    j:integer;         {Temporary loop variable.}

    blockfile:file;    {Our input file.}

    alldoc:array[1..64000] of char;      {Will hold all the text.}

    size:word;         {Size of the file.}

procedure displine;
{This procedure displays whatever line is currently pointed to by head.}

begin

      {Until we reach the end of the current line,}
      while (alldoc[head]<>#10) do begin

            {Only print it if it's not a line-feed or carriage return.}
            if alldoc[head]>#13 then begin

                  {Use the double * to select a color.}
                  if (alldoc[head]='*') and (alldoc[head+1]='*') then begin

                     bright:=not bright;

                     {Skip the selector for display.}
                     head:=head+2;

                  end;

                  {Makes sure we are printing with the right color.}
                  if bright then textcolor(11) else textcolor(7);

                  {Print the current character}
```

```
            write(alldoc[head]);

            {Return to default color.}
            textcolor(15);

        end;

        {Go to next byte.}
        inc(head);

    end;

    {Skip this character, it's a line feed.}
    if head<size then inc (head)

end;

procedure back1;
begin
{This procedure moves our head pointer to the previous line of text.}

    {Skip over the previous end-of-line characters.}
    if head>1 then head:=head-2;

    {Go back until we hit a line-feed.}
    while (head>1) and (alldoc[head]<>#10) do dec(head);

    {Go forward one to the next line.}
    if head>1 then inc(head);

end;

function fore1:boolean;
{This function skips to the next line of text. It returns false if it}
{encounters the end of the text and couldn't go forward.}

begin

    {Assume that it will work.}
    fore1:=true;

    {Go forward until the end of the line or the end of the text.}
    while (head<size) and (alldoc[head]<>#10) do inc(head);

    {Only at end of line, skip one to the next line.}
    inc (head);

    {If we are at the end of the text, then...}
    if head>=size-1 then begin

        {We can't move forward.}
        fore1:=false;

        {Go back to the beginning of the line.}
        back1;

    end;
end;
```

continues

Listing 16.2. continued

```
begin

     {Main program.}

     {Initialize our variables.}
     quit:=false;
     print:=false;
     redraw:=false;
     bright:=false;

     {Initialize the file.}
     assign(blockfile,filename);
     reset(blockfile,1);

     {Read the file in one big chunk.}
     blockread(blockfile,alldoc,64000,size);
     close(blockfile);

     {This assembly uses a BIOS routine to turn off the cursor.}
     asm
        mov ch,20h          {Turn off cursor}
        mov ax,0100h        {Subfunction one: set cursor size/shape}
        int 10h             {Video service interrupt}
     end;

     {Blue text background for status bars.}
     textbackground(1);

     {Clear the screen to blue}
     clrscr;

     {Bright white text foreground}
     textcolor(15);

     {The last line displays the control information}
     gotoxy(1,25);
     write('Keys: ',#24,'/',#25,' Arrows,',
           ' PgUp/PgDn, Home/End, P to Print, L to Log to Prn, Esc to quit');

     {Set the background color to black}
     textbackground(0);

     {Clear the main window to black.}
     window(1,2,80,24);
     clrscr;

     {Display the first 23 lines in our main window.}
     head:=1;
     for j:=1 to 23 do begin
        gotoxy(1,j);
        displine;
     end;
```

```
{Reset pointer to start.}
head:=1;


{Main program loop.}
while not quit do begin

      {Set the text window to the upper right status bar.}
      window(58,1,80,1);

      {Blue background}
      textbackground(1);

      {Display the current line, number of lines, and percent of text.}
      write(head/size*100:3:0,'% of file viewed');

      {Back to black background and normal window.}
      textbackground(0);
      window(1,2,80,24);

      {Wait until a key is pressed.}
      while not keypressed do;

      {We've got a key-what is it?}
      tchar:=readkey;

      {If it's escape, then quit.}
      if tchar=#27 then quit:=true;

      {If it's P then print everything.}
      if upcase(tchar)='P' then begin

         {First, display...}
         window(1,1,9,1);
         textbackground(1);

         {In flashing text...}
         textcolor(143);

         {The message "Printing"}
         write('Printing');

         {Now, for each character of text...}
         for j:=1 to size do begin

            {Skip the color commands.}
            if (alldoc[j]='*') and (alldoc[j+1]='*') then j:=j+2;

            {Print the character. The if ioresult simply ignores any}
            {printer errors. If you wanted to capture them, then you}
            {could have an else statement and take care of them.}
            if ioresult=0 then write(lst,alldoc[j]);

         end;
```

continues

Listing 16.2. continued

```
        {Done printing, erase the message and get normal window again.}
        clrscr;
        textcolor(15);
        textbackground(0);
        window(1,2,80,24);

    end;

    {L tells us to turn on or off logging the text to the printer.}
    if upcase(tchar)='L' then begin

        {Turn logging on, or if it is on, turn it off.}
        print:=not print;


        {If we just turned it on, then}
        if print then begin

            {Display the flashing message, "Logging"}
            window(1,1,8,1);
            textbackground(1);
            textcolor(143);
            write('Logging');
            textcolor(15);
            textbackground(0);
            window(1,2,80,24);

            {Print the currently displayed first line.}
            j:=head-1;

            repeat

                    inc(j);

                    {Skip color codes.}
                    if (alldoc[j]='*') and (alldoc[j+1]='*') then j:=j+2;

                    {Write character.}
                    write(lst,alldoc[j]);

            {Keep going until the end of line.}
            until alldoc[j]=#10;

            {Ignore printer errors.}
            j:=ioresult;
            {If you wanted to capture printer errors, you could insert}
            {if ioresult<>0 then begin}
            {and an error handler.}

        end

        {If we just turned logging off...}
        else begin

            {Clear the message.}
            window(1,1,8,1);
```

```
        textbackground(1);
        clrscr;
        textbackground(0);
        window(1,2,80,24);

    end;

end;

{If the character is ASCII 0, then it was an extended keystroke.}
if tchar=#0 then begin

    {Read the next key. This will be the scan code of the key.}
    tchar:=readkey;

    {Assume that we need to redraw the screen.}
    redraw:=true;

    {Figure out which key was pressed.}
    case tchar of

        {PgUp has a scan code of 73.}
        #73:if head>1 then for j:=1 to 23 do back1
        else redraw:=false;

        {PgDn has a scan code of 81.}
        #81:if fore1 then for j:=1 to 22 do tbool:=fore1
        else redraw:=false;

        {Up Arrow has a scan code of 72.}
        #72:begin

            {We will take care of drawing here.}
            redraw:=false;

            {If we're not already at the start of the text, then}
            if head>1 then begin

                {Skip back one line.}
                back1;

                {Call BIOS routine to scroll window down one line.}
                asm
                    mov ah,07h    {Video function to scroll down}
                    mov ch,1      {Top row of window (0-Based)}
                    mov cl,0      {Left column of window}
                    mov dh,23     {Bottom row of window}
                    mov dl,79     {Right column of window}
                    mov al,1      {Number of lines to scroll}
                    mov bh,15     {Video attribute for new line}
                    int 10h       {Video service interrupt}
                end;

                {Display the new line on line one of the window.}
                gotoxy(1,1);

                {Temporarily store the pointer so we can jump back.}
                thead:=head;
```

continues

Listing 16.2. continued

```
                    displine;
                    head:=thead;

            end;
    end;

{Down Arrow has a scan code of 80.}
#80:begin
        {We take care of drawing here.}
        redraw:=false;

        {Skip forward one line, only print if we aren't past}
        {the end of the file.}
        if fore1 then begin

            {Call BIOS scroll routine.}
            asm
                mov ah,06h    {Video function to scroll up}
                mov ch,1      {Top row of window (0-Based)}
                mov cl,0      {Left column of window}
                mov dh,23     {Bottom row of window}
                mov dl,79     {Right column of window}
                mov al,1      {Number of lines to scroll}
                mov bh,15     {Video attribute for new line}
                int 10h       {Video service interrupt}
            end;

            {Temporarily save current pointer.}
            thead:=head;

            {Read through to the start of the next line.}
            for j:=1 to 22 do tbool:=fore1;

            {Display the line.}
            gotoxy(1,23);
            displine;

            {Restore the pointer.}
            head:=thead;

        end;
    end;

{Home has a scan code of 71.}
#71:{Easy-just set the pointer to the start of the text.}
    head:=1;

{End has a scan code of 79.}
#79:begin
```

```
                {Go the end of the text.}
                head:=size;

                {Go back so there's something on the screen}
                back1;
                back1;
                back1;
            end;

            {It was another extended key, do nothing, no redraw}
            else redraw:=false;

        end;{case}

        if redraw then begin

            clrscr;

            {Save our position}
            thead:=head;

            {Draw 23 lines.}
            for j:=1 to 23 do begin
                gotoxy(1,j);
                displine;
            end;

            {Restore pointer.}
            head:=thead;
        end;

        {If logging is on, then write the top line to the printer.}
        if print then begin

            {Print the currently displayed first line.}
            j:=head-1;
            repeat
                inc(j);
                if (alldoc[j]='*') and (alldoc[j+1]='*') then j:=j+2;
                write(lst,alldoc[j]);
            until alldoc[j]=#10;

            {Insert printer error handler here, if desired.}
            j:=ioresult;

        end;


    end;

end;

{We're done with everything.}

{Clear the entire screen.}
window(1,1,80,25);
```

continues

Listing 16.2. continued

```
textbackground(0);
textcolor(7);
clrscr;

{Turn the cursor back on.}
asm
    mov cx,1314h
    mov ax,0100h
    int 10h
end;

end.
```

A few explanations are necessary here. One useful feature that I provided was the ability to change text colors to highlight things such as headings. Because we are loading the text from a separate file that should be viewable on its own, we can't embed any long codes in the file that could be distracting and confusing. For this reason, I limited it to simply selecting bright or normal mode; bright text is displayed in cyan, and normal text is in gray. The mode is toggled by placing double asterisks around the text to be highlighted. These will not look too strange in the text file when viewed separately, and they allow us to add a useful effect to the program.

Make sure, however, that you both open and close the highlighting mode on each line. Because the listing program operates on a line-by-line basis, each highlighted section should not cross lines. If you want to cross line breaks, simply highlight each line separately. Otherwise, the results will be unpredictable. The version of README.TXT, the example file, that is included on the CD uses the asterisks to highlight headings. Look at it to see how this works.

The strategy that I used for displaying the file is certainly not the only one possible. If you come up with a method that you like better, then use it. This is merely intended as a basis on which to build. Possible improvements for this program might be a help screen with expanded instructions, and a method of handling printer errors.

This program makes several assumptions about the format of the text when it is displayed. It assumes that the file has the following:

- Lines with a width of 79 characters maximum. (The screen can actually display 80 character lines. However, the display routines will automatically wrap to the next line if we put some text in the last column. This will have the effect of scrolling us down one line when we get to the last line of the screen, thus scrolling the top line off the screen. To avoid this, sacrifice one column.)

- Carriage-return/line-feed combinations at the end of every line. This is the standard end-of-line that is assumed by most printers, and the display program looks for both characters.

■ A blank line at the end of the file. Because we cannot readily determine where we are viewing relative to the last line, when we scroll the last line past the bottom of the screen it is displayed again. If it is a blank, this will not cause a problem, and it avoids some tricky coding elsewhere.

Thus, the text file should already be formatted to meet these requirements that our display program will place on it. To do this, we write another program that will pass through the text file and format it properly for us. Listing 16.3 is the program to format a text file to display.

Listing 16.3. Format a text file for display (TXTFORM.PAS).

```pascal
program text_format;
{This program formats text for use by the viewer, wrapping words.}

{We'll need to move the cursor.}
uses crt;

{We'll only use the first 79 columns. Otherwise it automatically wraps at 80}
const rmargin=79;

var docname:string;                      {The name of the file.}

    tarr:array[1..rmargin+2] of char;    {A temporary line buffer.}

    j,                                   {Temporary variable.}

    numbytes,                            {Number of bytes in current line.}

    indent:integer;                      {Level of indentation}

    df:file of char;                     {The output file (readme.txt)}

    tf:text;                             {The input documentation file.}

    ok:boolean;                          {Temp variable to decide when to stop}

{This procedure flushes the temporary line buffer to the file.}
procedure flush;
begin

    {Write each byte that is in use.}
    for j:=1 to numbytes do begin
        write(tf,tarr[j]);
    end;

    {Reset the characters in the line.}
    numbytes:=0;

    {Update our status indicator.}
    gotoxy(14,wherey);
    write(filepos(df)/filesize(df)*100:3:0,'%');

end;
```

continues

Listing 16.3. continued

```
begin
     {Initialize variables.}
     numbytes:=0;
     indent:=0;

     {The first parameter is the document name. If not, then give help.}
     if paramcount>0 then docname:=paramstr(1)
     else begin
          writeln('TXTFORM - Formats a text file, to display with README.');
          writeln('          Specify the name of the file as the parameter.');
          writeln('          The output will be in the file README.TXT');
          halt(1);
     end;

     {Initialize the files.}
     assign(df,docname);
     reset(df);
     assign(tf,'readme.txt');
     rewrite(tf);

     {Let the user know what we're doing...}
     write('Converting... ');

     {Main loop}
     while not eof(df) do begin

          {Read one character from the file.}
          inc (numbytes);
          read(df,tarr[numbytes]);

          {If it's a tab, convert it to spaces and keep track of the level}
          {of indent so that it indents all paragraphs.}
          if tarr[numbytes]=#9 then begin

             inc(indent);
             for numbytes:=numbytes to numbytes+7 do tarr[numbytes]:=' ';

          end;

          {If it's a carriage return, then...}
          if tarr[numbytes]=#13 then begin

             {New paragraph-reset indent.}
             indent:=0;

             {Read next byte...}
             inc(numbytes);
             read(df,tarr[numbytes]);

             {If it wasn't a line feed, then}
             if tarr[numbytes]<>#10 then begin

                {Put an LF in.}
                tarr[numbytes+1]:=#10;
                seek(df,filepos(df)-1);

             end;
```

```
      {Send this line to the file.}
      flush;
end;


{If we have reached the end of the line then...}
if numbytes>rmargin then begin

      {If the last character was whitespace, then we're OK.}
      if tarr[numbytes]<#33 then ok:=true

      {Otherwise we need to wrap it.}
      else ok:=false;

      {Don't quit until we're done.}
      while not ok do begin

            {Read back one character in the line.}
            dec(numbytes);

            {As long as we're not at the start of the line, then}
            if numbytes>0 then begin

                {If we've found whitespace, then we're done.}
                if tarr[numbytes]<#33 then ok:=true;

            end

            {If we're at the beginning of the line, and haven't}
            {found whitespace yet, then we can't wrap it.}
            else ok :=true;

      end;

      {If we stopped before the beginning of the line...}
      if numbytes>0 then begin

         {Then start the next line where we found a break, and}
         seek(df,filepos(df)-(rmargin+1-numbytes));

         {Put in a CR/LF.}
         tarr[numbytes]:=#13;tarr[numbytes+1]:=#10;
         inc(numbytes);

      end

      {If we went all the way to the start of the line,}
      {then just continue from where we left off.}
      else begin
            seek(df,filepos(df)-1);
            numbytes:=rmargin+2;
            tarr[rmargin+1]:=#13;tarr[rmargin+2]:=#10;
      end;

      {Send this line to the file.}
      flush;
```

continues

Listing 16.3. continued

```
                {If we're indented, start the next line with 8 spaces.}
                if indent>0 then for numbytes:=1 to indent*8 do
                    tarr[numbytes]:=' ';

         end;

    end; {End of main loop.}

    {Close our files.}
    writeln(tf);
    writeln(tf);
    close(tf);
    close(df);

end.
```

If a line in our input file is greater than 79 characters wide, the formatting program will automatically do word wrap. It will also remember the level of indentation that was used and automatically indent the split lines to the same level. Those are the two main functions of this program. It also guarantees that there will be a blank line at the end of the file and that all lines end in a carriage-return/line-feed combination. This way, you can simply use your favorite word processor to type the file, and export it to text format, without line breaks. The filter program will take care of the formatting, you can add highlights with double asterisks for emphasis, and you will have a great-looking documentation file!

Summary

In this chapter, we saw what components we need to put into our game documentation to make sure the users know what they need to do to have fun. When users read your documentation, they should be able to quickly find the information they need. By exploring one specific mainstay form of documentation in-depth, we've discovered the techniques and methods that can be applied to all of the many types of documentation.

Also, we developed a pair of tools to make the presentation of your documentation a little easier. Building on the information in this chapter, you should be able to write documentation that is useful and interesting, and present it in an impressive form.

Getting Your Game Published

by Brenda Garno

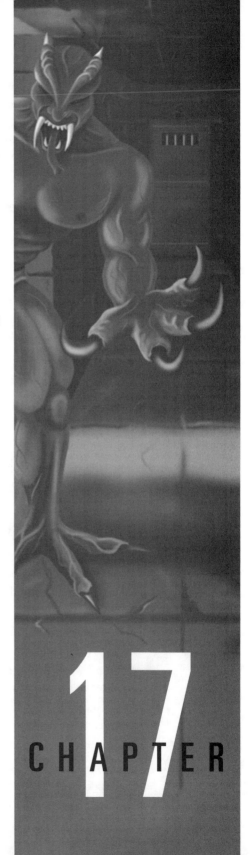

17

CHAPTER

Every developer who writes a computer game has the same goal: to see the game on the market. However, the process of attracting a software publisher is somewhat a gray area. There really aren't any established guidelines or codes for developers to follow, and the few publishers that actively seek developers often differ so much in their approaches that it's nearly impossible to determine a set of rules—unless, of course, you're on my side of the fence. In my 13 years at Sirtech Software, Inc., including eight years in product development and review, I have seen submissions float by every day. I see what works, and I see what doesn't.

By knowing how to approach a software publisher, you can increase your odds of acceptance.

This chapter will cover:

- Determining if your product is ready for a publisher
- Determining the right publisher for your product
- Determining what you need from the publisher and what you can offer
- Approaching the publisher
- Signing the non-disclosure agreement
- Sending the product
- Following up with the publisher
- Managing and reacting positively to rejection
- Negotiating agreements
- Managing the extra work that comes with acceptance
- Recommendations for filing

Is Your Product Ready for a Publisher?

Unless you're a noted game designer or developer, most companies will not accept your product when it's still in the "idea" stage—that is, when it's just a mound of paper that describes what you plan to do. Instead, publishers prefer to receive a tangible product, one that shows to some degree what your finished game will be. In my work, I've received good proposals in many forms:

- A program that shows how movement will be handled, along with screen shots of characters to be implemented at a later date.
- A lightning-fast, 3-D, smooth-scrolling engine—with terrible artwork. (The developer indicated in his letter that he needed our assistance with the artwork.)
- Screen shots of incredible artwork by a noted artist, complete with a list of employees who were committed to finishing the product. (All these employees had previously published products.)

In a nutshell, your product proposal is ready when it can be shown to someone and, without your coaching, he or she can understand:

- The mechanics of game play
- The intended genre and feel of the product
- The intended mechanics of its systems (movement, combat, magic, NPC interaction, and so forth)
- The intended "glitz" of the product (music, voice, and artwork)
- The storyline

However, while balancing your product against this list, try to remove as many items from the "intended" category as possible. A product with music is far better than a product proposal that lists, "We intend to implement a classical musical score that will make Mozart jealous." Often, it's not that much of a challenge to actually implement these things before the submission. To add voice, consider a local radio station disk jockey. Chances are, his or her voice is just as compelling as any of the high-priced "voice talent" available today.

Finally, before you decide to submit your product, subject it to the reality test (which is often the hardest test of all). Check out games that are currently on the shelf. Surf the Internet to see what games are consistently mentioned in posts. Then ask yourself if you can compete. It's the same question publishers will ask when your product appears on their desks. Give yourself the benefit of making your product the best that it can be by implementing the sophisticated systems and devices that others are using to land their games in the Top 100.

Determining the Right Publisher

Before you send your product proposal out to every software mogul on earth and his (or her) brother, spend some time investigating the industry to determine which publishers could best represent your product.

While that sounds perfectly logical, you'd be surprised by the number of strange proposals that publishers receive on a daily basis. My personal favorite is the gentleman who called and said, "I have a bridge game that's the best ever published." While that might be a great opening line for a company that specializes in publishing computerized card games, it hit me flat (our company specializes in role-playing, adventure, and strategy games).

In determining the appropriate publisher, consider the needs of your product with respect to this checklist:

- **Platform.** Has this publisher had success distributing and selling products published on this platform in the past? Sending your great DOS-based product to a company that publishes exclusively Macintosh products may hurt the ultimate distribution of your product and your royalties.
- **Genre.** Is this publisher known for this genre, and thus will its reputation benefit my product? A company that publishes shoot-em-ups probably is not your best bet for that educational adventure you have in mind.

■ **Overall Recognition.** Does this publisher have a respected name that will benefit my product?

■ **Distribution.** Do this publisher's products consistently appear in my local software store? Are they seen in mail order catalogs?

Determining What You Need

Needless to say, unless you're independently wealthy or have lots generous and talented friends, few game developers have the means to take a product from the idea stage to the software store without some help. Often, a developer just doesn't have the money or means to distribute, advertise, and market the product properly. Other times, the artwork may be somewhat lacking. Perhaps, you can't afford to license expensive sound drivers to make your product compatible with the dozens of cards on the market today. Whatever the case, taking inventory of your product's needs and your team's assets beforehand will save you time in the development and acceptance process. Most importantly, it will add to the professional image you're hoping to portray.

It's not necessary, nor is it recommended, to send the following "Game-Completion Task List and Cost Considerations" list along with the product to your prospective publisher. However, he or she will likely ask for it at some point. So preparing it ahead of the submission is highly recommended.

First, determine a reasonable release date. Then, unless you're wildly certain the release date won't slip, add a couple months as a buffer. Your publisher may want you to add a certain feature or introduce cinematics that will eat up your earlier development time. Next, consider whether you and your team will be leaving your current positions to work full time on the product if it is accepted. Obviously, you'll need some kind of advance on royalties or, if the publisher plans to buy the product outright, a salary of sorts to support you.

Then, against the following list, determine what you have and what you will need the publisher to supply. Because every game is different, you may not need certain items on the list or may have your own to add. Discuss everything with your current development team to make certain you have all bases covered.

Lastly, when calculating salaries and other development costs, be reasonable. You might want to earn lots of bucks for your programming or artwork, but your publisher isn't likely to pay them. Keep in mind that publishers employ artists, programmers, sound techs, and writers. They know what the going rate is for average, good, and great talent, and they will know if your scale is above the norm.

Game-Completion Task List and Cost Considerations:

1. Number of programmers required to complete project on time
   - Number of programmers you now have
   - Estimated cost of current programmers' salary
   - Estimated cost of additional programmers' salary
2. Additional cost for optional online/head-to-head programming*
3. Additional cost for optional Win95 programming**
4. Additional cost for optional Macintosh programming**
5. Additional cost for optional console programming**
6. Number of artists required to complete project on time
   - Number of artists you now have
   - Estimated cost of current artists' salary
   - Estimated cost of additional artists' salary
7. Number of storyborders/writers to complete project on time
   - Storyborders/writers you now have
   - Estimated cost of current storyboarders'/writers' salary
   - Estimated cost of additional storyboarders'/writers' salary
8. Percentage of music completed for project
   - Estimated cost to finish product soundtrack***
   - Estimated cost to finish/purchase MIDI drivers
9. Percentage of sound effects completed for project
   - Estimated cost to finish sound effects***
   - Estimated cost to finish/purchase sound drivers
10. Percentage of voice completed for project
    - Estimated cost to finish voice for project***
11. Documentation writer for project—estimated cost****
12. General administrative costs
13. Additional equipment required to complete project*****

Notes:

*   Numerous online providers are willing to work with developers to include their services within their forums. Contact providers, such as CompuServe, to see what kind of support they can provide you in your development.

**	Publishers will generally want to know what additional programming support you can provide for versions other than straight DOS. If you have the means or the contacts, fill in the required amounts.
***	Many musicians, voice actors and sound effects companies advertise their services online. You may determine costs for these services easily.
****	Most companies have on-staff writers who will be able to complete the documentation for you.
*****	If you require additional equipment to complete the project, prepare this in a separate list.

Depending on your publisher, you may be working against your ultimate royalties for the project. Thus, the costs may be coming directly from your pocket. Be realistic and shop around. Prices vary wildly. For instance, when shopping out a platform conversion, I was surprised to find a $100,000 difference among 12 different conversion houses.

Once you know what you'll need and have your product ready, it's time to open the line of communication with publishers.

Approaching the Publisher

The computer-game industry could learn a lot from the magazine and publishing industries. In publishing, there are very specific guidelines one must follow if he or she hopes to have an article or story published. In all honesty, these guidelines are designed to make the magazine or book editor's job as easy as possible. Yet, when one follows them to the letter, the chances of being accepted increase greatly.

In the game-publishing industry, though, there are no established guidelines, so (and this is coming from the keyboard of one who knows) developers often end up ticking off publishers with a sloppy approach that leaves a lasting impression. (Granted, if your product is the next DOOM, everything in the past will soon be forgotten regardless of how you submit it.)

In your first approach to publishers, however, I suggest you request guidelines for product submission. (Some companies already list their guidelines online). Because this isn't really the time to expound on your product, your letter or e-mail might resemble the simple one that follows:

Random Company
XYZ Street
Los Angeles, CA 00000

> Greetings:
>
> [Company name] has impressed me with its ability to market and distribute [genre] products. My development team currently has a product in development, [product name], that you may be interested in publishing.
>
> At your earliest convenience, could you provide me with submission guidelines and a non-disclosure agreement?
>
> Should you have any questions, feel free to contact me at [phone number] or by e-mail at [Internet I.D.].

Once you receive the guidelines, follow them to the letter. Should you receive no response, however, and if you feel strongly about submitting your product to a particular company, call them. Tell the receptionist that you would like to speak to someone in development about a product you wish to submit.

Once on the phone with development, don't waste time telling them about your product, just inquire about how they prefer to receive the submission. Also, ask them to mail you a non-disclosure agreement (covered in the next section). If no non-disclosure is available, seriously reconsider submitting your product to this publisher; non-disclosure is one of the few protections you should insist upon.

Signing the Non-Disclosure Agreement

A non-disclosure agreement is a standard contract that a publisher will ask you to sign before he or she looks at your product. In essence, this contract says, "We won't tell your secrets, and you won't tell ours." Most of the time, there's nothing more to it than that. However, be watchful of the following phrases:

- Anything that says, in effect, "developer may not submit product to another publisher while product is under consideration by publisher." If you sign this agreement, the publisher can keep your product on the shelf for years and *legally* prevent you from submitting it to another publisher for years.

- Anything that suggests "developer may not solicit other bids from other publishers for the product." Although submitting to multiple publishers may not please any one particular publisher, it is often your best bet toward getting a good price or a good royalty on your product. Don't shut off this avenue.

In most cases, the non-disclosure agreement a publisher provides will be fairly standard, two pages or fewer, and will be written in plain English. If you feel nervous about it, consult a lawyer. However, if you want to save time, don't have a lawyer draft a non-disclosure agreement for you. It's best to go with the publisher's version or to have the publisher's version modified.

Remember, at this point, the publisher has not seen your product. Again, unless your name is known or your development team has an ace in the hole, the publisher will seldom want to pay its legal team to review your agreement, especially if the product is still an unknown entity to them.

Even in the presence of a non-disclosure agreement, make certain you do the following:

- Secure everything with a general copyright (not registered) by including "Copyright (c) 199X by [your name]." Do not use the company name if it is not incorporated.

- In your cover letter, refer to the submission as "Proprietary Information" and mark each page of submission as such.

- As a safeguard, have a copy of your submission notarized by a notary public before sending it in. Note: A copy of the notary's statement should not be included with the submission, because it tends to look a bit pompous.

- Mail a copy of your entire submission to yourself before sending it in. When you receive it via return mail, do not open it. In this way, you will have government-dated proof that your idea existed before it was submitted.

> While the preceding items may lead you to believe that others are out to steal your ideas, that's not really the case. However, here and there in our industry's 15-year history, I have heard of some horror stories of one company stealing another company's idea. Therefore, you can never be too careful.

Sending the Product

Once you receive, sign, and return the non-disclosure agreement, you reach the critical stage—it's time to send the product in. Believe it or not, most product submissions are rejected within the first five minutes, regardless of the depth of the product.

Why?

In general, when you send your product into a publisher, he or she will look at the disks before reading anything you've enclosed along with them. At least 80 percent of the products that I receive are below par in many aspects: graphics, mechanics, engines, programming, and storyline. People who view products for potential publishing are trained to recognize faults in products and will fail them on the "reality test" (as outlined in "Is Your Product Ready for a Publisher" section of this chapter). They look at the enclosed material *after* they have had a look at the product.

So, before you send your product in, provide the following:

- An easy installation program, or at least a list that explains how to install and run the program. Put that list on the label of the disk. (For instance: "To install, PKUNZIP files into a directory and type GAME.") If you use an install program, name it INSTALL.EXE. It's the standard name that reviewers will look for. Include it on disk #1 of your submission.

- An easy setup program (if your game requires setup for certain soundcards or videocards). Call the program SETUP.EXE and include the notice on the disk's label. (For example: "Be certain to run SETUP.EXE before running GAME.")

- Notices of special hardware requirements if your program only works with certain boards, like a SoundBlaster AWE 32 for instance. Note this prominently.

Also, with your submission, include the following:

- A sheet that lists basic game commands. Attach it to the disks so that the product's reviewer will easily be able to understand the product and its mechanics.

- Complete "beta" documentation that tells the reviewer everything he or she needs to know about your product. (This documentation would be, essentially, a game manual. It need not be perfect, but it should answer all the reviewer's questions).

Most importantly, test the disks and your install program or instructions before you send your submission in. If ever there's a time when you don't want a botched disk copy, it's now. Test the disks, your instructions and your documentation against the product you're submitting. Then, run your disks against a virus checker. Infecting your potential publisher's network is not a good way to start off a relationship.

Along with your disks or CD-ROM, include a letter that indicates your purpose, assets, and potential failings:

> Ms. Product Acquisitions Manager
> Random Company
> XYZ Street
> Los Angeles, CA 00000
>
> Dear Ms. P.A. Manager:
>
> Enclosed, you will find our product, [Product Name], for your review. We are interested in working with [Company Name] to publish [and develop] this product. The installation instructions are included on disk #1 [are attached to the disks]. A brief manual is also included for your benefit.
>
> [Product Name] is a [genre] game based upon [brief storyline synopsis]. Our team [of x programmers, x artists, x writers, etc.] has included everything necessary for today's market: [features of the product]. However, although it features a [greatest feature], as

is evident in the product, we still require [X, Y and Z] to bring [Product Name] to its fullest potential. Nonetheless, we are confident that this product would be a welcome addition to [Company Name]'s lineup, and we would like to work with you to bring it to market.

[If your product has shortcomings, it's better to admit them than to be refused because you claimed you had every feature under the sun. On the other hand, if you have a top-of-the-line product, don't make concessions that aren't necessary.]

Once you've had a chance to review [Product Name] or if you have any questions, feel free to contact me at [phone number during the day and evening, e-mail and fax].

I look forward to your response.

In your letter and documentation, avoid the following sayings, all of which I have seen at one time or another:

- "Best game ever in this genre." Everyone's game is the best they've ever seen. Your love of your product probably won't cut it for the publisher. Besides, the "best game ever in the genre" is probably the one they've just published.

- "State-of-the-art." Everyone has a state-of-the-art something or another. The term just doesn't mean anything anymore.

- "Consider the licensing opportunities." Unless you own Marvel Comics or are otherwise wildly famous, your licensing opportunities are something your publisher will develop once your game takes hold. Until then, it doesn't mean a lot.

In essence, be humble, helpful, and eager. Don't exaggerate and make your product sound like the next DOOM unless it really is. Above all, include everything a publisher could possibly need to evaluate your program.

Following Up with the Publisher

Once your submit your product to a publisher (or multiple publishers), it may be several weeks before you hear a response. In the interim, be patient. Publishers typically receive dozens of products a week, and, depending on the development load, your product may sit on the shelf for weeks before it's even opened. (Smaller publishers typically take only a few days, though.)

Once three weeks have passed, however, a brief, reminder letter may be warranted, such as the following:

Ms. Product Acquisitions Manager
Random Company
XYZ Street
Los Angeles, CA 00000

Dear Ms. P.A. Manager:

On [date], I sent you our product, [Product name], and have yet to receive a response.

If there are any questions you may have about [Product name], feel free to contact me at [phone number during the day and evening, e-mail and fax].

Keep in mind that publishers may be releasing products that tie up their entire development department and will thus delay the acceptance of your submission. If you submit a product during the months of May, June, July and August (the prime Christmas-release development time), your product could take much longer to work its way through the channel.

In the end, though, six months is a generous amount of time to wait for acceptance or denial. If you've been on the shelf that long, it's a safe bet that your product will be there for another six. Either the company you're dealing with hasn't got its act together, or your product just didn't catch their eye. In that case, you might consider requesting return of your materials.

Managing and Reacting Positively to Rejection

Whether your product is rejected outright or sits on the shelves for months, rejection is something everyone in this industry will go through at one time or another.

If your product is rejected, be positive and attempt to find out why. Ask yourself questions: Is your artwork lacking? Your design? Your sound? Ask the publisher for feedback. Maybe the publisher simply didn't like the product or your approach. If you're lucky, they could point you in a more profitable direction.

Better yet, give yourself another reality check and submit it to another publisher. Some publishers, in fact, are willing to help up-and-coming development houses by providing assistance and advice. Check online for publishers' reps, and ask them their opinions.

Negotiating Agreements

If your product is accepted, the real work begins. Often, acceptance begins on one of two levels:

- Yes, we'd love to publish it just as it is
- Well, we'd be happy to publish it if you just made a few changes to fit into our marketing plan

More often than not, your product will fit into the second group. Be cautious about your acceptance. Just because you want to get a product published does not mean you should sell yourself short.

- Ask for the amount of royalties you will receive. If they want the product, now is the time to mention it. In my experience, the industry standard for royalties is 5 percent to 20 percent (the very high end) of gross sales. Before you consider this low, recognize that publishers have huge overhead in packaging, marketing, and administrative costs. Negotiate increasing royalties for every milestone you hit. Publishers may up your royalties after you've sold 50,000 units, 100,000 units, and so on.

- Ask the publisher what plans he or she may be able to offer you for a sequel to the product. Are they interested in a long-term relationship, or do they just want to shovel your product to the market?

- Ask about compensation for hint or strategy guides for the product. Will you receive a percentage of these sales?

- If the product is sold overseas or converted by outside development houses, what percentage royalty will you receive?

- Determine whether or not you're willing to give up worldwide rights for the product or if you'd prefer to negotiate agreements with international publishers on your own. (This is not recommended unless you happen to have contacts.)

Above all, once you've reached the agreement stage, get yourself a lawyer. He or she could be the difference in selling away your rights for life or turning a tidy profit. Have your lawyer review everything you receive. Also, if you sense you're on the receiving end of high profits, shop it out to other software companies before you ink the deal. You may be able to up your ante in the long run.

Recommendations for Filing

There are certain things that successful development companies do which keep them on the cutting edge and keep them in touch with software publishers.

- **Be online.** Whether on the Internet or one of the commercial services, developers know what's breaking, who's looking for talent, and who's offering free development kits. They also regularly talk to those who have been published, and they learn from their peers' experiences.

- **Be in touch with hardware suppliers.** Many suppliers offer free development kits to houses with products behind them. Others offer cards and developer kits at half price. Contact hardware suppliers for information on their programs.

- **Read the gaming magazines and learn what sells.** By reading a magazine from cover to cover, even if you don't agree with the reporting, you can form ideas of what consumers are willing to buy.

■ **Don't do what everyone else has done.** There are still ideas and genres waiting to be invented. Sir-tech proved that with Wizardry. Looking Glass proved it with Ultima Underworld. Microsoft proved it with Flight Simulator. id Software proved it with DOOM. And maybe you'll prove it with....

Summary

By following the suggestions in this chapter, you will be better equipped to properly market and sell your product and your development team to a publisher. You'll know what they expect to receive and, ultimately, what you may receive for your efforts.

In the end, though, it's the product that counts. A bad product will not find a publisher no matter how well you market it (although there are some products on the shelf that beg to differ). A good product, on the other hand, may attract competing publishers.

Though it all, keep everything in perspective and stick with it. Your product's strengths can be further strengthened and its weaknesses can be improved. Eventually, you will get published.

Appendixes

Beta-Testing Documents

by Andrew D. Lehrfeld

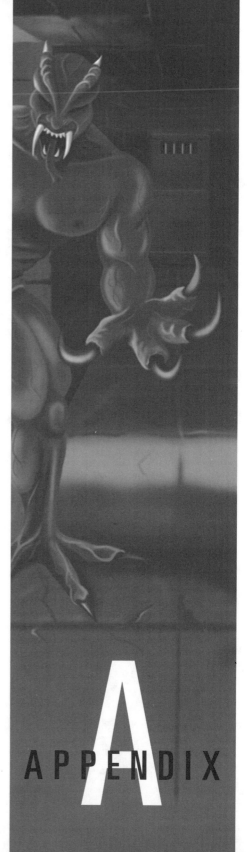

A
APPENDIX

Epic MegaGames

Application for Prospective Beta-Testers

Instructions:

To apply for a position on the Epic MegaGames Beta Test Team, complete this Application in its entirety and send it to Andy Lehrfeld, Epic's Beta Test Coordinator, at [71640,424]. You will receive a response via e-mail.

I. Name: CompuServe ID:

    Address: (You MUST have a CIS account in your own name
                                             to be considered.)

    City:

    State:

    ZIP (or postal code):

    Country (if other than USA):

II. Your computer brand:

    Type/Processor:

    Hard Disk Size:

    RAM:

    Video Card:

    Sound Card:

    Modem:

    Do you have a joystick?

    Do you have a CD-ROM?

    Do you own a laptop/notebook computer? Type:

    Operating systems you use:

III. How often do you logon to CompuServe?

    Which CompuServe forums are you a member of?

IV. Please tell us something about yourself personally; i.e., age, occupation, school, hobbies, interests other than computing, etc.:

V. Please describe any previous (or current) beta-testing experience:

VI. Please explain why you would like to beta test for Epic MegaGames, and why you believe you should be chosen for the Beta Test Team:

All applications will be carefully considered.

You are encouraged to provide as much information as you like.

Beta Test Team members are selected based on criteria that includes (but is not limited to) suitability of applicant's hardware/configuration to current testing needs, prior experience and/or related interests, personal profile, and written skills.

Thank you for your interest in the Epic MegaGames Beta Test Team!

:: Andy Lehrfeld :: :: Beta Test Coordinator ::

Epic MegaGames   *   Non-Disclosure Agreement for Beta-Testers

==

DESCRIPTION: This is a non-disclosure agreement that all Epic MegaGames beta- testers must complete. Please print this agreement twice. Sign both copies. Keep one for your records, and return the other to:

Epic MegaGames, Inc.
Attn: Beta-Testing
3204 Tower Oaks Blvd.
Rockville, MD 20852

YOUR INFORMATION:

Your full name: _____

Your mailing address: _____

City, ST, ZIP: _____

Country: _____

Your CompuServe ID (If any): _____

Your exact name on Exec-PC BBS (If any): _____

THE AGREEMENT: As a beta-tester for Epic MegaGames, I agree to the following:

1. CONFIDENTIALITY. I agree to keep the following confidential: information regarding Epic MegaGames beta-testing and upcoming products, including software, technology, game ideas, development team identities, and development plans.

2. COPYRIGHTS. I will respect the copyrights, trademarks, and all other rights belonging to Epic MegaGames and its associated developers. I will not copy, distribute, or upload any programs, files, or information I have obtained from Epic's private beta-test forums.

3. CONFLICT OF INTEREST. While I am an Epic MegaGames beta-tester, I will not design, develop, or participate in the design or development of competing products. If any situation comes up which could be a conflict of interest in this regard, I will notify Epic MegaGames that I can no longer participate as a beta-tester.

4. TESTING RESPONSIBILITIES: While I'm an Epic MegaGames beta-tester, I'll check in with the forum at least two times per week, actively participate in the testing of games, and post bug reports and game suggestions when requested.

Agreed,

_____

Signature of tester, or legal guardian if under 18 years old.   Date

---

```
==============================================================================
```

Beta-Testing Checklist   Copyright 1994 Epic MegaGames

CONFIDENTIAL

```
==============================================================================
```

This is a standard set of points for Epic beta-testers to look into when testing a new game. It covers everything from compatibility to gameplay and marketing. Please go through the list and answer everything that applies to you (with your hardware and software). Then, post your response in the Epic beta-test forum. If the large number of questions is intimidating, you can answer and post one section at a time. Thanks.

Compatibility points

_____

1. Memory managers & TSRs:

   A. Does the game work properly (no lockups, sound/music problems) with your memory managers?

      - EMM386

      - 386MAX

      - QEMM

      - Other memory managers (list them)

   B. List any special steps you needed to take to get the game working with your memory managers.

C. Disk compression programs (Stacker, SuperStor, DoubleSpace, etc).

Does the game work properly on a compressed drive? List any special steps you had to take to get the game working with your disk compression software.

D. Do you use any antiviral checkers? If so, did the game clash with them?

2. Other operating systems:

A. OS/2

- Does the game run under OS/2 without any special settings?

- If you were able to get the game running under OS/2 by using special OS/2 settings, please list them.

- Also note whether the game works under OS/2 with your sound card, and what steps you took to make it work.

B. Windows

- Does the game run under Windows properly with music/sound disabled?

- Does the game run under Windows properly with music/sound on?

- Is the game's performance OK under Windows? Does it work as well under Windows as under DOS?

- If you've found any tricks for getting the games working under Windows better, please share them! (For example, PIF settings, icons, configuration tips).

C. DR. DOS: Does it work properly? List any special things you had to do to get the game running in DR. DOS.

D. 4DOS: Does it work properly?

E. Novell Netware: Does the game work properly on a LAN with the Netware shell files loaded? Any problems?

F. Lantastic: Does the game work on a Lantastic network?

G. Other operating environments: If you use other DOS-compatible operating systems, tell us about your experience running the game!

3. Sound Cards

A. Sound Blaster card. Does it work properly with your Sound Blaster?

What version is your Sound Blaster (1.0, 1.5, or 2.0)?

B. Sound Blaster Pro. Does it work properly? Is the sound in stereo?

C. Sound Blaster 16 family cards. Does the game work properly with no noise or distortion? Does it work WITH the SB-16 driver?

Does it work WITHOUT the SB-16 driver?

D. PAS and PAS-16. Does it work? What special settings did you need to use to get the game working? What version are your PAS-16 drivers?

E. SET BLASTER environment variable. Did the game recognize your SET BLASTER command?

F. Gravis Ultrasound. If the game has native GUS support, did it work properly? If the game only supports the Sound Blaster, could you get music and sound using the SBOS drivers? What problems did you encounter, and how did you solve them?

G. If you have any other sound cards and you've found any special tips for getting the game running with them, please share the information with us! Also list any compatibility problems you had with Sound Blaster clones.

H. Did the game work properly with your normal IRQ, DMA, and port settings?

I. Was the audio quality of the sound and music OK?

4. Video cards. Did this game work properly with your video cards?

Describe any video problems you ran into (blank, distorted, noisy, or garbled picture, jerky graphics or scrolling) and tell us the brand, model, and chip set of your video card.

Gameplay points

———————————

A. Fun. Did you really enjoy this game? If you were stranded on a desert island with only this game and a beautiful lady (or a cute guy if you're female), would you play the game?

B. Frustration. Did you find anything in the game particularly annoying? What could we eliminate to make the game more fun?

C. Did you eventually get bored with the game? Where could we add variety to make it more interesting?

D. Did the game, your goal, and the controls make sense to you? What specific things did you have trouble figuring out?

E. Novice Testing. Go grab somebody who is a computer novice. We'll use them as a test case in this experiment. Sit them down in front of the game and see how they respond:

   - Did they understand how to play right away?

   - Did they enjoy playing?

   - What could we do to make the game more playable and enjoyable for this novice?

F. Kid testing. If you have access to a kid, get him to play the game and have him answer the previous three questions.

G. Does the game's story or underlying scenario make sense? Do you know who you are and what your purpose is?

User Friendliness

A. Did the user interface make sense to you?

B. What can we do to make the game's user interface (menu, controls, options) easier and more intuitive?

C. Do you think this game would make sense to a total novice? What problems do you think beginners will experience when trying to run the game?

D. Are this game's memory requirements sensible? Will people have trouble freeing up enough memory to run the game?

E. Were the game's menus simple and logical? Were you ever confused by the menus? Any ideas for improving them?

F. Did you ever feel lost or confused while playing the game?

Artistic Integrity

A. Graphics

   - Did you like the game's artwork?

   - Did you like the game's animation?

   - Did the game appear too bright or too dark on your monitor?

- Were the graphics too ¢ ᵕ ᶠ ᵎ ⁱ ⁱ ⁱ ᵕ ⁱ ⁱ ᵎ ⁱ ˎ ⁱ

- Were the graphics too ᵗ

- Was the style of all the artwork consistent? Did anything look like it clashed with the other art in the game?

B. Sound Effects

- Did you like the cool sound effects?

- Was the sound quality OK? Were the effects too noisy?

- Were the sound effects appropriate? Did they go along well with the action happening in the game?

C. Music

- How do you feel about the game's music?

- Was the sound quality of the musical instruments OK? Or did you notice that certain instruments were too noisy?

D. Audio Balance

- When you used the game's default music/sound volume settings, was the balance between music and sound effects good? Or were the sound effects too loud or quiet?

- When you first start this game, is it significantly louder or quieter than other games? In other words, did we goof up on the game's volume settings?

E. Pretend the game is a movie, and rate its content (sex/violence/language) as G, PG, PG-13, R, or X. Was the content of the game consistent, or did you feel that some aspects of the game (sex/violence/language) were out-of-place?

Text

___

By "text," we mean all written words in the game, including menu text, story text, ordering information, etc.

1. Did you enjoy all the written text in the game?

2. Was it short, concise, and to-the-point?

3. Did you find any spelling or grammatical mistakes? List 'em.

4. What parts of the text should be rewritten?

5. Font & typography checklist:

   - Were the fonts used in the game easy or difficult to read?

   - Was the text too bright or too dark? Describe any places where you noticed that the text colors were weird or hard to read.

   - Was the coloring of the text consistent? Or were too many different colors used?

   - Wherever text appeared in windows, were the margins too big or too small?

Marketing points
_____

Be as critical as possible here and tell it like it is! :-)

1. What is this game's competition?

2. How does this game compare to the competition? Better or worse?

3. If you downloaded the shareware version of this game, would you register it? Be honest.

4. What extra goodies would you like to see in the registered version that would make you want to buy it?

5. When you began playing the game, did it excite you? Were you *impressed* with it?

6. How long did you play the game? Do you want to play it more?

7. Would you recommend this game to your friends? Why or why not?

Recap
____

Finally, pretend you're a magazine reviewer. Pretend you've written an article and a review of this game. Now, write a one-sentence headline that captures the essence of the game!

-END-

:: Epic MegaGames Rules for Beta-Testers ::

To: All Beta-Testers

From: Andrew Lehrfeld, [SYSOP] Beta-Testers Section

Date: February 14, 1994

Epic MegaGames is a leading producer of quality computer games and software, and as such, expects that beta testers will conduct themselves in a professional manner consistent with the following rules and guidelines.

1. You have been granted access to a closed section and a closed library in the EPIC Forum. Section 16 and Library 16 are for Epic Beta-Testers ONLY.

    Access to these areas will be revoked if you violate the Epic Non-Disclosure Agreement that you signed. If you did not sign a Non-Disclosure Agreement, please leave a message for the SYSOP immediately.

2. As a member of the Epic Beta Test team, you are expected to participate actively in this Section. During periods when there is only one game in testing, you may find that visiting this Section two or three times a week is sufficient; however, during busier periods, you may want to visit once a day. You should become familiar with off-line readers, such as TAPCIS, which allow you to download all of the messages in this section, then read and respond to them while off-line. This will allow you to read and reply to messages without CompuServe connect charges.

3. When a new file is posted in Library 16 for testing, I will announce it in the message section. Download every game and play-test it thoroughly.

    (If you don't know how to unzip a compressed file, read HOW2UNZP.TXT in Library 16.) Post your messages, containing bug reports and your comments and suggestions, to ALL so that everyone in the Section can read and benefit from them. (When we have multiple games in testing at the same time, I may ask you to post your messages to the game's programmer instead.)

4. You are encouraged to contribute your thoughts to every message you see here, including bugs reported by others on the team. This Section is our "home base" for corresponding and communicating with one another. You are expected to contribute freely. This is the place — AND THE ONLY PLACE — to discuss your beta-testing activities for Epic. BE CAREFUL to post your messages only in the closed section, Section 16.

5. Please do not show the games you are testing to persons who are not on the Beta Test Team. I know it can be exciting to share a new game with a friend, but we want to minimize the possibility that information about our games in progress will spread to other software development companies. Epic will make available screen shots of upcoming games, and these can be used for promotion or sharing with a friend.

6. Games posted in the Library for beta-testing will be password-protected; that is, you will need to enter a password in order to play the game. In some instances, Epic may encode your password into the game in such a way as to render the game useless, or identify the offender, should an Epic game be illegally distributed by anyone here. DO NOT ALLOW BETA-TEST GAMES TO FALL INTO ANYONE ELSE'S HANDS. If an Epic beta-test file is found to have been uploaded onto a BBS, or otherwise distributed, the offender whose password was used to unlock the game will have his/her rights here revoked. Epic MegaGames may also choose to pursue other action.

7. Beta Test Team members who actively participate here will receive a free, registered copy of the game once it is completed.

(This file will be modified/added to as needed.)

DiamondWare's Sound ToolKit

by Keith Weiner

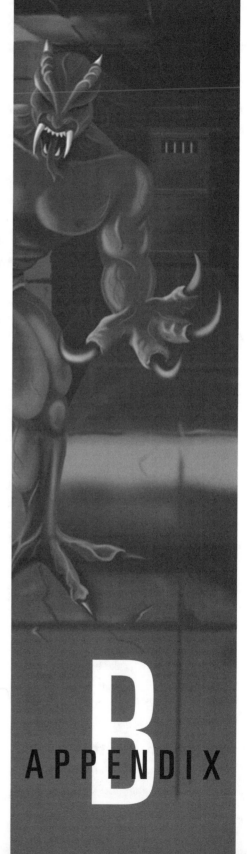

B

A P P E N D I X

All About the STK

DiamondWare's Sound ToolKit (STK) is a sound library written in 99 percent real-mode assembler (except for API "wrapper" functions). It supports FM music synthesis and digital audio on Sound Blaster and compatible hardware.

The STK can play up to 16 digital effects at the same time (a capability called polyphony). Unlike other sound libraries, there are no restrictions on calling INT 21h (DOS) functions.

It's linkable with any C/C++, Pascal, BASIC, or ASM program, which means adding the STK to a mostly completed program will be easy.

The STK is built tough. DiamondWare has acquired more than 30 sound boards, 50 books (including manufacturer's specifications), four operating systems, and five brands of CPUs to test the STK during development. All this testing means that programmers who use the STK won't field millions of tech-support calls saying "The sound doesn't work," or "It doesn't crash unless I enable the sound option."

The STK's autodetect capability is powerful. It can determine the hardware type, port, DMA channel, and IRQ level automatically—under every major DOS environment (including Windows DOS boxes, OS/2 DOS boxes, Novell DOS, QEMM, 386MAX, and EMM386), running on every major brand of CPU (including Intel, AMD, Cyrix, IBM, and Texas Instruments). The STK goes directly to the sound hardware, requiring neither environment variables nor user input. And, should you wish, you can override any setting.

The STK provides "mixer" functionality. The better boards (Sound Blaster Pro and upward) have chips onboard that can control the volume level of music and sound effects independently, as well as the total volume. For sound boards that don't have such a chip, the STK can do the mixing at the software level.

DiamondWare's STK supports an important subset of the MIDI specification, including true dynamic patch changes, velocity sensitivity, pitch bend, and aftertouch. Future versions of the STK will support more of the MIDI specification.

The STK doesn't allocate any memory dynamically. It doesn't make any INT 21h calls (except during autodetect and initialization). It doesn't require any outside code to link. It doesn't have to reprogram the timer hardware, though it comes with optional code to do this. The STK doesn't take hundreds of kilobytes of RAM. It doesn't pollute your users' install directories with scores of files. And it doesn't use a single line of code from a sound-board manufacturer or any other library vendor.

Its Limitations

The STK is a kit for Sound Blasters, SB-compatibles, and SB-clones. It will not work with the native modes of non-Creative Labs' sound boards. (Creative Labs is the major player in the sound-board market.) However, it has been designed and tested to work with their compatible modes (which are often only 90 percent to 95 percent "compatible").

It requires a 386SX or higher processor . This is not because it uses so much computing power (it doesn't), but because we've made extensive use of instructions and registers which are unavailable on the 286 and lower.

The STK can't play .VOC files (sound effects) that are larger than 64KB, although it supports easy sequencing of split-up .VOC files.

The STK needs interrupts in order to remain active. Disabling interrupts for extended periods of time will pause all sound playback until interrupts are enabled again. Music notes will hang, and digitized music will skip and repeat like a CD player trying to track a bad disc.

The STK does not support sampling rates under 4 KHz or over 24 KHz.

The STK does not manage resource files, nor play files from disk. You must manage your directory structure and load each file into a buffer before the STK can play it.

The STK can't change its settings (like volume levels) "in the background." If you want to do this, write some code that checks the current time, and slowly change the volume level. It's no harder than moving 20 space aliens, a player, and five bullets.

Prerequisite Knowledge

DiamondWare's STK is a programmer's library, not a game. As such, it's a highly technical product. While this appendix was written to tell you all about the STK, it can't tell you how to program. Before reading this appendix, you should be familiar with PC programming—including bitwise operations and linking with external libraries.

The STK was designed to work with C/C++, Pascal, and BASIC. Even if you will not be programming in C, several conventions and examples in this appendix are given only in C, so prior C experience will be helpful. For example, all function prototypes are given for C, Pascal, and BASIC; but in general, descriptions are given only using C terminology. Here is a guide for Pascal and BASIC users to aid in understanding C:

All subroutines are called "functions," although in Pascal and BASIC they may be "functions," "procedures," or "subroutines." A C struct, often called a "structure," is the equivalent of a Pascal "record" and a BASIC "TYPE."

C expresses bitwise OR as a pipe (¦), bitwise AND as an ampersand (&), logical OR as two pipes (¦¦), and logical AND as two ampersands (&&). C comments are either a double slash //Comment which is a comment until the end of the line (equivalent to BASIC's apostrophe or REM) or /*Comment*/ (equivalent to Pascal's (*Comment*)). BASIC programmers should ignore all underscores. (See Table B.1.)

There's one other important thing for Pascal and BASIC programmers to know about C. The ampersand (&) operator can also be used to take the address of a variable. For example:

```
dws_MSongStatus(&mstat);
```

This call passes the address of the variable mstat to the function dws_MSongStatus (which puts the song's status into the variable). This is equivalent to Pascal's var or BASIC's SEG (pass by reference) calling conventions.

In specific instances, Pascal and BASIC differences with C will be explicitly listed.

Table B.1. Syntax differences between C, Pascal, and BASIC.

Construct	C	Pascal	BASIC
bitwise or	|	OR	OR
boolean or	||	OR	OR
bitwise and	&	AND	AND
boolean and	&&	AND	AND
comment to end of line	//	N/A	' REM
open/close comment	/* */	{ } (* *)	N/A
address of	&	@	N/A

Sometimes in this appendix, Turbo Pascal is distinguished from other languages. This is because Pascal works with "units." A unit contains not only the linkable program code, but also the declarations that tell the compiler about that program code and the data types it requires. C and BASIC use a different model, in which the compiler is told to include some human-readable header file, which contains declarations of code and data types, but no more. The compiler produces an .OBJ file, which the linker puts together with other .OBJ files (and .LIB files, which are really just several .OBJ files in one) to make the final .EXE.

The Sound ToolKit is distributed with a single .LIB, which works with all Microsoft languages, Borland C/C++, and Turbo Assembler. Header files are provided for C/C++ and BASIC. Also included are unit files for Turbo Pascal versions 6 and 7.

All source files provided on disc were produced with tabs set to 2.

Linking

The STK has been designed so that calling it in a real-world program is relatively simple. However, the STK is a nontrivial component of your program, and there are some non-obvious things to know.

As mentioned previously, the STK works with C/C++, Pascal, and BASIC. Additionally, it should work with any other linkable language that supports the Intel/Microsoft .OBJ file format specification (such as assembler). If you are using such a language, you will have to port the C header files to your language. Link with DWS.LIB as you would with any other library.

By far the easiest way to use the STK is in large-model programs. In a large-model program, all function calls and all data references are made via 32-bit *segment:offset* addresses. The STK expects this convention.

It's possible to use the STK in mixed-model programs, where some code or data is "near" and other code or data is "far." As long as the STK's code and data is all "far," this can work. See your compiler manual for details on how to do this.

About Music and Sound

Sound, especially in the PC world, is a complicated topic. This section will serve as an overview of the subject. The STK provides functionality for the two primary means of sound programming: FM synthesis for playback of MIDI (.MID format) music, and digital audio for playback of digitally sampled (.VOC format) sound effects.

FM Synthesis

FM stands for "Frequency Modulation," which refers to how musical notes are created. In FM, a sound is created from two operators, which are simple sine waves. One operator, called the *modulator*, is used to modify the frequency output by the other, called the *carrier*. The resulting waveform is surprisingly rich (much more so than Amplitude Modulation). FM synthesis is a convenient method for playing music.

The waveform is put through an envelope, which alters the output volume during the four distinct phases of a musical note: attack, sustain, decay, and release.

On Sound Blasters, FM synthesis is performed by a Yamaha OPL-2 or OPL-3 chip in the digital domain. The total output of all voices is sent to a special Yamaha Digital-to-Analog Converter (DAC), which creates low-level analog signals.

Programmed properly, the FM synthesizer can produce fairly nice instrument sounds, including surprisingly good drums. The key phrase here is "fairly nice." If you want to create a mood, you can do it with FM synthesis. However, you cannot realistically reproduce the sound of most acoustic instruments. FM does a better job with "electronic" sounds.

Music is created by a musician, a computer, and sequencer software. Usually he'll use a (musical) keyboard controller to enter note data, although some musicians may type it in on their computer's keyboard.

The result of the musician's toil and effort, the .MID file, is a collection of note information, but it isn't sufficient to make music; it contains no information about what the instruments should sound like. A patch bank, which is a set of instrument-sound definitions, fills this gap. The "patch" nomenclature comes from the old days, when technicians plugged patch cords into racks of equipment to change synthesizer sounds. Today, patch is a synonym for a single musical instrument sound.

The OPL FM chip uses 11 parameters to describe an instrument. A single instrument patch is therefore 11 bytes (plus a header and some waste). Software such as Symphonix OPL Patch Editor/Librarian by Flashpoint Productions (included with the registered version of the STK) is the best way to tinker with patches.

Collections of patches are stored in instrument bank files (.IBK format). Although you can put any instrument at any index in the file, you're going to discover that only songs which are custom-written for that instrument bank file will play correctly. Other songs will probably sound totally unacceptable.

Enter the General MIDI standard, which specifies all 128 patches. (For instance, instrument 1 is Grand Piano.) Although for FM synthesis General MIDI compliance is not required, we strongly recommend it. When the industry moves to wavetable boards, your music will sound good on most boards. (Eventually, all sound hardware will support General MIDI and wavetable. But today's installed base is still mostly FM. Sales of FM hardware are still much greater than wavetable. Wavetable sales are projected to surpass FM sales in 1996. Wavetable installations will surpass FM no earlier than 1997. Considering this and the fact that many wavetable boards also include or emulate FM, we believe FM is far more important than wavetable right now. Good FM is currently a big market advantage.)

Potential Music Problems

The STK music playback engine may behave differently than you'd expect.

The following is a brief discussion of two bona fide features that may cause some unexpected problems.

The STK is extremely sensitive to velocity. If you play a song and the drums or an instrument sound faint (or loud), this is why. Change the output level of the instrument patch, or use your sequencer to bring up the volume of the problem track.

The STK will allow notes of bells and strings to "ring out" after they are "key released." If this is causing undesired effects, simply make your instrument patches "sustaining." The STK will shut such notes down immediately when they are released.

Digital Audio

In digital audio, an analog waveform is translated into the digital domain by sampling (in other words, measuring) the amplitude of the wave at regular intervals. The sampling rate is the frequency at which this is done.

As H. Nyquist proved, the sampling rate must be at least twice as high as the highest frequency in the waveform being sampled, or else aliasing occurs. When this happens, the sound takes on an unpleasant metallic overtone.

Let's say you're recording the sound of glass breaking, which includes some very high frequencies—we'll assume up to about 11 KHz. Unless you're using a low-pass analog filter (the Sound Blasters have several) to cut out high frequencies, you should sample at 22 KHz or higher.

> Sampling at very low rates will have undesirable side effects. Speech will be lisped, and in general, everything will sound dull.

Dynamic range, which is the difference between the softest and loudest sounds, is also important. 16-bit samples sound better than 8-bit samples because the extra byte enables more precision and more contrast between soft and loud.

It is important to record your sound effects at a low volume, if you plan on playing more than one or two simultaneously. You also can compress the dynamic range when you prepare the sound. This will help you avoid clipping (in other words, exceeding the dynamic range of the playback hardware).

Overview

Before you can bring sound into your program, you must convert the .MID and .VOC files into formats that are quickly and easily parsed at runtime. Use MID2DWM and VOC2DWD, respectively. See the Utilities heading in the Reference section for more information on how to use these programs.

The Autodetect

Before you can initialize the STK, you must know the sound hardware settings: base port, DMA channel, and IRQ level. The STK provides an autodetect routine to determine these.

Using the autodetect is easy. Create two structs, one of type dws_DETECTOVERRIDES, and the other of type dws_DETECTRESULTS. Set the baseport, digdma, and digirq fields of the overrides struct to 65535 (to autodetect them), or initialize them with their correct values. Either way, call dws_DetectHardWare, passing the address of both structs as parameters. The results struct will be filled in.

You must call dws_DetectHardWare even if you know these values in advance. The reason is that it stores information in the reserved field of the dws_DETECTRESULTS struct.

> If you write the settings to a disk file, make sure you write the entire struct. dws_Init requires the information in the reserved field and may crash if it's not there.

For more information about these and other structures, see "The Data Structures" in the "Reference" section later in this appendix.

Many sound boards (such as the Advanced Gravis Ultrasound and SBOS) require the user to load drivers from either CONFIG.SYS or AUTOEXEC.BAT files. These drivers must be loaded before any STK-enabled software is run. If their drivers aren't loaded, some boards may not respond, or worse yet, they could take on default values that conflict with other hardware. This last case is a major potential problem and could cause a crash.

In the overwhelming majority of cases, the autodetect will quietly do its job. It is robust, and there are only two known (obscure) failure cases. (If you find any others, please report them to DiamondWare!)

The first failure case occurs only when the STK is running in a Microsoft Windows Enhanced-mode DOS box. If the user has another card that is constantly doing DMA on an 8-bit channel, the STK will crash the machine. The only card known to do this is the NE2100 bus mastering ethernet adapter, which uses a 16-bit DMA channel 99 percent of the time. (It's an expensive, high-performance card; running it on an 8-bit DMA channel is like putting 85-octane gas into a sports car.) Other devices that use DMA, such as CD-ROM and SCSI controllers, do not perform DMA transfers unless they are in use, and they will not cause any problems with the STK.

The second failure case occurs only with Aria 16 and Aria 16se cards. If the Sound Blaster portion of the board is configured for IRQ 2/9, the autodetect will incorrectly return the IRQ used by the MIDI portion of the board, rather than that of the digitized portion.

Initializing the STK

After calling dws_DetectHardWare, you'll need a struct of type dws_IDEAL. Its fields are requests for STK services. Set each to the desired values. Then call dws_Init, passing the address of the dws_DETECTRESULTS and dws_IDEAL structs as parameters.

This struct is here for three reasons. The first is to tell the STK the initial sampling rate you want. The second reason is to conserve CPU cycles. The STK will run faster with fewer digital voices. The last reason is that future versions of the STK will offer more features (such as 16-bit, stereo, and so on). You may not want some or all of these services. Initialize this struct properly, and you will easily incorporate STK upgrades into your programs.

When the STK initializes, it resets the sound hardware to a 100-percent known state, including setting the mixer to maximum volume. It also sets up its own internal data structures, Interrupt Service Routines (ISRs), and so on. Few STK functions will work until you call `dws_Init`.

The Hardware Timer

Next, initialize the hardware timer. The STK must be called at a relatively high rate. The DiamondWare Timer (DWT) module will do the trick, or you can use your own code.

If you're going to use the DWT, call `dwt_Init`, passing it a rate constant as a parameter. The DWT will do all timing functions necessary to the STK (and keep time for your game, too). See `dwt_Init` in the Function Reference for complete information.

If you have your own code, initialize it now. Make sure it will call `dws_Update` once during each hardware-timer interrupt. The DWT will not interfere or even link into your application.

Playback of Music and Sound

To play a song, first allocate a buffer large enough to hold the .DWM file, and then read it in. Create a struct of type `dws_MPlay`; set the track field to point to this buffer, and the count field to the number of times to play. Now call `dws_MPlay`. The song will play in the background.

To play a sound effect, allocate a buffer, and read in the .DWD file. Create a struct of type `dws_DPlay`; set the snd field to point to the buffer, the count field to the number of times to play, ignore the priority field (for now), and set the presnd field to 0 (for now). Now call `dws_DPlay`. The sound will play in the background.

For more information on these structs and calls, see the "Advanced Tutorial" section, or "The Functions" heading and "The Data Structures" heading in the "Reference" section later in this appendix.

Note to BASIC users: Make sure that your buffers don't move around during "garbage collection."

The Rules of the Game

The STK can play one music track and up to 16 sound effects (at the same sampling rate) at the same time. Once a song or sound is playing, you can let it play without doing anything else. You can even make DOS calls.

In the mode used by the STK, the FM chip allows up to six musical instruments and five drums to play simultaneously. Drums can play and replay, still sounding good, but it's important that your music sound (and/or sustain) no more than six melody notes at a time. The STK player will automatically drop notes out (though it won't crash), but a musician would inevitably make a better decision as to which notes are important than any computer algorithm could.

There are five percussion instruments built into the STK, chosen as a reasonable compromise: bass drum, snare, high hat, tom tom, and top cymbal. All other drums are mapped to these five.

The STK will refuse to exceed the dynamic range of the hardware it's playing on. This means that if you try to play four sound effects that all use the full eight bits of dynamic range, you'll only hear the one with the highest priority. Until it ends, the others will not be played, although they will continue to advance silently. If the sound with the highest priority ends, any remaining sounds are added back in, to the limit of the dynamic range of the playback hardware.

Playback Status

The functions dws_MSongStatus and dws_DSoundStatus determine whether a song or sound is playing or finished. Each of these functions requires you to create a status variable for them to use. To get the status of your music, pass the address of the status variable to dws_MSongStatus. To query the status of a specific sound effect, pass the address of the status variable, as well as its ID (from the soundnum field of its dws_DPLAY structure) to dws_DSoundStatus.

Stopping Playback

Call dws_MPause or dws_MUnPause to suspend or restart music playback. Call dws_MClear to stop the current song. Make sure you stop music playback before you deallocate the song buffer.

Call dws_DPause or dws_DUnPause to suspend or restart all digitized sound playback. Call dws_DClear to stop all currently playing sounds. Call dws_DDiscard to stop a particular sound from playing; this function requires the sound's ID as a parameter (from the soundnum field of its dws_DPLAY structure). Call dws_DDiscardAO to stop all occurrences of a digitized sound; this function requires a pointer to the sound's buffer.

Each bit of the status variable is a flag. Perform a bitwise AND between the status variable and the playback condition you would like to test. For example, dws_MSONGSTATUSPLAYING & status evaluates to a 1 if the music is still playing, and dws_DSOUNDSTATUSPLAYING & status evaluates to a 1 if the sound effect is still playing. For a complete list of conditions, refer to both routines under "The Functions" heading in the "Reference" section.

Keeping Time

The DWT provides a double-word (32-bit, unsigned) timer, which begins at 0 when DWT is initialized and increments once per timer interrupt. Calling dwt_MasterTick returns the number of clock ticks since time began (when you called dwt_Init). dwt_Pause and dwt_UnPause suspend and restart the master clock, respectively.

They don't affect either music or digitized sound playback.

Tracking Errors

Most functions in the STK return a word (16-bit, unsigned) value. This is a boolean value, indicating the success/failure of the function. True (1) is success, and false (0) means that an error has occurred. In the case of an error, call dws_ErrNo to determine what happened.

dws_ErrNo behaves much like the errno variable in the C standard library. Initially it's 0, and it's only changed when a function encounters an error. It's important to check it after each call that fails, or else you won't know which one generated the error. Under "The Functions" heading in the "Reference" section, there is a list of errors for each function. You may assume this list is exhaustive; if an error isn't listed for a given function, then that function cannot generate that error.

Shutting Down

Before exiting to DOS, you must clean up. First, call dwt_Kill (or shut down your own timer module). Next, call dws_Kill. Finally, deallocate any buffers you may have allocated during execution.

There is a problem in Microsoft Windows Enhanced-mode DOS boxes when the sound board is set to IRQ 2/9 and Windows isn't configured for the sound board. The first time an STK-using program runs in this environment, it will work perfectly. But if the user exits the STK-using program and restarts it before restarting Windows, there will be no digitized sound (although FM music will play normally.)

Re-Entrancy

The STK is re-entrant. You can call its functions from your ISRs (interrupt service routines). Just make sure you heed the dws_BUSY error. If this occurs, make the call again later.

Tutorial

This tutorial will walk you through MINAPP.C, an application framework that fulfills the minimum requirements for implementing the STK in a program. It is intended for learning the basics; it does not check for STK errors at all. The source code for the sample applications PLAYDWD, PLAYDWM, and FINDSB are provided in C, Pascal, and BASIC on the accompanying disk. They include (more) robust error-checking and are highly commented. Please review them also.

Setting Up: Includes and Variables

```
#include <stdio.h>
#include <malloc.h>
#include "dws.h"
```

```
#include "dwt.h"

void main (void)
{
    FILE *fp;
    byte _ _ far *sound, *song;
    word mstatus, dstatus, msize, dsize;
    dws_DETECTOVERRIDES dov;
    dws_DETECTRESULTS   dres;
    dws_IDEAL ideal;
    dws_MPLAY mplay;
    dws_DPLAY dplay;
```

The standard C header file STDIO.H is included for the file I/O functions, and MALLOC.H is included to support dynamic memory allocation. DWS.H contains all the STK prototypes, #defines, structures, and type definitions. DWT.H provides the same, for the DWT.

MINAPP loads one sound effect, and one piece of music. sound, a pointer, holds the address of the sound effect buffer; song, another pointer, holds the address of the music buffer. dplay, a struct, holds all information needed to play the sound effect; mplay, another struct, holds information for playing the song. dov, dres, and ideal are structs required for initialization.

Loading Songs and Sounds

```
/* ALLOCATE MEMORY FOR SOUND FILE AND LOAD IT */
    fp = fopen("minapp.dwd", "rb");
    fseek (fp, 0L, SEEK_END);
    sound = _fmalloc (dsize=ftell (fp));
    fseek (fp, 0L, SEEK_SET);
    fread (sound, dsize, 1, fp);
    fclose (fp);

/* ALLOCATE MEMORY FOR SONG FILE AND LOAD IT */
    fp = fopen("minapp.dwm", "rb");
    fseek (fp, 0L, SEEK_END);
    song = _fmalloc (msize=ftell (fp));
    fseek (fp, 0L, SEEK_SET);
    fread (song, msize, 1, fp);
    fclose (fp);
```

These two sections allocate buffers to store the music and the sound, then read the files into them. MINAPP.DWM began life as MINAPP.MID and GM.IBK and was converted by MID2DWM. MINAPP.DWD began as MINAPP.VOC, and was converted by VOC2DWD.

Initializing the STK

```
/* AUTODETECT SOUND CARD */
    dov.baseport = 65535;
    dov.digdma   = 65535;
    dov.digirq   = 65535;
    dws_DetectHardWare (&dov, &dres);
```

```
/* INITIALIZE DIAMONDWARE STK SYSTEM */
   ideal.musictyp   = 1;
   ideal.digtyp     = 8;
   ideal.digrate    = 10989;
   ideal.dignvoices = 16;
   ideal.dignchan   = 1;
   dws_Init (&dres, &ideal);
```

Notice how all fields in the struct `dov` are set to 65535. This tells `dws_DetectHardWare` to autodetect the corresponding sound hardware parameters. The results of this are returned in the `dres` struct. We initialized the `ideal` struct to request the desired STK services. (In this case it is overkill, since we only need one digitized voice.) When we call `dws_Init`, the sound hardware and the STK are set up for business.

Optional Timer Module

```
/* INITIALIZE OPTIONAL TIMER MODULE */
   dwt_Init (dwt_72_8HZ);
```

A PC bootstraps (starts up) with a rate of 18.2 clock ticks per second, but the STK requires a higher rate. Just as importantly, the STK must be called during each clock tick. The DiamondWare Timer module will do this. We recommend 72.8 Hz, a good compromise between music quality and Windows DOS-box compatibility. (If you don't care about Windows DOS boxes, use 145.6 Hz.)

Preparing Songs and Sounds

```
/* PREPARE SONG FOR PLAYING */
   mplay.track = song;
   mplay.count = 1;

/* PREPARE SOUND FOR PLAYING */
   dplay.snd      = sound;
   dplay.count    = 1;
   dplay.priority = 1000;
   dplay.presnd   = 0;
   dws_DGetRateFromDWD (dplay.snd, &ideal.digrate);
   dws_DSetRate (ideal.digrate);
```

The `mplay` struct is set up so that a call to `dws_MPlay` will play the song once. The `dplay` struct is also set up. A priority of 1000 is arbitrarily chosen, but since no other sound effects will be playing in MINAPP, this field has no practical effect. The `presnd` field is also unused (set to 0), because this example does not sequence digital sounds. The current playback rate is set to the sampling rate at which the sound was recorded.

Initiating Playback

```
/* PLAY SONG AND SOUND ONCE */
    dws_MPlay (&mplay);
    dws_DPlay (&dplay);
```

A call to `dws_MPlay` starts the music, and a call to `dws_DPlay` begins playback of the digitized sound effect.

Wait 'Til the Fat Lady Stops Singing

```
/* MAIN LOOP */
    do
    {
        dws_DSoundStatus(dplay.soundnum, &dstatus);
        dws_MSongStatus(&mstatus);
    }
    while ((mstatus & dws_MSONGSTATUSPLAYING) ¦¦
        (dstatus & dws_DSOUNDSTATUSPLAYING));
```

We query the song and sound status. The status is placed in a bitfield variable, via its address. In the case of the music, we're interested in the `dws_MSONGSTATUSPLAYING` field; in the case of the digitized sound effect, we're interested in `dws_DSOUNDSTATUSPLAYING`. When this field is 1, it means that the song or sound, respectively, is playing.

Shutting Down

```
/* CLEAR ALL ALLOCATED MEMORY */
    _ffree (song);
    _ffree (sound);

/* DE-INITIALIZE STK */
    dwt_Kill();
    dws_Kill();
}
```

The buffers containing the music and sound effects are now deallocated. Normally, `dws_DClear` and `dws_MClear` would be called before freeing these buffers; but since we know that no sounds are playing at the moment, the calls are unnecessary. The DWT is deinitialized first by calling `dwt_Kill`, then the entire STK engine is shut down by calling `dws_Kill`. That's it.

Advanced Tutorial

Working with the Advanced Features

The example code fragments that follow illustrate sequencing and polyphony. We assume that the STK has been initialized. `sfx1` and `sfx2` are digital sounds in memory. The following shows how the two `dws_DPLAY` structures are set up:

```
dplay1.snd      = sfx1;
dplay2.snd      = sfx2;
dplay1.count    = 1;
dplay2.count    = 1;
dplay1.priority = 500;
dplay2.priority = 1000;
dplay1.presnd   = 0;
dplay2.presnd   = 0;
```

Each sound effect is set to play once, and the second sound is given a higher priority than the first. The presnd field of both structs is not set for sequencing.

Sequencing

The presnd field enables you to sequence sounds to play one after the other. The first sample of the second sound plays after the last sample of the first sound. The effect is that of a single sound, playing seamlessly.

This feature is useful if you want to break a long sound into several pieces that can fit into memory. Or a sound may have several different continuations, depending on player input. (For instance, a gun fires, continuing with either a scream or a ricochet, depending on whether the bullet hits.)

Set the presnd field of a dplay struct to the soundnum of the sound you want to sequence after, or use 0 if the sound is stand-alone.

> If you specify a non-zero sound number (which corresponds to a sound actually playing), the value returned in soundnum is the same as the value specified in presnd. The new sound will not play immediately but will wait until the first sound is done.

The priority field is not related to sequencing.

```
dws_DPlay (&dplay1);
dplay2.presnd = dplay1.soundnum;
dws_DPlay (&dplay2);
```

This plays dplay1 followed by dplay2. If you are sequencing more than two sounds, call dws_DSoundStatus to determine when it's safe to sequence each sound after the second.

Polyphony

To play multiple digital sounds, call dws_DPlay more than once.

The presnd field has no bearing on polyphony.

```
dws_DPlay (&dplay1);
dws_DPlay (&dplay2);
```

The sounds start simultaneously. dplay1, the first sound, has a priority of 500. dplay2 has a priority of 1000.

These numbers are arbitrary; it is the relationship between them that counts. Priorities of 1 and 2 will have the same results.

> If these two sounds together do not exceed the dynamic range of the hardware, they'll both play. However, if the total dynamic range used by both sounds exceeds 8 bits, then you will hear only the second sound (because its priority is higher). If the second sound is shorter, then the first sound will be heard when the second one ends. Until then, it will advance silently.

> When recording your sounds, record them at a low volume; and use sound processing software to compress the dynamic range, making the sound uniformly loud. This will maximuze the number of sounds that can play simultaneously. It's a good idea, no matter what library you use for sound playback.

Autodetection and Setup Programs

Finding the user's sound board is nontrivial because the user often doesn't even know what brand he owns, let alone its settings. So the STK asks the hardware directly.

It does a good job, but there are some potential problems. Sometimes the STK may be unable to find one or more sound-hardware parameters. (Almost always the problem involves finding the DMA channel.)

The capability field in the dws_DETECTRESULTS struct will tell you if the STK found everything it needed for music and for digitized audio. If both capability flags are set, then you have nothing further to do; music and sound will work.

However, only the dws_capability_FM flag might be set. This may be because the user has music-only hardware, or it may be that (for example) the STK was unable to find the DMA channel. To tell the difference, look at the baseport field of the dws_DETECTRESULTS struct. If this field returns as either 65535 or 388h, this means that no digitized-capable sound hardware is present (or the user's drivers aren't installed). If this field returns with any other value, it means that digitized hardware exists. Look at the digirq and digdma fields. If either or both of these are set to 65535, it means that the STK couldn't autodetect them (and the BLASTER environment variable was either not present or was wrong).

Planning ahead for this, you should have a screen where the user can type in port, DMA, and IRQ channel. Don't require him to do this, but make this option available. Take the settings you are given, and plug them into the dws_OVERRIDES struct. Then call dws_DetectHardWare again.

Don't simply look at the capability field of dws_DETECTRESULTS. Its Boolean flags simply indicate whether you figured out everything you needed to know about music and digitized sound. It can't tell you, for example, if you have a port and an IRQ level but no DMA channel. To determine this, look at the baseport, digdma, and digirq fields. If baseport is 65535 (or 388h), then you found no digitized capability. It's virtually certain that none is present. If baseport is 220h, digdma is 65535 and digirq is 7, then you couldn't determine the DMA channel. Ask the user! It beats dimming out your sound option.

We provide a new example program to registered users: SETUP.C, which handles the setup of sound settings and configuration files. It isn't pretty (using just printf and scanf), but it illustrates some important concepts.

Reference

This section of the manual is broken down into several headings: The Functions, The Errors, The Data Structures, The Utilities, and The File Formats.

The Functions

There are two headers provided with the STK. The first is for the sound library (DWS.H for C and DWS.BI for BASIC), and the other is for the DiamondWare Timer module (DWT.H for C and DWT.BI for BASIC).

For Turbo Pascal versions 6 and 7, there are two .TPU files provided. Additionally, although it's not strictly necessary, DWS.PAS (which also contains the timer module) is provided so you can see how everything is declared. The sound library header declares the constants for each error the STK can generate, some bitfield constants, the data structures used by the STK, and the prototypes of the functions.

This is a complete list, in alphabetical order, of functions provided by the STK and the optional timer module. Each function will be listed with a general description, as well as the declaration syntax (prototype) for C, Pascal, and BASIC (in that order), parameters, return value, possible error conditions, and related functions.

Most STK functions have a boolean return value to indicate success (true), or error (false). If an error occurs, call dws_ErrNo to determine what happened. Unless otherwise noted, the STK will perform no action during any call that returns an error, including modifiying structs—all return values are undefined.

Most errors are provided to help you integrate the STK into your application; once your program is stable, you should not expect to see any errors occur.

All functions and all pointers are far. All functions use the Pascal calling convention.

The Optional Timer Module

If you have written your own hardware timer code that reprograms the timer rate, then you don't need the DWT. Simply don't call your module, and it won't link into your application.

The DWT reprograms the hardware timer to run at a much faster rate than normal, while keeping the DOS and BIOS clocks happy by calling them at 18.2 Hz (as they expect). The DWT makes the call to dws_Update, which is required to keep the STK happy. And DWT will also keep time in a way useful for video games and multimedia applications. Even if the user has no sound hardware installed, you can still use DWT for its timing functions without any ill effect.

dws_DClear

Prototypes

```
word dws_DClear(void);
function dws_DClear : word;
DECLARE FUNCTION dwsDClear% ALIAS "DWS_DCLEAR" ()
```

Description

This function stops all digitized sounds from playing. It returns success, even if no sounds are currently playing.

Parameters

None.

Return Value

Boolean success.

See Also

dws_DPause, dws_DDiscard, dws_DDiscardAO, dws_DPlay

Errors

dws_NOTINITED, dws_NOTSUPPORTED, dws_BUSY

dws_DDiscard

Prototypes

```
word dws_DDiscard(word sndnum);
function dws_DDiscard(sndnum : word) : word;
DECLARE FUNCTION dwsDDiscard% ALIAS "DWS_DDISCARD" (BYVAL sndnum%)
```

Description

This function shuts off a single sound instance.

If you attempt to discard a sound that is not currently playing, this function will return success.

Parameters

sndnum is the sound you wish to discard from the sound's dws_DPlay structure.

Return Value

Boolean success.

See Also

dws_DDiscardAO, dws_DPause, dws_DClear, dws_DPlay

Errors

dws_NOTINITTED, dws_NOTSUPPORTED, dws_BUSY

dws_DDiscardAO

Prototypes

```
word dws_DDiscardAO(byte *snd);
function dws_DDiscardAO(snd : dws_BTPTR) : word;
DECLARE FUNCTION dwsDDiscardAO% ALIAS "DWS_DDISCARDAO" (BYVAL snd&)
```

Description

This function discards all occurrences of one sound effect (.DWD file) that is currently playing. If you are playing the same sound effect several times, this is an easy way to stop them all— useful before you deallocate the sound's memory buffer, for example.

This function requires that you specify the sound by the address of its buffer in memory.

> If any sound killed by this function has a sequenced sound waiting to play after it, the sequenced sound also will be killed.

Parameters

snd is a pointer to the buffer storing the .DWD sound effect.

Return Value

Boolean success.

See Also

dws_DDiscard, dws_DPause, dws_DClear, dws_DPlay

Errors

dws_NOTINITTED, dws_NOTSUPPORTED, dws_D_NOTADWD, dws_D_NOTSUPPORTEDVER, dws_D_INTERNALERROR, dws_BUSY

dws_DetectHardWare

Prototypes

```
word dws_DetectHardWare(dws_DETECTOVERRIDES *dov, dws_DETECTRESULTS *dr);
function dws_DetectHardWare(dov : dws_DOPTR; dr :dws_DRPTR) : word;
DECLARE FUNCTION dwsDetectHardWare% ALIAS "DWS_DETECTHARDWARE" (SEG dov AS
dwsDETECTOVERRIDES, SEG dr AS dwsDETECTRESULTS)
```

Description

This is the STK's hardware autodetect. It detects card settings, or verifies settings you put in dov. Upon return, dr will be filled with the autodetection results. DiamondWare recommends calling this function at the beginning of your program, each time it is run, so that if the user changes hardware settings between runs, your program will still work.

Parameters

`dov` is a pointer to a `dws_DETECTOVERRIDES` struct. Set every field with either a 65535 (to autodetect), or an override (user setting). User-setting values will be accepted on faith (sort of).

`dr` is a pointer to a `dws_DETECTRESULTS` structure, where the function will return its results.

The reserved array in this struct holds important information; If you write the contents of the struct out to a file, write the entire struct! `dws_Init` requires all of this information; without it, the STK could crash the computer.

The bitfield capability indicates supported features:

```
0                                      //no sound hardware
dws_capability_FM                      //music
dws_capability_DIG                     //digitized sounds
dws_capability_FM ¦ dws_capability_DIG //Both
```

Return Value

Boolean success.

See Also

`dws_Init, dws_Kill`

Errors

`dws_ALREADYINITTED, dws_DetectHardware_UNSTABLESYSTEM, dws_DetectHardware_BADBASEPORT, dws_DetectHardware_BADDMA, dws_DetectHardware_BADIRQ, dws_IRQDISABLED`

If the machine becomes unstable more than twice, please contact DiamondWare!

dws_DGetRate

Prototypes

```
word dws_DGetRate(word *result);
function dws_DGetRate(result : dws_WDPTR) : word;
DECLARE FUNCTION dwsDGetRate% ALIAS "DWS_DGETRATE" (SEG result%)
```

Description

This function returns the sampling rate to which the hardware is currently set.

Parameters

`result` is a pointer to the variable that will store the current sampling rate.

Return Value

Boolean success.

See Also

`dws_DGetRateFromDWD, dws_DSetRate`

Errors

`dws_NOTINITTED, dws_NOTSUPPORTED, dws_BUSY`

dws_DGetRateFromDWD

Prototypes

```
word dws_DGetRateFromDWD(byte *snd, word *result);
dws_DGetRateFromDWD(snd : dws_BTPTR; result : dws_WDPTR) : word;
DECLARE FUNCTION dwsDGetRateFromDWD% ALIAS "DWS_DGETRATEFROMDWD" (BYVAL snd&,
SEG result%)
```

Description

This function returns the sampling rate at which a .DWD file was recorded.

> This function will work before `dws_Init` is called.

Parameters

`snd` is a pointer to a buffer containing a .DWD file.

`result` is a pointer to a variable that will store the recorded sampling rate.

Return Value

Boolean success.

See Also

`dws_DGetRate, dws_DSetRate`

Errors

dws_D_NOTADWD, dws_D_NOTSUPPORTEDVER, dws_BUSY

dws_DPause

Prototypes

```
word dws_DPause(void);
function dws_DPause : word;
DECLARE FUNCTION dwsDPause% ALIAS "DWS_DPAUSE" ()
```

Description

This function pauses all digitized sound playback.

> All calls after the first will have no effect until dws_DUnPause is called. The STK does
> not maintain a "pause count."

Parameters

None.

Return Value

Boolean success.

See Also

dws_DUnPause, dws_Discard, dws_DiscardAO, dws_DClear

Errors

dws_NOTINITED, dws_NOTSUPPORTED, dws_BUSY

dws_DPlay

Prototypes

```
word dws_DPlay(dws_DPLAY *dplay);
function dws_DPlay(dplay : dws_DPPTR) : word;
DECLARE FUNCTION dwsDPlay% ALIAS "DWS_DPLAY"(SEG dplay AS dwsDPLAY)
```

Description

This function plays a digitized sound.

Parameters

`dplay` is a pointer to a filled `dws_DPLAY` struct, which contains:

snd	Pointer to a buffer with a .DWD
count	Number of times to play; 0 means repeat indefinitely
priority	Relative to other sounds; low priority snds may drop
soundnum	Unique ID; returned by the STK
presnd	ID of sound to sequence after; 0 means don't seq

Return Value

Boolean success.

See Also

`dws_DDiscard`, `dws_DDiscardAO`, `dws_DClear`, `dws_DSoundStatus`

Errors

`dws_NOTINITTED`, `dws_NOTSUPPORTED`, `dws_D_NOTADWD`, `dws_D_NOTSUPPORTEDVER`, `dws_D_INTERNALERROR`, `dws_DPlay_NOSPACEFORSOUND`, `dws_BUSY`

dws_DSetRate

Prototypes

```
word dws_DSetRate(word frequency);
function dws_DSetRate(frequency : word) : word;
DECLARE FUNCTION dwsDSetRate% ALIAS "DWS_DSETRATE" (BYVAL frequency%)
```

Description

This function sets the digitized sampling rate. If sounds are currently playing, this might sound weird. We recommend that you change rates only when nothing's playing.

Some sound boards don't support every rate allowed by the Sound Blasters. Many sound boards will produce an audible click when the rate is changed on the fly.

The STK supports sampling rates from 4 KHz to 24 KHz.

Parameters

frequency is the new sampling rate to use.

Return Value

Boolean success.

See Also

dws_DGetRate, dws_DGetRateFromDWD

Errors

dws_NOTINITTED, dws_NOTSUPPORTED, dws_DSetRate_FREQTOLOW, dws_DSetRate_FREQTOHIGH, dws_BUSY

dws_DSoundStatus

Prototypes

```
word dws_DSoundStatus(word sndnum, word *result);
function dws_DSoundStatus(sndnum : word; result : dws_WDPTR) : word;
DECLARE FUNCTION dwsDSoundStatus% ALIAS "DWS_DSOUNDSTATUS"(BYVAL sndnum%, SEG
result%)
```

Description

Internally, the STK stores each sound in a slot. Each slot can hold up to two sounds—an active sound and a sequenced sound (which becomes active when the currently active sound ends). The slot is identified by the ID of the sound playing in it.

This function queries the status of a slot.

Parameters

sndnum is the sound's unique ID.

result is a pointer to a variable to hold the returned status:

```
0                                         //no sound with this ID
dws_DSTATUSCURRENT                        //sound is currently playing
dws_DSTATUSSEQUENCED                      //sound is sequenced
dws_DSTATUSCURRENT ¦ dws_DSTATUSSEQUENCED //both
```

For a slot to contain a sequenced sound, it also must hold a playing sound. If you ever encounter a case where a slot contains only a sequenced sound, please report it to DiamondWare.

Return Value

Boolean success.

See Also

dws_DPlay

Errors

dws_NOTINITED, dws_NOTSUPPORTED, dws_BUSY

dws_DUnPause

Prototypes

```
word dws_DUnPause(void);
function dws_DUnPause : word;
DECLARE FUNCTION dwsDUnPause% ALIAS "DWS_DUNPAUSE" ()
```

Description

This function resumes digitized playback if it was previously paused by dws_DPause.

All sounds will continue where they left off.

All calls after the first will have no effect until dws_DPause is called again. The STK does not maintain a "pause count."

Parameters

None.

Return Value

Boolean success.

See Also

dws_DPause

Errors

dws_NOTINITED, dws_NOTSUPPORTED, dws_BUSY

dws_ErrNo

Prototypes

```
word dws_ErrNo(void);
function dws_ErrNo : word;
DECLARE FUNCTION dwsErrNo% ALIAS "DWS_ERRNO" ()
```

Description

This function returns the last error triggered by an STK function. Call it after any STK function returns false as its Boolean success indicator.

Successful STK calls do not affect the return value of dws_ErrNo.

Parameters

None.

Return Value

The last STK error.

See Also

None.

Errors

None.

dws_Init

Prototypes

```
word dws_Init(dws_DETECTRESULTS *dr, dws_IDEAL *ideal);
function dws_Init(dr : dws_DRPTR; ideal : dws_IDPTR) : word;
DECLARE FUNCTION dwsInit% ALIAS "DWS_INIT" (SEG dr AS dwsDETECTRESULTS, SEG
ideal AS dwsIDEAL)
```

Description

This function configures and initializes the hardware and the STK internals. Most STK calls won't work until after this call.

The exceptions are dws_Update, dws_DetectHardWare, dws_ErrNo, and dws_DGetRateFromDWD.

Parameters

dr is a pointer to a dws_DETECTRESULTS struct that has been filled in by a call to dws_DetectHardWare.

ideal is a pointer to a dws_IDEAL structure, which you must fill in with your requested settings. The programmer might not want the user's sound board running to its limit, and/or the user's sound board may not support every feature of the STK.

> The STK supports sample rates from 4 KHz to 24 KHz.

Return Value

Boolean success.

See Also

dws_DetectHardWare, dws_Kill, dws_Update

Errors

dws_ALREADYINITTED, dws_IRQDISABLED

dws_Kill

Prototypes

```
word dws_Kill(void);
function dws_Kill : word;
DECLARE FUNCTION dwsKill% ALIAS "DWS_KILL"()
```

Description

This function closes down the STK. You must call it before your program terminates.

> Make sure you cover every exit path from your program, including DOS critical errors! Failure to do so will leave the machine in a bad state. The sound board will make noise forever. The DMA controller will continue transferring. The sound hardware will continue to generate IRQ's. When the next program is loaded, it will overwrite the STK's Interrupt Service Routine (ISR)—and the machine will crash.

Parameters

None.

Return Value

Boolean success.

See Also

dws_Init, dws_DetectHardWare, dws_Update

Errors

dws_NOTINITTED, dws_Kill_CANTUNHOOKISR, dws_IRQDISABLED, dws_BUSY

If the STK can't unhook its ISR, it probably means the user installed a TSR that handles the sound board's IRQ. Whatever it accomplished(?), it's now preventing the STK from properly unhooking itself. Tell the user to get rid of it, and call dws_Kill again.

dws_MClear

Prototypes

```
word dws_MClear(void);
function dws_MClear : word;
DECLARE FUNCTION dwsMClear% ALIAS "DWS_MCLEAR" ()
```

Description

This function stops music playback.

Parameters

None.

Return Value

Boolean success.

See Also

dws_MPause, dws_MPlay

Errors

dws_NOTINITED, dws_NOTSUPPORTED, dws_BUSY

dws_MPause

Prototypes

```
word dws_MPause(void);
function dws_MPause : word;
DECLARE FUNCTION dwsMPause% ALIAS "DWS_MPAUSE" ()
```

Description

This function pauses music playback.

 All calls after the first will have no effect until dws_MUnPause is called. The STK does not maintain a "pause count."

Parameters

None.

Return Value

Boolean success.

See Also

`dws_MUnPause, dws_MClear, dws_MPlay`

Errors

`dws_NOTINITED, dws_NOTSUPPORTED, dws_BUSY`

dws_MPlay

Prototypes

```
word dws_MPlay(dws_MPLAY *mplay);
function dws_MPlay(mplay : dws_MPPTR) : word;
DECLARE FUNCTION dwsMPlay% ALIAS "DWS_MPLAY" (SEG mplay AS dwsMPLAY)
```

Description

This function starts playing a song.

Parameters

`mplay` is a pointer to a `dws_MPLAY` struct, which you must fill in. The fields are:

track	Pointer to a buffer that contains a .DWM file
count	Number of times to play; 0 means repeat indefinitely

Return Value

Boolean success.

See Also

`dws_MClear, dws_MPause, dws_MSongStatus, dws_BUSY`

Errors

dws_NOTINITED, dws_NOTSUPPORTED, dws_MPlay_NOTADWM, dws_MPlay_NOTSUPPORTEDVER,
dws_MPlay_INTERNALERROR

dws_MSongStatus

Prototypes

```
word dws_MSongStatus(word *status);
function dws_MSongStatus(result : dws_WDPTR) : word;
DECLARE FUNCTION dwsMSongStatus% ALIAS = "DWS_MSONGSTATUS" (SEG result%)
```

Description

This function returns the status of the music playback engine.

Parameters

result is a pointer to a variable to hold the returned status:

```
0                                                  //no song loaded
dws_MSONGSTATUSPLAYING                             //song playing
dws_MSONGSTATUSPAUSED                              //no song loaded,
                                                     STK paused
dws_MSONGSTATUSPLAYING ¦ dws_MSONGSTATUSPAUSED     //Song loaded but
                                                     paused
```

Return Value

Boolean success.

See Also

dws_MPlay

Errors

dws_NOTINITED, dws_NOTSUPPORTED, dws_BUSY

dws_MUnPause

Prototypes

```
word dws_MUnPause(void);
function dws_MUnPause : word;
DECLARE FUNCTION dwsMUnPause% ALIAS "DWS_MUNPAUSE" ()
```

Description

This function unpauses music paused by dws_MPause. The music will continue where it left off, except that any sustaining notes will not start until their next key on.

All calls after the first will have no effect until dws_MPause is called again. The STK does not maintain a "pause count."

Parameters

None.

Return Value

Boolean success.

See Also

dws_MPause

Errors

dws_NOTINITED, dws_NOTSUPPORTED, dws_BUSY

dws_Update

Prototypes

```
void __loadds __saveregs dws_Update(void);
procedure dws_Update;
SUB dwsUpdate ALIAS "DWS_UPDATE" ()
```

Description

This function keeps the STK going. Call it regularly and frequently.

If you're using the DWT, don't call dws_Update! Everything has been taken care of.

If you are using your own timer handler, you need to call dws_Update every time you get your interrupt. dws_Update will load the registers it needs and restore the caller's registers before returning. Note that this function is to be called, not jumped to. It returns with a retf, not an iret.

Parameters

None.

Return Value

None.

See Also

dws_Init, dwt_Init, dws_Kill, dwt_Kill

Errors

None

dws_XDig

Prototypes

```
word dws_XDig(word volume);
function dws_XDig(volume : word) : word;
DECLARE FUNCTION dwsXDig% ALIAS "DWS_XDIG" (BYVAL volume%)
```

Description

This function sets the digitized volume of the mixer.

dws_Init sets the digital volume to maximum.

Parameters

volume is the digitized sound level (0=min, 255=max).

Return Value

Boolean success.

See Also

dws_XMusic, dws_XMaster

Errors

dws_NOTINITTED, dws_NOTSUPPORTED, dws_X_BADINPUT, dws_BUSY

dws_XMaster

Prototypes

```
word dws_XMaster(word volume);
function dws_XMaster(volume : word) : word;
DECLARE FUNCTION dwsXMaster% ALIAS "DWS_XMASTER" (BYVAL volume%)
```

Description

This function sets the overall volume of the mixer.

> dws_Init sets the master volume to maximum.

Parameters

volume is the master sound level (0=min, 255=max).

Return Value

Boolean success.

See Also

dws_XDig, dws_XMusic

Errors

dws_NOTINITTED, dws_NOTSUPPORTED, dws_X_BADINPUT, dws_BUSY

dws_XMusic

Prototypes

```
word dws_XMusic(word volume);
function dws_XMusic(volume : word) : word;
DECLARE FUNCTION dwsXMusic% ALIAS "DWS_XMUSIC" (BYVAL volume%)
```

Description

This function sets the music volume of the mixer.

 dws_Init sets the music volume to maximum.

Parameters

volume is the music sound level (0=min, 255=max).

Return Value

Boolean success.

See Also

dws_XDig, dws_XMaster

Errors

dws_NOTINITTED, dws_NOTSUPPORTED, dws_X_BADINPUT, dws_BUSY

dwt_Init

Prototypes

```
void dwt_Init(word rate);
procedure dwt_Init(rate : word);
DECLARE SUB dwtInit ALIAS "DWT_INIT" (BYVAL rate%)
```

Description

This function initializes the timer hardware and DWT internals.

Call this only if you're using the DWT. Use the DWT only if you aren't reprogramming the hardware timer.

None of the DWT functions will work until this function is called.

Parameters

rate is one of four constants:

```
dwt_18_2HZ
dwt_36_4HZ
dwt_72_8HZ
dwt_145_6HZ
```

Return Value

None.

See Also

dws_Update, dwt_Kill, dwt_MasterTick

dwt_Kill

Prototypes

```
void dwt_Kill(void);
procedure dwt_Kill;
DECLARE SUB dwtKill ALIAS "DWT_KILL" ()
```

Description

This function closes down the DWT. If you used the DWT, you must call dwt_Kill before your program terminates.

> Make sure you cover every exit path from your program, including DOS critical errors! Failure to do so will leave the machine in a bad state. When the next program is loaded, it will overwrite the DWT's Interrupt Service Routine (ISR)—and the machine will crash.

Parameters

None.

Return Value

None.

See Also

dws_Update, dwt_Init

dwt_MasterTick

Prototypes

```
dword dwt_MasterTick(void);
dwt_MasterTick : longint;
DECLARE FUNCTION dwtMasterTick& ALIAS "DWT_MASTERTICK" ()
```

Description

This function queries the value of the master timer.

The master timer is reset to 0 in dwt_Init and is incremented at the DWT timer rate.

Parameters

None.

Return Value

Number of clock ticks since DWT was initialized.

See Also

dwt_Init, dwt_Pause, dwt_UnPause

dwt_Pause

Prototypes

```
void dwt_Pause(void);
procedure dwt_Pause;
DECLARE SUB dwtPause ALIAS "DWT_INIT" ()
```

Description

This function pauses the master timer.

This does not affect music or sound playback.

> All calls after the first will have no effect until dwt_UnPause is called. The DWT does not maintain a "pause count."

Parameters

None.

Return Value

None.

See Also

dwt_MasterTick, dwt_UnPause

dwt_UnPause

Prototypes

```
void dwt_UnPause(void);
procedure dwt_UnPause;
DECLARE SUB dwtUnPause ALIAS "DWT_KILL" ()
```

Description

This function unpauses the master timer, if it was previously paused by dwt_Pause.

> All calls after the first will have no effect until dwt_Pause is called again. The STK does not maintain a "pause count."

Parameters

None.

Return Value

None.

See Also

`dwt_Pause, dwt_MasterTick`

The Errors

This section discusses every possible STK error in numerical order. See the Functions section to find the complete list of errors which that be flagged by any given function.

0. `dws_EZERO`

   There was no error. You didn't need to call `dws_ErrNo`.

1. `dws_NOTINITTED`

   The STK was not initialized when you called an STK function.

2. `dws_ALREADYINITTED`

   This call cannot be made after the STK is initialized.

3. `dws_NOTSUPPORTED`

   The installed hardware doesn't support the requested feature (music or sound).

4. `dws_DetectHardware_UNSTABLESYSTEM`

   This system is now unstable. Please report this to DiamondWare.

5. `dws_DetectHardware_BADBASEPORT`

6. `dws_DetectHardware_BADDMA`

7. `dws_DetectHardware_BADIRQ`

   You tried to override the autodetect with an irrational value for base port, DMA channel, or IRQ level, respectively.

8. `dws_Kill_CANTUNHOOKISR`

   After the STK initialized, the user installed a TSR that hooked the sound board's interrupt vector. The STK can't shut down cleanly. Tell the user to kill the TSR. Then call `dws_Kill` again.

9. `dws_X_BADINPUT`

   You attempted to set a mixer level (digitized, music, or master) to a value outside the range 0-255.

10. `dws_D_NOTADWD`

    The buffer does not contain a valid .DWD file.

11. `dws_D_NOTSUPPORTEDVER`

    This .DWD file is the wrong version. Please reconvert using the VOC2DWD that came with this version of the STK.

12. `dws_D_INTERNALERROR`

    The STK encountered an invalid internal state. Please report this to DiamondWare.

13. `dws_DPlay_NOSPACEFORSOUND`

   You attempted to play a low-priority sound, but all slots were in use. Try increasing `ideal.dignvoices`. If this error occurs with that set to 16, you're playing too many sounds too fast.

> The following is a warning. It's reasonable to flag this error occasionally. But if it occurs immediately, or consistently, try calling `dws_DPlay` less often.

14. `dws_DSetRate_FREQTOLOW`
15. `dws_DSetRate_FREQTOHIGH`

   You attempted to set the sampling rate to an invalid frequency. The STK supports sampling rates from 4 KHz to 24 KHz.

16. `dws_MPlay_NOTADWM`

   The buffer does not contain a valid .DWM file.

17. `dws_MPlay_NOTSUPPORTEDVER`

   This .DWM file is the wrong version. Please reconvert using the MID2DWM that came with this version of the STK.

18. `dws_MPlay_INTERNALERROR`

   The STK encountered an invalid internal state. Please report this to DiamondWare.

19. `dws_BUSY`

   The STK is busy now. Please call again later. This error can only occur if you're calling the STK from an interrupt handler.

20. `dws_IRQDISABLED`

   You disabled IRQs (with the CLI instruction). IRQs must be enabled (with the STI instruction).

The Data Structures

In this section, the data structures are laid out in table form. This is done in the hope that it's easier to read than compiler declarations. Obviously, you can read the actual source files if you wish.

Note to Pascal programmers: The following types were created to allow the declaration of subroutines that take far pointers to their parameters. Declaring a function

```
function FooBar(var x: word);
```

passes a near pointer. The STK expects far pointers.

```
dws_DOPTR = ^dws_DETECTOVERRIDES;
dws_DRPTR = ^dws_DETECTRESULTS;
dws_IDPTR = ^dws_IDEAL;
dws_DPPTR = ^dws_DPLAYREC;
dws_MPPTR = ^dws_MPLAYREC;
dws_WDPTR = ^word;
dws_BTPTR = ^byte;
```

dws_DETECTOVERRIDES

Name	Size	I/O	Description
baseport	2	input	base address of sound board
digdma	2	input	DMA channel
digirq	2	input	IRQ level
reserved	10	N/A	undocumented

dws_DETECTRESULTS

Name	Size	I/O	Description
baseport	2	output	base address of sound board
capability	2	output	bitfield of supported features
mustyp	2	output	0=none, 1=OPL2
musnchan	2	output	*1=mono
musnvoice	2	output	*number of melody voices
dignbits	2	output	+8=8 bits
dignchan	2	output	+1=mono
digdma	2	output	+digitized DMA channel
digirq	2	output	+digitized IRQ level
mixtyp	2	output	mixer type (1 software, 2+ H/W)
reserved	44	N/A	undocumented

* Only if the hardware supports music.
+ Only if the hardware supports digitized.

dws_IDEAL

Name	Size	I/O	Description
musictyp	2	input	music type (0 none, 1 FM)
digtyp	2	input	digitzed type (0 none, 8 8-bit dig)
digrate	2	input	sampling rate, in Hz
dignvoices	2	input	number of voices (up to 16)
dignchan	2	input	1=mono
reserved	6	N/A	undocumented

dws_DPLAY

Name	Size	I/O	Description
snd	4	input	pointer to buffer with .DWD in it
count	2	input	# times to play (0=infinite loop)
priority	2	input	higher numbers are higher priority
presnd	2	input	soundnum to sequence after
soundnum	2	output	unique ID
reserved	20	N/A	undocumented

dws_MPlay

Name	Size	I/O	Description
track	4	input	pointer to buffer with .DWM in it
count	2	input	# times to play (0=infinite loop)
reserved	10	N/A	undocumented

The Utilities

PLAYDWM

PLAYDWM is a simple program to play .DWM music files. Full source is included with the STK. Usage is

```
PLAYDWM songname.dwm
```

You must type the full filename, including the .DWM.

PLAYDWD

PLAYDWD is a simple program to play .DWD sound effect files. Full source is included with the STK. Usage is

```
PLAYDWD soundfx.dwd
```

You must type the full filename, including the .DWD.

FINDSB

FINDSB is provided as both a simple example of how to use the STK and as a useful program in its own right. Full source is included with the STK. It will find and print out the user's soundboard settings. Usage is

```
FINDSB
```

MID2DWM

MID2DWM converts type 1 standard MIDI files from .MID format to .DWM format. It is strictly a command-line utility. Usage is

```
MID2DWM rate midifile[.MID] instrfile[.IBK] [outfile[.DWM]]
```

rate is the frequency at which STK will get its "heartbeat" call during runtime. In general, the higher the *rate*, the more natural the music will sound (to a limit). If your music was performed by a human, there are many nuances of timing that will be lost at lower rates.

> If your program is running in a Windows DOS box, 145.6 Hz will not work correctly. (Windows will simply refuse to call you that fast, and so the music will play slower than normal.)

The STK includes an optional timer module which is capable of four rates: 18.2, 36.4, 72.8, and 145.6 Hz. If you use your own timer code, then tell MID2DWM the rate at which it runs; MID2DWM will work at any rate. If you're using the code supplied in the STK, use one of those four rates only.

midifile is the name of the source file for the music in MIDI type 1 format. The extension, .MID, is optional.

instrfile is the name of the instrument patch bank file in .IBK format. The extension, .IBK, is optional.

outfile is an optional parameter to specify the name of the output file (if different from the source file). The extension, .DWM, is optional.

As a simple matter of managing the hundreds of files in your project, if you keep the default file extensions for each type of file, you'll make your life easier.

Examples:

```
C:\SOURCE\BANE\MUSIC mid2dwm 72.8 death gmptch
C:\SOURCE\BANE\MUSIC mid2dwm 36.4 death.mid gmptch.ibk dth1.dwm
```

MID2DWM can convert, and the STK can play, music files larger than 64K.

VOC2DWD

VOC2DWD converts digitized sound files from .VOC format to .DWD format. It is strictly a command-line utility. Usage is

```
VOC2DWD vocfile[.VOC] [outfile [.DWD]]
```

vocfile is the filename of the input file, which must be in VOC format. The extension, .VOC, is optional.

outfile is an optional parameter that specifies the name of the output file, if different from the input file. The .DWD extension is optional.

Examples:

```
C:\SOURCE\BANE\SFX voc2dwd scream
C:\SOURCE\BANE\SFX voc2dwd scream.voc sc1.dwd
```

You can use DOS wildcards to specify *vocfile*, as in:

```
C:\SOURCE\BANE\SFX voc2dwd *.voc
```

VOC2DWD will enable you to convert files greater than 64KB; however, this version of the STK will not play them back. A sequencing mechanism is offered to enable you to play long sounds, but they must be broken up while they're in .VOC format.

Although .VOC files can support all sampling rates via "extended blocks," some .VOC editors only save standard blocks. These blocks round to the nearest encodable rate, which can be off by up to 1 KHz. For example, an 11 KHz .VOC file will be saved at 10989 Hz if the sound editor only supports standard blocks. A difference of 11 Hz is negligible to the human ear, but 1000 Hz (which happens at higher rates) is not. VOC2DWD supports both kinds of blocks, and reports the true sampling rate during the conversion to help combat this problem.

Legal Stuff and Credits

DiamondWare's Sound ToolKit (STK) was designed and developed by DiamondWare, Ltd. and is marketed and distributed exclusively by MVP Software, Inc.

This software and documentation are Copyright 1994 DiamondWare, Ltd. All rights reserved. DiamondWare's Sound ToolKit, DiamondWare's STK, The STK, DiamondWare, and DW are trademarks of DiamondWare, Ltd.

DiamondWare can be contacted as follows:

FAX/BBS: (914) 638-6942

e-mail: `keith@dw.com`

MVP can be contacted as follows:

FAX: (616) 245-3204

e-mail: `74777.1116@compuserve.com`

DiamondWare's Sound ToolKit was designed and developed by Keith Weiner and Erik Lorenzen.

Example source code was developed by Erik Lorenzen and Keith Weiner, with language-specific help from David Johndrow (Pascal), and Don Lemons (BASIC).

This appendix was written by Keith Weiner, with major revisions by Eric Lund.

Included sample MIDI song is Copyright 1994 David Schultz, All Rights Reserved. Used by permission. May not be used without written permission from David Schultz. David is a professional musician and has produced music for several published games. You can contact David via CompuServe: `72143,3624`.

Proofreading was done by Joyce Peterson, David Ziegler, and Erik Lorenzen.

Miscellaneous utility programs that made the STK possible were written by David Ziegler.

The included FM instrument patch file is courtesy of Rob Wallace of Wallace Music and Sound. Rob is a professional musician and has produced music and sound for many published games. You can contact Rob via CompuServe: `71042,1410`.

Special thanks to Steve Blackwood, John Davis, Steve Estvanik, David Johndrow, Don Lemons, and David Schultz for testing.

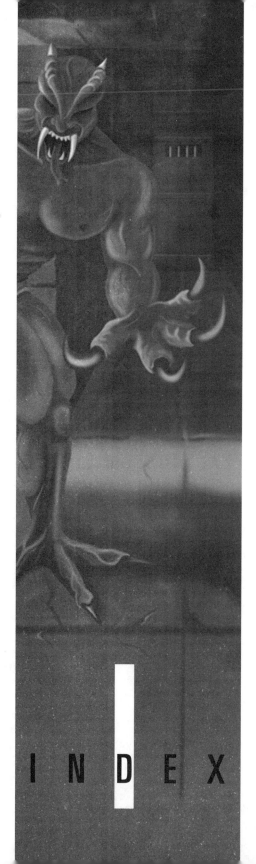

SYMBOLS

A

G

PLUG YOURSELF INTO...

MACMILLAN INFORMATION SUPERLIBRARY™

que • SAMS PUBLISHING • Hayden Books • que COLLEGE • NRP • alpha books • Brady • ADOBE PRESS

THE MACMILLAN INFORMATION SUPERLIBRARY™

Free information and vast computer resources from the world's leading computer book publisher—online!

FIND THE BOOKS THAT ARE RIGHT FOR YOU!

A complete online catalog, plus sample chapters and tables of contents give you an in-depth look at *all* of our books, including hard-to-find titles. It's the best way to find the books you need!

- STAY INFORMED with the latest computer industry news through our online newsletter, press releases, and customized Information SuperLibrary Reports.

- GET FAST ANSWERS to your questions about MCP books and software.

- VISIT our online bookstore for the latest information and editions!

- COMMUNICATE with our expert authors through e-mail and conferences.

- DOWNLOAD SOFTWARE from the immense MCP library:
    - Source code and files from MCP books
    - The best shareware, freeware, and demos

- DISCOVER HOT SPOTS on other parts of the Internet.

- WIN BOOKS in ongoing contests and giveaways!

TO PLUG INTO MCP: →

GOPHER: gopher.mcp.com

FTP: ftp.mcp.com

WORLD WIDE WEB: **http://www.mcp.com**

Home Page • What's New • Bookstore • Reference Desk • Software Library • Macmillan Overview • Talk to Us

Multi-Edit™
The Programmer's Editor of Choice - World Wide!

Confronted daily with managing large numbers of source files, integrating with multiple languages and compilers, and coordinating with other developers' work, you don't want to be burdened with inflexible editing tools. As a software developer you have your own personal habits and have established your own individual work style. You need an editor which will work the way you do, one which is able to adjust to your needs - Multi-Edit is your answer!

Small Footprint - Multi-Edit for DOS shrinks to just 3k when running compilers or other programs. Multi-Edit for Windows requires only 500k of RAM to run, while some Windows editors require several meg.

Powerful Extensibility - The powerful C-like macro language lets you extend Multi-Edit to suit your special needs. Multi-Edit for Windows provides a full DLL API, and extends the macro language so far that you can actually write Windows apps with it. You can extend Multi-Edit in your favorite language, or integrate its editing power into your apps!

Workgroup Support - Complete network support, including file locking, multi-user configuration, and MAPI/MS Mail integration*.

Complete Customization - Redefine the keyboard, customize the menus, modify the toolbars or create new ones, change every setting imaginable! All without touching any macros or .ini files.

- Edit up to 128 DOS, UNIX or Binary files of almost unlimited size.
- Interactive File Compare!
- Construct matching and templates
- Source code tagging and browsing
- Integrated Spellchecker
- Session manager lets you juggle multiple projects!
- Pop-up ASCII chart, text ruler and notebook.
- Multiple file Search and Replace (GREP)!
- Full regular expression support.
- Hex Editing!
- Syntax highlighting
- Unlimited Undo and Redo.
- Emulations for BRIEF, WordStar and others.
- Column blocks!
- Drag and drop editing*!
Much more!

* Multi-Edit for Windows Features Only.

Total integration - Turn Multi-Edit into your own personalized IDE. Integrate all your tools together. Compile, link and make without leaving the editor. Integrate into your existing environment through powerful DDE and DLL support*. Link in your compiler's (or any other Windows) help files for full context/language-sensitive help*. Unparalleled integration with most VCS systems, including PVCS, TLIB, SourceSafe, MKS-RCS and Versions.

for Windows®

multi edit

for DOS

Suggested Retail Price $199
for Windows *or* DOS.
(Buy both for $299 and SAVE!)
Special Pricing for Registered Multi-Edit DOS Users!

Sales Hotline:
1 (800) 899-0100

AMERICAN CYBERNETICS

1830 W. University Drive, Suite 112
Tempe, Arizona 85281
Voice: (602) 968 1945 • Fax: (602) 966 1654
CIS: GO_CYBERNET
Internet: sales@amcyber.com

Royalty-Free DOS Extender for C/C++
with a Windows™ linker, a dynamic overlay linker and more!

Why have a disk full of programming tools when one will do? Blinker is a DOS extender, a compiler-independent Windows™ linker, the world's fastest DOS dynamic overlay linker and a memory swapper to run multiple .EXEs, all in one product for one low price. Compatible with C, C++, CA-Clipper, FORTRAN, Assembler, and more, Blinker creates DOS and Windows programs in seconds, saving hours of valuable programming time.

Royalty-Free DOS Extender

In protected mode the extender provides direct access to 16Mb of extended memory and runs multi-megabyte programs in less than 200Kb of conventional memory, solving low memory problems caused by network shells and other TSRs. Full compatibility with DPMI, VCPI and XMS ensures your protected mode programs will run under Windows, DESQview and OS/2 as well as DOS. Blinker's DOS extender runs on any processor from a 286 with 1Mb of available memory up to the latest Pentium, and features a completely transparent VM system to access up to 64 Mb of virtual memory.

Dual Mode - A World First

Blinker is the only product to create dual mode programs, which detect at startup whether the runtime machine can run in protected mode. If not, **the same program** simply runs in real mode using

difference between a protected mode and a dual mode program. For the first time ever programs will automatically utilize all the available memory (up to 16Mb) on every PC from the smallest 8086 right up to the Pentium and beyond.

Make The Smart Choice!

Join over 50,000 programmers worldwide - order Blinker now to get the fastest link speeds available for DOS and Windows in one award-winning package with no runtime royalties on any programs you create. Blinker includes a 500 page manual, free technical support and a 30 day money back guarantee.

dynamic overlays, so you can concentrate on the code instead of the runtime environment. In real mode Blinker automatically manages overlays within 640Kb and increases execution speed using an EMS/XMS overlay cache. All this is completely invisible to the end user and there is no size

SRP $299

Children's
Software

It ain't what it used to be.

The old days of cheap graphics and speaker beeps are long gone.
Children's software is a different game now.

If you're looking for a good development company specializing in
non-violent children's educational & multimedia software, look no
further.

With clients like The Learning Company(R) and KinderSoft(TM), we know
how to build your next (or first!) children's software application. Give
us a call.

Add to Your Sams Library Today with the Best Books for Programming, Operating Systems, and New Technologies

The easiest way to order is to pick up the phone and call

1-800-428-5331

between 9:00 a.m. and 5:00 p.m. EST.

For faster service please have your credit card available.

ISBN	Quantity	Description of Item	Unit Cost	Total Cost
0-672-30717-0		Tricks of the DOOM Programming Gurus (book/CD-ROM)	$39.99	
0-672-30507-0		Tricks of the Game-Programming Gurus (book/CD-ROM)	$45.00	
0-672-30313-2		Programming Games for Beginners (book/disk)	$26.95	
0-672-30598-4		Teach Yourself Borland C++ 4.5 in 21 Days, 2nd Edition (book/disk)	$29.99	
0-672-30526-7		Mastering Turbo Assembler, 2nd Edition (book/disk)	$45.00	
0-672-30663-8		Visual C++ 2 Developers Guide, 2nd Edition (book/disk)	$49.99	
0-672-30523-2		Turbo C++ Programming in 12 Easy Lessons (book/disk)	$39.99	
0-672-30532-1		Master Visual C++ 2 (book/CD-ROM)	$49.99	
0-672-30292-6		Programming Windows Games with Borland C++ (book/disk)	$34.95	
		Shipping and Handling: See information below.		
		TOTAL		

❑ 3 ½" Disk

❑ 5 ¼" Disk

Shipping and Handling: $4.00 for the first book, and $1.75 for each additional book. Floppy disk: add $1.75 for shipping and handling. If you need to have it NOW, we can ship product to you in 24 hours for an additional charge of approximately $18.00, and you will receive your item overnight or in two days. Overseas shipping and handling adds $2.00 per book and $8.00 for up to three disks. Prices subject to change. Call for availability and pricing information on latest editions.

201 W. 103rd Street, Indianapolis, Indiana 46290

1-800-428-5331 — Orders   1-800-835-3202 — FAX   1-800-858-7674 — Customer Service

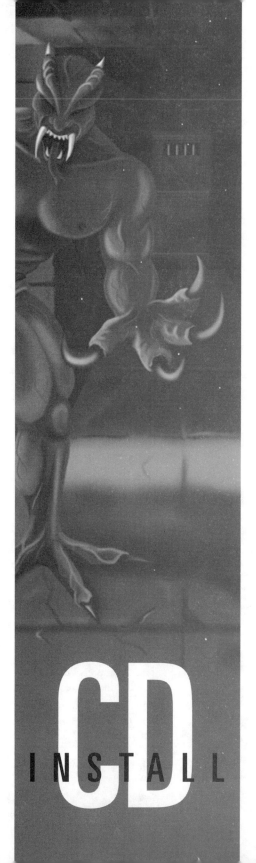

CD
INSTALL

What's on the Disc

The CD-ROM contains the source code and example programs discussed in the book, as well as many useful programming tools from commercial software vendors. Valuable software demos include the following:

- *DiamondWare's Sound Toolkit*—MVP Software's sound driver library
- *MultiEdit*—American Cybernetics' powerful DOS programming editor, now for both DOS and Windows
- *Blinker*—Blink, Inc.'s DOS extender, Windows & OS/2 linker, and DOS dynamic overlay linker
- *EZ-INSTALL*—The Software Factory's software installation aid
- *VGA Animate Game Developer's Kit*—Nexus Software's set of C programming tools for DOS graphics animation
- *UniVBE*—SciTech Software's full-featured graphics library for displaying high-performance graphics

How the CD-ROM is Arranged

The CD-ROM is divided into two main subdirectories, \SOURCE and \3RDPARTY. Code and examples from the book are found in the \SOURCE directory in subdirectories corresponding to the chapter in which they are discussed. For example, code from Chapter 3, "SuperVGA," is located in \SOURCE\CHAP03. The bonus software from various software vendors is located in the \3RDPARTY directory in subdirectories which indicate the name of the software vendor. For example, *DiamondWare's Sound Toolkit*, by MVP Software, is located in \3RDPARTY\MVP\STK.

Installing the CD-ROM

Insert the disc in your CD-ROM drive and follow these steps to install the software. You'll need at least 10MB of free space on your hard drive to install all the software.

1. From the DOS prompt, type `drive:INSTALL`, where `drive` is the letter of your CD-ROM drive. For example, type `R:INSTALL` if the disc is in drive R. Then press Enter. The installation program will provide choices to install software, source code, and examples from the CD-ROM to your hard drive.

2. Select one of the installation options by moving the highlight bar with your cursor (arrow) keys. Press Enter to make your selection. You'll be given the option to change the drive where the programs are to be installed after you make your selection.

3. You will be prompted to enter a drive letter. Enter a valid drive letter and press Enter. A subdirectory will be created on the drive you indicate labeled \MORETRIX. For example, if you type `C` and press Enter, C:\MORETRIX will be created and the software you chose will be installed in subdirectories of C:\MORETRIX.

4. You'll be asked to confirm the installation and will also be prompted after the installation is finished. The menu will return after the installation. Press ESC to exit the installation program and return to a DOS prompt.

For more information about the software, read the text files provided with each package and the README.TXT and 3RDPARTY.TXT files located in the root directory of the CD-ROM.